# PEOPLE FIRST

## An Introduction to Social Problems

**ALEXANDER LIAZOS**

*Regis College*

ALLYN AND BACON, INC.
Boston   London   Sydney   Toronto

*To Aphrodite Liazos (1880–1965), my grandmother, the past of my life; Melissa and Ariane, my daughters, the future.*

**Acknowledgments for quotations in text:**

*Pages 43, 205, and 385–386:* Erwin Marquit, *The Socialist Countries,* Marxist Educational Press, 1978, c/o Anthropology Dept., 215 Ford Hall, University of Minnesota, Minneapolis, MN 55455.

*Pages 88–89:* With permission from *Natural History,* December, 1969. Copyright the American Museum of Natural History, 1969.

*Pages 102–103, 113, 117, and 118:* Copyright © 1974 by Harry Braverman. Reprinted by permission of Monthly Review Press.

*Pages 114–115 and 119:* W. Lloyd Warner, *Yankee City.* Copyright © 1963 by Yale University.

*Pages 135–136:* Copyright © 1979 by Monthly Review, Inc. Reprinted by permission of Monthly Review Press.

*(continued on p. 438)*

Copyright © 1982 by Allyn and Bacon, Inc., 470 Atlantic Avenue, Boston, Massachusetts 02210. All rights reserved. No part of the material protected by this copyright notice may be reproduced or utilized in any form or by any means, electronic or mechanical, including photocopying, recording, or by any information storage and retrieval system, without written permission from the copyright owner.

**Library of Congress Cataloging in Publication Data**

Liazos, Alex, 1941–
  People first, an introduction to social problems.

  Bibliography: p.
  Includes index.
  1. Social problems.  2. Socialism and society.
3. Social justice.  4. Social values.  5. Equality.
I. Title.
HN65.L45     362'.042     81-12711
ISBN 0-205-07646-7 (pbk.)     AACR2

Printed in the United States of America.
10 9 8 7 6 5 4 3 2 1    86 85 84 83 82

# Contents

|  |  |  |
|---|---|---|
| | Preface | vi |
| 1 | **A PERSPECTIVE ON SOCIAL PROBLEMS** | 1 |
| | *Understanding Social Problems* | 2 |
| | *Socialist Critique of Capitalist Society* | 7 |
| | *Socialist Alternatives* | 13 |
| | *Conservative and Liberal Perspectives* | 17 |
| | *Conclusion* | 21 |
| 2 | **CLASSES AND INEQUALITY** | 23 |
| | *The Reality of Classes* | 23 |
| | *How Many Classes Are There?* | 30 |
| | *The Personal Costs of Classes* | 38 |
| | *Are Classes Inevitable?* | 40 |
| 3 | **THE ILLUSION OF DEMOCRACY** | 51 |
| | *Introduction* | 51 |
| | *Composition and Perpetuation of the Ruling Class* | 52 |
| | *Ruling-Class Control of the Economy* | 55 |
| | *Control of the Government* | 64 |
| | *What Difference Does It Make?* | 70 |
| | *Is Democracy Possible?* | 72 |
| 4 | **DOMINATION AND ELITISM** | 77 |
| | *The Pervasiveness of Domination* | 77 |
| | *Professional Domination in the United States* | 79 |
| | *Domination under Socialism* | 83 |
| | *Making People Gentle: Life without Domination* | 88 |

## 5 WORK: ART, NECESSITY, AND ALIENATION    95
*Introduction*    95
*The Meaning and Problems of Work*    97
*The Causes of Alienation*    114
*Liberal Reforms and Workers' Control*    120

## 6 IMPERIALISM AND HUNGER    135
*Introduction*    135
*The Development of Colonialism and Imperialism*    136
*The Nature of Modern Imperialism*    140
*Hunger and Starvation*    147
*Perspectives on Causes*    152
*The Effects of Imperialism*    153
*The End of Imperialism?*    161

## 7 THE DESTRUCTION OF COMMUNITY    167
*Community and Life*    167
*Capitalism and Community*    170
*"I Wanna Go Home": Appalachia*    174
*Contemporary Communities*    179
*Rising from the Ashes*    183

## 8 THE OPPRESSION OF WOMEN    189
*Biology, Culture, and Oppression*    189
*A Cultural Perspective*    191
*Women in the United States*    193
*Women in Socialist Revolutions*    205
*Changing Women, Men, and Society*    209

## 9 RACISM AND CAPITALISM    215
*Introduction*    215
*The Rise of Slavery, Racism, and Minority Exploitation*    217
*Minorities Today*    223
*The Personal Costs of Racism*    233
*Strategies for Change*    238

## 10 MOTHER EARTH IS SORE: THE DESTRUCTION OF THE ENVIRONMENT    245
*Awareness of the Environment*    245
*Ecology and Human Existence*    247
*The Destruction of the Environment*    249
*Growth, Profit, and the Environment—Other Perspectives*    262
*The Environment in Socialist Societies*    264
*Ecological Living*    267

| | | |
|---|---|---|
| 11 | **HEALTH AND ILLNESS:** | |
| | **THE QUALITY OF LIFE** | 279 |
| | *Introduction* | 279 |
| | *The Medical System: Profits and Big Business* | 280 |
| | *Sources of Health and Illness* | 292 |
| | *Can Medicine Heal Itself?* | 299 |
| | *Socialist Medicine* | 302 |
| | *Conclusions* | 307 |
| 12 | **CRIME: DANGER AT WORK AND IN THE STREETS** | 311 |
| | *What Is Crime?* | 311 |
| | *Extent and Effects of Crime* | 315 |
| | *Why Is There Crime?* | 319 |
| | *Controlling Crime* | 323 |
| | *Crime and Socialism* | 333 |
| | *Summary* | 343 |
| 13 | **EDUCATION: FITTING PEOPLE IN** | |
| | **AN UNFIT SOCIETY** | 345 |
| | *The Changing Scene* | 345 |
| | *The Rise and Functions of Public Education* | 347 |
| | *Class and Education* | 352 |
| | *The Culture of Education* | 362 |
| | *Education in Socialist Countries* | 367 |
| | *Changes in the United States* | 375 |
| | *The Integration of Learning and Life* | 376 |
| 14 | **EQUALITY, COMMUNITY, ECOLOGY:** | |
| | **TOWARD A HUMANE SOCIETY** | 381 |
| | *Social Problems Are Related* | 381 |
| | *Drugs, Prostitution, Alcoholism, and Other Forms of Deviance* | 382 |
| | *Principles for Socialist Struggle* | 383 |
| | *The Prospects of Socialism in the United States* | 388 |
| | *The Long Struggle* | 397 |
| References | | 399 |
| Glossary | | 427 |
| Index | | 431 |

# Preface

## TO THE TEACHER

In my many years of teaching I have rarely used the chapters of a book or text in the sequence presented by the author. Nevertheless, teachers may find it helpful to use Chapters 1-4 first, in that sequence, for these chapters lay the framework for the rest of the book. Later chapters do assume a knowledge of Chapters 1-4. The rest of the chapters can be easily used in a number of different sequences.

Some users of this book will agree with its perspective, others will not. I assume those who do not share its perspective will use the book to compare the socialist perspective with perspectives found in other texts. I encourage those who do hold a socialist perspective to supplement this text with some material presenting other perspectives. I encourage all users to use one or two other books that explore some problem at greater length.

## TO THE STUDENT AND TEACHER

An unusual feature of this book is the boxes found in thirteen chapters that provide short descriptions of particular struggles for equality and justice, often even for survival itself. In addition, each chapter ends with a general discussion of solutions to the problem in that chapter from a socialist perspective. All this material is not presented as a blueprint for others to copy. Rather, these are reports and discussions of what people in many places are doing to improve social conditions, intended as suggestions for all people to use in finding their own solutions. For me, the end-of-chapter discussions are tentative solutions and answers, in the process of development. The reports of struggles in China and other socialist societies are certainly not meant for people in this country to copy. These reports are meant for study and comparison, especially since those societies arose out of a feudal past, whereas the United States must struggle to solve the problems of an advanced capitalist society.

Throughout the book I use China as an example of the progress and problems of a socialist society. As I was writing the book, the current Chinese leadership made many significant changes from pre-1976 conditions in the economy, education, legal system, and other institutions. Thus, some of what I say is dated. Only time will tell how many of the changes will be corrections of mistakes committed during the turbulent years of the Cultural Revolution (1966–76), and how many will be significant departures from fundamental socialist principles.

I also want to say a few words about the personal, political, and intellectual development that led to this book. In many ways it is a logical outcome of the process that began with my article "The poverty of the sociology of deviance: Nuts, sluts, and preverts" (*Social Problems,* Summer 1972). It has been widely reprinted as an example of the radical perspective on deviance and social problems. But I did not at that time have a clear understanding of the nature of capitalist society and the need for socialism. It was only in the following years that I concluded that only as we struggle to create a socialist society can we even begin to confront and solve the human, social, and economic problems that beset us. It was a gradual but steady process.

I want to stress that while I am firmly convinced of the need for a struggle to create a socialist society, I have also come to see the enormity of that task. Achieving socialism will be difficult both because of the unrelenting opposition to change by ruling classes everywhere, but also because the institutions and values created by oppressive societies are deeply embedded in people's social and individual consciousness. The revolutionary overthrow of a capitalist or agrarian ruling class does not mean the immediate creation of an egalitarian, just, democratic, and humane society. Individuals and groups from the old society and from other capitalist societies will try to sabotage the new order. Moreover, existing values and institutions do not vanish overnight. Centuries of individualism, competition, and possessiveness will not disappear without a long struggle. The road to socialism and the struggle against ruling classes, ideas, and institutions will be long, difficult, and uncertain.

But we have no choice but to undertake that journey. That is the conclusion I have reached. At the start of the 1980s, with the legacy of many unsolved and worsening problems from the 1970s, many people have turned to conservative rhetoric and programs for solutions. I believe conservatism will be no more successful than was the centrist program of the 1970s (Nixon, Ford, and Carter) or the liberalism of the 1960s (Kennedy and Johnson). Much of the rest of the world has concluded socialism is the true alternative, and as I write there are socialist revolutions, in various stages, throughout the world. The United States is part of that world and the current crisis. Here I offer an explanation of that crisis and this country's part in it, and some possible solutions. Some of you may now share this explanation of the crisis, and probably fewer of you think socialism is the answer. You will probably not change very much even after you read this book. One does not become a socialist, or make any significant changes, in the course of an academic semester or the reading of a book. I do hope, however, that you can remain open and explore the socialist perspective, weighing its argument and evidence carefully and critically.

## ACKNOWLEDGMENTS

For years I have been reading the acknowledgments of other writers, and I must confess the lists of names have seemed long and unnecessary. Now that it is time for me to give thanks and identify my debts to others, I realize not only is it necessary to do so, it is also a great pleasure. Each in their own way, these people made this book possible. Not all of them share my perspective or conclusions, but they were still eager to help me each in his or her own way. I thank all of them deeply.

In the fall of 1976 I sent Peter Manning an outline of a proposed text, and he encouraged me to pursue the project. He also warned me that it would be more work than I thought. If I had known then what I found in the course of working on this text, I might never have undertaken to write it. Peter Manning also wrote some letters of introduction that opened the door.

During the various stages of its development, the manuscript was reviewed by many people: Robert J. Antonio, Charles Reasons, Peter K. Manning, Gerald Turkel, Richard Kronish, Robert C. Hanson, Jan DeAmicis, David Simon, Robert H. Mast, and Charles Petranek. Their comments, criticisms, and suggestions were very useful in improving the text. I did not follow all of their comments, for which I alone take responsibility. The suggestions of Turkel, Kronish, and DeAmicis, in particular, prevented some serious errors and enriched the text. Turkel I also thank for his suggestion that I emphasize people's struggles for justice and equality. This suggestion led to the "Struggles" features found in thirteen chapters of the book.

Gerry Starr sent me the story on the miners' strike, found in Chapter 2, and I thank him for it. My former students Elaine Crisafulli, Mary Latuca, and Linda Teuwen suggested articles and other material, and they generally encouraged me with the project.

The students at Regis College who took "American Society" with me in the spring and fall of 1979 used an earlier version of this text, and their generally favorable response gave me confidence to go on with the book. Roberta Colasanti and Karen Phillips were especially helpful. I thank them also for their tolerance to use a somewhat sloppy photocopied version.

In the course of a text an author summarizes and in other ways uses the works of many people. An author knows few of these people personally, and many of them may not agree with the way the author has used their work. I beg their tolerance and thank them.

I have made extensive use of government data, which are collected by people the author never gets to know. Here, in this small way, I wish to thank these people for myself and for all those who use their work.

The following journals have been invaluable both in educating me and leading me to a socialist perspective. They have provided me with endless sources of information, ideas, and encouragement that there is hope for the socialist view. It is my greatest pleasure to list these journals and to recommend them to anyone who wishes to study our society: *Monthly Review,* the *Guardian* (in New York City), *Radical America, Dollars and Sense,* the *Progressive,* the *Nation,* the *Insurgent Sociologist,* and *Crime and Social Justice.*

For many of us who came to adulthood in the 1960s, it was the struggles of millions of people throughout the world that taught us the nature of capitalist society and the need for socialism. Especially important were the struggles of black people in the United States and the revolutionaries in Vietnam, and the antiwar movement in the United States. The women's movement in the late 1960s and early 1970s led us to explore other forms of oppression. The people involved in these struggles raised consciousness and hopes.

It was Phil Olson at Clark University in the early 1960s who introduced me to the work of C. Wright Mills. Although Mills's work is not mentioned in the body of this book, the issues he raised were instrumental in beginning my education and liberation.

Dave Slaney, my friend and colleague at Regis College from 1972 to 1976, was the first person I talked to at great length when I finally and belatedly came to a socialist perspective. He continues to be a source of strength and enlightenment to me.

From 1975 to 1976 I was part of a study group on socialist criminology. It was at that time that I came to a clear and final understanding of capitalism and the hopes and problems of socialism. John Baumann, Jim Brady, Richard Quinney, and Richard Speiglman were my fellow students, and I take this opportunity to acknowledge my debt to them.

The title of this book, *People First,* is taken from a book with a similar title, *Food First,* by Frances Moore Lappé and Joseph Collins. Their book provided me with much information, especially for Chapter 6, "Imperialism and Hunger." I initially used the title *People Last,* a variation on *Food First,* and Gerald Turkel suggested I change it to a more positive tone. I am glad to follow his suggestion.

Sister Therese Higgins (president) and the trustees of Regis College granted me a sabbatical leave for the fall of 1978, during which I wrote a complete first version of this text. I could not have written it without that time off, and I am grateful to them.

Most of this text was written and revised at the Regis library and Cary Memorial Library (Lexington, Massachusetts). The staffs of both places were always helpful in finding books and information I needed. They did not all know what I was writing on, so I want to let them know of my debt.

Toni Miller, Janet Horrigan, and Patricia Ralph typed most of the manuscript. My debt to them is especially great because most of what they typed came from handwritten copy, which they deciphered with patience and accuracy. Had I needed to make a typed first draft, I doubt I would have ever finished the book. Many thanks to all three of you.

Alan Levitt of Allyn and Bacon knows why I am very grateful to him for agreeing to do this book. He was more than patient with my impatience during the years that the manuscript was revised and improved. Allen Workman, also of Allyn and Bacon, made many suggestions that improved the book as a text. Students have him to thank for many improvements. To both of you, many thanks.

I end with a personal note. In July of 1980 I handed the final manuscript to Alan Levitt. I then left on a long journey to visit my parents and other relatives in socialist Albania, from whom I was separated in 1947 at the age of six. In the four weeks in Albania I was preoccupied with seeing family and catching up with my past, so I did not spend much time studying the society there. I saw enough, however, to be able to say that despite any remaining problems, the Albanian people have made enormous progress in creating an egalitarian and just society. My parents and other older people told me tragic tales of suffering and death (including a sister of mine) in the days before socialism. Children and adults now live in a society where the essentials of life are guaranteed to all people.

So, in closing, I express my deepest love and gratitude to my family: to Aphrodite Liazos (1880–1965), my grandmother, who raised my brother Chris and me in the first difficult years of separation from our parents; to Theodore and Georgia Liazos, my parents, whose letters through the many years of separation sustained the family ties; to my other relatives in Albania, especially my brother Vangjel, who welcomed me so warmly (together with my parents) and taught me about life in Albania; and to my wife Karen and daughters Melissa and Ariane, who gave me strength during the time I wrote this book. Melissa and Ariane walk through the pages of Chapter 8. When they are old enough to read the book I hope they will also be forgiving enough to understand why I wrote about them.

# 1

# *A Perspective on Social Problems*

UNDERSTANDING SOCIAL PROBLEMS

*The Social Context of Our Lives*

As we go about our daily lives, we tend to focus mostly on our immediate surroundings and ignore much of what happens in the world beyond. Perhaps we must do so, if we are to avoid being overwhelmed by events seemingly so much beyond our control.

Yet, we cannot ignore that larger world for long. Sooner or later it touches us, our families, our friends, our neighbors, our communities. Companies move their plants to other locations (today, mostly outside the United States), and thousands lose their jobs; a nuclear plant leaks, and we are threatened; people in poor countries rise in revolt against their rulers, and the United States government may send troops in to stop the rebellion, threatening the lives of United States soldiers and adding to inflation, the cutbacks on social programs, and so on.

We then need to understand why such events happen, how they touch and shape our lives, and what we can do about them.

Some of us may not perceive any major problems in our lives. Others may see problems but don't know why they exist or how they can be changed. I hope to explore some major social problems, to see how they may shape our lives now or in the future, and to examine some solutions. You may not agree with my explanations, but I hope you will consider seriously the perspective I present and search for your own answers.

*Some Inequalities and Contradictions*

In this richest land in the world there are serious problems touching all of us. For example, old people have worked hard for many years. They have held jobs, raised children, paid taxes. But in the 1980s they not only face the usual problems of old age; many old people are threatened with the possibility of no place to live or with prohibitive rents. Many of their present apartments, in which they have lived for years and which they can afford, are being converted to condominiums (*Dollars and Sense,* March 1980, pp. 8-9).

> Marie Abbott is 72 years old and partially paralyzed on one side from a stroke. For the last 13 years she has lived in a nice apartment on Granite avenue in Dorchester's Cedar Grove area. She loves the apartment and all of her neighbors, most of whom are also elderly.
>
> Last week the residents of the apartment house received a letter from the management informing them that the building has been sold and the apartments would be converted to condominiums.
>
> Abbott, who is on a fixed income, said she could not afford to purchase a condominium and did not want to move. And even if she did want to move, "I don't know how I could," she said in an interview. "I'm crippled on one side. I can't walk. I can't even get on a bus. I'd just as soon die. I hope I do so soon. He (her doctor) told me I could have another stroke anytime" (Dwyer 1979, p. 17).

Marie Abbott's predicament, shared by many others, comes from a business decision. Apartment owners can make much more money by converting their apartments to condominiums than by keeping the present tenants. But how can it happen that business considerations win over the basic needs of old people? What does such treatment of old people tell about our society?

While there is a shortage of houses and apartments, and while the costs are rising beyond the means of millions, in many cities apartments are burned for profits. Rather than repair their apartments, landlords insure them at very high amounts and then hire arsonists to burn them. People have died during such fires. Some landlords and arsonists have been caught and convicted; most have not, and the fires continue to burn. How can destruction be more profitable than the meeting of human needs? How can people resort to arson to make money? Why do such irrational and destructive conditions exist? (*Dollars and Sense,* January 1980, pp. 7-9).

As we enter the 1980s, the prices of food, fuel, gasoline, housing, and other necessities continue to rise. People on welfare and millions of working-class Americans find they cannot pay their bills. Many must choose between food or fuel (see Chapter 2). For example, in May 1980, interviews with 108 old people in the Boston area showed that many of them had to set thermostats "far below healthy temperatures for people their age"; they would not see visitors because they were "embarrassed about cold houses"; and they had to scrimp on food so they could pay their fuel bill. It is indeed cruel "to be old, cold, hungry" after a lifetime of hard work (McMillan 1980).

A forty-year-old widow in Maine, suffering from kidney disease, tried to care for herself and four children on a monthly cash allotment of $568 (March 1980). But in February 1980, she had to spend so much of that $568 "on wood for the stove that the cupboard went bare, and for ten days she and her four children lived on rice and a 50-pound bag of potatoes that cost $3.25." She was ashamed that she often sent her children to school in ragged clothes. And she had to stop driving her son to the hospital for the treatments he needed to strengthen his leg that had never healed properly from a broken hip. She could not afford to buy gasoline (Thomas 1980).

While millions lack the necessities, others are urged to buy the superfluous. The October 1979 issue of *Smithsonian* magazine, which caters to the affluent, advertises such items as Greek fishermen caps, a "genuine Korean apothecary chest" for $199, and a "Senator Walking Stick" for $69—"replica of the gold-handled walking stick of Congressman Preston Brooks, used in the historic caning of Senator Charles Sumner in the U.S. Senate floor in 1856" (quoted in Kilian 1979, p. 68). A New York furrier had a sale, by invitation only, where a "raisin-dyed ribbed beaver" coat sold for only $3,500 (down from the usual $4,950), and a sable priced elsewhere for $110,000 sold for only $50,000 (O'Reilly 1980). Who produces such items? Who buys them? How can resources be wasted while millions cannot pay for food and fuel?

Problems and contradictions do not confront only the poor and the working class, however. Inequalities in material conditions are not our only problem. Everyone is affected by a polluted environment, for example. Dangerous chemicals at work and in the air, polluted drinking water, poisonous chemicals dumped illegally in the woods in the dark of night, nuclear wastes impossible to store safely, cancer-causing asbestos fibers in schools and at workplaces, lead in the air, diseases contracted at workplaces killing over 100,000 people yearly, additives in foods—the list is long (see Chapters 10 and 11). Is it ignorance that leads to the endangering of the environment, to illness and deaths? Is it people's "affluent" life-styles? Or are these problems the inevitable result of a profit-oriented system?

While corporations endanger the lives of their workers and other people with chemical poisons, they are not punished. At most, they pay small fines. Ordinary street criminals, who rob banks or stores, spend years in prison, but corporate officers, whose policies endanger thousands, go free. Why does the criminal justice system ignore the greater danger to our welfare? (see Chapter 12). Two hundred people died in Buffalo Creek, West Virginia in 1972 when a coal company dam burst and poured mud and water downstream. The company had been repeatedly warned to fix the dam but had not done so. It paid $14 million to the survivors, but no one spent even one day in jail (see Chapter 7).

There are problems in still other areas. In many city schools, thousands of students drop out before they finish high school. Many of those who stay in school feel alienated from these schools and vandalize them (see Chapters 12 and 13). The jobs they get upon graduation are alienating (Chapter 5).

After some progress in the 1960s, women and minorities stood still in the 1970s. At the start of the 1980s, full-time working women still make under 60 percent of the income men make. Most working women are in sex-segregated jobs: clerical, secretarial, sales, and similar occupations (see Chapters 8 and 9).

Outside the United States the world is in turmoil. In Iran, Nicaragua, Zimbabwe, and elsewhere there are revolutions and other political and social changes. Poverty and hunger are the daily experience of millions (see Chapter 6). How does this situation affect people in the U.S.?

I have implied answers to some of these questions. The following chapters will study each problem in some detail. Later in this chapter I will outline a social and political perspective that provides a framework for understanding these contradictions and inequalities.

## The Impact of Work

First, it is instructive to look at differing explanations of worker alienation.

Many studies in the 1970s showed that most people are unhappy with their work. Most jobs now involve less and less skill, people have little or no control over what they do, management increasingly divides the work into routine, repetitive, and smaller tasks, and, generally, work is impoverishing rather than enriching workers' lives. Office and factory workers, salespeople, service workers, and others all suffer from work alienation.

To study the effects of work, some researchers talked to people about their jobs, some watched them at work, and some became co-workers. Among the latter were Richard Balzer and Richard Pfeffer, who, independent of each other, got jobs in two different factories. The reports of what they found are remarkably similar, but their conclusions and explanations differ profoundly.

Balzer, in *Clockwork* (1976), describes his experiences as a worker at a Western Electric plant that made telephone equipment. He found that workers only endured their jobs and found no satisfaction in them. One worker told Balzer, "work is not something you enjoy, it's something you do." Most days people daydreamed, went for breaks as often as they could, prolonged meetings with questions, and did anything they could to make the time pass and not notice the work they were doing. But despite these outlets, some days time simply dragged on.

There were rules covering every situation imaginable: about smoking, talking, going to the bathroom, and so on. The workers felt humiliated because they were treated like children. The rules created a clear division between "we" (workers) and "they" (management). Indeed, by making all these rules the company essentially admitted no work would be done without them. The need for rules showed how workers really felt about their jobs. Workers were told "not only what to do, but what not to do, and when not to do it" (Balzer 1976, p. 92).

It is no wonder, then, that when work was over people ran to punch their time cards and run to their cars, even though when they started to drive their cars they would only sit in traffic, barely moving. In response, management made a rule against running and placed observers to enforce it, creating yet another rule and more conflict.

Why does management treat workers so as to humiliate and control them? Balzer says little about this issue, but he seems to think that management does not really understand how it affects workers. What would it take to change these working conditions? Balzer seems to argue that when management understands how it affects workers, it will make changes. But all evidence in Balzer's report argues otherwise. At meetings of management and workers, he tried in vain to show management how it treated and affected workers. This effort led to no important changes (for a discussion of Balzer, see Pfeffer 1979, pp. 328-72).

Richard Pfeffer worked seven months in a factory that made piston rings (*Working for Capitalism*, 1979). He drove a forklift and picked up trash hoppers which he emptied into outside garbage bins. The workers there were equally as unhappy as those at Western Electric. They too thought that there is an inherent conflict between "them" (management) and "us" (workers). They were demoralized and felt helpless. Pfeffer found, for example, that he could not do his work because management took its time fixing his broken-down forklift. Pfeffer could not control his work. The other workers had similar experiences. Since trying to do a good job was very frustrating, most workers gave up the effort after a while. But giving up left them feeling angry and helpless.

Fridays were the happiest days—workers got paid and looked forward to two days away from the job and its drudgery. While at work, workers were constantly counting time—until the next break, until lunch, until the end of the day, until the weekend, until vacation time, even until retirement. To describe their experience at the job, some used the same expression used by prisoners—"doing time."

Pfeffer found that routinely, workers were disciplined like children, felt humiliated, and lost their self-respect. But they kept quiet most of the time because of the fear of losing their jobs. This fear, and the fear of being branded agitators, was a social and political fact that pervaded the workers' life at the factory.

They won some struggles, but these victories turned out to be meaningless. They won the right to refuse compulsory overtime (previously, when management had asked them to work longer than eight hours or on Saturday, workers could be fired if they refused to do so). They needed the money, however, both for the necessities and for "luxuries" to which advertising attracted them, so most in fact took overtime work when it was offered them.

Similarly, workers had the right to appeal management decisions. But the appeal procedure was long and cumbersome, and people were discouraged from using it. Those who spoke up and made appeals were harassed, even laid off.

How does Pfeffer explain the helplessness and frustration he and his co-workers experienced? Unlike Balzer, he concludes that *management intends to rule and control workers.* Pfeffer says that management knows how its rules and regulations demoralize and control workers, and it means to do so. Management also understands the inherent conflict between itself and workers. Conditions cannot be different under capitalism. Thus, if changes are to occur, they will not come from an enlightened management. Workers must force management to make changes. Ultimately, in the view of this book, management must be abolished and workers must run their own plants.

The conflict between management and workers is not a personal one. Rather, the very nature and structure of work under capitalism require that production demands take precedence over workers' needs. Profits, not people, come first. Under such inevitably conflicting interests between workers and management, management must try to control the workers. The rules, the fears, the alienating work all result from the need to control workers in order to ensure profits for the corporation and its stockholders (see Chapter 3).

Many workers understand the reality of their exploitation by the corporations and they are cynical about any management reforms. In this view, such proposed reforms are not motivated by any concern for the workers' problems. Management "reforms" are tools to increase production and profits.

I will try to show throughout this book that this fundamental reality of conflicting interests underlies most social problems. Social problems exist, or are made worse, or cannot be solved, because in the organization of work, community life, schools, housing, the environment, and so on, human needs are secondary to profit considerations. In this society, the interests of a few people take precedence over the needs of the majority.

# SOCIALIST CRITIQUE OF CAPITALIST SOCIETY

*Classes, Class Conflict, and Exploitation*

An analysis of life in the United States or any capitalist society, and a discussion of its problems, must begin with the reality of different classes, with the upper (ruling) class dominating the rest. ("Upper class" and "ruling class" are used synonymously in this book.) All else follows from this simple and fundamental condition (see Chapters 2 and 3).

The reality, dominance, and injuries of class are no secret to most people. Nor is the fact that the rich benefit from this system. In twelve years of teaching, I have found that the best discussions center around the topic of social class. Students come alive as they do at no other time. Everyone mentions some example from his or her life. Everyone resents the system that benefits the rich at the expense of everyone else. What prevents people from taking the next logical step to socialism is the socialization process that labels socialism as "unpatriotic" and "un-American," and the eternal hope that they will be among those who will "make it."

Social classes are inevitably in conflict. The interests of the ruling class are met at the expense of the rest. The products and goods made by the labor of others are used to make profits for the owners of the means of production.

*The Dominance of Economic Institutions*

In capitalist societies, economic institutions dominate the rest: family, education, and so on. The needs of corporations dictate what happens to us in our daily lives: where we live, where we work, what we learn and how we learn it.

The economy is dominated by a small ruling class. To cite just two of the most basic facts: about 1 percent of the American people own about 75 percent of the stocks in major American corporations. In addition, a small number of people sit on the boards of directors of the largest American corporations (see Chapter 3).

This class dominates other institutions. Its members occupy most important positions in the executive branch of the federal government; they control political parties through donations and other means; they have access to governmental bodies in order to lobby for their interests, and so on.

The class that dominates the economy and the rest of society propounds the ideology of competition and the free market, but in fact much is done to sabotage competition, since competition lowers prices and thus decreases profits. In fact, fairly early (around 1900), the American economy became dominated by a few corporations, despite antitrust laws. Today in many industries four (or fewer) corporations make the products Americans buy. This condition gives enormous power to the ruling class and its corpo-

## Socialist Analysis of Capitalism

*The following analysis of the economic system in capitalist societies explores class struggle, exploitation of the workers, and competition.*

### 1. Class Struggle

No matter whether they're rich or poor, strong or weak, white, black, yellow, or brown, people everywhere must produce and distribute the things they need in order to live.

The system of production and distribution in the United States is called *capitalism.* Many other countries of the world have the same system.

In order to produce and distribute bread, clothes, houses, autos, radios, newspapers, medicines, schools, this, that, and the other thing, you have to have two essentials:

1. Land, mines, raw materials, machines, factories—what economists call the "means of production."
2. Labor—workers who use their strength and skill on and with the means of production to turn out the required goods.

In the United States, as in other capitalist countries, the means of production are not public property. The land, raw materials, factories, machines, are owned by individuals—by capitalists. That is a fact of tremendous importance. Because whether you do or do not own the means of production determines your position in society. If you belong to the small group of owners of the means of production—the capitalist class—you can live without working. If you belong to the large group that does not own the means of production—the working class—you can't live unless you work.

One class lives by owning: the other class lives by working. The capitalist class gets its income by employing other people to work for it; the working class gets its income in the form of wages for the work it does.

Since labor is essential to the production of goods we need in order to live, you would suppose that those who do the labor—the working class—would be handsomely rewarded. But they aren't. In capitalist society, it isn't those who *work* the most who get the largest incomes, it is those who *own* the most.

Profit makes the wheels go round in capitalist society. The smart business man is the one who pays as little as possible for what he buys and receives as much as possible for what he sells. The first step on the road to high profits is to reduce expenses. One of the expenses of production is wages to labor. It is therefore to the interest of the employer to pay as low wages as possible. It is likewise to his interest to get as much work out of his laborers as possible.

The interests of the owners of the means of production and of the men who work for them are opposed. For the capitalists, property takes first place, humanity second place; for the workers, humanity—themselves—takes first place, property second place. That is why, in capitalist society, there is always conflict between the two classes.

Both sides in the class war act the way they do because they must. The capitalist must try to make profits to remain a capitalist. The worker must try to get decent wages to remain alive. Each can succeed only at the expense of the other.

All the talk about "harmony" between capital and labor is nonsense. In capitalist society there can be no such harmony because what is good for one class is bad for the other, and vice versa.

The relationship, then, that *must* exist between the owners of the means of production and the workers in capitalist society is the relationship of a knife to a throat.

### 2. Surplus Value

In capitalist society, man does not produce things which he wants to satisfy his own needs, he produces things to sell to others. Where formerly people

*Source:* Huberman and Sweezy, *Introduction to Socialism,* 1968, pp. 23–27. Copyright © 1968 by Monthly Review Press, Inc. Reprinted by permission of Monthly Review Press.

*(continued)*

**Socialist Analysis of Capitalism** *(continued)*
produced *goods for their own use,* today they produce *commodities for the market.*

The capitalist system is concerned with the production and exchange of commodities.

The worker does not own the means of production. He can make his living in only one way—by hiring himself out for wages to those who do. He goes to market with a commodity for sale—his capacity to work, his labor power. That's what the employer buys from him. That's what the employer pays him wages for. The worker sells his commodity, labor power, to the boss in return for wages.

How much wages will he get? What is it that determines the rate of his wages?

The key to the answer is found in the fact that what the worker has to sell is a commodity. The value of his labor power, like that of any other commodity, is determined by the amount of socially necessary labor time required to produce it. But since the worker's labor power is part of himself, the value of his labor power is equal to the food, clothing, and shelter necessary for him to live (and since the supply of labor must continue, to raise a family).

In other words, if the owner of a factory, mill, or mine wants forty hours of labor done, he must pay the man who is to do the work enough to live on, and to bring up children capable of taking his place when he gets too old to work, or dies.

Workers will get then, in return for their labor power, subsistence wages, with enough more (in some countries) to enable them to buy a radio, or an electric refrigerator, or a ticket to the movies occasionally.

Does this economic law that workers' wages will tend to be merely subsistence wages mean that political and trade union action by workers is useless? No, it definitely does not. On the contrary, workers, through their unions, have been able in some countries, including the United States, to raise wages above the minimum subsistence level. And the important point to remember is that this is the *only* way open to workers to keep that economic law from operating all the time.

Where does profit come from?

It is not in the process of exchange of commodities but rather in the process of production that we will find the answer. The profits that go to the capitalist class arise out of production.

The workers by transforming raw material into the finished article have brought new wealth into existence, have created a new value. The difference between what the worker is paid in wages and the amount of value he has added to the raw material is what the employer keeps.

That's where his profit comes from.

When a worker hires himself out to an employer he doesn't sell him what he produces; the worker sells his ability to produce.

The employer does not pay the worker for the product of eight hours work; the employer pays him to work eight hours.

The worker sells his labor power for the length of the whole working day—say eight hours. Now suppose the time necessary to produce the value of the worker's wages is four hours. He doesn't stop working then and go home. Oh, no. He has been hired to work eight hours. So he continues to work the other four hours. In these four hours, he is working *not for himself,* but *for his employer.* Part of his labor is *paid* labor; part is *unpaid* labor. The employer's profit comes from the unpaid labor.

There *must* be a difference between what the worker is paid and the value of what he produces, else the employer wouldn't hire him. The difference between what the worker receives in wages and the value of the commodity he produces is called *surplus value.*

Surplus value is the profit that goes to the employer. He buys labor power at one price and sells the product of labor at a higher price. The difference—surplus value—he keeps for himself.

### 3. Accumulation of Capital

The capitalist begins with money. He buys the means of production and labor power. The workers, using their labor power on the means of production, produce commodities. The capitalist takes these commodities and sells them—for money. The amount of money he gets at the end of the process must be greater than the amount of money he started with. The difference is his profit.

*(continued)*

> **Socialist Analysis of Capitalism** *(continued)*
>
> If the amount of money at the end of the process is not greater than the amount of money he started with, then there is no profit and he stops producing. Capitalist production does not begin or end with people's needs. It begins and ends with money.
>
> Money cannot become more money by standing still, by being hoarded. It can only grow by being used as capital, that is by buying the means of production and labor power and thus getting a share of the new wealth created by workers every hour of every day of every year.
>
> It's a real merry-go-round. The capitalist seeks more and more profits so he can accumulate more capital (means of production and labor power), so he can make more and more profits, so he can accumulate more capital, so he can etc., etc., etc.
>
> Now the way to increase profits is to get the workers to turn out more and more goods faster and faster at less and less cost.
>
> Good idea, but how to do it? Machines and scientific management, that was (and is) the answer. Greater division of labor. Mass production. Speed-up. Greater efficiency in the plant. More machines. Power-driven machines that enable one worker to produce as much as five did before, as much as ten did, eighteen, twenty-seven. . . .
>
> The workers who are made "superfluous" by machinery become an "industrial reserve army" which can slowly starve, or, by its very existence, help to force down the wages of those who are lucky enough to have jobs.
>
> And not only do machines create a surplus population of workers, they also change the character of labor. Unskilled, low-paid labor—with a machine—can do work that required skilled high-paid labor before. Children can take the place of adults in the factory, women can replace men.
>
> Competition forces each capitalist to look for ways whereby he can produce goods more cheaply than others. The lower his "unit labor cost" the more possible it is to undersell his competitors and still make a profit. With the extension of the use of machinery, the capitalist is able to get the workers to produce more and more goods faster and faster at less and less cost.
>
> But the new and improved machinery which makes this possible costs a lot of money. It means production on a larger scale than before, it means bigger and bigger factories. In other words, it means the accumulation of more and more capital.
>
> There is no choice for the capitalist. The greatest amount of profits goes to the capitalist who uses the most advanced and efficient technical methods. So all capitalists keep striving for improvements. But these improvements require more and more capital. To stay in business at all, to meet the competition of others and preserve what he has, the capitalist must keep constantly expanding his capital.
>
> Not only does he *want* more profits so he can accumulate more capital so he can make more profits—he finds that he is *forced* to do so by the system.

rations: most people depend for their existence on the people who control these monopolies.

*The Poisoning of Human Relations*

Under this system, where the ruling class dominates all institutions to benefit itself, human relations and the quality of life are poisoned. Most of us do not suffer starvation or material deprivation (although millions do). But people do not live to eat and possess material objects; as humans, we have other needs that capitalism makes problematic. The values and institutions supported by capitalism pervade our lives, often destroying our relations with others. In a system where we are taught to compete and look out primarily for ourselves, daily life often becomes mean and suspicious.

As we shall see, racism, sexism, worker alienation, and poor medical care are inevitable under capitalism. They exist because capitalism operates for the benefit of the few, not to meet our common human needs. Details of these problems appear in individual chapters. Another problem is of immediate concern.

In 1976–77 I became impressed by the domination of the self-interest ethic in the United States. A number of stories in the *Boston Globe* made this point. Students admitted to cheating for better grades; owners of apartment buildings in Boston's Fenway section had fires set (often killing people) to collect insurance, after they had made huge profits by not repairing the buildings for years; top government employees worked few hours for full-time pay. Ex-GIs have told me they attend college classes, collecting government benefits, not to learn anything or get a degree, but because they can make money on the deal (one estimated it at $6 an hour). The list can go on. In class discussions, students tell me that, whereas they do not accept it for themselves, they think most other people act on the principle, "you're a fool if you don't cheat; everyone else does."

The revelations in the Watergate episode have confirmed what many of us knew or suspected. Nixon was correct in claiming he got punished for what many others did and do.

In a society dominated by individualism, where business crime abounds, where corporations move to where labor is cheap leaving jobless thousands of long-time workers, can we be surprised at the small-time cheating of GIs, students, and public employees? Human relations suffer when people lose trust in car mechanics who cheat repairing cars, students who cheat taking tests, and doctors who charge high prices for unnecessary treatment.

Capitalism lessens community, democracy, and trust in each other. The following from Dennison's *The Lives of Children* shows how competition invades and destroys even the play of children.

> Think of the ordinary games of boys—in sandlots, fields, parks, even stick-ball in the street. They are expansive and diverse, alternately intense and gay, and are filled with events of all kinds. The boys make much of one another's personalities, one another's strengths and weaknesses, and their witticisms fly back and forth with unflagging vivacity. They do not stop their game to argue a fine point, but rather the arguments are great features of the game; they are vociferous and long-drawn and run the gamut from sheer emotionalism to the most legalistic pedantry. What may seem to be a shouting match is in fact filled with close distinctions. (I heard a boy win such a match by introducing the word "immaterial." "Whatta ya mean immaterial!!" "It's immaterial, that's all!!" "Yeah?" "Yeah!" "Whatta ya mean it's immaterial!!" "It just doesn't matter, that's what!" "Oh . . ." If the other had lost his momentum before the mighty word, it was clear, too, that he was gaining the word.) Between innings the boys throw themselves on the grass. They wrestle, do handstands, turn somersaults. They hurl twigs and stones at nearby trees, and yell at the birds that sail by. A confident player will make up dance steps as he stops a slow grounder. If an outfielder is bored, he does not stand there pulling

up his pants and thumping his glove, but plays with the bugs in the grass, looks at the clouds, makes up a droll saying to shout at the duffer at bat—who immediately answers in kind. There is almost always a dog on the field, and no part of the competition is gayer or more intense than that between the boys and the dog, who when he succeeds in snapping up their ball, leads them off in a serpentine line that is all laughter and shouts, the dog looking back over his shoulder and trotting with stiff legs, until finally he is captured and flattens his ears as they take back their ball. No one has forgotten the score or who was at bat. The game goes on. Often birds and squirrels share the field, and sometimes a noisy crew of younger kids, who must scamper out of the way from time to time, and who shout childish versions of belligerent wit at their young elders. Everything is noticed, everything is used. The game goes on until darkness ends it, and the winners can hardly be distinguished from the losers, for by then everyone is fumbling the ball and giggling and flopping on the grass.

I have put all this in a generalized way, but the game I have been describing is actually one I witnessed recently in a New Jersey park. At the other end of the same park a Little League game was in progress. The coaches and officials were off-duty cops, doing their bit, yelling insults at the players, and the most vulgar kind of mockery. Everything was forbidden. "Keep yer eye on the ball, ya moron!"

But a game with cops is in a class by itself. The standard Little League game, no matter how gentle its officials may be, is an affair of uniforms and scoreboards, umpires and coaches, record books and publicity. And there in the stands, all around the boys, is an audience of adults (who should be doing something themselves), just waiting to be proud of them. How put-upon those boys are! They are strained and silent. They try to act manly and serious, and one sees at a glance that they are anxious and uncomfortable, and deeply resent having to prove themselves. The winners exult. The losers weep. What strange occurrences in the play of children! And who invented it? Not boys themselves, but nervous adults seeking to allay their own anxieties (George Dennison 1969, pp. 200–202).

Of course, not all relations under capitalism are distrustful. People manage to be kind to each other and to cooperate. I have known mechanics who were totally honest, but since dishonesty is so common, I find it difficult to trust even the honest ones. But whatever trust, cooperation, and honesty exist, they do so despite the system, not because of it.

The preceding critique of capitalism needs to be qualified in two ways.
1. This book provides a description of life in the United States from a particular perspective. This description may seen unreal to most of you. Oppression and exploitation are not what you think you experience daily. I must confess that at times I too think this portrait of United States society may be painted too darkly. Life cannot be that oppressive.

And it is not. Even under slavery, a condition that all agree is exploitative and oppressive, slaves do find daily joys. A good meal, friends, work in the field early on a summer day, talking with friends, watching children grow—these, and more, give joy. Moreover, at any given moment, slaves may not be conscious of their oppression. Life is not a constant hell. But surely, despite these mitigating realities, oppression and exploitation are the ultimate realities of slavery. The lives of slaves are defined and limited by their status as slaves. Most of their experiences are shaped by the slave relationship. The joys that do exist do so despite slavery.

So with life under capitalism. People in this system are not slaves, to be sure (although in some parts of the world a few people still live under conditions close to slavery). But the basic facts of capitalist society shape everyone's life: the inequalities of social classes and the importance of profits over people. Joys do exist, and I apologize for describing so few in this book. On some spring days I can walk on a beach or a mountain and feel at peace with the world around me; however, on other spring days I have been angered and depressed when I could not walk on miles of beach because they are private property.

2. I do not argue that capitalism causes all problems. Inequality and oppression have existed in many other societies. Many of our problems are inherited from precapitalist days. Rather, I argue that (a) capitalism causes many problems directly; (b) it intensifies others (sexism, for example); (c) it makes difficult or impossible the solution of many problems, even the ones it did not create. Conversely, I do not argue that socialism provides automatic answers to all problems. It does solve many and makes it possible for others to be solved through struggle.

## SOCIALIST ALTERNATIVES

In analyzing social problems, we focus on a double critique of capitalist society. There are, first, problems of material suffering and economic inequalities: for example, lack of access to higher education for the poor and working class, jobs that pay too little to support oneself and one's family, and poor medical care. Equally as important are problems in the declining quality of life and worsening social relations: for example, authoritarian education and alienating work. The socialist critique finds both kinds of problems are fundamental problems of capitalist society.

Socialist alternatives are seen by many people as utopian and impossible. This book intends to show that these alternatives are both necessary and possible (though not utopian, for socialism does not claim to create a society where all struggle and striving will end). I will present many examples from socialist societies, not to set up these societies as models to replicate exactly, but as possible examples that may be shaped to fit present needs and circumstances.

### *Community and Cooperation*

Socialism seeks to change the values that allow a few to profit by exploiting the rest. Society must be organized to meet the needs of all people. Production must be for use, to meet individual and collective needs, not to profit those few who control the economy. In order to accomplish these goals, we need to replace competition and self-interest with cooperation and community.

### The End of Deprivation

The first goal of socialism is the elimination of oppression and suffering—material, physical, social, and psychic. This would involve the end of social classes and the distribution of material goods for the benefit of all. It would mean guaranteeing to everyone the essentials of food, clothing, shelter, education, and medical care.

Closely related is the liberation of people so they can organize, in a collective way, to use their energies and creativity to improve material conditions. The increased production of food, manufacturing, and other goods that has been seen in Cuba, China, and elsewhere has relieved much hunger and starvation. In view of the fact that people of the nonsocialist third world countries are getting poorer, the material achievements of socialism are indeed impressive (Chen 1975; Cereseto 1977).

### Equality and Democracy

But material improvements are only the beginning of socialism. To be sure, they are a necessary beginning, without which little else can be accomplished. But socialism is not a system for making everyone rich; rather, it aims to create a true democracy of equals who focus both on providing the essentials of life for everyone and on improving the quality of human relations. In order to ensure the continuity of material security and to create the conditions for a humane society, all forms of domination and control must end: the domination of men over women, the rich over the rest, managers over workers, whites over blacks, adults over children, teachers over students, and so on. Socialism aims to eliminate all situations where people have power over others.

But equality of equals does not mean sameness. Some people will still like music, others walking, others painting, others writing poems, others fixing up their house, and so on. There are thousands of ways to be individuals within a community. But people should be unable to dominate others for material, prestigious, or psychic gains. If all of us are to be free, we cannot have a situation where "freedom" to some people means their domination of others. Nobody should be allowed to control and exploit other people. A person's "freedom" to make a million dollars is bought at the expense of exploiting many workers through low pay and domination of their labor.

### Age, Regional, and Work Equality

Socialism also aims to resolve other differences, dominant in capitalist societies: differences between city and country, between hand and brain work, between the old and the young. People in cities, those mostly working with their minds, and older people hold more power, prestige, and material possessions than do peasants, laborers, and young people. However, such conditions persist in socialist societies and need to be changed.

These changes do not mean people should become all alike. Obviously, in many areas a teacher knows more than a student, but a farmer also knows more than an outside expert, at least in some areas. But one person's ability to know or do something better than others should not mean his or her ability to control and dominate. It can mean teaching other people in a situation of equality of mutual respect and also learning from the other person. Nearly everyone knows something another person does not know, and teaching and learning can be mutual and reciprocal.

### Continuous Struggle

These goals may seem utopian. Socialism does not believe it is possible to reach a perfect society where people can rest without conflict and struggle. In fact, a fundamental socialist principle is the realization that the struggle for a socialist society is never-ending. Once people take over the state from capitalists, the struggle has just begun, and it must be continued for a long time. There will be periods when the struggle will be less intense, but people will always need to return to it.

People are not perfect. For example, regardless whether competition is innate, or whether it exists because it has been fostered for a long time, competition is rooted deeply in thought and value and must be struggled against. Old ways never die entirely, and they can reappear easily if people are not willing to keep fighting. Each society that has tried socialism shows again that socialism must be an act of struggle; people must win freedom themselves, not have it handed over.

### Popular Control

This struggle must always focus on people—all people—as the agents of change, not just a few experts. People's whole education—in and out of school—has fostered dependence on experts, on other people who claim to know what is best and how to attain it. Specifically, whether in the United States today or in a socialist society trying to uproot capitalist traditions, old people, women, students, workers, mental patients, and other groups know themselves what is best for them and are the ones to struggle to get it. Others may help, but they cannot be the ones leading the fight for liberation. This realization has spread in our society and there are now many self-help groups. This situation is not socialism, but it can be a sign in that direction.

*National Planning*

All institutions should ideally be controlled by the people within them. But a society cannot be a collection of unrelated groups and institutions. In order to make a decent society for all, national cooperation and planning are necessary. Community control and workers' control, as socialist goals, do not mean that each group will work for its own interests primarily. The object is cooperation with everyone to achieve results beneficial to all. For example, national planning means setting up a system of public transportation instead of private cars. Also, workers from different workplaces share new techniques and inventions. Finally, national planning means that all people, from all groups, actually participate in the creation of the national goals and plans.

According to socialism, private property should be abolished, and state communes and collective groups should control the means of production, not individuals. That tenet does not mean all property is owned collectively. There are three possible forms of property ownership in China (and most other socialist societies): (a) the private property of one's own possessions, such as clothing, bicycles, and furniture—also, many people own their own homes, and in the countryside families own garden plots of one-half acre each; (b) state property, owned and operated by the government—farms and factories may be owned this way; (c) communal and collective (most) property—most land is owned and operated by communes of 50,000 to 90,000 people, and they are largely self-sufficient. The means of production are controlled by the state or communes. It is in this sense that private property is abolished.

*Models of Socialist Societies*

Note that there are different models of socialist development. Many types exist in reality, of course, but all socialist societies have had to make some choices between two opposing tendencies, generally called the statist and democratic models. The statist model emphasizes the need to develop the economic conditions of society before there are struggles to do away with the state, create workers' control of workplaces, and create popular control of all institutions. Before there can be fully democratic institutions and before the need for powerful leaders and parties can vanish, the material conditions must advance and provide a comfortable life for all people. The democratic model, followed in this book, also stresses the importance of alleviating material deprivations and advancing economic conditions. But, in contrast to the statist model, this model sees profound dangers if power is not challenged from the very beginning; if, for example, workers do not begin to take direct control of the work process. Material progress must be accompanied by struggles to create democracy in all institutions, or new classes and ruling groups will arise (as they seem to have done in most places) (This issue is explored throughout the book, especially in Chapters 2, 3, 4, and 5).

*Dilemmas and Contradictions*

The rise of new ruling classes and the struggle for political democracy are continuing problems in socialist societies. As these problems are explored in later chapters, remember the following facts. In present socialist societies, there was no political democracy of any kind before the coming of socialism. Capitalist societies now have formal political democracy, but real political and economic democracy are problematic (see Chapter 3), and in most nonsocialist societies outside North America and Western Europe, even formal democracy does not exist. Economic inequalities have been minimized in socialist societies; whereas full economic and social equality are not imminent, the possibilities exist if people are willing to struggle.

The political process that will lead to socialism in capitalist societies is another fundamental dilemma. Up to now, socialism has been achieved only through armed struggle. Even when socialists have won elections (as in Zimbabwe in March 1980), these elections came about only after a long revolutionary war. Socialists won the election in Chile in 1970, but in 1973 the Chilean military, with assistance from the CIA, overthrew that government.

We cannot forget that the United States gained its independence only after a revolutionary war. (I am conscious of this fact as I write these words in the town library in Lexington, Massachusetts.)

## CONSERVATIVE AND LIBERAL PERSPECTIVES

The socialist perspective just discussed is probably new to most of you. Whether explicit or implicit, your present understanding of social problems is probably not socialist. Most of what you read and hear focuses on other explanations. This chapter concludes with a brief discussion of the political and social perspectives dominant in the United States. As you become aware of the conservative and liberal perspectives, the socialist perspective may be more understandable.

## Conservatism

The conservative perspective is the traditional view of capitalism, and of the kind of society a capitalist economy creates. First, there are certain values and assumptions about individuals and societies. Individualism is at the center of conservative ideology: in this view, each person should be primarily concerned with his or her interests; if all look out for themselves, then the interests of society as a whole also are satisfied.

Material possessions (materialism) are what individuals should strive to attain, for they are essential to a good life. These material possessions are to be obtained through competition, which is considered a basic human drive in all people. Private property and its protection at all costs are also basic, for they ensure the survival of individualism and of progress.

These conditions can arise and exist only in a free-market system of supply and demand, where people are free to produce what they want and find buyers for their product. If buyers do not exist, producers will go out of business, and they, or others, will produce what buyers want (demand). Through the operation of supply and demand all people's needs—as producers and consumers—are met free of government interference. Producers make goods because of the profit motive common to all people in a capitalist society.

This economic system coexists with a political system of minimal government interference. So long as people are left alone, with the government enforcing only economic contracts and some social laws through the legal system, then everyone's interests and needs will be met. Society will operate smoothly. (Summarized from Dolbeare and Dolbeare 1976, and other sources.)

Given these assumptions and values, conservatives tend to see social problems as caused by the interference with this economic and political system. For example, oil corporations and others have argued that the energy crisis resulted from government interference with the free-market system. Government regulations of prices, and laws meant to protect the environment that limit the places where drilling can take place, have reduced profits, thus reducing the capital companies have to search for more oil. If left alone, these companies say, they would satisfy the demand for oil through the free-market system, where if buyers are willing to pay the necessary price for producing goods, someone will provide them.

A related cause of social problems (say the conservatives) is people's tendency to have unrealistic expectations. Jacoby makes this point explicitly. He claims that even though poverty is being reduced, people's unrealistic expectations that it be totally eliminated, and soon, have created the problem. The problem is not poverty, but the raised expectations. Such utopian demands are encouraged, or created, by the mass media and dissatisfied intellectuals, who raise expectations, thus causing many social problems (Jacoby 1971).

A closely related conservative tendency is to see many conditions as natural and inevitable. Here, the problem is not the conditions themselves, but those protesting against them. This view is most obvious in the controversy about women's roles and place in society. A conservative position sees the problem in women protesting against their natural roles, not in any alleged oppression they suffer.

In short, conservatives see problems arising from government interference; or, they deny a problem exists; or, they see the problem in the protest against the condition, not in the condition itself; or, they see some conditions as inevitable and natural (such as sex roles and poverty).

Given the previous assumptions, the proposed solutions are obvious. These involve, first, removal of government interference with the free market system (of course, conservatives differ among themselves in what they consider as minimally acceptable government regulation of the free market and of society in general). In addition, it is necessary that people understand the nature of the free market and cease protesting against it. That is, people should be educated to understand that this is the best of all possible systems, and any "problems" will either go away in time or are unavoidable under any system (for example, some crime will always exist and the best thing to do is to lock the criminals up) (Wilson 1975).

*Liberalism*

Contemporary liberalism shares the basic values and assumptions of conservatism. It differs from conservatism in degrees and emphasis rather than in any fundamentally different values. Individualism, materialism, competition, the profit motive, and private property, all operating in a free market, are accepted as essential. Liberals differ from conservatives in seeing the need for some government intervention to curb abuses and help the victims of our system.

Liberals may disagree on the necessity of specific government programs, for example, the need for some government medical insurance to deal with the high cost of medical care. But in general they support government intervention for various ends: to help business, for example, through subsidies and other assistance—in this way, the economy functions better; to reduce the impact of some social problems (such as the inevitable unemployment under capitalism) and stabilize the system; and, generally, to promote harmony and the acceptance of capitalism.

Liberals see serious problems in society. The descriptions of these conditions often are vivid and moving (see the many works of Robert Coles, especially *Uprooted Children*). Liberals see the need for much reform, but the problems are seen as imperfections of a basically sound social system. Problems like racism, sexism, and pollution are not considered intrinsic and necessary to the system. Liberals attribute the problems to many causes, depending on the problem. Generally, causes of social problems are attributed to imperfect socialization, individual prejudices and faults, and not to any qualities of the system itself. For example, racism exists because individuals are taught to have biases against minorities, and education will remove the biases; pollution results from individual carelessness and greed and can be eliminated by some laws and education.

Liberalism's solutions follow logically. Government, groups, institutions, and individuals must work to perfect the system, but the system itself must be protected and its values (individualism, competition, and so on) must be perpetuated. Laws must be passed, for example, against race and sex discrimination; programs must be created to fight problems, such as the war on poverty; individuals must be educated to abandon biases and imperfections. All these changes and reforms, however, are to be sought within the system itself, through the political and legal processes now available. (Some specific liberal proposals are discussed in the book, and these generalizations will become clearer.)

Johnson summarizes well the differences between liberal solutions and the socialist solutions outlined above:

> As opposed to revolution, *reform* regards the foundations of the existing social order as essentially healthy. Reform's objective is to correct the flaws described as social problems, rather than to strike at the roots of the existing social order.... Reform raises the complications of "social surgery" in removing the unsound elements of social institutions without undermining the social order generally accepted by the members of the society (1973, p. 539).

## *Other Social Problems Texts*

If using some other social problems text in addition to this one, you will notice that it probably presents a liberal perspective. Most social problems texts propose liberal explanations as the causes of social problems, and, when they do discuss solutions, these texts espouse liberal reforms.

This is not to say these texts are all alike. Both the explanations and the suggested reforms vary, some being more serious critiques of American capitalism than others are. Neither liberal explanations nor their solutions, however, focus on the fundamental conditions of capitalist society. For example, all sorts of proposals are offered to humanize jobs, but they do not call for workers and a socialist state to take away the means of production from the corporations. Such texts recognize the problems of work but do not see them as inevitable under capitalism.

Two or three texts present a perspective similar to the one developed here. A few texts, while liberal, present a very thorough critique of life under capitalism, but they do not come to the conclusion that social problems are inherent in capitalist society. And at least one text takes a somewhat conservative stance (Nettler 1976). For example, Nettler does not agree with the conclusion of most texts that workers are alienated from their jobs.

In short, most social problems texts present some version of the liberal perspective.

# CONCLUSION

You may have noticed that I have not given a formal definition of "social problem." The search for such a definition has led to a long debate among sociologists and others, which will be referred to briefly here.

There seem to be two general perspectives on what makes a social problem. Some people argue that a social problem exists when society, a large group, or a powerful minority defines and perceives some condition as a problem and sets out to remedy it. Social conditions are not problems when no one defines them as problems.

Other sociologists argue that there should be some objective criteria in defining social problems. Social conditions can be damaging even if people are not aware of them as problems. This does not mean that people are totally ignorant of these harmful conditions (for example, unhappiness at work), rather, that they have not yet defined them as conditions that could and should be changed.

There is merit to both arguments, of course. Obviously, it is not until a group begins to work toward remedying a condition that they and other people become aware of a problem. It is another matter, however, to argue that a social condition presents no problem until some group begins to protest against it. Surely, for example, women did suffer and were oppressed in the 1950s and 1960s when there was no women's movement. The women's movement and its struggles did show the pervasiveness of sexism, but sexism existed before the women's movement.

The objective suffering of people *is* a problem. Two issues arise in making that statement: First, who decides what is an "objective" condition of suffering? Second, why do people who are suffering not define their condition as a problem that needs to be changed? I do not think that sociologists, or any other experts, can tell what conditions are objectively harmful. They can contribute to that debate, of course. But ultimately, it should be clear that it is the people living under some social condition who can tell whether they are suffering. Millions of workers were alienated from their jobs in the 1950s even before many other people became aware of alienation in the 1970s.

But why did those workers in the 1950s not protest against what their work did to them? That question leads to another social problem. It points to institutions that socialize people to accept certain conditions as unalterable facts of human existence. People may, in essence, be taught that work is boring by its very nature and may see no alternatives (see Chapter 5 for discussion of work that is not alienating).

Such manipulation of consciousness and imagination is inherent to capitalist society. This book hopes to expand the reader's awareness that life could be different and that people need not just accept social conditions.

I have come to certain conclusions about social problems through various sources: the struggles of minorities and women, the protest against the war in Vietnam, personal observation, participation in protest movements, and reading. This understanding is still growing, changing, and groping for solutions. This book represents my present view of the possibilities in American society and its relation to the rest of the world. I invite you to read it critically, debate it, and use it to help you understand your life, community, nation, and the world.

# 2

# *Classes and Inequality*

## THE REALITY OF CLASSES

In a biography of David Rockefeller, we read, "Anything that offended the eyes of the Rockefellers was removed. . . . A subbasement was constructed so that garbage trucks could enter a tunnel to pick up refuse without being seen" (Hoffman 1971, p. 96).

Ray Murdock, a garbage man, talks about his work: "When it's cold out the cans feel heavier and harder; when it's hot the stench penetrates the lungs and nostrils, and stays there. . . . I been working around garbage all my life and it still makes me puke. If I have too much of it on a hot day, with the bouncing in the truck, I puke my guts out sure as hell by noon-time" (Lasson 1971, pp. 17, 22).

In many cities of the world, poor people look through other people's garbage for things they can eat and use (de Jesus 1962).

Finally, "in Calcutta, India, . . . carts go through the streets every morning and collect the dead bodies that have accumulated from the night before" (Chambliss and Ryther 1975, p. 6).

These quotes offer a glimpse of social classes in modern societies. From banishing garbage from one's sight, to disposing of the garbage of others, to eating garbage to survive, to (the final degradation) becoming garbage one's self, these quotes show the profound differences that social classes create.

Issues of life and death are another reality of class societies, as the poor and working classes have always known. Working-class Americans resented antiwar demonstrations during the Vietnam War less because they supported the war than because the demonstrators were college students not in the armed forces, while working-class sons were dying in Vietnam (Levison 1974). Fallows reports that the 1970 graduates from Harvard did very well in avoiding the war. Six hundred of his classmates (out of 1,200) replied to a survey: only 56 had served in the armed forces, most far from the battle scenes. By 1974 most were in successful careers. Working-class men who fought in Vietnam suffered tremendously. Many died, more were wounded, many deserted and continue to suffer from prejudice, discrimination, and other problems (Fallows 1975, p. 8). As Ras Bryant said, "it's a rich man's war, and the poor people fight it" (Gitlin and Hollander 1970, p. 39).

These dramatic examples open the chapter because it is important to understand that classes are not mere sociological categories; they are not only statistics on incomes and jobs; they are not merely labeling devices. They are all these things and more, of course. But above all, classes refer to the differences in how we lead our lives; to the opulence of a few made possible by the insecurity, suffering, and struggle of many others; to much that people experience about themselves. In short, classes are not things that can be measured and counted. They are relationships among groups of people whose interests and experiences differ from each other (Thompson 1964, pp. 9–11).

## The Life of the Rich

The homes where rich people live are beyond the experience of most of us. For example, a whole-page ad in the *New York Times* (March 21, 1973), announced in bold letters: "If you can afford it, you should seriously consider purchasing a cooperative apartment at 733 Park Avenue now. Here's why." The features, as headlined: only one apartment to a floor; the unexpected luxuries ("five separate heating and cooling systems," "a buzzer for the maid," and so on); total security; and many others. The price started with the second floor at $190,000 "present total cash payment," $1,471 "estimated *monthly* maintenance" (italics added), and "estimated annual income tax deductions of $9,648; to figures for the twenty-seventh floor of $228,000, $1,648, and $10,751.

A girl described her family's three homes as "comfortable, comfortable places." They were "an enormous duplex apartment in Chicago, a ski lodge in Aspen, and a lovely old New England clapboard home by the ocean toward the end of Cape Cod" (Coles 1977, p. 53).

In a recent series of eight articles (April 16–23, 1978) the *Boston Globe* described ten suburban towns where the rich and near-rich of greater Boston live. In addition to describing the spacious homes, open spaces, and other amenities, the stories showed the determination of most town residents to protect these amenities by keeping out middle- and low-income families. Zoning regulations that prohibit apartment construction and require minimums of two or more acres of land per house are the most common means of keeping the character of a town unchanged.

*The Working People*

Insecurity, unemployment, and starvation did not end with the Depression of the 1930s. The recession of the mid-1970s has left its scars. Tony Longo saw "grown men that been working at the same job 15 years cry in the unemployment office. Because they are afraid of losing their house, or their marriage is breaking up" (Longo and Raines 1978, p. 92).

In late 1975, Alfred Prato, laid off from his job as a laborer in the New York City Parks Department, lived in fear of social and psychic disintegration. After twenty unsuccessful job interviews, he was afraid he might never get another job. "He worries constantly. 'It's with you 24 hours a day,' he said. 'When I got laid off, I weighed 172 pounds. Now I weigh 157.'... Five months of job hunting left Mr. Prato with nervous trembling in his fingers and the beginnings of a facial tic. He feels that he might disintegrate, were it not for his wife" (*New York Times,* November 3, 1975; reprinted in Edwards et al. 1978, p. 27).

The marginal existence of working people is obvious in many ways. Terkel was told of people who, during the Depression, eliminated visits to the dentist when they lost their money (1970, p. 502). But it is no different today. In the late 1960s, when Medicaid was instituted in New York, thousands of people eligible for assistance (those barely above poverty) went to dentists to fix teeth long left without care, for many on working-class incomes simply cannot afford dental care.

Rubin's *World of Pain: Life in the Working Class Family* (1976) describes working-class families in the San Francisco area in the early 1970s. The book is based on extensive interviews with the wives and husbands of fifty working-class families and, for comparison, interviews of twenty-five professional couples. Although her portrait of working-class life may be somewhat too dark, Rubin shows how working-class people's lives are pervaded with insecurity, and self-images are low, since their work and education, and the mass media demean them. For many, television becomes an escape from the degradations they suffer. One man told Rubin: "I'm watching, that's all. I'm not thinking about things or anything like that. I sit down and I'm just watching. That's what I do most nights. I come home and die in front of the TV" (p. 191).

The inflation and economic troubles of the late 1970s and early 1980s have made for more hardships for working people. They are not poor by government standards, but their incomes, between $8,000 and $20,000, often do not suffice for the necessities. For example, a New Hampshire couple made $14,000 in 1979, with both spouses working. It cost them $2,000 for a babysitter, $6,000 for food, rent, and car loan payments, and $3,000 for medical bills, utilities, diapers, and car maintenance. After deductions for taxes and Social Security, their take-home pay did not cover all these expenses. They could not pay for the fuel they needed, and they did not qualify for assistance from the fuel aid programs set up in 1979 by the state and federal governments; their income exceeded the eligibility level by $5,000 (Smith 1979).

This New Hampshire family typifies the plight of many working Americans.

## The Poor

Most poor people work—they work at jobs paying minimum wage where the work is dangerous, dirty, and tiring. John Dawson tells in graphic detail of the exploitation of temporary day-workers. Jobs provide no uniforms, or they injure you and the company avoids responsibility, or you are lied to about the job before you get it, and so on. At one job he had loading freight in a warehouse, "I worked there when it's thirty-one below zero on that T-[trailer]-section, where that wind, buddy, it was cuttin'" (quoted in Gitlin and Hollander 1970, p. 74).

John Dawson left the poverty of Appalachia for a job in Chicago. Others, who choose to stay in their communities, suffer at the hands of the coal companies (see Chapter 7). Caudill tells the story of a forty-five-year-old man, jobless and with his land ruined by the coal company, taken to court for not sending his kids to school. He said he couldn't send them because he couldn't afford shoes for them. He could not find a job anywhere. "If you think puttin' me in jail will help my young'uns any, then go ahead and do it and I'll be glad of it" (1963, pp. 359-61).

Poverty leaves permanent and powerful memories. Peggy Terry remembers "one time, the only thing to eat in the house was mustard. My sister and I put so much mustard on biscuits that we got sick. And we can't stand mustard to this day" (Terkel 1970, p. 64). Fried noodles, sardines, and other foods have had similar effects on other survivors of the Depression.

The recession of the mid-1970s had different effects on people's eating and nutrition. In such circumstances, a poor family cannot afford vegetables, fruits, or desserts; eats more starches than before; and eats hardly any meat. A middle-income family uses margarine rather than butter, eats more hamburger and less steak, and feeds their pet the cheapest pet food rather than a high-protein blend. A higher-income family is reported to have also made sacrifices: they fired their French cook and gave up their "special butcher" (Plaste, Dullea, and Taylor 1974).

Finally, the sweatshops still existed in the late 1970s. The U.S. Department of Labor investigated garment factories, hotels, restaurants, and other businesses, in New York City and elsewhere, that paid as little as $1.50 an hour (when the minimum wage was $2.90). Some of the workers were illegal aliens and felt they could not afford to complain to the authorities; the others, for various reasons, also had to work in these sweatshops (DeCormis 1979, p. 2).

## The Middle Classes

Few of you are likely to be among the very rich or among the poor; some of you probably belong to the working class, along with the majority of other Americans. But it is likely that most of you belong to what sociologists call the upper-middle and the middle classes. So, you may ask, how am I affected by living under capitalism? Beyond any sorrow felt for the plight of working-class and poor Americans, how can someone say that I suffer?

It must be admitted that many of you do not suffer in the obvious ways most Americans do. You and your family probably pay all bills, have all necessities and many luxuries, go out to dinner, live in a fairly large home, and do not experience any material deprivation. The inflation of the 1970s may have forced some of you to forgo some amenities you took for granted: perhaps you take less expensive vacations, or you eat less expensive cuts of meat.

Nevertheless, I think most people reading this book do suffer. It is true that most of the sociology literature is on the problems of the poor, the minorities, and the working class. However, it portrays a false image of capitalist society. Later chapters explore in some detail the ways in which most people are victimized by living under capitalism. Here are some brief examples.

In its search for higher profits, capitalism has poisoned the air, the earth, and the waters. Increasingly, people find that they get sick and often die from chemicals released in the environment. Up to 90 percent of the cases of cancer are estimated to be caused by environmental conditions; pollution affects everyone. Everyday, it seems, we discover new threats to our health and well-being—asbestos in factories and schools, drinking waters poisoned by chemicals dumped in the ground, and so on (see Chapters 10 and 11 for details).

As the sense and reality of community diminish, people live more isolated and fragmented lives. This isolation is more pervasive for middle-class Americans, for in the search for professional and managerial jobs they move more often than do working-class Americans, some of whom still live in real communities (see Chapter 7).

Capitalism, in its search for greater control of workers and workplaces, is now destroying the autonomy and skills of many jobs considered "white collar." Alienation at work is not limited to the factory. Many offices and professional jobs increasingly resemble factories, and many of these jobs will become obsolete.

In more or less obvious ways, capitalism injures everyone, not only by allowing economic inequities but by reducing the quality of life (through alienating work, a poisoned environment, diminished community life, schools that do not liberate the mind, impersonal medical care, and so on). The socialist critique of capitalism focuses on material inequalities and on capitalism's effects on the quality of life, on the way people relate to each other as human beings. In fact, it may be the strain of people's efforts to maintain a "high-class" standing in a competitive capitalist system that has the worst effects on human relationships. Consider the family described by this twenty-year-old woman in an essay for a midwest-college sociology class:

> The only way I can figure out how to discuss the influence of class on our lives is to discuss my mother and her outlook on classes, and how it has effected us (her kids) and the people around her.
>
> My mother, who is a writer for [a big city newspaper], is always, or always seems to be, acutely aware of the three social classes. She is constantly trying to keep up her reputation as being a "high class" woman and is always throwing names around of important people as if they were her best friends. You can also detect an almost artificial snobbish tone in her voice when she's talking to people that she is trying to impress. I guess she was always brought up trying to get to the top, and according to her, when you have a job or career, that's the most important thing that you'd want to do.
>
> As a result of these beliefs and the way that she feels about the job and people above her, she is *always* worrying especially about her kids and if they are going to get an important job that will impress her friends and other people, plus make them enough money to be comfortable and happy in the future.
>
> Due to always worrying and being tense, she has developed a nervous heart condition and has become a chronic workaholic. Being a workaholic she therefore doesn't know the first thing on how to relax. At dinner she talks about work or expresses her worries on how [we] . . . will turn out to be nothing but social and business failures. After dinner, during her free time, she's always finding work that doesn't need to be done and goes ahead and proceeds to take on a major operation that would ordinarily take two days in two hours, or vice versa.
>
> She is always exhausted and about once a year or so she usually ends up in the hospital. Needless to say she probably wouldn't end up in the hospital if she didn't work and worry so hard. But since she does it makes it pretty easy to believe that these illnesses that pop up are partly psychosomatic and her system's way to telling (almost forcing) her to take a rest.
>
> Her rewards from all this self-inflicted torture have been a big house [in a wealthy suburb] (another thing she always works in a conversation to impress

people), enough money to buy the things that she and her family both need and want and with more to spare. I suppose but don't really know that she has gotten the prestige and respect that she has always strive[n] for in the newspaper, but is still constantly striving for more and there is probably always that fear lurking in the back of her mind that everything she's worked for is going to be taken away or she is going to lose it somehow.

Despite all of these material things that she has gotten and all the prestige that she has won, she still isn't that happy. Even though she loves her kids and husband and knows that they love her, she can't seem to be contented with who they are (my father excluded) instead of what they will be. Therefore, even when she retires she'll still be worrying about us as much as she did when she was working, giving her no relief [for] all her worries. She'll also have no idea how to spend her spare time and won't be able to enjoy leisure time activities or just plain old sitting around without worrying about something. Which she has already proven on her vacations when she works harder than she does at work.

So even though she's happy in a materialistic sense she's not as happy as she could be in a number of other ways.

As to how her outlook on the social classes has influenced her kids, it's harder to write about since I am one of her kids. But I guess after all four of us have seen her practically work herself into the grave, we all tend to have an almost reverse attitude on how we look at social classes. Much to my mother's distress all of us refuse to play up to a higher class or treat a lower class any different than we'd treat each other.

Sometimes it even gets to the point that when someone asks us what we're doing now there is always that villainous impulse to reply that [we] have been working in a whorehouse and as of yet have not been seeking any other employment.

Most of the time I'd say that we as her kids having had the social class bull shoved down our throats all our lives have decided pretty much to ignore it (or try to ignore it; if that's not possible you usually end up making some socially unacceptable wisecrack about it). We all have jobs doing what we want to do and not what other people want us to do (much to the complaints of my mother saying we aren't going to get anywhere). And we pretty much have acquired a whole different set of values.

## *A Moral Perspective*

The foundation of the socialist critique of capitalism is a moral outrage that such conditions exist. It stems from the realization that the luxury and opulence of a few are gained at the expense of most of us. It comes from the realization that for most people life is insecure and presents a constant threat of deprivation. It also arises from an awareness that not only are the necessities of life either barely available or absent for so many, but also there is social and spiritual suffering and degradation for most of us. Socialism is based on the feeling and reality of powerlessness most people experience.

But the socialist critique goes beyond the realizations of inequality to assert that classes are not eternal and inevitable, that a better world can exist. At the end of the chapter, I will discuss the possibilities for a classless society.

## HOW MANY CLASSES ARE THERE?

The topic of social classes has been a central sociological issue. Sociologists, other social scientists, novelists, and most everyone else have thought about the criteria for and number of classes. Without pretending to summarize all that research and thinking, I do hope to clarify these issues by stating clearly a socialist perspective on classes, and coming to a tentative conclusion on the number of classes in the United States.

### *Criteria*

Sociologists have used hundreds of criteria to define classes and to assign people to one of these classes. Income and wealth, type of occupation, education, residence, prestige (status), power, and life-style have been the most prominent ones. A basic socialist critique of most sociological writing on classes is that it focuses too much on prestige, life-styles, and subjective judgments, rather than on the power and control (or lack of them) a class has over the major decisions and institutions of a society. The differences will become clear if we examine some specific lists of classes from the two perspectives.

### *Traditional Sociological Lists*

W. Lloyd Warner and his associates are among the most well-known sociologists of class. Beginning with their study of Yankee City (Newburyport, Massachusetts), they have studied classes in many contexts. In a very clear statement of their perspective, they write:

> Economic factors are significant and important in determining the class position of any family or person, influencing the kind of behavior we find in any class, and contributing their share to the present form of our status system. But, while significant and necessary, the economic factors are not sufficient to predict where a particular family or individual will be or to explain completely the phenomena of social position. Money must be translated into socially approved behavior and possessions, and they in turn must be translated into intimate participation with, and acceptance by, members of a superior class (Warner et al. 1960, p. 11).

Warner et al. claim that most communities have six classes: upper-upper (old family), lower-upper (new families joining the upper class), upper-middle, lower-middle, upper-lower, and lower-lower. In the study of Yankee City, the percentages of each class were: 1.4, 1.6, 10, 28, 34, and 25. What seem to be the central criteria, besides money, are manners, life-style, and reputation. Descending the class scale, money, prestigious jobs, size and location of homes, and leisure activities are given less weight by sociologists and their town informants. Thus, the lower-lower class are judged to be "lazy, shiftless, and won't work," and "are sometimes said to 'live like animals.'" The lower-middle class, the "top of the Common Man level, is composed of clerks and other white-collar workers, small tradesmen, and a fraction of skilled workers" (Warner et al. 1960, pp. 13–14).

In a recent text, Baldridge (1975), states that "in general, studies have shown that the public defines social classes by three major factors: (1) income and wealth, (2) educational levels, and (3) occupation" (p. 173). He then describes five classes. The upper class is "composed of the community's business and professional leaders, business executives in the major companies," lawyers, professors, doctors, accountants, and others (p. 175). Clearly, this is a confused list. How can the Rockefellers and other powerful capitalists belong to the same class as most professors or lawyers? There is little, if anything (except for years in school), that places me in the same class as David Rockefeller. This example illustrates well the confusion of most sociologists who focus on peripheral criteria instead of the objective realities of class.

The next class discussed is the "upper-middle class," composed of "people in minor managerial positions and in the lesser ranking professions, such as public school teaching and social work" (p. 178). The "middle class" is composed of those who make roughly the median income and who work in sales, offices, and factories (foremen and highly skilled workers) (p. 178). "The working class" is composed mostly of factory workers who make under the median income. Finally, the "lower class" is populated by the unskilled laborers, the unemployed, and those on welfare (p. 179).

This is a rather typical breakdown of classes. Most sociology texts give the same or a similar list. Together with these lists there appears a long series of generalizations about the life-styles of the different classes. Among the issues discussed are: socialization—the lower classes are said to be more rigid and strict with their children; leisure activities—the higher classes partake of higher refinement, like ballet and museums; and the lower classes watch television and play or watch sports; thought patterns—the lower classes are said to be less capable of abstraction than are the higher: their thinking is too "concrete;" and values—by claiming that the lower classes do not value work and success as much as the higher classes do, sociologists have dressed in academic garb an old prejudice about the laziness of the poor.

Levison claims that middle-class people simply have little or no contact with the working-class majority. "Contact is limited to a quick glance at a knot of construction workers sitting on a sidewalk eating lunch," or with various service people (Levison 1974, p. 43). The day before these words were written, I was with five other professionals (mostly electronic engineers) clearing rocks from the grounds of our childrens' nursery school. As two of us worked hard to dig a rock out, the three watching commented that this was a typical construction scene—two working, three watching. First, it did not occur to them that the two of us were bone tired from doing this kind of work for an hour, and that much physical labor is exhausting and cannot be done continuously. Secondly, their response was typical of the prejudices many professionals hold against working people. Most sociologists are not exempt from the prejudices of their class; these prejudices show up in comments on the working class. Many sociologists confuse differences in life-styles with the ranking of one life-style as better than another.

Hodges (reprinted in Popenoe 1974) collects most sociological prejudices and stereotypes in a few pages. The upper-lower class is seen as "authoritarian, anomic, misanthropic" (p. 275), whereas the upper-middle class is "flexible, trusting, democratic, tolerant, and non-dogmatic" (p. 277). In addition, they are "plainly more sophisticated and more discriminating" than the lower classes. They are the best devotees of the "fine" arts—opera, ballet, symphony orchestras, and so on (p. 278). What objective criteria makes ballet more sophisticated and discriminating than baseball? (A student once commented wryly that many who go to the ballet do so because they *think* it is the "cultured" thing to do, not because they enjoy it.) The class bias of sociologists (and others) reveals itself in these observations on the life-styles of different classes.

## *Marxist Lists*

In his time, Karl Marx argued that society was moving towards, and would soon arrive at, a division of two classes: bourgeoisie and proletariat (which have been variously called upper-class, rich, or ruling class; and workers, masses, or other names). Marx acknowledged the existence of the other classes—such as the petit bourgeoisie (mostly small businessmen) and the lumpen-proletariat (people we call poor or lower class), but he concluded that the only two classes that determined the course of society were the bourgeoisie and the proletariat—these two were in continuous conflict for control of the state and the economy.

Marxists and non-Marxists have debated this division ever since. Whereas most people calling themselves Marxists have written about new classes arising in the last century, it is probably true that for most of them the great division remains between the ruling class and the working class (the names used here from now on). Simply stated, the direction of society is controlled by the ruling class (about 1 percent of the population) and those they hire to work for them; that control comes at the expense of the vast majority of the rest of us. Those under the ruling class hardly lead similar lives; the differences between them are indeed real. A laborer making $6,000 a year is hardly in the same category as a college professor, an engineer, or a social worker. Their levels of comfort and security are indeed different. But from this perspective they also share some similarities: they are fairly powerless in relation to the dominance and control of the ruling class. They have little control over the major divisions and institutions of our society, as will be seen in Chapter 3.

Robert and Helen Lynd, in their studies of Middletown (Muncie, Indiana), also talked about two classes: the business and the working class. They admitted the oversimplification of this two-class division, but argued, as did Marx, that the essential division remains between these two classes (Lynd and Lynd 1929; 1937).

More recent Marxist descriptions are more elaborate. Here are three other writers' lists of classes, followed by the author's preferred way to describe the current situation.

Paul Sweezy begins his discussion of classes with a number of observations. The *family*, not the individual, is seen as the basic unit of class membership. People all begin life in the class of their parents. This reality is reflected further in the fact that most people marry within their class. Thus, one may argue that "a social class is made up of freely intermarrying families." And it is through families that property is passed on. A basic distinction between the upper class and the rest is the possession of property (today, possession of income-producing stock in major corporations and other income-producing property) (1951, p. 359).

After these preliminary observations, Sweezy discusses five classes. "The two decisive classes" are the owners of the means of production (those who control the stocks in major corporations)—the "capitalists' class"; and those who work the means of production whose labor the capitalists exploit—"the working class." However, other classes exist. There is the "lower-middle class"—who "stand somewhere between the capitalists and the workers and cannot easily be classified with either; government and business bureaucrats, professionals, teachers, journalists, advertising men, and so on." Finally, there are the "declassed" people—"bums, gamblers, thugs, prostitutes, and the like" (p. 361).

Sweezy concludes with two important comments. Social classes are not identical with economic classes (characterized by income, wealth, property, and occupation categories and differences). Although economic factors are decisive, they are not the only ones. Other considerations (e.g., lifestyles) are also important. In general, there is a ruling class of capitalists at the top, a working class at the bottom, and various groups in between who aspire to move to the top and are anxious to avoid falling to the bottom (pp. 361–363).

Two more recent discussions of classes are mostly elaborations of what Sweezy wrote. Barbara and John Ehrenreich describe four classes and their percentages: the ruling class—1 to 2 percent, the "professional-managerial class" (discussed below)—20 to 25 percent, the old middle class ("self-employed professionals, small tradespeople, independent farmers")—8 to 10 percent, and the working class ("craftsmen, operatives, laborers, salesworkers, clerical workers, service workers, non-college-educated technical workers")—65 to 70 percent (1977, p. 15).

The main point of the Ehrenreichs' paper is to show that in its evolution over the last hundred years, capitalism has created a new class, "the professional-managerial class" (PMC). This class includes "teachers, social workers, psychologists, entertainers, writers of advertising copy and TV scripts . . . middle-level administrators and managers, engineers, and other technical workers. . . . " The function of this class is "the reproduction of capitalist culture and capitalist class relations." People in the new class are members neither of the ruling class nor of the working class, but help to perpetuate capitalist institutions. Some people manage the workers of the corporations controlled by the ruling class; others offer some temporary comfort to the victims of capitalism (psychologists and social workers); others perpetuate capitalist beliefs (writers). A few people make it into the ruling class; most simply work for that class (1977, pp. 13–14).

Judah Hill provides another variation of the Marxist breakdown of classes. He calls the ruling class the "bourgeois class," composed of two sectors, monopoly and lieutenant. The difference between the two sectors is one of degree, the monopoly sector holding more power and wealth; the "petit-bourgeois class," consisting of the business, managerial, and professional sectors; the "proletariat," in which there are semiprofessional, office, service, and production workers, poor older people, and excluded sectors (mostly the unemployed); the "small-farmer class," with freeholder and tenant sectors (1975, p. 2).

Most Marxists think that the ruling class and the working class are the two main classes in capitalist societies. Other classes exist (such as professionals and the poor), but they function in relation to the first two classes.

## Ruling-Class Control and Working-Class Majority

But it is unimportant (probably even harmful) to have any definitive list of classes. Rather, it is important that we be clear about the following traits of this society (you can use these as you think best):

1. It is clear that there is a small percent of Americans who control the society. It may be ½ percent, 1 percent, or more. Chapter 3 will substantiate this claim.

2. It is equally clear that there are some poor people in the society (poor by anyone's standard)—those people who are chronically unemployed, work at the minimum wage, or are on welfare. For example, in 1977, 16.5 percent of Americans reported family incomes of under $7,000. They certainly are poor. What they do, how they feel, what others think of them are not helped by their low income. Another 18.1 percent made between $7,000 and $11,000—not far from poverty (*Statistical Abstract* 1979, p. 449). They also suffer from accusations that their poverty is their fault, that they waste their money, and so on. But occasionally a few facts arise (though they do not change many minds), showing the poor in a different light. Carol Foreman of the U.S. Department of Agriculture provided government studies showing that poor people spent a smaller percent of their income on alcohol, and were better food shoppers, than the middle class. A 1965 study showed "families with annual incomes under $3,000 got an average of 99 grams of protein for each food dollar spent. Families with incomes of more than $10,000 got 72 grams of protein per food dollar" (United Press International 1977).

3. There are self-employed people (outside the ruling class) who vary tremendously. Some own businesses that provide a comfortable income ($100,000 and up); others probably make less than many workers. There are owners of marginal businesses (small grocery stores, diners, candy stores, and so on). Some self-employed people associate and identify with people from the working class; others aspire to enlarge their businesses and make a comfortable living. Some make it; most exist on hope. It is the perpetual dream of many Americans to own their own businesses, but the reality of corporate America is harsh: over 80 percent of new businesses fail (see Chapter 5). Those who succeed often do so at great cost to themselves and their families.

4. There is another distinct group of Americans, usually labeled the "new middle class," sometimes the "new working class," and labeled the "professional-managerial class" by the Ehrenreichs. These are the lawyers, doctors, psychiatrists, psychologists, social workers, engineers, managers, technicians of all kinds, and professors and teachers. The author agrees with Sweezy and the Ehrenreichs that these people are a growing group in the society, made necessary by the increasing need of capitalism to control the society by other means than force. Not only objectively, but subjectively too, the identity and class membership of this group are unclear. One example may clarify. Teachers on all levels (especially in colleges and universities) have long resisted forming and joining unions. This resistance lay clearly in their unwillingness to identify with the working class—unions are working-class institutions. Probably not many ever believed they belong to the ruling (upper) class. The fact that over the last fifteen to twenty years teachers have formed and joined unions (especially in larger cities) may signify that status and prestige symbols no longer suffice to mask low incomes and powerlessness.

At any rate, this group is diverse and not easily classifiable. Even the daily experiences of people in the same profession vary: some people teach at Harvard and advise presidents, while others teach at community colleges, enjoying little money and prestige; some nurses are married to doctors or are high administrators, while others perform the unpleasant task of emptying bedpans (Ehrenreich and Ehrenreich 1977, p. 14).

The last two groups (the self-employed and the new middle class) exemplify best Sweezy's comment that between the capitalists and the working class fall those avoiding the bottom and striving for the top.

5. Then there is the rest—the vast majority. Whatever label is used, the reality remains the same. The money made provides for food and shelter at a minimal level, and for some other necessities. But there are no luxuries and in addition, people are increasingly losing control over their jobs (see Chapter 5). The following income figures show that, even by government statistics, most people now are working class.

Annually, the U.S. Department of Labor publishes three family budgets for a hypothetical family of four: a father of thirty-eight, a wife who is not working outside the home, a boy of thirteen, and a girl of eight—thus, no college expenses yet. These budgets are national averages, higher in some localities and lower in others (see Table 2.1). For fall 1978, the "lower" budget was $11,546, the "intermediate" $18,622, and the "higher" $27,420. The lower may be seen as the very minimum level for what sociologists consider the working-class life-style; the intermediate as the minimum for middle-class life; and the higher as the bare beginnings of a comfortable life. Family incomes seen in Table 2.2 show that for 1977 (the last year for which there are figures) over half the families did not make the intermediate budget, which is the bare beginning of middle-class life. Adding about 10 percent to the 1977 median income of $16,009 in order to allow for inflation, the median family income for 1978 was about $17,500, over $1,000 below the intermediate budget of $18,622. Of families on higher budgets, where some comforts are affordable, about 80 percent of those families did not reach the middle-class life-style. In 1978, the $27,420 higher-budget figure was 8.8 percent above the 1977 one. Adding 8.8 percent to the $25,000, which only 22.4 percent of families reached in 1977, yields $27,200; thus, equal to the higher budget, which seems to allow for a comfortable but not affluent lifestyle.

The living standards of most Americans have remained unchanged since 1967, and actually have declined since the early 1970s. In 1967, average weekly take-home pay was $90.86. In February 1980, in 1967 dollars (what a dollar could buy in 1979 compared to 1967), average take-home pay was $84.60 ($200.17 in 1980 dollars) (*Dollars and Sense*, May–June 1980, p. 10). But in 1976, the "average family had $790 less in real purchasing power than in 1973" (Raines, quoted in Longo and Raines 1978, p. 88; for inflation in the 1970s, see the entire issue of *Dollars and Sense,* October 1979).

**TABLE 2.1** Annual Costs of Budgets for a Four-Person Family, Autumn 1978

|  | Lower | Intermediate | Higher |
|---|---|---|---|
| Urban U.S. average | $11,546 | $18,622 | $27,420 |
| Boston | 12,501 | 22,117 | 33,596 |
| New York | 12,063 | 21,587 | 34,252 |
| Chicago | 11,829 | 18,794 | 27,169 |
| St. Louis | 11,150 | 17,897 | 25,847 |
| Atlanta | 10,495 | 16,897 | 24,666 |
| Houston | 10,906 | 17,114 | 24,787 |
| Los Angeles | 12,193 | 17,722 | 26,525 |
| Seattle | 12,506 | 18,671 | 26,567 |

*Source:* U.S. Department of Labor 1979a.

**TABLE 2.2** Families by Total Money Income, 1977

| Family income | Percent of families |
|---|---|
| Under $3,000 | 3.6 |
| $3,000–4,999 | 5.7 |
| $5,000–6,999 | 7.2 |
| $7,000–9,999 | 10.9 |
| $10,000–11,999 | 7.2 |
| $12,000–14,999 | 11.3 |
| $15,000–24,999 | 31.7 |
| $25,000 and over | 22.4 |
| Median income—$16,009 | |

*Source:* U.S. Bureau of the Census 1978, p. 32; and *Statistical Abstract* 1979, p. 449.

These figures on income, and the increasing loss of skill and control most people experience on their jobs (see Chapter 5), show that most Americans are not leading an affluent, white-collar life. Some suffer physical and material deprivation, and their suffering is not to be minimized. For most people, however, the problems are a constant struggle to make ends meet, a sense of insecurity over the possible loss of income or job, indebtedness, a job one hates, and so on.

Two points should be stressed. (1) Classes refer to human relations—to the way some people relate to others, as subordinates or bosses, as employers or employees, as possessors of prestige, as rich or poor, as powerful or powerless. Classes are not abstract entities; they influence most of our daily experiences. And (2) Classes also change over time. The rise of the "new middle class" has already been referred to. Other important changes include the disappearance of small farmers, independent craftspeople, and the self-employed people.

Equally important changes are the economic necessity for wives to work, the increasing use of part-time workers in many businesses (thus lowering wages), and the decrease in real income. All these factors change human relations, the way people live and feel. Undoubtedly, more changes will occur. The constants will be the attempt by the ruling class to direct these changes so that they will continue to hold power and the efforts by working people to resist ruling-class control.

## THE PERSONAL COSTS OF CLASSES

In the following chapters I will show how our communities, our health, and our work are shaped by capitalism and the ruling class. Here I want to discuss something more personal: how our self-images, self-confidence or lack of it, and perceptions of other classes vary according to our class. This is the ultimate effect and destructiveness of life in a class society. I do not want to say, however, that all meaning in life is lost under capitalism. Only that *much* is lost—and it need not be. And what meaning we do create is gained through greater cost than need be.

Consider the children of poor Americans. Coles portrays the harsh life of the children of migrant workers; he speaks of their lives as "extraordinarily cruel" because of the constant moves, the demanding work done by parents and children, the hardships of poverty incomes, and, above all, "the need always to gird oneself for the next slur, the next rebuke, the next reminder that one is different and distinctly unwanted . . . (1970, p. 52). These children's parents face the impossible task of socializing them to accept these sufferings and degradations, and since they have no good explanation, they often get angry at their children for asking "why, why, why." In time, by age five or six, the children have learned the harsh facts, and they have internalized them, as seen in the blurry, indistinct self-portraits they draw, compared to the portraits they draw of children from other classes and races (Coles 1970).

Memories of poverty live on, even in the unconscious. Longo says: "I remember being hungry when I was a kid, putting cardboard in my shoes, going to school with cardboard in my shoes. And people laughing at me. Always wearing the same clothes, people would always be laughing. That ain't going to happen to my kids. (Raines: did that hurt you?) It still freaks me out. It's right there" (Longo and Raines 1978, p. 92).

Poor people also suffer as adults. Caudill reports from the Appalachians that many older workers who could not find jobs and had nothing to survive on, had to "manufacture" a disability (and find a doctor to certify it) so they could collect the meager welfare to avoid starvation. Resorting to such lies did not allow these people to retain their dignity. Others too thought less of them. An unemployed forty-five-year-old man not only feels useless, but he also "senses that his children have already commenced to hold him in contempt" (Caudill 1963, pp. 278-85).

But the poor, even though they suffer the most, are not the only victims. Most working-class people endure shame and a sense of failure; if people survive spiritually, they do so only through struggle or through delusion (what Longo calls "hoping, not living") (Levinson 1974; Rubin 1976). Collins, writing about her father, a commercial artist who never got the chance to draw the pictures he longed to paint, points to this destruction of the self (as did Arthur Miller in "Death of a Salesman").

> Year after year the disease got worse. Debilitated by the constant anxiety of personal inadequacy—the dominant mode of self-apprehension among men in a class-stratified society which yet appears permeable—my father became more and more irritable, harassed and despondent. His worry grew into an obsession. Most of the arguments between my father and mother erupted over money. They always ended with his shouting at her, "Well, somebody in this house has to worry about the bills!" and my mother collapsing in tears that were her strength. Soon my father's body conformed to the obsession, his shoulders becoming rounded, his wide chest, the symbol of manliness and pride, curving into a hollow.
> 
> Yet in all those years I never saw him cry, never saw him get angry at anyone or anything else, except at members of the family as a kind of reflex, for he was a loving man. The brunt of his rage was turned in upon himself. In a society in which advancement and economic success appear to depend on merit, and respect hinges on advancement, to fail is to doubt the integrity of the self (Collins 1978, p. 86).

The poor suffer from the worst degradation; the working-class majority manage to survive but live in insecurity and the knowledge that they have not succeeded in life; the new middle class (professionals, managers, and others) lead a confused, often anxiety-filled life, for they struggle to move to the top with little chance of success. Everyone suffers in some way.

What about those at the top? "The first thing you notice about gentry is a sense of assurance. Even the *children* have it . . ." (Burnham 1978, p. 14). Coles talks of "entitlement." Upper-class children seem to expect, in the same way as they expect the sun to rise in the morning and set in the evening, social position and wealth and other people to serve their needs. They come to think of themselves as superior, as seen in their self-portraits. "Especially noteworthy is the care [rich children] take with themselves as they draw. So often poor children treat themselves cursorily; they quickly sketch a rather unflattering self-portrait. Sometimes they are unwilling to complete what they have started—as if they are unsure of life itself. . . . The girl mentioned above spends a half-hour drawing herself, moves her eyes toward a mirror every once in a while to check on how she actually does look, and is eventually quite proud of what she has drawn. She regards herself—though she has learned to be affectingly modest—as a rather attractive person. No wonder she once posed herself, in a picture, beside a giant sunflower. She was in no way overshadowed by the flower; if anything, it adorned her own luminous presence" (Coles 1977, pp. 54–60).

There is nothing mysterious about this process. The children reflect what they see, hear, and experience. They hear their parents talk about important decisions they make; they see people who attend to their every need and desire; they are raised by a governess while their parents are out having fun and expect to do the same when they grow up; usually, they see no other world. These children are taught to need privacy and avoid crowds. A girl who wanted to see Santa Claus in Boston Common was put off by the crowds of children, their behavior, and the meager presents they received (Coles 1977, p. 57).

As adults, many show an ignorance of the daily lives of most people. A rich New Yorker said: "Oh, you won't have any trouble parking on Saturday. Everyone will be out of town for the weekend." Even during the Depression the ruling class was protected from harsh realities. The following is a typical statement (found in *Hard Times*) of wealthy people: "We didn't know the Depression was going on." Thus, Burnham can say with some justification: "The essence of the propertied class is an avoidance of the outside world, a shying-off from pain. Therefore, the necessity for privacy among the aristocracy, who build, with their private islands, private estates, private schools and servants and clubs, walls of privileges that serve as much to imprison as to protect them" (Burnham 1978, pp. 11 and 13; Terkel 1970, p. 80).

Perhaps most, if not all, of you will so far have felt a twinge of self-recognition, the rekindling of memories of experiences that evoked similar feelings. Issues of class are profoundly personal. They are for me. I have known people of all incomes and occupations (except the very rich). I have worked in the dirtiest, most low-paying of factories. As a child in Greece, I grew up in poverty. I was ashamed of being poor, of wearing used clothes, of living in half a room. As the years have worn on, I have become more aware of classes in many other ways. I detest the prejudices, of sociologists and others, against the poor and the working class; I cannot be with people who I know serve to increase the profits of corporations, without being enraged; the destruction and humiliation of class society never escape my senses.

## ARE CLASSES INEVITABLE?

### Perspectives on Classes and Inequality

In her book *Social Inequality,* Duberman says that even though the degrees of inequality in societies have varied, "in all types of societies, from the primitive hunting and gathering tribes to the highly industrialized democracies or communistic nations, inequality is unavoidable. True, total equality is unattainable, and to strive for it as a goal can only result in frustration and failure" (1976, p. 20). Most people have been socialized to believe something like Duberman's conclusion. Is inequality inevitable? Must the poor and other classes always be with us?

What is the argument for the eternal existence of classes? Most people who make that argument present some version of the functionalist theory of inequality. According to this theory, those who have more money, power, and prestige than others possess these things as rewards for contributing to the welfare of society. Doctors make more money because they contribute more to the survival of society than, according to this view, garbagemen or assembly-line workers or most other people. Doctors and others must receive these rewards to compensate them for their rare skills, their long training to develop such skills, and the sacrifices they make, for example, being on call most of the time.

Many more examples could be given. The essence of the functionalist perspective is that those who receive higher rewards deserve them because they contribute more to the survival and well-being of society than other people do.

There are variations of the functionalist theory. Duberman summarizes Lenski's argument in *Power and Privilege* (1966): "First, people are motivated basically by selfish interests, and altruism exists only infrequently, when very little can be gained or lost by proffering it. Second, . . . [since money, power, and prestige] are always and everywhere in short supply, people always are competing to obtain more than their fellow. Third, human beings are not equally endowed by nature to fight for scarce good and services" (1976, p. 23).

Duberman does say that in hunting-and-gathering tribal societies, there is only minimal inequality. But such relative equality is explained by the relative poverty of the whole society: there is only enough to eat for mere survival, and food can only be obtained by the work of everyone. As soon as surpluses arise, in food and other possessions, and as soon as it no longer is necessary for everyone to work to guarantee survival, inequalities arise. Duberman claims increasing inequality in both agricultural and industrial societies (1976, pp. 6–12).

The essence of the socialist response is that classes and inequalities are neither necessary for the survival of a society, nor inevitable. They arise because some people use power and coercion to benefit themselves. And in fact some societies have moved to reduce inequalities considerably. A brief response to the functionalist argument follows.

First, it is not true that those who receive higher rewards (in money, prestige, and power) contribute more to the survival of society. There are those who merely inherit wealth, and inheritance is the essence of the ruling class. For example, an accountant, lawyer, or economist who helps a corporation reduce its taxes by manipulating tax loopholes is not only not contributing to the well-being of most people, he or she is causing harm by leaving other people to pay the taxes corporations do not pay.

Second, do doctors truly make more sacrifices than mine workers and many others, who may lose health or life in their jobs?

Third, there is the question of inherited abilities. Chapter 13, on education, will attempt to demonstrate that, with rare exceptions, people have similar abilities. Rather, most people are capable of many things and certainly there are more than 300,000 or so people who could become doctors.

Finally, a simple distinction is often missed. *Equality* is not *sameness*. I may be more musical than you, and you a better carpenter than I. We are different. Are we unequal? By what scale is one quality better than the other? From my perspective, socialism argues for the equality of all people —in terms of prestige, power, and the necessities of life. But it does not argue for the colorless similarity of all. Differences are not inequalities.

*Reduced Inequalities*

Most tribal societies were largely egalitarian societies. Many anthropologists and others do not accept this conclusion, but the work of some anthropologists presents a convincing argument that before their destruction by industrial capitalism, tribal societies guaranteed everyone the material and social essentials of life (Radin 1953; Lee 1959; Bodley 1976).

In contemporary times, socialist societies have taken up the struggle to eliminate social classes and begin the long road to communist equality. No socialist society claims to have eliminated classes entirely, or even largely. Socialism aims not only to eliminate material inequalities, but to reduce and eliminate differences in power and prestige.

To a large degree, inequalities of income have been reduced in all socialist societies. Certainly, none shows discrepancies such as those found in the United States, where many in the ruling class have annual incomes in the millions, many managers and professionals make $100,000 and over, and many other people suffer from poverty, even making under $5,000. In addition to the reduced income inequalities, socialist societies (especially China, Cuba, and Albania) guarantee to everyone at low or no cost the essentials of housing, food, medicine, and education. Prices are remarkably stable. In China, for example, "in 1969 the prices of medical supplies were reduced by 37 percent. The price of medicines is now [1972] only 20 percent of what it was in 1950. Prices of transistor radios were cut by a big margin in 1970" (Fan and Fan 1975, p. 309). On November 1, 1979, some prices (meat, eggs, milk ) were increased by about 30 percent, but workers were given wage increases to cover the higher prices. Other prices (grains, cloth, coal) were not increased (*Beijing Review,* November 9, 1979, pp. 4–5).

However, in the USSR, the minimum wage was 60 rubles per month in 1968 and the average wage was 112.6 rubles. In 1973, manual workers made 145.6 rubles per month, engineering and technical workers 184.9, and nonmanual workers 118.5. But the ratio of the highest to the lowest was considerably more unequal. A government minister made 1,050 rubles per month in 1969, nine times the average. To that must be added "cars, houses, holiday facilities and special shops" available to the government elite. Some have even claimed that a few people in the USSR make 80,000 rubles per month, making for a 300:1 ratio of highest to lowest, but still less than the 11,000:1 ratio found in this country. Generally, it seems that in the USSR the essentials are guaranteed and income inequalities are lower than in capitalist societies (Lane 1971, pp. 73–74; Yanowitch 1977, p. 30).

But classes exist, nevertheless. Engineers, professionals, factory managers and directors, and party officials earn more and enjoy more material comforts than do workers. Also, power is distributed very unevenly. The bureaucracy controls the goods produced. Sweezy has concluded: "The Soviet Union is now the world's second industrial power with a high level of popular education and a vast trained intelligentsia, and yet its working class has no access to political power, is barred from any form of self-organization, and probably has less influence on its conditions and methods of work than the working class of advanced European capitalist countries" (1977, p. 6). These inequalities are perpetuated through the family by the fact that "the child of a bureaucrat typically gets a better education than the child of a worker or peasant. Thus the children of bureaucrats grow up to qualify as members of the ruling class" (Gandy 1976, p. 13).

Cuba, China, and Albania have made greater progress in reducing inequalities of income and have taken some steps to eliminate power and prestige hierarchies. Important also has been the struggle to eliminate material incentives for hard productive work, and to socialize everyone to work for the benefit of the whole society and for the enjoyment of the work itself (see Chapter 5). The movement to moral incentives has been highly uneven, however, even though it has made some progress (see Zimbalist 1975; Ehrenreich 1974; and Bettelheim 1974). The cultural revolution in China (see Chapter 4) was an effort, not completely successful, to bring real power to the hands of the people—or, rather, to enable people to struggle to gain that power, for it is not given up easily by those who possess it. The move to workers' control and other changes described in this book have been important ways to eliminate the destructive effects of society: to give dignity and self-confidence to everyone.

With few exceptions, in China highest-to-lowest pay ratios are 3:1 and 5:1. In one factory, Bettelheim found the work paid from a high of 102 yuan per month to a low of 30. Except for older technicians who were allowed their former wages of 225, most engineers and technicians made about 150.

Marquit cites a study by Granick in the early 1970s that compared the ratio of

> the salary of directors of large enterprises to the average earnings (including bonuses) of all employees. The averages for these ratios from Granick's data are as follows: Hungary, 4.4; Slovenia (the most industrialized part of Yugoslavia), 3.2; Rumania, 3.9; GDR (East Germany), 3.2; USSR, 3.6. A rough estimate for China is 2.2; in Albania the ratio is 1.7. By contrast, Granick gives the ratio 18.9 for the United States (without stock options) (1978, pp. 100–101).

There are serious economic problems in China, as was learned in the late 1970s. The Chinese themselves are openly discussing some of them. There is some unemployment, for example, especially in large cities. Also, while for most Chinese rent, water, and electricity cost only 5 percent of their income, and while there are no more slums or shacks, housing is a problem. Most families live in crowded three-room apartments. There is increasing evidence that income and privilege differences still exist (DuRand 1979; Jin 1979; Mathews 1979a, 1979b).

An American reporter who visited Shanghai in 1945 (before the Communist revolution) and in 1978 provides a vivid contrast between a class-driven society and one showing the improvements made under socialism:

*The Streets, 1945*
The next day you drive through the streets. Lepers claw at you, beggars beat on the pavement and call out in hoarse voices; big Sikhs, fierce in their beards and turbans, direct traffic.

You see a little boy, perhaps 10 or 12, sitting on the curb, his face swollen. He is crying. You walk over and see that he is holding in his arms a dead baby. You wonder if this is a trick by a street-wise kid to get money, but he does not beg and you are told by old China hands later that it is common not only to live in street but to die there.

*Today*
In four days you have not seen a beggar. The Sikhs are gone, replaced by blue-uniformed Chinese, usually sitting in elevated boxes, regulating traffic lights. Their bow to imperialism—or is it to authority, as represented by a cavalcade of automobiles?—is to clear the way for the VIP's by turning the traffic light red for the cross street. You have noticed, from time to time, slums of appalling poverty. In a market near the hotel, a woman picks through greens tossed to the pavement near a vegetable stall. A block away a woman goes through one trash can to another selecting items.

But these are isolated instances. Walks in areas chosen at random uncover surprisingly little trash. Narrow lanes, paved with small stones, have been washed. If only Somerville or Roxbury were so clean.

You see no urchins living on their street sense. The young people who follow you with such curiosity are vibrantly healthy. They may dress alike, but they are clean (Phelps 1978, p. 2. Courtesy of the *Boston Globe*).

Cuba presents a similar picture. Professional workers, like doctors, were allowed to keep their pre-1959 wages, and some make up to 1,000 pesos a month (but not so those who began working after 1959). But for most workers, the top wage is 300, the salary of some managers. The minimum, for unskilled laborers, is 85 pesos a month. Manual laborers make 100 to 125 pesos; factory workers can make 200. In most workplaces, the range of highest to lowest rarely exceeds 3.5:1, and can be as low as 2:1. "With rents fixed at no more than 10 percent of the household head's salary, and food costs fixed at about 25 pesos a month per couple, there is usually money left over from most wages" (Ward 1978, pp. 17–18; Zimbalist 1975, pp. 10–11).

The exodus from Cuba of over 100,000 people in the spring of 1980 may seem to contradict this view of the advances of socialism. By all available evidence, however, the Cuban émigrés were not escaping from poverty and deprivation (unlike the refugees from Haiti). No one is starving in Cuba, and housing, medical care, work, and education are available to all. What Cubans do not have is a consumer society: cars, color television, and the luxuries of consumer capitalism. People left Cuba neither to escape from suffering nor to search for freedom. They came to the United States to find wealth, unaware of the worsening economic conditions here. Moreover, this desire for luxuries was fueled by some wealthy ex-Cubans now living in the United States who visited Cuba in 1978 and 1979 and showered their relatives with lavish gifts. The exodus does not show the failure of socialism; it does show that Cuba is still a poor country where mistakes are often made, where the failure of the tobacco and other crops because of blight in 1979 and 1980 created temporary difficulties; and where consumerism for the few is to be avoided in favor of providing necessities for all people (Kelley 1980; Kinzer 1980; Suhor 1980; Winn 1980).

So the picture of socialist societies is uneven. On the one hand, the essentials of life are either free or very inexpensive, and the differences in income are considerably lower than in capitalist societies. Also, at least in some socialist societies, there is an ongoing struggle to return real power to all people. But on the other hand, clear income differences exist; some enjoy privileges denied to most people. There are also differences in power and prestige. In some places, there seems to be a definite ruling class; in others, there is an ongoing struggle to avoid such a powerful class.

What about the United States? Are classes becoming more or less rigid? The answer is complicated. For some time, the working class has made gains, both in winning greater wages and in establishing minimal guarantees at work.

But the struggle has been long, bitter, and violent. No gain was made without sacrifices. Three books give a glimpse of the nature of the struggle. Brecher's *Strike*, Rose's *Violence in America*, and Terkel's *Hard Times* give convincing evidence of the enormity of resistance to worker's unions. As one example, *Hard Times* makes clear the long and bitter confrontations of the 1930s before the auto workers established their union. From the 1870s to the present, working people have had to fight for any gains they have made. Strikes—often violently resisted by companies and their representatives—have been the most common weapon of working people. But other means have been used: sitting in and taking over plants, slowdowns and sabotage, and political actions.

These limited gains, made at great costs, can also be undone. The distribution of income has not changed much in the last thirty years. The poorest 20 percent of American families still divide among themselves about 5 percent of the income, as in 1950; the top 20 percent divide over 40 percent of the income. But whereas the relative distribution of income has remained

## STRUGGLES: Striking Miners

*In the winter of 1977–78, the United Mine Workers of America (UMWA) went on strike. On February 6, 1978, Arnold Miller, the president of UMWA, agreed to a contract with the coal companies. As the story below shows, this contract gave away many of the gains the miners had won through the years. The workers rejected the contract and in time won a better contract, one that minimized their losses. The following account explains how they were able to get a better contract.*

On February 6, UMWA President Arnold Miller and the BCOA announced agreement on a contract. Miller called it "the best agreement negotiated in any major industry in the past two years." It was the best—for the bosses. It gave in to every one of their demands.

- Automatic twenty-dollar-a-day fines for any miner who honored a picket line.
- Firing of any miner who has "picketed, threatened, coerced, fomented or otherwise been involved in the cause of an unauthorized work stoppage."
- Elimination of the UMWA Health and Retirement Funds, to be replaced by commercial health insurance with miners paying up to $700 a year for services that had been free to them for decades.
- Drastic curbs on the power of union safety committees, which under the 1974 contract had been authorized to pull miners out of an area of "imminent danger."
- Strict penalties for "absenteeism."
- Imposition of speedup "incentive pay" schemes and seven-day workweeks.

Also included were a host of other union-crippling provisions that had never even been publicly discussed.

*Source:* Reprinted from Nancy Cole and Andy Rose, *The 110–Day Coal Strike: Its Meaning for All Working People* (New York: Pathfinder Press, 1978), pp. 11, 12, 20, 22. Reprinted by permission of Pathfinder Press. Copyright © 1978.

- Elimination of the cost-of-living escalator for wages.
- A thirty-day probation period for new miners, during which they would be deprived of many union rights.
- Cutting in half (from ninety days to forty-five) the much-needed training period for new miners.
- Elimination of royalties paid to the union benefit funds on nonunion coal sometimes purchased by unionized companies, giving them a green light to step up this practice.
- Increasing from 1,000 to 1,450 the number of hours a miner must work in a year to qualify for pension credit—another measure to crack down on wildcats and "absenteeism."
- And, with a final twist of the knife, even the benefits paid to widows of UMWA members were cut back.

When the news of these provisions reached the coalfields in early February, the union ranks exploded with outrage. Thousands of miners joined in meetings and rallies to discuss and protest the contract terms. Meetings of local union officials in district after district repudiated the settlement.

Hundreds of miners boarded buses to Washington to demonstrate February 10 at the national UMWA headquarters, where the union bargaining council—composed of district presidents and members of the international executive board—was to vote on the agreement.

"This is a company-written contract," declared Doug Arrington of District 28, one of the protesters.

"It's going back twenty years," said Bob Smith, a miner from Cumberland, Kentucky.

One member of the bargaining council said they had received a stack of telegrams "twelve feet high" opposing the deal.

The council got the message. On February 12 it officially voted by thirty to six to reject the settlement, which one council member dubbed the "ball and chain" agreement. . . .

*(continued)*

**Striking Miners** *(continued)*

There were two keys to the miners' success in fighting back: union democracy and working-class solidarity.

With the defeat of the corrupt, procompany regime of Tony Boyle and the election victory of Miners for Democracy in 1972, miners established a series of democratic rights they had never enjoyed before.

Perhaps the most important single gain was the right to vote on their contracts. And not only to *vote*. Miners wrote it into the UMWA constitution that every member has the right to a copy of the actual contract language—not a "summary."

They have the right to discuss it with others and hear an explanation from their officers at a local meeting, mull it over for another forty-eight hours, and *then* vote.

This simple democratic procedure proved to be a tremendous obstacle to the coal operators and the government.

But the power shown by the ranks of the UMWA stemmed from much more than simply the formal, constitutional provision for a vote. It comes back to the question of rights. Through a decade-long struggle for control over their own union, miners have developed a firm belief that they have a *right* to decide for themselves.

That's why the miners didn't rely only on the formal democratic mechanism. They organized mass meetings of up to 3,000 miners—with or without official sanction—where the various contract offers were discussed point by point.

Where any miner could get up at an open microphone and voice his or her opinions.

Where they could discuss how to make the strike more effective.

Where they could remind the union officials loud and clear of what they would or would not stand for.

The miners didn't accept the notion that they should subordinate their fight to government dictates, no matter what the pretext. "Usually when a president talks about patriotism, it's the miners' rear end that's getting picked on," said Jim Bailey, a local vice-president from Harlan County, Kentucky.

The miners had confidence in themselves. The quiet assertion voiced by miner after miner—"We're not as dumb as some people think we are"—captured the essence of that confidence. Workers can think for themselves, decide for themselves, and act for themselves. . . .

All the support activities for the miners were initiated by rank-and-file workers and local union leaders. In some cities they succeeded in drawing together strike support coalitions that also won the endorsement of district-level officials and city or county labor councils.

Especially after Carter's threat to cut off food stamps for the strikers and their families, unionists rallied behind the need of the miners for material relief. Local unions and individual workers contributed hundreds of thousands of dollars. Caravans were organized from Baltimore, Detroit, Chicago, and other cities with food and clothing for the beleaguered strikers.

These actions helped prompt some gestures of solidarity from top union officials. The day after Carter invoked Taft-Hartley, UAW President Douglas Fraser came forward with a $2 million donation to the UMWA relief effort. Later the United Steelworkers and the Communications Workers each gave $1 million, and other unions chipped in as well.

But far more important than the amount of material aid was the political impact of the solidarity actions.

They gave the miners a chance to explain their demands and expose the lies of the companies.

They let the miners know they were not fighting alone.

They put the bosses on notice that further escalations of the attack on the miners could provoke wider and more powerful protests.

In many union locals, the coal strike was the first time in years that the idea of taking action in support of another union had been raised—even the simple act of passing a resolution of support or sending a token financial contribution.

An old tradition began to be reborn. The tradition that "an injury to one is an injury to all." The tradition of labor solidarity.

the same, the absolute dollar difference has increased. In 1970 dollars, the poorest 20 percent averaged $1,956 in 1958 and $3,085 in 1968; the highest 20 percent averaged $15,685 and $21,973. Thus, the difference between the poorest and the richest groups increased from $13,729 in 1958 to $18,888 in 1968 (Upton and Lyons 1972, p. 4). In addition, in 1950 and 1972, the top 1 percent of families held over 20 percent of the wealth (*Statistical Abstract* 1977, p. 464). Finally, for the last five years or so, the real income of most American families has decreased, while corporate profits have been hitting record highs (for example, oil industry profits were 80 to 20 percent greater in 1979 than in 1978). As Green shows, in the 1978 strike miners fought hard to minimize losses of benefits they had earned at great suffering and death. For one example, "the miners' health fund developed a consumer-controlled system of free clinics designed to deliver preventive medical care." In their initial proposal, the companies dismantled the clinic system and established pay deductibles of up to $700 per year. By continuing the strike to 110 days, the mine worker reduced the deductible, and made some other gains and minimized some other losses. But the gains were made after a long, bitter strike (Green 1978, pp. 4-5).

In the 1970s, union workers were generally able to offset the effects of inflation better than nonunionized workers. From 1967 to 1978, real wages of miners increased 19.5 percent, and of manufacturing workers 8.7 percent. Workers in nonunion places lost real wages or made very small gains. Those working in wholesale and retail trade lost 2.8 percent in real wages from 1967 to 78, and those in finance, insurance, and real estate lost 3.7 percent. Service workers gained 4.2 percent. Thus, unions do provide some protection for working people (*Dollars and Sense*, October 1979, p. 15).

Protest continues. The rising percentage of personal income going to taxes and the decreasing percentage of corporate income created the tax revolt of the late 1970s. Most people now see the cause for rising taxes as government expenditures for social services, rather than the corporate control of the economy. But people do clearly sense that something is wrong, that they suffer (*Dollars and Sense*, October 1978, pp. 3-5). This crisis of lowered living standards in capitalist societies is worldwide, and so are protests. For example, there is worker turmoil in Italy over declining living standards (Barkan 1979).

It is evident that the struggle to reduce and eliminate inequalities—in income, prestige, and power—and to abolish the personal injuries caused by social class, will be long and uneven. New socialist societies are faced with the deep-rooted inequalities and traditions inherited from the capitalist past. But new forms of inequalities and classes can and do arise under socialism on the way to communism. They present a momentous challenge and must be struggled against (Hinton 1972; Sweezy 1977).

Perhaps Duberman is right, to a degree. But the dream of equality (not sameness) is a noble one, that presents the possibility for the liberation of all people and is worthy of being pursued. Even without creating total equality, the vast inequalities of capitalism can be reduced, and the struggle can give meaning, dignity, and self-respect to the oppressed millions. We may clean up our environment, make work a humanizing rather than a destructive experience, and live in communities rather than as strangers and competitors.

In the steep mountains of southern Albania is Llongo, the village where I was born and where my parents and other relatives still live. When I visited there in 1980 my mother and other people over sixty recalled my childhood when we went hungry for many days, without even bread to eat. My mother cried when she remembered that an older sister died at the age of four because my parents could not find the proper medication. Conditions have improved drastically since the arrival of socialism in 1944. I saw healthy children who eat all they need. They live in a society where medical care is free, where work is available to everyone. Whatever other problems socialist Albania may have, whatever inequalities may persist, there is no doubt that socialism has created a good life for people, ending the misery and suffering of my childhood.

# 3

# *The Illusion of Democracy*

INTRODUCTION

Those of us who argue that a small ruling class dominates the economy and the government are not revealing any secret. Many people, especially in the working class, agree. Such statements appear in everyday conversation and in many books (see Lasson 1971; Gitlin and Hollander 1970; Terkel 1970, 1974).

The aim of this chapter is to provide evidence that the ruling class exists; to show how it exercises its power; and to argue that though this power is extensive, it is not total, so struggles toward a real democracy are not hopeless.

The statistics reprinted in this chapter (and others) are important as a base for understanding what is happening. Economics is intimately connected with our daily lives; it is not an obscure, difficult subject. The author hopes the reader will bear with him in reading these statistics, for they are part of the story.

The socialist perspective on the ruling class can be stated plainly. The ruling class owns 25–30 percent of the wealth, makes 20–25 percent of the yearly income, and controls 60–70 percent of the corporate stocks (Domhoff

1974b, p. 82; Zeitlin 1978). It rules "through its members who (1) do the job themselves, (2) hire and fire those who do, or (3) pay for the upkeep of political machines to do the job for them" (Sweezy 1951, p. 368).

But ruling-class control involves more than the placing of its members in powerful positions. Through the years the ruling class has shaped political, economic, and social institutions. These institutions function to maintain capitalism and ruling-class power. Thus, even if socialists were to be elected to political office, their effectiveness would be limited so long as they functioned within the institutions created by the ruling class, and so long as the ruling class controlled the economy. In order to create a socialist society the state must be taken away from the ruling class, the institutions shaped by the ruling class must be changed, and control of the economy must fall from ruling-class hands.

As many people have pointed out, power is not absolute. If it were, cynicism and fatalism would prevent any change. But history shows that changes and revolutions do occur. The ruling class constantly seeks to consolidate and increase its power, but its own limitations and inherent contradictions, working-class opposition, and revolutions throughout the world limit that power. As Dreier argues, it is important to study both the ruling class and its power, and to focus on power struggles (Dreier 1975, p. 233). Leaders of the ruling class can be forced to make compromises or lose their power. To keep its control of the society, the ruling class makes concessions it would not make on its own were it nor for the organized struggles of the people throughout the world. Most of the time, such concessions ("reforms") can be the beginning steps to a challenge of the very nature of capitalism (Sweezy 1951; Domhoff 1967, 1970).

## COMPOSITION AND PERPETUATION OF THE RULING CLASS

The ruling class is not easy to study. For obvious reasons, its members do not want to expose their power and their exercise of it. Except for the most powerful members (such as the Rockefellers and DuPonts), they are not highly visible. In addition, many who do not belong to the ruling class but who work for it are often confused as members. (In time, of course, some of these people, or their children, do enter the ruling class. It is always open to new members with ambition and ability, for such people strengthen the class.) Given these difficulties, it is still possible to study the ruling class, both through careful analysis of government documents, business reports, and other similar documents, and through talks with ex-members or close employees of the ruling class. A number of social scientists in the last twenty years, most notably Domhoff and Mills, have been students of this class.

*Definition.* The ruling class consists of those families whose members dominate the society's economic and political institutions and who control a highly disproportionate amount of the wealth. Athletes and entertainers may make half a million dollars or more a year, but they are not in the ruling class (although some of their children may marry and integrate into it). It is power that defines the ruling class. People who make major decisions that affect millions of others, such as concerning the United States role in the Vietnam war, are what is meant by the upper class. This group controls most of the wealth, the major corporations, and the government. (Some members of the ruling class are not active in politics or business.)

The entire ruling class does not have periodic conventions where it conspires to manipulate the society. Small groups may meet on specific occasions, but the essence of ruling-class activity lies elsewhere: it is the sameness of values, interests, and experiences that unite people into an upper class that rules. The institutions described below make it possible for the ruling class to exist and perpetuate itself (Morris 1977).

How do we find its members? They are white, mostly of northern or western European descent, and those who exercise the power are mostly men. Domhoff has argued that ruling-class members can be found in: membership lists of *Social Registers* of different cities, membership lists of exclusive clubs, and alumni lists of certain private preparatory schools. Also, some may be missing from all of these lists but still belong to the ruling class if they are on the boards of directors of major corporations, hold powerful corporate positions, or they marry someone who meets any of the above criteria. Usually, most members are found in more than one list. (Hill 1975, p. 5; Domhoff 1967, 1970, 1974b).

How many people are included? Estimates vary, but 1 percent of the United States population is the highest given. According to Hill (1975, p. 5) .25 to .50 percent (about 500,000–1,000,000 people) belong to the ruling class. The make over $400,000 per year per family, and have a net worth of $50,000,000 or over. The adult white men of these families hold most of the powerful positions in the society.

Before looking at the institutions of the ruling class, note who does not belong to this class. There are people in the "lieutenant sector," whose power is substantial but less than those in the ruling class. They own large, but not major, businesses. Their power is delegated to them—they are the managers of the corporations. They may run the government—they are presidents, governors, senators. (Hill included cabinet members, but as will be seen, most of them do come from the upper class.) Hill estimates their number at 1 percent (two million people) and their income in the $50–200,000 range (as of 1975) (1975, pp. 7–8).

Professionals are also not in the ruling class. Rose (1967) includes doctors. Certainly doctors make high incomes, and a few may come from, or join, the ruling class. But most of them hold no major powerful positions. Indeed, in time the ruling class may sacrifice the doctors by opting for some form of national health insurance or even socialized medicine to control the increasing unrest over the high cost of medicine, since such unrest may become more generalized against the whole capitalist system.

## The Institutions of the Ruling Class

All sociologists agree that people of the same class tend to intermarry, attend similar schools, have fun doing similar things, belong to similar organizations, hold similar values, and undergo the same socialization process. The ruling class is no different. In fact, being fewer, and having more resources, people in this class should find it easier to form a cohesive, clearly defined class. They intermarry, are exposed to the same experiences, and spend much time with each other.

As children, they are rarely raised by their own parents. Nurses, governesses, and maids take care of their needs. From early in life, they learn that they are born to be waited on and to give orders to others.

When they go to school, these children attend exclusive preparatory schools (of course, not all children in these schools are from the ruling class—many are prospective members, or children of parents with high aspirations). These schools serve many functions. First and foremost, they introduce to each other children from different parts of the country, who begin life-long friendships and acquaintances. All people make friends in school; the rich are no different. Second, boarding schools continue the molding of ruling-class values and personality. Burnham, who attended such schools, says:

> The final step in the care and training of the propertied class occurs in the boarding school, a fact that is so completely understood all over the country that parents from Lake Forest, Illinois, or Pebble Beach, California, automatically send their children East to school....
>
> The first thing that strikes the visitor is the extraordinary richness of Foxcroft, visible in the tennis courts, gardens, stables, orchards, and servants, in the boxwood walks and 18th century brick house, in the classrooms, art rooms, photo labs, and dorms....
>
> We accepted the wealth as natural. We didn't even see it. Just as we accepted the grooms who brought our horses to us, already saddled and bridled, and the gardeners trimming the formal walks, clipping the hedges and mowing the grass. We did not speak when passing them, but grunted, eyes grounded in pride or shyness, as they touched their caps (Burnham 1978, p. 16).

Despite many societal changes, old school ties remain strong. Arnold cites the schools attended by people such as the Saltonstalls, Kennedys, and Roosevelts and shows the emotional and social significance people attach to their school friendships. Ted Kennedy is said to attend Graduates' Day at Milton Academy whenever he can (Arnold 1978).

Ruling-class children continue their education in exclusive colleges. Although not as many now attend Ivy League and similar colleges, many do, and the rest go to other top schools (major state universities, for example). Ten generations of Saltonstalls have graduated from Harvard. And a study of 476 top executives showed 86 percent had attended Yale, Harvard, or Princeton (Arnold 1978; Domhoff 1967, p. 18).

Ruling-class men and women also tend to marry each other. This fact is fairly well known, and hardly surprising, so nothing needs to be explained. It is important to note, however, that a high rate of intermarriage within a group is the best evidence that a class exists (Domhoff 1970, p. 76).

In addition to meeting each other in business and government, ruling-class people have other ways to meet after they leave school. They meet at clubs, summer resorts, and charitable and cultural organizations and in such recreational activities as foxhunts, polo matches, and yachting (Domhoff 1967, p. 16).

Especially important are clubs and camps. There it is possible to meet each other, have fun together, exchange ideas, meet experts from outside the class, and so on. Domhoff studied two camp retreats still open only to ruling-class men. The list of one (Bohemian Grove) is an "all-star team of the national corporate elite." The people in these clubs and camps sit on the boards of directors of major corporations, in advisory groups for the government, and in the government itself. We cannot underestimate the importance of these clubs, retreats, and other nonbusiness activities. People who have fun, play, and talk together become closer to each other. In these settings deals are made and ideas explored. One can meet people of one's own class, some from distant places, to make class ties truly national (Domhoff 1974, especially pp. 35-39).

The names of the schools, clubs, and corporations that support this argument are found in the sources cited. It becomes more convincing as we turn to statistical evidence showing that the ruling class I have just described controls the economy, government, and other institutions.

## RULING-CLASS CONTROL OF THE ECONOMY

The ruling class owns a great deal of wealth and most of the stock of the top corporations, runs those corporations, and is expanding its control to new areas.

*Income and Wealth*

Inequalities increase as we move from income, to wealth, to certain kinds of wealth. I have found no statistics on income for the top .5 percent or 1 percent; there is a statistic for the top 5 percent of families, which in 1978 showed they made 15.6 percent of the income for that year. That statistic may not include unreported capital gains and other untaxable income (*Statistical Abstract* 1979, p. 452; *Dollars and Sense,* October 1979, p. 11).

Wealth is much more concentrated. One table shows that, in 1972, the top 1 percent held 20.7 percent of the wealth; another table shows 25.9 percent (this figure includes real estate, corporate stock, bonds, cash, trusts, and so on). Most figures show that about 25 percent of the wealth is held by the richest 1 percent of families (*Statistical Abstract* 1979, p. 470).

But for specific forms of wealth—the wealth which produces income and controls corporations—the concentration is highest. Whereas the New York Stock Exchange reports that in 1972 there were 31 million people owning stocks in publicly held corporations ("You and the Investment World" 1972, p. 30) in 1972, .5 percent of Americans held 49.3 percent of corporate stock and 80.8 percent of money in trusts; 1 percent of Americans held 56.5 percent and 89.9 percent (*Statistical Abstract* 1979, p. 470). (Other estimates give 70 percent of corporate stock to 1 percent of Americans.) For the ruling class, most yearly income is not from salary, but from dividends from stocks and bonds. People making half a million dollars and over receive at least three-quarters of it from stock dividends; this income is usually inherited wealth (Anderson and Gibson 1978, p. 120).

In 1969, 50,000 people held stock worth over one million dollars, and 5,000 held stock over five million dollars. Just these 50,000 people held 18 percent of "personally held corporate stock" (Burnham 1978, p. 12).

It is control of such income-producing wealth, in major corporations, that gives the ruling class its control over the economy. And through manipulation of the tax system they manage to hold onto most of that wealth.

People have been looking for ways to reduce their heavy tax burdens. In this climate business interests pushed for Proposition 13 in California in 1977, which was passed by the voters. It reduced property taxes on homes and businesses. But it appears that, in the long run, it will be businesses and corporations, not the average taxpayer, who will benefit. The distribution of the $7 billion tax cut in the year following passage of Proposition 13 reveals the following: 24 percent went to owners of owner-occupied residential property; 12 percent to owners of renter-occupied residential property; and 28 percent to owners of commercial, industrial, and agricultural property. Thus, business got greater benefits than did home owners. (Because people could no longer deduct real estate taxes from their income taxes, 14 percent of the $7 billion went to the state of California and 22 percent to the federal government). In addition, for reasons explained in an article in *Consumer Reports,* the gap in benefits will increase even more in favor of business. Many services, such as park maintenance and libraries, have already been reduced. Proposition 13 has meant great tax benefits for businesses and reduced services for the public (*Consumer Reports* 1979).

Since the 1950s individual income taxes have increased and corporate taxes have decreased. In 1954, corporate taxes were 30.3 percent of federal revenues, but only 13.8 percent in 1976. In 1953 working people paid 9.2 percent of their income in taxes, but in 1974 they paid 16 percent of their income. Corporations, on the other hand, paid 43.3 percent of their profits in taxes in 1953, but only 31.8 percent in 1974. The tax system has shifted to favor even more the ruling class and corporations (Ciancanelli 1978, p. 201; Stern 1972).

Most people own little or none of this income-producing wealth, or indeed, any wealth. Their jobs are most people's only income. Even if people sold most of their possessions (homes, cars, furniture) they would hardly survive a year without the income of jobs. Not so the ruling class.

*Control of Major Corporations*

The ruling class controls most of the stock in corporations. Moreover, a few corporations control the economy, and these corporations are run by a few people.

A quick look at Tables 3.1, 3.2, and 3.3 shows that fewer than 200 corporations control most of the assets, sales, and profits in the industrial and manufacturing field. Table 3.2 shows that the 100 largest industrials own about two-thirds of the assets of the 500 largest industrials, and these 100 corporations have assets over seven times the value of the 500 second-largest industrials. Table 3.3 is the most revealing. One hundred ninety-nine manufacturing corporations, each with assets of one billion or more, controlled over 58 percent of assets and profits of all United States manufacturing corporations in 1978. That is clear evidence that the economy is dominated by a small fraction of all corporations.

Other fields show a similar dominance by relatively few corporations. There were 13,000 commercial banks in the United States in 1970, but a hundred of them had 50 percent of all deposits; ten had 25 percent; and just three had 13 percent (Etra and Leinsdorf 1974, p. 25). A recent study by Corporate Data Exchange is even more revealing of the power of financial institutions. It shows that "financial power in the United States is becoming concentrated increasingly in huge money-center banks like Citicorp, Chase Manhattan and J. P. Morgan." These banks are becoming more coordinated and united ("interlocked") as they hold more and more of each other's stocks (Rich 1980).

**TABLE 3.1** Sales of Largest Industrials, 1978, in Billions of Dollars

Largest 500—1,218.7
Largest 100— 820.5

*Source: Statistical Abstract of the United States* 1979, p. 571.

**TABLE 3.2** Assets of Largest Industrials, 1978, in Billions of Dollars

Largest 500— 898.5
Largest 100— 598.9
Second largest 100—152.2

*Source: Statistical Abstract of the United States* 1979, p. 572.

**TABLE 3.3** Assets and Profits of Manufacturing Corporations, by Asset Size, 1978, in Millions of Dollars

|  | Number | Assets | Net Profits |
|---|---|---|---|
| All corporations | NA | 1,086,350 (100%) | 81,314 (100%) |
| Corporations with assets of $1 billion or more | 199 | 632,866 (58.3%) | 47,644 (58.6%) |
| Corporations with assets of $25 million to $1 billion | 2,192 | 301,055 (27.7%) | 21,759 (26.8%) |

NA—not available
Source: Statistical Abstract of the United States 1979, p. 568.

Even more revealing are figures showing that in most manufacturing industries, just four corporations control most of the market for that product: 94 percent of telephone equipment, 98 percent of locomotives, 81 percent of cigarettes, 79 percent of typewriters, 71 percent of tires, 63 percent of computers, and 60 percent of steel are produced by four corporations in each case (Babson and Brigham 1975, p. 40).

These powerful corporations are controlled by a few people. The board of directors makes all important decisions for a corporation, and these boards are populated by a few thousand people. Indeed, many people sit on more than one board of directors, thus creating the possibility for all sorts of cooperation between corporations in different fields, or even supposedly in competition with each other.

Consider some details. Domhoff found that in 1963, 53 percent of the 884 people on the boards of the top fifteen banks, top fifteen insurance companies, and top twenty industrials were members of the upper class (as he defines it; see earlier part of this chapter). These directors, in addition to making these companies' major decisions, also own enough stocks to control them; that was the case in 141 of 232 largest corporations (Domhoff 1967, pp. 49–51; for similar findings in 1968, see Useem 1978).

But the extent of the power of a few thousand ruling-class people becomes most obvious in the prevalence of interlocking directorates—two or more companies with a common director on their board. The reprinted story from Reuter explains the latest situation very clearly. It shows that most large corporations have directors on each other's boards. Thus, they can cooperate for each other's benefit.

This national condition of interlocking directorates may become clearer by looking at three specific cases. Boston Edison Company has fourteen directors—eight sitting on the boards of other large local businesses,

> **Panel hits close ties between top firms**
>
> WASHINGTON (Reuter)—A Senate committee study, in a searing criticism of the US business establishment, recommended yesterday that interlocking directorates between corporations with more than $1 billion in assets be prohibited. . . .
>
> The study examined two basic kinds of interlocking directorships, direct and indirect.
>
> A direct interlock occurs when two companies have a common director. An indirect interlock exists when two companies each have a director on the board of a third corporation.
>
> The study showed that 123 of the 130 corporations examined on average had some connection with about 65 of the other companies. The 13 largest firms not only were linked together, but accounted for 240 direct and 5547 indirect interlocks, each being attached to an average of more than 70 percent of the other 117 corporations.
>
> The 13 largest companies ranked by assets were American Telephone and Telegraph Co., BankAmerica Corp., Citicorp, Chase Manhattan Corp., Prudential Co., Metropolitan Life, Exxon Corp., Manufacturers Hanover Corp., J. P. Morgan and Co., General Motors Corp., Mobil Corp., Texaco, Inc. and Ford Motor Co.
>
> The study said the boards of Citicorp, Chase, Manufacturers Hanover, Morgan, Prudential, Metropolitan, AT&T, Exxon and GM "looked like virtual summits for leaders in American business."
>
> The study found that leading competitors in the fields of automotives, energy, telecommunications and retailing met extensively on the boards of their corporate customers and suppliers and also on the nation's largest financial institutions.
>
> The patterns of director interrelationships, the study said, implied a potential for antitrust abuse and possible conflicts that could affect prices, supply and competition, and could also have an impact on the shape and direction of the economy.
>
> Source: Boston Globe, April 23, 1978, pp. 41, 45.

the three major banks and the two biggest insurance companies (Babson and Brigham 1975, p. 14). The First National City Bank, second largest in the nation, is interlocked with seven of the top ten industrials, six of the top fifteen insurance companies, two of the largest four retailers, and the two largest utilities (Etra and Leinsdorf 1974, p. 29). Finally, in his study of United States Steel directors, Domhoff found "the 16 men studied were also directors or trustees for 20 major industrials, 18 banks, 11 insurance companies, 9 railroads, 8 utilities, 5 universities, and 3 charitable foundations" (1967, p. 55; see also Sonquist and Koenig 1975).

Some people are not alarmed by these figures. They point out that old-style capitalism has disappeared. It is no longer the rule that one family owns most of the stock in and runs a large corporation (although this situation still occurs). But the change in the form of control does not mean the ruling class has lost its control. For example, instead of the Rockefellers owning all of Exxon, they own large blocks of stocks in many corporations. A few thousand people still are running the corporations, and a few people own most stocks. The diversification of stock holdings has had positive effects for the ruling class. For one thing, it protects each family from financial catastrophe—if one company fails, they still own stock in other corporations. It is more dangerous to hold most stock in one company than to spread holdings around. Secondly, such diversification strengthens the ruling class as a whole. It lessens competition between capitalists, for their opulent life-style depends less on the profitability of one corporation than on the profitability of the whole economy. So intelligent ruling-class people see that they must work to strengthen control of the economy in the hands of the ruling class as a whole. This new form of capitalism is better for the whole class (Hill 1975, p. 5; Domhoff 1967, p. 40; Zeitlin 1974).

*New Forms of Control*

Capitalism, like any social system, changes through time. Specifically, the ruling class is always looking for new ways to increase its power and wealth. Food and land had been two areas largely uncontrolled by the ruling class, but the situation is changing rapidly.

A major reason for the increase in food prices in the 1970s has been the increasing dominance of production of specific foods by a few corporations. Four corporations control the following percentages in these foods: 90 percent breakfast cereals; 70 percent dairy products; 65 percent sugar; and 80 percent canned goods. Campbell Soup *alone* controls 90 percent of the canned soup market. "In most food products—not many, *most*—two to four corporations already have seized control of the market. In this vast nation of 220 million people, only fifty manufacturing firms now control the means of food production" (Zwerdling 1980, p. 25).

United Brands (formerly United Fruit Company) controls 50 percent of the banana market and has been trying to achieve the same control in lettuce. Once such control is achieved, it enables a corporation to raise the price without much fear of competition (Zwerdling 1975).

In the late 1970s, large food corporations were buying out medium and small ones at an increasing pace. *Business Week* called these moves "The Great Takeover Binge." For example, Procter & Gamble was not in the coffee business until the early 1970s. It then brought out a regional company making Folger's Coffee and proceded to spend millions of dollars on advertising, driving out of business many local coffee companies as it sought to catch up with Maxwell House in the national market. What happens is that consumers pay higher and higher prices in order to finance the takeovers and the advertising campaigns of huge corporations.

A look at the food (and nonfood) products Procter & Gamble makes will show the tremendous control exercised by this one corporation: Pringle's potato chips, Duncan Hines cake mixes, Crisco oil, Ivory soap, Crest, Charmin, Pampers, Tide, and Cheer. Another company, Beatrice Foods, has bought and now controls over 400 companies—among them the makers of Canada Dry, Dannon yogurt, Sunbeam bread, Miracle White fabric softener, and Samsonite luggage (Zwerdling 1980).

The production of meat is also becoming concentrated in a few hands. In 1973, the five biggest meat packers controlled about 40 percent of sales in the United States. In 1969, 1 percent of feedlots handled over 50 percent of all beef sold (the figure is certainly higher today). In addition, "5 companies buy 90 percent of all broiler chickens" (Babson and Brigham 1975, p. 22; Browning 1975, p. 42).

There are as yet no two or three giant supermarket chains controlling the market nationally, but "in most of 200 leading cities and towns, a cartel of four or fewer supermarket chains already controls food sales, and the monopoly hold is fast increasing" (Zwerdling 1980, p. 24).

More details could be given. But the general direction of food production is clear: more and more foods are raised or produced by a few corporations, which are thus enabled to increase prices (and profits).

Also, land formerly used for residences, recreation, and farming is coming under corporate control of the few. Indeed, corporations in nonagricultural fields are buying up land: Mobil Oil has bought timber companies and coal companies; Westinghouse, Chrysler, and others are discovering there is money to be made in exploiting land for food, minerals, and expensive recreation communities. Browning explains how land is bought and sold both as a profitable investment and as a tax shelter (Browning 1975, pp. 17, 100-103).

The land giveaway began long ago. Between 1875 and 1900, the railroad companies were *given free* 130 million acres (twenty-five times the size of New Jersey) of public lands. The railroads were expected to dispose of the land soon, but they still hold 20 million acres of it (Browning 1975, pp. 9-10).

More detailed investigation shows the enormous control of the land by corporations. In one West Virginia county, 76 percent of the land is owned by out-of-state corporations. In California in 1969, of 11.8 million acres of crop land, 6.1 million were owned by corporate farms. Big Sky, a huge recreational community in Montana, is owned by outside corporations—52 percent by Chrysler, which also owns land in many cities (Browning 1975, pp. 12, 27, 57-58).

The land is destroyed and abused in the search for corporate profit. Coal strip-mining operations are moving west, to exercise there the same techniques that destroyed the Appalachians (see Candill 1963). By 1970, 59 million acres of public lands in the mountain states had been leased to corporations for mineral exploration. Unless there is a strong fight to stop them, corporations will destroy land and many communities in the West. Browning reports a West Virginian man's account of an area of one hundred square miles, once "solid farmland," now totally stripped, with not one person living on it.

Steiner, in *The Vanishing White Man*, reveals the creation of "new Indians"; white ranchers whose land is being taken away by corporations and the government. Land they thought was theirs is not: the government owns rights to mineral exploration, rights that it is leasing to corporations. In searching for minerals, corporations are given the right to dig in and deface the land. As land was taken from the Indians, it is now taken from ranchers. Some see the bitter irony of what is happening to them.

## Conglomerates and Multinationals

In the old days of capitalism, a company made and sold one product, usually within its own nation. In the last thirty to forty years, however, things began to change, and now most major corporations make more than one product and operate in many lands.

ITT is one well-known conglomerate (a maker of many products and provider of many services). It produces over one hundred different goods. Conglomerates are becoming the rule: hardly any major corporation now limits itself to one product or service. Ford Motor Company owns Philco (television), Chrysler owns land, and Tenneco owns farms. Indeed, the enormous power of conglomerates is seen in their control of food and publishing.

Tenneco, the thirty-fourth largest corporation in the United States, is involved in

> manufacturing, oil and natural gas, packaging and shipbuilding, and now agriculture. Tenneco has assets of $4.3 billion and 1970 gross revenues of $2.5 billion. Farming and land development profits hit $22 million in 1970, not including appreciation on the 1.8 million acres of land it farms or controls in the Western United States" (Baker and Taylor 1972, p. 332).

In addition, corporations such as Greyhound, DuPont, and Atlantic-Richfield are moving to fatten their profits by investing in the production of beef (Rowen 1972).

In the last ten years, publishing has been succumbing to conglomerate control too. It has long been the case that larger publishers would buy smaller ones. Now, these merged publishing companies are themselves owned by nonpublishing corporations. Hardly a major publisher is independently owned. For example, Gulf & Western (oil) owns both Paramount (motion pictures) and publisher Simon and Schuster, which owns Pocket Books. CBS, RCA, and Time, Inc. all own large publishing houses. Whereas the conglomerate owners have not yet, by and large, tried to influence what kinds of books get published, there is no assurance that this situation will continue. As Levin points out, book publishing may go the way of television and other media, where profit considerations are primary (Levin 1978; *Dollars and Sense,* December 1978, pp. 6–7).

Oil corporations, in addition to buying publishing companies and department stores, are beginning to dominate the nuclear energy industry:

> The major oil companies dominate the nuclear industry. In the 1960's they saw the limits of the world's oil reserves—and the end of their corporate lives if they stuck exclusively to oil. . . .

As a result of their buying binge, 10 of the largest oil companies now hold half the nation's uranium reserves. They also own 40% of the industry's milling capacity, which is used to process ore into yellowcake powder. The reserves and the mills are the foundation on which the entire nuclear power and weapons pyramid is built. . . .

Exxon's interest in nuclear energy is pervasive. The biggest oil company in the world is also fourth in U.S. uranium reserves, sixth in milling capacity and one of eight fabricators of fuel rods (DeCormis 1979a, p. 6).

Finally, food production, like other products, is going multinational (multinational corporations have branches in two or more countries). Pineapples, traditionally thought of as Hawaiian, no longer always are. To avoid union wages and higher land costs, many companies have moved to Thailand and the Philippines, where they pay workers as little as ten cents an hour (Kellogg 1974).

The extent of the control of food production by multinationals may be seen if we examine one of them, Del Monte. The following figures show that their operations are extensive and widespread, their power considerable.

As the world's largest canner of fruits and vegetables, the San Francisco-based Del Monte epitomizes the worldwide sweep of the American food business. In addition to canning and selling more than 200 products from applesauce to zucchini, it owns and operates 132,700 acres in the United States, Canada, the Philippines and Kenya and employs 40,000 people. Nearly 25 per cent of its canned food sales and 35 per cent of its fresh fruit sales come from international markets. Its direct investments abroad total $60 million and it has sales organizations in 100 countries.

It is a completely integrated company. In the United States it has fifty-four processing plants, thirteen can factories, thirty-eight ranches and farms, one ocean terminal, one air freight forwarding center and ten distribution centers. Overseas it has processing plants or plantations in Belgium, Brazil, Canada, Costa Rica, Ecuador, Guatemala, Hong Kong, Italy, Japan, Kenya, Mexico, Panama, the Philippines, Puerto Rico, South Africa, the United Kingdom and Venezuela. It has two can factories abroad, nine tuna seiners and tranships, and five banana transport ships (Baker 1973, pp. 457–58).

*Advertising*

The ruling class and its corporations have created an economic system where the search for profits demands increased production of goods every year. But what should be done with these products? Beginning in the 1920s, advertising was created to stimulate the desire for them.

Advertising demanded a major shift in motivation, from thrift and saving to consumption. This process is not merely the consumption of essentials; it also involves an assault on people's self-image so they feel inadequate unless they use the new products of corporate capitalism. All sorts of sexual, personal, and social insecurities are exploited by advertising; people think they must buy the products to feel better. People are made to feel deprived unless they own and use cosmetics, machines, fancy and expensive cars, and so on (Henry 1963; Ewen 1976). The chapter "Advertising as a Philosophical System" (in Henry) is a devastating critique of advertising's conscious manipulation of people's insecurities and fears.

In addition to solving the problem of selling goods (which people buy on credit, often denying themselves essentials, or work long hours to get the money), corporations have used advertising to quiet social unrest. Ewen shows that even in the 1920s workers still resisted the long hours and degrading working conditions. By increasing salaries somewhat, and by turning people to consumerism, corporations basically tried to buy off the discontent and prevent the rebellion of workers. Workers were made to feel as if life was good to them. As Chapter 5 will show, the attempt was only partly successful. Work alienation persists.

## CONTROL OF THE GOVERNMENT

Perhaps the ruling class may be expected to control the economy and create powerful corporations. But we may balk at the statement that the ruling class controls the government, too. Do we not elect politicians periodically?

The following summary of considerable research on this issue shows otherwise. Different wings of the ruling class control both the Democratic and Republican parties. They do so through party membership, elected and appointed office, and campaign contributions (Domhoff 1967, ch. 4; 1978b).

### *The Executive*

Most social scientists agree that the executive branch of the federal government is the most powerful. The cabinet and other executive positions have been mostly the province of ruling-class men.

Domhoff shows that in the period 1932–1964, the vast majority of secretaries of state, defense, and treasury (the most important cabinet posts) have come from the ruling class. In a more extensive study, Mintz found that of the 205 people who served in presidential cabinets during 1897–1973, nearly 90 percent belonged to the "social or business elite" (as she defines them), who are, at most, 1 percent of the population. Freitag, also covering the period 1897–1973, found similar connections: 76.1 percent of cabinet officers were "interlocked" with big businesses. They had served on boards of directors of, or held major offices in, major corporations, and they also were appointed to the cabinet. Another 11.7 percent were "unknown lawyers (possible interlocks)" and 12.2 percent had no connections with business. The percentages are approximately the same for both Democratic and Republican administrations (Domhoff 1967, p. 97ff.; Mintz 1975; Freitag 1975).

President Carter's cabinet and other top executive positions continued the same trend. No outsiders there. Carter's cabinet was indistinguishable from Nixon's. Carter's people came from corporate headquarters and top law firms: the twelve cabinet secretaries had seventy years in public office, thirty corporate directorships, and an average income of $211,000. Even "newcomer" Juanita Kreps sat on eight boards of directors, including Eastman Kodak and the New York Stock Exchange. Deputy secretaries also came from similar backgrounds (Morris 1977).

Indeed, we find that over 200 of Jimmy Carter's top cabinet appointees graduated from Ivy League colleges, as did some of his White House assistants, such as national security adviser Zbigniew Brzezinski (*Intelligence Report* 1978).

It is clear, therefore, that for a long time most secretaries and other top officials of the executive branch of the federal government have been members of the ruling class.

Although President Reagan's cabinet secretaries are somewhat more conservative than those who worked for Jimmy Carter, they come from similar class and business backgrounds. Before they joined the government, most of them were top corporate officials or corporate lawyers. For example, Donald Regan, secretary of the treasury, was chairman of Merrill Lynch, a large stock-brokerage firm, and William French Smith, attorney general, was a senior partner in a law firm whose clients are large corporations (*U.S. News and World Report,* January 19, 1981, pp. 18–21).

For a long time most top officers of the executive branch of the federal government have been members of the ruling class.

*The Trilateral Commission*

The enormous presence of the ruling class in Carter's administration is revealed also through its relationship to the Trilateral Commission (TC). Created in 1973, TC is composed of sixty members each from Western Europe, North America, and Japan. The members came from major corporations in banking, industry, and the mass media; from establishment think tanks (organizations seeking solutions to the problems of capitalism); and token unions. The initiative for TC came from David Rockefeller; he also chose most key members and staff experts. The commission was created to solve some new major problems faced by capitalism, problems arising in the wake of inflation, competition between capitalist nations, and the spread of socialism. "The real function of trilateralism was and is to get imperialist powers to work together for a global order which puts the Third World [nations outside Western Europe, North America, and Japan] *and* the socialist countries in their proper, subordinate place" (Sweezy and Magdoff 1977, p. 22; Frieden 1977; Lydon 1977; Novak 1977).

Capitalism is a worldwide system, and problems must be addressed on that level. TC is an effort of major corporations in major capitalist nations to solve problems, but it is not a conspiracy: "its power is significant—a concentrated power based on a "commonality of interests rather than a blood oath" (Frieden 17).

This powerful commission was intimately tied to the Carter administration. Carter himself and Vice-President Mondale were members of TC, and at least twenty-five important positions were occupied by trilateralists.

In this fashion the ruling class dominates and controls the government (or at least tries to) in many ways. As the world changes, so does the ruling class's strategy for domination.

## *Congress and Legislation*

A number of studies have shown that not only has the ruling class controlled legislation obviously beneficial to its interests (most notably tax policy), it has also shaped much of the "reform" legislation since 1900. Kolko and Domhoff examine many reform laws. For example, Domhoff shows that legislation to enable workers to unionize did arise, in part, from the strikes and other protests of working people. But the legislation was finally passed because the more liberal wing of the ruling class realized unions could function to limit the militancy of workers—they could help to stabilize capitalism in the long run (Kolko 1963; Domhoff 1970, 1978b).

With some exceptions, senators and congresspeople do not come from the ruling class (Senators Edward Kennedy and Charles Percy are two current—1979—exceptions). So the ruling class does not control Congress that way. However, most congresspeople and senators do come from the professional, managerial, and business world, and their ideology and interests are closely connected to those of the ruling class. Moreover, as research has shown, both presidential and congressional elections have been heavily financed by contributions from the ruling class and the rest of the business world (Zweigenhaft 1975; Domhoff 1967, 1978b; Nichols 1974).

## *Regulatory Agencies*

To control some of the abuses of early capitalism, Congress created various regulatory agencies. First of all, contrary to popular belief, many of these agencies were wanted by major capitalists themselves. Secondly, the agencies' ties with those they are supposed to regulate have hardly inhibited the operations of most industries.

Studies of agencies such as the Food and Drug Administration and the Interstate Commerce Commission done by Ralph Nader and his associates have shown the failure of agencies to regulate. In fact, some regulators come to the agency after having worked in the industry they are to regulate,

> **The Powers That Be**
>
> *The following case history illustrates how members of the ruling class manipulate politicians and political institutions to control and expand their wealth.*
>
> The most famous tax-break case of the past thirty years involved the billionaire Du Pont family of Delaware and a Washington lawyer. In 1961 the Justice Department succeeded in convincing the Supreme Court to break Du Pont family control of both General Motors and the Du Pont Corporation in a court case that had been dragging on since 1949. The Court ruled that Du Pont Corporation and the family holding company, Christiana Securities, would have to sell their GM stock. Leaders within the family decided to sell the stock to individual members of the family. This assured that the family's potential influence would lurk in the background of GM decision-making. But there remained the problem of paying taxes on the profits made from selling the stock.
>
> In order to avoid or greatly reduce the tax, the family hired Washington lawyer Clark Clifford, who had made his mark as a Democratic advisor to President Harry Truman before developing a lucrative private practice based upon corporate clients. Clifford and his aides decided that the Du Pont problem required special legislation. They wrote a bill which would allow the Du Ponts to pay the tax on the profits at the maximum capital gains rate of 25 percent rather than at ordinary income tax rates. According to one estimate by the Treasury Department, this reduced the tax liability from $45 per share to $7.25 per share. To assure passage of the bill, Clifford and others arranged for a family spokesperson, Crawford Greenwalt, president of Du Pont Corporation, to meet with every member of the Senate Finance Committee and the House Ways and Means Committee. This personal lobbying, along with the efforts of the Democratic senator from the Du Ponts' home state of Delaware, led to the passage of the bill. For his help and advice, Clifford was paid $1 million over a ten-year period in yearly "retainer fees" of $100,000.
>
> Special tax legislation usually does not require such elaborate lobbying and large retainer fees. More often it is quietly tacked on to one or another piece of general tax legislation by a single legislator or a staff aide.
>
> *Source:* Reprinted from G. William Domhoff, *The Powers That Be* New York: Random House, 1978 pp. 27–29.

and even more commissioners and staff "use their jobs as stepping-stones to higher paying posts in the industries they oversee" (Babson and Brigham 1975, p. 16, quoting *Wall Street Journal;* see also Domhoff 1978b, ch. 2).

*Advisory Commissions, Social Clubs, and Open Doors*

The discussion so far about how the ruling class dominates the government has come from fairly public knowledge, accessible to interested people. More hidden, but equally important, are the advisory commissions and study groups, whose members come from the major corporations, and who recommend policy to Congress and the executive branch; the many ties between these groups and social clubs; and the open-door policy practiced by government agencies, who invite corporations to present their problems to sympathetic ears. These people meet informally at parties and social clubs, where many important decisions are discussed or even made. Political power is exercised quietly in informal settings (Burnham 1978, p. 18).

Consider a few details. Before it disbanded itself in 1973 because it would not make its meetings public, the Industry Advisory Council to the Department of Defense met regularly with defense officials to discuss mutual interests and concerns; for example, what weapons the department wanted and needed. On the IAC board were the presidents or chairmen of thirty corporations, all among the top one hundred military contractors —people who sold equipment and weapons to the Department of Defense. This was a very cozy arrangement (Roose 1975).

The Council on Foreign Relations (CFR) is another important private advisory group. Here, top corporate leaders get together with academics (such as Henry Kissinger) and others to study and explore the problems of American capitalism in United States foreign relations. Many CFR positions eventually become government policy, and members serve the government in many ways. They are appointed to government positions, serve on special presidential commissions, become government advisers, testify before congressional commissions, and write books and articles (Domhoff 1974b, p. 97; 1978b, ch. 3).

Domhoff, the foremost student of the American ruling class, has also shown that there is a great overlap between the members of the federal executive, policy groups, and social clubs and corporate directors and officials. In some cases, the same people occupy positions in all these institutions; in other cases, the same corporation has representatives in these institutions; in all cases, these people are members of the ruling class, or their hired experts (Domhoff 1974b, especially pp. 102–103; 1978b, ch. 3).

In addition, the executive branch invites corporations to drop in any time to discuss their problems, especially problems with the government. Such hospitality is not publicized (could the average person drop in to discuss such problems?), but it is assumed by all corporate leaders. It becomes known only when the government is forced to open its workings to public exposure.

The ITT hearings of spring 1972 were one such occasion. The Nixon administration was accused of receiving a bribe (a donation to the Republican Party) in exchange for "fixing" (dropping) an antitrust case against ITT. The hearings exposed the extraordinary hospitality of government agencies. Corporation presidents and representatives repeatedly testified that all it took was a phone call for them to see a government official (Committee on the Judiciary 1972).

The director of ITT's Washington office testified that he set up an appointment with Secretary of the Treasury John Connally. He explained that such appointments "are not difficult to get. You call the secretary as a rule and get an appointment." Richard Kleindienst, in the Justice Department, had told another ITT official, "well, the door is always open" (vol. 3, pp. 951–52, 1069).

Such relationships are not surprising. Government officials often come from the corporate world and return to it after their service is over. When in government, they deal with business people they know or whose basic perspective they share. So explicit conspiracies and deals, even though occasionally made, are not really the issue. It is simpler: shared interests, values, and views. It concerns a class—a ruling class—whose interests and power dominate both the economy and the government. Members of this class occupy and control most key positions both in the economy and government.

*Local Government*

The national (and multinational) corporations determine what happens to the nation's economy, and the federal government dispenses most money and power, but that is not the entire picture. But most American communities have a local ruling class, the people who own large local businesses, banks, and newspapers. Some people have argued that there is no local ruling class (see Dahl 1961), but there is increasing evidence that individual cities also have ruling classes (Domhoff [1978a] disputes Dahl's findings on New Haven).

But such local elites are increasingly losing power. National corporations are constantly buying large local businesses and making them subsidiaries (see Warner 1961 for an account of one such takeover, in Newburyport, Massachusetts). Also, large national corporations are heavily involved in major cities. For example, New York City has been controlled both by local real estate dealers and contractors, and by national institutions and ruling-class leaders (e.g., the Rockefeller family and Chase Manhattan Bank, First National City Bank). These local and national corporations make decisions largely beneficial to themselves, leading New York and other cities to crises in their finances and in the quality of life. First National City Bank has millions on deposit from working people, but uses hardly any resources for their needs, such as housing. Instead, the bank invests its money on luxury buildings and loans to major corporations. And it was the Rockefellers who pushed for the World Trade Center, a 110-story office building. Thus, New York has plenty of office space but no housing for working people (Newfield and DuBrul 1977; Etra and Leinsdorf 1974, p. 30).

Finally, local politics are primarily controlled by a local elite, mostly in real estate, banking, and other interests. Even the liberal mayor John Lindsay was financed by New York real estate interests and made decisions favorable to them. Local politicians are not members of the national ruling class, and they can be heavily influenced by national corporations. But neither are they average working people (Newfield 1973; Sweezy 1969, pp. 117-19; Domhoff 1967, ch. 6.)

## The Ruling Class in Other Institutions

The power of the ruling class is most obvious in its control of the economy and the government, but it has also sought to shape the nature and functions of public education (Bowles and Gintis 1976). In addition, the mass media control what people see and hear (Ewen 1976). Foundations, created by corporate profits, have allowed the ruling class to support and advance ideas and research they find acceptable (Domhoff 1967, p. 74; Horowitz and Kolodney 1969). The criminal justice system has also been shaped by the ruling class (Liazos 1974; Quinney 1974; Tigar and Levy 1977). The ruling class also tries to influence how we think, both by trying to propagate certain ideas as acceptable and by branding others as unacceptable (Domhoff 1978, Ch. 5).

These areas are mentioned simply to suggest the broad influence and domination of the ruling class. They pervade and try to control most institutions. Later chapters explore some of these issues.

## WHAT DIFFERENCE DOES IT MAKE?

By this time, many of you have probably raised an important question. If important positions in the economy and government are occupied by people from a small group, does it follow that they make all decisions solely to benefit themselves? Even more, how is it possible to know what goes through their minds, what they say to each other, when they make important decisions?

Of course, it is not possible to know how these people make decisions. Sometimes mistakes are made, inadvertently exposing governing methods (the Watergate scandal is an example), but much of the time decisions are made at meetings that are not open to anyone.

Examine the assumption that the upper class rules for the benefit of the whole society. For example, reform legislation has been passed through the years. Does this not show that the ruling class is not entirely self-interested?

First of all, even a benevolent ruling class is still a ruling class. Ordinary people still have no power, and any benefits given may be taken away. Secondly, much reform legislation turns out to benefit the ruling class, and the part that benefits ordinary people is a concession made to prevent greater losses to the ruling class.

Another objection to this portrait of the ruling class may be that it is not a closed group, that ordinary people have a chance to join. But studies have shown otherwise. According to a study by Domhoff, only 5 percent of those in the ruling class rose there from the bottom. Most of the rest came from ruling-class families, with some from middle-class backgrounds. But these newcomers, whatever their background, entered the ruling class only after they had accepted its values and interests. Indeed, to strengthen itself, the ruling class wants capable newcomers who have accepted capitalism and its values (Mills 1956; Domhoff 1970, p. 73).

But does it make any difference to the rest of us what the backgrounds of ruling people may be? Even if it were totally reconstituted by new members each generation or were made up entirely of ethnic and racial minorities, women, or any combination of these—if people are exploited and ruled by a small minority, it matters little who they are. People would still be ruled and exploited. The competition and insecurity now rampant would still reign supreme. Would the average black person, or woman, or working-class man, be any less ruled if the rulers rose from their ranks?

Finally, the ruling class does not rule only, or primarily, by placing its members in the government and the economy. Even if socialists were elected to powerful government positions, they could make few significant changes. As the socialists found out in Chile (1970-73), control of the government is not sufficient if the institutions created by the ruling class are left largely intact, if the ruling class controls much of the economy, if members of the ruling class are left free to sabotage socialism. Thus, by focusing on the means by which individual members of the ruling class occupy government and business positions, Domhoff is somewhat misleading. Capitalism is a system that has developed over time, and it is the institutions, values, and habits that need to be changed, not the individuals who come from the ruling class. (I am indebted to Richard Kronish for pointing out to me this weakness in Domhoff's analysis.)

But these are academic questions. There is a small ruling class, largely unchanged from one generation to the next, that controls most of the wealth, and holds most power, wielding it largely for its benefit. A look at some important government decisions shows that they benefit mostly the ruling class.

First, in 1970, 75 percent of the taxes collected on personal income came from people making under $10,000 a year. Secondly, half of the federal budget goes for defense, and most defense contracts are awarded to a few large corporations. Third, of the 32 percent spent on welfare and education, much of it really ends up as subsidies to national and local businesses. Fourth, farm support programs have benefited mostly the large corporate farms. Fifth, the federal government provides loans and guarantees to large corporations and subsidizes airports and other facilities useful mostly to the ruling and upper-middle classes. And finally, large corporations receive free the right to use the public airwaves for television, a guarantee of huge profits (Chambliss and Ryther 1975, pp. 270-73).

There is more evidence. Industrial customers use 50 percent of all electricity produced, but pay only 28 percent of the total light bill. Is there better evidence that the powerful few who run the economy arrange things for their own profit? (Babson and Brigham 1975, p. 14).

Finally, the central point of Babson and Brigham's pamphlet "Why Do We Spend So Much Money?" is to show that as fewer and fewer corporations control the economy, prices and profits inevitably increase. As they need not fear competition, corporations can raise prices. Competition may be said to be the American way, but it is bad for business and profits.

For example, in 1979 the big oil corporations manipulated petroleum supplies to raise gasoline and home heating-fuel prices. While they were importing more petroleum in the first five months of 1979 than they did in the comparable 1978 period, oil corporations were: (a) selling more gasoline outside the United States, (b) refining less petroleum than they had in previous years, (c) holding petroleum out at sea by having oil tankers move at ten knots an hour instead of sixteen or seventeen. Thus, in a few months the oil companies managed to raise prices by over 50 percent and increase profits tremendously (Cook 1979; Tyler and Neumann 1979; Gannon 1979; Gannon shows that the conspiracy to fix and raise prices began in 1972).

So the ruling class under capitalism, as ruling classes everywhere, rules for its own interests, depriving people of material necessities, dignity, and liberty. But must it be ever so? Is a true democracy possible?

## IS DEMOCRACY POSSIBLE?

*The Limits of Ruling-Class Power*

As stated earlier, the ruling class is powerful but not omnipotent. In addition to its own internal divisions, it must confront the opposition of the working class, both on a national and international level. Concessions must be made or power may be lost. In reflecting on the threat to ruling-class power during the 1930s Depression, Joseph Kennedy said: "I am not ashamed to record that in those days I felt and said I would be willing to part with half of what I had if I could be sure of keeping, under law and order, the other half. Then it seemed that I should be able to hold nothing for the protection of my family" (quoted in Domhoff 1967, p. 153).

And recently, Samuel Huntington, in a report for the Trilateral Commission, wrote that we need "a greater degree of moderation in democracy" (quoted in Novak 1977, p. 59). The bluntness of this comment, and the report as a whole, worried many commission members who objected to its publication. It shows an obvious concern that the working class is threatening the power and wealth of the ruling class; the ruling class is worried and wants this threat controlled (see Bowles [1977] for an elaboration of this point).

The limited power of the ruling class, and the reforms they are forced to make may be interpreted in two ways. Domhoff has argued that such reforms have not changed the essence of ruling-class power. For example, he argues that despite all compromises by the ruling class, workplaces are as undemocratic as ever, and people suffer as much work-related injury and death (1970, p. 167). Reforms make some improvement in working-class life, but they represent no threat to the power of the ruling class; indeed, the appearance of change may prevent the struggle for real change.

A different perspective on reforms is exemplified by Dreier (1975) and Ackerman (1978). They agree that many reforms present no challenge to ruling-class power, but some others do. Some reforms co-opt, but others can lead to socialism. They are not socialism itself but they serve to improve people's lives and to teach what is possible and where the ruling class is vulnerable.

*The American Scene*

Probably the first necessity in the struggle to create democracy is the realization that major decisions affecting society are made by people, not by some impersonal power beyond control. Aronowitz (1974), after discussing some decisions that have shaped American society after World War II (the Federal Housing Act, the interstate highway program, the concentration of agriculture into fewer hands, and so on), argues that none of these was inevitable. Federal agencies, congress, and the president made them in response to the needs and power of the ruling class and its interests. All could have been made differently, to benefit everyone, not just the ruling class.

It is important to demystify the process by which major decisions are made. Thus, people can begin to reduce their feelings of helplessness and can study which reforms can lead to real democracy.

There have been some reforms and changes that have the potential to lead to socialism and control by the people. In this day, Marx saw the fight that led to the ten-hour workday as a significant political victory for the working class, not merely as a ploy by the ruling class to buy off the workers. It was good in itself (it reduced the suffering of twelve- and fourteen-hour days), and was also a political victory, for it showed workers what they could do if they struggled as a united, organized class (Dreier 1975).

The Occupational Safety and Health Act and the mineworkers' campaign to improve working conditions and provide increased benefits for those suffering from black lung, both raise the issue of workers' control (see Chapter 5). Not only may they provide concrete benefits, but workers can begin to see the reality of controlling their work environment. Such control is the beginning of democracy.

Dreier mentions other examples. Ackerman (1978) discusses the real problems of both extreme positions: either always giving in to limited reforms and compromises, or opposing all reforms on principle. He argues that each case must be studied carefully, to find out if it would give the mere appearance of change or promises real change and education. Dreier and Ackerman show that other successful revolutions have not rejected all reforms and compromises, seeing both as necessary steps on the way to socialism.

Domhoff made a different proposal for socialism in America: people should first get together and develop some programs for a socialist America, and then run in Democratic primaries for all levels of office. In doing so, people could present and debate openly their socialist proposals. Since other attempts at socialism (such as third parties) have not worked, Domhoff believes something new is needed, and he outlines some advantages of his proposal (for one, by working within the Democratic party, you avoid the likelihood of immediate rejection by the voters, since this party is seen as part of the American way). Although Domhoff's proposal should be studied and debated, it has serious limitations, as already discussed above (Domhoff 1974a).

*Democracy under Socialism*

The successful socialist revolutions, and those now underway, clearly show that the ruling class is not omnipotent. Both on national and international levels, the ruling class has suffered many defeats.

But what happens after a successful revolution has taken over the state and eliminated the power of the capitalist ruling class? This is a central problem of socialist society. To protect the revolution from the threats of its enemies (internal and external), to meet the immediate crises of starvation and poverty, to free a people who have been oppressed and degraded for centuries, and to begin developing the economy, a strong central government and a bureaucracy are needed. But there is a danger that this government will lead to the formation of a ruling class, even if in new form. As argued in the previous chapter, some socialists have concluded that in the Soviet Union, and in some other socialist societies, a new ruling class has arisen. Conrad reports that in East Germany there is a rising protest against the control of the ruling class (a class similar to that in the USSR). Most of the protest is Marxist and aims to take power away from the new ruling class, to reduce income inequalities, and so on (Sweezy 1978; Conrad 1979).

In China, Mao Zedong was very worried about the dangers of a new ruling class, and urged the Chinese people to challenge constantly leaders and experts. The cultural revolution of the late 1960s and early 1970s was meant as an experiment and struggle to achieve true demcracy. It made some progress in popular control of institutions, but it failed because the leaders of the cultural revolution soon began directing and ordering people, rather than creating conditions where people understood and accepted the goals of the revolution and began to rule themselves. Bettelheim poses the issue: "Is power wielded *by* the working people, or is it wielded *for* them . . . ?" (1978, p. 105). The struggle for mass democracy was uncertain; only in time will it be possible to tell how deep its roots took in Chinese society. For now, the official line of the leaders following Mao's death clearly opposes the goals of the cultural revolution (see Chapter 4 for a longer discussion of the revolution and its aftermath; see also Hinton 1972; Chen 1975; Bettelheim 1978; all of *Monthly Review* May 1979).

Zimbalist (1975) shows the same concern for democracy in Cuba. People are searching for ways to have all decisions made by the people affected by them—decisions that affect neighborhoods and workplaces, and decisions on the national and international levels. A visitor to Cuba in early 1979 writes:

> No major policy goes into effect, no factory output quota is set, no new housing is allotted without detailed public discussion—in neighborhood organizations, union meetings, or workplace assemblies—of all the factors and choices involved. As Roberto, our driver, indicated, this process of collective sharing and evaluation of the facts is basic to the Cuban concept of democracy.
>
> By way of contrast, elections of individual officials are of distinctly secondary importance. Since 1976, Cubans have been electing local governments, and the local delegates have in turn been electing the higher echelons. But a young office worker, whom I asked about the significance of this change, insisted that Cuba had been democratic even before these elections.
>
> What is important about the new local governments, he said, is that they have the power to deal directly with many local problems. So citizens with complaints about, say, housing now have someone to confront in person with their needs, rather than being dependent on a bureaucrat in a distant Havana ministry.
>
> On the whole, Cubans assume on the basis of experience that their government works in their interest. They generally refer to "the revolution" rather than "the government." What they meant by democracy is not US civics-course-style checks and balances, but ways of participating in the process of the revolution (*Dollars and Sense,* February 1979, p. 9).

On April 8, 1979 there were local elections in Cuba, as reported in the *Guardian:*

> Nearly 97% of the country's eligible voters turned out to elect 10,660 delegates to the Municipal Assemblies of People's Power. About 90% of the delegates were selected in the first round of balloting, the rest in runoff elections April 15. They will take office May 6.
>
> The municipal assemblies, elected every two and a half years, are responsible for overseeing the running of local production units, services, schools clinics, recreational facilities, etc., in the country's 169 municipalities (which include rural areas surrounding the towns). The assemblies are also responsible for electing delegates to the provincial assemblies (every 2.5 years) and the National Assembly, the highest organ of state power and lawmaking (every five years).
>
> Cuba's People Power electoral process is structured to insure a high degree of voter participation at the grass roots. It begins in the neighborhoods, where several hundred voters meet and discuss who should be nominated to repre-

sent them—anyone over 16 is eligible. The neighborhood, of which there are several in each voting district, usually nominates one candidate for the district, who runs against nominees of other neighborhoods. By law, there must be at least two candidates in every district. This year, some 75% of the electorate participated in the neighborhood nominations (*The Guardian,* May 2, 1979, p. 12).

It still seems, however, that despite these changes the party and government leaders make major foreign policy decisions and hold major power in making other decisions. There is clearly a move toward democratic institutions, to popular control, but a long struggle and much work lie ahead before there will be complete democracy.

The following chapters explore in greater detail the possibilities for real democracy.

Both in the struggle to achieve socialism in capitalist societies and in the struggle to create democratic institutions under socialism, it is important to avoid fatalism and utopian thinking. Fatalism guarantees people will never fight for their freedom; utopian thinking discourages people easily by underestimating the need for a long and continuous struggle for democracy. Democracy is something that must be earned, it will not be given. For if it is *given,* it can also be taken away.

# 4
# *Domination and Elitism*

## THE PERVASIVENESS OF DOMINATION

In capitalist societies, the ruling class has power over the rest of the people. It uses its power to control, dominate, and exploit them.

Although some societies have been characterized by little or no domination, it has been pervasive in many societies. For example, in Greek peasant society (typical of most Europian peasant societies), children and women were controlled and oppressed by adult men. Other forms of domination have been common.

But domination pervades most human relations under capitalism. Parents and adults dominate and control their children. Experts of all kinds —teachers, managers, doctors, scientists, lawyers, judges, politicians, professionals, and bureaucrats—all dominate the people they claim to serve. They use their positions for their own advantage (both collectively and as individuals) and in time forget that their jobs were created to serve the needs of their clients.

The development of industrial capitalism has meant the proliferation of different forms of domination by experts. Although domination is not unique to capitalism, it flourishes there. Since capitalism has been the prevalent system over the last four centuries, domination has become an important problem. It is certainly characteristic of American society, and it will be very difficult to destroy, even under socialism.

To say, for example, that the relationship of teacher to student is negative and destructive because of the element of domination is not to deny that some people know more than others, which they can teach to them. Nor can anyone deny that some people may be better leaders than others. Nor, finally, can anyone deny the obvious differences in abilities between people. I refer to something different. In relations of domination, the person who knows more, or has more of some ability or quality, uses that ability (or, really, the mystique of it) to oppress others, to keep them inferior, to exploit them, and in some way not allow them to gain equality.

Power and authority differ. Under authority, I use my ability (whatever it may be) to teach or help others. They are able to choose, willingly, whether to follow my advice. In ordinary teaching relationships, I hold the power to grade—thus, students do not learn entirely willingly. But I can teach without any such power—people may choose to come to me, acknowledging my greater knowledge in a subject, and I can teach it to them, if they really want that knowledge. I have some expert ability, and by sharing my knowledge I help others learn and grow—I liberate them in some way. Coercion and power need never enter the relationship. As argued earlier, differences need not result in inequalities.

Doctors can heal in very different ways than they now do. They can explain, share as much of their knowledge as patients can and want to know, and openly admit their ignorance in many cases. They need not keep patients ignorant and subordinate. The fear and ignorance pervading relationships with experts, professionals, and bureaucrats are not essential to those relationships, they are tools for domination.

Domination is essential to capitalism. In a society divided by classes, where competition, individualism, material values, and the exploitation of one person by another are central values, domination must arise. In a capitalist system, no one can "succeed" and outdo others without also trying to dominate them. How can someone win if he or she must share with competitors? How can doctors demand high prestige and pay without creating an aura of rare knowledge and abilities? How can experts justify their position without excluding lay people from the special knowledge they supposedly possess? The rewards of higher positions (money and prestige) can only be justified if those holding them can keep them away from others, thus creating the mystique of their special abilities. But if competition were not central, if there was equality, there would be no need for domination and exclusion. Then people would use their abilities to help others and people would share—not hide and dominate.

Domination by experts has not been total, of course. People always have been able to provide for themselves: they raised children before pediatricians came to the scene, and they dealt with emotional problems before there were psychiatrists. In addition, various self-help groups have arisen in recent years: ex-mental patients organize to help themselves with problems they share; people set up informal schools to teach each other without grades, tests, and degrees; neighborhoods organize to fight the demolition of their homes that were decreed by expert urban planners to be slums; women's groups struggle to liberate childbirth from the control of hospitals and doctors; and people generally realize more and more that they must organize for their own interests against the power and control of experts of all kinds.

The belief in the superiority of experts is a problem because it pervades most social relationships. It is rooted in social relations and will take longer to change than will material inequalities. It relates to the quality of human relations, to the creation of social conditions that allow freedom for all. This chapter will explore what some socialist societies are doing in this area and the problems they face. Many people in the United States are struggling also to create freeing and egalitarian social relations.

An example from Chapter 5 (on work) may clarify the issue of domination. Two related issues are raised:

First, there is the material exploitation of workers—whether jobs are available and whether workers' labor is exploited for the benefit of the ruling class.

Secondly, there is the quality of the work experience—who decides how work is to be organized and carried out. The focus is on how domination by experts affects the control of the process of work. Will managers and experts decide what is to be produced (or how a service will be provided) or will all workers conceive, plan, and then carry out all the work?

For example, will workers stand on one spot of an assembly line and install the same part in cars as they come by every minute, because management has decreed that is the way to make cars? Or will the workers decide what automobiles to make and how to make them (perhaps differently than in an assembly line) and then set up the plant to produce them? Indeed, in a true socialist society the workers making cars, together with other groups and communities, could decide to stop making cars because of energy and environment problems and switch to producing parts for mass-transit vehicles. And whether they made cars or trains, workers could arrange the plant themselves and make the work enriching rather than alienating.

## PROFESSIONAL DOMINATION IN THE UNITED STATES

"Professionalization is one major feature of the more general process of bureaucratization that characterizes modern society" (Boughey 1978, p. 227). Most occupations not yet known as professions aspire to that title. Why do professions have such high prestige? Are they beneficial to the society (to ordinary people)?

## What Is a Profession?

Different definitions could be given. Professionals would like people to think that the following are the measures of professions. Professionals claim to have special knowledge, theory, and techniques. This knowledge and the values that accompany it are gained after long training and socialization. Lay people do not possess such knowledge or techniques because they lack the abilities and long training of professionals. Because of such special skills and knowledge, which they use to help their clients, professionals claim (and usually receive) prestige, authority, and high rewards. In addition, they control the government bodies that regulate their profession—thus controlling the standards and norms of their work, with little or no outside interference. Professionals have the power to decide who can and who cannot join their profession. They also claim to set up and administer professional codes of ethics that protect clients from abuse (Hall 1975, pp. 70-76; Krause 1971, p. 77).

There is some truth to these claims. At least some individuals in each profession do live by its professed standards and ethics. The long training surely gives people some special knowledge and skills.

But the claims are unjustified if we consider professions as a whole and examine how they work in practice. The special knowledge claimed by professionals is exaggerated in order to mystify and control the public. Their knowledge is often not so profound, nor so difficult that most people could not learn it. The long training required of professionals (becoming even longer in some cases) is not so much necessary to acquire difficult knowledge and skills, as it is meant to impress the public with the hard work and special abilities that supposedly accompany long training. In short, this claim is public relations. Indeed, as George Bernard Shaw said, it may well be that "all professions are conspiracies against the laity" (quoted in Gross and Osterman 1972, p. 9; see also Krause 1971, p. 78).

The codes of ethics and standards created to protect the public more often work to protect the professions from outside criticism. Incompetent, unethical, and even cruel actions by professionals are hidden from public view, because the professionals claim only they know what is necessary or proper for clients.

To impress the public with their claimed superior knowledge, professions develop special languages (jargon) that only they can understand. Such jargon often restates the obvious and hides ignorance. The social sciences abound with jargon that only confuses people (despite my best intentions, I am sure this book contains some jargon; years of professional training cannot be overcome easily). Jargon is a weapon for power and control, common to all professions: doctors, lawyers, teachers, and others. I can never forget the time my wife was having false labor while pregnant with our second child. After a week of contractions coming in short intervals, she visited her doctor (an extremely competent and kind person, whom we liked). He attempted to explain the cause to her. But in fact what he did was give a name (jargon) to her symptoms (something like "irritable uterus"), which of course merely restated what she already knew and explained nothing. But it is not the nature of the professional (and of lay people's expectations) to admit ignorance. (See Boughey 1978, pp. 227–29.)

*Professional Insulation*

This long training and socialization to enter a profession often act to insulate professionals from the realities of other people's lives. It is not a question of malice or exploitation, but of ignorance.

Chapter 7 discusses a flood that destroyed Buffalo Creek, West Virginia. After the flood, experts and professionals from the Department of Housing and Urban Development (HUD) came to the region to set up temporary trailer camps for the homeless people. It never occurred to HUD experts to ask people whom they would like to live next to. They did not think that people had social ties they would like to retain. So, people from many different neighborhoods were placed in the same camp, thus helping erode the sense of community even more (Erikson 1976, pp. 148–49).

But professionals harm people from intent as often as from ignorance. Chapter 6 cites *Food First* many times. One of the clear messages this book conveys is that agricultural professionals work to enhance the power and control of large corporate farms, not the peasants and farmers. New seeds developed by large scientific institutes are appropriate for the needs of corporate farms, not of small farmers. Professional scientific knowledge is not "neutral"; it is used for the benefit of powerful groups and institutions (Lappé and Collins 1977, p. 123).

This point needs to be emphasized: the ruling class and powerful institutions use the expertise and knowledge of professionals for their own ends. In *The Rape of Our Neighborhoods,* Worthy shows how time and again colleges, hospitals, urban-renewal departments, and other institutions use the power and mystique of professional experts to take homes and land away from people for institutional expansion. Experts are presumed to know what cities and communities really need, to know what is a "slum" and must be destroyed. What replaces these "slums" and homes taken away from people are structures beneficial to the upper classes. Often I drive by what was the West End of Boston, once a bustling ethnic neighborhood and in its place now stand luxury apartment buildings, hospital buildings, and empty land for parking.

*Doctors*

In surveys of occupational prestige, doctors have had the highest rating. Also, except for top managers of corporations and people in the ruling class, they have the highest income. But as people are now becoming more aware, the medical profession has much incompetence, arrogance, mystification, protection of incompetent doctors, and unnecessary operations (see Chapter 11).

A few findings will be presented here from Millman's study *The Unkindest Cut* (1977), especially its Chapters 5 and 6. Millman shows in some detail how doctors, in the hospitals she studied, kept information from patients, not for the patients' benefit, but to save face. A doctor who did not get the proper tissue sample did not tell the patient the truth, but said the sample showed no disease. As one doctor told Millman, ["we"] try to "protect ourselves, no one else" (p. 145).

The following case, related by a doctor, shows that professional needs often take precedence over patients' needs.

> There's a fellow who just died up in the Intensive Care Unit this morning who shouldn't have had heart surgery when he did. He had an infection and was spiking fever and the surgery should have been postponed. He probably had endocarditis (an infection of the heart tissue) at the time of surgery, and it should have been postponed, but the surgeon needed to do a case this week in order to keep up the minimum case load required to maintain the thoracic service.
>
> I couldn't say anything about the case. I did the catheterization on the patient, but he developed the infection afterwards, and at that time I was no longer involved in the case (pp. 134-35).

The hospital would not fire incompetent doctors. Millman was told they would be watched if they stayed on the hospital staff, but if they worked unwatched elsewhere they could do more harm. It never occurs to anyone in the hospital to try to revoke their licenses. A service chief said: "Once a doctor gets his license to operate, no one's going to stop him from doing anything. It's easier to practice medicine than to keep a driver's license" (p. 132).

Within the medical profession doctors do not argue against obvious (to them) wrong decisions by other doctors. One justification for such noninterference holds that one does not argue with others outside one's specialty. Another justification is that one does not question those in higher authority. Even more, "members of the same specialty explain that they must mind their own business to be able to work with their colleagues" (Millman, pp. 128, 133).

## *The Spreading of Professionalism*

Recent United States history has seen the proliferation of professions and their domination of many institutions. What people have been doing for themselves and each other is being taken over by professionals and experts.

For example, midwives delivered babies for thousands of years. Beginning in the late nineteenth century, however, doctors gained control and outlawed midwifery (which now is again possible in some states). What had been a natural part of life, a skill mastered by many women, became a specialty totally controlled by doctors (Ehrenreich and English 1973; Shaw 1974; Chapter 11 of this book).

Child-rearing also was taken over by experts. Pediatricians and psychological professionals conspired to deprive parents of their confidence in child-rearing and transformed child-rearing into a field of expertise. Ironically, most of these experts have been men who have had little to do with raising their own children, or any children, and who, in their own lives, have the same problems raising children that everyone does. What people in all cultures had always been able to do became a mysterious and difficult body of knowledge available only to experts (Lasch 1977; Ehrenreich and English 1978).

Childbirth and child-rearing are but two areas taken over by experts. Many more fields are being taken over by groups requiring long, special education, licenses, and degrees. Lay people are prohibited from practicing in these areas of expertise.

The development of capitalist institutions and ruling-class control deprived workers of their crafts and of much knowledge. These same institutions have led to professional domination that "turned the citizen into a client." Lasch argues that "both the growth of management and the proliferation of professions represent new forms of capitalist control, which enable capital to transcend its personal form and to pervade every part of society." As a worker must be told what to do every step of the way, so parents must be told how to raise their own children. Just as advertising strives to convince people that store-bought spaghetti sauce is superior to the sauce cooked at home, child experts try to convince people that the experts' knowledge of child-rearing is superior (Lasch 1977, pp. 156–57).

## DOMINATION UNDER SOCIALISM

The coming of socialism does not mean automatic freedom from domination by political leaders, managers, professionals, experts, specialists, and bureaucrats. True freedom of speech and thought, real daily participation by all people in the institutions where they work and live, can only come with protracted and continuous struggle. It would be a mistake to think otherwise.

### *The Cultural Revolution in China*

In no contemporary society is there true democracy. Nowhere are all institutions controlled and run by the people in them on a daily basis. In all societies there are many types of inequalities between most of the people and leaders, experts, professionals, and others who claim to possess greater abilities and knowledge than do most people ("the masses," in socialist terminology). Domination by experts is rooted in modern capitalist societies, and socialist societies do not appear to have overcome that problem.

Supporters of the cultural revolution in China (from 1966 to 1976), Chinese and others, claim that it was a mass experiment to end domination. It is examined here because it is the only modern experiment in mass democracy. It may be that this Chinese experience is not relevant to the United States, given the political, economic, and social differences between the two societies. In China, for example, 80 percent of the people still live in villages and work the land, whereas only 5 percent of Americans work on the land.

Despite differences, however, some comparisons do exist. For example, a description of socialist work organization and socialist medicine suggests that the principles of organization can also apply to industrial capitalist societies. How a factory is organized, and who runs it, with what goals, reveals both what is missing under capitalism and what must be done to make work a humanizing experience.

In other areas too the cultural revolution is relevant to this society. The United States, China, and other societies confront the same problem: people are taught to accept expert advice without questions; manual labor is less respected than mental labor (indeed, often it is seen as degrading); and institutions are not run by the people in them, rather, by leaders, experts, professionals, managers, and other elites. At least some people in China sought to confront these issues during the cultural revolution; since the United States faces most of the same issues, there are lessons in the successes, failures, and experiences of China's cultural revolution. (The following account draws from the following authors: Hinton 1972, 1979; Pfeffer 1973; Ehrenreich 1974; Chen 1975; Gamberg 1977; Bettelheim 1974, 1978; Lotta 1978; Selden 1979; and all of *Monthly Review* for May 1979).

*Goals and Methods*

The cultural revolution sought to question and overturn all relationships of domination and oppression. People struggled to create decentralized, locally controlled institutions and to eliminate inequalities between mental and manual labor, between the city and the peasantry, and between leaders and masses.

In factories, people in cadres (small leadership groups) and managers were required to do physical labor one day a week; workers, on the other hand, began to learn how to run the operations, to do more than physical labor. In schools, students were urged to challenge their teachers, not merely to repeat what they were told.

There was an effort to re-educate cadres in all organizations. Many were sent to special cadre schools in the countryside, where they worked in the fields and studied the socialist principles of equality, class struggle, and mass participation. The Chinese believed that "the arrogant air of an official disappears by half, the moment he carries a hoe on his shoulder." It was apparent, of course, that not all people went willingly to cadre schools and many did not change. Many went though the motions only because it was expected of them. Factory managers also came to avoid physical labor (Gamberg 1977, pp. 221-33; Ehrenreich 1974, p. 24).

Workers in offices, factories, and farms were encouraged to criticize publicly the leaders of their organizations. For example, workers wrote anonymous posters and put them up on walls. Those criticized had to respond, and often there were long debates and struggles between workers and cadre leaders.

Another important trait of the cultural revolution has been the deprofessionalization of many activities and the accompanying growth of self-help and mutual help. As discussed in Chapter 7, Chinese neighborhoods and communes are organized in a series of groups, from small to large. The smallest groups, about eighty people each, provide many services. For example, disputes are settled by local group leaders, and people in a group help each other in times of crisis. In general, social services are not provided by professionals, rather, by neighbors. Nonprofessionals, who often run these self-help groups, learn by doing and grow in confidence. Self-help groups in China stem from necessity and are sponsored and encouraged by the whole society and its leaders. The revolution encouraged this demystification of the expertise of doctors and other professionals and the turn to self-reliance and decentralization. In short, people were taking over (Sidel 1976, pp. 223-28; 1974, pp. 151-53).

The following excerpt shows how, when freed from professional domination, peasants and workers can make important contributions to society.

> A nationally publicized example of the ideal method and approach is that of Yao Shih-chang, a production leader from Shantung province. Almost half of the brigade land was devoted to peanuts. After failing to increase production by copying methods which had given fair results elsewhere, Yao Shih-chang decided to apply dialectics to peanuts, pin-pointing the main contradictions to resolve them. He started by going to the fields at night, literally to watch the growth process. His first discovery came just before dawn one morning when flowers opened on the first of his test clusters. More early-morning vigils and he discovered that this was a law—the flowers all opened just before dawn. Knowing that the pods begin to form as the flowers begin to wither, he continued watching the flowers, hanging a label on each stem with the date on which the first flowers appeared, continuing his night-watch over sixty nights, by which time he had accumulated a vast amount of peanut lore, the test plants being covered with labels. He discovered that the time between the opening of the flower and the ripening of the nuts was sixty-five days, and that the first pair of branches produced 60 to 70 percent of the nuts, the second layer 20 to 30 percent, while the mass above produced nothing except empty pods.
> 
> The following season, by pruning off the unproductive upper branches and changing cultivation methods to provide maximum nourishment for the first

and second branches, Yao Shih-chang managed to boost output from 3.65 tons per acre in 1958, when the Great Leap Forward inspired him to start his experiments, to an average of 8.5 tons on the whole 330 acres devoted to peanuts, with up to 15 tons in some places (Burchett and Alley 1976, pp. 191-92).

The cultural revolution sought to translate this peasant's motivation into all of China's workplaces. When knowledge and investigation are not widespread, there arise the conditions for great inequalities. Keeping knowledge in the hands of experts tends to increase their power and to make workers subordinate. The mystique and the reality of greater expert knowledge must be struggled against. When all the people gain knowledge, they can begin to grow and control their lives. Through their work and contributions they can also improve living conditions (Andors 1977, p. xxii).

The cultural revolution sought both to liberate the masses from domination and to improve living conditions. When former housewives provide primary health care after three to six months training, they accomplish two goals. First, they provide more medical care to more people, thus improving living conditions. But they also expand their knowledge and self-confidence, and medicine loses some of its mystique. People begin to understand that medical care is a human activity done by people who develop skills through study and training, but who are still ordinary people and by no means omnipotent (Sidel 1974, p. 152).

*Why Did the Cultural Revolution End?*

For now, the cultural revolution in China has ended. There is no more talk of workers running their factories. Also, managers, teachers, scientists, and cadre leaders no longer are required to do manual labor. As domination by cadre leaders and experts resumes its previous forms, there are increasing material inequalities between them and the masses. Stores sell color television sets for $1,600, obviously affordable only by the elite; some cadre leaders now have access to special shops, villas, and airplane rides (Lederer 1978; Reuter 1978; Bettelheim 1978).

Why has the cultural revolution ended? One view holds that the leaders of the cultural revolution did not carry out their principles consistently. Inequalities and domination are increasing in China because the cultural revolution did not develop fully the initiative, control, and participation of all people. In that context, cadre leaders, whose class interests conflict with those of the mass of people, have reasserted control. The new order, in work, education, agriculture, and so on, benefits the bourgeoisie under socialism.

In 1966, at the start of the cultural revolution, the Chinese communist party pointed out the need for all people to speak out without fear, to have real and total freedom of speech. But in many ways the leaders of the cultural revolution did not practice that principle. Often, they used Mao's prestige to make a political argument. Such use of Mao's authority discouraged critical analysis and thinking by all people. By 1971, instead of mass movements, there were criticism campaigns organized by party officials. The political role of the people decreased. The leaders of the cultural revolution often imposed their views, rather than educating people through analysis, study, and discussion. Intellectual activity (as in numbers of books published) was restricted unnecessarily. Often young people were coerced to go work in the country, instead of being educated on the need to do so. Leaders appealed to the people for support by attacking the other side merely by labels and cliches, instead of explaining in detail the issues and principles involved. In short, after the first years of the cultural revolution, authority and domination became common. The education and liberation of the masses became secondary (Bettelheim 1978; Selden 1979, p. 32).

A different socialist perspective holds that the leaders of the cultural revolution were either wrong in their goals or pronounced those goals as an excuse to create anarchy and take power in China. The current leaders in China blame the leaders of the cultural revolution for all problems in the present and recent past, from juvenile delinquency to housing shortages (see most issues of *Beijing Review* for 1979). Critics have argued that during the years of the revolution there were tremendous abuses of power; many workers took advantage of the need to criticize managers and they did little or no work; discipline in work and education eroded so deeply that China was near total anarchy and faced critical shortages of material goods (Ch'en 1979; Leiken 1979; MacEwan 1979; Hinton 1979; Sweezy and Magdoff 1979b; Yates 1979).

*The Meaning of the Cultural Revolution*

The arguments about what went on in the years 1966-1976 will continue for a long time. Certainly, both supporters and critics of the cultural revolution exaggerate (MacEwan 1979; Selden 1979, pp. 31-32). Some abuses of power, some disorder, surely existed. Even supporters admit as much. On the other hand, it seems clearly unjustified to blame all of China's troubles on the cultural revolution. Indeed, some evidence exists that shows production increased during those ten years (Bettelheim 1978, p. 78).

Only time will reveal the meaning of what happened during those years. It is quite possible that events did not match the rhetoric and the ideals. Very possibly the rhetoric covered confusion and disorder (Hoxha 1979). Despite these valid doubts and criticisms, the cultural revolution and its goals must be studied, for to date it is the only mass experiment to have tried to lessen domination and end inequalities. The principle involved applies to all societies: how can people struggle against domination and the inequalities that follow from it? And how can people know who holds power and control? A society where material goods are distributed equally among all people, with no privileged elite, would be a society run by all people (MacEwan 1979, pp. 47-48).

## MAKING PEOPLE GENTLE: LIFE WITHOUT DOMINATION

Issues of professional domination, ruling elites, and class privilege have been around a long time. During the Jacksonian era (1830s), American voters "voted the licensing laws for lawyers and physicians out of existence" and the times were generally against professional power and privileges (Krause 1971, p. 26). But professions reasserted control and in time became dominant. Can societies work without professionals, leaders, and experts? Is their power inevitable?

### Curbing Power

Richard Lee went to the Kalahari Desert "to study the hunting and gathering subsistence economy of the !Kung, and to accomplish that it was essential not to provide them with food, share my own food, or interfere in any way with their food-gathering activities." But at the end of his year's stay, to compensate for his "stinginess," he decided to provide a feast for the whole group. He bought what he knew they considered a delicacy: a big, fat cow, obviously full of meat. But when he told some !Kung which cow he had bought people responded in dismay. "Do you expect us to eat that bag of bones?" they said. They warned Lee that "there are many fierce ones here, and with such a small quantity of meat to distribute, how can you give everybody a fair share?" Fights seemed to be inevitable (1969, pp. 22, 23, 26).

Lee could not understand what was happening. When the feast day arrived, he feared for the worst. But the cow had at least two inches of fat on it and was full of meat. Everyone laughed and had a great time. Lee did not see what the joke was.

After a while he asked a !Kung friend [/gaugo] for an explanation:

"Why did you tell me the black ox was worthless, when you could see that it was loaded with fat and meat?" "It is our way," he said smiling. "We always like to fool people about that. Say there is a Bushman who has been hunting. He must not come home and announce like a braggart, 'I have killed a big one in the bush!' He must sit down in silence until I or someone else comes up to his fire and asks, 'What did you see today?' He replies quietly, 'Ah, I'm no good for hunting. I saw nothing at all (pause) just a little tiny one.' Then I smile to myself," /gaugo continued, "because I know he has killed something big. . . ."

"But," I asked, "why insult a man after he has gone to all that trouble to track and kill an animal and when he is going to share the meat with you so that your children will have something to eat?"

"Arrogance," was his cryptic reply.

"Arrogance?"

"Yes, when a young man kills much meat he comes to think of himself as a chief or a big man, and he thinks of the rest of us as his servants or inferiors. We can't accept this. We refuse one who boasts, for someday his pride will make him kill somebody. So we always speak of his meat as worthless. This way we cool his heart and make him gentle" (Lee, 1969, pp. 28–29).

So the !Kung knew well the dangers of power and developed ways to stop people from exercising it. Native Americans were also wary of power. Pelletier's grandfather told him: "To have power is destructive. You'll be destructive if you have power because if people don't join you, then you will destroy them." Thus, power was temporary, to be used for specific tasks. Pelletier's tribe had no permanent leaders (Pelletier 1970, p. 22).

Mao had the same concern. As Pfeffer states it: "Elites . . . tend to become self-serving, as power in a class society inevitably tends to corrupt powerholders" (1972, p. 162).

Cubans also work to combat elitism. Thus, students in top scientific schools do the same work as others (they clean toilets and do other manual labor), and they know they attend the top schools because of collective efforts (Wald 1978, p. 365). But the problems of elite reassertion of control remain so long as there are experts and professionals. Self-help and decentralization are the only ways to control (if not entirely eliminate) professional domination.

*Self-Help*

Mutual aid and self-help have existed throughout history. People get together to help each other survive physically, emotionally, socially. In the United States today there is an explosion of self-help groups; drug addicts, alcoholics, the handicapped, mentally ill people, women, and people with many other kinds of disadvantages get together to help each other. Worldwide, the move to self-determination and nationalism (and socialist revolutions, the most significant move toward self-determination) reveals the struggle people wage on their own to change their lives. "In our day, when material deprivations or physical dangers are not as acute as in the past, we find that self-help movements are also generated by the human need for emotional sustenance, through day-to-day interaction with the like-minded"(Katz and Bender 1976, pp. 23, 14).

Self-help occurs within community settings. Where community exists, or where people strive to re-create community, self-help is part of that process. In a community, people show responsibility and concern for one an-

### STRUGGLES: Mental Patients Help Themselves

*The Mental Patients' Association (MPA) in Vancouver, Canada is a self-help group (the following account pertains to MPA in the mid-1970s). It operates a drop-in center and five cooperative residences with a capacity for forty-nine people. The organization is run by its members. In the passages below, the author explores how closely MPA meets the seven criteria she thinks a true self-help group should possess.*

1. *The service must provide help with needs as defined by the clients.* MPA clearly fits this description. MPA was organized by ex-patients who recognized that their needs were not being met by the existing mental health system. I believe that only in a service founded by clients can this criterion be met. When the service is formulated without input from clients, needs will be predefined, and clients will have to fit that structure in order to use or benefit from the service. At MPA, new needs are continually presented, and the organization has grown in response to these needs. Experiments have been tried—some successful, others not. At one point there was a rural residence, but, in the words of one member, "at the farm . . . there was no support from the community for a self-help group. The distance from MPA prevented the development of the kind of support coordinators and residents needed. We gave up the idea that fresh air and the country life had some magic curative effect." The group has been free to change in response to needs because there was no master plan to fulfill. Flaws can be recognized and dealt with because there is no bureaucracy to defend an unsuccessful plan. Ideas fail or succeed based only on whether or not they work.

2. *Participation in the service must be completely voluntary.* MPA meets this standard completely. Usually, the initial contact with the drop-in center is made by the prospective member. In the residences it is sometimes a hospital social worker who makes the first inquiry, but the prospective resident makes all the arrangements. No one can "place" a person at MPA. . . . People who are involved in a compulsory activity know that they do not control it, no matter what they may be told.

3. *Clients must be able to choose to participate in some aspects of the service without being required to participate in others.* No one at MPA has a "program." Each member chooses for him or herself what aspect of the organization to participate in. Some members partake only in the "service" aspects without getting involved in decision making. Many residents never go to the drop-in center. Some members wouldn't dream of missing a business or general meeting, others attend infrequently. A few people are seldom seen except at the free Wednesday night dinners and Saturday morning breakfasts. *MPA does not keep records on members.* No one keeps track of a member's utilization of activities and services. Members are seen as responsible people who do not have to be compelled to do things "for their own good." . . .

4. *Help is provided by the clients to one another and may also be provided by others selected by the clients. The ability to give help is seen as a human attribute and not as something acquired by education or professional degree.* MPA was started as a self-help organization, one in which people turned to one another and everyone was equal. An important and significant diference between MPA and many other "self-help" organizations is that MPA did not develop under professional sponsorship, nor did it employ or consult outside "experts." The people who founded MPA were largely skeptical about the abilities of mental health professionals. Decisions about whether or not to consult professionals were felt to be purely personal ones. MPA *as an organization* takes neither a propsychiatry or an antipsychiatry position. Some members see mental health professionals as useful and helpful; others do not.

*Source:* From "Inside the Mental Patients' Association," *On Our Own,* by Judi Chamberlin. Copyright © 1978 by Judi Chamberlin. Reprinted by permission of the publisher, E. P. Dutton.

*(continued)*

**Mental Patients Help Themselves** *(continued)*

I attribute the lack of a position on psychiatry to a short-circuiting of the consciousness-raising process that led to the formation of the organization. Because MPA got involved in service delivery so early in its existence, major attention had to be paid to practical matters rather than theoretical (or personal) ones. Meetings necessarily became focused around immediate issues. Because service delivery costs money, enormous amounts of energy went into fund raising. Members could easily agree on the importance of fund raising, running the drop-in center, and setting up the residences. Coming to a group position about psychiatry was time-consuming, served no immediate practical purpose, and was potentially divisive. Opinions about psychiatry vary widely within MPA. . . .

5. *Overall direction of the service, including responsibility for financial and policy decisions, is in the hands of service recipients.* MPA has avoided splitting off certain kinds of decision making to a small group within the organization. This is one of its greatest strengths. Membership control is meaningless if policy decisions come from above. It is impressive to observe participatory democracy in action.

An[other] example of MPA's democratic process was the 1976 funding crisis. MPA, which had previously received federal government funding, was in the process of switching over to local and provincial funding. The residence program was to come under a new program that would impose regulations about length of stay and would remove the residents' financial independence. The residents of the houses voted to reject the funding and to seek another, less restrictive funding source. When no other source could be found, the residents, faced with the possibility of losing their homes completely, voted to accept the funding on an interim basis. Anything short of this is not true membership control.

6. *Clients of the service must determine whether participation is limited to ex-patients or is to be open to all. If an open policy is decided upon, special care must be taken that the nonpatients do not act oppressively toward the ex-patients.* MPA has, since its beginning, been open to anyone who wants to join. This position has significant strengths and weaknesses. A positive effect of open membership is that MPA does not define the needs of ex-patients and nonpatients differently. Everyone is seen as benefiting from participation. However, some members feel that MPA has not been sufficiently sensitive to mentalism, which needs to be dealt with as an ongoing problem. Although the open membership policy was not set up with this result in mind, what has evolved is that most of the nonpatients in MPA are coordinators—people put on salary by the organization. One of the unintentional results is that nonpatients are seen as more competent, less needy people, since their role in MPA is largely giving help to others rather than getting it for themselves. Ideally, open membership should lead to the recognition that *all* people, not just those who have been labeled mentally ill, benefit from caring and emotional support, but, in order to reach this ideal, I believe there must be an ongoing consciousness-raising process. This has not happened at MPA.

7. *The responsibility of the service is to the client, and not to relatives, treatment institutions, or the government. Information about the client must not be transmitted to any other party without the consent of the client, and such information must be available to the client.* MPA's policy of keeping no individual records is significant. . . . Record-keeping implies that some people need to keep track of other people; and a two-class system is created. . . .

other and share values, interests, and activities. Self-help arises in community settings and enhances the sense of community.

Three characteristics of self-help groups are relevant here. "Self-help always involves other persons and refers to . . . 'face-to-face' interactions."

Personal participation is a key characteristic; bureaucratization "is the enemy of the self-help organization." And "typically, self-help groups start from a condition of powerlessness" (Katz and Bender, pp. 9–11).

Katz and Bender describe many varieties of self-help. Self-help under socialism in China differs from self-help under capitalism. In China, it is part of an entire society trying to live cooperatively, running institutions for the benefit of the people in them. Without reference to socialist principles, self-help can be of limited (but important) use. Under socialism, it is a fundamental tool of the struggle against bureaucracy, professional domination, and class privileges (Sidel 1976).

But under capitalism, if self-help is not part of a larger political struggle, it may serve to "reduce costs to the capitalist state. Self-help is most progressive when it is tied to political demands" (Gerald Turkel, personal communication). As "heal thyself" is an inadequate strategy in a capitalist society where the sources of illness are social and political (see Chapter 11), so self-help is not sufficient as a long-term solution to the problems of capitalist society.

For example, tenants of Co-Op City in New York rebelled against increased rents and won the right to manage that public apartment complex. But because of economic difficulties (because the city and federal government tax and distribute funds to benefit the ruling class), the people of Co-Op City were short of money to manage it and were forced to raise their own rents. By itself, self-management cannot overcome the material and social inequalities of capitalist society (Mattera 1979, p. 59). (For a socialist analysis of self-help, see Withorn 1980.)

Ultimately, only the people can liberate themselves. Pelletier tells of all the people in his tribe working together to do what was needed (give a party or help a neighbor) without the direction of leaders and experts. In fact, they did nothing when others tried to direct and organize them (1970, p. 27).

There is evidence that free people can also be productive people. *Food First* shows repeatedly that free peasants do grow more food than corporations (p. 368). Bettelheim cites data to show that during the ten years of the cultural revolution in China production increased at a faster rate than it did in previous years. The production of machinery, "taking $100 = 1957$ as the base year, rose from 257 in 1965 to 1,156 in 1975. These figures are taken from a source so unfriendly as the CIA's handbook" (p. 78).

## Changes in the United States

The power of institutions and professionals is becoming somewhat limited. In *The Rape of Our Neighborhoods,* Worthy shows that organized citizens can limit institutional expansion. In many professions, people are calling for changes to end the domination of the professional mystique.

## Individualism and Cooperation

It is a paradox that to assure freedom, individuality, and noncoercion, people need to take collective action and responsibility for others. Dorothy Lee has argued that people can become individuals only in a group structure of cooperation, responsibility, and rules (1959). When we read a recipe from a book or someone teaches it to us, is our individuality repressed? Or are we provided with the means to express our interests, to do something we enjoy? Without cooperation from others, without the responsibility to help others, can anyone grow and become an individual? It is only *coercion* that denies our freedom, not cooperation and responsibility (Lee 1959:15-26; see also Gamberg 1977:25).

Domination can end only through collective struggle. We must struggle against domination and inequality, and we must do so thrugh a long cooperative effort to achieve freedom and the opportunity to learn and grow.

# 5

# Work: Art, Necessity, and Alienation

## INTRODUCTION

In every society, most people work. It is no different for us in the United States today. Whether we get paid for our work or do housework, or do volunteer work in some capacity, we engage in activities that enhance the physical and social survival of ourselves and others. Therefore, when work becomes a problem or a burden, we are all affected by it. Even if our own work is enriching, our parents, spouses, relatives, or friends may suffer from alienation and therefore we too are touched.

There are societies where everyone, even young children, does some physical work—hunts, gathers, sows and reaps, and fishes—to get the necessities of life. There are other societies where a few people produce the food, others make cars, refrigerators, and other products, and still others manage those who work with their hands. In some societies work is a cooperative effort, often accompanied by singing and rituals. In other societies, work is a daily drudgery of noise, isolation, and competition (where, however, people still humanize the work somewhat, by socializing on and off the job, joking, or sabotaging the work to get a break). In still other societies, people are struggling to create new forms of work arrangements so that some will not control the labor and movements of others.

The Industrial Revolution changed the nature of work. To some, the problem was the loss of craft and independence; to others (the owners of factories and capital) the problem was the resistance of workers to the new type of work.

Most of us today have never known any other way of organizing ourselves as a society to produce what we need. We may hate the jobs we must do, but we have been deprived of our collective history, so we do not know that workers 100 to 150 years ago fought bitter battles against the industrial system that robbed them of their crafts and the use of their minds. Sociologists and others maintain that things are better now than ever before. We have been told that most of us have better jobs than our ancestors, for the American labor force is becoming both more skilled and more middle class ("white collar").

The 1950s, now romanticized in the mass media, were the supposedly "happy days" for American workers. A few problems were acknowledged: some jobs did not pay well, and some geographic areas and minority groups did suffer from unemployment. But not only were more workers joining the white-collar ranks, factory workers were becoming middle class. Galbraith claimed that what few problems remained were isolated exceptions to general affluence and contentment (1958).

These celebrations did not coincide with the daily reality of workers' lives. Personal accounts of work written in the 1950s show a much different reality. Harvey Swados, a novelist who worked in factories from the 1930s to the 1950s, was one of the dissenters to the myth of the happy worker.

> The worker's attitude toward his work is generally compounded of hatred, shame, and resignation. . . .
> Almost without exception, the men with whom I worked on the assembly line last year felt like trapped animals. Depending on their age and personal circumstances, they were either resigned to their fate, furiously angry at themselves for what they were doing, or desperately hunting other work that would pay as well and in addition offer some variety, some prospect of change and betterment. They were sick of being pushed around by harried foremen (themselves more pitied than hated), sick of working like blinkered donkeys, sick of being dependent for their livelihood on a maniacal production-merchandising setup, sick of working in a place where there was no spot to relax during the twelve-minute rest period. (Some day—let us hope—we will marvel that production was still so worshipped in the fifties that new factories could be built with every splendid facility for the storage and movement of essential parts, but with no place for a resting worker to sit down for a moment but on a fire plug, the edge of a packing case, or the sputum- and oil-stained stairway of a toilet.)
> The older men stay put and wait for their vacations (1957, pp. 107, 111).

The liberal paeans to work in the 1950s did not last long. The general re-examination of American values and institutions that took place in the

1960s also affected workers. They saw that most jobs lacked something fundamental. In addition to the concerns about not enough jobs and low pay, people became more aware of the daily humiliations they had to endure. They may not have talked about "alienation," but they experienced it daily.

One of the first reactions of working people was a great increase in strikes, many occurring against the advice and authorization of union officials, and many demanding better working conditions, not just a pay increase (Gorz, in Hunnius et al., 1973, p. 332).

This worker insurgence and renewed concern with working conditions frightened the liberal establishment in universities, foundations, corporations, and government. They sought explanations and solutions. Profits were threatened when workers began to quit jobs with increasing frequency and to go on strike rather than accept intolerable working conditions. The 1972 strike in the Vega factory in Lordstown, Ohio, has become a symbol of the worker rebellion. The plant was new, with younger workers. When the assembly line was speeded up from the usual sixty to one hundred operations per hour, workers went on strike against the speed-up (but when they went back to work, in essence it was on company terms).

In the early 1970s there were many books, studies, and media stories on worker alienation. These discussed causes and solutions of this worker alienation. The Department of Health, Education and Welfare commissioned an impressive study, *Work in America* (1973). Senator Kennedy conducted congressional hearings, entitled "Worker Alienation, 1972" (Committee on Labor and Public Welfare, U.S. Senate, 1972). *Newsweek* ran a cover story, "The Job Blahs: Who Wants to Work?" (March 26, 1973), with a picture of Charlie Chaplin from *Modern Times*.

The problem was real, and the reaction was a sign of its seriousness. To the workers, the problem was to eliminate and change conditions they had endured for a long time. To the employers, the problem was the workers and their threat to profits; employers sought ways to pacify them.

The following pages explore the meaning and problems of work, the causes of alienation under capitalism, liberal reforms and workers' control, and, finally, socialist attempts to eliminate alienation and return art, creativity, and freedom to work.

## THE MEANING AND PROBLEMS OF WORK

*Why Work?*

We work because we must, to obtain food and shelter. We share these needs with other creatures. But the way we do our work is not predetermined. As creative beings, we give additional meaning and significance to what we must do. We transform necessity into art. Work can become another human experience shared with others. It can challenge our ingenuity, leading to joy, not drudgery.

Let us look at some examples. Many of us enjoy gardens; they add meaning to our lives. But millions of Americans still earn their living working the land, providing us with the very stuff of life. They make a meager living, however, a bitter commentary on capitalism, which pays the least to those who do the most necessary work. And the work is dangerous. The damp weather causes rheumatism, arthritis, and bad backs; pesticides cause respiratory diseases; and the intense summer heat gets depressing when you are faced with endless rows of lettuce and hurting back (Roberto Acuna, in Terkel 1974: 36–37).

Biffle, who has worked the fields early in the morning picking onions, says, "Your body gets into a strong, smooth rhythm and you take pleasure in the economy and strength of your movements." But as the day wears on, and as you see how little money you make, tiredness, exhaustion, and soreness set in. After six hours of work and thirteen sacks of onions, Biffle made $4.55. Working in the fields as a hired hand, for the profit of landowners (individuals, corporations, conglomerates), makes the producing and gathering of food a physical and emotional drudgery (1975, p. 270).

But as Roberto Acuna points out, "working in the fields is not in itself a degrading job." If the hours were shorter, and the pay and conditions better, it could be pleasant (Terkel 1974, p. 38).

And indeed, farm work has been different. Camara Ley describes his boyhood experiences in an African village, working with the men in the fields.

> Once the signal had been given, the reapers set out. With them, I marched along to the rhythm of the tom-tom. The young men threw their sickles into the air and caught them as they fell. They shouted simply for the pleasure of shouting, and danced as they followed the tom-tom players. . . .
>
> The movement of the sickles as they rose and fell was astonishingly rapid and regular. They had to cut off the stalk between the last joint and the last leaf at the same time that they stripped the leaf. They almost never missed. This was largely due to the way the reaper held the stalks so as to cut them. Nonetheless, the speed of the sickle was astonishing. . . .
>
> My young uncle was wonderful at rice-cutting, the very best. I followed him proudly, step by step, he handing me the bundles of stalks as he cut them. I tore off the leaves, trimmed the stalks, and piled them. Since the rice is always harvested when it is very ripe, and, if handled roughly the grains drop off, I had to be very careful. Tying the bundles into sheaves was man's work, but, when they had been tied, I was allowed to put them on the pile in the middle of the field.
>
> "Sing with us," my uncle would command.
>
> The tom-tom, which had followed as we advanced into the field, kept time with our voices. We sang as a chorus, now very high-pitched with great bursts of song, and then very low, so low we could scarcely be heard. Our fatigue vanished, and the heat became less oppressive (Ley 1954, pp. 56, 58, 61).

As he was harried by customers and orders, a Greek pizza house owner once told me, with sadness and longing, "we used to dance in the fields" during the reaping of the harvest. Under the right conditions, work can be joyful and playful, as among the Tikopia:

> As the turmeric is being cleaned the young people pick out and chew an occasional root; the small girl takes a special delight in this, not so much for its aromatic flavour as for the sight of the bright yellow saliva which she dribbles out into a little cup made from a roll of banana leaf. The whole atmosphere is one of labour diversified by recreation at will, and exhibits what even the cold-blooded objective scientist may be allowed to call touches of essential humanity, little humorous asides which, trivial in themselves, constitute nevertheless part of the flesh and blood of the native social relationships. Thus Pa Nukunefu as he digs the turmeric clears away the weeds before him and throws them to the side of the plot. Suddenly he takes a handful and tosses it out into the trees on the slope below him, so that the dirt from the roots sprinkles through the foliage on to the heads of his wife and daughter, who are working a little way down. They look up in some astonishment, see him grinning, and laugh too (Firth 1936, p. 94).

As these examples illustrate, anthropologists have shown that in many societies people work in groups, sharing their experiences, and fusing work, play, creativity, and sometimes religion, into one experience. The picking of lettuce is not in itself either liberating or degrading. Through the exercise of muscles and minds, we take necessity and infuse it with creativity, fun, play, sharing, and cooperation to increase physical survival and make for individual and social enrichment.

## Unemployment

But in industrial societies, the chance to work to feed and clothe oneself has become questionable. We produce few, if any, of the goods we consume. We work for wages to buy the things we need and want. Over 90 percent of us work for corporations and the government. That means we must search for work. Some of us find the work we want to do, but most of us do what we must to earn the paycheck, and many have only part-time jobs.

Many people have no work. Through the 1970s official unemployment was around 7 percent and 7.8 percent in May 1980 (*Monthly Labor Review* May 1979, p. 71; Pine 1980). But that is a very deceptive figure. Many people have shown that real unemployment is at least twice this figure. Counting those who really want to work but cannot find jobs or have part-time jobs, and including people in the military, who do not produce usable goods or services, in 1970 there were "nearly 40 million persons out of a real labor force of 104 million who are either military-dependent or out of work" (Anderson 1974, pp. 219-20).

Official unemployment statistics do not include people who have been out of work for several years (for example, married women) who now need a job; people out of school looking for a job who have not had a job before; people who have part-time jobs but would work full-time if they found a job; and people on welfare, prisoners, and older people whom employers won't hire (*Work in America* 1973, p. 156).

The official statistics also understate the unemployment of specific groups and areas. Black people, especially young blacks; people in areas like Appalachia; and others have real unemployment over 50 percent (see Rich 1976).

Behind the statistics on unemployment there are human tragedies. For example, a study of five communities where large employers closed their plants and moved elsewhere to make higher profits, shows the effects of joblessness. After being without work for a year or longer, people began to lose confidence in themselves, to feel useless, to get depressed, to have family problems, even to lose some of their skills. People in their forties and fifties did not want to be cut off their community roots, so they did not go looking for work elsewhere and were condemned to joblessness. After a while they stopped looking for work, at which point they were not considered part of the labor force, thus lowering the official unemployment rate. The human suffering continued, however (Young and Newton 1980, pp. 81–83).

Why are there not enough jobs? Why are people's energies unused when so much needs to be done? The answer lies in the nature of capitalism. Capitalism must have unemployment. It needs a large reserve of people who are often out of work and people who are part-time workers in order to keep wages down. (Many American corporations, such as Dunkin' Donuts and McDonald's, have no full-time employees except for the manager; they hire mostly teenagers. This way they pay the minimun wage or slightly above, they need not pay for benefits like medical insurance, and they avoid unions (Nadler 1980 b). When employment is nearly full, employees need not compete with each other for scarce jobs; to attract workers, companies must pay somewhat decent wages. But under these conditions, company profits decrease. To prevent such a condition, there must be more workers than jobs, and workers cannot ask for higher wages because they know they can be replaced by those who have no jobs. Thus capitalism has a need for irregularly employed and part-time workers (Gordon 1975).

But if workers' wages are kept low in order to increase profits, who will buy the products of the corporations? This is one of the inherent instabilities of capitalist economies, leading to the regular ups and downs and to the search for other solutions: neocolonialism, advertising, and consumer credit.

Another reason for unemployment in the United States is the export of American jobs to other countries where workers are paid a fraction of what American workers make. When workers unionized in the industrial northeast, raising their abysmally low wages somewhat, many firms moved south, in search of cheap, nonunion labor. Textile-mill cities of New England—Lowell, Fall River, and others—still suffer from the legacy of runaway corporations through official unemployment statistics of over 10 percent. And corporations still move out of New England to cheaper labor areas (Bass 1979). Since the 1950s American corporations have been moving production facilities to Mexico, Hong Kong, Singapore, Korea, and other countries.

The effect is double exploitation, both of American and foreign workers. Zimmerman documents the effects of runaway corporations. First, there is loss of thousands of jobs, affecting specific areas very severely. For example, General Electric moved its clocks and timers plant from Ashland, Massachusetts, to Singapore, laying off 1100 workers. Second, "unemployment from runaway shops hits black, latin, Asian, and women workers hardest" because they work in labor-intensive industries, which are the ones most commonly moving overseas. Third, "employers are using the threat of runaway shops to blackmail workers into accepting lower wages," and Zimmerman gives many examples of this. And fourth, runaway shops are used to break strikes and force speed-ups and higher production from workers (1973, pp. 4–10; also Grossman 1980).

Thus, to ensure high profits, United States corporations exploit both American and foreign workers.

*Low Pay*

For most of us, the size of the paycheck is the primary consideration in any job. Auto workers endure terrible working conditions because the pay is relatively good. But the question remains, how well do most jobs pay?

The best way to judge the adequacy of wages and salaries is to compare them to family budgets (see Chapter 2). An intermediate-level family budget for 1978 was $18,622 ($358 per week), and a high-level budget was $27,420 ($527.30 per week). In March 1978, the "usual weekly earnings of full-time wage and salary workers" reveal some interesting statistics. These figures are only for men who work full-time; women part-timers, and those who are unemployed part of the year make less. Table 5.1 shows that 58.2

**TABLE 5.1** Usual Weekly Earnings of Full-Time Wage-and-Salaried Male Workers, March 1978

| Weekly earnings | Percent making those earnings |
| --- | --- |
| Under $100 | 1.4 |
| $100–149 | 11.0 |
| $150–199 | 13.9 |
| $200–249 | 16.9 |
| $250–299 | 15.0 |
| $300–399 | 22.9 |
| $400 plus | 18.9 |
|  | 100.0 |

*Source:* U.S. Department of Labor 1978c.

percent of male full-time workers made under $300 ($58 below the minimum figure for an intermediate-level budget); and 81.1 percent of male full-time made under $400 ($527.30 is the minimum for a higher-level budget. So the vast majority of male workers (about 90 percent) do not make enough to afford the higher-level standard of living, not even with their wives working, as discussed in Chapter 2.

*Death and Injury at Work*

People who work in white-collar jobs may never realize that dangerous working conditions are a daily threat to millions of American workers. It is a common perception that things have improved since Upton Sinclair's *The Jungle* described the slaughterhouses of Chicago around 1906. Here, as in many other areas under capitalism, perception and reality do not coincide. By every known statistic, injury and death still abound in the jobs of working-class Americans. Through the 1970s, over 14,000 people died every year from accidents in workplaces; 100,000 to 200,000 died from illnesses contracted at work; and 10 to 20 million were injured at work. Even the conservative figures reported by employers to the United States government show 5.3 million injuries in 1977 (of injuries that require more than first aid). Among workers' serious health problems are: gas and fume poisoning; high noise levels; and illness from contact with vinyl chloride and varnish. One of every twelve workers in the private sector is the victim of job accident or illness every year. This figure excludes some accidents; a 1975 study found that in small plants 40 percent of the accidents were not reported (*Dollars and Sense* April 1980, p. 9; Levison 1974, pp. 77-78; U.S. Department of Labor 1979b, p. 11).

Congress did pass the Occupational Safety and Health Act (OSHA) of 1970, but the act has made no difference: 115,000 workers a year still die from work accidents and disease. The government does not have nearly enough inspectors to check on every workplace regularly ("1200 inspectors to oversee the nation's five million workplaces"), and the fines levied on companies convicted of violations average $25.87—no deterrent to dangerous working conditions. It costs much less to pay the fine than to remove the dangers. Lives and health are sacrificed for the sake of higher profits. And even this weak OSHA law and its limited enforcement are being fought by corporations who seek to dismantle the agency set up to enforce the law. In addition, in the spring of 1980 a bill in the Senate proposed to remove 85 to 90 percent of workers from OSHA coverage (Stranahan 1976; Turner 1976; Levin 1977; *Dollars and Sense* April 1980, p. 8).

Another condition of work under capitalism is cited by Braverman:

> The economies sought in the organization of masses of labor can be seen, to take a single instance, from the following: Leffingwell calculated that the placement of water fountains so that each clerk walked, on the average, a mere

hundred feet for a drink would cause the clerical workers in one office to walk an aggregate of fifty thousand miles each year just to drink an adequate amount of water, with a corresponding loss of time for the employer. (This represents the walking time of a thousand clerks, each of whom walked only a few hundred yards a day.) The care with which arrangements are made to avoid this "waste"gives birth to the sedentary tradition which shackles the clerical worker as the factory worker is shackled—by placing everything within in easy reach so that the clerk not only need not, but dare not, be too long away from the desk. . . .

"Save ten steps a day for each of 12,000 employees," said Henry Ford of his system of having stock-chasers bring materials to the worker instead of having the workers move around freely, "and you will have saved fifty miles of wasted motion and misspent energy." All motions or energies not directed to the increase of capital are of course "wasted" or "misspent." That every individual needs a variety of movements and changes of routine in order to maintain a state of physical health and mental freshness, and that from this point of view such motion is not wasted, does not enter into the case. The solicitude that brings everything to the worker's hand is of a piece with the fattening arrangements of a cattle feed-lot or poultry plant, in that the end sought is the same in each case: the fattening of the corporate balance sheet. The accompanying degenerative effects on the physique and well-being of the worker are not counted at all (1974, pp. 310–311).

These findings show that much work is indeed dangerous to well-being. Work affects the quality and the length of workers lives. See Chapters 10 and 11 on the health problems caused by working conditions and the damage to the environment (Ashford 1976; Berman 1978; Clary and Thompson 1978).

*The Degradation of Manual Labor*

Most people have heard of the untouchables of India—the leather workers and others who worked with their hands who, because they dirtied their hands, were considered defiling and dangerous. Merely touching them was considered dangerous by the upper classes. Similar attitudes to manual labor were common in many ancient civilizations: Greece, Egypt, and China.

People tend to think that attitudes and actions have changed, but evidence shows otherwise. Capitalism perpetuates the degradation of those who work with their hands, the division of hand and mind. This division lowers wages and raises profits, since manual labor pays less (Levison 1974, ch. 1).

Evidence is both statistical and personal. A 1961 survey of "distribution of prestige ratings" of occupations showed that all thirty occupations at the top of the prestige scale involved mental work, none manual labor. On the other hand, twenty-six of the thirty at the bottom of the scale were manual labor jobs. At some level, we have been persuaded that the work most of us do carries little respect (Popenoe 1977, p. 224). This feeling was expressed by six male workers interviewed by Lasson and others. All expressed the desire that their sons go to college so they would not work at the jobs the fathers held. The driver of a garbage truck said, "My kids are going to college all right. I want them to be able to make twice the money I make and do half the work. I don't mind the job, but it's not for my kids" (Lasson 1971, p. 23).

During the years of the cultural revolution the Chinese tried to eliminate the low prestige of manual labor. But the bias against manual labor is deep, found in all stratified societies. According to a minor Chinese official the highest prestige jobs in China in 1979 were, first, official positions (in cadres), followed by "intellectuals, like professors and lecturers." This official said his job did not pay much more than workers' jobs, but it carried more prestige (Beecher 1979, p. 1).

The low prestige of manual labor is embedded deeply in individual consciousness and social institutions. This bias has a long history in many societies. Peasant, capitalist, and other societies all include the bias against working with one's hands, and socialist societies face a long struggle in order to diminish it.

## Work as Identity

Given that most people have jobs low in prestige, pay, or both, and given that many jobs are dangerous and alienating, there is the further problem of how these realities affect our identity—how we and others think of ourselves and our character. *Work* is necessary and can be creative and joyful; but the low prestige and meaning attached to *jobs* are arbitrary.

Reports have shown that most workers do not think much of themselves. The jobs people hold tend to define them. A doctor or college professor does not socialize with a janitor—janitors are stereotyped as dull people. Usually the first question asked of nonstudents is "what do you do?" meaning, what kind of job do you have? It is indeed true that "our jobs ... are our credentials" (Ruben 1976).

But that is not a necessary condition. *Jobs under capitalism* are degrading to identity; *work* is not. In rejecting the enslaving and degrading conditions found in capitalism, do not confuse the issue by declaring all work destructive. Jobs need not be an identity card. Creative work need not be the sole basis for defining one's self. Cooperation, commitment to equality, relationships with others could and should be as important. But work, as necessity and art, remains important too (see Appleseed 1976).

One of the problems of work in modern societies is the need to work in order to keep busy, to fill time, as well as to find an identity. Anthropologists have shown that "most people, in most times, have not worked hard" (Norbeck, 1971). The work of Richard Lee shows that the !Kung of the Kalahari desert in the early 1960s only worked twelve to nineteen hours a week to provide for their material needs. Native Americans were labelled "lazy Indians" because they were not addicted to working long hours, either as an identity or escape, or to gather material possessions. In the long run, it will be necessary to confront these problems of work (Norbeck 1971, p. 49).

*Alienation*

Most of us know what capitalism does to us. In addition to the exploitation of our labor for the profit of others, the problems of finding work, the dangers to our bodies, there is also the destruction of mind. It is the removal of all thought and creativity from our daily labors that alienates us.

Alienation is a general condition of life under capitalism. "By alienation is meant a mode of experience in which the person experiences himself as an alien. He has become . . . estranged from himself. . . . In Marx's system alienation is called that condition of man where his 'own act becomes to him an alien power, standing over and against him, instead of being ruled by him' " (Fromm 1955, pp. 56–57). In work, alienation results from the loss of control over the product of our labor; others tell us what to do and they use our labor for their profit. Thus, the product of our labor is alien to us, outside of us.

Philosophers, sociologists, and others have debated whether workers are indeed alienated. They have questioned the Marxist claim that people find their jobs destructive and degrading. Many sociologists have concluded that most people are relatively happy with their jobs.

Nettler has summarized most of the surveys done over the last 25 years on workers' attitudes about their work. It is said that in western industrial societies only one-eighth of the workers report dissatisfaction with their jobs (1976, p. 176). Nettler summarizes a recent survey:

> A more recent test of the "work-alienation" hypothesis is contained in the results of the Survey Research Center's 1971 poll of a representative sample of American adults on the "quality of their lives" (Campbell et al. 1975). In keeping with the reviews by Hoppock and others . . . 90 percent of the respondents say that it is "very true" or "somewhat true" that their "work is interesting," 75 percent say that "the pay is good," 93 percent find that their jobs give them "a lot of chances to make friends," 81 percent that at work "the physical surroundings are pleasant," and 77 percent that "the job security is good."
>
> As regards self-fulfillment, 76 percent say that it is "very true" or "somewhat true" that "I have an opportunity to develop my own special abilities," and 79 percent that "I am given a chance to do the things I do best" (1976, p. 181).

Blauner's following comment may explain the findings of relative happiness with work: "The average worker is able to make an adjustment to a job which, from the standpoint of an intellectual appears to be the epitome of tedium" (quoted in Braverman 1974, p. 29). In short, workers learn to live with boring jobs.

But other studies and reports find profound alienation with work. Surveys reported in *Work in America,* when summarized, show such alienation. Specifically, by asking people if they would choose the same job were they starting their work life from the beginning, researchers found that except for professionals, most people would not do the same work again. Only 43 percent of white-collar workers and 24 percent of blue-collar workers would choose the same work. The authors of the report interpreted these findings as showing alienation (p. 16).

Other, more personal accounts of workers reveal the meaning and feeling of alienation. Studs Terkel's *Working* unearths deep wounds and buried dreams.

> This book, being about work, is, by its very nature, about violence—to the spirit as well as to the body. It is about ulcers as well as accidents, about shouting matches as well as fistfights, about nervous breakdowns as well as kicking the dog around. It is, above all (or beneath all), about daily humiliations. To survive the day is triumph enough for the walking wounded among the great many of us.
>
> It is about a search, too, for daily meaning as well as daily bread, for recognition as well as cash, for astonishment rather than torpor; in short, for a sort of life rather than a Monday through Friday sort of dying. Perhaps immortality, too, is part of the quest. To be remembered was the wish, spoken and unspoken, of the heroes and heroines of this book.
>
> For the many, there is a hardly concealed discontent. The blue-collar blues is no more bitterly sung than the white-collar moan. "I'm a machine," says the spot-welder. "I'm caged," says the steelworker. "A monkey can do what I do," says the receptionist. "I'm less than a farm implement," says the migrant worker. "I'm an object," says the high-fashion model. Blue collar and white call upon the identical phrase: "I'm a robot." "There is nothing to talk about," the young accountant despairingly enunciates (pp. xiii–xiv).

The workers themselves are no less eloquent in pouring out their feelings and thoughts:

> *Sharon Atkins, Receptionist*
> The machine dictates. This crummy little machine with buttons on it—you've got to be there to answer it. You can walk away from it and pretend you don't hear it, but it pulls you. You know you're not doing anything, not doing a hell of a lot for anyone. Your job doesn't mean anything. Because *you're* just a little machine. A monkey could do what I do. It's really unfair to ask someone to do that (p. 59).
>
> *Eddie Jaffee, Press Agent*
> The occupation molds your personality. Publicity does that to people too. Calling an editor on the phone, asking favors, can be humiliating. Being refused a favor disturbs me, depresses me. That's why I could never resign myself to being a press agent. Many are not aware they're being turned down. They wouldn't develop colitis like I did. That's the way I act, emotionally, with my gut. That's why I went to the analyst (p. 128).

*Enid Du Bois, Telephone Solicitor*
We didn't have to think what to say. They had it all written out. You have a card. You'd go down the list and call everyone on the card. You'd have about fifteen cards with the person's names, addresses, and phone numbers. "This is Mrs. Du Bois. Could I have a moment of your time? We're wondering if you now subscribe to any newspapers? If you would only for three short months take this paper, it's for a worthy cause." To help blind children or Crusade of Mercy. We'd always have one at hand. "After the three-month period, if you no longer desire to keep it, you can cancel it. But you will have helped them. They need you."

I did as well as I wanted to. But after a while, I didn't care. Surely I could have fast-talked people. Just to continually lie to them. But it just wasn't in me. (The disgust was growing in me every minute. I would pray and pray to hold on a little longer. I really needed the money. It was getting more and more difficult for me to make these calls.)

What really did it for me was one call I made. I went through the routine. The guy listened patiently and he said, "I really would like to help." He was blind himself! That really got me—the tone of his voice. I could just tell he was a good person. He was willing to help even if he couldn't read the paper. He was poor, I'm sure of that. It was the worst ghetto area. I apologized and thanked him. That's when I left for the ladies' room. I was nauseous. Here I was sitting here telling him a bunch of lies and he was poor and blind and willing to help. Taking his money (pp. 239-42).

*Phil Stallings, Spot Welder at an Auto Plant*
I don't like the pressure, the intimidation. How would you like to go up to someone and say, "I would like to go to the bathroom?" If the foreman doesn't like you, he'll make you hold it, just ignore you. Should I leave this job to go to the bathroom I risk being fired. The line moves all the time. . . .

I don't understand how come more guys don't flip. Because you're nothing more than a machine when you hit this type of thing. They give better care to that machine than they will to you. They'll have more respect, give more attention to that machine. And you *know* this. Somehow you get the feeling that the machine is better than you are. (Laughs.) . . .

Proud of my work? How can I feel pride in a job where I call a foreman's attention to a mistake, a bad piece of equipment, and he'll ignore it. Pretty soon you get the idea they don't care. You keep doing this and finally you're titled a troublemaker. So you just go about your work. You *have* to have pride. So you throw it off to something else. And that's my stamp collection (pp. 222-25).

The classic assembly line, as used in automobile production, is seen as the typical working-class job. Many such jobs do exist, but, as Levison shows, different working-class jobs present different problems.

Some jobs, such as doormen and guards, "are simply dull or repetitive without being physically arduous." Other jobs, such as garbage collecting and loading and unloading trucks, involve heavy, dirty work, but the workers are not tied to an assembly line. Then there are the classic assembly-line jobs, in the auto industry, electronics, textiles, canning, and so on. Here the problems of alienation are most severe. Next higher in alienation are skilled machine operators who are not tied to an assembly line. Truck and bus drivers are in the same position as skilled factory workers. "Finally, there are the skilled craftsmen, the carpenters, electricians, auto mechanics, etc., who have considerable knowledge and whose jobs involve a good deal of independent judgment." Levison concludes that despite these differences, most of these people are alienated from their work; they describe it as "being treated like a machine and not a man" (Levison 1974, pp. 58–59).

Levison is mistaken in one respect: alienation is not limited to working-class jobs. Many middle-class workers experience alienation, and, as Braverman shows, many white-collar jobs are becoming more like those in a factory.

Roth has shown that, in time, most survey interviewers and research assistants feel they are tools working to achieve success for others and thus resort to various forms of cheating. They write answers to questions they did not ask, simply skip questions, feel bored so they rush through an interview, and so on. Both factory worker and interviewer are tools for someone else's end; they do not control their work (1965).

Nevertheless, why do some sociologists claim most workers are relatively happy with their work, and others report findings of daily humiliation and deep wounds? There are two possible explanations.

The opposing conclusions rise out of different kinds of research. Those studies showing relative worker contentment use survey methods—a researcher sends out hired interviewers who ask workers prearranged questions. The setting does not allow for a gradual acquaintanceship of the two people talking, for reflection, for revelations of deep feelings. Books like *Working*, on the other hand, are the result of many long personal encounters. Terkel talked to the workers himself. He did not "interview" people; they just talked, sharing experiences and emotions. The setting (bars, homes, and so on) and the situation's informality allowed for the surfacing of inner feelings. "The talk was idiomatic rather than academic. In short, it was conversation. In time, the sluice gates of dammed-up hurts and dreams were opened" (p. xxv). People explored their lives and unearthed buried feelings. "On one occasion, during the play-back of the tape-recorded talk, my companion murmured in wonder, 'I never realized I felt that way' " (p. xxiii).

The second explanation for the differing conclusions on worker alienation is equally significant. It refers to the difference between what people learn to endure because they see no other choice, and their intrinsic needs, what people would like to do if they could. Hobart Foote, a utility man in an automobile factory, said of younger workers: "And those other people when they settle down one of these days, they'll be what we call old-timers. He'll want to work. Number one: the pay's good. Number two: the benefits are good" (quoted in Terkel 1974, p. 235). Foote meant he had learned to adjust to the work, to endure the humiliations he described, because he must; he had a family to feed. But he does not *want* to work. It is the difference between "I like what I get" and "I get what I like" (Lewis Carroll, *Alice in Wonderland*). Foote revealed what he really felt about his work when he said later that, after seventeen years, he had thirteen more before he could retire. "Thirteen more years with the company, it'll be thirty and out. When I retire, I'm gonna have me a little garden. A place down South. Do a little fishin', huntin', sit back, watch the sun come up, the sun go down. Keep my mind occupied" (p. 239). He is like a person waiting for his prison sentence to end. What does it tell about a man's work when he spends the prime of his life waiting for work to be over? Does he want to work? Does the pay compensate for the destruction of his hopes and dreams?

*Working* and other books are also inspiring because of their abundant evidence that workers' dreams and hopes persist. Most people in *Working* expressed the desire to do something that is creative, freeing, useful, and meaningful. Sharon Atkins, receptionist, wants to refinish furniture; Louis Haywar, washroom attendant, wants to write; everyone wants something more than a job. Nora Watson, in a few words, captured the essence of the problem missed by countless social-science research studies:

> I think most of us are looking for a calling, not a job. Most of us, like the assembly line worker, have jobs that are too small for our spirit. Jobs are not big enough for people (Terkel 1974, p. xxix).

From her talks with many workers, Garson reached a similar conclusion: "It was positive things I saw that touched me the most. Not that people are beaten down (which they are) but that they almost always pop up. Not that people are bored (which they are) but the ways they find to make it interesting. Not that people hate their work (which they do) but that even so, they try to make something out of it" (1975, pp. xiii, xx).

The need to produce, to create, to find satisfaction in work, is not easily destroyed, even by capitalism. It may be repressed, but it cannot be destroyed. Creativity and thinking will surface again and again.

*Aspects of Jobs*

Some of you may reflect on jobs you or people you know have had and realize that you liked these jobs. Why, then, talk so much of alienation? It is important that we clarify the aspects of any given job we like or dislike:

*Money.* Some jobs, for example, writing commercials, pay very well. People may like these jobs for that reason. But the work itself may be very alienating. Other jobs, such as auto worker, may pay enough to keep body and soul together, even to permit some comforts, but the work itself is destructive of body and mind. Liking the job because of the pay is not the same as finding the work itself fulfilling.

*Prestige.* Some jobs are considered prestigious, and people like them for that reason. Jobs such as president and manager are more prestigious than working in a factory or washing dishes, and people "like" these jobs because of the prestige reflected on them. Also, the power to control the work of others seems to give prestige to these positions. The work itself, however, may be full of pressures and compromises and leave its scars on emotions and feelings.

*Friendships.* Many of us make friends where we work. We like some of the people we work with and look forward to seeing them regularly—even see them evenings and weekends. But these satisfactions are not intrinsic to the work itself; they arise despite the work and working conditions (such as rules that prohibit talking while on the job or that allow two minutes to go to the bathroom). When people say they like their job, they may mean that they and their co-workers have defied dehumanizing working conditions and created a human reality despite all obstacles.

*Work.* Finally, of course, we may in fact like the work itself (often, again, despite all pressures to not to become involved and creative). The work may allows us to think about what we do, to be creative, and to plan and control our day. There can be satisfaction in the quality of a product we make or the service we provide because we have control over it and can use our minds. Under capitalism, there are fewer such jobs every year, as the drive toward the minute division of labor continues inexorably. Some people manage to find and create jobs they like, such as the mason and the firefighter in *Working*. A few others leave the money and prestige of some jobs and seek work they find satisfying, many returning to farming, for example. (Such solutions are possible for a few; but if work is to become meaningful and enriching for all, the only solutions are collective and cooperative efforts in a socialist society. A few people going to Vermont to farm will not liberate the vast majority in factories and offices.)

Any given job may possess none, one, or more of these qualities. We should be clear on the reasons we like or hate any given job.

## *The Myth of the White-Collar Majority*

A very prevalent belief among social scientists is that in work and income most Americans now are "middle class" and "white collar," and that most American workers are becoming more skilled and more educated (for example, see McNall 1975, p. 52).

It is true that Americans are becoming more educated, at least in the number of years spent in school. And by the policy of requiring more years of schooling for certain jobs while leaving the jobs unchanged, people can claim that jobs need more education and skill. But for most people, in fact, jobs are becoming more routine, detailed, and repetitive, and require less use of one's mind.

First, it is only by statistical and verbal manipulation that one can claim most workers are white collar. Look at the following categories of jobs, and the numbers of people in them, for March 1980.

As Table 5.2 shows, it appears that blue-collar and farm workers comprise about 36 percent (35 million) of the workforce. White-collar workers seem to be over half of the workforce, and service workers the rest. But who of the following list is a service worker who is in a different category from the traditional blue-collar worker—"janitors, porters, ushers, elevator operators, doormen, and even shoeshine boys . . . guards, watchmen, cooks, housekeepers, hospital and other attendants, barbers, police, and firemen" (Levison 1974, pp. 22–23). Even among the white-collar group it is playing with reality to include clerk typists, who do nothing but type all day long what others give them and key-punch operators with doctors, lawyers, and managers. These people share much more with factory workers than with managers and professionals. In 1976, of 5.5 million sales workers, 420,000 were "gasoline service station attendants" and 2,750,000 were "retail trade sales workers." By what realistic criteria are such workers on the same level as doctors, lawyers, and other professionals, all lumped together as white-collar workers? In terms of salaries, too, there are great discrepancies. In March 1978, average salaries of file clerks ranged from $6,621 to $10,095; for secretaries, the average salaries ranged from $9,801 to $14,430. Compare these average salaries to those of engineers: from $15,928 to $42,104 (Griffin 1978, p. 16; U.S. Department of Labor 1978d).

Secondly, even clerical work which supposedly gave people white-collar and middle-class status is becoming increasingly similar to work in a factory. In a superb chapter Braverman (1974, ch. 15) has shown the inevitable drive under capitalism to make office work routine, detailed, and totally controlled by management. Three examples will show this process.

Efficiency experts have timed every possible motion, up to the thousandth of a second, and have tried to save time by reorganizing every move (pp. 321–25). Efficiency experts have invaded even social services. People who come in to social work agencies are placed in one of four categories, and social workers are dictated the maximum amount of time they can give to each type of client (Patry 1978).

**TABLE 5.2** Employment by Occupations, March 1980 (in Thousands)

| | |
|---|---:|
| White-collar workers: | 50,302 |
|     Professional and technical | 15,397 |
|     Managers and administrators (except farm) | 10,755 |
|     Salesworkers | 6,113 |
|     Clerical workers | 18,037 |
| Blue-collar workers: | 31,670 |
|     Craft and kindred | 12,767 |
|     Operatives, except transportation | 10,579 |
|     Transport equipment operatives | 3,558 |
|     Nonfarm laborers | 4,767 |
| Service workers | 12,981 |
| Farmworkers | 2,733 |

*Source: Monthly Labor Review,* May 1980, p. 69.

The computer field, the second example, is a new area in white-collar work. It is considered a very highly skilled job requiring much education and training. Yet, in a few years computer work has been transformed to daily drudgery. The vast majority of computer workers are key-punch operators. The following excerpts from *Automation in the Office* show how close to assembly-line work is the life of key punchers:

> Mrs. Duncan described all key-punch girls as "nervous wrecks." "If you happen to speak to an operator while she is working, she will jump a mile. You can't help being tense. The machine makes you that way. Even though the supervisor does not keep an official production count on our work, she certainly knows how much each of us is turning out—by the number of boxes of cards we do." Mrs. Calvin, a former operator of a different company, reported the same kind of tension: "If you just tap one of them on the shoulder when she is working, she'll fly through the ceiling."
>
> Both women reported that absenteeism was very high among their group. Mrs. Duncan remarked, "Someone is always saying, 'I don't think I'll come in tomorrow. I just can't stand this any longer.'" Although the girls do not quit, they stay home frequently and keep supplies of tranquilizers and aspirin at their desks. The key-punchers felt that they were really doing a factory job and that they were "frozen" to their desks as though it were a spot on the assembly line.
>
> The factory atmosphere is unmistakably present. Not only are the office machine operators often required to punch a time clock, but they are not permitted to converse while at work. They are subject to dismissal with as little notice as a week or at most a month. (Hoos 1961; quoted in Braverman 1974, pp. 333–35). (For material on computer workers, see also Greenbaum 1976.)

Computers, the wonders of the age, in fact continue to mean degraded jobs for many white-collar workers. Beryl Simpson, an airline reservationist, talks about her work:

> They brought in a computer called Sabre. It's like an electric typewriter. It has a memory drum and you can retrieve that information forever. Sabre was so expensive, everything was geared to it. Sabre's down, Sabre's up, Sabre's this and that. Everything was Sabre.
>
> With Sabre being so valuable, you were allowed no more than three minutes on the telephone. You had twenty seconds, busy-out time it was called, to put the information into Sabre. Then you had to be available for another phone call. It was almost like a production line. We adjusted to the machine. The casualness, the informality that had been there previously was no longer there. The last three or four years on the job were horrible. The computer had arrived (Terkel 1974, pp. 82–83).

The work of secretaries also, especially in large organizations, is being subdivided and organized into repetitive and minute tasks. In the past, a company, for example a bank, had twenty-five secretaries, each working for a different person. Under the new system only about half that number are still employed. None, however, works for any one person. Each works for everyone. Each becomes a "specialist." Some do typing only. They type from taped messages that are recorded by telephone connection. If I am an executive and I want a letter typed, I pick up the phone, call a number, and record a message at the other end. Then someone else types it. I and the typist never see each other. The finished letter is brought to me by a messenger, and I sign it. The secretaries become chained to their typewriter and tape machines. Other secretaries only answer telephones, others only make appointments, and so on. Routine and impersonal jobs replace the jobs of secretaries as usually known. Work becomes alienating, but company profits go up because fewer secretaries are needed under the new system (Braverman 1974, pp. 344-47).

The American labor force is said to be more skilled than ever before. "Semiskilled and skilled operatives and craftsmen have increased proportionately, while the proportion of unskilled labor has decreased" (Julian 1977, p. 481). In his closing chapter, Braverman shatters one more myth of academic sociology. He argues that the "average skill" may be up in comparison to 1900, but that that average is derived from adding the skills and knowledge of the few who know everything about the process of production to the very limited skills of the workers who are kept ignorant of the process. In fact, relatively, most workers today are more ignorant and unskilled than those in 1900; they are losing old crafts and skills and never learn new ones (p. 425).

Much of the upgrading of workers' skills is the result of statistical and definitional manipulation. Since 1930, all those who operate machines have been called "semiskilled," thus removing them from the old category of laborer. As Braverman argues eloquently:

> It is only in the world of census statistics, and not in terms of direct assessment, that an assembly line worker is presumed to have greater skill than a fisherman or oysterman, the forklift operator greater skill than the gardener or groundskeeper, the machine feeder greater skill than the lumberman or raftsman (pp. 428-29).

In reality, jobs that can be learned in a few days (65 percent of assembly-line jobs are learned in less than a month), and in which people are told exactly what to do, cannot be called skilled. People working on farms in 1900, now classed as unskilled, in real life knew more (about the soil, the weather, the habits of animals) than the workers today who are considered more skilled. And as computers are entering the workplace, more workers are losing their skills and control over their work. Engineers and managers dictate more of the details of a job; machinists become observers rather than participants (*Dollars and Sense* December 1979, pp. 15-17; Shaiken 1979).

(The special work problems of women and minorities are discussed in Chapters 8 and 9).

## THE CAUSES OF ALIENATION

The causes of alienation will now be explored in more detail. Work has become alienating because most of us work for others who control the process of what we do. The body works but the mind vegetates. Work is also alienating because employers use workers' labor for their profit. Employers arrange the work process solely with the aim of retaining and increasing profits, paying little attention to the human costs of such working conditions.

*Historical Changes in Work*

Most people do not realize that the organization of work today is a recent phenomenon, shaped to fit the needs of capitalism; these conditions are seen as inevitable.

A few studies of American communities in the 1920s and 1930s document the changes in work. At that time the transformation of work to its present form was almost complete, but people had a living memory of different conditions. Two of the best studies are *Middletown* (Muncie, Indiana) (Lynd and Lynd 1929, ch. 1) and *Yankee City* (Newburyport, Massachusetts) (Warner 1963, pt. II).

Consider the statistics on self-employment. In the early 1800s, about four-fifths of working Americans were self-employed; after that, the figures decrease drastically: only one-third in 1870, one-fifth in 1940, one-tenth in 1970, and 8.5 percent in 1974. This means that people who were independent farmers, store owners, and craftsmen went to work for others. For most people today, working for others is all they have ever known. Instead of learning the skills of farming or of a trade over years, people can spend years in school and then get a job they can learn to perform in a few days (Braverman 1974, p. 53; Julian 1977, p. 82).

The changes in the making of shoes provide a clear case study of what has happened to work over the last three centuries. This description is found in Warner's study of Newburyport, Massachusetts.

*From Cobbler's Bench to Assembly Line*
During the first years of the settlement of Yankee City and New England and in the earliest phase of shoemaking, families made their own shoes. The second phase of the first stage was characterized by the itinerant shoemaker who, owning his own tools, made shoes in the kitchen of his customer, using materials supplied by the customer. In the process, the shoemaker was assisted by his customer's family and received his compensation largely in the form of board and lodging. Many families in Yankee City and in the outlying communities, particularly those dwelling on the north bank of the river, became proficient in the art of shoemaking at this stage. They made their own shoes during the winter months, passing down the art in the home from generation to generation. This section of New England has, therefore, a strong tradition of shoemaking.

The next stage began (*circa* 1760) when the shoemaker set up a small shop and made shoes to order for his local customers. These shops were known as "the ten-foot shops," and the customer's order was known as "bespoke." During the first part of this period, the shoemaker still made the complete shoe, but his relation with the market became indirect. The entrepreneur appeared. He was a capitalist shoemaker, hiring workers in their homes to make boots and shoes for him to sell at retail or wholesale. In the second phase of the period the central shop developed where materials were sorted. The parts were cut in the shop, distributed and served in the homes, then collected and the soles joined to the uppers in the shop. Machines were used scarcely at all. The processes of shoemaking were divided, and workmen specialized in one or more operations. Jobs were thus defined within the industry; for the most part, the worker no longer faced his customers.

During this period the market remained local, and the interests of the merchant-master and the journeyman were the same. When improved land and water transportation brought about an expansion of the market, the merchant became an increasingly dominant figure. The bargain became one of price as well as quality, and the interest of the merchant to produce cheaply in order to undersell competitors began to conflict with the maker's desire to earn as much as he could from his labor.... In 1852 a sewing machine for stitching uppers was invented, and the following decade saw the mechanization of many other processes. This development intensified the split in interests between the owner-control group and the operatives; it also established the subordinate position of the latter, which they have occupied ever since.... The security of the workers as craftsmen was threatened by the new developments. The shoe workers did not make the machines they were suddenly forced to operate, and they had no way of predicting what jobs would next be mechanized. The owning group had in the machines an effective weapon to lessen the value of the worker's craftsmanship (Warner 1963, pp. 275-77).

Since the 1850s, the trend has been one of further subdivision of work, more routine tasks and less control by workers, and total control of the planning of the making of shoes by management. One need not romanticize the life of the cobblers in order to see that their work was more meaningful than that of the modern operatives in a shoe factory. (Having taken over total control of conception and planning, management moved production out of New England to cheaper labor markets, when workers unionized. Few shoe factories remain in New England.)

People resisted this drastic change in their lives. Working in factories, under the conditions and control of employers concerned only with profits, was not accepted readily by formerly independent people. There was much resistance. Indeed, many of the first people who worked in factories were forced into such work. In England, where industrialization began, most industries got their workers from prisons, workhouses, and orphanages. Indeed, "the modern industrial proletariat was introduced to its role not so much by attraction or monetary reward, but by compulsion, force and fear." Factory work was resisted by most people; early capitalists turned to captive populations (Pollard, quoted in Braverman 1974, p. 66). These conditions of slave labor were "the forerunner of the company town in the United

States in the recent past as one of the most widely used systems of total control before the rise of industrial unionism" (p. 67).

The coming of industrial capitalism affected people's lives in many ways. People felt demeaned because of their work. In addition, when fathers and mothers had to work away from home in factories, the time spent with their children and families decreased drastically. Ties with family, friends, and community were weakened as people had to relocate where industrialists moved their factories (Lynd and Lynd 1929, ch. 1).

Over the last thirty years there have been more changes in the United States labor force. Industry is reducing the number of skilled jobs. Some are being automated; others are being moved overseas (as are many unskilled jobs). American workers are increasingly forced to take unskilled and service jobs, which pay much lower than skilled industrial jobs. Tables 5.3 and 5.4 show clearly this movement in the workforce. Major American cities are being transformed into workforces of low-paying service, clerical, and sales workers (Schurmann and Close 1979; Goodman 1979; Braverman 1974, ch. 17).

*Conception and Execution*

At the center of alienation is the loss of control over what we do and how we do it. As human beings, we need to think, plan, and imagine the work we do and then carry it out. We need to conceive and to execute our work. So long as we retain control of our work, we are engaged in a human activity. As soon as we begin to lose the thinking function and perform only the physical labor, we lose part of our humanity.

Capitalists have always sought to control the work process. Centralizing production in factories was the first step; employers later would dictate to workers the methods they should use to carry out their work. However, it was not until Frederick Taylor, the father of "scientific management," that a detailed theory for the total control of workers' labor was developed. According to Braverman, "Taylor raised the concept of control to an entirely new plane when he asserted as an *absolute necessity for adequate management the dictation to the worker of the precise manner in which work is to be performed*" (italics in original) (1974, p. 90).

While working for Bethlehem Steel Company (around 1900), Taylor found that men loading pig iron averaged twelve-and-one-half long tons per man per day. But careful study, Taylor claims, showed they could load forty-seven to forty-eight. The task was to persuade the men they could load the higher tonnage and "to see that the men were happier and better contented when loading the new rate..." (quoted in Braverman 1974, p. 103).

They chose Schmidt, a man who was strong and sturdy and "mentally sluggish" to be the first who would try to produce the higher rate. He was told that if he agreed to carry out his work exactly as he was told, his wages

**TABLE 5.3** Employment by Industry, 1949, 1978, and 1979 (in Thousands)

| Industry | 1949 | 1978 | 1979 |
|---|---|---|---|
| Mining; construction; manufacturing; transportation and public utilities | 21,566 (49.5%) | 30,240 (35.2%) | 31,727 (35.5%) |
| Wholesale and retail trade; finance, insurance, and real estate; service | 16,330 (37.3%) | 40,050 (45.5%) | 42,143 (47.1%) |
| Government | 5,856 (13.2%) | 15,476 (20.3%) | 15,612 (17.4%) |
| Total | 43,754 (100%) | 85,763 (100%) | 89,482 (100%) |

Source: *Monthly Labor Review,* May 1979, p. 73; May 1980, p. 73.

**TABLE 5.4** Average Weekly Earnings, by Industry Division, 1949 and 1979

| | Average weekly earnings | |
|---|---|---|
| Industry | 1949 | 1979 |
| Mining | $65.56 | $364.64 |
| Construction | 65.27 | 341.69 |
| Manufacturing | 53.12 | 269.84 |
| Transportation and public utilities | NA | 326.38 |
| Wholesale and retail trade | 40.80 | 164.99 |
| Finance, insurance, and real estate | 45.48 | 191.66 |
| Services | NA | 175.27 |

NA—not available
Source: *Monthly Labor Review,* May 1980, p. 77.

would increase from $1.15 a day to $1.85 (a 60 percent increase in pay for a 300 percent increase in production). Taylor continued the explanation:

> "Well, if you are a high-priced man, you will do exactly as this man tells you to-morrow, from morning till night. When he tells you to pick up a pig and walk, you pick it up and you walk, and when he tells you to sit down and rest, you sit down. You do that right straight through the day. And what's more, no back talk. Now a high-priced man does just what he's told to do, and no back talk. Do you understand that? When this man tells you to walk, you walk; when he tells you to sit down, you sit down, and you don't talk back at him. Now you come on to work here to-morrow morning and I'll know before night whether you are really a high-priced man or not."
>
> Schmidt started to work, and all day long, and at regular intervals, was told by the man who stood over him with a watch, "Now pick up a pig and walk. Now sit down and rest. Now walk—now rest," etc. He worked when he was told to work, and rested when he was told to rest, and at half-past five in the afternoon had his 47½ tons loaded on the car. And he practically never

failed to work at this pace and do the task that was set him during the three years that the writer was at Bethlehem (quoted in Braverman 1974, pp. 105-106).

In a footnote, Braverman comments:

> Georges Friedmann reports that in 1927 a German physiologist, reviewing the Schmidt experience, calculated that the level of output set by Taylor could not be accepted as a standard because "most workers will succumb under the pressure of these labors." Yet Taylor persisted in calling it "a pace under which men become happier and thrive." We should also note that although Taylor called Schmidt "a man of the type of the ox," and Schmidt's stupidity has become part of the folklore of industrial sociology, Taylor himself reported that Schmidt was building his own house, presumably without anyone to tell him when to stand and when to squat. But a belief in the original stupidity of the worker is a necessity for management; otherwise it would have to admit that it is engaged in a wholesale enterprise of prizing and fostering stupidity (p. 108).

The total control of the work process continues, despite the talk about humanizing the work place. Most people, in factories and increasingly in offices, find that Taylorism is accepted and practiced implicitly, as the method of organizing work under capitalism. Management controls and dictates each step of the work process.

Scientific and technical knowledge of course is necessary. There is, however, the issue of power and control. When the owners, experts, and managers are the only ones possessing such knowledge, then they control the workers and the work process. Then they can dictate to the workers what they must do. As Andors summarizes the intent of the cultural revolution in China, "scientific and technical knowledge must become the property of the workers." Knowledge is power. With it, workers can liberate themselves, control and run workplaces, increase their knowledge and creativity, and also increase production. The issue is not the need for knowledge; it is control of knowledge and of the workers—by whom; for whose benefit. (Andors 1977, p. xxii; Braverman 1974, ch. 4).

Braverman goes on to explain that some division of work exists in every society. However, nowhere is it carried to the extremes found in the capitalist division of labor, where both the degree of the division, and the conception and control of it by management, dehumanize workers (Braverman, especially pp. 72-73, 78, 125).

Braverman's analysis of the work process, where management controls the workers, has been criticized as one-sided (Sattel 1978). His view is said to show workers as objects controlled by management, neglecting the struggles workers have waged to resist such control. In part, this is the same issue raised in Chapter 2: does the ruling class have near-complete power and control? But Braverman is aware of the enormous resistance by workers against management control, as seen above. Other studies have shown this resistance. For example, retail sales clerks have cooperated and have formed a work culture to resist the attempt by management to control in detail the selling process (Benson 1978). Braverman may be read to imply total management control; rather, it is more accurate to say that he describes the intent of management, which has met much success, but he is surely aware of working-class resistance.

*The Technological Imperative*

New machines and technology have been part of the alienating work process—for example, machines that workers operate, performing minute tasks hundreds and thousands of times daily. But the nature of this technological process has been confused by sociologists and popular writers, who state that technology is an impersonal force that cannot be controlled. The most workers can do is adjust to it (Toffler 1970).

This is another area of confusion, where the role of capitalism and profit seeking have been obscured (Braverman 1974, p. 16; Clairborne 1971). Warner's study of the shoe industry in Newburyport, Massachusetts is an example of the confusion. In one place Warner writes about the "inevitable advance of industrial technology," but a few pages earlier, he has shown that the technology described is not inevitable; it was planned by management to subjugate workers, lower wages, and increase profits.

> Designers and engineers invent new and cheaper ways to make shoes and design machines to perform the new processes. Since the shoe-factory workers holding high-skilled jobs are a potential threat to management's control of shoe operatives, inventors apparently are encouraged to break down complex jobs into series of simple, easily standardized operations. An important result of their work, therefore, is to eliminate more and more of the skilled jobs from shoemaking, tending to accelerate the leveling of technological jobs in the shoe factory to a common low order of skill (1963, pp. 299, 292).

The forms and uses of technology are not inevitable. Technology could be developed by workers, controlled by them, and used for human liberation. The forms of technology under capitalism result from the needs of capitalists to control and exploit workers.

*Profits over People*

Many times earlier I have shown that profits are the primary consideration of capitalist management. Dangerous working conditions are not eliminated because it is much cheaper to pay a small fine than fix them; companies move from old sites, often leaving people jobless who have given them the best part of their lives, because the companies have found another site with cheaper labor; farm workers, many of them children, pick crops at starvation wages to assure high profits for agribusiness.

A proponent of capitalism spoke plainly in *Working*. Larry Ross, ex-president of a conglomerate and now a business consultant, told Terkel: "But the warm personal touch *never* existed in corporations. That was just a sham. In the last analysis, you've got to make a profit" (1974, p. 537).

## LIBERAL REFORMS AND WORKERS' CONTROL

Most people who look at work and working conditions agree that something must be done to change conditions. In the United States, there is the more recent phenomenon of generational differences, with younger workers less willing to tolerate daily assaults on their identity and humanity. Many people quoted in the book *Working* noted the readiness of younger workers to protest against alienating work. In part, this attitude comes from a generation not dominated by the memories of the Depression, and therefore not intimidated by the threat of joblessness (Terkel 1974, pp. 78, 161, 278, 327, 334, 524).

Management is very worried. Most are more concerned with the threat to their control and profits, to the need for production, than they are concerned with the alienating conditions and their effect on the workers. Something must be done to protect capitalism. Despite protestations by Jenkins and others that moves toward humanizing the workplace are motivated by concern for the workers themselves, not by the threat to profits, history shows otherwise. Before the resistance of workers, management did not worry about humanizing work. And *Work in America* seeks to assure management by emphasizing that there can be both satisfying work and higher productivity (Braverman 1974, p. 32; Jenkins 1973, p. 3; *Work in America* 1973, p. 94).

In the United States the reforms and experiments in work are still very limited. Few workers and companies are involved. The vast majority of working people still toil under Taylor's principles. Indeed, as Braverman has shown, these principles are spreading to white-collar work.

But in other parts of the world, the reorganization of work is becoming a reality. The following pages describe some of these efforts to make work human again.

The following discussion focuses on efforts to deal with alienation. But the other problems of work—low pay, unemployment, dangerous working conditions—also require solutions. These problems will be largely solved as soon as the exploitation of labor for profit is ended under socialism. Under capitalism, these problems will persist for most people. Alienation is much more difficult to end, even under socialism.

## Capitalist and Socialist Principles

Many of the current and proposed changes in working conditions assume similar forms in socialist and capitalist societies. In both instances, there is talk of workers becoming involved with their work, of contributing to the daily process of production with their minds as well as their hands. There are two fundamental differences, however. In socialist societies, the struggle to restructure work is taking place within the context of a new society, and the aim is for actual and total control by the workers. This is a profound change from what had existed and has not been nearly completed in any socialist society. The struggle to liberate workers has begun and has made notable progress in some socialist societies, however.

## Reforms under Capitalism

These reforms are varied. Hardly any aspect of work has been left untouched. Raskin (1977) summarizes some of the efforts at reform:

> The expressions of job reform are infinite. In some places committees representing the workers are called in to help decide the basic layout of the factory and the types of equipment that will be used. Autonomous work teams rotate jobs, map production schedules, assign time off, propose departmental budgets, and take over most of the responsibilities of first-line supervision.
>
> In many cases workers designate foremen from within their ranks, leaving their former bosses free for more challenging duties. Even such sacrosanct managerial prerogatives as the power to hire or fire are now occasionally entrusted to departmental work groups. In line with this trend, some companies are permitting workers to establish their own pay systems.
>
> The rigidities of the old five-day, 40-hour work schedule with every worker punching in and out at the same time, have been relaxed. In many enterprises, including such robotized bureaucracies as the Social Security Administration in Baltimore, flextime arrangements now allow workers, especially mothers with small children, plenty of latitude about when they come to their desks and when they go home (p. 11).

In relation to "participative management," *Work in America* includes the following tasks in which workers will participate:

- Their own production methods
- The internal distribution of tasks
- Questions of recruitment
- Questions regarding internal leadership
- What additional tasks to take on
- When they will work (1973, p. 103).

Some related reforms include the following: workers setting their own wages; a team of workers producing a whole engine, rotating jobs, not working on an assembly line; and reorganizing the work day, week, and year, so that workers can put in the same number of hours but schedule them at their own convenience (for example, work eight hours from 7 to 3, 8 to 4, or 9 to 5) (McNall 1975, p. 77; Lawler 1977; McLean 1975).

Finally, in some European countries, in addition to most of the reforms above, there have been efforts and laws to include workers in the boards of directors and other management groups. The theory is that the workers will be more responsible and more involved if they join in the running of the company (Garson 1975; Jenkins 1973, ch. 8).

*Work in America* reports the following example of changed working conditions in the United States.

> Until 1967, Texas Instruments contracted for its cleaning and janitorial services. But the firm's engineers evaluated the plant as only "65 percent clean." Apparently, the contractor's ability to do the job well was aggravated by a quarterly turnover rate of 100 percent. Preceded by careful planning and training, the following actions were taken in a test involving 120 maintenance personnel:
> 
> - Cleaning service teams of 19 people were organized and were given a voice in the planning, problem solving, and goal setting for their own jobs.
> - They were thoroughly trained in the job requirements and techniques, and were provided with adequate equipment to do the job.
> - They were held accountable for the overall job. The means of getting the job done were left to them. It was also the team's responsibility to act independently to devise its own strategies, plans, and schedules to meet the objective.
> - They were taught how to measure their own performance and were given the freedom to do so, both as individuals and as teams.
> 
> These were the outcomes:
> 
> - The cleanliness level rating improved from 65 percent to 85 percent.
> - Personnel required for cleaning dropped from 120 to 71.
> - Quarterly turnover dropped from 100 percent to 9.8 percent.
> - From the fourth quarter of 1967 until the fourth quarter of 1969, costs savings for the entire site averaged $103,000 per annum (1973, pp. 100–101).

In another example, the Eaton Corporation, manufacturer of engine valves, has changed working conditions in some plants. Initially, prospective employees are given a tour and are encouraged to ask questions about their work and the plant. Once they are hired, there is no probationary period (a practice common to most factories). At work, there are no punch cards, time clocks, or buzzers. In general, office and production employees are treated the same way (Scobel 1975, pp. 166–67).

Workers are involved in the planning of the work. "Office and factory supervisors hold departmental meetings at least once every two weeks to discuss issues that the employees themselves raise. . . . the manager invites some factory and office people to his weekly staff meetings." There is also "worker participation in decision making." In one plant, workers voted to work a ten-hour–four-day week, and Eaton went along. Elsewhere, workers have nominated and selected their own supervisors (pp. 167–68).

What have been the results of these changes? "About one-third of the people seek some involvement in their equipment repairs" and three-quarters "want to learn more about the whole production process." Absenteeism and turnover have been reduced drastically while work production has gone up; workers have taken care for the plant; there have been no complaints of discrimination or unsafe working conditions; it is said that workers are so full of energy when they go home that they go dancing and bowling; there is decreased aspirin consumption; workers have voluntarily planted trees and shrubs to make a picnic area; and guitar-playing workers are said to have sung about "a workplace havin' a soul" (pp. 168–72).

The next section will comment on these experiments from a socialist perspective. Here, two things must be said. First, liberal reforms do not change the reality of ultimate control. The authors of *Work in America* point this out very plainly: "Not all of a company's decisions, of course, are turned over to the workers when they participate in management. Upper-level managers continue to run the company, handle major financial transactions, and coordinate all the functions" (p. 104). Gyllenhammer, describing the Volvo experiment with work, also shows that management retains ultimate control (1977, pp. 111–12). Even radical and progressive union leaders do not want to challenge ultimate management control. Gary Bryner, president of the Lordstown local of the United Auto Workers, told Terkel, "The workers' idea is not to run the plant. I don't think they'd know what to do with it. They don't want to tell the company what to do, but simply have something to say about what *they're* going to do" (Terkel 1974, pp. 264–65).

Jenkins reports a case where workers were given real control of their work. At Polaroid, "in the early 1960s, there was a project in which a group of some 120 machine operators were put in an unusual routine. Instead of spending all day at the machine, they spent one hour in special training, two doing coordinating work, and five running the machine, thus gaining an unusually intimate understanding of what they were doing." By all accounts, the workers carried out very successfully a very difficult operation. But the company ended the program. Why? The workers presented a threat to management control; they showed they did not need managers. Corporations and the media lost interest in work alienation when it became obvious that the central issue was *control*, which management cannot relinquish under capitalism (Jenkins, 1973, pp. 314–15; Smoot 1977).

Even where workers have formal control of the plant, as is the case in Yugoslavia and in some United States corporations, they do not have actual control. The experience of Yugoslavia and other places shows that management does not give up ultimate control.

From a socialist perspective, liberal reforms suffer from two basic faults: they do not attempt to bridge the gap between conception and execution, and the workers do not really run their workplaces. But what if, despite these shortcomings, most workers became happy, should the examples of Eaton and other corporations become widespread? What if most workers went home full of happiness and energy, and their lives were filled with joy, love, and friendships? Why would socialist criticisms matter?

This is a serious issue that must be addressed at many levels. First, assuming that Scobel (part of the management at Eaton) is reporting accurately, no one can tell how long Eaton workers will remain happy. Second, it cannot be predicted whether these changes could be installed in most United States companies. But most important, in the long run a solution cannot work unless it deals with the real roots of a problem. If the basic problems are divorce of mind and body, and lack of control over the entire work process, then no attempted solution that does not attack these problems can make work human and liberating. Time will show, as it has shown in relation to other reforms in the past, that the above liberal reforms are no solution.

*Worker-Owned Companies*

In the United States today, there are a few companies that are owned entirely by the workers. Some plywood firms in the Northwest have been worker-owned for a long time; former farm workers combined their resources and efforts and now run their own farm; an asbestos mine, about to close, was bought by the workers and operated by them; and laid-off workers of a printing company that closed down have opened their own plant, which they own cooperatively (Bernstein 1974; Bennett 1979; Zwerdlung 1974; Boyles 1979; Greene 1979).

It appears that in most of these cases the workers bought out plants that were failing, closing, or closed, and kept them open in order to keep their jobs. Whereas in some plants the workers make ultimate decisions (plywood factories), in others it is an ongoing struggle, and in others the management retains actual control. The workers report various degrees of satisfaction. Generally, they express greater satisfaction than other workers or than they did themselves in their former jobs, and they are more productive than most other workers (Bernstein 1974).

A number of recent reports have shown, however, that the workers who owned the Vermont asbestos mine did not have control. As one report put it, "employee ownership isn't workers' control" (*Dollars and Sense*, May–June 1979, p. 6). Problems arose because:

> When the mine's ownership changed, the power relations within the mine did not change with it. The "white hats," as management-level employees are called, continue to manage the operation in a day-to-day sense, as well as dominating the elected board of directors. There was no move to set up a new system of workplace democracy or workers' control (Cluster 1978, p. 26).

## STRUGGLES: Workers Run a Restaurant

*In 1971, some people in Brattleboro, Vermont set up a community restaurant. It was organized as a cooperative, but many problems arose since the workers were not consulted on the decisions made by the board of directors and the manager. Fritz Hewitt was manager in 1976–77, but quit the job because problems persisted. At that point the board decided to sell the restaurant. Hewitt describes the developments from that point.*

They figured the staff would go along with it. Well, at first we capitulated. We felt doomed. Then one of the managers ran into Dave Ellerman of the Industrial Cooperative Association and told him our woeful story. He said, "Hey, you don't have to let it go!" and rushed right up to meet with us. His outline of how a worker-managed cooperative could work really appealed to us, but we were worried about commitment and logistics.

For two months we went back and forth from, "Yes, we want to keep it" to "How are we going to get it together to do it? Who'll do it?" and then "*I'll* do it!" and "Yeah, well all right, *I'll* do it too!" The demagogic fervor was running wild! As soon as someone would come up with a ringing speech for one point of view or the other, all the sheep would trot over there.

But Ellerman kept after us, and it all began to take shape. We realized we could probably sell worker management to the membership. A huge split between the workers and the board-owned business was a pipedream. Everyone lost perspective; it became an ego battle and the whole thing boiled along with uncomfortable little border wars.

Then there was a very passionate membership meeting in spring '77 where both sides yelled at each other across the room and the newspaper reporters took it all down. After some very stirring pro and con speeches, the staff quietly handed everyone printouts of a carefully thought-out plan for worker management. We made commitments to the membership for paying them back their shares, and presented a six-part management—office, kitchen and floor with two people in each area—to replace the old one-manager system. Six of the staff committed themselves to running the place for 18 months.

We made clear that the workers' cooperative proposal didn't mean the sale of the restaurant to a specified, nameable group of individuals. It suggested reorganization from a consumers' coop to a workers' coop with some community input. The voting membership or "ownership" rights would be held only by the people who work day to day in the restaurant. The shares function under this system only as membership cards or certificates issued upon acceptance as a worker-member, and are forfeited when the person stops working in the cooperative.

The most important fact was that we could not just turn around and sell the restaurant if things didn't work out. Since the equity had been built up by the community, we would have to come back to them to make a decision like that.

The members finally voted to go with worker management. All existing stock was converted to Class A non-voting, and a new class of voting stock that could be owned only by employees was created. A few members bowed out by turning in their stock, but only a few. We ended up paying back less than $2,000 out of nearly $8,000 owned by the original membership. Since the members were behind us, we got a well-known, functioning business for a very small amount of investment capital. We were most appreciative of that vote of confidence. It meant we were able to pay back what we owed in several months from the restaurant income and workers' investments and get on with the business of running the business.

From that time on things changed drastically. There was suddenly no we/they; no one to blame and carp about anymore. We *were* the they, and only *we* were responsible for how the business ran. Everyone took a new interest in cash flow—people wanted to know what we made everyday.

Staff meetings were held weekly to work out the problems of democracy among 25 people. They were considered part of our 40 hour work week. We operate on a two-thirds vote. We do listen to everyone, even to the extent that new staff members can come

*(continued)*

*Source:* Reprinted from Fritz Hewitt, "Reaching Common Ground," *New Roots* 6 (May–June 1979), pp. 26–28.

### Workers Run a Restaurant (continued)

in, with no idea of what's going on, and with a speech send us back two years in history to some system that didn't work before. It's all moving more in a spiral it seems—it moves forward but at the same time you see some repetitions.

The committees are really working hard now and save staff meetings many hours of time by doing the research and making concrete proposals. That way everyone gets to participate. Used to be that the committees, when there were any, were all the same people. Well, I and others had to give up our mother hen attitudes and learn to keep our hands down and *not* volunteer. Now there's a lot of excellent talent coming along and our services are not as needed. It's good to know the place won't fall apart anymore if certain key people leave.

One of the main problems of democracy is determining what it's necessary for the group to talk about and what individuals can decide. Individuals are making decisions without bringing it up at staff meeting, which may be avoiding a cooperative responsibility. But at least we don't have things kicked around forever. The important thing is that for the first time people are trusting each other's judgment. We're all responsible for the place together, so it's not the feeling of "Aha! Now I can do what I want." Decisions are made when the person feels they have a good idea of what the group would want.

In terms of hiring and firing, which can be a sticky issue, we've appointed a hiring committee. New people go through a training period of three months during which they look us over and we look them over. After that, staff meeting votes whether to accept them into the cooperative. If they're accepted they pay $5, as we all did, which is a membership or voting stock certificate. Before worker management one person did all the hiring and the training period was only two weeks.

Another thing we've instituted is evaluations of people's work. At first it was painfully hard to criticize, and for two meetings no one said anything critical at all. But when the evaluations started working, things got much less tense and better generally.

One thing we're about to get together are the internal accounts. This means everyone will invest $50 which will go up and down in value as the business does. If people leave, they get paid back their internal account over several years.

Perhaps it's too early to make any grandiose claims, but from all current indications, it appears that we are overcoming the problem of high turnover of both staff and management, and the consequent lack of expertise that beset the Common Ground for its first six years.

You know, it's funny, the staff talks about "the restaurant" almost as a separate entity, like a precious endowment. In a way, it's like a land trust where people don't "own" the land. The Common Ground isn't owned, but it's here to be improved, used and loved. I get the feeling people are really beginning to take root and flourish.

---

The workers, even though they owned the mine, did not come to control, understand, and plan the operations of the work process, any more than do workers in socialist societies.

Finally, these are isolated examples with no real commitment to bridging the gap between conception and execution, they make few efforts to redesign the actual work process, and, above all, they take place in a capitalist context. They are not part of a struggle to make the whole society and all institutions democratic.

Bernstein, in comparing favorably the plywood factories with Chinese practice, forgets about the great differences of the contexts within which workers control their plants. He shows that many, probably most, workers do not participate in the running of the plant in any active way. In time, they become like workers in any other plant; indeed, some worker-owned plywood plants have been sold to private corporations. Work conditions and worker actions cannot be democratic in an unjust society run on authoritarian principles. When schools, government, mass media, and other institutions are controlled by, and run for the benefit of, the ruling class, how can democracy flourish in isolation at the workplace? We are socialized not to be active participants, not to cooperate with others to take control of our lives. In addition, when other institutions are not run democratically, isolated attempts at democracy face a constant crisis of survival (Bernstein 1974, p. 26).

### Socialist Struggles in Capitalist Society

Under capitalism, there can be no real workers' control and transformation of work. Efforts at such transformation must remain glimpses of possibilities until the state is taken over by the workers and the struggle for nonalienating work begins.

The groups mentioned in the previous section did not carry out their efforts with socialist goals. There are some groups, however, that are consciously working to create the beginnings of a socialist society. Case discusses a number of demands that workers have made, or can make, that would begin to raise the issue of workers' control and the move to a socialist society. Workers can demand that their plant not pollute the environment; psychiatric aides can demand better care and more funds for patients; teachers can focus on working conditions such as class size and demand their voice be heard. Case concluded that "the *potential* of workers' control is that it provides a vision through which the specific demand can move to the general: demands for a say about working conditions or organizational policy can point toward the ultimate goal of popular control over the economic system" (quoted in Hunnius et al. 1973, p. 468; Babson and Brigham 1978).

Worker collectives have been formed all over the United States. In November 1975 there were about fifty in the Boston area. They tend to be small (ten or fewer people) and concentrate on small-scale production or services: bookstores, restaurants, printing presses, carpenter shops, and so on. They are worker-owned and worker-controlled and have an egalitarian organization—no presidents or managers. Jobs usually are rotated so that no one does the difficult or boring jobs all the time. Decisions are made on a consensus basis—no formal vote is taken. An issue is discussed until no one has major objections to the proposed decision. Of course, the problem of some people having more influence still exists and must be struggled against. (From author's notes of a November 20, 1975 meeting of People for Self Management; also Vocations for Social Change 1976).

## Work in Socialist Societies

Work under socialism means workers' control, the uniting of the conception and execution of work. It involves a profound change, where no managers exist—rather, where all workers are managers. But such new work arrangements cannot arise instantly; thus a transition period is necessary where managers do exist. During this period a long struggle must be waged to limit management power and transfer it to workers. One means used has required managers to work alongside workers one day a week; another technique has placed limits on managers' income in relation to workers' income (see Chapter 2).

The socialist context of workers' control includes national planning. Up to now, these national plans have been drawn by political leaders and experts. Until workers also take on real power in the formation of national plans and priorities, there can be no workers' control. Participation only in the running of one's plant is not sufficient (Zeitlin 1970, p. 68).

Such socialist planning raises the real possibility and actuality of threats to individual liberty. How much power and control do workers have if they must produce what a national plan requires? The answer is complicated. Workers should struggle to take active part in, and eventually control, the national plan. To the extent they do, it is not a dictated plan they follow, rather, a collective creation in which they played a part. National, rational planning is freeing, because it creates a society that meets everyone's needs, liberating workers from oppression and suffering. People can begin to be creative individuals only once the constant threat to their existence has ended. Some rules and plans are necessary in any society. "Do your own thing" was a necessary reaction to the oppression of capitalism, but it is not a prescription for society. There must be rules prohibiting the exploitation of and harm to others. What distinguishes socialism is not the existence of rules; rather, it is the function of these rules and the question of who makes them and through what process. Complete freedom is impossible and destructive.

If the society as a whole decides that the rational and healthy thing to do is make bicycles and develop public transportation, a single group of workers cannot be allowed to produce polluting and inefficient cars. The work and products of all workers affect the larger community, and, under socialism, the larger community must relate in some way to workers' control. People in each workplace can use initiative and cooperation to make their work freeing and useful. But they cannot function in isolation. In this sense, workers' control differs profoundly from worker-owned enterprises under captialism.

Socialism does not guarantee workers' control. In the Soviet Union and East European socialst societies the workday and workplace of most people resemble those in the United States and other capitalistic societies. To be sure, there have been material improvements and the elimination of much exploitation. But the work most people do is what others conceive and direct (Braverman 1974, ch. 1; Yanowitch 1977, ch. 5).

Cuba, after many trials and errors, now seems committed to a real liberation of work and workers. Gradually, managers are becoming less powerful and their lifestyle resembles that of the workers; workers are gaining confidence as they take over some controls; and boring jobs are being eliminated or shared (Zeitlin 1970; Zimbalist 1975). An American visitor to Cuba in early 1979 visited "a cigar factory in Havana that seemed to be in a constant state of meeting. The topic was arrangements for the forthcoming two-week shutdown and paid vacation period (one of two in the course of the year). While work continued, various workers left their posts and came forward to a microphone to make their points" (*Dollars and Sense,* February 1979, p. 9).

Yugoslavia has been committed to formal workers' control since the early 1950s. Theirs is the most widely known effort at workers' control. Jenkins summarizes its essential features:

> The key instrument of worker control is the workers' council, one of which must exist in every enterprise. In companies employing less than 30 persons, all employees are members; in larger companies, there are from 15 to 120 members, directly elected by the employees on a one-man–one-vote principle. The council holds all the formal power; it approves all important management decisions, appoints management personnel, sets salary scales, decides on hiring and firing, establishes capital investment programs, carries out long-term planning, and in general runs the company. The members of the council are elected to two-year terms, serve without extra compensation, and continue in their regular jobs while they are serving on the council.
>
> There also is a managing board, consisting of from three to ten members selected by the workers' council, which maintains closer contact with management personnel and which takes a more active role in the company's day-to-day operations (Jenkins 1973, pp. 96, 98).

To insure greater direct participation of workers, small units have been created within large enterprises.

But the promise of workers' control in Yugoslavia suffers from some weaknesses. There seems to be little effort to change the work itself, to reunite conception and execution. And despite laws and formal guarantees, directors and managers retain most power and influence in the running of the enterprises. According to Jenkins, however, things are improving. Also, in many ways, Yugoslavia is drifting back to capitalism. For example, investments by capitalist societies are allowed within its borders, and the country is moving back toward the market system instead of toward more national planning (Jenkins 1973, pp. 100–107; Supek 1975).

During the years of the cultural revolution the Chinese made some progress toward workers' control. The changes did not begin with the cultural revolution, of course. Changes were started in parts of China before 1966.

> Established in 1960 after the Soviet Union withdrew its technicians [the Taching oil field], was built on the same kind of enthusiasm and energy which Americans show along a rapidly rising river when the levee needs reinforcing. Although the work was arduous, there was no question of bonuses. After a mass struggle, technicians were integrated into the work teams and all problems were discussed by everyone. The result was not only an extraordinary collective spirit but technical innovation helped boost the field's production at a phenomenal rate without costly imports of sophisticated equipment (Steinberg 1978, p. 31).

During the cultural revolution, efforts were made throughout China to create institutions leading to workers' control. Bettelheim describes developments in the General Knitwear Factory in Peking. "In 1971 it employed 3,400 people, 60 percent of whom were women." Every effort was made to reduce danger and improve working conditions; for example, fans were installed near hot dryers, and great quantities of ice were used to reduce the heat (1974, pp. 13-14).

Before the cultural revolution, bonuses and higher wages were used to induce more and better efforts from workers. The "revisionist line . . . stressed production, bonuses, the importance of experts and technicians" (p. 19). When Bettelheim visited in 1971, he found that there was a campaign to motivate workers to "serve the people" (work for the common good, not just individual interests) and decrease the power of experts and managers. There was a mass movement to re-educate factory cadres.

Various institutions were created to make these changes. One was the "worker management teams," elected by the workers, which had five areas of concern:

> (1) ideological and political work; (2) production work and technical revolution; (3) financial and material matters (cost control, investments, etc.); (4) work safety; and (5) general welfare. They function as intermediaries between management and the masses and act as a control on the managerial bodies, as well as on the party members and administrative departments (p. 23).

The members of the workers' management teams were full-time production workers.

According to Bettelheim, "the workers make every effort to find collective solutions to whatever problems come up (including quality control)." In small teams, they discussed all plans and passed on all suggestions. No decision ever was made without consultation with the workers. Under this system that involved everyone and sought for means to pass power to the workers, the workers achieved many innovations in machinery and work processes (pp. 25, 28).

In his second chapter, Bettelheim shows in detail how national economic plans were drawn. Although by no means did workers control them entirely, they played a significant role. Bettelheim tells of workers making raincoats who decided to observe their use on a farm. By doing so, they learned to improve the raincoats so they would be more useful to the people who ultimately wore them. Generally, the unity of practice and theory (workers and experts) made for many innovations. Each enterprise had to cooperate with others for the benefit of all, not be concerned solely with meeting its quotas the easiest way. Bettelheim also cautions: "The Chinese reject as illusory the belief that there are magic organization formulas guaranteed to prevent any regression in a bourgeois direction" [control by experts, politicians, and managers] (p. 43).

There is a controversy about what in fact went on during the cultural revolution, and about how workplaces should be run during a socialist transition. A common criticism of the cultural revolution holds that during those years there was near anarchy in factories. Instead of changing rules, many leaders of the cultural revolution sought to eliminate them. According to this argument, some discipline is necessary. For example, workers who run trains must get to their jobs on time, or riders will be inconvenienced and transportation of needed materials and goods delayed. Leiken argues against confusing "exploitative discipline" with "strict discipline under socialism [that] does not exploit the people: it serves their interests" (1979, pp. 36-37).

No doubt some, perhaps many, abuses took place during the cultural revolution in China. But while no one doubts the need for rules and discipline, the issue is who makes the rules and by what process? This is the issue that people faced during the cultural revolution and which, it appears, the Chinese leaders now are avoiding. The new economic principles of the Chinese leadership call for workers to follow strict discipline, not to waste even a minute. These principles are not stated as a temporary necessity, or even as a reaction against the excesses of the cultural revolution; rather, they are stated as objective economic laws. Such claimed "laws" are conditions leading to alienated labor (Sweezy and Magdoff 1979b, pp. 13-14). DuRand discusses some changes that are said to be leading to workers' self-management. Still, it does not yet appear that Chinese workers control their workplaces (1979).

In addition, the changes of the cultural revolution were probably not as profound as claimed at first by enthusiastic visitors to China and by the Chinese themselves. Cadre leaders, teachers, managers, and scientists were said to be happy to work in the fields or alongside factory workers in order to change the leaders' elitist attitudes and reduce their power. It seems now that many, perhaps most, of the elite did not really change their values, embrace the need for all to do manual labor, or change their elitism to egalitarianism. Observers were deluded into thinking that such profound changes can take place in so few years. Obviously, the struggle is much longer and more difficult than formerly thought.

*Some Principles for Liberated Work*

These principles are brought together in brief form to conclude this section of the problems and promises of work.

1. Control of the workplace and the work process must be achieved by workers themselves; liberation is an act by people, not a gift bestowed.
2. At the center of workers' concerns must be the release of everyone's potential and creativity.
3. This struggle must proceed within the context of national planning which, through cooperation, aims to meet all people's needs.
4. A basic commitment of reorganized work must be to give dignity to physical labor. This dignity will come about as everyone shares in doing some necessary manual labor.
5. The power of experts and managers must be reduced steadily. Whether it can be abolished entirely is a question no one can answer, given our present knowledge. But this power must be reduced or there is no hope for change.
6. Work, home, and community must be integrated. In order to save energy, promote close relationships, and humanize work, people must live and work in the same community, preferably within walking or bicycling distance of each other.
7. Specialization pervades all our institutions; it creates an aura of authority and mystery, it keeps people ignorant; it leads to the avoidance of manual labor. Future generations will have to examine critically the need for specialists in all areas, and decide how much specialization is needed, and what loss in some very special knowledge is acceptable in exchange for widespread knowledge of basics and essentials.
8. Little has been written about size in relation to reorganized work. Yet in every known case where workers really control the work process, the group is no larger than about 300. In Israel, kibbutzim are not allowed to grow larger than 300; in Yugoslavia, larger plants are subdivided into smaller units to allow for more personal and direct control of the work, and for better personal relationships with other workers; in China, the various sizes of groups insure direct participation for all. Bernstein says that 300–400 workers is the maximum group size that allows for direct management, because larger plants do not allow for communication and personal contacts. Small is indeed beautiful and necessary to restore relationships to a human scale (Hunnius et al. 1973, pp. 240-55; Bernstein 1974, p. 33; Schumacher 1973).

### A Final Thought

It is impossible to return to the working conditions of the Tikopia and others described earlier in the chapter. The increase in population, technological changes, and the connections between the two make such a return impossible. But technology can be used wisely. We can learn the lessons of nature and use creativity and cooperation to make technology a tool for liberation, not oppression. To return joy and fulfillment to work, we must struggle to retain some old forms of work and create new forms and conditions. But if we are freed from the shackles of profit and capitalism, from destructive traditions, our chances of success are good. We must try, or we will continue to suffer daily humiliations and slow destruction of our humanity.

# 6

# *Imperialism and Hunger*

INTRODUCTION

In this book *imperialism* is used to describe the world capitalist system and its capacity for economic, political, and cultural exploitation. Under capitalism, wealth flows from the poorer to the richer countries, and societies have various degrees of economic development and wealth.

> The overall structure can best be understood in terms of the center-periphery metaphor. The transition from the center to the periphery is not clear-cut or abrupt but rather takes the form of concentric rings which merge into each other. At the center is the hegemonic power—in the present historical phase the United States of America—with the greatest concentration of wealth and military power. Around it are grouped the secondary imperialist powers —Germany, Japan, Britain, France, Holland. Next come the less powerful developed capitalist countries—the Scandinavian countries, Belgium, Switzerland, Austria, Italy, Greece, Spain, Portugal, Canada, Australia. Beyond this is where the periphery begins. The inner ring of the periphery consists of what may be called regional subimperialist countries—Mexico, Brazil, Israel, Saudi Arabia, Iran (until recently), perhaps India. And finally there are the outer rings of the periphery comprising the great majority of underdeveloped Third World countries in Asia, Africa, and Latin America.

All of these taken together make up a coherent whole, with lines of authority and subordination running from the center of the center clear out to the edges of the periphery. Generally speaking there is a reverse flow of money and its counterpart, real wealth, from the outer edges of the periphery through the intermediate rings to the center and finally the center of the center. The whole constitutes on the one hand a pyramid of power and wealth and on the other hand a system of exploitation of weaker by stronger at every stage of the transition from center to periphery and from bottom to top (Sweezy 1979, p. 2).

Although in this metaphor, wealth moves from the periphery to a core, two other features of imperialism must be noted. Not everyone in the poorer peripheral nations suffers; the upper classes in these nations align themselves with the imperialist nations, and they thus benefit from imperialism. Conversely, not everyone in the dominant central nations benefits from imperialism. In the long run, for most of us, imperialism is harmful. This book will show that imperialism leads to militarism, unemployment, inflation, and other destructive forces.

Within each country of the system, rich, poor, and those in between, there is a ruling class that tends to exploit the rest of the people. People in Latin American countries, for example, are exploited both by their own ruling classes and by United States corporations; indeed, these two often cooperate. Thus, it is helpful to think of the class struggle as international—between the ruling classes of capitalist societies and the rest of the people in these societies. Most of the people in the peripheral countries are poorer (and more exploited) than are the people in the core countries, but there too most people are exploited by the ruling class.

Therefore, in this analysis, wealth flows from the periphery to the center, but most of the people in one society do not exploit most of the people in the other societies. Rather, imperialism is a system where the ruling classes of capitalist societies dominate the people in those societies. The ruling classes in the core nations are most powerful, and the mass of people at the periphery are more exploited than the masses at the center (Hoxha 1979, pp. 252-338).

Imperialism is a problem for most of us at the center of the capitalist system. With various degrees of difficulty, socialist societies have managed to escape from that system. People in the center also can struggle against imperialism. The opposition that helped stop the Vietnam war was an example of what can be achieved; more such actions are possible.

## THE DEVELOPMENT OF COLONIALISM AND IMPERIALISM

### *Imperialism, Racism, and Slavery*

Imperialism and racism have been part of world history since the fifteenth century. The destruction of feudalism in Europe led to commercial, and later industrial capitalism, and ultimately the destruction of other societies and cultures.

The first victims of capitalism were Europeans. For example, in England, the land used by peasants for grazing and farming was taken away from them by people interested in producing wool for commerce. Thus, the "land enclosure" acts created many unemployed peasants who went to the cities and became a source of cheap labor (Cox 1976, p. 21).

English capitalists then shifted their attention overseas. Ireland was colonized by the British, as totally as any society ever was (for example, the Irish were forbidden to speak Gaelic and forced to speak English). The Irish potato famine of the 1840s, which led to starvation and emigration, resulted from the theft of the best lands by the British—a practice soon copied throughout the world.

The United States itself began as a nation in revolt against the colonial status imposed on it by the British. The colonists refused to continue in the system that required them to produce cheap raw materials and buy from England expensive manufactured products. The United States, Europe, and Japan impose this fate today on the countries at the periphery of the capitalist system.

With the rise of colonialism, racism appears. Racism emerged when Western capitalists moved to exploit the rest of the world; it provided a justification for the exploitation of non-European peoples. "Inferior" people deserved to be exploited and forced to change; left alone, they would never become "civilized." Racism as an ideology thus developed to justify colonialism (Cox 1976, pp. 26, 28).

The slave trade led to racism and was very important in the creation of capitalism. Some historians have argued that the slave trade provided "the capital which financed the industrial revolution in Europe" (but "mature capitalism," no longer in need of slavery, later destroyed the system), (Williams 1944, p. 1). Slavery was an economic institution. There was a need for labor and it could not be found any other way. Native Americans were the first slaves; white indentured servants followed them as a source of labor. For reasons explained by Williams, neither of these groups provided adequate labor. It was only then that the slave trade from Africa began. Slavery was an economic necessity and led to a racist ideology that claimed that black Africans were inferior (Williams 1944; Cox 1976).

*Stages of Imperialism*

In this chapter, we focus on present forms of imperialism. These forms have developed from previous ones, and thus we need to know something about the history of imperialism.

There have been three general stages of imperialism. *Colonialism,* in its classic form, consisted of the appropriation of land, labor, and resources from colonies in Africa, Asia, and elsewhere. Gradually, imperialism abandoned colonies (or never had them—as in Latin America) and exploited other nations through *trade*. This stage involved buying minerals, foods, and other materials at very low prices and selling them as expensive manufactured items. The trade stage of imperialism continues, along with the third stage—the *investment* of capital in poor countries. Although investment in poor countries began in the late nineteenth century, it became important in the imperialist system in the middle of this century. Its chief attractions are cheap labor, low taxes, and the likelihood of high profits.

Colonialism was the first, and classic, form of imperialism. Bodley has detailed the colonial exploitation and destruction of tribal societies throughout the world. Although Bodley is not consistent in showing the process as a logical outcome of capitalism and imperialism, his very specific account leads naturally to this conclusion (1975).

First and foremost, land was taken away from tribal people. We may know of this theft in the United States, but it happened throughout the world—in Asia, Africa, and Latin America. (In 1979, classic colonial remnants existed in South Africa, where whites owned 87 percent of the usable land; in Rhodesia; and some other places.) To assure the destruction of tribal societies, colonialists forbade communal land ownership, realizing capitalism would not allow for it. A United States commissioner for Indian affairs said, in the 1830s, "common property and civilization [capitalism] cannot coexist" (Bodley 1975, pp. 30, 88).

Not only was land taken, but cultures were destroyed and people killed. In the Belgian Congo, about eight million people were killed or died through disease and starvation, just in the years 1885-1908. Bodley cites worldwide figures totalling twenty-eight million killed through slaughter, disease, and starvation. In addition, many millions were "recruited" for work into virtual slavery (1975, pp. 34, 35, 39).

The remaining people and land were exploited further. Tribal societies had been self-sufficient, growing or gathering all their own food. But through various mechanisms (such as taxation), colonists forced tribes to cultivate one or two crops for sale (to the colonists). This is the reason that today some nations still grow predominately one or two crops: coffee, cocoa, sugar, and so on. When millions were forced to stop growing their own food and cultivate crops for the colonists, physical and social destruction soon followed. Lappé and Collins summarize the process well:

*Colonialism*
- forced peasants to replace food crops with cash crops that were then expropriated at very low rates;
- took over the best agricultural land for export crop plantations and then forced the most able-bodied workers to leave the village fields to work as slaves for very low wages on plantations;
- encouraged a dependence on imported food;
- blocked native peasant cash production from competing with cash crops produced by settlers or foreign firms (1977, p. 85).

Tribal people did not take well to forced labor, and colonists had to resort to the courts to exact that labor. When people refused to work by running away and other means, they were punished. Imprisonment in irons, corporal punishment, floggings, jail sentences for those "accused of deserting or neglecting their duties," and other forms of punishment were widespread (Bodley 1975, p. 130).

The colonists then forced the surviving tribespeople to abandon their cultures. Through one-sided education, missionaries, and laws that forbade tribal customs and forced people to abandon their established ways of making a living, the colonists tried to destroy tribal cultures. Bodley gives some details (1975, ch. 6).

Thus the nations we know today were created out of stable, self-sufficient societies. The people did not ask to be "modernized"; all resisted the process, many dying in their resistance. Although Bodley claims that the old cultures are dead, he is partly too pessimistic, as we see in the resurgence of Native American cultures (most of which never died, but were simply ignored).

### Anthropologists, Missionaries, and Medicine Men

Physical force and starvation were the primary means used to control tribal people, but they were not the only ones. Indeed, some people thought other means were more efficient.

Anthropologists, although many did not mean to, were helpful to the colonists.

> Successful rule ultimately depended on census data, elaborate records, and administrative bureaucracy, but it also required the accurate data on native customs which were provided by anthropologists working under direct government supervision or with the support of national and international research institutions (Bodley 1975, p. 61).

Missionaries always followed in the steps of armies and traders, and they did much of the work of changing the local cultures (Turnbull 1962). Gates, a Baptist minister who later worked for the Rockefeller medical philanthropies, said in 1905:

> Quite apart from the question of persons converted, the mere commercial results of missionary efforts to our own land is worth, I had almost said a thousandfold every year of what is spent on missions.... Missionary enterprise, viewed solely from a commercial standpoint, is immensely profitable. From the point of view of subsistence for Americans, our important trade, traceable mainly to the channels of intercourse opened up by missionaries, is enormous. Imports from heathen lands furnish us cheaply with many of the luxuries of life and not a few of the comforts, and with many things, indeed, which we now regard as necessities (Brown 1977, p. 26).

Medical philanthropies (often in the same place as missions), also did much to subjugate tribal people. In his study of the Rockefeller-financed public health and medical activities, Brown shows their clear imperialistic drive. Support for public health was recognized as great public relations. In addition, Rockefeller Foundation reports repeatedly stressed that better health increased worker productivity (Brown 1977).

Public health was seen as more effective than guns. The president of the Rockefeller Foundation said:

"Dispensaries and physicians have of late been peacefully penetrating areas of the Philippine Islands and demonstrating the fact that for purposes of placating primitive and suspicious peoples" *medicine has some advantages over machine guns* (quoted in Brown, p. 29) (emphasis added).

To be sure, many of the Europeans and Americans who worked in Africa, Latin America, and Asia really meant to help the people in those societies. But they were unaware of their ethnocentrism and the consequences of their actions. In the process of providing medicine or religion for the local people, the colonists also undermined the tribal cultures. Later, however, developers from Europe and the United States seem to have recognized clearly that they could use force, medicine, religion, and other means to dominate tribal societies.

## THE NATURE OF MODERN IMPERIALISM

Colonialism and imperialism have existed for a long time, but the means of exploitation have varied. The dominant colonial-imperialist nations have changed over time also.

In the West, racism, imperialism, and exploitation were begun by the Spanish and Portuguese. It was only later that England became the dominant colonial power (although France and others were also powerful colonizers). After a long period of predominance, England was slowly replaced by the United States; this change became obvious and final after World War II. The United States has dominated for about three decades, but we now are living through a period where the European Common Market nations and Japan are challenging United States power.

Thus, capitalism is threatened not only by socialist and nationalist revolutions in the nations at the periphery; it is also threatened by rivalries between imperialist powers. To a lesser degree, dominant nations may also be challenged by rising capitalists in some of the poor nations, such as the OPEC (petroleum) nations.

As of the early 1980s, however, most large multinational corporations (MNCs) are based in the United States and are run by its citizens. The automobile and oil companies and most other large United States corporations are multi-national. Many have incomes larger than some nations. The income of General Motors (annual sales of $30 billion in 1973) exceeds the income of Greece or Turkey. These companies' power and future prospects are immense:

> Of the 300 giant MNC's, two-thirds call the United States home. These 200 corporations account for 80 percent of all direct U.S. foreign investment; they have estimated annual sales of $200 billion. And they are just getting under way. Some experts predict that, whereas in 1969 the 300 top MNC's accounted for 15 per cent of the free world's GNP, by 1990 they will account for half of it. Concentration of power and control of resources will intensify, and the numbers of people dependent on MNC's for their livelihood will increase accordingly. Experts believe that by 1990 it won't be unusual for an MNC to hire a million people (Sherrill 1973, p. 489; Barnet and Müller 1974).

The managers of the MNCs have developed an ideology of the world as one entity, the parts dependent on each other, to justify the MNCs' wealth and exploitation; however, the foreign operations of United States MNCs have become integral to their profits and growth (Barnet and Müller 1974, p. 18).

### Minerals and Raw Materials

Classic colonialism involved the outright taking of minerals and agricultural products that were often produced with slave labor. At the present historical period, the dominant nations continue to benefit by buying products cheaply and selling expensive manufactured products. (Petroleum has been an exception since 1973.) Coffee, sugar, bananas, tea, some grains, and other foods are grown in poor countries for sale to imperialist powers. It may be true, however, that the United States could survive without these products (England, Japan, and other countries depend much more on imports of foodstuffs than does the United States).

The story is different with minerals and energy sources. The U.S. Department of the Interior predicts an increasing dependence on imports of such minerals. Certain of these minerals are also very important to the production of planes, appliances, and autos, and the United States is becoming increasingly dependent on imports from countries at the periphery. In the late 1960s, this country imported 80–100 percent of thirty-eight strategic materials it used (of a group of sixty-two). Other capitalist countries are also very dependent on imported energy sources (Gedicks 1977, p. 3; Magdoff 1969, p. 50).

Since the mid-1970s, as socialist revolutions have arisen in Africa, the United States has become very involved in that area. In addition to the military and political aspects of this policy, raw materials have been an important consideration. "The United States depends on imports of oil, uranium, diamonds, copper and other materials for its industrial strength, and Africa has vast quantities of each. . . . Africa harbors vast quantities of conventional raw materials such as oil, gold, uranium, copper and iron along with more exotic—and strategic—metals such as platinum, germanium and cadmium" (Holstein 1978, pp. 47, 50).

Government data reveal our dependence on imported minerals, metals, and fuels. Table 6.1 shows that the percent of United States production, in relation to world production, decreased from 1960 to 1977. It follows that the United States imported a greater percentage of these materials in 1977 than in 1960. Most of these imports come to the United States from countries on the periphery and from Canada, a nation dominated by United States multinationals (*Statistical Abstract*, 1979, p. 754).

The production of and profits from these minerals and metals have been dominated by a few MNCs. Seven companies control most of the petroleum production and distribution, and the story is similar for copper production (outside socialist countries). Poor countries have traditionally been forced to sell these resources and many others cheaply and to pay high prices for the manufactured products derived from them (Gedicks 1977, p. 8).

United States multinationals have invested in peripheral nations because their mineral deposits are of a higher grade than the deposits in core countries and because their labor costs are lower. But since the 1960s the MNCs in the United States have been losing control over mineral resources,

**TABLE 6.1** Metals, Fuels, and Minerals—United States Production as Percent of World Production, 1960, 1975, and 1977

|  | 1960 | 1975 | 1977[a] |
|---|---|---|---|
| Fuels |  |  |  |
| Coal | 15 | 18 | 18 |
| Crude petroleum | 34 | 16 | 14 |
| Nonmetals |  |  |  |
| Nitrogen | 26 | 20 | 21 |
| Sulphur | 56 | 23 | 20 |
| Metals (mine basis) |  |  |  |
| Bauxite | 7 | 2 | 2 |
| Copper | 23 | 18 | 18 |
| Iron ore | 17 | 9 | 7 |
| Silver | 15 | 12 | 12 |
| Zinc | 12 | 8 | 7 |
| Metals (smelter bases) |  |  |  |
| Aluminum | 40 | 29 | 30 |
| Copper | 25 | 19 | NA |
| Iron (pig) | 24 | 15 | 15 |
| Zinc | 24 | 9 | 7 |

[a]Preliminary figures
NA—Not available
*Source: Statistical Abstract of the United States* 1977, p. 747; 1979, p. 753.

primarily because of nationalist and socialist movements in the peripheral nations. To counter this threat, the United States multinationals have resorted to four policies: (1) they have concentrated new mine production in stable core countries; (2) they have re-entered peripheral nations where they believe local governments have created a climate favorable to capitalist investments (Chile is a good example); (3) they have strengthened their control over the transportation, processing, and marketing of minerals, the part of the process where most of the profit is usually found (e.g., in the production of petroleum); and (4) they are mining the sea (Pollin 1980).

Some people have argued that the United States is not very dependent on imports from poor countries. According to Szymanski, two-thirds of "U.S. material imports are from other advanced capitalist countries" (but petroleum is imported mostly from poor countries). Only for seven minerals did the United States import over 25 percent of its consumption from poor countries. In addition, most minerals imported from poor countries are available in the United States and other capitalist countries—but for a greater price, sometimes three to four times their present cost. So the United States does have other sources of supply. But Szymanski argues that the military costs for maintaining the sources of cheap minerals and metals may exceed any profits made. Capitalism faces a serious contradiction if in the long run military costs outweigh economic benefits. In addition, of course, poor countries are beginning to raise the prices for their goods (Szymanski 1977, pp. 47–50).

In a reply to Szymanski, Magdoff has argued that (a) the strategic importance of many of these minerals and metals is great, and our economy could not do without them; (b) the reduction in some imports, cited by Szymanski, is probably due to the stockpiling of these minerals by the United States government; (c) finally, and most important, the theoretical argument that there are other (more expensive) sources for these materials outside the poor countries ignores the driving force of capitalism: profits. Paying three to four times the present cost of these materials would reduce corporate profits, cause increased prices, wreak havoc with capitalist economies, and lead to their loss of power and control (Magdoff 1977).

Although in the long run military costs may outweigh economic benefits, corporations make profits in the short run. Costs may also be passed on to customers. The MNCs may not be able to avoid the consequences of these contradictions in the long run, but they are doing well now.

*Trade*

The United States has limited trade relations with poor countries. In 1972 the United States sold only 25 percent of its exports to such countries. The economic benefits from this trade come mostly from obtaining strategic materials and making investments and loans (McCarthy 1974, p. 53).

This statement must be qualified in two ways. First, these exports often return huge profits. United States MNCs often overprice the goods they sell to poor countries, from 30 to 700 per cent higher in comparison to domestic prices. Some drugs have been sold at prices eighty-two times higher than the "established international prices" (Barnet and Müller 1974, pp. 158-59).

Second, trading involves more than exports of United States products to other countries. Increasingly, United States MNCs manufacture products in their overseas subsidiaries (Europe, Asia, and Latin America) and they sell them in the United States and other nations in the capitalist system. Thus trading with poor countries is more important to United States MNCs than McCarthy's figures indicate. Countries at the periphery with heavy United States-MNC investments (Brazil, Hong Kong, South Korea, Mexico, and others) increased their exports of manufactured goods from 18 percent to 60 percent a year from 1960 to 1971 (Barnet and Müller 1974, p. 128).

United States multinationals also sell (to poor and richer countries) products that the MNCs manufacture in their foreign subsidiaries. In 1976, United States firms with foreign subsidiaries exported from the United States goods worth $76.6 billion, but their foreign subsidiaries sold goods worth $212.8 billion ($161 billion sold in the countries in which the MNCs are located; $14.1 billion exported to the United States; and $37.7 billion sold to other countries). Magdoff does not show how many of the foreign subsidiaries manufacture and sell in poor countries, but it seems from other data in this chapter that many do (Magdoff 1979).

*Investments and Loans*

United States multinationals have expanded their overseas investments tremendously. The book value of these investments grossly understates the real market value; the former has increased from $7 billion in 1946, to $78 billion in 1970, to $168 billion in 1978. In addition, United States banks have also expanded their overseas operations. In 1960, eight United States banks with a total of 131 branches had $3.5 billion in assets. By 1978, 137 banks had opened 761 branches overseas, with assets of $270 billion. Even with inflation, the expansion of investments and bank operations overseas shows the increasing involvement of United States multinationals in other countries (Kolko 1974, p. 32; Edwards et al. 1978, p. 416; *Statistical Abstract* 1979, p. 850; Sweezy and Magdoff 1980, pp. 7-10).

These investments are concentrated in Europe and Canada (about 75 percent); about 25 percent are in the poorer countries. United States firms control large percentages of the European markets, for example, 30 percent of the auto market. United States-MNC involvement is heavy in some countries that are neither major capitalist countries nor poor ones; Canada and South Africa are the primary examples. In South Africa, "about 350 American companies, including General Motors, Ford, Mobil, and General Electric, have investments . . . of an estimated 1.7 billion dollars and major banks such as Citicorp and Morgan Guaranty have made loans of about $2.2 billion" (Holstein 1978, p. 50). Canada can be viewed as a United States colony.

> The Herb Gray Report shows these percentages of nonresident ownership in Canada: 99.7 per cent of rubber products; 87 per cent of the transport equipment; 84.5 per cent of the tobacco industry; 81.3 per cent of chemicals and chemical products; 72.2 per cent of machinery; 64 per cent of electrical products; 55.2 per cent of primary metals; 51.6 per cent of nonmetallic mineral products; 46.7 per cent of metal fabricating; 39.2 per cent of textiles and clothing; 38.9 per cent of paper and allied industries; 31.3 per cent of food and beverages. It's little wonder that Canada sometimes feels like a kind of latter-day East India Company experiment, only this time the government is owned by U.S.-based MNC's (Sherrill 1973, p. 490).

Many of these investments, especially in poor countries, are not financed by capital exported from the United States. In Latin America, from 1960 to 1970, 78 percent of manufacturing operations of United States MNCs were financed from local capital—by borrowing from local banks. Thus, it can hardly be argued that the United States helps poor countries by exporting capital to them (Barnet and Müller 1974, p. 153).

And the profits made by borrowing from local banks are exported to the United States. A United Nations study for 1960–1968 showed that United States MNCs in Latin America took out "79 per cent of their net profits" (Barnet and Müller 1974, p. 153).

In addition, very often United States MNCs do not start new businesses; rather, they buy out already existing capitalist operations (because of the enormous power of United States MNCs, local capitalists cannot compete with them and are forced to sell out). Three hundred thirteen of 717 (46 percent) of manufacturing subsidiaries of 187 United States MNCs were local firms that they had bought out (Barnet and Müller 1974, p. 139).

People in nations at the periphery do not benefit from MNC investments in their lands. Kaiser Aluminum's investments in Ghana are an example. Kaiser signed a contract to process in Ghana some of the bauxite Kaiser mined in other countries. In exchange, the government of Ghana dammed a river and built a huge hydroelectric plant, displacing 6,000 people. Other results were: Kaiser could buy electricity at one-fifth what it cost Ghanaians; the waters gathered by dams to run the hydroelectric plant increased the incidence of schistosomiasis (a debilitating parasitic disease); local employment increased only by 2,700 people; and Kaiser refused to mine Ghanaian bauxite to use in its smelter plants. Kaiser's investment, therefore, did not benefit the people in Ghana; indeed, it seems to have made many of their lives worse (*Dollars and Sense* November 1979, pp. 15–17).

Such manufacturing investment in poor countries is fairly recent. Traditionally, investments have been mostly in producing oil, minerals, metals, and foodstuffs. The shift to manufacturing investment has become a necessity both to increase profits and to outweigh the cost of using American workers. The shift is especially noticeable in labor-intensive industries (where labor is a large part of the cost), for example, the assembling of television sets. "For a TV built in the U.S. the labor cost was $56 (in 1970); built in their [Zenith's] new plant in Taiwan the equivalent cost was $4.50, nearly 12 times less" (Kolko 1974, p. 39).

United States electronics firms have moved many of their operations to Southeast Asia because of cheap labor (almost all female). In 1979, as payment for testing 3,500 chips per day, one worker began at 80 cents *a day*. After three months a worker made 92 cents, and later one dollar (Grossman 1980, p. 35). Table 6.2 compares 1970 United States hourly wages with foreign ones for the same year.

**TABLE 6.2** Differential Hourly Wage Rates* in Selected Industries —Underdeveloped Nations vs. U.S.A.

|  | Average hourly rate (in dollars) | |
| --- | --- | --- |
|  | Underdeveloped nations | U.S.A. |
| Consumer electronic products | | |
|   Hong Kong | 0.27 | 3.13 |
|   Mexico | 0.53 | 2.31 |
|   Taiwan | 0.14 | 2.56 |
| Office-machine parts | | |
|   Hong Kong | 0.30 | 2.92 |
|   Taiwan | 0.38 | 3.67 |
|   Mexico | 0.48 | 2.97 |
| Semiconductors | | |
|   Korea | 0.33 | 3.32 |
|   Singapore | 0.29 | 3.36 |
|   Jamaica | 0.30 | 2.23 |
| Wearing apparel | | |
|   Mexico | 0.53 | 2.29 |
|   British Honduras | 0.28 | 2.11 |
|   Costa Rica | 0.34 | 2.28 |
|   Honduras | 0.45 | 2.27 |
|   Trinidad | 0.40 | 2.49 |

*Hourly wage rates for a given country and the U.S.A. are for comparable task and skill levels.

*Source:* Reprinted from Barnet and Muller 1974, p. 127. Copyright 1974 by Richard L. Barnet and Ronald E. Muller. Reprinted by permission of Simon and Schuster, a Division of Gulf & Western Corporation.

The move of operations overseas is motivated neither by benevolence for the new workers (to provide them with jobs), nor malevolence toward American workers (to punish them for unionizing). Profit remains the driving force of capitalism. The following figures show clearly that overseas profits have become essential to the operations and growth of United States MNCs.

In 1950, United States nonfinancial corporations made $21.7 billion profits from their domestic investments and $2.1 billion from foreign investments. In 1965, domestic investments yielded $36.1 billion and foreign $7.8 billion (Magdoff 1969, p. 183). In 1950, United States corporations made 7.3 percent of their profits from foreign investments, on 5 percent of their invested capital. In 1972, they made 24.4 percent of their profits from foreign investments, on only 9.8 percent of invested capital. Thus, foreign investments have a much greater return of profit than do domestic ones (Edwards et al., 1978, p. 477).

Looking at profits in another way, we find that from 1966 to 1978 United States multinationals sent $50 billion out of the United States. During the same years, however, their overseas investments produced an income of $203 billion. Some of that money was reinvested abroad, "but $132 billion came back to the United States in the form of dividends, interest, royalties, fees, etc." (Sweezy and Magdoff 1980, p. 7).

For specific corporations, foreign profits are even more important. Of 178 large companies in eleven industries (1972), 90 earned at least 25 percent of their profits overseas; 38 earned 50 percent or more (Kolko 1974, p. 33; see also Barnet and Müller 1974, pp. 16-17 for more details. For example, by 1973, "America's seven largest banks were obtaining 40 percent of their total profits from abroad, up from 23 percent in 1971").

Latin America is especially profitable. A study showed that United States investments there have a 79 percent rate of return, ranging from a low of 38 percent to a high of 962 percent. Drug firms especially make enormously high profits (Barnet and Müller 1974, p. 160; Lall 1977).

American businessmen see Latin America as a great place for investment and profit. But capitalism, in its drive for profits, overlooks the torture of political prisoners (as in Chile and Argentina), the suffering, and the hunger that abound in these countries (Petras 1977, p. 22).

## HUNGER AND STARVATION

Hunger does exist in the United States. Occasional congressional hearings and television documentaries expose it. This situation is puzzling, for the United States has more than enough food to feed everyone. It is possible to see hunger as a direct result of the inequality of capitalism.

But hunger overseas is less puzzling to most people. Many people have argued that it is the direct result of not enough land, too many people, unfortunate weather, and ignorant uses of the land by people in poor countries.

It may seem that if only these people stopped having so many children and followed American know-how, there would be no hunger.

The truth is different. Hunger in the world today is due mostly to capitalism, its colonial inheritance, and modern imperialism, as two recent works have shown. The discussion below relies largely on Lappé and Collins (*Food First* 1977; henceforth FF) and Cereseto (1977).

*How Many Are Hungry?*

Tribal societies were equalitarian. Food and other necessities were shared by everyone; if the tribe had food, no one went hungry (Radin 1953). Colonialism changed this pattern. There has been a deterioration of diet and health throughout the world. Not only are people eating less, but they are eating worse foods, full of sugar and other nonnutritious substances (Bodley 1975, ch. 8).

Today, by many estimates, 50 percent of the world's people in nonsocialist countries suffer from malnutrition. Sixty-two percent of the children in Santiago, Chile, suffer from malnurition. One study concluded that "malnutrition is the primary or contributing cause of death in 57 percent of all deaths in Latin America of one- to four-year-olds." In the last thirty or so years, many, many people throughout the world have eaten less than their parents did (Barnet and Müller 1974, pp. 122, 179; Petras 1977, p. 16).

Hunger exists not because there is a lack of food. Despite the waste of land documented in *Food First,* right now there is enough food in the world for everyone to eat 3,000 calories a day—more than enough (FF, p. 13). But the world's food is not distributed equally, not only between nations, but also within nations. From 1952 to 1972, 86 percent of the people in poor countries "lived where food production kept pace with or exceeded the rate of population growth" (FF, p. 112). Despite world population increases, there has been a 5 percent per capita increase in grains (1953 to 1973) (Cereseto 1977, p. 35), but starvation has increased, because prices also are higher and people have no money to buy food.

Poverty and unequal distribution are at fault. Whereas the average caloric intake in one state in India is 98 percent of the required daily minimum, 50 percent of the people in all of India consume much less (Cereseto, p. 46).

Population density is not at fault. Even Bangladesh, where it is supposed too many people live on very little land, grows enough food. But there the rich eat twice the protein of the poor, some food is exported, and the rich grow nonfood (jute) for export, while by and large the poor own no land (FF, pp. 19–20).

The world does grow enough food. But this increased production goes to support the life-styles of the urban rich and middle class: earnings from food sales are used for luxury products; grains are fed to livestock for meat the poor cannot afford; some grain gets exported; and some gets dumped to keep prices and profits high (FF, pp. 135–36). Thus the paradox: there is more food but more people are hungry.

The United States, which has had a food surplus (especially in grains), has been using it for political and military purposes. Most of the food we give to other countries goes to military and right-wing dictatorships. These governments use the money they would have paid for the food to buy military equipment. Food is used to support governments that oppress their own people. Utimately, no one country can feed the world's hungry people. They must take control of their own lands and grow their own food (Freund 1979).

*The Uses of the Land*

Land, throughout most of the world, is not used to feed people. Indeed, much land is simply not used at all. There are estimates that only 44 percent of the world's arable land is used for farming. For example, Del Monte (a United States multinational) owns 57,000 acres in Guatemala, but only 9,000 of those acres are cultivated (FF, pp. 16, 82).

Yet, throughout the peripheral nations of the capitalist system, 30 to 60 percent of rural residents are landless. More and more land is now owned by fewer and fewer people, who use it for profit-making crops (FF, p. 129).

These larger farms, owned by a few people and the multinationals, are being cultivated by machines with the use of chemical fertilizer. *Food First* and other works give abundant evidence that mechanization, chemical fertilizers, and pesticides have not increased the productivity of the land. Small farms can still produce more per acre—but small farms are not profitable to corporations. This is so even in the United States (FF, pp. 156–57). The "green revolution" of wonder seeds that was to eliminate hunger has produced more profits for large farmers and corporations. These seeds were suited for cultivation in large, mechanized farms. Poor farmers cannot afford the technology for the new seeds. Lappé and Collins conclude:

> Once it is manipulated by people, nature loses its neutrality. Elite research institutes will produce new seeds that work perfectly well for a privileged class of commercial farmers. Genetic research that involves ordinary farmers themselves will produce seeds that are useful to them. A new seed, then, is like any other technological development; its contribution to social progress depends entirely on who develops it and who controls it (FF, p. 123).

As more land is being concentrated in fewer hands, more of it is being used for cash export crops, and unemployed peaseants leave and crowd the cities (Cereseto 1977, p. 38). In Mexico, as the acreage devoted to local consumption has decreased, and the cash crops for export increase, imports of corn, soybeans, and other staples have also increased—and so has infant mortality due to malnutrition (up 10 percent from 1966 to 1976). In many countries, 50 to 70 percent of the arable land is used for coffee, sugar, tea, and other cash crops. A study in Niger showed that in villages where peasants grew peanuts and other export crops they ate less well than in villages where people grew food crops for their own consumption (FF, pp. 36-37, 101, 170).

In addition, the deserts of Africa are expanding not because of nature's whims, rather because of the use of the land for raising cash crops and the change from traditional methods of growing food. Where crops were rotated, and some land left fallow, deserts did not appear. Cash cropping destroyed such land-conserving methods. Algeria is reclaiming much of its desert through reforestation (as did China) (FF, pp. 98-107).

Ironies abound. While the Sahel (desert) countries in Africa were experiencing famines in the early 1970s, they were exporting meat for European consumption. In 1974, 23 percent of Senegal's foreign exchange went for the importation of refrigerators, air conditioners, cars, and televisions (FF, pp. 102-3).

*Changed Diets*

In addition to the causes for hunger outlined above, changes in traditional diets have contributed to malnutrition and disease. Processed food simply is not as beneficial and nutritious as the food people formerly ate. Reduction in the production of traditional crops (such as lentils and rice) that eaten together complemented each other and yielded more usable protein, followed from the growing of "green revolution" seeds and cash crops and led to protein hunger. The power of advertising has also been used by multinationals to change dietary habits. In Mexico people now eat white bread and drink soft drinks (FF, pp. 141-42; Barnet and Müller 1974, pp. 183-84). Because of the publicized importance of roughage for digestion and health, corporations that originally removed the roughage from grains now add new roughage—sawdust—and increase the price of bread. (Only July 16, 1981, I examined the list of ingredients in bread at a local supermarket and discovered that one brand, for example, contains "finely powdered food grade cellulose . . . refined from a naturally abundant wood source.")

The latest case of malnutrition due to changed dietary habits involves infant formulas. Breast milk is more nutritious and provides important immunities—it is also free. Yet MNCs have been using the modern techniques of advertising and promotion (free samples, visiting nurses employed by the MNCs, and so on) to convince poor women to switch to infant formulas. Not being able to afford them, but stuck with them once breast feeding was stopped, poor mothers have had to water down the formulas. Malnutrition and disease were inevitable. Some poor countries have awakened to the dangers and limited or prohibited the sale of infant formulas (FF, pp. 310 ff.; *Dollars and Sense* May-June 1978, p. 12-13).

## Food for People

Although the world has widespread poverty and starvation, socialist nations have been feeding their people. No better example can be given than a comparison of China and India. Both have large nonindustrial populations and both became independent in the late 1940s. China went the socialist route, India did not. Today, poverty and hunger abound in India; not even the most fanatic antisocialist can make that claim for China. India, with more arable land than China (and fewer people), and half of that land in tropical regions allowing for two crops a year, produces fewer grains than China: 184 kilograms per year per person, versus 264 in China. In addition, unlike India, food prices in China have been stable.

How has China grown enough food? The communes have reorganized and strengthened rural life and the economy; millions of people have worked to build reservoirs, terrace the land, and stop the spread of deserts through reforestation; communes are diversified and some even meet their own industrial needs (for example, build tractors to meet their own specific needs) (Cereseto, pp. 41ff.; FF, pp. 93ff.).

China has demonstrated that famines are not natural calamities—they are social creations of inequality, poverty, and profit making. In 1972-73, China had its third year of drought—but no starvation. Reservoirs and planning produced enough food for everyone (FF, p. 95).

## Too Many People?

Finally, hunger is attributed to too many people. The causes and solutions of "overpopulation" are badly understood.

In India and elsewhere, peasants have many children for good reasons. They need more children, and for Indians this means sons especially, to work the little land they own and produce enough to feed themselves. In addition, children provide protection in old age (Cereseto 1977; FF, pp. 63-68).

Thus, mechanical solutions (such as birth control and vasectomies) cannot slow down the population increase when they do not eliminate the causes. There has been no case of decline in population growth when there was not also an increase in social equality and elimination of poverty and exploitation (FF, p. 70). People will use birth control once life has become more secure. China provides a case study.

However, recent evidence in *Beijing Review* (an official government weekly from China) modifies some of the conclusions reached by Cereseto, Lappé and Collins, and others. China has not slowed down its population growth as much as we had thought. Its population increased from 550 million in 1949 to 975 million in 1978. So far, people have met their material needs because of increases in production and more equitable distribution of goods. But a continued large population increase will tax China's resources and must slow down.

Why has it not slowed down? The *Beijing Review* authors focus on the attitudes persisting from presocialist days. People want large families; they also want a son if their first two or three children are daughters. Also, there has been no organized campaign to limit population growth. Such a campaign now is under way to educate people on contraceptive methods, to encourage their use, and to distribute them freely. In addition, laws have been passed that benefit couples with fewer children, preferably one child. Those with one child get free day care and other benefits.

It is clear that in addition to social and political changes there is a need for organized campaigns to slow down population growth. It seems the only way to insure the long-run self-sufficiency of each nation and the world (Chen 1979; Ouyang 1979; Zhou 1979; all in *Beijing Review* November 16, 1979).

To summarize, overpopulation is not the primary cause of hunger. People are poor and hungry in most countries because they are exploited both by their own ruling classes and by imperialist nations.

## PERSPECTIVES ON CAUSES

The causes of poverty in most nations of the world are imperialism and capitalism imposed from outside, and vast inequalities within poor nations. The sources cited so far provide the evidence for this socialist perspective.

But there are other perspectives. One perspective that might be called "conservative" blames the poor nations for their poverty. It takes different versions, but all end up by blaming the victims for their condition. One version is blatantly racist, claiming the poor (who are also largely nonwhite), are inferior, lazy, unmotivated, and so on. Other versions are more sophisticated, but essentially still racist (Singer and Bracken 1976).

Theories of "underdevelopment" focus on the limited life-styles of poor peasants, and ignore the evidence showing that people managed well before the rise of capitalism and imperialism. They had no cars or television (poor people still do not), but they were not hungry, landless, and forced to live in urban shantytowns (Bodley 1975).

Another formulation, for example by Robert McNamara, president of the World Bank, states many of the facts of increasing poverty and inequality, but never speculates on the causes. McNamara does say the rich nations are doing little to help the poor ones, but that is as far as he points to a cause. Imperialism is never mentioned, and McNamara ignores the dismal failure, up to now, of the solutions he recommends (McNamara 1977).

The socialist view, in summary, traces imperialism to capitalism's drive for greater profits. Poor nations have been sources for such profits, and for resources to make for profits at home. In addition, competition within and between imperialist countries, insecure markets for their products, and so on, drive corporations to seek control over resources, to conquer foreign markets, to find sources of cheap labor, and so on (Magdoff 1969: 35-36; Barnet and Müller 1974: 129ff).

## THE EFFECTS OF IMPERIALISM

Behind the figures for multinational assets and sales, cheap labor costs, raw materials, and cash crops are people—people who like all of us are trying to survive. Although the effects of imperialism are more devastating for people in peripheral countries, most of us in the United States also are affected.

*Inequality and Oppression in Poor Countries*

Hunger is a reflection of inequalities in all areas of life.

Conditions in Chile have deteriorated since the overthrow of the socialist government in 1973. People make less money, there is more unemployment, hunger threatens daily. Property is being repossessed by the rich, corporations, and multinationals. Public enterprises are being sold cheaply to private businesses. Production has decreased in all areas. In short, the quality of life is fast worsening for most people (Petras 1977, pp. 14-15).

Throughout the poor countries, unemployment is very high. By government standards that underestimate the number of people without work, or only working part-time, 30 percent of the people in poor countries were unemployed in 1972. United Nations statistics show equally high unemployment. In many countries, over 40 percent of the people have no jobs (Kolko 1974, pp. 123-24; Barnet and Müller 1974, p. 166).

An expected result of high unemployment is cheap labor. When people face starvation, they will work for very low wages under primitive conditions.

Hunger, unemployment, and low wages can exist while a country's total yearly income increases. Statistics may show that per capita income has gone up. But that is an average, combining the high incomes of the few and the poverty of the many. In fact, income distribution, inequality, and poverty are worsening in most poor countries. Brazil and Mexico, two countries where the economy as a whole has improved, are good examples. "In the early 1950's, the richest 20 per cent of the population had ten times the income of the poorest 20 per cent. By the mid 1960's the rich had increased their share to seventeen times what the bottom 20 per cent received. A 1969 United Nations study reports that in the Mexico City area the richest 20 per cent of the population lived on 62.5 per cent of the area's income while the

> *In the following dramatic description, Barnet and Müller show vividly the degree of suffering among most people in the peripheral nations of the imperialist system.*
>
> The symptoms of underdevelopment are easy enough to identify. All underdeveloped countries share in lesser or greater measure certain characteristics. A modern Gulliver might describe the typical underdeveloped country this way: "What a curious contradiction of rags and riches. One out of every ten thousand persons lives in a palace with high walls and gardens and a Cadillac in the driveway. A few blocks away hundreds are sleeping in the streets, which they share with beggars, chewing-gum hawkers, prostitutes, and shoeshine boys. Around the corner tens of thousands are jammed in huts without electricity or plumbing. Outside the city most of the population scratches out a bare subsistence on small plots, many owned by the few who lived behind the high walls. Even where the soil is rich and the climate agreeable most people go to sleep hungry. The stock market is booming, but babies die and children with distended bellies and spindly legs are everywhere. There are luxurious restaurants and stinking open sewers. The capital boasts late-model computers and receives jumbo jets every day, but more than half of the people cannot read. Government offices are major employers of those who can, but the creaky bureaucracy is a joke except to the long line of suppliants who come seeking medical help or a job. (For suppliants with money for a bribe the lines shorten miraculously.)
>
> "Nationalist slogans are prominent, but the basic industries are in the hands of foreigners. The houses behind the walls are filled with imported cameras, TV's, tape recorders, and fine furniture from the United States or Europe, but the major family investment is likely to be a Swiss bank account. There appear to be three groups in the country distinguishable by what they consume. A tiny group live on a scale that would make a Rockefeller squirm. A second group, still relatively small in number, live much like the affluent middle class in the United States—the same cars, the same Scotch, the same household appliances. The vast majority eat picturesque native foods like black beans, rice, and lentil soup—in small quantities. The first two groups are strong believers in individual development for themselves and their family, but they see no solution for the growing plight of the third group. So they fear them, and their walls grow higher. For the third group disease, filth, and sudden death are constant companions, but there is an air of resignation about them. Life has always been full of pain and uncertainty and it always will be. The only development they see is the same journey from cradle to an early grave that their fathers and their grandfathers took."
>
> *Source:* Barnet and Müller 1974, pp. 133–34. Copyright © 1974 by Richard L. Barnet and Ronald E. Müller. Reprinted by permission of Simon & Schuster, a Division of Gulf & Western Corporation.

poorest 20 per cent attempted to survive on 1.3 per cent of the income" (Barnet and Müller 1974, pp. 149–50). Similar, and worse, conditions existed in Brazil and in other poor countries (see also Petras 1977, p. 15, for conditions in Chile).

Galeano, comparing living conditions in Latin America in 1978 to those in the early 1970s, found them worsening:

> The system has multiplied hunger and fear; wealth has become more and more concentrated, poverty more and more widespread. That is recognized by the documents of specialized international organizations, in whose aseptic vocabulary our oppressed territories are "countries in process of development" and the pitiless impoverishment of the working class is "regressive income distribution" (1978, pp. 14–15).

Brazil illustrates Galeano's conclusion. While the economy as a whole is growing, the wealth is going to a few people and the vast majority of the 120 million Brazilians experience declining living standards. In São Paulo, over half of the seven million people

> live more than 50% below the minimum subsistence level as defined by the state itself.
> The plight of children mirrors this condition. Forty children . . . are buried each day in São Paulo's cemetery—dead from poverty. Fifteen years ago, when the military usurped power, infant mortality was about 50 per 1000. Today it is 80. . . . Some 600,000 boys and girls between the ages of 6 and 16 live by begging, stealing and prostitution. . . . In one industrial suburb, 80% of the families could not afford to buy enough food to survive (Bini 1979, p. 12).

Even some people from the ruling classes of the peripheral nations of the imperialist system cannot deny the abject poverty there. President Marcos of the Philippines told a gathering of delegates from imperialist nations: "It is very difficult to escape the feeling that we have gotten nowhere in the past 20 years" (quoted in DeCormis 1979b).

The poor also suffer from poor health. Hunger is not its only cause. Bad working conditions and crowded living quarters and neighborhoods also worsen health. In addition, drugs to cure the illness are often not available. MNCs produce drugs for profits, at high prices, so most people in poor countries cannot afford them. There is no profit in inexpensive, useful drugs (Lall 1977, p. 28).

Indeed, United States multinational drug firms may soon join European ones in selling to people in Latin America, Asia, and Africa drugs they cannot sell at home. These are drugs considered unsafe for human use. Is there any better evidence that corporate profits win over human welfare? (Bader 1979).

Many other products banned in the United States are sold overseas. For example, children's clothing containing the flame-retardant Tris, suspected of causing cancer and banned in the United States, has been sold in other countries. Dangerous chemicals not produced or sold in the United States are produced and sold in other countries. And pesticides, which in time backfire by producing presticide-resistant insects (see Chapter 10), are marketed all over the world (Weir 1979; Dowie 1979; Lamb 1980; Chapin and Wasserstrom 1980).

Those who protest the exploitation of the world's poor (both by their own ruling classes and by MNCs) are repressed. Torture and political persecution, under military dictatorships open to MNC investments, abound in countries like Chile, Argentina, Brazil, the Central American countries, and South Africa. This repression is aided by the C.I.A. and the American military (see Petras and Morley 1975; Petras 1977; Agee and Wolf 1978, 1980).

## Neocolonialism

In effect, poor countries are still colonies of the imperialist nations. They sell their resources cheap, their economies are controlled by MNCs, they are heavily in debt, and their cultures are assaulted by the advertising of the MNCs.

In 1960, three tons of bananas sold for enough money to buy a tractor; in 1970, it took eleven tons to buy it (FF, p. 183). The process of declining prices for raw materials has continued. In 1974-75, prices decreased by 30 percent, while manufactured goods became more expensive and inflation in general went up. Just to stay even, poor countries must produce more (Gedicks 1977, p. 8).

In addition, the economies of many countries are dominated by MNCs. By 1970 most of the Chilean economy was controlled by United States corporations. From 50 to 100 percent of the petroleum, machinery, and other products were in the hands of foreign corporations. Even 80 percent of the copper, Chile's most important resource, was controlled by United States corporations (Petras and Morley 1975, p. 9). Even when a country tries to free itself from foreign control, it suffers for many years. Replacement parts for automobiles, machinery, and other products must still be imported. When Chile and Cuba went socialist, the United States cut off supplies of replacement parts. Cuba, with the assistance of the USSR, overcame this problem, but Chile did not, and it became one of the causes of the overthrow of the socialist government.

Another aspect of neocolonialism is the heavy debt incurred by poor countries, who borrow from capitalist governments, international institutions such as the World Bank, and United States and other capitalist banks. This situation, not widely known, is growing more critical. "Net lending to developing countries reported by U.S.-based banks, which was only $882 million in 1971, rose to $2,131 in 1973, $6,648 in 1974, and $6,878 in 1975" (Payer 1977, p. 4). Borrowing from European sources rose from $1,475 million in 1971 to $11,530 million in 1975. Estimates of total debt by poor countries vary from $130 to $200 billion (for 1977). In 1979, poor countries in the southern hemisphere had a foreign debt of $275 billion. The annual payments of this debt (by non-oil-producing poor countries) are staggering: $9 billion in 1973, $28 billion in 1974, and $38 billion in 1975. Most countries cannot meet the annual payments and so must borrow further. Most of this debt is owed by a few countries such as Mexico and Brazil (Payer 1976, pp. 4-7; DeCormis 1980).

Chile is one country that borrowed heavily during the 1960s. When the socialists came to power in 1970, the government was heavily in debt, and the payments were coming due. This debt, plus other conditions, made it possible for the United States to put a concerted economic squeeze on Chile and eventually help overthrow the socialist government (Petras and Morley 1975).

When poor countries find it difficult to make their payments, they are given more credit and old debts are refinanced, but only under certain conditions. As happened to New York City, these countries find that their economies are placed under virtual control of foreign banks. Their governments agree to regulate their spending and economic policies to meet conditions set up by the banks. Such policies usually result in lowered living standards for most people (Payer 1976, p. 8; Barnet and Müller 1974, p. 135).

Another result of neocolonialism is the destruction of local cultures and traditions. The United States has a tremendous psychological influence on many people. Its products and life-styles are portrayed, through advertising, as the gateway to success and happiness. I grew up in Greece and experienced this psychological pull. Chewing gum, lipstick, and white bread were seen as the things one must consume in order to be sophisticated and modern. For example, Greek peasant women may wear nylon stockings, which are useless and inefficient for their life-styles, but the women have been convinced they need the stockings to be modern. The marketing of infant formula for the same reasons was discussed earlier. Here are two more examples of the uses of advertising to manipulate poor people:

> Albert Stridsberg, an "international advertising specialist" writing in *Advertising Age,* says that we must rid ourselves of "the conventional range of ideas about what will minister to the poor man's physical needs. The psychological significance of his spending his money on a transistor radio may be more important than the physical benefit generated by spending the same money for basic foodstuffs." It is an interesting theory, especially when applied to a country like Peru where, it is estimated, a substantial number of all babies born begin life with serious, and possibly irreparable, brain damage due to malnutrition.... One message that comes through clearly is that happiness, achievement, and being white have something to do with one another. In *mestizo* countries such as Mexico and Venezuela where most of the population still bear strong traces of their Indian origin, billboards depicting the good life for sale invariably feature blond, blue-eyed American-looking men and women. One effect of such "white is beautiful" advertising is to reinforce feelings of inferiority which are the essence of a politically immobilizing colonial mentality (Barnet and Müller 1974, pp. 177–78).

*Imperialism at Home*

The suffering of millions in poor countries is undeniable. But imperialism also affects people in the United States. No one knows how many jobs have been lost by multinationals moving their operations outside this country. A search of various government publications, filled with many minute details on the United States labor force, reveals nothing on jobs lost to runaway shops. Zimmerman (1973) provides some details, and Sherrill (1973) reports government unconcern for these lost jobs. We know that labor-intensive products are being made increasingly overseas, some, like televisions, almost entirely. Some people may think that products made overseas are cheaper, so most of us gain. Not so. Prices have stayed the same or increased.

One of the difficulties of tracking down the number of lost jobs comes from MNC practices. "A multinational corporation can produce components in widely separated plants in Korea, Taiwan, and the United States, assemble the product in a plant on the Mexican side of the border and sell the goods in the U.S.—perhaps with a U.S. brand name" (Andrew J. Biemiller, AFL-CIO lobbyist, quoted in Sherrill 1973, p. 490).

## Militarism

To protect its multinational interests overseas, the United States has needed a standing army. From a defense budget of barely a billion dollars in 1939, the United States now spends over $100 billion on the military. Excluding the war years (Korea and Vietnam), the military budget (in 1972 dollars) has increased from $29.4 billion in 1950 to $70.4 billion in 1980 ($125.8 billion in 1980 dollars) (*Statistical Abstract* 1979, p. 364).

The cost of military actions needed to protect multinational companies' interests was most obvious during the Vietnam war. Fifty-five thousand died, mostly from the working class. Hundreds of thousands of others were injured (physically and emotionally), and most are still suffering. Unemployment among Vietnam veterans is higher than for other people their age. Also, much of the inflation of the early 1970s resulted from heavy government borrowing to pay for the Vietnam war. The war has left many scars still unhealed.

In itself, Vietnam was not very important to capitalist interests. The value of its resources was outweighed many times by the money the United States government spent fighting the war. Nevertheless, as part of a region of 200 million people (including Indonesia), with vast resources, Vietnam was very crucial. The Vietnam war was fought as an example to stop socialism and economic independence in poor countries. When the United States government became involved, it underestimated the determination of the Vietnamese, and it could not foretell the cost of the war. As the cost became prohibitive in many ways, the government gradually withdrew. The cost of protecting investments and economic interests in one country may be higher than the value of those investments and interests, but "the underlying purpose is nothing less than keeping as much as possible of the world open for trade and investment by the giant multinational corporations" (Magdoff 1969, p. 14; Petras and Morley 1975, p. viii).

Total military commitments, like that in Vietnam, have become too costly politically and economically, but the United States still needs to protect its multinational investments. The 1979–80 crisis in Iran may be used as a pretext to plan for a quick strike force to quell revolutionary situations anywhere in the world. In early 1980, plans were well under way for a force of 50,000, to be ready by 1983 or 1984, that could be flown anywhere in a few days to protect right-wing dictators and the imperialist system (Kelley 1979).

In addition, in 1980 the Carter administration was using the Soviet invasion of Afghanistan and the alleged general Soviet military threat as an argument to increase significantly the military budget (forgetting that this increase was being planned even before the Soviet invasion). The Center for Defense Information in Washington argued, however, that Soviet military expansion has been limited and that the Soviet Union has even suffered considerable setbacks in its foreign and military relations with other countries. But the United States is using the Soviet Union, as it did Iran, as a reason to increase military spending and possibly to reinstitute the military draft in order to suppress socialist and nationalist revolutions that are threatening United States investments in other countries (Sweezy and Magdoff 1980; Klare 1980; Lasch 1980).

Direct military intervention is not common. It costs too much and creates bad publicity. Much more important are covert activities by the CIA and other government agencies.

Chile has been a case study. Unknown to most people, in 1964 the United States government spent $20 million and employed over 100 CIA agents to help elect Eduardo Frei, whose policies were less threatening to MNC interests than were those of the socialists. In 1970 the United States could not stop the election of the socialists, so it went on to spend $40 million for "destabilization" activities. The most damaging were two strikes, by truck drivers and copper-mine workers. Other boycotts and demonstrations were also financed by United States money (Petras and Morley 1975, pp. xvi, 20–21).

Some people may argue that these were the actions of CIA agents acting on their own. But as ex-CIA director William F. Colby testified to Congress: "The agency didn't do anything without the knowledge and consent of the 40 committee" (chaired by the President's representative, in this case Kissinger). Colby could have added that the agency took no major action without the direction and command of the President and his cabinet (Petras and Morley 1975, p. xiii).

CIA activities throughout the world have been exposed in the last few years. However, the MNCs depend on other forms of government action. The United States government often helps to finance foreign regimes. Brazil is a good example. The United States "pumped in $2 billion since 1964 [1964–71] to protect a favorable climate of investment that amounts to about $1.6 billion" (Senator Frank Church, quoted in Petras and Morley 1975). Some of that aid went to train the Brazilian police, some as economic aid. Generally, MNCs seem to assume government actions will protect their interests. Payer thinks that banks that lend heavily to poor countries assume that their (the banks') governments will not allow the poor countries to default on their debts and go bankrupt. However, in the long run bankruptcy may possibly be prevented (Petras and Morley 1975, pp. 61–62; Payer 1976, pp. 10–11).

*Who Suffers?*

Two final examples show how imperialism affects people in this country. In the mid-1970s, while banks would not loan money to United States cities (especially New York), they were happy to loan to military dictatorships. "First National City and Manufacturers Hanover Trust [of New York City] handed the junta [in Chile] $680 million at a time when they said there was no money for New York City schools" (Petras 1977, p. 20).

Also, not only are the costs of imperialism heavy, its benefits elude most people. In the mid-1970s, profits from direct foreign investments were but 1 percent of national income, but they were 25 percent of corporate profits, and 50 percent or more of the profits of some corporations (e.g., Exxon, Mobil, IBM, and Coca-Cola) (MacEwan 1976, p. 488).

Some socialists have argued that at least some working-class Americans have benefited from imperialism. It may be that, in the short run, imperialism creates a temporary affluence in the core countries that benefits many, if not most, people. But if this were true in the 1950s and early 1960s, it is not any longer. The Vietnam war caused inflation, waste, death, and other problems in the United States. In addition, United States workers suffer as many industrial jobs are being exported, and cities are being transformed into large workforces of clerical and service jobs that pay much less money than industrial jobs do (see Chapter 5). This change in the nature of the workforce, central to modern imperialism, is not beneficial to most workers.

In effect, there is no gain for most people from the actions of multinationals. MNCs and the imperialist nations are helping to perpetuate a world of hostility and wars, where people fight each other instead of cooperating for the common good.

> There is a more subtle but even graver problem for Americans. As multinational corporations expand into the underdeveloped world, American consumers are rapidly being made dependent on a whole range of imported agricultural products. Once this shift is made, there will no longer be hundreds of thousands of farms in the United States supplying the vegetables, fruit, meat, and even flowers Americans buy. *The food needs of American consumers will be made dependent on the active maintenance of a distorted land use system in underdeveloped countries.* We will be forced to translate our own legitimate food requirements into opposition to those of countries where hundreds of millions go hungry. Agribusiness, by putting American consumers at odds with the interests of the world's hungry, creates a type of interdependence no one needs (FF, p. 294).

## THE END OF IMPERIALISM?

Imperialist countries and multinational corporations are becoming increasingly powerful. But there are also increasingly effective struggles taking place to destroy imperialism.

*Socialist Revolutions*

Of the books cited here written in 1973 and before, none predicted the imminent success of socialist revolutions in Africa (Angola, Mozambique, Guinea Bissau) or Nicaragua. Therefore, predictions are unwise.

Nevertheless, the last thirty years show an increase in the struggle, and success, of socialist and liberation revolutions throughout the world. As this is written (early 1980), there are ongoing revolutions in the news (especially in Africa) and many others hardly ever mentioned but still very real. Some of these revolutions may last for decades, as did the struggle in Vietnam; others may succeed sooner.

In the late 1970s, there was an emerging opposition to military dictatorships and other oppressive governments in Latin America. The opposition varied. There was armed insurrection, as in Nicaragua, that led to the overthrow of Somoza in 1979; there were mass organizations opposing the government; and there were "sporadic activities, occasional strikes, and protests confined to limited sectors of the population" (Petras 1979a, 1979b). The opposition forces grew from two sources: working people saw the need for a struggle to end their exploitation, and the middle class had begun to resent being dominated by military dictatorships and multinational firms.

Socialist revolutions do not always succeed in breaking away completely from the imperialist system. Angola, faced with severe shortages of food and other materials when the forces of the revolution took over in 1975, and unable to operate immediately the oil fields developed by Gulf Oil, was forced to deal with Gulf and allow it to continue operating within Angola:

> In the long run, the Angolan government is determined to reduce its dependency on multinational corporations. A national oil company has been set up to acquire technical expertise and to train Angolans in all aspects of the industry. Full nationalization and complete control of the oil industry is clearly the eventual goal.
>
> However, in the short run the government has been bargaining from a position of weakness, and may have had little alternative to renewed dependence on Western multinationals, particularly Gulf. And regardless of long run intentions, such dependencies often become more, rather than less, difficult to break with the passage of time. Continued dependency on the developed capitalist world is one important reason why the achievement of socialism in Third World countries is never an easy or straightforward process (*Dollars and Sense,* May–June 1979, p. 17).

## STRUGGLES: The Liberation of Angola

*Most former European colonies received political independence in the 1950s and 1960s. Most of them continue to be exploited by imperialism and neo-colonialism, but in some places people have waged or are waging struggles of liberation. Angola, one of the oldest colonies, won independence from Portugal in 1974. The following account shows the growth of the revolutionary socialist movement for the liberation of Angola.*

The Popular Movement for the Liberation of Angola (MPLA) was founded in 1956. MPLA stood for the total independence of Angola and for the building of a socialist society led by peasants and workers. MPLA sought to unify the people in a struggle to free Angola from all forms of foreign domination. They taught that only by winning total independence could the Angolan people take full control of their resources. MPLA made clear that while Portuguese colonialism was the direct enemy, the fight had to be against all the forces which had economically invaded Angola, especially the United States.

MPLA understood the result of 500 years of colonization. Under the Portuguese, all Angolans, regardless of their tribe, suffered a common oppression. As contract laborers, they slaved side by side. They were forged into a unified people, a nation. MPLA explained that any program that stressed going back toward tribal allegiances would divide the people, making them more vulnerable.

MPLA recognized how the subjugation of women weakened the struggle. They stressed the need to fight for the total liberation of Angolan women. . . .

MPLA began armed struggle in Angola on February 4, 1961. Armed mostly with *caetanas* (machetes), militants of MPLA attacked the prison in Luanda to free 1200 political prisoners. The attack failed and the Portuguese retaliation was brutal. This repression did not stop MPLA and the rising revolutionary spirit in Angola. . . .

*Source:* Reprinted from People's Press Angola Book Project, *With Freedom in Their Eyes* (San Francisco: People's Press, 1976), pp. 23, 27, 31, 32, 33, 40.

To carry out the armed struggle, MPLA focused on organizing the enormous popular force in every village and town.

One man was a hunter who joined the guerrillas and taught them his skills. Women led in reorganizing the field work so that there was more food and their innovations were brought to other regions. A cattle herder drew detailed maps of the little-known trails and river-crossings. Villagers deceived Portuguese patrols, leading them away from supplies. A woman developed better ways to teach the Portuguese language so that people of different tribes could talk with one another. Young people with sharp eyesight and hearing became guides for the fighters. A village developed new ways of carrying supplies strapped to their backs. "Everyone teaches one and wins them to the cause." This is people's war.

MPLA's military arm, the Popular Armed Forces for the Liberation of Angola (FAPLA), led the military struggle. In 1963, it began guerrilla actions in Cabinda, the strategic northern province. Soon, FAPLA was fighting throughout the country.

This mobilization of the people reduced the Portuguese advantage of having more and better weapons. Portugal responded by waging war of massacre, bombing and mass arrests. Each atrocity brought more militants to MPLA.

The process of building armed struggle depended on education. Success rested on the peoples' agreement with the MPLA program, their trust in the leadership, and their active participation.

During this period, a FAPLA fighter explained, "Our political officers and activists go to the village to teach the people about the politics of our struggle. When they reach a village, they call the people together and talk to them about MPLA and the armed struggle we are waging against Portuguese colonialism. The people know they are exploited and oppressed by the Portuguese; we don't need to tell them much about that. They want to know how they can fight against the Portuguese and win. We never recruit by force; all of our militants are volunteers." . . .

*(continued)*

### The Liberation of Angola *(continued)*

MPLA formed mass organizations that brought together parts of the population with common concerns. The National Union of Angolan Workers, the Organization of Angolan Women, and the youth organization, the Pioneers, helped to reach out to everyone, involving them and stimulating their participation in liberating Angola. . . .

By 1974, the Portuguese people had suffered under a fascist dictatorship for 48 years. The fascists depended on their profits from the colonies to maintain economic stability in Portugal. The liberation wars undermined the Portuguese economy. An army of 200,000 cost one-half the national budget. The economy slumped, and one and a half million people left Portugal to find work.

Within Portugal, opposition to the wars grew. Desertions from the army increased. Groups inside Portugal carried out armed actions in support of the liberation movements. Within the army, junior officers influenced by the African liberation movements formed the Armed Forces Movement. Their goal was to end the wars and bring political democracy to Portugal.

On April 25, 1974, the Armed Forces Movement overthrew the fascist regime. One of their first acts was to negotiate independence for the colonies. The overthrow of fascism in Portugal did not mean the defeat of all those who still hoped to hold on to the colonies, but it weakened them, and gave much support to the African movements. Imperialism was deprived of its caretaker in Angola, leaving it up to the US to prevent total independence. Under the leadership of MPLA independence now seemed certain.

*Author's note: When Angola became independent from Portugal, South Africa and the United States (through the CIA) provided money, arms, and personnel to other groups within Angola to prevent the MPLA from taking power. With the assistance of Cuban troops and arms from the Soviet Union, the MPLA finally prevailed by early 1976, although South Africa still engaged in periodic bombings and invasions of Angola.*

## *Other Struggles against Imperialism*

Armed struggles are the ultimate, and in some cases the only effective, means of destroying imperialism. But other actions are possible.

Labor unions can also act against imperialism. For example, in June 1978, a longshoremen's union refused to load arms headed for Chile, and pledged to fight to prevent arms shipment to that country. Such arms were clearly meant to repress the Chilean people, not for United States national defense.

There are cases of international cooperation among unions. When a multinational company moves operations to another country to find cheaper labor, the union workers of the parent country may cooperate with the workers of the poor country. They help them unionize and in the long run prevent the exploitation of workers everywhere (Zimmerman 1973, pp. 37–38).

To fight against the rising poor countries, United States corporations are beginning to turn elsewhere for cheap resources. Puerto Rico, Native American lands, and United States public lands generally have become the new targets for exploitation. But opposition has arisen both among Puerto

Ricans and Native Americans. Both groups are using legal battles, demonstrations, organization of the poor, and other means to prevent corporate exploitation of their resources (Gedicks 1977, p. 10).

It is also possible for poor countries to develop their own petroleum resources. The technology for drilling is available to governments, at modest cost, from independent drilling companies. Once they find oil, these governments can borrow money, often at low cost, to develop their finds. Tanzer (1978) shows that Mexico, India, and Vietnam each has developed its own petroleum finds and kept the profits itself instead of handing them over to the multinationals. In urging the government of Puerto Rico to develop its own resources, Tanzer cites the fact that eighty poor countries have set up their own corporations to deal with petroleum. Some carry out the entire process of exploration and development; some do most of it; some are able to get better concessions from the MNCs. Even the United States government is considering getting into the field of "oil exploration."

Lappé and Collins cite many examples of poor countries that have eliminated widespread hunger. China and other socialist countries are the primary examples. By involving more people than the MNCs to participate and experiment in the production of food, socialist societies have had enormous increases in their food production. The Chinese have limited the bad effects of weather and have developed their own food technology.

The solution has been to give control of the process to the people themselves. In Tanzania, many problems in food growth and storage were solved this way. In Mozambique, the socialist government "is successfully restoring a peasant food economy that had been destroyed by Portuguese colonialism." In Honduras, peasants are organizing to fight the cattlemen taking over their lands (FF, pp. 367–68, 394, 395).

Payer proposes that poor countries heavily in debt to imperialist nations should default on their debts. They will thus get out of dependence on capitalism and orient their economies to meeting their people's needs. Default, Payer says, need not mean catastrophe, for a country still has its people, land, buildings, and other physical properties (she assumes no military invasion from imperialist nations, which may be too optimistic). To mean anything, of course, defaulting on debts must be accompanied by radical political and economic changes (Payer 1976).

What can people do to eliminate world hunger? Lappé and Collins outline some suggestions in their last chapter. First, we must learn much more about the real conditions and causes of hunger. Second, we must realize we cannot solve the problem for other people, but we can help remove the obstacles put in their way by MNCs and capitalist governments. For example, people can work to limit military actions and CIA activities.

Poor people will continue to struggle for their own liberation, but help may make their struggle shorter, and it can educate and liberate others too. People in this country begin to change our own life-styles, for example, eating less or no meat. This step will not feed the hungry of other nations (and it may be used by the ruling class to create austerity at home), but it may also be the beginning of individual and collective freedom from corporate control.

### Cooperation between Poor Countries

Ever since oil-producing countries formed OPEC (Organization of Petroleum Exporting Countries) and got a higher price for their oil, similar organizations have arisen. Many people see this as an important instrument to stop exploitation of poor countries. As capitalist nations compete with each other for the scarce resources of the poor ones, the bargaining position of the latter improves.

However, as long as a country still depends on one or a few cash crops or minerals, and as long as it has wide disparity between classes, there will be problems. Some countries produce luxuries for the markets of the imperialist nations, and raising their prices through collective agreements has its limits. After all, it would be possible to live without coffee, bananas, cocoa, and so on. The solution is for these countries to raise their own food, not produce luxuries for us.

An even more important issue involves the larger profits leading to higher prices for the peripheral countries' resources. What guarantee is there that the new money will benefit the average citizen in these countries? Greater profits can be used to support the affluence of a few, as they have been up to the present. We must remember that the world's poor are exploited both by the imperialist powers *and* their local allies in poor countries. These local capitalists are capable of using their countries' increasing wealth for their benefit only.

### After Capitalism, What?

According to many socialists, the collapse of world capitalism and imperialism is inevitable. The contradictions found in the nature of capitalism (such as military costs to protect economic interests), and the suffering of the world's poor that will lead to their uprising, will destroy capitalism.

But, as Kolko argues, what will follow is not inevitable. Whether there will be another world war, or fascist governments everywhere, or socialist revolutions—that is the issue confronting us today. Today, of course, there are both fascist governments and socialist revolutions (Kolko 1974, p. 180).

Certainly, liberal proposals are no solution. McNamara argues that capitalist nations must help poor ones because "the rich and powerful have a moral obligation to assist the poor and the weak." But he says, just before this, "There are, of course, many sound reasons for development assistance: among others, the expansion of trade, the reduction of social tensions, and the promotion of international stability" (1977). He proposes that capitalist nations use 3 percent of their income to stop what may be viewed as socialist revolutions. But this 3 percent will not come from corporate profits, it will come from our taxes.

McNamara argues that aid is important, but that the poor nations must eliminate their poverty themselves. He ignores all the evidence presented here that shows the imperialist nations and the rich in poor countries have created and perpetuate a system that keeps people poor. Charity from capitalist nations is no solution; people must take over their own destinies. To limit death and suffering, all people must struggle to understand the causes and effects of imperialism and end it.

# 7

# The Destruction of Community

## COMMUNITY AND LIFE

From February 6 to 8, 1978, about thirty inches of snow fell in eastern Massachusetts. Drifts piled the snow over six feet high in places. Streets were impassable, and the whole region closed down for a week, with driving banned. People were caught without food and in other predicaments. Radio and television stations stepped in to give helpful advice. For example, emergency numbers for medical care, fuel, and food were constantly read over the air. People were reminded to call on any elderly neighbors and make sure they were safe.

People who called in to radio stations with comments and questions were put on the air. I remember a caller from Lexington (where I live) saying over the radio that she had extra food and that any of her neighbors who needed it could have it. This story served as a shock of recognition. It reveals both the absence of community and our longing for it. For in any real community, people from Lexington would not need to call radio stations in Boston, ten miles away, to offer food to neighbors. Such assistance and caring would be done automatically, if people knew their neighbors and had ongoing ties with them. Nor would people need to be reminded to check on elderly neighbors.

The storm emergency caused an outpouring of the communal spirit repressed by modern social conditions. People helped each other in unprecedented ways. Forced to stay out of cars, people began to walk and discovered neighbors whom they saw rarely or never. Many people said how satisfying it was to rediscover neighbors and the pleasures of walking. The emergency ended in a week, and people went back to their old routines, left with a pleasant memory. Community once more became an unreality for most people.

Next door to our house in Lexington lives a woman of eighty-three. She and her husband, now dead, have lived in that house for over sixty years. The husband and his father built the house in which my family lives. They now know very few of the neighbors, and they socialize with none (except for us). Their social contacts are with family and friends scattered throughout the area. One of their daughters and her husband have lived with them since their marriage. The other daughter and her children come over frequently. Were it not for the unusually close family life they lead, the old people would be very isolated. At one time, a true neighborhood feeling existed there. People would stop by the house for coffee, whether they were going shopping or just out for a walk. But most of the old neighbors have moved or died and now no one visits. Indeed, in the whole neighborhood, except for some relatives who live near each other, there is very little socializing.

But in some places communities still exist. These areas are few and constantly assaulted, but people manage to preserve them. For community is the essence of life. In East London in the 1950s, there was a working-class community where family and neighborhood ties were close. Bethnal Green, a working-class area in London, was rich with family and community ties. In one week, Mrs. Landon, a resident of Bethnal Green, met sixty-three people she knew in the street, some many times. Thirty-eight of them know each other. In her many years of living in this area she had built up a gradual series of social ties. She met people at school, at work, and through relatives and other friends. In fact, hardly anyone in Bethnal Green seemed a stranger (Young and Willmott 1957, pp. 105-107).

For others, community ties are being destroyed. But they fight to keep ties and relations. Millions of people have been displaced from Appalachia; they now work in Dayton, Cincinnati, Chicago, Detroit, and elsewhere in the Midwest. On Friday afternoon, many begin drives of 600 miles and longer to drive back home, to spend some time with family and old friends.

This decline in community ties affects the quality of our lives; we suffer when we live with few and limited community relations. Such poverty in social relations affects everyone, the professional and upper-middle classes as well as the working class.

Following an attempt to show how capitalism, in its search for profit and growth, inevitably destroys or weakens community ties, this chapter (and other chapters) will give examples of struggles to save or restore community life.

## What Is Community?

We are social beings. We live in families and communities. Beyond the family, the community is the most basic form of social organization.

What makes a community? A community may be defined as "a group of people living on the same piece of land, sharing the same aspirations and interests, participating in the same activities, feeling the same pride, love, and fears, and united by a strong sense of loyalty" (Iwańska 1962, p. 205). This definition includes a number of important elements. People in a community share values, interests, and activities; they feel concern and responsibility for each other; they help each other; in some sense they understand that unbridled individualism and concern with self-interest destroy community; and because of this commitment to each other and to the same interests and values, they stay on the same piece of land for a long time. Such stability makes for easy and warm personal relations (as will be seen in the example of Buffalo Creek before the flood). In addition, for a group of people to be a community, their group must be small in size in order to make possible ties that are personal, meaningful, frequent, and deep (see Chapters 5, 10, and 14).

If there is no sharing of values and interests, no commitment of people to each other, geographical stability and small size alone will not make a community. But when people do feel a sense of belonging and sharing, they are unlikely to move away willingly. This chapter will show that capitalism has forced people to move away from their communities; it has destroyed the bonds of socializing and mutual concern created over time. Other examples will show that through self-help, through struggles to stop the physical destruction of their neighborhoods, and other struggles, people are working toward community.

## Love, Work, and Community

Sigmund Freud was asked once what he thought made for a happy and fulfilling life. "Love and work," he replied. The answer is interesting because it does not focus exclusively on sexual and emotional relations as the foundation for a happy life.

But it also shows a profound lack of understanding, for without community, love and work, even if they are possible, have little meaning. More than most anthropologists, Dorothy Lee has shown that all meaning in life derives from social ties within a community. Without such a community, life becomes empty. (Today, remnants and variations of community survive, along with the longing for it.) Shared values and activities receive their meaning in a context with others, with people whom we know, who have a commitment to the community above everything else. Today we live in societies rampant with competition and individualism, and we tend to forget the elemental truth that we are *social* beings (Lee 1959).

Capitalism has been destroying communities for a long time. This destruction occurs in many ways. For example, competition and individualism drive people apart. When capitalism created an economic system that forced people to move in order to find work, stability and commitment to community became difficult (see the example of Appalachia below).

But the forces created by capitalism had begun to destroy communities centuries ago.

## CAPITALISM AND COMMUNITY

Wherever capitalism moves, it destroys communities. The previous chapter showed how cultures and communities throughout the world were assaulted by imperialism. But the assault began at home. Where peasants and craftspeople had created living communities, people were forced to move, lost their lands and skill, and soon lost their ties to family, friends, and neighbors. Industrial capitalism has no use for people cooperating for the common good, and without cooperation there can be no community.

### *Examples from History*

In a sense, the history of capitalism can be seen as the history of the destruction of community and communities. A few examples illustrate this view.

Braverman cites the example of weavers. When their craft was destroyed, their labor exploited, all for the profit of rising capitalists, their culture and community disappeared.

In the middle of the nineteenth century weavers lived in incredible poverty and degradation. Only a short time before, when they still practiced their craft, they led a rich community life. They passed their leisure time in family groups in gardens and parks; they had many hobbies, including botanical and entomological societies. There were "weaver-poets, biologists, mathematicians, musicians, geologists, botanists..." (E. P. Thompson, quoted in Braverman 1974, p. 135). What had been a thriving community of science, culture, and family and social activities, became a slum.

The Lynds studied Muncie, Indiana at the beginning of its industrialization. People they talked with in the 1920s had vivid memories of community life and were experiencing its decline. One of the first effects of industrial capitalism is the separation of work from home and neighborhood. "This trend towards decentralization of workers' dwellings means that instead of a family's activities in getting a living, making a home, play, church-going, and so on, largely overlapping and bolstering each other, one's neighbors may work at shops at the other end of the city, while those with whom one works may have their homes and other interests anywhere from one to two-score miles distant." Night work in factories disrupted home and community life. People were aware of these changes, as they told the Lynds: "Neighbors used to be in each other's houses much more than they are now." "Mother couldn't understand when she came to live with us why people didn't run in more and neighbor as they used to." "People used to drop over in the evening, but now they invite them way ahead of the date and make a party of it" (Lynd and Lynd 1929, pp. 65, 55, 274, 279).

Gallaher studied Plainville, Missouri, in 1955. Comparing it with another study done in 1939, he found many changes. Farming had become commercialized. People once had borrowed from each other and exchanged work, but by 1955 they would hire someone else to do the work for them. Cooperative relations now were commercial transactions. Collective work of the past, such as threshing, now was done by machines (Gallaher 1961, pp. 198–99, Iwańska 1962).

At about the same time (mid-1950s), Vidich lived in a small upstate New York town. In their report of his research, Vidich and Bensman also show the decline of community. One of the changes was the decline of the town center as shopping centers displaced it. People began to drive everywhere to shop. Over time, to use the image of some writers, all of America has become a huge shopping center. The socializing, gossiping, watching of neighbors, renewing of ties, and establishing of many types of relationships with store owners and others that were typical of town centers and neighborhood stores, have become uncommon. During the Depression of the 1930s neighborhood store owners would sell on credit to unemployed customers, people they had known for years. Would the modern supermarket extend the same courtesy to its customers? (Vidich and Bensman 1958; Terkel 1970)

*Commercialism and Community*

Many studies show conclusively that as commercialism and mobility come to small towns, suburbs, new towns, and even rural areas, the quality of life worsens.

A 1944 study compared two California towns. One had a few large commercial farms, the other many small family farms. The differences are striking. The small farm community supported:

- about 20 percent more people and at a higher level of income;
- a working population that was mostly self-employed in contrast to the large-farm community where less than 20 percent were self-employed (and nearly two-thirds were agricultural wage laborers);
- many more democratic decision-making organizations and much broader representation in them;
- better schools, parks, newspapers, civic groups, churches, and public services;
- twice the number of small businesses and 61 percent more retail businesses (Lappé and Collins 1977, pp. 242–43).

All these characteristics point to a real community. Since 1944, of course, the trend has been to large commercial farms.

Iwańska studied such a town in 1956–57. The people expressed love and longing for community, but all their actions (heavy use of cars, commercial farming, and so on) were destroying it. They did not see that their values of success, mobility, and individualism were destructive of the very thing they wanted. It never occurred to farmers to buy expensive machinery collectively and share its use. The land had no emotional or personal meaning to them, nor did community ties. They said they would sell their land, if they could make a good profit and move somewhere else to make a living (Iwańska 1962).

Roseto, Pennsylvania, in 1961 was a small town where people maintained close family ties and a strong community and placed greater emphasis on human relations than on mobility and monetary success. Despite their high-cholesterol diet (Italian cooking), their heart-disease rate was one-third the national average. Ten years later, the town had become "Americanized": family ties were weakening; people commuted to work miles away; they were more concerned with success and money. The heart-disease rate rose to three times the national rate—with the same diet as ten years before.

> "We have found, here and elsewhere, that many heart-attack victims are essentially loners who have nowhere else to turn when the pressure is on," said Bruhn. He contends that cholesterol, while significant, does not play the major role in heart attacks.
>
> "In Roseto," he said, "family and community support is disappearing. Most of the men who have had heart attacks here were living under stress and really had nowhere to turn to relieve that pressure. These people have given up something to get something, and it's killing them" (Chambliss and Ryther 1975, p. 153).

Finally, East Londoners who moved to a new town in the outskirts of London gained newer, roomier homes—but lost their community. The wives, who did not go out to work, experienced intense loneliness. In the old neighborhood, everything was within walking distance and going shopping meant meeting many people; now, without a car to drive to the shops miles away, the women were isolated. They found their neighbors "keep to themselves," and, in time, they also kept to themselves. The contrast with their old neighborhood is striking (Young and Willmott 1957, ch. 10).

*Capitalism, Not Industrialism*

The following two sections discuss how capitalism continues to destroy the communities that remain. The last section presents examples of the resurgence of community.

Before exploring those issues, it is important to be clear on the causes of the destruction of community. Many writers seem to attribute the cause to some impersonal force, such as "technology" or "industrialization." For example, Stein writes of the "trend" to "increased interdependence and decreased local autonomy." Leisure, recreation, work, and innovation are centralized. This trend is seen as impersonal, not as the work of capitalists and capitalist institutions who increase their control and profit from such centralization (Stein 1960, p. 108; Gallaher 1961; Iwańska 1962). (For the example of China, where decentralization and local control are the rule, see Burchett and Alley 1976.)

The creation of central work places (factories) that removed people from their neighborhoods was not dictated by technological necessity.

> At the beginning of the industrial revolution, when cottage workers were first brought into factories, their skilled jobs were immediately divided into less skilled tasks which were arranged sequentially. The sequential arrangement is efficient not because of machinery but because, if a foreman can keep up the pace of just one worker, all the others along the line are automatically bound to that pace.
>
> As a matter of historical fact, the machinery used in those early factories was often developed well after this division of labor had been established.
>
> The destruction of skills, then, actually preceded the invention of modern industrial machinery. The machinery was created later specifically to suit an arrangement of production which is by no means universal, eternal, or even more efficient (Garson 1975, p. 212).

From the beginning of capitalism to the present, communities have not been destroyed by impersonal forces. The decisions of capitalist groups and institutions are the main cause. The motive is control and profit.

United States history since the 1940s shows that a series of deliberate government policies has caused further deterioration in community. The auto industry has worked to sabotage mass transit (see Chapter 10); the federal government and the auto makers created the interstate highway system, which destroyed mass transit even more; and as a result, shopping centers and the separation of work from home have become permanent realities of our lives. Furthermore, federal housing policies favoring one-family homes in the suburbs, industrial dispersal away from the cities, and the concentration of agriculture into a few hands, and similar policies have all made true communities less possible. Highways and so-called urban renewal (detailed below) also came about because of decisions for the benefit of corporations and the ruling class, not through impersonal forces (Aronowitz 1974, pp. 30–31).

But other people do not want to leave family and friends; they stay when they lose their jobs. For example, in the mid-1970s five rural communities in the western United States and Hawaii experienced severe unemployment. Their "economic survival depended on one company or one industry [mining, timbering, growing pineapples, farming] which had made decisions to leave the areas." It is not that the companies were losing money; rather, they expected to make more profits in their new locations because of cheaper labor. The people who lost their jobs, many in their 40s and 50s, did not want to move away to look for new jobs, but in time some were forced to move elsewhere. Of those who stayed on, many became depressed and lost pride and self-confidence as they remained without a job. In time, of course, their children will have to move away. The profit imperative leads not only to "human obsolescence," it also eats away at community life (Young and Newton 1980).

The destruction of community life in Appalachia also came about because corporate profits took priority over regional economic planning for the benefit of the people there. Corporations moved in, bought forest and mineral rights far too cheaply (often at fifty cents an acre), took out the profits, and paid little or no taxes. In time, because of the mechanization of coal mining and because of lower demand for coal, employment in the mines decreased drastically. Unemployed miners led to more local unemployment, since they had no money to spend. Some people struggled to make a living locally; millions, including new high school graduates, left for cities in the Midwest. Community life deteriorated drastically.

But it did not have to be that way. The profits from forestry, coal mining, and other uses of the land could have stayed in Appalachia. Then, rational economic planning could have created local jobs for those left unemployed because of mechanization and lower demand for coal. There was nothing inevitable in the destruction of Appalachia. It was the capitalist hunger for profits that led to unemployment and social dislocation.

Today, corporations move their plants to other countries not because of impersonal industrial forces, but because they are looking for cheap labor and higher profits. The resulting unemployment in the United States forces some people to move away from their communities to find work. Thus, community ties are weakened.

## "I WANNA GO HOME": APPALACHIA

Nothing shows better the destruction of community by capitalism than the history of Appalachia.

### *The Plunder of a Region and the Destruction of a Community*

Briefly, beginning in the late nineteenth century, corporations moved to Appalachia and began to exploit the people. Corporations have used their power to enforce highly unjust contracts, and they have taken the local wealth out of the region. Over time, corporations increased profits by mechanizing the mines (thus creating massive unemployment) and by extracting coal by stripping it from the surface (not mining it underground). Stripping has destroyed the land and has caused floods, since treeless land cannot hold water (Caudill 1963).

Unwittingly, people practically sold their lands through leases which they thought allowed companies only to dig coal underground. Courts have ruled that coal companies can do whatever they wish to land—even totally strip it—in their search for coal. When one man sued the company that had plowed up his land, the judge told him:

> The truth is that about the only rights you have on your land is to breathe on it and pay the taxes. For all practical purposes the company that owns the minerals in your land owns all the other rights pertaining to it (Caudill 1963, pp. 308-309).

By the 1950s, poverty and unemployment in Appalachia were pervasive. During the Depression of the 1930s, despite poverty, people stayed on because "they felt a powerful attachment to the familiar hills, valleys and institutions surrounding them" (p. 177). But in time the continuing poverty forced people to leave. In many counties, over 75 percent of the high school graduating class left within a year. The effects were drastic.

> In community after community one can visit a dozen houses in a row without finding a single man who is employed. Most are retired miners and their wives who live on social security and union pension checks. Hundreds of other houses are occupied by aged widows, some of whom have taken in a grandchild or other youngster for "company" in their old age....
>
> One may walk the streets of camps and wander along winding creek roads for days and rarely find a young man or woman (Caudill 1963, p. 333).

In many Appalachian counties today, most people survive on some form of public assistance (p. 340). They feel degraded and dispirited. Any sense of community begins to erode in the face of millions leaving while those behind survive in abject poverty. These conditions result from the corporate plunder of a region's wealth, the creation of a new local economy, and the brutal dismissal of workers in order to increase profits through mechanization.

Swados visited a town whose mine had closed. Most workers were determined to stay on, but, without jobs and money, their life-styles began to change. They had once gone fishing and socialized with each other, but they now kept to themselves or moved away. They were discouraged and felt their world was falling apart. The company had closed the mine purely for economic considerations without concern for the human effects (Swados 1959).

What happens to those who leave? Do they find better lives? Hardly. As discussed above, they long for their old home, neighbors, and community. "And in the taverns of Northern industrial cities former hillbillies for months sipped beer to the lament, 'I wanna go home, I wanna go home' " (Packard 1972, p. 5). In Chicago, where thousands have moved, they endure poverty and exploitation. They get low-skilled jobs paying minimum wages; they live in crowded slums; hospitals degrade them through endless waits; many live on welfare. Thus, people in Appalachia are twice exploited: corporations ruin their region and communities and force them to move, and in the big cities they are exploited as cheap labor. There is hardly any sense of community possible under these conditions (Gitlin and Hollander 1970).

## The Violent End of Community

Appalachian communities break up gradually as the effects of corporate exploitation unfold. At times, however, the end of community comes suddenly and violently.

In April 1977 many parts of the region were flooded. Stripped mountains, with no trees or vegetation, could no longer hold the rain waters. When heavy rains fell in early April, there were catastrophic floods. Primack wrote: "Entire towns have effectively ceased to exist in parts of eastern Kentucky, Tennessee, West Virginia, and southwestern Virginia. Thousands of people are homeless, and many of them protected by little if any flood insurance" (1977). These floods resulted directly from strip-mining, and thus from profit orientation, not from a natural disaster.

But the most violent destruction of community in Appalachia took place in Buffalo Creek, West Virginia, on February 26, 1972 (the following account is based entirely on Kai T. Erikson's *Everything in its Path: Destruction of Community in the Buffalo Creek Flood*, 1976). Buffalo Creek is about seventeen miles long, and the area is populated by about 5,000 people. At the top of the creek, a coal company created a lake about twenty acres across and forty feet deep. It was dammed by wastes of "mine dust, shale, clay, low-quality coal, and a vast assortment of other impurities" (p. 25). Following heavy rains that winter, the dam simply collapsed and the sludge and water poured downstream. In the next few minutes, over 200 people died, many more were injured, houses and buildings totally demolished, and what had been a vibrant community (one of the few that had managed to survive in Appalachia) was destroyed, probably for a long time. (The destructiveness of the raging mud and waters [pp. 21–48 of Erikson's account] cannot be summarized. It is impossible to read these pages without feeling some of the horror the victims experienced.)

The company had been warned many times that the dam was unsafe. On the morning it collapsed, even though company officials saw that it was dangerously porous and ready to go, they did not warn the people in the creek below.

Erikson talked with many survivors, and he read 40,000 pages of testimony from the suit filed against the company. These sources show that a true community had existed, but was now replaced by fears, anxieties, and a loss of communal feeling.

Two years after the flood, people still suffered from recurring nightmares and terror. Whenever it rained, children would begin to cry and be overtaken by terror. Depression, anxiety, and insomnia were common. People ceased to care about themselves, their family, and their neighbors.

> Well, I've got a nervous condition due to the flood. I am tense. I lose my temper easily. I have bouts of depression every now and then. I can't stand loud noises—they tear my nerves all to pieces. It seems like I've lost all confidence in myself. I am afraid to be alone. I'm afraid of storms. I have nightmares. I am just not the same person I was before. . . . When I have those bouts of depression, everything seems dark. I feel like there is nothing to live for. It is a terrible low (p. 136).

People not only lost relatives and friends, they also lost the houses and other physical evidence of their past life that provided the sense of continuity and history we all need to survive as individuals and as a community. "My old home is gone and I can't tell where it used to be" (p. 197). (Reading this account reminded me of the visit I made to my home town in Greece in 1969, after fourteen years away. I went to visit the building where I had lived from the ages of seven to fourteen, a time when I made friends and formed some sense of identity. The building was gone, replaced by a bus depot. I felt emptiness, a sharp pain. A part of me had disappeared forever. I understand the pain of the victims of Buffalo Creek.)

The people also suffered from the loss of something precious, equal to life itself. They were eloquent in their descriptions.

> We all just seemed, in that vicinity, like one big family. We raised our children with our neighbor's children, they was all raised up together, and if your children wasn't at my house on a weekend from Friday to Sunday, mine was at your house with your children. And that's the way we raised our children, we raised them together, more or less like brothers and sisters. The whole community was that way. . . .
>
> What's a neighbor? Well, when I went to my neighbor's house on Saturday or Sunday, if I wanted a cup of coffee I never waited until the lady of the house asked me. I just went into the dish cabinet and got me a cup of coffee or a glass of juice just like it was my own home. They come to my house, they done the same. See? . . .
>
> If my car wouldn't start, all I'd have to do is call my neighbors and they would take me to work. If I was there by myself or something, if my husband was out late, the neighbors would come over and check if everything was okay. So it was just a rare thing. It was just a certain type of relationship that you just knew from people growing up together and sharing the same experiences (pp. 146-47, 187-88, 190).

The flood ended that life-style. Typical comments were: "It was almost like a ghost town now." "It's like a graveyard, that's what. A cemetery."

> It's kind of sad around there now. There's not much happiness. You don't have any friends around, people around, like we had before. Some of them are in trailer camps. Some of them bought homes and moved away. Some of them

just left and didn't come back. It's like teeth in an old folk's mouth down there now. . . .

The people who are here don't get out and do things like they used to. Before the flood, the men worked on old cars or got together and talked for hours at a time. Now it's just for a few minutes at a time, and it seems everyone wants their children to stay close home (pp. 196, 224).

The very quality of life was shattered. Rich, easy, constant, and pervasive community ties were destroyed as surely as the homes were. But, unlike homes, ties cannot be rebuilt in a year or two.

Without labeling them so, Erikson discusses some apparently negative aspects of the community at Buffalo Creek (or of any community, it seems). Whereas individuality is a quality of life in America, there individuals seemed to be submerged in the communal whole. People were so much alike they appeared the same. This is a comment pervasive in much of the literature on community (pp. 192–93).

I think Erikson and others are fundamentally mistaken. For indeed, it is in a community that one can develop a distinct personality. When we live among relative strangers, then material possessions, titles, jobs, and so on become the characteristics identified with our selves. But in a true community these surface characteristics do not matter. People know each other as whole persons.

Erikson himself provides evidence refuting his earlier comment. He says that in an established community, people make allowances for individual quirks and traits that seem deviant to strangers. If people know another person deeply, they are not bothered by apparently "deviant" acts or traits (p. 207). Young and Willmott make a similar observation about East London: "In a community of long standing, status, in so far as it is determined by job and income and education, is more or less irrelevant to a person's worth. He is judged instead, if he is judged at all, more in the round, as a person with the usual mixture of all kinds of qualities, some good, some bad, some indefinable. He is more a life-portrait than a figure on a scale" (1957, pp. 161–62).

Some other observations are relevant to this discussion of community. Many people in Buffalo Creek continue to fear more floods. The ongoing strip-mining makes their fears very realistic (p. 238).

Future victims of floods and other disasters will suffer from the ignorance of experts who come to help them, as did the victims of Buffalo Creek. Government officials who assigned people to trailer camps did not think to group them by their old neighborhoods. The separation enhanced the reality of a lost community (p. 148). Living themselves without community, the outside experts had no sense of what the Buffalo Creek community had meant to the victims of the flood.

It's important to remember that, if only in a less dramatic and sudden fashion, millions have undergone the same loss of community. Displaced farmers, unemployed and degraded craft persons, the victims of urban renewal and highway construction who have lost their homes—these and others all share the experiences of the people in Buffalo Creek.

And these victims were not helped much by the $13.5 million settlement they won from the coal company. It may have helped in material ways, but it could not recreate the bonds, ties, and relationships built slowly over the years.

The words of a Buffalo Creek survivor sum up the loss:

> All I can call the disaster is murder. The coal company knew the dam was bad, but they did not tell the people. All they wanted was to make money. They did not care about the good people that lived up Buffalo Creek (p. 183).

## CONTEMPORARY COMMUNITIES

*Mobility and Isolation*

The United States is a nation on the move. We move mostly as single individuals and nuclear families, not in large groups. Each time we move we sever ties in the community we leave, and we must find new ties. Even though the physical environment may stay the same, the comings and goings disturb the network of social relationships. Although most people move at some time, those most likely to move are younger and middle class (Packard 1972, pp. 10-12).

Table 7.1 shows the extent of mobility. Indeed, in one year, 1975-76, 17.1 percent of the population moved. Here is another figure that is very hard to believe: only 20 percent of adult Americans settle to live within a fifty-mile radius of where they were born (Kimble 1970, p. 490). No true community is possible when we move so much. Human ties take time to develop, and we are severing them before they can begin to grow.

Of course, we are not totally without ties. If we were, we would die—life without any contact is spiritual, and often physical, death. Many studies of the 1950s show that people had most contacts with their conjugal family. Work and neighbors provided few social contacts (Greer 1958). A

**TABLE 7.1** Mobility Status of the United States Population: 1970-1975

| | |
|---|---|
| Same house (nonmovers) | 51.5% |
| Different house in U.S. (movers) | 41.3 |
|   Same county | 24.2 |
|   Different county | 17.1 |
|     Same state | 8.4 |
|     Different state | 8.6 |
| Abroad or not known | 7.2 |

*Source: Statistical Abstract of the United States* 1977, p. 37.

later study, while trying to show people are not so isolated in urban societies, also shows the poverty of human relations. People, especially middle-class professionals, quickly form ties with their new neighborhood (although they too depend on relatives for long-term problems). They also-join various associations. But since they are likely to move again, these ties are limited and not very deep. Certainly they do not resemble the community in Buffalo Creek and other places (Litwak and Szelenyi 1969).

Cars, of course, enable families and friends who live miles away from each other to keep in some contact. But it is not the daily contact people have with family or friends who live in their neighborhood. Cars and single homes are profitable for corporations, since these two things use energy and thus raise profits. But they destroy environment and community. The obsession with privacy and private possessions, fostered by capitalism, ultimately isolates people.

> We seek a private house, a private means of transportation, a private garden, a private laundry, self-service stores, and do-it-yourself skills of every kind. An enormous technology seems to have set itself the task of making it unnecessary for one human being ever to ask anything of another in the course of going about his daily business. Even within the family Americans are unique in their feeling that each member should have a separate room, and even a separate telephone, television, car, when economically possible. We seek more and more privacy, and feel more and more alienated and lonely when we get it (Slater quoted in Sidel 1974, pp. 157–58).

Such loneliness is the inevitable result of capitalist values and corporate control. When profits, competition, and individualism dominate, concern with people and their communities slowly but surely erodes. What is profitable and materialistic wins over social ties and human relations (Lee 1959).

## City Neighborhoods

In the 1950s and 1960s, large parts of many American cities underwent a process known as "urban renewal." Usually a city, using federal and city money and many special laws, forced out residents and businesses. People were paid something for their property, but hardly enough, and most were not provided with new homes or apartments. They moved to old slums, crowding them further. The official explanation was that the areas where buildings were torn down were slums. Some were, but many more were ethnic and working-class communities that did not fit the city planners' designs for "progressive" neighborhoods (see Gans 1962 for one example).

After existing buildings were torn down with public money, the areas were sold cheaply to private developers. But the new apartments and businesses were not rented to the old residents. If not used for highways, urban-renewal areas were populated by professionals and other upper-middle-class people. In short, urban renewal meant the forcible removal of poor, minority, and working-class people from their communities to provide profit for business and convenient homes for the higher classes.

That kind of brutal destruction of communities soon gained a bad name and it was stopped. Many people thought that the rape of communities for the benefit of outsiders had ended. But capitalism never gives up. There is now a new form of "urban renewal." Governments no longer force people out. The marketplace does. The term "gentrification" has replaced "urban renewal." Where once they fled to the suburbs, professionals and managers are now rediscovering the joys of city life. But with housing limited, they are taking over established working-class and ethnic communities. This trend has become a stampede that continues into the 1980s (Richards and Rowe 1977; Henry 1978; Mattera 1979; Williams 1980a).

Speculators move into these neighborhoods, buy the houses cheaply, renovate them a little (or not at all), and sell them to upper-class professionals. The poor and working class can no longer afford houses and apartments, with prices four times or more higher than a few years back. An old established community like Boston's North End is steadily being gentrified; rents are becoming way beyond the reach of old residents, and, whereas the West End was bulldozed out of existence, the North End will be gradually but surely destroyed by the capitalist marketplace: another example of profits over people.

> The most recent area to be hit by gentrification has been the North End, which a decade ago was 95 percent Italian, predominantly blue collar. Today, it is 65 percent Italian and more than 40 percent of the 12,000 residents are white-collar workers. In another ten years, one resident predicted, "we'll be lucky to have 30 percent Italians here."
>
> "It's the ruin of the neighborhood," said a 72-year-old lifelong North Ender who now lives in an elderly housing project. "An outsider bought my building. He says I can stay if I want to pay the new rent. He knows I can't afford it. It makes me sick. Most of the people I know feel the same way. They look out and see our streets being taken over by outsiders with money. That's the problem. Money buys everything" (Henry 1978, p. 9).

City neighborhoods have also been destroyed for expansion by hospitals, colleges and universities, museums, and other power-hungry institutions. In *The Rape of Our Neighborhoods,* William Worthy shows both the determination of institutions to expand at any cost and strategies to fight them. This book is an education for all of us who have been socialized to believe in the benevolence of hospitals and universities.

Institutions expand not for the benefit of the community, but for "glamour, prestige, and power." With an excess of hospital beds, hospitals still seek to buy whole city blocks, tear down the houses, and erect new buildings and garages. They try to buy up property quietly; they proceed secretly, never announcing the whole expansion plan. Unless community residents catch on to the game early and oppose expansion vigorously, it is soon too late (as in the area near Boston's Symphony Hall, where the Christian Science Church forced out old residents and businesses). Institutions, bureaucrats, and experts fear popular resistance and try to keep things quiet with an aura of expertise, authority, and benevolence (Worthy 1976, pp. 51, 66–67, 39).

When residents begin to oppose expansion, institutions have a three-step plan. First, ignore the opposition. When it will not go away, blame the conflict on radicals and outside agitators. When that does not still opposition, resort to dirty tricks. The apartments of residents who will not move out are often burglarized; fires are set; heat is turned off; and so it goes. Most of us find it difficult to believe that hospitals and universities resort to such tactics to force residents out; however, Worthy's documentation is detailed and overwhelming. When people get in the way of powerful institutions, war is declared upon them. Wars involve sly tactics as well as force and violence (pp. 28–32).

Harvard University is a prime example of an institution that wrecks neighborhoods as it expands. Worthy provides extensive information on its tactics. For example, when the state of Massachusetts was stopped by 3,000 demonstrating residents from buying a city block to use for a mental health center, Harvard moved in quietly and bought the homes one by one. It continues to expand, and be resisted, in many parts of Cambridge and Boston (pp. 44–46).

The problem of powerful institutions destroying communities is international. Worthy reports the fight of 103 families in France who refused to move to make way for a military base (p. 32).

Thus, urban renewal, highways, gentrification, and expanding institutions have all destroyed viable city neighborhoods. Whatever benefits the ruling class, powerful institutions, and professionals and managers wins over the needs of working people. Whatever remnants of community exist are assaulted continually. Power-hungry institutions, profit-oriented corporations, and alienated professionals cannot understand the grief people feel over lost homes and neighbors.

*Disintegration of Community*

Nothing reveals better the loss of community than the quality of our lives during our last days. Instead of being surrounded by relatives, friends, and neighbors, most old people live in various degrees of isolation. Curtin, in *Nobody Ever Died of Old Age,* explores the living situations of old people: in nursing homes, retirement communities, flophouse hotels, and in homes and apartments isolated from family and neighbors. They suffer not only from poverty and limited income, they are also deprived of much human contact. Without community and work, isolation and loneliness haunt the days of most old people (1972).

When death comes, that too is a lonely experience. Throughout history, people have died in their own homes, surrounded by family and friends. Now, too often, people die in hospitals or nursing homes. Birth, life, and death derive their meaning from social contact. Now, death has become meaningless and terrifying for many old people.

## RISING FROM THE ASHES

As long as there are people, there will be at least some remnants of communities (although many people will live in near-total isolation), and there will be the longing and striving for community.

It may be that existential loneliness is inherent to the human condition:

> All that each person is, and experiences, and shall never experience, in body and in mind, all these things are differing expressions of himself and of one root, and are identical: and not one of these things nor one of these persons is ever quite to be duplicated, nor replaced, nor has it ever quite had precedent: but each is a new and incommunicably tender life, wounded in every breath, and almost as hardly killed as easily wounded: sustaining, for a while, without defense, the enormous assaults of the universe (Agee 1941, p. 56).

Such loneliness may be the fate of all of us. But surely it can be mitigated and controlled, and life can have meaning, if we live in real communities. Existential loneliness need not mean social isolation. The erosion and destruction of communities are made by people, and can be undone.

I do not mean that communities of past eras were utopias. Whether in tribal societies, peasant societies, or cities and towns, all contained problems, inequalities, and oppressions. Communities in European peasant societies oppressed women and children, among others. On the other hand, most communities in tribal societies were much more egalitarian (Radin 1953; Turnbull 1961).

Our goal cannot be to return to the conditions of old communities (even if we wanted to, it would be impossible; the world has changed too drastically). But we can recapture some of the old qualities of stability, neighborhood, concern for our neighbors, security, and so on. In striving for community, we should remember some fundamental realities and truths.

### *Necessities for Community*

All of us need to live in groups of manageable size. Whether it be 500, 1000, or more, at some point a group (neighborhood, work, or school) becomes too large for our senses and abilities to know and experience. Indeed, community is synonymous with smallness. We must find ways to create small, personal groups or community cannot exist. (The organization of Chinese neighborhoods seems to take size into account; see below. See also Chapter 5.)

Home, work, play, school, health care, and shopping should all be within walking distance. Walking to work and other destinations allows for social interaction. Seeing the same people each day creates stability, continuity, and familiarity. Furthermore, health and satisfying work are possible only in a context of family and friends. Democracy and individuality can only develop in integrated communities. Chapter 14 will attempt to show that social problems can only be solved in small, integrated neighborhoods. Crime, mental illness, alienation, isolation of old people, ecological catastrophe, and so on can be confronted only in communities built on a human scale and incorporating all aspects of life.

The burden of this chapter has been to show that capitalism destroys community. A new way of organizing society must be tried. For us today only socialism makes it possible (not certain, by any means) to re-create communities. Only where cooperation and the common good guide people's actions can we build communal ties.

## China

China is attempting to create authentic communities. About 80 percent of the Chinese live in rural communes, each with about 50,000 people. Each commune is subdivided into brigades, and brigades are broken up into teams. Thus, most people work in fairly small groups (Burchett and Alley 1976, ch. 1).

Each commune runs its own schools, its own health system, and, increasingly, tries to meet many of its industrial needs (making and repairing its own tractors, for example). Thus, the Chinese are making a real effort to integrate all areas of life.

In cities, people are organized in neighborhood committees, with residents' committees as the smallest local subdivision. The functions of these committees include: "supervising social services and welfare tasks (e.g., employment offices, nurseries), transmitting governmental edicts, channeling complaints upward, mediating local disputes and family squabbles, reporting suspicious activity or persons, and especially looking after the welfare of the young, old, and housewives who were not served by committees at their places of work." In Shanghai neighborhoods, each apartment building of about eighty people has its own group. At this level, disputes are settled and services are provided. "If, for example, a woman delivers a baby and her husband is working out of the area, others in her block will help to care for her other children and help her to buy food. Or if an elderly widow needs to be brought to the hospital and has no family to assist her, her neighbors, group leaders, or members of her residents' committee will come to her aid" (Sawyers 1977, pp. 44-46; Sidel 1976, p. 223).

It is important to remember that these forms of community in China are being created in a socialist context. People seek both personal happiness and the chance to make contributions to their community. There must be a commitment to more than personal happiness and fulfillment. (I stress that achieving personal happiness is very difficult without community.) There must be cooperation for the common good. In such communities—policeless states—people feel safe; they feel a common bond with their neighbors (Sidel 1974; Burchett and Alley 1976).

*The United States*

Although true communities cannot be created without socialism, much can be done to create at least partial communities and to preserve what exists. Such struggles may function as the steps to a socialist society, as discussed earlier in Chapter 1.

Packard makes some recommendations that, while helpful, ignore the political context of capitalism. Without collective struggle, they cannot be attained. Packard mentions the need for corporations and the government not to move their employees as often as they do now. He suggests we work near home, and, even though he recognizes the difficulty of doing so, he ignores the reasons why we cannot work near our homes: the total lack of integrated communities. He also recommends policies that would help working-class people stay in their communities. For example, corporations could build plants where people are, as in the rural South (Packard 1972, pp. 277-79, 287). But corporations build plants solely on profit considerations: if they move, they tend to go to low-wage, nonunionized areas.

The solution lies in groups fighting against capitalist institutions that continually encroach upon neighborhoods and communities. It also lies in our realization that the decisions and acts (outlined above) that destroy communities are not impersonal, inevitable forces. They are made by people (Worthy 1976; Aronowitz 1974, p. 31).

Worthy quotes Simone Weil—"The strong are never absolutely strong"—and adds, nor are "the weak absolutely weak" (p. 25). With will, knowledge, and determination, powerful institutions can be challenged. Indeed, it was public resistance to urban renewal and to expansions of hospitals and other institutions that created a new climate where Congress voted limits on hospital extensions. The secrecy of institutions is waning. Community participation is now the rule on any decision to expand. Worthy thinks we have come a long way since the days of the early 1960s. He may be too optimistic, but surely we do know more and have made progress since the 1960s. In his book Worthy outlines the lessons of past community struggles, which will be indispensable for any group seeking to protect its homes, parks, and stores from destruction by expanding institutions. Community newspapers that have arisen in most Boston neighborhoods have been instrumental in fighting for the protection and benefit of local residents. They

## STRUGGLES: Art and Community

*There are many ways to create community. One example involves artists and neighborhood residents cooperating in painting a mural. The following is one account of the community mural movement.*

Community mural projects, although they cannot start a community process, can build or advance one; they often serve as catalyst for community action.

Community murals have a distinctive relationship to social change: they are concrete public expressions of a community's values, problems, or goals; they are created with intense community involvement and they may be seen as a form of political praxis.

Whether painted in abstract or figurative styles, community murals reflect and articulate values and concerns felt by the community. In both subject matter and style, many relate directly to a specific locality, a particular building, a dominant cultural ambience, and occasionally, even, specific local events. For example, in a mural painted by the Lil' Valley gang with artist Bill Butler in East Los Angeles, (1972), there is a universal dimension of violence, tragedy, history and peace. For knowledgeable community residents there is an additional level of meaning that comes from the recognition of a turtle and the balance-scales with the cross in between as visual representations of the names of two individuals killed in a gang war. This mural served as a symbolic peace settlement between two warring gangs. This and many other mural histories recounted in our book illustrate vividly that community art can become a form of symbolic social action and implies further social action.

Those familiar with the stories of individual murals know that these walls have emerged from the social struggles of the 1960s, and have, whatever their variety and changes in direction, continued to be rooted in a larger arena of social and political praxis. The issues may be national or ethnic identity, housing, labor, racism, sexism, education, health, sports, or economic cutbacks, but the common spirit has been and remains one of art as an expression of struggle, one of building people's solidarity, creating community, raising political consciousness, combatting racism in all its forms. While some publicity was finally given the community demands around San Francisco's International Hotel in 1977, the fact is that the struggle had been going on for many years and included as one of its first organizing weapons a huge and impressive mural a block long on one side of the Hotel. Similarly, whether one talks of the Chinatown mural in Philadelphia created to prevent a freeway from going through, or the "Wall of Respect" in Chicago, or Dewey Crumpler's Washington High School murals in San Francisco (1965-71), which were actually *demanded* by the students, one will find throughout the history of this young movement a constant emphasis on concrete struggle against specific acts of oppression. . . .

Whatever role the artist plays, and whether a wall is executed by an individual or a team, the community is intimately involved at almost every stage, from the gaining of wall permissions, to the celebration of the mural at its completion. Funding for the work is, on a national average, over fifty percent grassroots donations. All the work—moving scaffolding and supplies, scraping, painting, etc.—as well as later developments in the community around the wall or the issues it addresses—actively involves local people. . . . Artes Guadalupanos de Aztlan of Santa Fe, New Mexico, grew out of a Chicano environment and problems relating to drugs, unemployment, etc. Its members are not professionally trained artists, but its murals include some of the most visually forceful in the nation. Its emphasis on community interaction has included its participation in city politics, an alternative school project, an alternative people's health clinic, etc.

The high degree of community participation characteristic of the mural movement has led some neighborhood youth to turn toward the study of art, to forego the escapist route of drugs, etc. But the new

*(continued)*

*Source:* Excerpted from pp. 7, 8, 10, 11 in James D. and Eva S. Cockcroft, "People's Art and Social Change: The Community Mural Movement," in *Radical America*, Vol. 12 #2, March-April 1978. 38 Union Sq., Somerville, MA 02143.

> **Art and Community** *(continued)*
> grassroots interest in art extends far beyond actual participants in mural projects. As early as 1971, it was possible to hold "seminars" on mural painting in Chicago's Cabrini-Green housing projects. Anyone who has done any type of community-organizing work will easily appreciate the level of interest represented by over two hundred people, adults and children, crowding in to see slides and discuss mural painting.

tell the truth about what is happening, often and early, and help community groups fight to keep their communities whole. They do not win all the time, by any means, but they often do and they keep the spirit of resistance alive (Worthy 1976, pp. 259–69; Weisel 1978).

In the end, we have no choice but to believe in "the wisdom of ordinary people when they are unburdened by manipulative leaders" (Worthy, p. 258). Local struggles by ordinary people rarely make news, but socialist consciousness begins when people struggle to save their own homes and neighborhoods. The destruction of Vietnam has the same cause as the destruction of neighborhoods. In time, people will see that.

There is no need for optimistic or pessimistic conclusions. People's awareness of their real needs for home and community and of the deprivation of these, will lead to the struggle against expanding institutions and capitalist human relations. The success of the struggle is uncertain, but it will be waged. No utopia awaits, but surely we can create more satisfying human relations than we now have.

For most of us over the last hundred years the loss of community has been less sudden and less visible than in Buffalo Creek. We have been taught and forced to choose "progress," for example, to change to commercial farming where farmers buy their own machinery instead of sharing it and working on each other's land.

Capitalism forced progress upon us, but we are beginning to see what such progress has cost. We have been taught to be individuals, to look out for ourselves, to want our own private cars and private everything. But with privacy comes less social contact, less concern for others, less sharing, less dependence on neighbors and friends. To survive and lead meaningful lives, we need to hold on to the communal ties we do have and to restore what we have lost. Many people are beginning to struggle for community.

# 8

# *The Oppression of Women*

## BIOLOGY, CULTURE, AND OPPRESSION

"Wherever women are needed economically it is quickly decided that they are biologically or even spiritually destined" (Baxandall, Gordon, and Reverby 1976, p. 75, discussing the opening of nursing to women in the nineteenth century). Generally history shows that it is not biology (physical or mental traits) that has oppressed women. It is social, political, and economic conditions that have shaped women's lives.

This chapter will try to show some of the many ways women are exploited through sexism. Men too, however, are victimized by sexism: forced to repress emotions, and directed away from many satisfying activities because they are considered "women's work," in the same way women are prevented from attempting many jobs because they are considered "man's work." In other ways, too, both men and women are victimized by sexism.

There are three central issues in the study of sexism: (1) the causes for the oppression of women; (2) the real changes women are undergoing in their social and economic roles; and (3) the lesson we can learn from the experiences of both capitalist and socialist societies, that in order to become equal citizens, women must be liberated in all areas—in the economy, at home, in politics, and so on. Partial liberation is no liberation.

## Biology

Margaret Mead showed that temperament is not a biological inheritance. In one society both men and women are nurturing, gentle, and nonaggressive. In another, both men and women are aggressive and competitive. And in a third society, roles are reversed: women are productive and assertive, and men are concerned with their appearance and with gossiping (1935).

As discussed below, women have always done much work, including hard physical labor. In Greek peasant society, most of the agricultural labor was women's work, as it was in many other societies. Today, both in the United States and in other societies, women do much physically demanding work. A look at what women have in fact done throughout history does not lead to the conclusion that women are biologically incapable of doing any work men do. It is society's assumption of weakness (social weakness), not physical weakness, that oppresses women (Mitchell 1971, p. 201).

This is not to deny differences between men and women. Rather, we should be aware that we do not know exactly what these differences are, since women are different more because of social inequalities—unequal treatment—than because of biology. My four-year-old daughter is physically stronger than most boys her age. If at twenty she is weaker than most men her age, will it be because of her biology, or because of the socialization she gets in the next sixteen years? Ehrenreich and English point to the same issue:

> We need to know much more about occupational health hazards specific to women, about actual emotional patterns accompanying menstruation and pregnancy, about the potential hazards of various contraceptive methods, and about many other areas ignored or distorted by medicine. But in our concern to understand more about our own biology, for our own purposes, we must never lose sight of the fact that it is not our biology that oppresses us—but a social system based on sex and class domination (1973, p. 89).

Many biological differences exist between people, of the same or different sexes. Most differences are not socially significant. We choose to make some important. For example, some people argue that nature made woman the parent who can nurse, and that fact limits women's mobility; they must stay closer to home. That need not be. In socialist societies, working mothers are given two thirty- to forty-five-minute extra breaks to nurse their children. Biology does not imprison us; it sets limiting conditions (for women *and* men), but these need not mean inferiority or inequality.

## Sameness and Equality

Some women anthropologists have argued that women are not necessarily inferior (or have lower status) because they play different roles. And it is certainly true that women's contributions to human survival have been as important as men's. Why then have they been the social unequals of men in most societies? Despite the argument by Chiñas (1973, p. 11) that role differences need not mean social inequality, that has usually been the case. Must such inequalties persist? Can they be overcome? The rest of this chapter will explore some of these issues.

## A CULTURAL PERSPECTIVE

We in the United States have inherited much of European tradition and culture. In that tradition, women have been unequal to men and oppressed for a long time. In the Christian and Judaic religions, women have been relegated to lower positions. However, we must not think this tradition applies to women's place in all societies.

### Men and Women

Women have been highly oppressed in some societies, less in others, and not at all in still others. In addition, in most societies those women who have powerful personalities have overcome the limits placed on women in general. Moreover, housework, which oppresses women today, was less of a problem in tribal societies. Because of fewer possessions, housework was simpler (Hammond and Jablow 1976, pp. 83, 130; Chiñas 1973).

It seems that public, political positions have been held mostly by men, and women have held private, household positions. Generally, tasks and roles have been divided by sex—but not along the same lines in all societies. What women cannot do in one society, they must do in another (Hammond and Jablow 1976, p. 6; Chiñas 1973).

In hunting-and-gathering societies (such as many Indian tribes, the Bushmen of Southwest Africa, and the BaMbuti), women were essentially equal to men. In terms of their power, the importance of their work for the society's survival, abilities, confidence, and self-perception, they were not an oppressed minority. In such small egalitarian societies (where there are no classes or rulers), individual abilities are more important than sex roles (Hammond and Jablow 1976, p. 130).

The !Kung are one hunting-and-gathering society where women seem equal to men.

> In the hunting and gathering context, women have a great deal of autonomy and influence. Some of the contexts in which this egalitarianism is expressed . . . are: women's subsistence contribution and the control women retain over the food they have gathered; the requisites of foraging in the Kalahari which entail a similar degree of mobility for both sexes; the lack of rigidity in sex-typing of many adult activities, including domestic chores and aspects of child socialization; the cultural sanction against physical expression of aggression; the small group size; and the nature of the settlement pattern (Draper 1975, p. 78).

Draper goes on to show that those !Kung women whose families moved to sedentary, village life soon became unequal to men. Instead of moving about to gather food in the desert, they were now housebound (the men worked the fields and had contacts with the outside world). Once housebound, the women trained their daughters for the same role, while the boys joined their fathers on the outside. Whereas in the desert boys and girls played together, here they were separated very early. In short, Draper shows clearly that women's roles are shaped by material, economic, and social conditions. If women are to be equal to men, we must pay attention to (and change) material conditions.

The economic contributions of women have varied. In most hunting-and-gathering societies, women have contributed (by gathering) 60 to 80 percent of daily food (by weight) (Draper 1975, p. 82; Hammond and Jablow 1976, p. 69). At other times, women have made all the clothing and were the craftspeople. During colonial times in America, women produced most items used by families.

Thus, women have made indispensable contributions to human survival, as important as, at times more important than, men's contributions. Yet, "whatever the nature of women's work or its economic value, it is never invested with glamor, excitement, or prestige" (Hammond and Jablow, p. 73).

## Sex Roles

All anthropologists agree that in every society some tasks are only women's work, others only men's work, and a few can be done by either women or men. But this fact must be qualified. The divisions are not based on any natural abilities, for sometimes what women cannot do in one society, they must do in another. Moreover, the divisions are less rigid in some societies than in others. Among the !Kung, men and women do some of each other's work. Men build the huts (women's job) when there are no women around. But women never carry meat from the hunting site to the settlement, and men never clean children's feces. Women gathering food watch for animal tracks and inform the men when they see any. And boys and girls of all ages play together (Draper, pp. 87–93).

It appears that the only tasks universally assigned to men in tribal societies have been hunting and warfare. Even hunting presents some problems. "Occupational lines are rarely as clearly maintained in reality as they are drawn in theory. Women on gathering expeditions automatically kill small game to bring back to the campsite along with the wild plant foods they collect. Aranda women even wield their digging sticks to bring down the large animals they encounter. . . . Landes describes Ojibwa women who, having learned the appropriate skills from male relatives, crossed the occupational lines to become successful hunters and trappers" (Hammond and Jablow 1976, pp. 70–71).

Among the !Kung, it is obvious that women possess the stamina, intelligence, and courage to hunt. Yet they do not. So too in many other societies. Individual women have become hunters. Why then is hunting a male occupation?

*Strong Women*

In many societies, women have not been the meek, withdrawn, and quiet people they are in peasant societies and other places. !Kung women have high self-esteem. They go into the desert in groups, without men. They acquire much detailed knowledge about hundreds of plants before they become gatherers. They gather the food and determine its distribution (Draper, pp. 83-85).

In most societies, women practice some crafts. Craftsmaking in groups becomes an occasion that is psychologically satisfying and that improves women's self-image. Chiñas found the Zapotec women were strong. Even though excluded from public roles, they work outside the house. They cooperate with each other, develop communal bonds, and always protect each other, especially from male aggression. There is no jealousy or fighting over men (Chiñas 1973, pp. 105, 111-12).

In most societies where women have been oppressed and assigned low status, they have not tolerated it willingly. Hammond and Jablow cite many examples of women fighting against the restrictions placed on them (pp. 44-45).

In short, women have not been equally oppressed in all societies, and hardly oppressed in some. The material and economic conditions of hunting-and-gathering societies and their egalitarianism have made women the social equals of men. When social classes arose, when some people owned and controlled more than others, women's position began to worsen. Stratified societies have been detrimental to all women—and to most men.

## WOMEN IN THE UNITED STATES

A brief historical account will help to clarify the place of women today in the United States society and economy. History shows that women's place in our society has changed in some ways but remained constant in others. (The following account is based on Ehrenreich and English 1973; Blau 1975; Baxandall, Gordon, and Reverby 1976.)

*Women in United States History*

In colonial America, women's lives and work were more varied than today. Men did most of the agricultural work and dominated some crafts. But women did equally important work. In addition to the household chores, they made shoes, soap, clothes, and many other items. This work was done with the cooperation of husband, children, and other women. Thus, the woman in the home was not isolated; the husband was not gone all day as he is today. Home and work were integrated and included the whole family. Women typically developed many skills.

Moreover, women were not entirely excluded from outside occupations. Many women, especially widows, worked in taverns and other businesses. Generally, before 1800, only a few middle-class women were full-time housewives as we understand the term. The rest worked very hard doing much more than housekeeping (Sacks 1976, p. 29).

The coming of industrialism (1820s on) began to change women's lives. For a long time most women lived as they had during colonial times, but steadily more and more of them saw their lives transformed. The primary change was the removal from the home of husband and children. He went to work in factories and other places, and the children went to school. Women were left alone to do housework.

Some women did leave the home for outside work, mostly single and widowed women. Most workers in the textile industry were women. Slave women, of course, went on working in the fields and homes of their owners. For these women, freedom in 1865 meant little, for they went on working in the fields (as sharecroppers) and as maids.

In the early years of manufacturing (first half of the nineteenth century), most men were still busy on the farms, so women (and children) were the only readily available labor supply. At first, they were single women of Yankee settler families, but soon they were immigrant women. At any rate, it is important to note that women were drawn into factories and manufacturing work from the very beginning of industrialism.

By the late nineteenth century most women were taken out of the paid labor force, but not all. Poor immigrant women, black women, and widows, for example, still worked in textile mills and other places. In 1900, 20 percent of women over sixteen were in the labor force (for more details on working women in the late nineteenth century, see Baxandall, Gordon, and Reverby 1976, p. 83).

It is confusing to talk of women in general for the nineteenth century, however. The lives of middle- and upper-class women differed drastically from those of working-class and black women. The women of the upper classes were seen as fragile, sick, and incapable of physical and mental straining. Working women, on the other hand, were not seen as fragile, nor as sick, even though they suffered from illness and deprivation under the conditions in which they lived. Working women were seen as sickening, as "dangerous and polluting." Medical arguments about the inherent weakness of women kept them from education and voting. Such arguments disqualified women as doctors (women had formerly been healers for most people), but qualified women of the upper classes as patients (Ehrenreich and English 1973, p. 12).

The health care for the "fragile" women was bed rest, surgery, and other treatments that incapacitated them. Rebellious women were kept in their place. The "cult of invalidism" was used as a way to control women of the upper classes. Poor women, on the other hand, suffered from real illnesses that went untreated, from poverty and exploitation.

In the early 1900s, more women entered the labor force. Many were active in some of the major strikes of that time, although unions in general did not want women in their ranks, seeing them as competitors for men's jobs who would lower men's wages. But the demands of the capitalist economy began to create "women's" jobs. As the corporations began to grow, after 1890, they needed more clerical workers, and they turned to women for a plentiful and cheap source of labor.

Even though at this time fewer than 25 percent of women were in the labor force, the rest were not just keeping house. Many women (especially blacks) did farm work and some home manufacturing. Others took in boarders to supplement their income, and thus they had more washing, cooking, and cleaning to do. This monetary contribution to family survival has been ignored (Baxandall, Gordon, Reverby 1976, p. 150). A major change began to take place in the 1920s. In order to find markets for their increasing production, corporations turned to advertising. Women were the major targets. They became consumers, losing most of their role as producers. Home production declined drastically as clothing and other needs (the desire for some products, of course, was a *created* need to increase corporate profits) were manufactured in factories. Increasingly, women were consumers, not producers. This situation was a long way from colonial times.

The 1940s began the gradual but steady absorption of women into the labor force. Till then, working wives were considered a blow to masculine self-esteem. In addition, most jobs available to women were unpleasant and paid poorly, so women preferred housework. Most of those women with outside jobs needed them for survival.

World War II created labor shortages and accelerated the trend of more women working. In 1940, 28.5 percent of women were working, up from 23.6 percent in 1930. By the war's end, 36 percent of women were in the labor force. During the war years wages increased, up to 40 percent higher for many women. The kind of women in the working force also changed. The number of working wives doubled, and black women began getting manufacturing jobs. In addition, women now were getting skilled, higher-paying jobs such as precision toolmakers, crane operators, lumberjacks, and drill press operators (Szymanski 1976, p. 41; Baxandall, Gordon and Reverby 1976, pp. 280–81).

Since the 1940s, working women have been typical. Married women, many with young children, have been entering the labor force. At the same time, women have been limited to a few sex-segregated jobs, and their earnings (in relation to men's) have not increased.

After the war, some women were sent back home, but that was a temporary stage. The inflation of the late 1940s, the need for more money for families to buy the usual necessities and some new necessities of the emerging consumer society, and other conditions began to make women regular workers. The percentage of women in the labor force has increased every year, and now 50 percent of women are in the labor force (as compared to about 78 percent of men). But in relation to men, today women make less money than they did in the 1950s. They must work because of increasing inflation and the consumption ethic created by advertising and corporate profits. Today, it is normal for married women to hold a job outside the house.

*Socialization for Sex Roles*

Even this brief discussion of women in history should show that women's (*and men's*) lives are shaped by economic and cultural conditions, not by biology. In the United States, we have moved from women doing all types of work in colonial times, to their isolation in the house, to their integration in the labor market. Each period demands that women be raised to fit into the dominant social conditions. Women and men must be socialized to play their roles. Today, women work outside the home, but usually in sex-segregated jobs, at lower pay. In some ways, women must now be raised to become the primary caretakers at home *and* to fit into the jobs demanded by a capitalist economy.

Socialization begins at birth. Boys and girls are treated differently. For example, girls are perceived as softer, and weaker. Parents tend to handle boys more vigorously. It is such treatment that makes boys tougher and better in sports and physical activity.

At age two and a half, boys often are drawn to what are labeled "girls' toys." But they are soon taught to hide such liking. Harrison tells of "a small boy who once went to the pathetic extreme of fashioning a stuffed airplane to take to bed to 'cuddle', thus, presumably, preserving his orthodox masculine image while satisfying his need to nurture and to gentle." Harrison goes on to list some typical actions that foster sex roles:

> A fire engine rushes past your house. Whom do you call to see it? Your daughter, or your son?
>
> You drive past a wedding party. Whose attention do you call to it? Your son's, or your daughter's?
>
> You are given flowers. Whom do you ask to arrange them prettily in a vase? Your son, or your daughter?
>
> Out walking with your children, you pass a woman with a small baby. With whom do you share your pleasure in the infant? Your son, or your daughter?
>
> A building is under construction. To whom do you point out the crane, the workers, the details of construction? Your daughter or your son?
>
> Relatives come to visit. Do they hug and kiss your daughter and tell her how pretty she looks? Do they shake hands with your son, toss him up in the air, and jocularly mess up his hair? Why?

Your small son asks for a doll, a toy even, or a jump rope. How do you react?

Your daughter and your son both ask for trucks for Christmas. Who gets the 29¢ truck in the Christmas stocking? Who gets the $9.95 truck under the tree?

Would a stranger be able to tell the sex of each of your children from their respective Christmas lists? (1974, pp. 4-7).

Further on Harrison describes some ways by which teachers in school reinforce stereotypes. For example, a teacher to whom a girl goes with her carpentry problem hammers in the nails properly for her, but the teacher tells a boy with the same problem to do it himself (pp. 9-11). (Both my observation of my own daughters and reading convince me that sex roles become entrenched long before children go to the first grade.)

In the school she studied in 1970, Harrison found that second-grade girls were interested in rockets, but they hid this interest when they were with boys. Such fears begin with the use of toys and the reactions of others. They become reinforced at school where, for example, women are still almost entirely absent from history books (1974, p. 28).

Children's books reinforce the image of women as unequal to men. For example, as I read books to my daughters (ages five and three in 1979), I was astounded by the nearly total absence of women and girls. Not only were most human characters in the books male, so were most animal characters. Cats, dogs, bees, butterflies, and birds either are given male names or are referred to as "he." So by the age of three, both my daughters had many times looked at a book they had not seen or heard before, seen an animal whose sex is not obvious, and called the animal "he." Generally, both of them now use "he" when they want to refer to people in general. When I ask them why they do so, they can offer no explanation; like the air around them, sexism simply exists and is taken for granted. We try to fight against sexist language, but the battle is hopeless (although at times, when I point out some things to them, my daughters do change pronouns and characters' names); individual actions can make limited difference. Obviously, changes must be made at the societal level.

Early in life girls begin meeting experiences that make for low confidence and self-esteem. This is so even though in the early years girls do better than boys in most activities; even in math, before age twelve, girls, on the average, are better than boys (in high school, boys do better in math). But they *perceive* boys as more capable, showing the early creation of low self-esteem (Harrison 1974, pp. 141-43; Freeman 1970, pp. 243, 247). Thus the women in a study by Seifer, women in their 40s and 50s who had worked for their family and community, thought there was little importance in what they did. They were reluctant to talk about themselves. These were working-class women, and their class lowered their self-esteem further still. "I began to see how a society that values material wealth and status symbols devalues those who lack them and how that societal devaluation turns inward into low self-esteem" (Seifer 1976, pp. 32-33).

Television programs and advertising also play a major role in socializing girls and women. Most ads still show women in silly and superficial situations, expressing ecstasy over shiny floors and clean clothes. Women's sexuality is still used to sell products. Thousands of such commercials, beginning with sex-typed toys on children's shows, take their toll. Women are trained in their role, mostly as passive consumers. Television advertising manipulates and exploits women as passive consumers and sex objects. Corporations, which dominate TV, create a passive woman consumer parallel to the passive worker. Both are dominated in order to increase profits (Caldwell 1977; Baxandall, Ewen, and Gordon 1976, pp. 7-8).

Medicine also contributes to the socialization and oppression of women. There is no longer the cult of invalid women (upper classes) and the fear of sickening ones (poor women). Today, psychiatry and its ideology oppress women. First, women's real illnesses are often dismissed as unreal, as "psychosomatic." A recent study reported in the Journal of the American Medical Association showed the sexist behavior of doctors: A team of researchers from the University of California at Davis "examined the medical records of 52 married couples to find out how the doctors responded to such common complaints as backache, headache, dizziness, chest pain and fatigue—which may signal more serious illness. In all cases the doctors ordered more X-rays and diagnostic tests for the men than for the women" (Lessinger 1979, p. 10). Secondly, women are seen as dangerous to men. Mental illness, delinquency, and so on are attributed to domineering or uncaring mothers. "The ambitious woman can be blamed for 'emasculating' men, and the devoted mother can be blamed for 'infecting' her sons with guilt and dependency." Pediatricians and psychiatrists warn working mothers that their children will suffer irreparable damage without constant mothering. Either way, at work or at home, a mother runs the risk of neglecting or smothering her children. Ehrenreich and English caution us, however, not to see medicine as a cause of women's oppression, for it "does not invent our social roles, it merely interprets them to us as biological destiny" (Ehrenreich and English 1973, pp. 80-83).

## Women Working

The argument can be stated briefly. Women are becoming a permanent part of the labor force. As they work, they gain some power in relation to men. But they continue to be oppressed because their pay is still low (in relation to men) and because they are limited to a few jobs and job categories. Women are becoming a permanent, exploited part of the capitalist economy.

Table 8.1 shows the steady increase in women in the labor force. By 1978, over 50 percent of women sixteen and over were in the labor force, compared to a decreasing percentage of men—fewer than 80 percent. If the trend continues, by the year 2000 or so women will have the same labor force participation rate as men.

**TABLE 8.1**  Labor Force Participation Rates

|      | Men  | Women |
|------|------|-------|
| 1900 | 85.7 | 20.0% |
| 1950 | 86.8 | 33.9  |
| 1960 | 82.4 | 37.1  |
| 1965 | 80.1 | 38.8  |
| 1970 | 79.2 | 42.8  |
| 1975 | 77.3 | 43.7  |
| 1976 | 76.9 | 46.8  |
| 1978 | 77.2 | 50.5  |
| 1979 | —    | 51.0  |

Source: *Statistical Abstract of the United States* 1979, p. 392; Szymanski 1976, p. 41; U.S. Department of Labor 1978a, 1980.

But these figures tell only part of the story. Even more revealing are the kinds of women who work. In May 1978, almost 57 percent of working women were married, compared to 24.1 percent who were single, 4.4 percent separated, 5.7 percent widowed, and 9 percent divorced (Goff 1978). The greatest increase in female labor force participation has been by married women. Forty-seven and six-tenths percent of all married women were in the labor force in 1978; the many working women with children reveal the profound changes in our society. As Table 8.2 shows, young mothers have contributed heavily to the increase in the numbers of working women. And although many mothers of young children work part-time by choice, most working women work full-time. In 1978, 79 percent of women age twenty

**TABLE 8.2a**  Labor Force Participation Rate of Married Women, Husband Present, March 1978

| In labor force       | 47.6% |
|----------------------|-------|
| No children under 18 | 44.7  |
| Children 14–17       | 57.5  |
| Children 6–13        | 57.0  |
| Children 3–5         | 47.9  |
| Children under 3     | 37.6  |

Source: U.S. Department of Labor 1978a.

**TABLE 8.2b**  Labor Force Participation Rate of Women, by Age, 1979

| 16 years and older | 51.0% |
|--------------------|-------|
| 16–19              | 54.5  |
| 20–24              | 69.1  |
| 25–54              | 62.2  |
| 55 and over        | 23.2  |

Source: U.S. Department of Labor 1980.

and over in the labor force were full-time workers (*Statistical Abstract of the United States* 1979, p. 397; Leon and Bednarzik 1978).

When women work outside the house, they tend to get jobs in only a few areas, jobs that continue women's caring role. They work in service occupations, such as retailing and waitressing, and in clerical positions, nursing, and teaching. In most of these occupations, women are the vast majority of the workers. Over 60 percent of women workers, black and white, are concentrated in sales, clerical, private household, and service occupations. There are also racial differences among women workers, and these have changed over time. In 1967, only 16.6 percent of black women workers were in clerical occupations, but in 1976 26 percent were (*Handbook of Labor Statistics* 1977, pp. 58–61).

Some manufacturing jobs, especially in electronics, have become predominantly women's jobs, paying low wages. Indeed, United States electronics corporations that have moved their operations to Southeast Asia employ women there too, paying them as little as *a dollar a day* (Grossman 1980).

In the 1970s there were only slight changes in the occupational distribution of women workers. Comparing 1972 to 1978, we find the following percentages: clerical, 34.7 (1972) to 34.6 (1978); service, 21.1 to 20.7; management and bureaucracy, 6.6 to 9.3; and professional and technical, 12.7 to 13.3. The last two categories show some increase in the 1970s, but most women still work in clerical, service, and related occupations (*Dollars and Sense*, January 1980, p. 17).

Table 8.3 shows the changes and growth in female occupations. Note that most women in professional occupations are noncollege teachers, nurses, and helpers of men professionals. Of all scientists and engineers, only 10.8 percent were women in 1978. Of over one million engineers, only 1.6 percent were women. Of mathematicians, 18.3 percent were women; of life scientists, 22 percent; of economists, 11.2 percent; of psychologists, 27.3

**TABLE 8.3** The Female Occupational Structure (All Employed Workers)

|  | *1900* | *1940* | *1974* |
|---|---|---|---|
| Professionals | 8.1% | 12.8% | 14.9% |
| Managers | 7.3 | 4.5 | 5.2 |
| Clerical and Sales | 8.2 | 28.8 | 41.7 |
| Service | 35.5 | 29.4 | 21.4 |
| Craftsmen | 1.5 | 1.1 | 1.5 |
| Operatives | 23.8 | 19.5 | 13.0 |
| Nonfarm Laborers | 2.6 | 1.1 | 1.1 |
| Farm Workers | 13.1 | 2.8 | 1.2 |
| Total | 100% | 100% | 100% |

*Source:* Szymanski 1976, p. 45; his sources; *Historical Statistics of the U.S.; Manpower Report of the President,* 1975.

percent; and of sociologists and anthropologists, 34.6 percent (*Statistical Abstract* 1979, p. 625). Thus, within science and engineering itself, women are basically excluded from engineering and concentrated in the social sciences (economics excepted).

It is clear that women, as much as ever, still work in a few, female-dominated occupations. Many of these jobs (clerical and sales notably) are considered white-collar occupations, but they actually are low-paying, and they are becoming more detailed, routinized, and similar to assembly-line work. We might expect women in clerical jobs to resist the assembly-line organization of their work, but executives also are resisting it. It seems they want to be waited on by their secretaries, and routinization of clerical work eliminates the amenities of personal secretaries (Baxandall, Ewen, and Gordon 1976, p. 4; Braverman 1974, ch. 15).

Generally speaking, most women, like most men, do routine and oppressive work. Telephone operators and service representatives are watched constantly and are under tremendous pressure. (Many men escape their frustration with such work through sports and drinking; women may escape by shopping, for example, buying wigs to change their personality [Langer 1970]).

Not only are women concentrated in a few occupations, but they earn substantially less than men. Many people argue that women work to buy luxuries and that they do not need the money. Studies have shown this is not so. Also, given the still-existing prejudice against working mothers, women with children would not go to work if they did not need the money. The lower the husband's income, the more likely the wife is to work. Thus, in 1968, 47 percent of women whose husbands made between $5,000 and $7,000 worked; but only 18 percent with husbands making over $25,000 worked (many of these women were no doubt college-educated with professions and careers). "In 1976, 84% of the women in the labor force either supported themselves, or were married to men earning under $15,000 per year" (Szymanski 1976, pp. 50–51; Zaretsky 1978, p. 215).

In relation to what men earn, women have lost ground. In 1955, men's median weekly earnings were 56 percent higher than women's median weekly earnings. By 1974, however, men's earnings were 75 percent greater than women's. In 1977, full-time women workers had a median income only 58 percent of full-time the men's median (down from 59 percent in 1970). Table 8.4 shows the differences by occupational categories for May 1978. They continue to be substantial (U.S. Department of Labor 1976, p. 1; *Statistical Abstract* 1979, p. 461).

What accounts for these differences? First, women are directed to lower-paying occupations.

> These differences between the earnings of men and women suggest that women are being paid less for doing the same job. Undoubtedly this is true in some instances, but other factors are also significant. First, women are concentrated in those occupations which are less skilled and in which wages are rela-

**TABLE 8.4** Median Usual Weekly Earnings of Full-Time Wage and Salary Workers, by Occupation and Sex, May 1978

|  | All races | |
|---|---|---|
|  | Men | Women |
| White-collar workers | $325 | $185 |
|    Professional and technical workers | 344 | 246 |
|    Managers and administrators except farm | 361 | 212 |
|    Sales workers | 283 | 129 |
|    Clerical workers | 255 | 165 |
| Blue-collar workers | 253 | 146 |
|    Craft and kindred workers | 285 | 164 |
|    Operatives, except transport | 236 | 145 |
|    Transport equipment operatives | 252 | 148 |
|    Nonfarm laborers | 202 | 143 |
| Service workers | 189 | 123 |
|    Private household workers | — | 59 |
|    Other service workers | 189 | 126 |
| Farm workers | 142 | 121 |

*Source:* U.S. Department of Labor 1978c.

tively low. Second, women working on full-time schedules tend to work less overtime than men. Third, although women are as well educated as their male counterparts in terms of median years of schooling completed, there are differences in the kinds of education, training, and counseling they receive, which directs them into traditional and low-paying jobs. Fourth, women on the average have fewer years of worklife experience than men. Studies have shown, however, that even after adjusting for some of these and other factors such as age, region, and industrial concentration, much of the male-female earnings differential remains unexplained—representing a maximum measure of discrimination. . . . In 1974 the earnings gap was largest among sales workers, where men were more often in high-paying commissioned, nonretail jobs while women worked primarily in retail trade. Men's earnings exceeded women's by 142 percent. The earnings differential was smallest among non-farm laborers (38 percent). Among professional and technical workers, men earned 55 percent more than women. Here, doctors, lawyers, judges, engineers college educators, or architects were likely to be men, while noncollege teachers, nurses, librarians, dietitians, and health technologists were usually women (U.S. Department of Labor 1976, p. 2).

Since most women are working in such jobs, most of the income difference is explained by job segregation. But even within the same occupation, doing the same work, women make less.

When a comparison is made of the salaries of fully employed women in the same highly skilled, detailed occupations, the gap narrows but does not disappear. The median salaries of women scientists in 1970 were from $1,700 to

$5,100 less than those of men in the same fields. The gap was greatest in chemistry, where women earned a median salary of only $10,500 as compared with $15,600 for men (U.S. Department of Labor 1976, p. 2).

This sexual division of labor, with women concentrated in low-prestige and low-paying jobs, increases the profits of corporations. Clearly, were women to gain equality to men, were all jobs equally occupied by women and men, and were the millions of women workers to be paid as much as men, corporate profits would decrease. Therefore, to insure higher profits, corporations do not want to eliminate sex differences; in fact, they perpetuate and strengthen them through hiring policies, training, and other means (Szymanski 1976, pp. 44, 47–48).

We should not be misled by the publicity given to the few women who become managers and break out of job segregation. Whatever may happen to some women, statistics clearly show that the vast majority of women still work in a few (female) occupations at low pay. Conditions are not only not improving, they are worsening. Thus, the economic oppression of women workers is becoming a permanent feature of capitalist societies.

A recent survey of 150,000 women showed clearly that the economic pressure on women to work in the current capitalist system is a serious problem for most of them.

> In contrast to the popular image, America's average working woman describes herself as frustrated, working in a dead-end job with no chance in sight for advancement or training opportunities. She is underpaid, under-utilized and afforded little or no respect for the work she contributes.
>
> She is troubled by inadequate child care facilities, and spends her working days obsessed with guilt because she is not home with the children. Yet she can't afford to quit because her income is vital to the management of the home.
>
> Her husband does not object to her job, but he is of almost no help with household chores. When a child is sick and requires the attention of a parent, it is she, four out of five times, who stays home while her spouse goes off to work. She desires job counseling (Lipinski 1979, p. 29).

And while both wife and husband are out working, our society has made no effort to catch up with the reality that both men and women must work. Schools operate only part-time, so parents must arrange a place for the children to be for the rest of the time. There is little, and expensive, day care available for preschool children. Indeed, most children of working parents are not in day care: "... 68% of all three to six year olds with working mothers in 1975, according to the latest Census Bureau figures. Husbands and wives take jobs at different times of the day and night so that one is always home, a grandmother or other relative comes in to stay with the child, or the child is transported to a relative's home for care" (*Dollars and Sense,* January 1979, p. 6).

Women are subjected to other forms of discrimination. Sexual harassment at the workplace has been common since at least the late nineteenth century. "It is consistent, systematic, and pervasive, not a set of random isolated acts. The license to harass women workers, which many men feel they have, stems from notions that there is a 'woman's place' which women in the labor force have left, thus leaving behind their personal integrity" (Bularzik 1978, p. 26).

Around 1900, single working women were equated with prostitutes, since a respectable woman's place was in the house. The situation may no longer be as degrading, but women in all types of work have been, and continue to be, harassed. Waitresses, secretaries, models, factory workers, and professionals all experience harassment.

Harassment includes staring, verbal abuse and obscene suggestions, touching, attempted and actual rape. Supervisors are often the worst perpetrators of harassment, but men co-workers also harass women. Finally, although all working women have been harassed in some way, "physical violence was [found to be] more common and expected by women in menial jobs" (pp. 30, 37, 38).

Harassment exists in numbers difficult to believe. Kirchheimer, in reviewing Lin Farley's *Sexual Shakedown: The Sexual Harassment of Women on the Job*, summarizes many studies on sexual harassment: "More than 90 percent of women surveyed in all the studies listed sexual harassment as a serious job problem; 70 percent said they had experienced it; and more than 50 percent said they had left jobs because of it" (1978).

A survey of federal government women workers in 1979 also showed extensive harassment. Of 150 women questioned, 93 had been harassed. "Some 73 had been the object of degrading remarks or jokes, 46 had been patted or touched and 44 had received promises of special treatment from supervisors in exchange for sex. Nine women reported being sexually assaulted" (Bedell 1979, p. 2).

Most women have reacted individually. Either they feel they are at fault for attracting the attention of men and thus do nothing, or they devise individual strategies for protection, which at times include leaving the job. Some groups have been formed to combat harassment, but not many, and they have not proved very effective or long-lasting (Bularzik pp. 34-35). (For a detailed description of the sexual harassment of cocktail waitresses in the early 1970s, see Spradley and Mann 1975.)

In conclusion, I want to stress a few important features of women's work. Women are becoming permanent members of the work force, but they still get low wages and are restricted to a few sex-segregated jobs. Most jobs women hold are not interesting and exciting (neither are most men's jobs). Most women's jobs are oppressive and degrading. Indeed, jobs of middle-class women (teaching, nursing, and so on) are becoming collectivized, routinized, and controlled by management, so middle-class women are really moving closer to the working rather than the ruling class. When women work side by side with men, they continue to serve them (getting coffee, for example) and they are reminded of their subordinate status by overly familiar forms of address and sexual harassment (Sacks 1976, p. 46; Garson 1975; Terkel 1974).

## WOMEN IN SOCIALIST REVOLUTIONS

Socialist revolutions do not guarantee the liberation of women. They eliminate the worst forms of oppression and at least make total liberation possible. But a long, continuous struggle is necessary before true liberation can be achieved. We can learn much from the experiences of women in socialist revolutions. These experiences show the many aspects of women's oppression and teach us the need for struggle in many areas. After looking at the bitter past of women in prerevolutionary societies and the enormous progress women have made under socialism, this chapter will detail some important remaining problems.

*The Prerevolutionary Legacy*

Most socialist societies were formerly peasant societies, where women's oppression was severe. For example, in the USSR's Central Asian region, women

> were bought and sold like chattels, married off at the age of 10-14. The slightest act of disobedience to husbands was met with savage cruelty. Even after death, the woman had to be lower than her husband—her grave was required to be dug deeper than that of her spouse. Less than one woman out of a thousand was literate. The women were so heavily veiled that even their eyes were hidden. Their national dress included two sleeves sewn together behind their backs as a symbol of their subjugation to God and husband. Their liberation did not come easily. Hundreds were killed savagely in the 1920s during the campaign to throw off the veil, many by being thrown off the roofs of buildings (Marquit 1978, pp. 157-58).

Today, "women constitute 42% of the Uzbek labor force, more than 45% of the elected officials and more than 33% of the PhDs" (p. 158).

In another example, most writers agree that nowhere were women more oppressed than in prerevolutionary China. Foot-binding was a physical expression of their subjugation, but many women were sold in much the same manner as slaves, and women were always under male control: father, husband, and son. But Gordon writes that equally oppressing to these women (as elderly Chinese women reveal when they talk of the old days) was the poverty common to most Chinese people, women and men. Poverty and oppression were their lot, and the end of poverty was as significant to Chinese women as will be their liberation as women (Gordon 1973, p. 28).

As Marquit notes, there was tremendous resistance to the liberation of women. The long, bitter past did not disappear because of legal and economic liberation. In China, when divorce became legal and forced marriages were abolished with the coming of socialism, "100,000 women died from murder or suicide." In response, women organized in groups and often beat recalcitrant men (Gordon, p. 30).

In short, socialism quickly ends legal oppression; economic oppression is ended less quickly, although much progress can be made; social oppression is the most difficult to fight. Women still do most of the housework, and the most powerful positions in the economy and the government are occupied by men. It is because women are still oppressed by housework and other remnants of sexism that complete equality has not been achieved. It is here that the struggle will be long and bitter (Marquit, p. 159).

*Progress and Revolution*

The material, social, and political improvements in China have helped women too. Women's position improves when general social conditions do. Women cannot gain full equality when there are social classes.

The movement for liberation begins with work. In most socialist countries, women constitute 40 to 50 percent of the labor force (in Cuba, with a more recent socialist experience, only 26 percent of the labor force are women). Although many jobs are still sex-segregated, there is a concerted effort to change that condition. In technical education, engineering, and college education in general the numbers of women are increasing (1960–1974 statistics), and in many cases women have achieved equality. In one of the top science schools in Cuba, 50 percent of the students are female. In the USSR, more men are entering medicine (traditionally a women's occupation) and more women are becoming engineers. In 1974, 40 percent of engineering students were women (Marquit 1978, pp. 158–65; Wald 1978, p. 362).

Because of some persisting job segregation, women earn less than men. However, in no socialist society do women have a median income only 54 percent of men's median income. Usually, women make 70 percent or more of what men make.

On the job, women receive substantial benefits. Pregnant women receive two to six months of paid maternity leave. And "in all socialist countries, nursing mothers receive time off for feeding their babies with no loss in pay." Usually, women get two free periods a day, of thirty to forty-five minutes, to nurse their babies who are in nearby nurseries (Marquit, pp. 160, 170). (This is an example showing that biology need not dictate social behavior.)

Women have also begun to move into public life (one of the roles traditional to men, as anthropology has shown). In socialist countries, women are

16 to 32 percent of the members of parliamentary bodies, 23 to 48 percent of local and regional people's councils, and 15 to 31 percent of Communist party members. In contrast, women are 4 percent of the legislators in the United States, 5 percent in France, and 7 percent in Germany (Marquit, p. 177).

The direction of change is shown by the changes in one country, Albania. Before socialism a backward peasant society where women were indisputably subjugated, Albania seems to have made enormous progress. Women constitute 46 percent of the workforce. Their educational attainment almost equals that of men. In politics, women have not gained equality, but they are clearly making progress. From 27 percent to 43 percent of the membership of various levels of political bodies are women (*New Albania* 1979, p. 17).

But the progress is more general and significant. Prostitution, so pervasive in prerevolutionary China and Cuba, has been eliminated. Some individual cases are found, but "prostitution as a social phenomenon . . . has vanished." Writing of China, Diamond notes that birth control is encouraged by all levels of government, there is more child care, and there is a move to train women for leadership positions. For Cuban women, Wald notes the end of prostitution, equal pay for equal work, education made available for boys *and* girls, economic independence and the easing of divorce laws, and the government campaign for men to share housework. In China illiterate women start their own neighborhood factories and quickly pick up extremely complex techniques. They gain enormously in self-confidence and begin the road to true liberation. As anywhere else, women's freedom in China increases when they earn their own money. Gordon stresses that in China women are not treated as sex objects. They wear the same simple clothes that men do. The double standard for sexual behavior does not seem to exist (Marquit, p. 176; Diamond 1975, p. 394; Wald, p. 35; Gordon 1973).

The equality and confidence of !Kung women are evident in the way they walk and carry themselves. Gordon notes the same phenomenon among Chinese women: "young Chinese women walk differently than women in the West, with larger, more swinging steps. Their jaunty, confident stride is the walk of women who are not self-conscious" (p. 33).

Before considering some of the persisting inequalities, we should note that, under socialism, the liberation of women is the goal of state and society. Liberation means more than formal legal equality, for that is true in capitalist societies (at least in the United States). Under socialism, in China and Cuba, for example, the problem of men sharing the housework is political, to be dealt with by the government and in groups. At work and in neighborhoods, women get together to struggle to raise consciousness and improve pay. The disparagement of women by men is exposed and discussed. All these actions become part of the total revolutionary struggle (Croll 1976, pp. 42, 45–46, 50; Gordon, p. 37).

## Persisting Inequalities

In relation to their starting points, socialist countries have made enormous progress in liberating women. But in relation to the goal of total equality, much remains to be done.

In China, women are unequal in pay, access to education, and responsibility for housework. They are also under pressure to have sons. In communes, women do the less prestigious and lower-paying work (Diamond 1975, pp. 374, 387). The Chinese are very aware of these problems. Davin summarizes a *People's Daily* editorial in 1973:

> It criticized the failure to train women cadres in proper numbers, unequal pay for equal work in rural areas, unwillingness to accept women as workers in some factories, and the surviving feudal influences in marriage. It urged that nurseries should be well run, families planned, and household work shared between men and women in order to enable women to take a more effective part in political activities, production, work, and study. Thus in spite of all the progress made by women in China it is officially recognized that their struggle is far from complete (1976, p. 197).

(See also Sidel 1974, pp. 154–55, and Sung Ching-Ling 1975, pp. 35–36 for similar conclusions.)

Women's oppression is most severe in the home. Chinese and Cubans cite no figures, but all note that most housework is still done by women. In the USSR, a survey of steel, machine tool, and textile workers showed women had fourteen fewer hours of free time a week than men did. In the German Democratic Republic, where women are 50 percent of the labor force, they do thirty-seven hours of housework a week, and men only six. Soviet women have been integrated into the workforce where they have substantial equality, but they have only one-third to one-half of men's free time. Social services are limited and men do not share the housework (Cleverdon 1975, p. 30; Marquit 1978, p. 161; Yanowitch 1977, ch. 6; Schwartz 1979).

In political life, women have made substantial gains, but not at the very top. In China, they dominate in local government bodies that are close to home. In the central committees of Communist parties, studies show women were 8 percent in Poland and 10 percent in China (up from 4 percent in 1956). At the very top political positions, women are absent (Gordon 1973, p. 31; Marquit, p. 178; Croll 1976, pp. 47–48).

Women will be limited in public life, in politics, and the professions until the oppression of housework ends. During the child-bearing years especially, the same years that men work to establish themselves in their professions, women simply have less time. For the very highest positions, people must put in many hours of work, and women cannot give so many hours. Day care has been only a partial solution (Marquit, pp. 166–67, 179). (Again, the socialist situation is much better than in the United States. For example, in Minnesota only .5 percent—one-half a percent—of high school principals are women; 27 percent are principals in the USSR).

What is the solution? Are women to copy men in working inordinately long hours advancing their careers? If so, what happens to the children? Increasingly, the avenue to the top will be open to only a few women—as it is open to only a few men. The solution requires changes for all people—men and women—and a society with no ruling class, where all people rule.

The progress in the workplace has been mixed. In China, for example, women have been very active in local community work and in neighborhood factories and shops. Such activity enables women to work and to continue their work as housewives. It integrates home and work. At first glance, such an arrangement seems ideal, until we realize the danger that it may become permanent and institutionalized. If it does, women will be still defined by the role of housewife more than that of worker. Neighborhood factories and shops were a good means to begin the liberation of women, but if liberation stops there, women will not gain equality. For what many Chinese women do is support men's work. They work close to home, thus still being defined as the primary caretakers; they make small items for factories run by men (automobile headlights are one example) and get paid less than men (Burchett and Alley 1976, pp. 87-88, ch. 5; Davin 1976, pp. 196-97).

## CHANGING WOMEN, MEN, AND SOCIETY

Women have been oppressed wherever there are social classes. When inequalities in power and possessions exist, women have suffered from extreme inequality. A division of labor that degraded women existed before capitalism. Capitalism did not invent sexism, but it has strengthened it and is making the economic and social exploitation of women a permanent necessity of its social structure. In the kinds of jobs and pay women get, in forms of socialization and consumption, capitalism has created its own form of sexism (Szymanski 1976, pp. 31-33; Baxandall, Ewen, and Gordon 1976, p. 2).

### *Beyond Economic Liberation*

Mitchell concluded that there are four aspects to the oppression of women: "production, reproduction, sexuality, and the socialization of children." Unless women are liberated in all four, they will not gain full equality (1971, pp. 199, 212).

Participation in the economy is necessary for women's liberation but is not sufficient by itself. Socialist experience tends to contradict, in part, Szymanski's conclusion that only in the United States (and other capitalist societies) are women no longer oppressed at home but rather mostly in the economy. The economic oppression of women that has been the case for centuries has created an ideology, a psychology (in women and men), and institutions that go beyond economic exploitation (although such material conditions gave rise to sexism and continue to provide a base for it) (Croll 1976, p. 40).

The institutions of all societies (especially capitalist ones) do not allow most men to be free, creative, and full human beings. Most women (and most men) will not be liberated if liberation means women are to copy men in competitiveness and the search for power. That way lies inequality for most women and advancement for a few. Men and women must both change their roles, and both must struggle for a society that is liberating for all.

Women must become stronger and men more sensitive to emotions. As Harrison said so well, sensitivity does not exclude strength and assertiveness, and strength does not include violence (1974, p. 125).

The experience of the Israeli kibbutz shows the complexities of freeing people from traditional roles. Women in kibbutzim no longer raised their children and no longer cooked for their families. They held jobs. But all service work (such as cooking and raising children) was done by women. These activities became "jobs" but were still women's work. The highest prestige went to men's jobs, and men did not do "female" work. Unhappy with their low status, kibbutz women sought a partial return of more traditional nuclear-family life. Economic liberation had not been complete liberation (Cleverdon 1975, pp. 30-32).

Day care in itself is not freeing for women as a group. So long as children are raised mostly by women, traditional sex roles will continue. Men and women must raise their children—both in day care sites and at home. Child care must pay more and have higher prestige. Also, when parents have young children and both must work outside the home, the economy must be restructured so that both parents can work less than full time in order to care for the children and share the housework.

All housework must be shared by women and men. Housework cannot be "socialized." Some of it can be eliminated by machines, but there are economic and ecologic limits to the elimination of housework through machinery. The solution lies both in sharing and in having fewer possessions (as noted above, in tribal societies women were less oppressed by housework since they had fewer possessions to care for).

Making some women (or men) "housework specialists" without increased salary or prestige would be just another form of oppression. The freedom of some cannot be bought at the expense of others. Indeed, freedom is not possible for only a few; it must exist for all.

We cannot copy the !Kung, but we can learn from them. !Kung women approached full equality (Draper argues they *were* equal) because of the nature of the whole society. All people worked. There were no leaders, no powerful people (women or men) who could oppress others and who could "succeed" at the expense of the rest.

When men succeed because they devote all their time to a career, and when women do not achieve similar success because more of their time goes to care of children and housework, the solution is not for women to find ways to get others to do the housework and raise the children. The solution is for men not to be allowed to succeed at the expense of others. The very criteria of success and the organization of society must be changed. Women and men must have jobs that are truly fullfilling, and classes and inequalities must be struggled against. In the long run, a society that liberates women can only be a society that liberates all people. The rest of the book will detail the changes in work and political institutions that can create such a society.

## Changes in the United States

Before we can talk about changes, we must be clear where we are. According to Seifer, the ten working-class women to whom she talked did not see men as their enemies. They saw no advantages in leading "men's lives." Rather, they sympathized with the men for their low pay and boring, difficult jobs. Difficult as it may be to accept, for many women marriage has been seen as an escape from the terrible jobs they have held (especially around 1900) (Seifer 1976, p. 30).

Women today do not work because they seek "freedom." They work because they need to—as do men. In this context, their problems are economic. The issues of better jobs, higher wages, and better working conditions apply to women and men. For women as workers, capitalism is the problem, and its solution is a common struggle with men. Working-class women are actual allies with working-class men. And in fact women see it that way, for most women support specific demands for equality (equal pay, opening all jobs to women, and so on) (Baxandall, Gordon, and Reverby 1976:334; Szymanski 1976).

Working women are not liberated. They are exploited, first of all, on the job. Then, since day care is scarce (both in quality and quantity), they have problems arranging for caring for their children (since the children are still their responsibility). Nobody seems to know what millions of working women do with their children.

It is true that working wives get more power within their families. Having their own money gives them more confidence and bargaining power. Also, they do less housework than nonworking wives, twenty-six hours a week versus fifty-five hours, and their husbands help them (the husbands do not *share*). Combining work outside and at home, women put in sixty-six hours, more than the fifty-five hours of nonworking wives (Szymanski, pp. 36-37, 43).

Despite all the problems women workers encounter, women's constantly increasing participation in work outside the home is bound to affect other areas and institutions. For example, who will care for the children? Can schools continue to have as many days off when both parents work full time? As little girls grow up and see their mothers and other women working, will their self-images and expectations improve? As men and women take it for granted that both must work, will there be an eventual full sharing of housework? Such sharing is emerging very slowly; how long will it be before housework is shared? In another area, if women gradually gain equality at work, can male social and political institutions resist change?

Their increasing participation in the workforce is the most important and most visible change in women's lives. In the long run it should have the profoundest ramifications. But unless we are careful, women may become a permanently segregated and low-paid part of the workforce (as the data cited above indicate). Changes are inevitable, but not inevitably positive. We must struggle to insure positive changes.

In various contexts, women are working to gain control of their lives. For example, the women's self-help movement in health care is growing. Women are seeking to gain the knowledge and technology of medicine without the ideology (Ehrenreich and English 1973, p. 84). But like all struggles under capitalism, these are difficult to continue and people active in them wear out (for one example, see Galper and Washburne 1976).

Dave Slaney (a sociologist and personal friend) once told me, "You can't have socialism in one family." We were talking about the difficulties of ensuring that girls are not affected by a sexist society and the things we can do as parents. As my daughters are growing (ages four and one-half and two and one-half as I write), I begin to see the truth. In our neighborhood, girls, beginning at age four or five, seem not to play with boys. They play mostly "girl" games. My wife and I try to choose nonsexist books and to change the language of sexist ones. We talk about girls and boys and their essential similarities. Sometimes I think some benefit will result from all these efforts, but mostly I feel pessimistic.

Harrison details the two-year struggle at her children's (private) schools to fight sexism. It was an enormous undertaking. By 1972, some changes had taken place. Here are some, as related by second-, third-, and fourth-grade teachers.

> "It used to be that when a girl complained she couldn't handle the saw at the woodworking bench, I'd call upon a competent child to help her, to make the activity less teacher-directed. Nine out of ten times, of course, the 'competent child' was a boy, who wanted to get to the bench anyway. Now I'm much more likely to get that girl to do it herself, even if it involves struggle. I tell her she doesn't have to do it all in one day. The idea is not that all girls have to be whizzes at woodworking, but that they learn not to lean on or be intimidated by the superior strength or ability of boys."
>
> "I'm not even aware of all the things I do now, but I see the difference in the kids. Even the smallest girls now play kickball in outdoor games, the same ones that used to group together, and 'tell secrets,' and withdraw from physical activities. A lot of the girls wanted to play soccer, but were scared to compete with the boys. I started to play soccer with them, and that helped. Some

## STRUGGLES: Organizing Office Workers

*In the 1970s much attention was given to various aspects of the women's movement. Little was written about the lives of most working women, however. The following accounts describe the organization and some of the successes of a group working to improve conditions for the largest group of working women, office workers.*

Working Women, National Association of Office Workers, is a pioneer in workplace change, breaking new ground in the women's movement, and acting to improve the quality of working life for the nation's 20 million women office workers.

Our roots are in the first meeting of ten women in downtown Boston, nearly six years ago. At that first gathering, women discovered they had many experiences in common. Whether employed in banks, insurance companies or universities, the office environment often denied women satisfaction of such basic needs as adequate pay and job security. Women were consistently frustrated in attainment of esteem and self-actualization on the job.

So, in 1973, women decided to reach out to other office workers and to change the conditions of their employment, and the working women's movement of today was born.

Six years later, the original office workers' groups have established firm local identities, demonstrated their ability to win stronger enforcement of anti-discrimination laws, change unfair employment practices, and raise the issues to the public.

Working Women, sponsored by organizations in Boston, Cleveland and San Francisco, helps establish new groups of women office workers, provides training for staff, produces resource materials, counsels groups on-site, and more. Working Women also coordinates regional campaigns to end discrimination, directs national events, and conducts programs of public outreach.

Today, Working Women has members in forty states and is affiliated with groups in a dozen cities acting together to make lasting changes in the lives of working women.

The organization [9 to 5, another women's organization] has clout. It has the makings of a new, major national movement. It has already scored significant achievements, especially when one considers that, for its first year, according to Cassidy [director of 9 to 5], the members couldn't decide whether it was worthwhile to charge dues and recruit new members.

Even today, 9 to 5 is unsure whether it is really a labor organization, a feminist group, a special interest group or a greatly oversized career development association.

Why have women office workers [proved] so susceptible to organization? "It comes down to the way you're treated," says Pat Cronin, 29, a publishing company employee and currently the elected "chair" of 9 to 5. "When you see incompetent men brought in from outside the company to fill important positions while perfectly competent, trained women are sitting right there. When you see some women spending their whole lives earning less than most men earn the first year they work, it reinforces the fact that something has had to be done."

At 9 to 5, the motivation has not come from feminist ideology, whatever the personal feelings of some of the members. "We've got people who want to join who come in referring to 50-year-old women as 'girls,' and nobody jumps up to correct them," says Cassidy. "Many people ask us for help, saying things like, 'I'm not one of those women's libbers, but my boss is being unfair.' The last thing we want to do is turn them off by being strident."

The practical problems women office workers face are enough, says Cassidy, to generate members

*Source: A New Movement of Working Women* (pamphlet). Reprinted with permission of Working Women, National Association of Office Workers (Cleveland, Ohio, 1979); and Phil Plampied, "9 to 5: Dealing Successfully with Problems of Women Office Workers, *The Washington Star*, December 2, 1978. Copyright 1978 Time Inc. All rights reserved.

*(continued)*

214   THE OPPRESSION OF WOMEN

> **Organizing Office Workers** *(continued)*
> for 9 to 5 and give the organization an urgent sense of purpose. Of these, the statistically documented wage differential between men and women is the most basic. . . .
> In Boston, prodding government agencies has been a major part of 9 to 5 strategy. It was the intervention of the Massachusetts attorney general's office that won the $750,000 discrimination payback at Houghton Mifflin. Now, the attorney general is helping 9 to 5 members sue Houghton Mifflin again (for a different class of employee), as well as the publishing companies Addison-Wesley and Allyn and Bacon.

of the boys made fun of the girls for being inept, and that scared them off again. . . . I didn't treat that as a boy-girl thing; we just had long talks about how people related to others whose skills weren't as developed as theirs. I think it made the boys feel easier too, not to have to insist on their physical superiority."

"I now assign chores like housekeeping, clean-up, messengering, mopping, straightening up, without regard to sex. I used to say, 'Is there a strong boy who'll help me carry chairs?' A seventh-grade girl pointed out to me that that was silly; she said, 'We're just as capable of carrying chairs as boys are. And you're not asking them because they're stronger. You're asking them, to make them feel stronger.' She was right of course."

I heard this story about a girl in my class: she went to her doctor's office, and a little boy who was getting an injection was crying. The boy's father said, 'Boys have to be brave.' Jenny, the Woodward girl, said, 'I don't think boys have to be brave all the time, boys can cry.' The nurse humored her and said, 'That's right, honey, girls are really stronger, aren't they?' And Jenny said, 'No, girls aren't stronger; girls can cry and girls can be brave. Boys can cry and boys can be brave. It's what you feel like.' Jenny is seven" (pp. 166–69).

The long-term effect of such changes is unknown. Nevertheless, we have no choice but to struggle on all fronts, for, until women are free, men cannot be. Freedom cannot be achieved under capitalism, but the struggle for women's liberation can be the beginning of the road to a socialist society, with liberation for all people in all contexts and institutions.

# 9

# *Racism and Capitalism*

INTRODUCTION

Racism is a problem for people of all ethnic and racial backgrounds. Minorities suffer because of economic exploitation and personal degradation; those in the majority suffer because racism divides working people and prevents them from working together for a just society.

This chapter will try to show how racism arose and continues as an economic institution to meet the needs of capitalism and also that racism results in profound personal injuries. We must remember that racism is part of a system of exploitation, where blacks and other minorities suffer today, just as still other ethnic minorities have been exploited in the past.

Whenever societies come in contact with each other, conflicts frequently result. Sometimes there are wars. Often, as the Athenians did, the victors enslave the loser. Ethnocentrism is common—people of each society tend to consider their culture superior to the culture of other societies. At the very least, people of each society prefer their way of life.

But racism as it has existed in the Western world since the fifteenth century (see Chapter 6) is a unique phenomenon because of its worldwide nature; it has dominated world history in that time, as this section will try to show.

There are three broad levels of explanation for racism and minority oppression today. Probably the most common explanation focuses on cultural and ethnic conflicts; racism is considered an extreme form of ethnocentrism. (Most sociology textbooks espouse a version of this explanation.) Differences between customs, traditions, and life-styles—and between competing economic interests—cause tension, conflict, and sometimes war.

Another explanation focuses on individuals in each society or group and how they become prejudiced against people in the other group. When we are born into a society or ethnic group, we inherit its culture. Part of that culture is attitudes and prejudices against other ethnic groups. Thus, I was raised in Greece, where hatred of Turks and distrust of Jews are part of Greek culture. Learning Greek culture included prejudices against Turks and Jews. For most whites reading this book, cultural learning has included various attitudes against blacks and other groups. All of you probably remember certain common sayings of your parents and others.

This second explanation tells how we learn prejudice in our culture, but it does not help us understand how and why that prejudice arose. The mechanisms by which prejudice perpetuates itself are not the same as its origins. This explanation also does not show how racism can continue for five centuries merely by parents passing it on to their children, without regard for social, economic, political, and material conditions. These are the foundations for racism.

The socialist perspective on racism focuses on historical and contemporary conditions that have given rise to slavery, racism, the continuing exploitation of many minorities, and individual prejudices. Slavery and racism, I will argue, were economic institutions. They arose to serve the needs of European and American capitalists in their exploitation of people throughout the world. Capitalism meant racism; capitalism became possible, largely, because of the exploitation of people everywhere. To justify such exploitation, theories of other peoples' "inferiority" arose in time.

In looking at contemporary racism, socialists take two different views. While all agree on the historical uses of racism for capitalist profits, some argue that capitalism today has no use for racism, but it has created a monster which it does not know how to destroy. Others (I include myself here) argue that racism is still useful to capitalism. Blacks and others make lower wages, thus creating higher profits, and racism divides people of different groups, thus making it difficult for them to unite and fight for their common social and economic interests.

Two key points are often forgotten. Although blacks have been the most exploited group, they have not been the only one. Native Americans, European immigrants from all nations, Mexican-Americans, Puerto Ricans, Chinese, and others have all been exploited as cheap labor. We cannot ignore them. Secondly, capitalism plays no favorites. Whites of the dominant culture have been—and still are—exploited in many ways. Just as one example, people of Appalachia (see Chapter 7) have been utterly devastated by the coal companies. As discussed in Chapters 2 and 3, most of us are victimized by capitalism. Minority people have simply been the most oppressed of an exploited population.

## THE RISE OF SLAVERY, RACISM, AND MINORITY EXPLOITATION

Slavery and racism originated in specific economic and political conditions, which we need to understand in order to see why we have racism today, to understand who benefits by racism, and to educate ourselves on what we must do to end it.

Slavery was central to the rise of capitalism, both because of the profits made from the slave trade, and because of the greater profits produced by cheap labor (the following account is based on Baron 1971; Cox 1976; Williams 1944; and Meier and Rudwick 1970).

Capitalism left its first mark on English and other European cultures. When settlers came to the United States, slavery was not the first institution of cheap, exploitable labor; white indentured servants from Europe were the first source. These were poor people, some convicted of crimes, who had had their passage to America paid in exchange for a period of seven (sometimes more) years of labor owed to whoever had paid for their passage. At the end of the indentured period, they were free.

From 1654 to 1683, 10,000 servants sailed from Bristol alone for Virginia and the West Indies. European convicts became one source of white labor for the new colonies. Williams argues that the status of servants became worse in time, coming close to slavery (1944, pp. 10, 16).

But indentured servants apparently did not provide an adequate supply of labor for the plantations of the English colonies and the West Indies. Also, their servitude was not permanent. Native Americans were used for a time as servants and slaves, but they also did not solve the labor problem. They could not accustom themselves to the discipline of the work, and they could always run away to their native lands.

So merchants and plantation owners turned to Africa for cheap, plentiful, and permanent labor. According to some historians, slavery itself developed gradually. The first blacks from Africa used for labor were indentured servants. As commercial farming grew in its need for more workers, slavery, and racist laws and beliefs to justify slavery, came into existence.

The profitability of slavery was obvious to contemporaries. In the words of a nineteenth-century economist:

> The most-approved judges of the commercial interest of these kingdoms have ever been of the opinion that our West Indian and African trades are the most nationally-beneficial of any carried on. It is also allowed on all hands that the trade to Africa is the branch which renders our American colonies and plantations so advantageous to Great Britain; that traffic only affording our plant-

ers a constant supply of Negro servants for the culture of their lands in the produce of sugar, tobacco, rice, rum, cotton, pimento, and all plantation produce; so that the extensive employment of our shipping into and from our American colonies, the great brook of seamen consequent thereupon, and the daily bread of the most-considerable part of our British manufacturers, are owing primarily to the labor of Negroes (in Baron 1971, pp. 5-6).

Similarly, merchants in the United States profited immensely from the slave trade:

> Merchants in all sections of the mainland provinces participated in the slave trade, but pre-eminent were those from the Massachusetts and Rhode Island seaports. Rhode Island entered the slave trade much later than Massachusetts, probably around the beginning of the eighteenth century. By mid-century Newport and Providence surpassed their rivals in Boston and Salem. From then until the official closing of the slave trade in 1808, the traffic flourished in Rhode Island and formed the basis of some of the greatest fortunes in the state (Meier and Rudwick 1970, pp. 30-31).

Slavery was beneficial only to merchants and large plantation owners. Slave labor in the sugar plantations of the West Indies resulted in the creation of a small class of rich whites, millions of exploited slaves, and the eventual destruction of a class of small white farmers. (Indeed, in the United States, black indentured servants and slaves staged periodic uprisings from 1663 on, sometimes together with poor whites.) After the slave trade and slavery were abolished by the British in the early nineteenth century, the plantation owners of the West Indies began importing cheap labor from other sources, chiefly from India (a colony of the British Empire). And British merchants continued to import sugar and other products from the slave plantations of Brazil and other places. Thus, slavery was not inherently connected to blacks. It was an economic institution of capitalism, which exploited people everywhere (Williams, pp. 24-29).

After slavery was instituted, racist laws and beliefs began to develop to justify slavery. Elaborate theories on the natural inferiority of blacks followed the creation of slavery as an economic institution under capitalism. In addition, there were some free blacks, and if they were allowed to be considered equal to whites, they might serve to repudiate the racist theories justifying slavery. Thus, plantation owners worked to pass laws against all blacks, focusing on race, not merely slavery, as a justification (Baron, pp. 9-10).

Slaves were used on sugar and other plantations. Around 1800 the need for slavery was increased with the invention of machines for the spinning and weaving of cotton, and the use of steam and water power for the production of cloth. Industrial capitalists needed cotton, which was grown by slaves in large plantations.

Recently there has been much controversy on the profitability of slavery and on the effects it had on the slaves. These issues are beyond the scope of this book. But a few things can be said about how slaves reacted to their condition and what slavery did to them.

Periodically, there were slave uprisings and rebellions. They began in 1663, and sometimes poor whites joined the rebel slaves. More often, individual slaves tried to escape to free states. While in slavery, malingering and self-inflicted injuries were used to avoid work. Sometimes even suicide was chosen over enslavement.

Frederick Douglass, a slave in the 1830s who escaped to freedom, has left a clear description of the daily horrors of slavery. Only fear would make slaves work, so owners tried to "inspire this fear" (1854, p. 216). To prevent any advancement, slaves were not allowed to learn to read and write. Whites who taught them, as well as other slaves, were stopped from doing so. In addition, slaves were forbidden from speaking their native African language or practicing their culture (the Irish, colonized by the British, were forced to stop speaking Gaelic, another example of how capitalism destroys native cultures). Despite severe persecution, Douglass managed to learn how to read and write (1854, pp. 145–47).

For most slaves, slavery meant daily anguish. Douglass provides a graphic description of how slaves who resisted were "broken" to adjust them to their fate (pp. 205–247). Beatings and starvation were common. The songs of the slaves attested to their condition. Their spirituals were "tones, long, loud, and deep, breathing the prayer and complaint of souls boiling over with the bitterest anguish. Every tone was a testimony against slavery... (p. 99). (During 1845–46 Douglass visited Ireland, which was suffering from a famine, and wrote, "I heard the same *wailing notes,* and was much affected by them" (italics in original)... (p. 98).

But slavery was not maintained entirely by force and fear. Cunning and manipulation were used. Douglass, writing of the occasional holidays slaves were given, shows how the owners used such free time to strengthen slavery.

> To enslave men, successfully and safely, it is necessary to have their minds occupied with thoughts and aspirations short of the liberty of which they are deprived. A certain degree of attainable good must be kept before them. These holidays serve the purpose of keeping the minds of the slaves occupied with prospective pleasure, within the limits of slavery. The young men can go wooing; the married man can visit his wife; the father and mother can see their children; the industrious and money loving can make a few dollars; the great wrestler can win laurels; the young people can meet, and enjoy each other's society; the drunken man can get plenty of whiskey; and the religious man can hold prayer meetings, preach, pray and exhort during the holidays. Before the holidays, these are pleasures in prospect; after the holidays, they become pleasures of memory, and they serve to keep out thoughts and wishes of a more dangerous character. Were slaveholders at once to abandon the practice of allowing their slaves these liberties, periodically, and to keep them, the year round, closely confined to the narrow circle of their homes, I doubt not that

the south would blaze with insurrections. These holidays are conductors or safety valves to carry off the explosive elements inseparable from the human mind, when reduced to the condition of slavery. But for these, the rigors of bondage would become too severe for endurance, and the slave would be forced up to dangerous desperation.... It is plain, that everything like rational enjoyment among the slaves, is frowned upon; and only those wild and low sports, peculiar to semi-civilized people, are encouraged. All the license allowed, appears to have no other object than to disgust the slaves with their temporary freedom, and to make them as glad to return to their work, as they were to leave it. By plunging them into exhausting depths of drunkenness and dissipation, this effect is almost certain to follow. I have known slaveholders resort to cunning tricks, with a view of getting their slaves deplorably drunk. A usual plan is, to make bets on a slave, that he can drink more whisky than any other; and so to induce a rivalry among them, for the mastery in this degradation. The scenes, brought about in this way, were often scandalous and loathsome in the extreme. Whole multitudes might be found stretched out in brutal drunkenness, at once helpless and disgusting.... When a slave is drunk, the slaveholder has no fear that he will plan an insurrection; no fear that he will escape to the north. It is the sober, thinking slave who is dangerous, and needs the vigilance of his master, to keep him a slave (pp. 253-56).

This is the best analysis I have seen of how oppressors try to manipulate oppressed people. You surely can think of many parallels, past and present.

The Civil War freed the slaves in law but not in fact. There was a brief period when blacks made some legal gains, but the failure to provide them with an economic foundation (land and jobs) returned them to virtual slavery. The 1877 Compromise assured their fate: the Northern capitalists allowed the Southern plantation owners and the new industrialists to use blacks as cheap labor. Plantation owners of the period speak of blacks as good and cheap workers (Baron, p. 13). Economically, most blacks became sharecroppers and were in constant debt to the owners of the land.

The Jim Crow laws segregating blacks and denying them the vote began to be passed in the late nineteenth century. They too made blacks into virtual slaves. In addition, lynchings, prisons, and chain gangs (doubly exploited labor), blacks' continued economic dependence (true of many poor whites too), and their socialization as obedient workers served to keep black people oppressed.

A word about education for blacks: many whites wanted to keep them uneducated, but the more "enlightened" new industrialists (North and South) saw the value of limited education. It would provide blacks with some skills, and the proper attitudes for obedience, to make them better workers. Liberal education was out, but practical education would produce dependable workers. Thus, industrialists worked to provide education for blacks. Rockefeller was among them. Many contemporaries saw the practical advantages to themselves of a trained black labor force. Anderson concludes that "the industrialists were interested in education as a subtle and systematic form of coercion that would subjugate blacks and create an inexpensive labor force. Also, a key concern of the industrialists was to manipulate labor to their advantage through creating a docile, tractable black working force that would be insurance against the spread of unionized white labor" (1975, p. 22).

One way to fight unionization of white workers was the use of blacks as strikebreakers. Baron argues that blacks were not used often as strikebreakers (other whites were), but racist conditions made those cases very noticeable. But the reality and perception of blacks as strikebreakers, and even more the conscious manipulation of laws and race relations by the ruling classes of the South, worked to defeat any populist alliance of poor whites and blacks. For a while around 1900, there was the promise of an alliance between poor whites and blacks, working together to advance their common interests. Remember that most whites too were poor, many of them sharecroppers. White workers and farmers were given a "bargain": racial superiority over blacks in exchange for consignment to low wages, poverty, and exploitation (Baron, pp. 14, 19; Woodward 1957, pp. 60–64; Agee and Evans 1941). This was not an openly recognized condition, of course, either on the part of the ruling class or the white workers. The creation of this economic, legal, and social system had the *effect* of dividing black and white workers (see below) and discriminating against blacks. Only in this sense did white workers "gain" socially and psychically; they were still exploited economically.

So blacks entered the twentieth century oppressed by laws and economic institutions. Richard Wright's *Black Boy* exposes the fears and oppressive conditions of daily life for blacks in the first three decades of this century. It is a description very similar to the description of slavery provided by Douglass. We see how Wright, as a little boy, learned about discrimination and the conditions blacks had to endure. He saw violence; his uncle was killed in the middle of the night and the family had to run away. Like the slaves, he was supposed to smile constantly, not to show any serious thinking. Degradations, fears, and poverty were daily realities. Lynching, and the fear of it, provided the harshest reminder of blacks' oppression. As some people have said, this time was one of the darkest hours in the history of black people in the United States.

During this period (late nineteenth to early twentieth centuries) anthropologists, sociologists, psychologists, and other social scientists wrote many papers and books supposedly proving the natural inferiority of blacks, East and South Europeans, Asians, Mexican Americans, and others. Such questionable findings seemed to justify the continued discrimination of "inferior" people and were also used to close immigration from East and South Europe and Asia.

Ironically, the ending of immigration in the 1920s may have helped to speed up the migration of blacks to northern cities. The labor shortages of the two World Wars and the mechanization of farming were the two primary reasons for the migration of blacks out of the rural South, but the ending of cheap immigrant labor made it necessary to find a new source. Blacks became that source (Greer 1976). But while blacks did get industrial jobs, they were kept in the lowest job categories. Some U.S. Steel Corporation officers consciously placed job quotas on blacks, keeping them out of many jobs:

> When we got [up to 10 percent black] employees, I said [to the employment manager], "No more colored without discussion." I got the colored pastors to send colored men whom they could guarantee would not organize and were not bolsheviks.... It isn't good to have all of one nationality; they will gang up on you.... We have Negroes and Mexicans in a sort of competition with each other. It's a dirty trick, but we don't have the kind of work that will break a man down.... Negroes are nice, simple people. I don't approve of using them for skilled work—not that they couldn't do it, but we have enough competition within the skilled groups. Let the Negroes scramble for the unskilled jobs (quoted in Greer, p. 51).

Thus, 80 to 90 percent of black people were working the land in 1900, but in 1940 50 percent lived in urban areas, and in 1970 "fewer than 5 percent of America's 22.3 million blacks [worked] the land" (Piven and Cloward 1971, p. 214). Whereas for years black people were exploited as farm workers, today they are exploited by capitalism in other ways, as discussed below.

### Other Minorities

Although black people are unique in having been exploited from the beginning of capitalism, they are not alone. United States capitalism used many other groups for cheap labor.

Michael Gold writes that "America is so rich and fat, because it has eaten the tragedy of millions of immigrants" (in Miller, ed., 1972, p. 214). But slaves, Native Americans, Mexican-Americans, and others are part of this tragedy. A superb collection edited by Wayne Miller, *A Gathering of Ghetto Writers,* shows that each immigrant group (whatever their reasons for coming to the United States) was exploited: at work, in the ghetto, and against each other. Immigrant workers were old at forty, and accidents were a daily experience (Greer 1976).

The Irish were the first European immigrants to be exploited by United States industrial capitalism (they came to escape the famines created by British imperialism). From 1830 to 1870, there were many planned and spontaneous riots and rebellions by Irish workers. When the Irish began to unionize, factory owners turned to Italian immigrants, who were not yet organized. Miller's collection shows many instances of how capitalism pitted ethnic groups against each other (pp. 7, 28).

Other groups were exploited in different ways. Native Americans, of course, were the first. Their lands were stolen in many ways. That story is well known by now. Less well-known is the continued theft of Indian lands today (see below) (Brandon 1974).

Also, Jacobs and Landau, in their documentary history *To Serve the Devil* (1971) explore the oppression of Chicanos (Mexican-Americans), Hawaiians, Chinese, Japanese, Puerto Ricans, as well as blacks. (See below for brief discussion of Chicanos and Puerto Ricans.)

## MINORITIES TODAY

In 1976, there were 23.8 million black Americans, about 11 percent of the United States population. In addition, there were 10.5 million Hispanics (in 1973): 6.3 million Chicanos (Mexican-Americans) and 1.5 million Puerto Ricans, with the rest being "persons of Central or South American, Cuban, and other Spanish origin." Finally, in 1970 about 800,000 people considered themselves "Indian" (*Statistical Abstract* 1977, pp. 30, 33).

Most minority statistics on employment and income relate to black people, so these will be considered first, along with some other important conditions of minority living today.

*Occupations and Income*

How many black people do work? In 1960, 80.1 percent of black men were in the labor force, and 47.2 percent of black women (82.6 and 36 percent for white men and women). But by 1978, 70.8 percent of black men were in the labor force, (as compared to 78 percent of white men). Both percentages of men workers went down, but black men much more. In 1978, 52.8 percent of black women were in the labor force (and 48.8 percent of white women). Thus, the percentage of black men workers has decreased substantially, the percentage of white women workers has increased even more, but white men and black women stayed about the same (*Statistical Abstract* 1979, p. 392).

What about unemployment rates? They have gone from 10.2 percent in 1960 (for "black and other," except whites), to 8.2 percent in 1970, 13.9 percent in 1975, 13.1 percent in 1976 and 1977, 11.9 percent in 1978, and 13.9 percent in May 1980. But the rate of black unemployment has been about twice that of white unemployment (varying from 1.8 to 2.3 percent) (*Statistical Abstract* 1979, p. 404; Pine 1980). But these figures do not tell the whole story: they hide the millions of blacks who have given up hope of finding a job, have stopped looking for one, and thus are no longer listed as unemployed; they also hide the very high joblessness of young blacks. While official statistics showed that 28 percent looking for work did not find it in 1979, a Labor Department study of 17,693 youths showed that the unemployment rate among black youths was 38.8 percent. Specific cities show catastrophic rates. In 1975, in Charlotte, North Carolina, an estimated 90 percent of young blacks were jobless (Elam 1980; States News Service 1980; Thomas and Scott 1979; Rich 1976).

Table 9.1 shows the kinds of work minority people do. Since 1960, they have moved into some white-collar jobs, mostly in clerical positions (from 7.3 to 16.9 percent) and other low-paying jobs. Managerial and administrative jobs are still held mostly by white people.

In one company, U.S. Steel, blacks have one-third the chance of holding white-collar or managerial positions. Against laws and court rulings, U.S. Steel continues to promote whites systematically over blacks, even when the blacks are more qualified (Greer 1976, pp. 58–61).

In terms of individual income, black men make considerably less than white men. Black women, on the other hand, make almost as much as white women (but both black and white women make considerably less than men, as discussed in the last chapter). Tables 9.2a and 9.2b show details. Table 9.2a shows that in May 1978 the median weekly income of black full-time

**TABLE 9.1** Employed Persons, Percent Distribution by Occupation and Race, 1960 and 1978

|  | White | | Black and other | |
| --- | --- | --- | --- | --- |
|  | 1960 | 1978 | 1960 | 1978 |
| White-collar | 46.6 | 51.8 | 16.1 | 36.2 |
|   Managers and administrators | 11.7 | 11.4 | 2.6 | 4.8 |
|   Clerical | 13.7 | 18.0 | 7.3 | 16.9 |
| Blue-collar | 36.2 | 32.9 | 40.1 | 37.2 |
|   Operatives | 17.9 | 14.6 | 20.4 | 20.5 |
| Service workers | 9.9 | 12.3 | 31.7 | 24.1 |
| Farmworkers | 7.4 | 3.0 | 12.1 | 2.4 |
|  | 100% | 100% | 100% | 100% |

Source: *Statistical Abstract* 1979, p. 416.

**TABLE 9.2a** Median Weekly Earnings of Full-Time Wage and Salary Workers, by Race and Sex, May 1978

| Race and sex | Median weekly earnings |
| --- | --- |
| White |  |
|   Both sexes | $232 |
|   Men | $279 |
|   Women | $167 |
| Black |  |
|   Both sexes | $181 |
|   Men | $213 |
|   Women | $156 |

Source: U.S. Department of Labor 1978c.

**TABLE 9.2b** Median Usual Weekly Earnings of Full-Time Wage and Salary Workers, by Occupation, Sex, and Race and Hispanic Origin, May 1978

| Occupation | All races Men | All races Women | White | Black | Hispanic origin[a] |
|---|---|---|---|---|---|
| White-collar workers | $325 | $185 | $245 | $216 | $192 |
|   Professional and technical workers | 344 | 246 | 296 | 251 | 249 |
|   Managers and administrators except farm | 361 | 212 | 325 | 281 | 256 |
|   Sales workers | 283 | 129 | 234 | 168 | 169 |
|   Clerical workers | 255 | 165 | 174 | 182 | 165 |
| Blue-collar workers | 253 | 146 | 237 | 186 | 185 |
|   Craft and kindred workers | 285 | 164 | 283 | 237 | 233 |
|   Operatives, except transport | 236 | 145 | 197 | 168 | 157 |
|   Transport equipment operatives | 252 | 148 | 260 | 200 | 228 |
|   Nonfarm laborers | 202 | 143 | 198 | 172 | 177 |
| Service workers | 189 | 123 | 153 | 137 | 136 |
|   Private household workers | (b) | 59 | 54 | 94 | (b) |
|   Other service workers | 189 | 126 | 155 | 141 | 141 |
| Farm workers | 142 | 121 | 144 | 110 | 144 |

[a] Data on persons of Hispanic origin are tabulated separately, without regard to race, which means that they are also included in the data for white and black workers. At the time of the 1970 Census, approximately 96 percent of their population was white.
[b] Median not shown were the universe is less than 75,000.
Source: U.S. Department of Labor 1978c.

workers was 78 percent of the median for white full-time workers (76.2 percent for black men, 93.4 percent for black women). Table 9.2b compares some specific job categories by race. For example, black blue-collar workers made a weekly median income 78.5 percent of what white blue-collar workers made.

In terms of family income, in 1977 the median income for all families was $16,060. It was $16,782 for white families and $9,485 for black families (*Statistical Abstract* 1979, p. 454). That is 57 percent of the income of white families. Table 9.3 shows interesting changes in the relation of black to white family income. Relatively, black family income went up from 1947 to 1952, went down until 1958, and then made significant increases from 1958 (51 percent) to 1970 (64 percent). It has continued to decline since and seems to have leveled off at 60 percent. The effects of unemployment and underemployment on family income are significant. In 1977, black families made 57 percent of what white families made. But comparing families that had a "head full-time worker, employed year-round," black families made 73 percent of what white families did *(Statistical Abstract* 1977, p. 445; 1979, p. 454). But greater unemployment, discrimination keeping them from better-paying jobs, lower labor force participation rates, and probably more part-time work, combine to make black family incomes even lower than this 73 percent.

**TABLE 9.3** Black Family Income as a Percentage of White Family Income

| Year | Percentage |
|------|------------|
| 1947 | 51 |
| 1952 | 57 |
| 1958 | 51 |
| 1963 | 53 |
| 1967 | 62 |
| 1970 | 64 |
| 1971 | 63 |
| 1972 | 62 |
| 1973 | 60 |
| 1976 | 59 |
| 1977 | 57 |

Source: Thurow 1976, p. 8; Statistical Abstract 1977, pp. 441, 445; 1979, p. 454.

Old blacks suffer the heritage of the low-paying jobs and unemployment of their working years. When they retire, they are three times more likely to be poor than are whites (Hicks 1977, p. 141).

Data show clearly that black people made economic gains in the 1950s and 1960s but have not in the 1970s. In 1955, black full-time, full-year men workers made 56 percent of white full-time, full-year men workers; 61 percent in 1968; 66 percent in 1973; and 62 percent in 1977. For black women in relation to white women, the figures were 56 percent in 1955; 77 percent in 1968; 86 percent in 1973; and 90 percent in 1977 (Thurow 1976, p. 6; *Statistical Abstract* 1979, p. 460).

Because in the 1970s there were no rebellions in the black ghettoes, many people probably thought that the economic and social problems of black people had been either solved or reduced. The uprisings in Watts, Detroit, and elsewhere were thought to be a thing of the past. In the spring of 1980 events in Miami indicated that profound problems persist. Fires and violence in that city were sparked by a specific incident: a jury found four white police innocent after they had beaten to death a black man they had arrested. The more important and continuing causes, however, were joblessness, poverty, low incomes, discrimination, neglect by the government, and general racism. Miami was a warning that black people have made little progress, that they are still oppressed from racism and exploitation (Williams 1980b; Bradlee 1980).

*Other Minorities*

The data presented in the preceding section pertain mostly to black people. Some government statistics are about black people only, others distinguish only between "white" and "other," "other" including many groups some of which will be discussed here.

*Native Americans.* There are about one million Native Americans (depending on the definition they or others use), not a large number, but their historical and contemporary significance is enormous. In the last ten years much has been written on the theft of their lands and the destruction of their cultures by expanding United States capitalism. But the focus has been almost entirely on the past. Today, Native Americans are still being robbed by various corporate interests. Their water rights are attacked by corporate farmers, mining companies seek to explore and therefore devastate their lands, and white ranchers own land on reservations and seek to control even more (Brandon 1974, p. 439; Regal 1976). With their best lands taken away, those Native Americans seeking to hold on to their cultures on reservations face enormous poverty. Conditions on the Oglala Sioux reservation are typical of other reservations:

> Only eight per cent of the reservation is suitable for dryland farming. There are very few other jobs of any kind within reach. . . . One-third of the people had a family income, counting welfare and any other nickels and dimes from any source, of less than $999 per year; nearly one-half of the people were on some kind of welfare (average amount less than $25 per month per person); half of the people were still living in one- or two-room mud-caulked log houses and some hundreds in tents winter as well as summer; nine out of ten homes had no electricity, nineteen out of twenty no running water, with most householders transporting water a quarter-mile or more (Brandon 1974, p. 433).

*Chicanos (Mexican-Americans).* The exploitation and discrimination of Chicanos has a long history. A late chapter, the Mexican-American War of 1846, opposed by some Americans then as the Vietnam war was opposed in our day, resulted in the annexation of Mexican land by the United States. From the beginning, Chicanos have been discriminated against in "jobs, housing, voting, education, civil rights, organizations, and social activities." Their best lands were taken away from them and they have been forced to take low-paying jobs, first in agriculture and later in urban areas (Burma and Leon 1978, p. 122).

In the nineteenth century, Chicanos were the Negroes of the Southwest. Although legally free, their lives were no better than those of the slaves in the South. Historically, they have been poorer than the poorest Mississippi blacks. Prejudice against them was pervasive. They were seen as "treacherous, childlike, primitive, lazy, and irresponsible" (Jacobs and Landau 1971, vol. 1, p. 239). (In the 1950s, in Worcester, Massachusetts, where hardly any Chicanos lived, prejudice against them still showed itself. In a restaurant where I worked, whenever we wanted to comment on people's laziness and slowness, we would call them "speedy González.")

In California in the nineteenth century, beatings and lynchings of Chicanos were frequent. Even though outright physical and social persecution abated in the twentieth century, economic discrimination and exploitation continued. When corporate farming came to the Southwest early in this century, white tenant farmers were replaced by Chicano workers who provided very cheap labor. But when the Depression came in the 1930s and Mexican nationals were deported from the United States by the hundreds of thousands, many Chicanos (American citizens) also were deported. In a racist climate, Mexican-Americans were not treated as United States citizens.

Today, the Chicanos are this country's second largest minority. There were about 7.15 million in 1978. Of these, 77 percent lived in urban areas, and of them 43 percent lived in central-city ghettoes. Most Chicanos live in Arizona, California, Colorado, New Mexico, and Texas (*Statistical Abstract* 1979, p. 33; Burma and Leon 1978, pp. 105-106).

Some are farmworkers still. Their battles to unionize themselves (late 1960s-1970s) were long, bitter, and violent; some people lost their lives during strikes. But with unions came modest wage increases.

Most Chicanos, however, now live and work in cities. Generally they hold low-wage jobs. Income data reveal their poverty. In 1975, the median annual income of Chicano working men was $6,777, compared to a median annual income of $12,590 for all United States men workers. For women, the difference was $3,202 versus $7,504 (Burma and Leon, p. 109; *Statistical Abstract* 1977, p. 411).

In the 1970s and 1980s, illegal aliens have become a political issue in the United States. Many of them are Mexicans who cross the border. They are the latest example of an exploited minority. Whereas the official stance of the federal government is to discourage illegal aliens, and some are arrested and deported, in fact the government and business want them for cheap labor. They do the menial jobs (farming, cleaning, some factory work, restaurant work, and so on) most Americans will not do at the prevailing low wages. Unlike United States citizens, Mexicans cannot collect welfare or other benefits, so they must work at minimum or even lower wages—their main attraction to business and government. So, they will not be deported because they could not be replaced easily. Nor will they be allowed to enter legally, since then they would be eligible for Social Security, insurance, and other benefits. This situation represents the ultimate form of exploitation, comparable to the exploitation of blacks in South Africa (Burnett 1979; *Dollars and Sense* April 1980, pp. 6-7).

Milton Friedman, a conservative economist and believer in unfettered capitalism, acknowledges openly the exploitation of illegal aliens:

> Mexican immigration over the border is a good thing. It's a good thing for the illegal immigrants, it's a good thing for the citizens of the United States, but it's only a good thing so long as it's illegal. That's an interesting paradox to think about. Make it legal and it's no good. Why? Because so long as it's illegal the people who come in do not qualify for welfare, they don't qualify for social security, they don't qualify for all the other myriads of benefits that we pour out from our left pocket into our right pocket. So long as they don't qualify, they migrate to jobs. They take jobs that most residents of this country are unwilling to take *(Saturday Evening Post,* October 1978; quoted in Burnett 1979, p. 46).

*Puerto Ricans.* In many cities of the northeast United States, Puerto Ricans are a large minority. They are one of the latest groups to migrate to United States cities. In 1978, there were 1.82 million Puerto Ricans in the continental United States, with about 800,000 in New York City alone. With 3.21 million people in Puerto Rico itself, the Puerto Ricans in this country represent one-third of all Puerto Ricans. Such great emigration from a society results from profound social dislocations and causes further dislocations in the new country. Why have Puerto Ricans left their native land in such numbers? How do they live in their new homes? (*Statistical Abstract* 1979, pp. 33, 887).

A brief look at Puerto Rican history explains the migration. The United States captured Puerto Rico from the Spanish in 1898 as part of its general imperialist expansion in the 1890s (Cuba, the Philippines, and other countries were also brought under its domination). Businesspeople and the federal government saw such expansion as "the only solution for internal economic problems of overproduction and insufficient markets for surplus commodities and capital" (Jacobs and Landau 1971, vol. 2, p. 276).

Puerto Ricans became United States citizens in 1917, but they were not allowed to govern themselves. Moreover, until 1948, when they did take over their school system, educational content was controlled from the United States and English was the primary language in schools. This situation was part of the general degradation of Puerto Rican culture.

By the 1930s, the Puerto Rican economy was dominated by United States corporations. Much of the land was turned over to cash crops (primarily sugar), and people had to pay high prices for imported food. As a result, there was widespread poverty (Jacobs and Landau 1971, vol. 2, pp. 276–85).

To deal with this poverty, "Operation Bootstrap" was launched in the 1940s. Foreign corporations were encouraged to invest in Puerto Rico and provide jobs for people. But the multinationals came because of plentiful cheap labor and large tax breaks from the government, not to provide decent jobs to people. A few rich people and a small middle class benefited from Operation Bootstrap, but most people have not. Huge corporate profits leave the island, minimum wages have been kept low, and unemployment remains high (20 percent in 1977, an official statistic that always underestimates real enemployment) (United Nations 1978, p. 93).

In 1940, 50 percent of the people in Puerto Rico worked in agriculture, but only 4.4 percent did in 1972. These displaced people were not absorbed by the Puerto Rican economy and began migrating to New York City and elsewhere. They were running away from poverty, but the promised land of New York delivered less than the promise (Marden and Meyer 1978, p. 264).

Only about 70,000 people had migrated to the United States by 1940. The increasing poverty in Puerto Rico, the demand for labor during the war, and the introduction of cheap air fares led to increased migration. In 1970 there were 1.43 million first- and second-generation Puerto Ricans in the United States, and 1.75 million in 1976. Most live in New York and New Jersey, with smaller but increasing numbers in Connecticut, Massachusetts, California, Illinois, Pennsylvania, and Ohio.

Puerto Ricans have been doubly discriminated against. Unlike rural black migrants from the South, they spoke no English. Unlike European immigrants, they were seen as nonwhite. Generally, they have encountered all the prejudice, discrimination, and economic exploitation that have been the fate of all immigrants and minorities. The slums where Puerto Ricans live resemble those of the Irish, Italian, black, and other immigrants before them. There is "poverty, drug addiction, escapist spiritualism, sweatshops, alcoholism, and general despair that remain endemic to ghetto existence" (Miller 1972, p. 63).

Puerto Ricans work in low-paying occupations, such as restaurants, the garment industry, greenhouses, and farmwork along the east coast. Income figures are difficult to get, for in statistical reports Puerto Ricans are usually grouped either with "black and other" or "Spanish." This latter category includes Chicanos, Cubans and other people who migrated from Latin America. At least some Cubans and others came to the United States with professions, so their income exaggerates the income of the "Spanish" workers. But one statistic, for New York City in 1970, may reveal the poverty of Puerto Ricans. Median family income was $5,575, compared to the $9,682 for white New York families (about 58 percent) (Marden and Meyer 1978, p. 270). Since black incomes did not catch up with white incomes in the 1970s, we can assume that Puerto Rican incomes also did not catch up. (This discussion of Chicanos and Puerto Ricans has been based largely on Jacobs and Landau 1971; also on Miller 1972, Burma and Leon 1978, López y Rivas 1973, Marden and Meyer 1978, Burnett 1979.)

## A Socialist Perspective

Socialism provides a key to understanding this long history of the exploitation of immigrants and minorities.

This chapter has tried to show that capitalism created slavery and racism as a means to increase production and profits. (Chapter 6 showed the international exploitation of people throughout the world by multinational corporations.) Blacks and other people are still exploited today through lower incomes, high unemployment rates, and confinement to the worst jobs (Kinlock 1979, Ch. 7).

But not only are minority people exploited by being paid lower wages, many have also become "useless" people. Capitalism has created a group who act as surplus labor, to be used when needed, at cheap wages; it has also created a group for whom there are no places in a capitalist economy. Many black men simply never enter the labor force, more now than ever before.

In the early part of this century, unemployment for blacks was no higher than for whites. Blacks were desirable workers (for the lowest jobs, of course), especially since they worked for considerably lower wages. Also, at a time when workers were unionizing, blacks just leaving the rural South had not yet developed a consciousness for organizing and were often preferred by employers. They were, at times, also used to break strikes (Bonavich 1976).

But 1930s federal legislation, which helped unions become established, began to change the employment conditions of black workers. Blacks could no longer be used as well to undercut the wages of whites. In order to counteract the somewhat higher wages brought by unionism, corporations resorted to three solutions. They exported many jobs so they could use cheap overseas labor; they sought cheap labor within the United States by moving plants to nonunion areas; and they mechanized. In each case, jobs that had been occupied largely by black people were either relocated or mechanized out of existence. Thus, since about 1950 the unemployment rate of blacks has been twice that of whites.

Therefore, the claim by many social scientists that black people are consigned to unemployment or the worst jobs because of their "culture of poverty" is entirely wrong. Black people are not out of work because their values do not fit them for our society and economy. Many social scientists have argued that black parents do not teach proper values to their children (especially sons), who then cannot strive for and hold jobs. Black men have no jobs or low-paying jobs not because of what their fathers did not teach them, but because there are few good jobs. Bonavich has shown how the changed capitalist economy has increased black unemployment. In addition, World War II with its labor shortages created a demand that made it possible for black people to achieve their "most dramatic improvement" (Baron 1971, p. 29) ever in the urban industrial economy. Black workers improved both in income and in access to desirable jobs. These improvements took place because jobs were available, not because the culture, values, attitudes, skills, or anythng else of black people had changed. Changed economic conditions put an end to more improvement (Ryan 1976; Liebow 1967). (The related issues of education, the I.Q. controversy, and the abilities of black people are explored in Chapter 13.)

Useless people can be social dynamite, of course. To control the dangerous possibilities, capitalism has developed various mechanisms. First, there is the appearance (with little reality) of token improvements. Some blacks and others do improve their status and hope is created, but the underlying social and economic conditions do not change.

Welfare is another weapon for pacification and control. Surplus unemployed and underemployed people cannot be left to die of starvation; the situation would be too dangerous. Welfare has been expanded when the poor have rebelled, but mostly its levels of subsistence have been kept low to insure that people take the lowest-paying jobs in preference to welfare (some jobs, of course, are so degrading and low-paying that welfare is preferable; capitalism has no perfect solutions to its problems). But the costs of welfare

are paid by the taxes of working people, since the ruling class and corporations write and manipulate laws to avoid taxation (see Chapters 2 and 3). Capitalism creates useless people but uses the money of working people to control them, and thus racist attitudes increase (Piven and Cloward 1971).

The legal system is another means of control (see Chapter 12). George Jackson wrote that black men who live past the age of eighteen learn to "accept the inevitability of prison." The political and economic institutions of capitalism create prisoners and control them as the slaves used to be. Violence, intimidation, terrorism, and fear are used to keep inmates (usually 50 percent black) in line. The ones who resist the most, such as Jackson, are put in isolation; they never leave this situation whole—either they come out dead (Jackson's fate) or they are made totally submissive (1970, pp. 9, 25-27).

Some socialists have argued that capitalism no longer needs racism, that it is no longer profitable for the ruling class. After showing that black workers have made considerable gains in relation to whites, Szymanski concludes that capitalism no longer needs to exploit black workers as cheap labor:

> It would appear that the ever stronger need of the corporations for a homogeneous working force, which would maximize the number of potential workers in each job classification, hence decreasing wages and increasing the flexibility of its labor forces, has exerted itself over the older principle of racial discrimination. The profit opportunities involved in a homogeneous labor force seem to have come to outweigh the profit possibilities of using blacks as strike breakers and menial laborers (1974, p. 722).

Other socialists have agreed and added that, in fact, capitalists would rather destroy the racism and racist attitudes of the American people since these threaten the stability of the society, thus undermining the control of the ruling class.

Conceding the decreasing direct profitability to capitalism of cheap black labor, we must keep in mind a number of complicating conditions. First, as I have shown, since 1970 black workers have made no improvement in income relative to white workers. Second, the historical and contemporary legacy of capitalism consists not only of exploited black workers, but also millions of others useless to capitalism. Capitalism profits by not doing anything to provide jobs for these people. Blacks are the victims of the profit making system as much as all the other minorities used for cheap labor. Finally, racism continues to divide the working class. It focuses the resentment of the white working class on blacks and other minorities as the cause of their condition and deflects their attention away from capitalist institutions. The taxes of the average worker are used to support the surplus people created by capitalism, and racism inevitably comes about (Greer 1976; Reich 1972; Baron 1971). (I explore this issue further in the next section.)

Although capitalism has changed some of the ways in which it exploits minority people, under capitalism, racism will continue to exist.

## THE PERSONAL COSTS OF RACISM

Racism started, and continues to function, as an economic institution of capitalism, but it has become more. The exploitation of minorities has led to much personal and cultural degradation and destruction. We should never forget that capitalist institutions and values pervade all of life.

As a form of self-justification, capitalist institutions seek to destroy the cultures and personalities of people they exploit. The Irish were forbidden to speak Gaelic and in time lost this language. Tribal people throughout the world were forced to convert to Christianity; their own religions were denounced as barbaric. Native Americans also were forced to stop practicing their religions and speaking their languages, and their children were sent to boarding schools where their cultures were ridiculed. Immigrants also were victimized, as their children became ashamed of their parents' culture; success in America meant becoming "Americanized" (Miller 1972).

Native Americans have struggled to keep their cultures alive. But cultural survival on the reservations has been attained at enormous cost. Poverty has been rampant, since their best land has been stolen from them.

Rodriguez, a Chicano, describes how in order to get an education in the Anglo (white) culture, he had to give up his own culture and separate himself from parents, relatives, and community. His experience was not unique. People in all immigrant groups have paid a high price for "success" (Rodriguez 1975; Miller 1972).

Many people of minority groups have come to despise their looks, language, names—everything associated with their groups. A young Italian boy is typical of many minority children:

"I enter the parochial school with an awful fear that I will be called Wop. As soon as I find out why people have such things as surnames, I match my own against such typically Italian cognomens as Bianchi, Borello, Pacelli—the names of other students. I am pleasantly relieved by the comparison. After all, I think people will say I am French. Doesn't my name sound French? Sure! So therefore, when people ask my nationality, I tell them I am French. A few boys begin calling me Frenchy. I like that. It feels fine."

"Thus I begin to loathe my heritage. I avoid Italian boys and girls who try to be friendly. I thank God for my light skin and hair, and I choose my companions by the Anglo-Saxon ring of their names. If a boy's name is Whitney, Brown, or Smythe, then he's my pal; but I'm always a little breathless when I am with him; he may find me out. At the lunch hour I huddle over my lunch pail, for my mother doesn't wrap my sandwiches in wax paper, and she makes them too large, and the lettuce leaves protrude" (quoted in Miller, p. 33).

Malcolm X describes the painful process ("conking") he used to straighten his hair and comments:

> How ridiculous I was! Stupid enough to stand there simply lost in admiration of my hair now looking "white," reflected in the mirror in Shorty's room. I vowed that I'd never again be without a conk, and I never was for many years.
>
> This was my first really big step toward self-degradation: when I endured all of that pain, literally burning my flesh to have it look like a white man's hair. I had joined that multitude of Negro men and women in America who are brainwashed into believing that the black people are "inferior"—and white people "superior"—that they will even violate and mutilate their God-created bodies to try to look "pretty" by white standards (Malcolm X 1965, p. 54).

Such were the depths of degradation for minority people. For blacks, slavery and racism meant an effort at total subjugation of their personality. Many were destroyed by this process, and those who resisted it (like Frederick Douglass and Richard Wright) did so because of unusual courage and at some cost. The whole of *Black Boy* shows how Wright could not make "Subservience an automatic part of my behavior," but for many others subservience had become automatic.

> I began to marvel at how smoothly the black boys acted out the roles that the white race had mapped out for them. Most of them were not conscious of living a special, separate, stunted way of life. Yet I knew that in some period of their growing up—a period that they had no doubt forgotten—there had been developed in them a delicate, sensitive controlling mechanism that shut off their minds and emotions from all that the white race had said was taboo. Although they lived in an America where in theory there existed equality of opportunity, they knew unerringly what to aspire to and what not to aspire to. Had a black boy announced that he aspired to be a writer, he would have been unhesitatingly called crazy by his pals. Or had a black boy spoken of yearning to get a seat on the New York Stock Exchange, his friends—in the boy's own interest—would have reported his odd ambition to the white boss (pp. 215–16).

### *Life in the Slums*

Slums and ghettoes have always mushroomed under capitalism. In these places, people pay the price of exploitation. The *favelas* (shanty towns) of Brazil and the ghettoes of New York and other cities are current examples, but all minorities have been ghettoized. The Irish were forced to resort to alcoholism, prostitution, and the "misuse of religion" to escape their oppression in nineteenth-century America. Need, degradation, and ignorance have led some minority women to prostitution (Miller, pp. 18–22).

Jackson, speaking of black people, says they have tried to escape the pain of their "neo-slavery" through religion, drinking, and drugs and by hiring themselves out as janitors, athletes, and singers. Some have wanted to rebel but have seen little they could do (pp. 51–52).

Writing about 1940s and 1950s black youth living in slums, Malcolm X saw the same conditions and reactions.

> What makes the ghetto hustler yet more dangerous is his "glamor" image to the school-dropout youth in the ghetto. These ghetto teen-agers see the hell caught by their parents struggling to get somewhere, or see that they have given up struggling in the prejudiced, intolerant white man's world. The ghetto teen-agers make up their own minds they would rather be like the hustlers whom they see dressed "sharp" and flashing money and displaying no respect for anybody or anything. So the ghetto youth become attracted to the hustler worlds of dope, thievery, prostitution, and general crime and immorality (p. 311).

The demoralizing effects of ghetto life and unemployment continue today; drugs and delinquency and bitterness abound. In the Charlotte, North Carolina ghetto in 1976, Rich found:

> The acrid, depressing stench of cheap marijuana blends with the gloom of corroding lives.
> Black teenagers in housing projects like Dalton Village, Earle Village and Boulevard Homes, sitting in groups in cars or concrete apartment steps, are mistrustful of strangers, fearful of police harassment, angry idle, frustrated, not really sure if they are the criminals, as adults say they are, or the victims (Rich 1976, p. 594).

The effect on people's relations with each other has been devastating. Jackson, writing from prison, told his father:

> How do you think I felt when I saw you come home each day a little more depressed than the day before? How do you think I felt when I looked in your face and saw the clouds forming, when I saw you look around and see your best efforts go for nothing—nothing. I can count the times on my hands that you managed to work up a smile (p. 62).

The tragedy has been multiple. It has included people like George Jackson's father who worked as he was supposed to but never could manage well, and was destroyed; it has included the unemployed; it has included the drug addicts and alcoholics; it has included those who stole and robbed, mostly from their own people; it has included the intelligent people who become pimps and drug dealers instead of doing creative and useful work.

*The Spread of Racism*

Racism, obviously, is harmful to blacks and other minorities. It is also harmful for white people, however, as I will try to show. That most white Americans have some prejudice against blacks and other nonwhite minorities, is undeniable. But how much prejudice there is, and whether it is increasing or decreasing, we cannot say with much certainty. Outwardly, at least, the school-busing controversy and worsening economic conditions seem to have increased prejudice.

Some years ago, John Howard Griffin, in *Black Like Me,* described for white readers the prejudice and discrimination experienced daily by blacks (1959–1960). A white man, Griffin made his skin black and lived with blacks *and* whites. He learned what most blacks need not learn since they experience it daily (and unlike Griffin, cannot escape it). Racism at the personal level results from the racism created by capitalism. Griffin saw whites' hatred, fear, condescension, violence, and discrimination against black people.

Since then, two decades have passed with new laws, economic programs, and educational efforts to improve the condition of black people. Have things changed? Economically, only slightly. Some of the worst forms of racism are not as pervasive, but in many American cities black people cannot live in (or even walk through) some white neighborhoods, and whites sometimes are attacked in black neighborhoods. According to polls and other evidence there are still "strong negative feelings about black goals, little change in stereotyped attitudes and a growing willingness of whites to publicly downgrade the abilities of blacks." Whereas most blacks still feel they are discriminated against, most whites say that this is not so (Dreyfuss 1978).

A commonly held belief in social science is that poor and working-class whites are more prejudiced against blacks than are middle-class whites. Every sociology textbook I have seen makes that statement. But Levison, writing about the late 1960s and early 1970s, disputes that conclusion.

He cites three types of evidence. First, 1968 surveys showed that blue-collar and white-collar whites had the same attitudes and opinons on civil rights. Secondly, in the United Auto Workers and other unions predominantly white locals have routinely elected blacks as stewards, vice presidents, and presidents. (In fact, blacks have made more progress in labor unions than in any other American institution, including higher education.) And thirdly, in votes for open housing and in primaries where the pro- and anti-black candidates were clearly identifiable, working-class whites voted more for civil rights than have middle-class whites (1974, pp. 142-49).

## Racism Hurts Everyone

In 1836, Frederick Douglass, still a slave, worked in the shipyards of Baltimore. His wages were lower than those of the white workmen. Resenting him for keeping their wages low, the whites beat Douglass brutally. Years later, in 1855, Douglass gave the best analysis I know of the way slavery (and racism) are used by the ruling class to divide blacks and whites and exploit both, an analysis that has not been equalled since.

The slaveholders, with a craftiness peculiar to themselves, by encouraging the enmity of the poor, laboring white man against the blacks, succeed in making the said white man almost as much a slave as the black slave himself. The difference between the white slave, and the black slave, is this: the latter belongs to one slaveholder, and the former belongs to all the slaveholders, collectively. The white slave has taken from him, by indirection, what the black slave has taken from him, directly, and without ceremony. Both are plundered, and by the same plunderers. The slave is robbed, by his master, of all his earnings, above what is required for his bare physical necessities; and the white man is robbed by the slave system, of the just results of his labor, because he is flung into competition with a class of laborers who work without wages. The competition, and its injurious consequences, will, one day, array the non-slaveholding white people of the slave states, against the slave system, and make them the most effective workers against the great evil. At present, the slaveholders blind them to this competition, by keeping alive their prejudice against the slaves, as men—not against them as slaves. They appeal to their pride, often denouncing emancipation, as tending to place the white working man, on an equality with negroes, and, by this means, they succeed in drawing off the minds of the poor whites from the real fact, that, by the rich slave-master, they are already regarded as but a single remove from equality with the slave. The impression is cunningly made, that slavery is the only power that can prevent the laboring white man from falling to the level of the slave's poverty and degradation (pp. 309–311).

Others saw a similar exploitation of ethnic conflicts. In the 1880s, some Irish writers argued that immigrants and other minorities must unite along class lines, not compete against each other because of their different nationalities—otherwise, they would make no progress. But cooperation has not been the case, and ethnic and racial conflicts have been common in our history (Miller 1972, p. 2).

Some social scientists have tried to document how racism hurts both blacks and whites. In one study, Reich found that "where racism is greater, income inequality *among whites* is also greater" (italics in original). That is, where racism exists, most white people earn much less than the few white people who control most of the wealth (1972, p. 74). Others have come to similar conclusions. Thus, racism oppresses blacks, but it is also an obstacle to white working people. (The statistics supporting this argument are too complicated to summarize here.)

Racism causes white working people to blame black people for the good jobs they do not get and for other misfortunes. But the cause is not black people, it is the capitalist society of inequality and limited opportunities. For example, if all blacks in medical schools had not been admitted and were replaced by whites, only 7 percent of the rejected whites would get in (Dreyfuss, 1978).

Racism has come to pervade much of our society. In prisons, authorities instigate fights between black and white prisoners in order to control both of them. The anger and oppression of both black and white prisoners is turned against each other instead of against the society that turned them to criminals and sent them to prison (Jackson 1970, p. 29).

A final insight from Frederick Douglass: not only are blacks and most whites hurt by racism, but "slavery is a greater evil to the master than to the slave. . . ." Douglass shows how slaveowner after slaveowner became cruel, suspicious, and unfeeling. They treated slaves in ways that were not natural. To perpetuate slavery, they had to suppress much of their humanity. When Douglass moved to Baltimore, his mistress there was kind and generous to him. But Douglass shows how, under the imperatives of slavery, she soon began to distance herself (she stopped teaching him how to read and write) and, although not brutal to him, no longer considered him a human equal to her (pp. 105–111).

Slavery has ended, but racism today is no less harmful to all of us. Not only economically, but in our daily relations with each other, in allowing racism to separate us and assure our common exploitation under capitalism, we all suffer. The argument that the working class benefits by racism is limited and shortsighted. Some few individual white workers may benefit in the short run by being given a job or a promotion over black workers, but the vast majority of white people do not benefit. Douglass hoped that someday blacks and whites would see their common interests and humanity; we have made little progress to that goal.

## STRATEGIES FOR CHANGE

Since racism was created and is still maintained by a capitalist economy and society, under capitalism minority people (like everyone) cannot be truly free.

Centuries of racism have unavoidably left most of us with some prejudice and fear of minorities. We must struggle against such prejudice and fears in addition to ending the economic basis of racism. We cannot underestimate the struggle needed to erase the prejudice implanted in all of us. But only in a socialist society can the struggle truly begin.

### Historical and Contemporary Struggles

Historians have long debated the extent of slaves' opposition to their enslavement. How do we quantify this opposition? We can tell with certainty that there were slave rebellions of small and large scale, some with the cooperation of poor whites.

For a while after slavery, freed blacks made some progress: "the black generation from 1865 to 1900 was perhaps the greatest achieving generation of all; . . . it was in the first years of this generation that freed slaves

## STRUGGLES: The United League of Mississippi

*Meaningful social change requires a long and constant struggle. Victories disappear if the struggle ceases. This reality is evident in the following description of the United League of Mississippi, an organization still working in the 1980s for justice and equality for black people, an equality they supposedly won in the 1960s and 1970s.*

Founded in 1967 as the United League of Marshall County, the organization now has chapters in many towns and counties across the northern half of the state and into neighboring Tennessee, with a membership of more than 50,000.

...the United League employs three tried and true tactics—the ballot, the bullet and the boycott. A great deal of League effort goes into helping elect Black candidates to local and county offices across much of the state, offices that frequently guard the front-lines of white domination. Last November, for example, thousands of Black voters armed with United League sample ballots and protected against harassment by United League pollwatchers unseated reputed Klansman Kenny Smith as sheriff of Marshall County. The new Sheriff is Osbourne Bell, the first Black ever to hold that office.

Marshall County's November election also brought in a Black superintendent of education. In nearby Holmes County, two Black justices of the peace, a court supervisor and a superintendent of education were elected, though League activist Joseph Smith narrowly lost his bid for sheriff.

When necessary, the United League has also proved that it will not flinch from meeting the Klan bullet for bullet. League militants make no secret of the fact that they carry arms and have shown in several shoot-outs that they are ready to use them. After several Blacks were killed in the Marshall County town of Byhalia in 1974, for example, Black residents asked United League President Alfred "Skip" Robinson to help establish a local chapter.

*Source:* Reprinted from Andrew Marx, "The United League of Mississippi," *Dollars and Sense,* Somerville, MA, October 1980, pp. 12–14.

"People took their guns," Robinson recalled recently, "and we laid it out to them [the mayor and the police]. We told them that if any more people were killed, it would be a life for a life. We said the last Black had been killed in Byhalia. And there has not been another since."

A stroll through downtown Byhalia offers striking evidence of the power of another favored United League tactic—the boycott. Most of the downtown area is up for rent. Shuttered and vacant shop windows face each other across streets whose commercial life drained away during an 18-month boycott organized by the United League. Residents now do their shopping at new stores that sprang up along the highway outside of town.

Several of these new businesses are owned by Blacks, a development that gives the United League considerable pride and satisfaction. Far removed from polemical skirmishes over "Black capitalism," League militants welcome any step that adds to the independence and economic leverage of the Black population. Robinson explains, "All the system is corrupted, and we should be organizing to come up with something better. But we're going to be stuck with capitalism for at least 10 or 15 years. And until we can replace it with something better, we've got to be part of it in order to survive.". . .

It's all part of the battle to survive, part of "what Blacks, poor whites, poor Chicanos need to be doing" if they are not to lose out in the "civil war" Robinson fears may be coming. As they wage a daily struggle against local police and KKK terror, and against "the Klan in three-piece suits" who sit in the corporate boardrooms and political offices, other United League activists share that fear.

"There could be a big shootout," one young Vietnam veteran commented. "I hope it doesn't happen. But sometimes I have the feeling it will take a real shootout to wake people up that we have to live and work together just to survive. It's hard. But I've got a little daughter, only four years old. And I don't want her to have to go through what I've gone through."

and previously free blacks cooperated closely in politics, education, and economics; and . . . the Black family was a great creative force in these accomplishments" (Reddick 1976, p. 39).

There was also the brief hope of populism when poor whites and blacks cooperated for their common good. But racism divided them and this hope vanished. There have been other examples of interracial cooperation. In the 1930s, when the CIO (Congress of Industrial Organizations) fought against racism, the difference in income between black and white workers decreased, and not at the expense of white workers. Black workers at U.S. Steel made significant gains, earning 83 percent of what their white coworkers made. But after the CIO became less militant in fighting racism, black workers made no more gains; they still earn 83 percent of what white workers make (Greer 1976, pp. 55–56).

There have also been many black groups trying to improve the condition of black people. In this century, there has been the NAACP (National Association for the Advancement of Colored People), organized in 1909, and other groups of various degrees of militance for change and improvement. But some individuals and groups have despaired of making any change and have called for separation from white America. The Marcus Garvey movement (1920s and 1930s), calling for the migration of black people out of the United States, appears to have had a stronger appeal than many of us have been led to believe. Lately the Black Muslims have had a considerable following (see Malcolm X's autobiography for the ideology and goals of the Muslims up to the early 1960s). They have saved many blacks from the depths of crime and degradation.

But for better or worse, most black people realize they must live within the United States, and they are searching for solutions. Neither separatism nor socialism capture the imagination of most black people. Most of the efforts are aimed at improving the condition of blacks within the current capitalist economy. The tactics for change have been many: legal changes in courts and legislatures; protests, sit-ins, demonstrations; boycotts of stores and rent strikes. The growing corporate economy has destroyed the black-run businesses and organizations that once flourished within most black communities. They simply could not survive under the competition of corporate giants (nor have most businesses owned by whites; see Chapter 5) (Reddick 1976, p. 36).

*Reforms*

The alternatives for the future of minorities are many. There may be a change for the worse, as capitalism goes through economic crises. Maintaining the status quo is an equally good possibility. Some liberal reforms may occur, but in the currently stagnating economy, it is difficult to hope for much progress. Separatism is another alternative, but little is heard of it these days. Socialism, also little discussed, has been espoused by some groups, and remains the only hope. But what is the problem with liberal reforms?

Capitalism's response to the crisis of the 1960s contained many elements. The ruling class did not worry about the small black bourgeoisie, but they repressed the black revolutionaries:

> Through an elaborate system of sanctions, rewards, penalties, and persecutions—with, more often than not, members of the black bourgeoisie acting as hatchet men—any Negro who sought leadership over the black masses and refused to become a tool of the white power structure was either cast into prison, killed, hounded out of the country, or blasted into obscurity and isolation in his own land and among his own people (Cleaver 1968, p. 87).

The ruling class also bought off black political leaders in various ways (Frappier 1977, pp. 21-22). Many so-called reforms for improving the lives of black people have in reality been efforts to silence black leaders. Many federal programs of the late 1960s (Model Cities, for example) hired leaders of the black communities and, in time, integrated them into elective politics and the federal bureaucracy. In short, they became part of the governing institutions, but with very little power, and thus also became ineffective (Piven and Cloward 1971, pp. 274-76).

In the early 1970s there was "black capitalism," a federal program under the Nixon administration which, together with banks and other corporations, claimed to provide equality under capitalism for black people. In reality, black capitalism gave no more than the appearance of change; the amounts provided to help develop black-owned businesses were miniscule. Most of the money loaned by banks to black people went to set up service and retail business, which, in today's economy, provide little power and low-paying jobs. The data on black- versus white-controlled businesses (black-owned ones accounted for 0.3 percent of United States business income) show black capitalism is a poor solution (Frappier 1977, pp. 30-33).

Even though some leaders of the ruling class may see the importance of alleviating the conditions of black people, not much has been done. David Rockefeller wrote:

> Today, there is a growing realization that management is not doing the job it should for the stockholders simply by earning as large a profit as it can this year, unless at the same time it is helping to shape an environment in which the business can continue earning a profit four or five or ten years from now (quoted in Frappier, p. 27).

Rockefeller and Chase Manhattan Bank urged more private-business help for black people, but, given their imperative for making profits, the corporations were not about to rush to invest in the slums. The profit motive prevents any significant commitment of money for real change. Only the appearance of change can be afforded to prevent rebellion or revolution. The reality of change is impossible under capitalism.

Not all reforms are dominated and manipulated by the ruling class (although in time some reforms are co-opted). The United Farmworkers union under Cesar Chavez has been a militant force for change, involving great struggle and even bloodshed. In part, the liberal elements of the Democratic party (such as Robert Kennedy) saw the need to end the exploitation of farmworkers and supported their struggle. As noted in Chapter 3, the ruling class is divided on tactics; some support considerable reform to gain long-term stability. But even these reformers do not want to challenge the foundations of capitalism.

Other reforms aim to be more fundamental. Burnette and Koster list nine changes that would improve the lives of Native Americans. Following are some of their recommendations:

> 1. Abolish the BIA [Bureau of Indian Affairs] and replace it with a secretary of Indian affairs, an autonomous organization outside of the Department of the Interior. This would eliminate the tremendous conflict of interest between Interior's stewardship over the Indians and [its] responsibility for timber, minerals, water, grazing, parks, and other resources. 2. The Department of Indian Affairs should be staffed by ten Indians, elected by the Indians who reside in the present geographic areas now known as area offices. These ten Indians would act to protect the best interests of their people and would be answerable to the reservation and urban communities.... 5. Legislation should give the individual Indian new freedom to manage his property under the trusteeship of the government.... 8. Congress should enact a "New Indian Finance Act" and appropriate $500 million for the purpose of lifting the Indians to an economic level equal to that of their non-Indian counterparts (1974, pp. 287–88).

Even if these changes could be instituted (an assumption I do not make), although the lives of many people would improve, in the long run there would be no significant change. Under capitalism, profit, destruction, and robbery of powerless people are inevitable. No laws and reform programs in the past have stopped the theft of land and domination of Native American cultures, and we cannot assume such laws would be more effective today.

William Ryan's *Blaming the Victim* (1971, 1976) shows how one person's thinking can change. In the first edition, Chapter 10 made recommendations for change but offered no challenge to the foundations of racism. By 1976, Ryan saw his suggested reforms were limited. He had called for community control, but in the 1976 appendix to Chapter 10 says this is of little value if the lifeline to the community is controlled by outsiders. Moreover, Ryan fears community control can be divisive, reactionary, and racist; it encourages the stressing of differences from other communities (1976, pp. 336–37).

Ryan concludes that history has shown only collective actions can create real gains for people. He cites a study that shows it is not individual striving that makes for economic gains—rather, only union membership and general elimination of low wages help people. Ryan discusses some groups today that wage collective efforts for everyone's benefit. For example, Fair Share in Massachusetts has fought for lower electricity rates and a just property tax (eliminating all reductions for business). These actions create some gains for all working people and a sense of unity and common purpose, and they help us see the external causes of our problems (1976, pp. 337-339).

But Ryan never mentions socialism. It would seem to be the logical and inevitable outcome of what he says, but it is not discussed.

*Socialist Struggles*

Individual black people have espoused socialism. W. E. B. DuBois and Paul Robeson are among the more well-known, but many others have joined socialist organizations. They, like other socialists, were persecuted and suffered greatly.

Some black people are active in socialist organizations today. In addition, recently there have been two black groups with a socialist organization. The Black Panthers, despite their many troubles and sabotage by the F.B.I., did espouse and struggle for socialist principles. Their free breakfast programs, community schools, and free health clinics showed that serving people's needs could replace profit and exploitation.

From 1967 to 1973, the League of Revolutionary Black Workers (LRBW) in Detroit was an organization with a socialist ideology. Rising from the 1967 ghetto rebellion, many black workers within the United Auto workers organized themselves to oppose exploitative conditions inside the plant.

> At their height in the 1968-69 period, the in-plant organizations which composed the LRBW were able to organize hundreds of black workers and command the respect of thousands more. The League's political influence spread far beyond the geographical confines of metropolitan Detroit. The LRBW itself became involved in a number of community-organizing projects, owned and operated a modest printing plant, set up an independent legal-defense operation, and was in the process of developing a revolutionary alternative to the United Fund—the International Black Appeal—on the eve of its demise in the early 1970's (Allen 1977, p. 70).

Allen, a member of LRBW, thinks the organization failed because it started too many projects and the leadership lost contact with the rank-and-file members. But while it existed, it was in part a socialist group organizing black people to resist capitalist oppression (Denby 1978 provides another account of LRBW).

Some other struggles can be preludes to socialism. Many of the reforms discussed above, at least before they are co-opted or destroyed, can make some improvements in people's lives and enhance their consciousness of the possibilities for a better society. In the South and other places, even racist whites (some in the KKK) find themselves working with blacks in unions for higher wages and better working conditions. But as history has shown (see Chapters 2 and 3), unless these reforms expand and lead to a socialist consciousness and strategy, they will not make any real changes in the lives of most minority people (or any working people). Unless people of all ethnic and race groups cooperate for a socialist world, all of us will continue to be exploited by capitalist institutions.

# 10

# *Mother Earth Is Sore: The Destruction of the Environment*

### AWARENESS OF THE ENVIRONMENT

Previous chapters have shown how the growth of capitalism has destroyed cultures and groups of people. Capitalism has also been destroying nature. In *Victims of Progress,* John Bodley describes in great detail the destruction capitalism has visited upon tribal lands and people. People who had lived in balance with their environment had their cultures changed, often forcibly, and tremendous damage was done to their land. Ecological wisdom that had matured over thousands of years was sacrificed in the search for profits.

Ecological destruction became a serious problem with the rise of imperialism and capitalism. But the pace has quickened terrifically in the last thirty or forty years. As the energy shortage makes plain, we have begun to pay the price for ecological waste and pollution, and conditions seem destined to become much worse before there is any change.

Concern with the environment seems to have become another fad, now faded, even though the issues are as serious as they ever were. A poll taken at different times asked: "Which three of these [given] problems would you like to see government devote most of its attention to in the next two years?" In 1965, 17 percent of respondents chose "reducing pollution of air and water" as one of their three choices; 53 percent did in 1970, the height of the environmental movement. Concerns were soon to change, however, and by the mid-1970s polls showed economic worries were considered much more important than concerns with pollution (Rosenbaum 1977, p. 7).

Capitalism had made pollution another occasion for profit making. Publishers rushed to put out books on the subject, and corporations began developing pollution control devices—to clean up the pollution they had created. The crisis had become another commodity. Most people were diverted by the faddish approach and were made to feel guilty, for, after all, isn't it "we" who pollute the environment? The common root of economic deprivation and insecurity, of racism, poor health, and ecological destruction was never exposed. So, *U.S. News and World Report,* after citing some minimal gains in environmental protection (a few lakes and rivers had become less polluted), attempted to strike what they thought was a proper balance. Economic considerations (such as jobs and energy consumption) must be balanced with ecological regulations, they argued—as if the survival of our environment and of much of our life can be an issue for compromise and "balance!" (Weisberg 1971, p. 5; *U.S. News and World Report* 1976).

The tragedy of the environmental movement has been its membership. Those who suffer most from dangerous pollution, chemicals, and working conditions—the poor and the working class in cities and factories—have not been in the movement. It has been populated mostly by upper-middle-class people with elitist concerns. They define ecology, primarily, as the preservation of enclaves of land in their natural condition. Most people, however, cannot use these preserved lands. The daily environmental dangers of unsafe working conditions are not of as much concern to the environmental movement, which also did not examine the real causes of pollution in the economic system. Even the antinuclear movement of 1977–78, seeking to stop the dangerous and expensive growth of nuclear energy, found itself opposed by many unions and working people. They had become convinced that nuclear energy means more jobs. It does, but only in the short run. In the long run, nuclear energy both is dangerous to the environment (and therefore to all of us) and creates fewer jobs.

The environmental crisis is directly related to most other social problems. All these problems arise from the domination of an economic system that places profit for the few over the common good. The environmental destruction detailed below relates to work, where many of us are exposed to dangerous chemicals and other pollutants; to health, since many diseases are now seen as the result of environmental conditions; to imperialism, as capitalism rushes to exploit limited minerals and energy resources; and to the domination of experts, who know many specific things but have lost sight of ultimate human values and limits. Some of these connections have been discussed already; others will be explored in Chapters 11 and 14. We must be aware that environmental problems are part of our entire existence under capitalism; in a sense, they represent the ultimate problem under capitalism: the quality of life and its survival. Other societies in the past damaged their environment, but not until capitalism arose did the continued existence of life itself become problematic.

Environmental destruction affects all of us, sometimes in the short run (dirty air; polluted waters); other effects take many years to appear, for example, cancer caused by asbestos takes about twenty-five years to strike after exposure to asbestos dust; nuclear radiation's effects will be with us for thousands of years.

Everything we do has consequences. Sooner or later, what we do now will affect both ourselves and following generations. Chemical dump sites, nuclear wastes, pollution of waters, and exhaustion of limited energy sources (all discussed below) illustrate this principle.

As we come to see the profound dangers to ourselves and to life itself, the protest movement against these dangers should grow.

But the protection of the environment also points to a potential conflict with the need for freedom and privacy. As we decide the necessity of a policy (e.g., recycling; a limit of two children per family) how do we enforce it? If after discussion, education, and persuasion some people still do not follow the policy, what do we do next?

## ECOLOGY AND HUMAN EXISTENCE

Ecology is not a narrow area. It is not only polluted rivers and lakes. As Barry Commoner has shown, ecology refers to the totality of our relation to the environment (which includes people), the quality of life, and how we manage to make a living from the earth, water, and air around us. The problem of modern ecological disaster arose out of the imbalance of the three systems in which we live.

> The ecosystem—the great natural, interwoven, ecological cycles that comprise the planet's skin, and the minerals that lie beneath it—provides all the resources that support human life and activity.
>
> The production system—the man-made network of agricultural and industrial processes—converts these resources into goods and services, the real wealth that sustains society: food, manufactured goods, transportation, and communication.
>
> The economic system—the recipient of the real wealth created by the production system—transforms that wealth into earnings, profit, credit, savings, investment, taxes; and governs how that wealth is distributed, and what is done with it (Commoner 1976, pp. 2–3).

The economic system depends on the production system, which depends on the ecosystem. Without the ecosystem we cannot survive. Therefore, to insure our survival we should understand, respect, and protect the air, earth, and water around us. The environmental crisis has arisen because the economic system and the production system no longer operate within the bounds of the ecosystem. To insure high profits for corporations (the capitalist economic system), technologies have been created, such as gas-guzzling cars (production system) which both deplete the earth's limited resources and pollute air, earth, and water (Commoner 1976, pp. 2–3).

We can see that our relations to the environment are many and are affected by many aspects of our life-style. Besides the pollution caused by auto emissions, pesticides, and other chemicals, the kind of food we eat (sugar and processed foods) affects us as much as does polluted air. Also, the energy we use to move about and manufacture products exhausts non-renewable, limited supplies and pollutes the environment. Our use of the land is still another aspect of our relation to the environment. The noise of auto, plane, and industry; the additives in our foods (some people argue food additives make many children "hyperactive"); the waste we throw away—all these are aspects of ecological imbalance. Ultimately, these destructive ways of relating to the environment take their toll on our physical, emotional, and social health.

In a society dominated by the quest for profit and by the exploitation of people and nature, we have become cynical and focus on specialists who "do" things. Ultimate questions of the meaning and beauty of life are considered impractical and unscientific. But the value and meaning of life also are part of ecology; for they refer to the fact and quality of our existence. Here, tribal societies can teach us much. For as Bodley argues in *Victims of Progress* (1975) and *Anthropology and Contemporary Human Problems* (1976), tribal societies lived in ecological balance with their environment for thousands of years. Industrial capitalism, on the other hand, is threatening life itself—our very survival.

Stan Steiner's *The Vanishing White Man* is an expression of contemporary Native American tribal wisdom. Any definition of ecology must deal with that wisdom. Frank DiLuzio, former manager of the Los Alamos Scientific Labs of the Atomic Energy Commission, told Steiner:

> "The Indian philosopher will listen to a bubbling brook and it will be gentle on his ears and he will talk about these beautiful sounds he hears. And he will listen to the wind whistling through the trees and describe it in beautiful words—and that will be his philosophy.
>
> But the Westerner will look at the same bubbling brook and the first thing he will think of will be to put that damn water to work. He will want to build a dam there, and put in some power turbines" (1976, p. 23).

Alvin Dashee of the Hopi expresses that culture's value of the quality of human life:

"In our way, the highest value is the human value, the value of the human being. That is priceless. That is something no one can weigh, as a value in dollars. No one can weigh what the human soul is, what human values are worth, what friendship is worth, what love is. That is the Hopi way" (quoted in Steiner, p. 6).

From the beginning, the Hopi, among other Native Americans, foresaw the ultimate destructiveness of imperialism and capitalist exploitation: "As we have known you white men, you have been cannibals. You have always been devouring everything on earth for yourselves. Even people. Even the animals. Even the earth. You have never respected anything, or anyone, on earth" (Talahaftewa, quoted in Steiner p. 11). David Monongye told Steiner: "Long ago we prophesied that the *bahana* [white people] would destroy the earth and destroy the air and destroy himself. So we have been expecting that" (p. 9).

## THE DESTRUCTION OF THE ENVIRONMENT

The destruction foretold by the Hopi has now become part of our daily life. Some of it we experience as harmful, but we may have become so accustomed to other aspects that we do not even perceive them as dangerous. This section will detail both kinds of environmental destruction.

*Air, Water, and Earth*

The amounts of pollution and waste, both absolutely and in relation to thirty to fifty years ago, are enormous. From 1946 to 1968 the real value of the United States gross national product (GNP) went up 126 percent, but the amount of pollution increased ten times faster. The amount of waste produced by each American family doubled between 1920 and 1970. Each one of us discards a ton of waste every year, and this is increasing. About 48 billion metal cans and 26 billion bottles were discarded annually in the early 1970s. Enormous quantities of paper and plastics are used up for packaging goods (Commoner 1971, p. 146; Anderson 1976, p. 123).

Phosphates polluting water have increased greatly. In 1910, 17 million pounds were used; 40 million in 1940; and 300 million in 1970. Equally enormous increases took place in the use of other polluting substances. Indeed, many polluting substances were only introduced after 1946 (because they were more profitable to corporations than the substances they replaced): DDT, detergents, and synthetic plastics are some examples (Commoner 1971, p. 128).

The pollution produced in any given country is not the only threat. We may ban DDT in the United States, but DDT used in other countries finds its way to the seas, and thus into the fish we eat. Or, imported meat may contain DDT, if the animals were exposed to it elsewhere. Other dangerous chemicals, banned in the United States, often are used in food that is later imported here from other countries. Environmental pollution knows no national boundaries; it is a worldwide phenomenon (Lappé and Collins 1977, p. 48; Weir 1979).

Consider some specific aspects of pollution. Air pollution includes carbon monoxide (mostly emitted by the private car and its combustion engine), sulfur oxides, hydrocarbons, particulate matter, and nitrogen oxides. Three-fourths of these air pollutants are produced by gasoline-consuming vehicles, electric power plants, and industry. In 1977 transportation (mostly private cars) contributed 83.5 percent of carbon monoxide, 40.7 percent of hydrocarbons, and 39.6 percent of nitrogen oxides (*Statistical Abstract* 1979, p. 212; Rosenbaum 1977, pp. 30–32).

In the West, in the Four Corners intersection of Arizona, Utah, Colorado, and New Mexico, there has been a great deal of coal mining (much strip-mining) and electricity produced from coal. The effect on the air has been dramatic; the sun has literally darkened from the smog, sulfuric acid, and nitrogen oxides. The effects are not merely esthetic. Air pollutants may be blocking sunlight, cooling off the earth. Since the 1940s, worldwide temperature has fallen 2.7 degrees F (Steiner 1976, pp. 9, 27).

The use of freon and other gases in refrigerators and air conditioners is threatening the ozone layer that protects the earth from the sun's ultraviolet rays. Because of destruction of some of the ozone layer, skin cancers increase, and the temperature of the upper stratosphere "could fall as much as 10 degrees Celsius" (*Washington Post* 1978; Shabecoff 1979).

As dangerous as air pollution has been, water pollution is even more of a problem. The air can still cleanse itself most of the time. Polluted bodies of water stay polluted, sometimes even after the pollution sources are eliminated. Only 1 percent of the earth's water is available in fresh (unsalted) form, and most of it is polluted. The sources of pollution are many: artificial fertilizers, manure from commercial feed lots (it takes 2,500 to 6,000 gallons of water to raise one pound of meat), industrial and municipal wastes, and, if the use of nuclear energy increases, water will be required to cool off the turbines, thus raising the water temperature and killing many fish (Anderson 1976, pp. 28, 127; Rosenbaum 1977, pp. 32–34).

Air pollution sometimes pollutes waters. "Acid rain," "an insidious and invisible form of pollution caused by the burning of fossil fuels—coal and oil—from as far away as Ohio, Pennsylvania, or West Virginia," falls in northern New England and kills fish in lakes, trees, and other life. The acidity of the water overwhelms the life around it (Dumanoski 1979; Lansford 1979).

The ocean, too, is becoming polluted. Industrial wastes, garbage and other wastes dumped by municipal governments, "atomic wastes, chemical and biological warfare agents, explosives, and a large amount of crude petroleum" all have made the oceans less hospitable to marine life. For a long time, both the nuclear-power industry and the government have looked to the oceans as the place to dump nuclear wastes. It is only now that the government, alarmed by leaking from barrels dumped in the sea in the 1950s, is beginning to study the effects of nuclear waste disposal in the sea (Weisberg 1971, p. 68; Ackerman 1980). Oil spills are very common. We read about the catastrophic ship crashes that produce huge oil spills, but most ships dump some oil into the sea, if only when they are cleaned. Life in the sea is smothered by oil. Mostert quotes Sir Francis Chinchester, who toured the Mediterranean by yacht in 1970:

> "I have just returned from a 4,600-mile try-out sail in my Gipsy Moth V to the Mediterranean and back. Time after time we sailed through patches or slicks of oil film on the surface. Seas coming aboard the yacht left clots of black oil on the deck and stained the sails. I noticed signs or effects of oil at intervals all the way from the Solent to Gibraltar and in the Mediterranean itself between Gibraltar and Majorca. I mention this because I think it is probably more noticeable from a small low yacht than from a steamer. Does it mean that in time, if it continues to increase, the oil effect will kill life in the sea?" (quoted in Mostert 1970).

Detergents have been a major source of water pollution. Soap has been used for thousands of years without producing any pollution problems; detergents, on the other hand, have caused pollution everywhere they have been used (corporations produce detergents rather than soap because of higher profits; see below). Detergents are not biodegradable and water cannot absorb them (Commoner 1971, p. 55).

Pesticides are still another source of pollution. During the years 1950–1967, pesticide use increased 168 percent "per unit agricultural production." But pesticides are indiscriminate. They kill off harmful insects, but equally as much kill the insects' natural predators. Once the predators are gone, the harmful insects can (and often do) multiply; so the farmers become hooked on pesticides. They must continue, and increase, their use. Some insects develop a resistance to pesticides and multiply in fantastic numbers (Commoner 1971, p. 151; Satchell 1979).

Ironically, the benefits of pesticide use are debatable. Nearly half the pesticides spread on United States land goes to golf courses, parks, and lawns; not farmland. Of pesticides used in agriculture, over half goes to non-food crops (cotton mostly). And crops are not protected. From 1945 to 1975 the use of pesticides increased twelve-fold while the percentage of crops lost before harvest doubled. In short, pesticides do not seem to protect crops (Lappé and Collins 1977, pp. 49–50).

In poor countries, pesticides are not used on food grown for local consumption, rather, on cash crops for export to other countries (Lappé and Collins, p. 50).

Reductions in the productivity of cotton and other crops have followed much pesticide use. The insanity of pesticide use is seen in orange groves. In order to produce a perfect-looking orange, growers use great quantities of pesticides to eliminate the thrip, an insect which scars the orange skin but does not reduce crop yields or nutrition. For such debatable gains, water and earth are polluted, and fish and birds are killed (Lappé and Collins, pp. 51-57).

## The Uses of Energy

In addition to these substances, the way we use energy also pollutes the environment. Moreover, the enormous increases in use are exhausting available energy sources and creating a crisis.

Prior to the revolutionary introduction of coal and oil, energy use was minimal, with humans and animals providing most of the energy for work and transportation. It has been estimated that people in tribal societies used 4,000-12,000 kilocalories per capita daily; "state-organized cultures," 26,000; early industrial societies 70,000; and the United States in 1970, 230,000. In the United States, from 1920 to 1970, there was a 3,040 percent increase in energy use (from 57.5 billion to 1.648 trillion kilowatts). This is an enormous escalation in energy consumption which cannot continue for long (Bodley 1976, pp. 59-60; Steiner 1976, p. 56).

Energy sources are few. Crude oil (petroleum), natural gas, coal, wood, nuclear energy, geothermal sources, and solar energy are the main ones. Of those, petroleum, natural gas, and coal have been predominant, with nuclear energy having come into prominence in the last few years (only 2 percent of our energy came from that source in 1974). All three sources present two important problems: they are nonrenewable, and they are enormously polluting. Oil and coal are in-ground sources of energy that developed slowly over 500 million years, but we are exhausting them rapidly. Estimates of existing oil reserves vary, but whether we have enough (at present consumption rates) for ten, twenty, or a hundred years, it is clear that there is a limited supply (Anderson 1976, p. 156; Rosenbaum 1977, p. 40).

The United States has enormous coal reserves, but they too are finite and cannot last forever. Moreover, increasing reliance on coal is an environmental menace. In addition to work-related disease and death, land is destroyed when it is stripped (stripping has become the common way to get coal out of the ground). Coal usage also requires immense quantities of water, thus creating a critical shortage in water supplies. Rivers and streams are poisoned by the runoffs of stripped mountainsides.

As of now, "most of our remaining energy reserves are on or under public land." The government has leased most of these public lands to a few corporations and, driven by the search for profits, these corporations are stripping and destroying the land (Barnes 1975, p. 125).

Nuclear power presents problems also. Its huge turbines use enormous quantities of water in order to cool off, and this water is heated up considerably, destroying much marine life. The explosion at Three Mile Island made us aware of the danger of nuclear plant accidents, but since 1943 there have been over 1,400 accidents that released radioactivity into the atmosphere. In addition, since no safe method has been found to dispose of radiactive wastes, nuclear energy is very dangerous. Indeed, transportation of nuclear wastes from their sources to disposal sites is beginning to arouse concern about accidents along the way. In short, both alternatives to petroleum—coal and nuclear energy—are highly polluting and dangerous (Floss 1979; Lens 1980).

We simply use too much energy—for example, wasting it in private cars. Much of the life-style developed by capitalist technology is wasteful: 6.3 times more energy is needed to make the aluminum cans we now use than was needed to make the steel cans of some years ago. Such waste of energy also means more pollution. Lobsters and crabs are flown all over the United States, using much energy, for consumption by affluent people. Our entire food-distribution system, where most onions, or most lettuce, or most of many foods, are grown in one area and then transported to the rest of the country is enormously energy-wasteful (Weisberg 1971, p. 44; Commoner 1971, p. 174).

We have become so enslaved to continuous increases in energy consumption that often more energy is used to find and develop new energy sources than the energy we can get from such sources. In short, we use too much energy, wasting much of it; our resources are dangerous to the environment, and diminishing; and the only safe alternative, solar energy, is being ignored (more about this in the next section).

*Domination by the Private Car*

The use of private cars and trucks as our major means of transportation has led to great wastes of energy and has also had severe consequences for our health, land use, social relations, and communities.

The first point is that the car and other modern conveniences do not necessarily improve the quality of life. Rather, they compensate us for something we have lost. "Cars, telephones, telegrams, and letters represent not so much a new and higher standard of life as [they do] a means of clinging to something of the old. [When] you could walk to your enjoyment (or work), you did not need a car. Where you cannot walk, and public transport is inconvenient or too expensive, you need a car" (Young and Willmott 1957, p. 159).

In the 1930s, the United States still had a diversified transportation system. In time, the auto companies destroyed it and replaced it by cars and trucks (more below). Today, the private car and trucks dominate. Some data show the increasing dominance of the car:

> In 1973 Americans registered 125 million cars, trucks, and buses; they junked 8 million and turned out 12.6 million new ones. They drove their cars over 1,000 billion miles over 3.8 million miles of roads, drove trucks 260 billion

miles, and buses (only) 5 billion miles. In the meantime, the number of railroad locomotives in service shrank from 42,000 in 1950, to 29,000 in 1972, passenger train cars from 38,000, the number of passenger-miles declined from 31.8 billion miles to 8.6 billion miles, and freight tonnage remained virtually the same but dropped from carrying 57 percent of total freight volume in 1950 to 38 percent in 1972. Operated track mileage was reduced by 40,000 miles, while highways were growing by 500,000 miles (Anderson 1976, p. 20).

The domination of the car can be seen in still other figures. In 1975, 65 percent of working people went to work alone, by car or truck; 19.5 percent carpooled; only 6 percent took public transportation; and the rest used other means (for example, walking) or worked at home (*Statistical Abstract* 1979, p. 653).

Indeed, the car has become much more than a means of transportation. It invades and changes every area of our life. We eat in it, watch movies from it, bank and mail letters from it. We watch TV and listen to the radio in it. We go camping and sleep in it. We also make love in it and many of us die with it. Estimates show that American men twenty- to fifty-nine-years old spend one-third of their free time commuting. This situation shows a deterioration of life such that "little basic experience today takes place without the automobile" (Weisberg 1971, p. 108).

Cars and trucks dominate despite their high energy inefficiency. Mass transit (especially electric trolleys) and railroads are much more energy-efficient in moving people and goods. Trucks burn six times more fuel and pollute the environment six times as much, carrying the same freight as do railroads. Moreover, highways take more land than railroads (400 to 100 feet) and use up 3.6 times more energy to build (Commoner 1971, p. 171).

A list of the energy efficiency of all transportation forms shows cars and airplanes to be the least efficient:

> ...(1) electric inner-city railroads; (2) electrified trolleys; (3) diesel-operated railroads; (4) diesel-operated buses; (5) diesel-operated trucks; (6) the private car; (7) airplanes. But the development of the transportation industry over the past several decades has moved in a direction quite the reverse of the listing based on the efficiencies (Alperovitz and Faux 1977, p. 59).

Waste of energy is not the only price we pay for the private car and the truck. Deaths and injuries are the most obvious consequences. More people have been killed by car (1.7 million) than in all the wars the United States has been involved in (1.05 million people). Air pollution; noise; open land turned into streets, highways, and parking lots; a reduced tax base because of land taken over by highways; and probably most important, reduced social interaction and changes in community life—these have been the costs (Weisberg 1971).

There is serious damage to our health because of this pollution. Much death from cancer is connected to air pollution. Specifically, death from "arteriosclerosis, heart disease, and cerebrovascular disease ... [is] 79 percent higher in polluted areas than in those with relatively non-polluted air" (Weisberg 1971, p. 117).

Lead, dangerous to adults and especially to children, has gotten into the air because of the car (and some other uses, as, until recently, lead paint). Those exposed to heavy concentrations of exhaust fumes have near-toxic levels of lead. We know of the severe consequences to children exposed to lead paint, which they chew, but lower levels of lead ingested through breathing probably also have long-term effects (Commoner 1971, p. 74). A study compared the amount of lead in a skeleton from Peru estimated to be 1,600 years old with the amount of lead in the bodies of United States citizens today. It concluded that today we are "subjected to lead exposures that increase the concentration of biologic lead 500-fold above natural levels" (Cooke 1979a).

The dangers of the car are many. Bernstein (1977) writes about benzene, added to gasoline as an antiknock agent, that is carcinogenic (increases the chances for getting cancer). There are no safety standards against its release in the air. Generally, Congress and the Environmental Protection Agency have postponed putting into effect auto emission standards, thus cars are continuing to endanger our health.

Finally, private cars have speeded up the decline in community. When people live in one area but work and shop miles away, the weakening of social bonds and community ties begun by capitalism (see Chapter 7) grows worse. Long hours commuting mean people spend less time with their children and with each other. Shopping in distant supermarkets prevents developing ties with neighborhood stores. The list is endless.

Given that it causes such energy waste, health dangers, and diminished human contact, why has the private car dominated? There are two related reasons. Reliance on private means of transportation and commuting long distances to work are a logical outcome of capitalist-style social organization, reflecting the individualism, isolation, and decline in community life begun long ago when industrial capitalism arose. But also, the private car and truck have taken over the movement of people and goods because the auto and oil corporations have planned it so. Simply stated, the corporations make huge profits from the sale of private cars and trucks, and from the higher sales volume of gasoline and other products to operate these vehicles.

There is convincing evidence for that conclusion. In the late 1930s, General Motors bought out and dismantled the electric transit system of Los Angeles. They did not stop there, however:

> By 1949, General Motors had been involved in the replacement of more than 100 electric transit systems with GM buses in 45 cities including New York, Philadelphia, Baltimore, St. Louis, Oakland, Salt Lake City, and Los Angeles. In April of that year, a Chicago Federal jury convicted GM of having criminally conspired with Standard Oil of California, Firestone Tire and others to replace electric transportation with gas- or diesel-powered buses and to monopolize the sale of buses and related products to local transportation com-

panies throughout the country. The court imposed a sanction of $5,000 on GM. In addition, the jury convicted H. C. Grossman, who was then treasurer of General Motors [and] had played a key role in the motorization campaigns.... The court fined Grossman the magnanimous sum of $1 (Snell 1973, p. 311).

In time, through heavy advertising and other means use of the private car exceeded the use of buses (which were not as efficient as electric-powered trains). The development of the National Highway Trust Fund in 1956 sealed the fate of the railroads. They began declining when diesel engines replaced electricity as the energy used, since the electric locomotive is much more efficient than the diesel engine. When the federal government, pushed by the powerful oil and auto lobby, taxed gasoline to develop the interstate highway system (1956 on), the future of railroads became doubtful. Transport of passengers and goods switched to the private car (airplanes for long distances) and to trucks (Snell 1973).

Taxes collected for the Highway Trust Fund can only be spent to build highways. The federal government covers 90 percent of the cost of any interstate highway developed within a state, and states rushed to use that money. And in the late 1970s, despite the energy inefficiency and costs of the private car, the federal government was shrinking the railroad system (Baldwin 1979). There was no such funding available for mass transit (in the mid-1970s, there has been a modest increase of funds for subways and other forms of mass transit, but nothing approaching the scale of the Highway Trust Fund). "From 1945 through 1970, states and localities spent more than $156 billion constructing hundreds of thousands of miles of roads. During that same period, only 16 miles of subway were constructed in the entire country" (Snell, p. 321). Federal aid to state and local governments continues to reflect the supremacy of the highway, with some increase in mass transit funding (see Table 10.1).

The auto and oil corporations are very powerful. Not only do they control the transportation system, but they are more powerful than any other sector of the economy. Table 10.2 shows how much wealth is controlled by the top corporations directly related to oil and autos. These figures do not include the tire and steel companies, which sell many or most of their products to auto companies, or sell products to operate cars and trucks

**TABLE 10.1** Federal Aid to State and Local Governments for Transportation, 1965–1977 (Millions of Dollars)

|  | 1965 | 1970 | 1972 | 1974 | 1976 | 1979[a] |
|---|---|---|---|---|---|---|
| Airports | 71 | 83 | 106 | 243 | 269 | 565 |
| Highways | 4,008 | 4,333 | 4,678 | 4,489 | 6,272 | 6,807 |
| Railroads |  |  |  |  | 2 | 94 |
| Urban mass transit | 11 | 105 | 179 | 348 | 1,262 | 2,191 |

[a]1979—estimates.
Source: *Statistical Abstract of the United States* 1979, p. 290.

**TABLE 10.2** Large Manufacturing Corporations—Sales and Profits, 1970 and 1978 (in Billions of Dollars)

| Industry | Sales 1970 | Sales 1978 | Profits before taxes 1970 | Profits before taxes 1978 | Profits after taxes 1970 | Profits after taxes 1978 |
|---|---|---|---|---|---|---|
| 1. Total (170)[a] | 304.9 | 842.4 | 29.3 | 88.2 | 16.6 | 43.9 |
| 2. petroleum refining (15) | 61.4 | 242.7 | 8.5 | 29.5 | 5.2 | 11.4 |
| 3. motor vehicles and equipment (9) | 48.9 | 140.7 | 2.2 | 10.6 | 1.3 | 5.6 |
| 4. columns 2 and 3 combined (24) | 110.3 | 383.4 | 10.7 | 40.1 | 6.5 | 17.0 |
| 5. column 4 as a percentage of column 1 | 36.2 | 45.5 | 36.5 | 45.5 | 39.1 | 38.7 |

[a]Figures in parentheses represent number of corporations.
Source: *Statistical Abstract of the United States* 1979, p. 568.

(Weisberg 1971, p. 99). By 1978, the oil and auto corporations accounted for 45.5 percent of net sales of these top 170 manufacturing corporations, up from 36 percent in 1970 (*Statistical Abstract* 1979, p. 568).

In large part, we have come to depend on polluting and inefficient cars and trucks because the powerful oil and auto corporations have created that dependency. They have literally torn up electric trolley tracks and lobbied to shape federal and local legislation to develop the highway system instead of railroads and subways.

*The Rape of the Land*

Previous chapters have discussed the devastation of the land brought about by corporate exploitation (see data in Chapter 3 showing the increasing control and use of most land by a few corporations). For the sake of reducing labor costs and increasing profits (in the short run), agribusiness has turned to chemical fertilizers, insecticides, and other energy-wasting methods.

The devastation began with the rise of capitalism and imperialism. Soil erosion, destruction of lands, and increase of desert areas followed the system of cash cropping imposed by imperialist nations. That process continues, and is now spreading throughout the United States. Strip-mining is moving to the western states, where it uses immense quantities of the limited water supplies. Ranchers are finding out that when corporations buy underground mineral rights from the government, the corporations can strip the earth to get to those minerals (Bodley 1975, pp. 160–62; Steiner 1976, p. 252).

A government report on the environmental impact of strip-mining in the western United States shows the devastation likely to visit the land:

> The report makes it clear that surface drainage patterns may be disrupted; water sources might be eliminated; streams may be silted in and contaminated with toxic materials; big game wintering grounds and migration routes, and

wildlife habitat in general, would be destroyed; archaeological sites would be destroyed; geological features and scenic resources would be destroyed or "disrupted"; and miles of impassable "high walls" might be left. Where underground mining takes place, surface collapses might occur. Contamination by radioactive fly ash would occur in the vicinity of the coal-fired electric generating plants. Local communities would be disrupted by a temporary influx of outsiders. A variety of other detrimental impacts can be predicted. In summary, the "grand scale of the operation impacts significantly on the environment" (Bodley 1976, p. 78).

Bodley writes of what may happen, but we need not speculate. Most of these things have happened in the Appalachians (see Chapter 7).

*The Price of Environmental Destruction*

The effects of environmental destruction have a heavy cost. Hardly any aspect of our lives, as individuals or in groups, is unaffected by our relation to the environment. As we mistreat it, we suffer. Soil depletion lowers food production; deforestation leads to soil erosion and less recreational land; pollution damages health; and "depletion of fish and wildlife costs us in terms of food, ecological balance, and biological richness" (Anderson 1976, p. 141). Future generations will pay a high price, much higher than we do, from present ecologic damage. A fraud has been perpetrated upon us in the name of "progress" and growth.

The changed diets enforced on people because of changing technology, farming techniques, and new life-styles have been taking their toll. Bodley cites evidence:

> Twenty years ago, Dr. T. L. Cleave, Surgeon-Captain of the British Royal Navy, linked together a whole list of seemingly diverse diseases, including dental decay, peptic ulcers, obesity, diabetes, constipation, and varicose veins, into a single category which he called the "saccharine disease." Using historical data and research on primitive peoples, he argued that all of these conditions are caused at least in part by the extensive use of concentrated carbohydrates such as sugar and white flour by modern industrialized populations. This radical change in diet over the patterns that man had evolved during many thousands of years altered body chemistry and greatly slowed transit times in the digestive tract by reducing dietary bulk, thereby creating many pathogenic conditions (1976, p. 215).

Heart disease, diabetes, and hypertension, mostly absent in tribal societies, increased many times with the advent of new diets. Teeth too have been affected. Peoples who hardly ever had problems with their teeth (such as the Eskimo) now suffer from many cavities and gum diseases (for details, see Bodley 1975, pp. 152–54, 157–58).

Modern techniques of raising most foods are dangerous. Additives and preservatives have unknown effects, which may be long-term. Beef cattle, the staple of the American diet, are raised under inhumane conditions:

> Formerly, beef cattle were grazed for one to two years before they were ready for slaughter. The kind of grass and corn they were fed determined the taste and tenderness of the roasts and steaks that eventually reached the dinner table. Now grazing hardly exists at all, replaced by chemical hormone stimulation that can enable cattle to be stuffed with up to twenty pounds of feed daily.... Most of the fattening of commercial beef now takes place in such commercial feedlots, and their ownership is among the most concentrated of any element in the food industry (Browning 1975, pp. 41–42).

We must not think only of the dangers to ourselves, but also of the degradation we heap on other living things. Chicken and cattle are born, live, and are killed indoors, in confined quarters, and most never see the outdoors. They are produced like cars, assembly-line style. We transform living beings into commodities, depriving them of all contact with the world into which they appear. We never think of how such treatment affects them —and us. We degrade life.

Environmental pollution leads to health dangers. United States industry introduces 700 to 2,000 new chemicals a year without testing their effects on health and the environment. In 1980, the Environmental Protection Agency considered 65,000 chemicals dangerous enough to be tested. For some of them, of course, we cannot know the effects. It is estimated, for example, that up to 90 percent of cancers are caused by environmental factors; industrial chemicals such as vinyl chloride are a large part of those factors. Nitrate, found in chemical fertilizers, is another example. It gets into underground waters, and a study in Illinois showed that during the months when nitrate levels in water increased, female infant mortality went from 2.5 per 1,000 births to 5.5 per 1,000 (Jacobs 1980; Huebner 1977; Commoner 1971, p. 93).

The poisoning of water by nitrate, hardly noticed in the 1960s, was a forerunner of what we are now learning has been a criminal assault on the environment and on our health. We are paying a frightful price for the growth of our economy through the invention of chemicals. Corporations have been producing wastes and dumping them throughout the United States. For example, in 1980 trucks were stopping in New Hampshire forests in the middle of the night and dumping barrels filled with poisonous and dangerous wastes. Nadler (1980) described this dumping as "chemical garbage strewn across the U.S." (p. 5). There are an estimated 30,000 to 100,000 illegal dumps. We are just beginning to find out the effects of dumped chemical wastes (Nadler 1980; Brown 1980; Elam 1979).

Probably the best known chemical dump site is in the area of Love Canal (near Niagara Falls, New York). The Hooker Chemical Company dumped twenty-two kinds of chemicals, eleven of them carcinogens, in the 1940s and 1950s. The site later was covered and was sold to the town for $1. Then, schools, homes, and parks were built over that site—but people were not told what lay underneath their houses and schools. By 1978 the buried chemicals began to take their toll. Miscarriages and birth defects began to appear at abnormally high rates. In 1979, ABC News reported that in 187 homes still occupied in the area, "there were 34 miscarriages, 20 birth defects, 41 cases of respiratory diseases and three suicides—all well above the national average." More effects were revealed in 1980. A study of thirty-six adults in the area showed that eleven of them had very rare chromosomal aberrations, which, most scientists in the field think, often are linked to cancer and genetic damage in offspring (Galdston 1978; Elam 1979; Molotsky 1980).

Woburn, Massachusetts, an old industrial town near Boston, may also be suffering from the indiscriminate dumping of chemicals. Some residents began to suspect that something was wrong when they learned that their town had the state's highest cancer rate. Officials began to find that chemicals had been buried in various sites throughout the town: arsenic, lead compounds, chloroform (which entered the city water), radioactive wastes, and animal hides "impregnated with chemicals and slowly decomposing into the air and water." Woburn, like so many other places, had been slowly poisoned for a very long time (Knight 1980).

Woburn is hardly alone in having had its waters contaminated. Throughout the nation, town after town has had to close many of its wells as testing of water has revealed dangerous contaminations. In most cases, the sources that contaminated the waters have not been found. Dangers lurk everywhere, from sources no one suspected. For example, the Environmental Protection Agency estimates that there are about 300 million pounds of PCBs (a highly toxic group of chemicals) buried throughout the nation. They percolate into the water table gradually and then enter the food chain. In time, PCBs will enter our bodies. In fact, about 50 percent of people in the United States have PCBs in their bodies in various concentrations (Pollard 1979; Toedtman 1979; Gatto 1979; Rosenthal 1979; Arnesen 1979; Langner 1979; Mitchell 1980; Jacobs 1980, p. 45).

Government and industry have been very slow in reacting to the dangers we face. For example, it took more than two years of often bitter protest for President Carter to give assistance to Love Canal residents so they could move away temporarily. But over two years after the initial findings, both the government and Hooker Chemical Company still refused to buy the homes in Love Canal so that the people could buy houses in other places. Generally, both government and industry avoid responsibility and act in limited ways, often long after the danger has become obvious. It is clear that only organized and committed people will be able to get any action from the government and from polluting corporations (Nader and Brownstein 1980; Warren 1980; Jacobs 1980).

Corporations have found it cheaper to expose workers to the hazards of steel mills and pay them low pensions when they retire at fifty because of disabilities contracted at work, than to modernize the coke batteries (Lynd 1973, p. 31).

The dangers are more than physical, however. Many workplaces, arranged for high production levels, affect mental health. The health director of a Volvo plant advises workers to spend no more than two years on the assembly line. "After two years, they will be threatened with lasting mental or nervous damage that may disable them for the rest of their lives" (quoted in Weisberg 1971, p. 163).

The benefits of increased food production are debatable. The effects of food produced in a capitalist economy are evident in other ways. Water pollution and pesticides have invaded rivers, lakes, and seas and in the process killed many fish, thus reducing a significant source of food, especially in poor areas (as in Asia) (Anderson 1976, p. 130; Lappé and Collins 1977, p. 54).

Generally, we have become more vulnerable because of corporate technology and the concentration and specialization it encourages. Almost all things we eat and use are produced in other places and transported great distances, using much energy. We have become ignorant of the very process of life. A brief film from *Sesame Street* illustrates: a little girl, talking to a woman, asks where potatoes come from, and both say, from the store. They then proceed to trace potatoes from the store to the local distributor to the farm. The need to explain what should be an obvious fact shows how far we have come in our alienation from the process of life. Most onions we use in the United States are grown in one Texas county, most raisins in one California county, and so on. Distant conditions, such as bad weather, the decision to use the land for something else, or the ability to raise prices because of the monopoly agribusinesses enjoy, affect the price and the quantity of food available in local stores. In two years (1976-78), raisins more than doubled in price.

The United States has become the ultimate consumer society. With 6 percent of the world's people, in 1970 we consumed 40 percent of the world's production and 35 percent of its energy. And much of this production is of throwaways. In the period 1946-68, the greatest production increase was in nonreturnable soda bottles, up 53,000 percent. Other drastic changes have included the substitution of vinyl for leather and polyester for cotton. In the process, there were great increases in energy consumption and in pollution. But has the quality of our lives really improved because we now use vinyl rather than leather? What have we gained? We can see what we have lost (Bodley 1976, p. 67; Commoner 1971, p. 143).

It is often said that new products make life easier. We believe so much in the ideology of growth that we fail to look at the evidence:

> Aboriginal Australian women, for example, were found to devote an average of approximately 20 hours per week to collecting and preparing food, . . . while women in rural America in the 1920's, without the benefit of laborsaving

appliances, devoted approximately 52 hours a week to their housework. Some 50 years later, contrary to all expectations, urban, nonworking women were putting in 55 hours a week at their housework, in spite of all their new "labor-saving" dishwashers, washing machines, vacuum cleaners, and electric mixers (Bodley 1976, p. 66).

You may argue that we have chosen a consumption life-style. But how much choice do we really have? If we are denied community and meaningful human relations and work, we become very vulnerable to the advertising that promises happiness. If we were not thus deprived, heavy advertising would not be needed to convince us to buy what we need. Advertising has come about to create, not meet, needs. More money is spent on corporate advertising and sales promotion than is spent on all public and private education. Corporate advertising is polluting our minds (and because of increasing prices, we pay for having our minds polluted) (*Ramparts* editors 1970, p. ix; Bodley 1976).

## GROWTH, PROFIT, AND THE ENVIRONMENT—OTHER PERSPECTIVES

Thus life is being threatened by the capitalist drive for growth and profits.
Hardly anyone would deny that there is an ecological and energy crisis. But the explanations for that crisis vary.

The classic conservative capitalist view argues that there are enough energy sources, and enough energy would be supplied if only government regulations and restrictions were eliminated. Friedman makes that point very clearly:

> From an economic point of view oil is not an exhaustible resource.
> 
> In any economic sense, oil—or, more generally, energy—far from being an exhaustible resource, is a producible resource at more or less constant or indeed declining cost because of the improvements in the technology of drilling and exploring and so on. You can find more oil, and therefore if the future price tended to rise above the present prices, that would give somebody an incentive to go out and find more and add to the supply (Friedman 1978, p. 21; also McManus 1977).

The liberal perspective sees an energy shortage and pollution but places the blame on all of us: on our values, life-styles, and culture. The Council of Environmental Quality sees among the principal causes

> ... the nation's dedication to unlimited industrial production and economic growth, an affluence that stimulates an apparently insatiable appetite for consumer goods, a burgeoning population, and technology. Other analysts add to the list our belief that nature is property to be used at its owner's discretion, our faith that science can solve any social problem before it becomes catastrophic, and our fierce dedication to private rights over public ones. A major

alteration in the American life style seems to be the price of environmental clean-up, and Americans have a powerful incentive to resist paying it (summarized by Rosenbaum 1977, p. 57).

Others blame Christianity, for it is said to place human beings in the center of the universe and show little respect for the environment. But many people have looked at Christianity as pacific rather than aggressive in its view of the environment. And Japan, with a very different religion, also has been destroying the environment (Anderson 1976, pp. 119-20).

### A Socialist Perspective

Denying the existence of the problem, or diffusing responsibility to all of "us" and to vague beliefs and values, will not suffice to help us understand the dangers we face.

Capitalism is not alone it its assault on the environment. Socialist countries have a mixed record in their relation to the environment. Many past civilizations have also destroyed much of their environment, depleting the soil, deforesting the land, and creating deserts. Ancient Greece used up all its wood and had to import wood. Occasionally, some tribal societies overexploited their environment. So I am not arguing that only capitalism is unecological (Anderson 1976, p. 122; Corwin 1979).

But no past examples of environmental destruction were so widespread. The scale of damage to the environment under capitalism is so unprecedented that the effects on the environment and on us have reached a new level. And so long as profit remains the primary consideration in capitalism's relation to the environment, no solution to the crisis is possible.

The escalation of violence against the environment has been sharp since the 1940s. Commoner argues in both his books, *The Closing Circle* (1971) and *The Poverty of Power* (1976) that corporations, in their search for more profits, have developed a technology that is more profitable but also more polluting than the technology it replaced. Increased production is not the cause for the escalation in pollution; in the years 1946-68, the increases in the production of food, steel, and clothing were only slightly greater than the population increase. It is the kinds of technology and goods developed to meet our needs that have changed (Commoner 1971, pp. 139, 144).

The profit made on detergents is 50 percent of sales, and it is 30 percent on soap. The same situation appears to hold with the production of larger cars, which, though more polluting than smaller ones, return much higher profits (p. 264). In another example, it is obvious that collecting immense amounts of animal manure and using them for fertilizer would be both more economical and ecological. But there would be no profits for the corporations producing chemical fertilizers or for the oil companies that provide the petrolcum to make the fertilizer (Commoner 1971, pp. 259-64).

Similarly with land use: speaking of Randall Sheffield, a Kentucky farmer, Frank Browning writes that "he knows that if he abuses the land, he will himself suffer disastrous consequences." It is different for corporations that farm and exploit the land for profit.

> Erosion, leaching of the soil, chemical poisoning may turn high short-term yields but may ruin the land for generations to come. For the diversified investment fund, that is someone else's problem, for then the land can be exploited in another manner or the investment shifted out of that particular piece of property. And then the land, like a used automobile, becomes scrap. Or, as a BankAmerica officer Lee Prussia replied in answer to a question about the ecological effects of the Bank's agribusiness policies: "A financial institution, historically and traditionally, has not been responsible for these kinds of decisions. We need not take a stand on issues of ecology" (1975, p. 30).

Under capitalism, any technology, no matter what its consequences, that increases profits is preferred to any other technology that returns lower profits. In their review of *The Poverty of Power,* Alperovitz and Faux summarize the logical development of capitalism that leads to environmental destruction. In order to survive, corporations must keep growing and expanding. In order to expand, they need capital (money), which they must get from profits (if they borrow in order to expand, they repay the loan from future profits). The key to higher profits is lower labor costs; this is accomplished by buying labor-saving technology which replaces workers. This technology is usually much more energy-consuming and polluting than previous technology. "Thus, chemical farming replaces organic farming, diesel buses replace trolleys, plastic handbags replace leather ones." Therefore, polluting technology arises not by itself or to meet human needs, but to meet the needs of a capitalist economy (1977, p. 59).

## THE ENVIRONMENT IN SOCIALIST SOCIETIES

Although the threat to the environment in a socialist society is smaller, it is present, and a long, careful struggle to change priorities and life-styles even further will be necessary.

More than capitalism socialism does have the potential to stop environmental destruction, since profit and growth are not inherent in a socialist society. After initial and equally distributed growth in the production of goods to meet basic needs, socialism does not demand continuous growth in technology and material goods. People should begin to find meaning not in consumption, but in social relations, in expression of their talents, and in useful work (Anderson 1976, p. 7).

But in reality socialist countries have damaged their environment. Especially since they typically begin as very poor societies needing vast improvements, they have been tempted to emulate western technology—quick results but long-term destructiveness. The USSR, for a large part, has followed that route. China, since the death of Mao and the rise of leaders very anxious to industrialize the society, are borrowing much western technology (or want to), and China too may wreak havoc upon its environment.

Let us take a closer look at two socialist societies, the USSR and China.

*USSR*

The Soviet Union is not dominated by the private car, economically or environmentally. In all of the Soviet Union, there are only 5 million cars, in contrast to 100 million cars and 26 million trucks in the United States. It has developed an extensive mass transit system, and as a result has avoided the pollution caused by auto emissions. In addition, it uses little chemical fertilizer, 33 kilos per hectare versus 183 for Western Europe. It has also not resorted to the mass use of insecticides.

In other ways, it has avoided many of the problems experienced in capitalist societies—work places, such as mines, have eliminated most of the dangers (for example, from dust). When Lake Baikal became seriously polluted because of industrial development, a coalition of Soviet scientists, students, and conservationists were able to save it, at least for the time being (Anderson 1976, pp. 240-41; Marquit 1978, pp. 106, 252).

On the other hand, there is much timber cutting causing erosion stripmining in the USSR. There is considerable water pollution. Urbanization is growing, creating disparities between city and country, and also leading to greater pollution and demand on resources. Nuclear plants in the Soviet Union appear to be less safe than plants in this country. Indeed, there are persistent reports that there have been serious accidents in some of the Soviet plants. The CIA is reported to have known about these accidents but did not publicize them in order to deflect opposition to nuclear plants in the United States. A consumer society of sorts is developing in the Soviet Union. Economic growth is being used to satisfy consumer wants, not to create better social relations and more satisfying work (this aspect of the USSR is discussed in other chapters) (Anderson, pp. 235-41; McMahon 1979).

On balance, the Soviet Union shows much environmental destruction, but also some attempt at limits. Anderson concludes that it can turn toward true environmental conservation more easily than the United States can (p. 241).

*China*

Out of both commitment to a safe environment and economic necessity, the People's Republic of China has been much less wasteful and polluting than have capitalist societies.

Few things are wasted in China. Most wastes are converted to useful products. Chemical factories try to reuse all their wastes by converting them to different forms. Increasingly, not only do factories not dispose of their wastes into rivers and other waters, but city sewage is used as fertilizer. Lung Chiang (in Fan and Fan 1975, pp. 339–340) describes the cleaning up of a very polluted river, where eventually fish returned in abundance. Thousands of people organized to construct new waterways so that sewage would be diverted to farmland, where it could be treated and used for irrigation and as a fertilizer. Elsewhere, 90,000 people dug 400,000 tons of "organic mire from a river to use as fertilizer" (Fan and Fan 1975, pp. 339–40; Anderson 1976, p. 249).

There is very little junk; no discarded cars (few cars at all, thus avoiding air pollution), no nonreturnable bottles, none of the tonnage of garbage found in capitalist societies. Everything that can possibly be saved, is. "Multipurpose use" (their expression for recycling) is widespread. Chinese farming uses mostly organic fertilizer, with only 30 percent of the total fertilizer used being chemical. Generally, farming has developed through intensive labor and agricultural experimentation that is the province of all workers, not only a few experts (see Chapters 4, 5, 6, and 7 for more details) (Fan and Fan, p. 333; Anderson, pp. 247–50; Orleans and Suttmeier 1970).

As seen in Chapter 5, China is a society where local autonomy prevails. Eighty percent of the Chinese people live in rural communes, decentralized forms of social, political, and economic organization. Each commune attempts to meet most of its needs, thus (among other benefits) avoiding the need for expensive, energy-consuming transportation of goods to distant places. Among the goals of most communes is the development of their own industry, so they can meet their own needs for machinery, such as tractors. Generally, unlike in capitalist societies, urbanization has not taken over; the city does not rule over the country in China. City life and city people not only dominate the economy and culture of capitalist societies, they are also enormous consumers of energy and polluters of the environment. By avoiding urbanization and private-car domination, the Chinese are also avoiding environmental disaster. (People in China get around by public transportation, bicycles, and walking.)

There are now even more extensive experiments in China combining agriculture, industry, and commerce. Some rural communes have begun to use their own raw materials to produce industrial goods. For example, on some communes milk is made into powdered milk, tea is packaged, and wheat is ground and baked into bread. Not only have the income and welfare of the people improved, but also the differences between industry and agriculture and town and countryside have been reduced (*Beijing Review*, November 30, 1979, pp. 6–7).

In September 1979 China passed a comprehensive environmental-protection law. It stipulates that economic growth must not occur at the expense of the environment. It calls for national planning to protect the environment. Pollution from all sources must be controlled and prevented. For example,

> The law stipulates that no enterprise or institution which might pollute the environment can be built near residential areas in cities and towns or beside protected water areas, places of historical interest, scenic spots, hot springs, resorts or natural areas under protection. Those already existing should adopt measures to control their pollution or be moved to other places within a specified period (*Beijing Review,* November 9, 1979, p. 24).

Progress is not measured by consumption standards, by millions of gadgets, private cars, and other material goods. Improvements in the quality of life (such as free education and free, or inexpensive, humane health care) and in social relations (cooperation for the common good, enhanced community life, improved status of women) are better indicators of progress. Such progress and growth do not endanger the environment (Anderson, p. 245).

## ECOLOGICAL LIVING

Capitalist exploitation and destruction of the environment must end, or life itself cannot survive. Already, many species are becoming extinct because of the pollution visited upon nature (Thomas 1978). If the world were to emulate American patterns of consumption, all resources would soon be exhausted, we would run out of energy, and air, land, and water would no longer be able to cleanse themselves. If everyone achieved our life-style and consumption standards, the world would need from 75 to 250 times the iron, copper, tin, and other resources it now uses (Weisberg 1971, p. 70).

Clearly, there will be changes. But if we continue in the present path, these will not be the kinds of changes we can look forward to. Change can also occur if we learn to understand the limits nature places on us (and also the opportunities) and struggle to live and grow within them in a socialist context. This chapter concludes with a look at the ecological wisdom of tribal societies, some general principles for ecological living under socialism, and some of the immediate and longterm alternatives for changes in American society that must occur if we are to learn to live in cooperation with each other and with nature and to find meaning in each other, in human relations, not in consumption.

### *Tribal Ecology*

No tribal society has ever freely chosen to become "civilized." Such societies have rejected the Western capitalist model of growth. In case after case, tribal peoples have resisted Western imperialism and its values and lifestyles. You may ask, is not the fact that capitalist countries eventually won over tribal societies proof of the superiority of capitalism? They won only in a perverse, short-run perspective. The present environmental and social crisis is proof of the dangers of capitalist economy and culture (Bodley 1975, pp. 14–16).

In contrast to industrial capitalism, which has come to a crisis point after only four or five centuries and which has led to the suffering and exploitation of millions of people, tribal societies survived thousands of years, because they lived in harmony with nature. They knew and understood the limits of nature. Frank Tenorio, a Pueblo Indian, speaks:

> "There is something suicidal in the non-Indian's belief in ever-expanding development and his belief in his ability to be able to continually reform nature through technology. The Southwest, in terms of water supply, can only support a limited number of people; that is a fact of life. The fact is that the Great Spirit put only so much water on this earth, and that is a fact the white man refuses to confront" (quoted in Steiner 1976, p. 89).

Knowing these limits, tribal societies created institutions to function within them. Customs to limit wealth—limits on property ownership; use of the land for meeting only the basic necessities—all assured that the environment would not be exploited and destroyed (Bodley 1976, pp. 48–52). Tribal societies continue to struggle to live within these limits. The Cheyenne, after almost losing their land to strip miners, were able to assert their respect for and understanding of Mother Earth. "The coal dispute is over on Northern Cheyenne. They have forsaken the billions. They have decided to leave the land alone. 'We're for some progress,' said tribal sociologist Gail Small, 'but only at our own pace and for the benefit of the people. This whole country seems based only on greed and progress, but what is progress? Mother Earth is an integral part of our religion. Do we want strip mines here?'" (Levey 1978).

It is not that tribal societies were not able to produce more goods or exploit nature. The most technologically simple among them, such as the Australian Aborigines (who worked only twenty hours a week), did not spend their lives getting from nature. The stereotype of the "lazy" Indian stems from the Indians' appreciation of nature and of its limits, and their refusal to exploit it (Bodley 1976, p. 51).

Thomas Bell, a white man trying to escape "progress," points to the cost:

> "Money cannot buy sunsets. Money cannot buy the bugle of an elk that I heard a few days ago in the woods. Money cannot buy the natural beauty of life people may find if they know what they are looking, or listening, for. So many people don't know what they are looking, or listening, for that they will never find it. And they think they can buy it" (quoted in Steiner, p. 109).

The values and drives encouraged by industrial capitalism are depriving us of such beauty. They make it increasingly difficult for us to find value and meaning in nature and each other.

*Toward Social and Ecological Balance*

We cannot for a long time, if ever, return to the conditions of tribal societies. There are too many of us. The issue is, can we find ways to live in harmony with the environment and not destroy ourselves and other living beings?

If we are to survive with the possibility of finding joy and meaning in life, we must follow certain principles that have been shown to be the only viable alternative to present catastrophe. Some could be implemented soon, but in their totality these principles require a total change in our way of life. They demand the end of capitalism and the creation of a socialist society, one not imitative of capitalist values and conditions. These principles do not come from any one person; they embody the experience and understanding of people throughout human history. Together they constitute a socialist response to the current threat to life capitalism poses.

I enumerate them for clarity, not in any order of importance. They all relate to each other; they are parts of one principle, the struggle for human survival.

1. We must begin by understanding and accepting the limits nature places upon us. We are not greater than nature, we cannot conquer it; we are part of nature. For example, for a long time people acted as if water appeared magically from the tap. We are learning that water is limited and precious, although we have been and continue to pollute it, to use enormous quantities in industry, and to squander it at home (von Ranson 1980).

2. We must find meaning in social relations, not in consuming material goods or in exploiting others and nature. After we guarantee to all people the essentials of life, we can find meaning and joy in art, useful work (of which there is much to be done, including, for a long time, the cleansing of the environment), study and contemplation, social activities, and so on.

A survivor of the Depression of the 1930s told Terkel, "Security to me is not what we have, but what we can do without" (1970, p. 55).

3. We must reduce urbanization, end city dominance, and revitalize the country. A close study of the Chinese communes and of our own history will show how to begin to think about, and implement, living on the land without giving up the true benefits of city life.

4. We must create true communities, where our activities—work, home, play, shopping—are integrated. If we walk to work and to stores, we will reduce energy consumption, reduce air pollution, be healthier, and have more human contact. We must end our increasing isolation from each other. For example, instead of each family having its own small yard, we must be-

gin to plan (for this will take generations) for many people to share one large park. Such a plan would require, and would enhance, cooperation and human contact (Weisberg 1971, p. 178).

5. Decentralization and the reduction in size of all human groups and organizations are essential. "Central to the socialist transition is the decentralization of power, production, and population" (Anderson 1976, p. 233). There must be local and regional production of food and manufactured products. Energy to transport goods would be saved, we would diversify our lives, and we would enjoy the better taste and nutrition of local fresh food. In New England people would not have tomatoes in the winter, imported from Florida and Mexico, but there would be plenty in the summer—and they would have some taste. If we grew our own grapes and raisins, costs would go down and quality up, and we would not be helpless (as we are now) when faraway weather conditions or corporate greed raised the prices.

6. As I argue throughout this book, we must have an egalitarian and democratic society, without the political, economic, and expert domination now pervading our society (see Chapters 3 and 4). Many people maintain that constant economic growth (under capitalism) is the only way to raise the living standards of poorer people. But not only does the system not work that way, since the profits of growth are kept by the ruling class and a few others, but poor and working people are the chief victims of growth's companions: pollution and work dangers. Moreover, growth solidifies inequalities. Oil has brought billions of dollars to poor countries, but the wealth has not been spread around; it has enriched the few (Anderson pp. 30–38).

7. We must produce for real needs and not create consumer needs that only increase corporate profits. We can live very well with soap; we do not need to pollute the waters with detergents. We can move about by walking and by riding bicycles and public transportation, without depending on the private car, now triumphant because of auto and oil corporation dominance.

8. We must use our bodies more. Our health would increase and energy consumption would decrease. But if we walk or wash dishes, the decrease in energy use will not be profitable to a capitalist economy, so the need to eliminate profit as a consideration is paramount. Also, in order to use our minds and bodies, work must change (see Chapter 5).

9. We must change our eating habits (part of which involves growing our own local food, principle number 5). For example, meat eating is enormously wasteful. For every gram of protein we get from meat, ten grams of grain and other protein are required to raise it. This is a great waste of protein. (See Frances Moore Lappé, *Diet for a Small Planet*.) The tremendous health problems we have because of the processed, sugared, and chemicalized food we eat have already been mentioned. (If food were grown locally, it would need no preservatives and chemicals.)

As you see, these principles are closely connected. One depends on the other, and they all depend on a society operating for the good of all people, not for profit and exploitation.

You may think of more principles we must implement if we are to create a happier, safer world. I do not think any one of us can exhaust the exploration of what we must do for a better world. At most, I hope to have offered some glimpse of what is desirable and possible.

You may find this discussion utopian and unrealistic. But Anderson reminds us that just because a large, egalitarian, comfortable, and ecological society has never existed before is no argument that it cannot. "Obviously, the future has never existed before" (p. 271).

This chapter concludes with some programs, technologies, and research being created now that can start us on the way to that future. We can begin the future now.

*Practical Alternatives*

Some proposals do not question the viability of capitalism. Most of these seem to focus on ways to find energy sources that will allow us to continue our present rate of energy consumption, instead of reducing consumption and protecting the environment.

Some people still deny that there is a crisis. One newspaper story in 1978 argued there was no imminent energy shortage, that it was at least twelve to fifteen years away. With the development of known oil reserves and exploration for more, we could have more oil, this argument goes. But for how long? Fifty, a hundred, two hundred years—there is a limit (Greider 1978).

Another proposal (hotly debated in the 1978 New Hampshire governor's race), would allow electric companies to raise the capital they need by charging extra to their customers now for energy the companies will produce later (by building nuclear plants). In other words, we would pay to build plants so that the electric companies could profit later by selling us electricity. That plan, as some people have said, is socialism for the corporations and capitalism for us (Commoner 1976, p. 260).

Liberal proposals focus on the actions of individuals: picking up litter; driving cars less often; using less electricity. Useful as these actions are, they do not get to the essence of the problem, which is social and which requires social, total, political changes. We cannot, as individuals, liberate ourselves from dependence on the car. We cannot decide to walk or bicycle to work or to take public transportation where none exists, when communities are organized so that work, home, entertainment, and shopping are not close to each other.

In addition, such proposals are also misleading. Rockefeller may call for consumers to use less electricity, but corporate consumption is more the problem. In New York City, households consume 25 percent of electricity, but corporate offices consume 44 percent (Barnet and Müller 1974, p. 344).

Proposals for more and new sources of energy are no solution. "Nuclear fission, coal burning and gasification, and shale oil" (extracting oil from shale rocks) are the main proposals for more energy. All require enormous amounts of water, thus exhausting and polluting our limited supplies of water.

> There are now 176 potential sites for coal gasification, each requiring about 25,000 acre-feet of water per year to operate. One acre-foot of water equals 325,851 gallons, so what it all adds up to is the prospect of the consumption of almost 1½ trillion gallons a year. To put this figure in more understandable terms, coal gasification may require roughly three times as much water as the total annual flow of the California Water Project, one of the world's largest (Perelman and Gardner 1975, p. 123).

Nuclear power, coal, and shale oil are also more energy-inefficient than are the present sources of energy (Alperovitz and Faux 1977, p. 59).

The laws protecting the environment have been weakened and often not enforced. In 1969, the Environmental Protection Act created the Environmental Protection Agency (EPA). The law was a strict one, requiring major projects that might affect the environment (such as nuclear plants) to make an environmental impact statement, showing the EPA there would be no damage to the environment. But through the years, especially in 1972, Congress has passed bills to weaken the work of the EPA, especially by exempting many types of projects from making environmental impact statements. Despite federal subsidies and tax breaks, corporations continue to oppose and postpone pollution controls. Over 50 percent of regions had not met air and water pollution minimum standards by 1977. Such pollution affects working people mostly, for they live in crowded cities which have the worst pollution. Business opposition seems to have succeeded: federal support for environmental protection is declining, harming millions of working people (Marine 1973; England 1978).

Even the limited restrictions on dangerous chemicals and working conditions are not safe from corporate attack. The chemical corporations are waging a fight to stop regulation of dangerous chemicals. On the one hand, they engage in propaganda: one ad claims, "without chemicals, life itself would be impossible," ignoring the great difference between natural chemicals and synthetic ones produced by industry. On the other hand, corporations argue that risks at work are just another part of the inevitable risks of life. Above all, corporations are using their power to cripple and stop government regulation of their plants (Noble 1979).

Nevertheless, despite the limits of liberal solutions, while we work for a socialist, international solution, much can be done to begin changing the economic and political system and our life-styles, so we may avoid eventual catastrophe.

To begin with energy: much more can be done to reduce consumption by planned, systematic efforts to insulate homes and buildings. We can commit ourselves to recycling (which now probably is less profitable than production of new materials, thus not appealing to corporations). "The energy required to produce a ton of steel from urban waste, including separation, transportation, and processings, is only 14 percent of that needed to produce a ton of steel from raw ore. For copper the figure is about 9 percent, and for aluminum only 5 percent" (Morris 1978, pp. 269, 280).

Returnable bottles also would save energy now required to produce throwaway ones, and they would also make for a cleaner environment. Bottling companies have fought against such bills, because, according to capitalism's inner logic, throwaways have meant profit. Indeed, in my lifetime, the nonreturnable bottle became a reality almost unnoticed. There were certainly no consumer outcries against nonreturnable bottles in the late 1950s. But bottling corporations introduced them and, before any of us realized what was happening, the throwaway bottle had become part of our lives. Bottling companies now spend millions to fight against referenda banning throwaways, and they have won about half of these elections.

In addition to energy consumption, a major shift to solar energy is both realistic and necessary. It is free, renewable, requires minimum or no transportation, and needs little capital. With solar, we use as much energy as we need, at the temperatures we need, without waste, radiation, or any pollution. Most homes have enough roof space to collect solar energy adequate to their needs. Other data show that even our present wasteful energy uses could be met with solar energy (Alperovitz and Faux 1977, p. 59; Commoner 1976, pp. 131–35; Morris 1978).

It has other advantages. It does not require huge plants in order to be economical, for small-scale uses, even private homes, are as economical as large-scale ones. Many people fear that reduced energy consumption and solar energy would mean fewer jobs, but energy conservation and reliance on solar and other renewable energy sources actually would create more jobs than does current energy use (Morris, pp. 274–76).

Despite its minute support from the federal government (see Morris for details), solar energy is slowly spreading, especially as the price of oil continues to rise. There are local efforts to change to solar energy, and there is increasing use of solar energy in California. Due to tax write-offs, state government research, and the work of many citizens' groups, solar energy is becoming a reality. Costs are decreasing, and it is estimated that by 1981 as many as 200,000 homes will heat their hot water with solar energy. There are legislative proposals calling for all new buildings to install solar energy, and predictions that by 1985 "40 percent of existing buildings will have solar heat" (Morris, p. 276; Mann 1978).

There are two problems with the concept that solar energy is our salvation. First, if corporations step in and take over the business of constructing and installing solar energy units, costs will be high. This take-over has in fact already begun. While down-playing the promise of solar energy, oil corporations and others seem to be playing it safe by investing in solar power. Of nine major firms producing solar cells, eight are owned by large corporations, five by oil companies. The largest eight oil companies, now moving in to the solar energy field, already control 64 percent of oil reserves, 60 percent of natural gas, and 45 percent of uranium reserves. Such control is bound to make for expensive solar equipment (see Chapter 3). Moreover, we will lose the opportunity for local decentralized power if the oil companies come to dominate the solar industry (Munson 1979; Denman and Bossong 1979).

Secondly, it is not true that solar energy will allow us to continue our present rate of energy consumption. The equipment to capture the sun's energy is made from limited minerals; also, we cannot assign all our land space to capture enough energy to sustain current energy demands. We must change our life-styles, reorganize our communities, and consume less.

There can, however, be major changes in the growing of food. Besides moving away from heavy meat consumption, other changes are possible. For example, city sewage could be treated and returned to the land, where it would fertilize farms instead of polluting the waters. Chapter 6 discussed more proposals. In *Food First*, Lappé and Collins mention crop rotation on the same land (thus preventing exhaustion of nutrients), mixed planting, introduction of natural predators instead of pesticides, and weeding by hand (pp. 57–59; Commoner 1971, pp. 188–89).

By the mid-1980s we may witness the conversion of sewage and sludge into composted manure. Congress has passed a law that decrees that after December 31, 1981, "cities may no longer dump their sewage wastes—raw and untreated—into the Atlantic or Pacific." And by 1985 communities will no longer be able to bury solid wastes in dumps (sanitary land fills). Thus, we shall have to turn to composting sewage and sludge and to recycling solid wastes. Indeed, such efforts are already under way. One plan is for composted New York City sludge to be brought by railroad to a place two hours away, there to fertilize land for fast-growing trees which can be used for energy. Composted sludge and sewage have been used as fertilizer in many parts of the world, and finally we may return to it (Schwerin 1979).

Organic farming, free of pesticides and chemical fertilizers, is possible. Farmers in the United States and elsewhere are returning to organic methods, mostly because chemical farming was too costly and was ruining their land. This development is not organic farming on a small scale. Zwerdling visited grape fields, pineapple groves, and grazing lands involving thousands of acres, representing business investments of from $3 to $6 million, where no chemicals were used. Organic farming is best for the land, and right now, great quantities of food are being raised organically in the United States, costing no more than food grown with chemicals (Zwerdling 1978).

A long-term, planned change of our economy and culture will be necessary to free us from the domination of the car, but some changes are beginning to occur in this area. A number of experiments banning cars from city streets, either on a partial or total basis, have been attempted. Uniformly, people have liked the changes and the environment has improved: cleaner air and quieter streets have been evident. In addition, people in the area begin to walk more and to sit in outdoor benches and cafes, and children play in the streets without the need for constant parental supervision (Dean and Breines 1975).

Many groups are working to implement changes. The workers of one steel mill bargained to include work safety in their contract and then were able to insist on regular inspections to ensure safe working conditions. When the company delayed or refused inspections, the workers not only had the contractual right but trained themselves to do their own inspections (Lynd 1973).

Some communities in the United States are taking action to reduce their energy consumption. Davis, California has taken various steps; a building code regulates the geographical position of new homes, in order for them to receive maximum heat from the sun. Electricity consumption has been reduced by about 10 percent since the code was passed in 1973. To encourage bicycle riding, extensive bicycle paths have been built. To reduce the use of the private car, expanded bus service has been instituted. Since narrow, shaded streets are ten degrees cooler in summer, the town is planning to narrow its streets and plant more trees. Thus, electricity and air conditioning should be reduced. Finally, there is a campaign to encourage solar heating (Ridgeway 1979).

Seattle, Washington also has revised its building codes to save on heating and lighting waste. In addition, it is encouraging the use of public transit, exploring alternative local energy sources, and instituting an extensive conservation education campaign for all residents. There is extensive citizen involvement and input in this campaign (Ridgeway 1979).

In Berkeley, California, as more "street commerce was converted into department stores," houses torn down to make way for "plastic apartments," and more open spaces turned into parking lots, some people revolted. They took over a piece of land that had been planned for conversion into high-rise dormitories and which was then being used as a parking lot and turned it into a people's park, where children could play and people could rest (Weisberg 1971, pp. 165-66).

And in western Massachusetts some people are working to create local food self-sufficiency. Instead of building malls on the fertile plains of the Connecticut river, it makes more sense to grow food on them rather than import it from California. For example, soybeans are being grown, and more

## STRUGGLES: Protesting Nuclear Power

*Protests against nuclear weapons and nuclear power began years ago, but for most of the 1970s the media and most people paid little attention to the issue. But increasing problems with nuclear power, especially the near tragedy at the Three Mile Island plant in March—April 1979, created the conditions for organized opposition to nuclear power. The following news account describes the beginning stages of this expanding protest movement.*

Metropolitan Edison Co., the utility which brought you the Three Mile Island disaster, is seeking to siphon thousands of gallons of radioactive waste water into Pennsylvania's Susquehanna River. At this juncture, only a court order stands between a clean drinking water supply and deadly contamination.

A court order and a movement. And, even more than that, an international antinuclear movement.

On June 2–4, thousands of people across the U.S. and around the world, separated by oceans and cultures, descended on nuclear plants and utility offices to demand an end to nuclear murder.

The demonstrators' tactics were as varied as their backgrounds: they parachuted onto sites, left calling cards of black coffins at utility company doors, scaled fences, climbed cranes, occupied plant sites, blocked entrances and roads in nonviolent civil disobedience, and fought with the cops.

The protests were part of the International Demonstration Days Against Atomic Energy, the first internationally coordinated action linking the dangers of both commercial nuclear power and the vast arsenals of nuclear weaponry.

In the U.S.—from Shoreham, N.Y., to Miami, Fla., from Tulsa, Okla., to Dallas, Texas—some 50 demonstrations, marches and occupations took place in at least 26 states. In all, thousands of protesters, mothers and fathers with young children and rank-and-file unionists, were carted off into buses toward the local jail and countless more thousands participated.

Source: Excerpted from Dennis Schaal, "Antinuke Posse Chases Industry," *The Guardian* (June 13, 1979), p. 3.

"The international protests are a dramatic way to indicate that the antinuclear movement involves millions of people in every state and country," Rex Friend of the Sunbelt Alliance in Oklahoma City told the Guardian June 5.

*Continued Organizing*

Activists around the country were looking to the June 2–4 protests as a means of proving to the nuclear industry and government that the May 6 protest of 110,000 people in Washington was no fluke, that antinuke militants intend to continue organizing and expanding in their local communities.

In general, the June 2–4 protests, in contrast to the May 6 demonstration, were much more militant in character, employing mass arrests, and in political tone, drawing the connection between corporate greed and nuclear perils and tying the antinuclear struggle into the disarmament movement.

"In general, the June 2–4 actions were certainly more rooted in the local communities, were closer to people's concerns and hearts and were more militant because of it," Bob Moore, Mobilization for Survival (MfS) national secretary, noted June 6. "A large number of the actions made the connection with nuclear weapons. And it was a real show of strength on the grassroots level."

"Not only is the antinuke movement getting larger," explained Ed Josephson of the N.Y.-based SHAD Alliance, "but it's getting broader and broader. It will take a while to make its way up to the trade union bureaucrats, but at the grassroots level there really is a lot of sentiment against nuclear power."

The largest antinuclear demonstration in the country took place June 3 in Shoreham, Long Island. Some 15,000—20,000 demonstrators slogged through the sands of Brookhaven Town Beach to denounce nuclear proliferation and to demand the permanent construction halt to the 80%-completed Shoreham plant.

As the rally segment of the SHAD-sponsored event was drawing to a close, more than 600 demonstrators, organized into affinity groups based on consensus decision-making, marched up to the fence

*(continued)*

> **Protesting Nuclear Power** *(continued)*
> surrounding the 80-acre construction site, perched on a hill about 60 miles east of New York City. Deploying conventional ladders and home-made varieties fashioned out of rugs and wooden slats, they scaled chain-link fences, where most were arrested on criminal trespass charges, a misdemeanor. . . .
>
> Perhaps, the tenor of the international protest could be summed up by Josephson of the SHAD Alliance: "The antinuke movement was growing even before Harrisburg. The SHAD Alliance is really less than a year old. If we can pull off a demonstration of 15,000 in the pouring rain in that short a time, this proves the depth of the antinuclear sentiment."

could be (soybeans are used to make tofu, a cheese-like bean curd rich in protein). Energy is thus saved, land is used for growing food, and jobs are created (Anderson 1979).

In the late 1970s, some groups organized and succeeded in slowing down the growth of nuclear energy. The Clamshell Aliance of New England has held demonstrations and engaged in legal action to stop construction of the nuclear plant in Seabrook, New Hampshire.

The near disaster at Three Mile Island in March and April of 1979 increased the concern about nuclear power. The dangers of nuclear radiation have become more obvious as news accounts reveal unusually high incidences of cancer and other diseases among those exposed to radiation in Utah and other places (see Chapter 11 for details). We are also finding out that the government knowingly kept people ignorant of the dangers to which they were exposed. People's concern with health and their anger against government lies may lead to a growing movement that will stop nuclear power, both in the United States and overseas. But such opposition will not be easily tolerated by the nuclear industry and the government. They are actively trying to stop all dissent to nuclear power. Active dissenters have been persecuted. Some have been attacked and beaten (while going to their cars in no connection with any demonstration, for example); one was shot and killed (Solomon 1980; see various issues of the *Progressive* and the *Guardian* from May 1979 to January 1980 for extensive coverage of the Three Mile Island incident, antinuke protests, and government repression).

There have been many referenda, requiring work by many people, to legislate against nonreturnable bottles. Some referenda have won, others have lost.

In East Boston, people have been fighting to stop the growth of Logan Airport, which has not only taken parks and other lands, but also damages people's hearing because of the noise. This fight, like others, has met limited success. Business and corporate needs triumphed. (In 1978, as Logan flights go over some of the suburban communities, thus polluting them with noise, suburbanites were belatedly joining the fight to limit this noise.)

All these are vital struggles to protect our lives, environment, and communities. Most people active in them are not socialists and do not share the socialist perspective. They act out of immediate necessity to protect themselves and improve their lives. In time, some may come to see the ultimate cause of social and environmental threats. For our separate struggles to improve our communities will not, by themselves, bring significant and long-lasting changes unless national and international capitalism is ended and profit considerations are replaced with human needs. Capitalism is a world system, and we must find ways to stop it on that level. Capitalism's threat to the environment and to life spans the whole earth.

# 11

# *Health and Illness: The Quality of Life*

## INTRODUCTION

Health is not simply the absence of illness, nor is it a gift bestowed by doctors and the medical system. Health refers to the quality of our lives, as determined by our body, our mind, and our physical and social environments. It is shaped by the food we eat, the air we breathe, the work we do, the human relations we enjoy (or lack), and, also, the kind of medical care we get.

Previous chapters have explored some of the issues related to health and illness. The working conditions of millions of Americans make them ill and kill hundreds of thousands of others. Chapter 10 described some of the dangers to health brought about by the destruction of the environment. The third section of this chapter (based on Lynch's book *The Broken Heart*), will try to show that it is the class system itself that damages our health and often kills us. Issues of health and illnesss touch the very essence of the quality and meaning of life and society.

First, the worsening conditions of medical care in the United States will be described, followed by an exploration of the basic sources of health and illness. Next, present and proposed reforms to confront the crisis of the medical system are discussed. The fifth section examines the theory and practice of medicine under socialism, which focuses on prevention, the availability of basic care to everyone, and the involvement of all people in the management of their health and illness. The chapter concludes with a summary of principles regarding health, illness, and the quality of life.

## THE MEDICAL SYSTEM: PROFITS AND BIG BUSINESS

No one denies that today the medical system is going through a severe crisis. There are two related issues: one involves the enormous increases in the cost of medical care; the other raises questions about the quality of care, the human relations involved, and their effects on patients. Let us first look at the cost of medicine.

### Paying for Medical Care

The cost of living has increased steadily in the last thirty years, and dramatically in the last ten. But the cost of medical care has increased even faster than the cost of other goods and services.

In 1950, "personal consumption expenditures" were $192 billion, and in 1977 $1,206.5 billion, up 6.3 times from 1950. Medical care expenses increased from $9.1 to $118 billion, up thirteen times from 1950. In short, between 1950 and 1975 medical care increased almost twice as fast as the rest of personal consumption expenditures (*Statistical Abstract* 1979, p. 440).

Table 11.1 shows the dramatic increase in medical care as a percentage of the Gross National Product (GNP), the total of goods and services produced in any given year. We spent almost twice as much of our GNP on medical care in 1978 (8.6 percent) as we did in 1950 (4.5 percent); $12 billion in 1950, $139.3 billion in 1976.

In individual terms, whereas in 1950 the per capita costs (private and public) spent for services and supplies were $75.66, they had increased to $820.68 by 1978 (*Statistical Abstract* 1977, p. 95; 1979, p. 101).

Although the government has assumed a steadily greater portion of these rising costs, do not forget that the government is spending our tax money. In reality, paying for medical care has become a great burden for each of us.

Why has the cost risen so sharply? Simply, medical care has become a very profitable big business. Doctors, corporations that make drugs and supplies, hospitals, and nursing homes are all reaping huge profits.

Doctors' income has increased much faster than that of any other professional group. Their median income is more than twice that of lawyers (Ehrenreich 1978, p. 57). In 1977, the median net earnings for all self-employed physicians was $52,500 ranging from $46,000 for general practition-

TABLE 11.1  National Health Expenditures: 1950–1978

|      | Percent of GNP | Average annual percent change |
|------|----------------|-------------------------------|
| 1950 | 4.5            | 8.8                           |
| 1960 | 5.2            | 8.3                           |
| 1965 | 5.9            | 8.5                           |
| 1970 | 7.2            | 15.5                          |
| 1972 | 7.8            | 11.9                          |
| 1973 | 7.7            | 10.3                          |
| 1974 | 7.8            | 11.5                          |
| 1975 | 8.4            | 15.0                          |
| 1976 | 8.6            | 14.0                          |
| 1977 | 9.0            | 14.2                          |
| 1978 | 9.1            | 13.2                          |

Source: Statistical Abstract of the United States 1977, p. 94; 1979, p. 100.

ers to $71,700 for orthopedic surgeons. Doctors, moreover, have begun to incorporate themselves, and the median net earnings of incorporated physicains are much higher. In 1977, they had a median of $78,300, from the $62,500 for pediatricians, and $63,400 for general practitioners to the $98,800 for general surgeons (*Statistical Abstract* 1979, p. 109).

These are median incomes, which means that 50 percent made over those figures, many considerably higher. In part, doctors' incomes have increased because they have increased their fees. In the two years from 1974 to 1976, the fee charged by my family's pediatrician for a fifteen-minute visit increased from $11 to $16. But doctors increase their income by other means, also.

A physician told reporter Ronald Kotulak: "There are thousands of doctors who take urine specimens and blood samples and throw them in the ash can" (1977). Others demand repeated visits when they are not needed. A letter to the editor of the *Boston Globe* described the four visits needed for a broken finger. The first two, to set the broken finger of the letter-writer's daughter and to check its progress, seemed fair enough. But asking the patient's parents to bring her back merely to look at the finger, pronounce it healing properly, and then asking for another return visit, were obvious padding. When the parents did not keep the fourth appointment, they were called by the doctor's wife and told to come in. The total cost came to $150 (Guillette 1978). A California surgeon who reviews claims for a nonprofit insurance company said that of those claims he checks, half "prove to be grossly inflated. How else would you describe a $400 charge by a plastic surgeon for suturing a lacerated chin? . . . Or two separate and full billings by a neurosurgeon and an orthopedist who had teamed to do a disk-and-fusion procedure—and then an additional bill from each doctor for assisting the other?" (quoted in Klaw 1975, p. 18). Reporter Kotulak was told by a physician that doctors could live very well by practicing honestly, but that many cheat to make $200,000 and up. The physician also charged that doctors are too profit-oriented. They read more business journals than medical journals. *Medical Economics* is the most-read journal, filled with advice on tax shelters and investments.

Unnecessary surgery is the most costly form of cheating. It costs heavily in money and lives. According to the physician interviewed by Kotulak "every specialty has its guaranteed income operation." Tonsillectomies, hysterectomies, and appendectomies are the most common operations performed when there is no medical need. A study by the U.S. House of Representatives found much unnecessary surgery. It estimated that, in 1974, there were 2.38 million unnecessary surgeries, at a cost of $3.92 billion. Even more tragically, an estimated 11,900 people died from these surgeries. (The findings are based on the known 0.5 percent mortality rate from elective surgery and 0.25 percent from all surgery.)

The House study found there are six types of unnecessary operations:

- Category I. Completely discretionary operations for asymptomatic non-pathologic, non-threatening disorders;
- Category II. Operations where no pathologic tissue is removed;
- Category III. Operations where indications are a matter of difference in judgement and opinion among experts;
- Category IV. Operations to alleviate endurable or tolerable symptoms;
- Category V. Operations formerly performed in large numbers, now considered outdated, obsolete, or discredited;
- Category VI. Operations done primarily for the personal gain of the surgeon, wherein the weight of informed opinion would deny any indication to the present (Subcommittee on Oversight 1976, p. 9).

An additional piece of evidence on the effects of surgery comes from a strike of doctors in Los Angeles in 1976. During the strike, the death rate declined week by week. In the first week that surgeons went back to work, the death rate in the area increased, from 14 to 26 per 100,000 people (Drummond 1980, p. 38).

Estimates of over two million unnecessary surgeries a year may not seem believable: how can doctors operate on people merely to increase profits? Some examples prove the point. A young pediatrician did not join a fee-for-service (private, profit-making) medical group when he was told he would have to "produce an average of two tonsillectomies a week for the group's general surgeon" (Klaw 1975, p. 8). Another doctor saw five siblings and removed the tonsils of all five, one of whom almost died from ensuing complications. "Laboratory tests determined that the operating physician had removed healthy tissue from each of the five children" (Subcommittee on Oversight, pp. 10–11). At least some of these doctors may rationalize that since private insurance policies or the government are paying for the operations, the patient is not really cheated.

It may seem that such high charges for medical care simply reflect the shortage of doctors and the demand for their services. But there is no shortage of surgeons. In fact, there are too few general practitioners and too many general surgeons, who perform too many unnecessary operations and pad their bills (Klaw, p. 22).

Most people think that getting second opinions on the necessity of an operation would decrease the number of surgeries. Drummond, however, doubts it. He cites a study done in 1945, in which out of 1,000 children examined, 611 were found to need tonsillectomies. The other 389 went for second examinations with other pediatricians, who advised 174 of them that they needed the operation. A third round of examinations for the remaining 215 resulted in the recommendation that 89 more needed their tonsils removed. It seems that second opinions, when they come from the same kind of doctors giving the first opinions, do little to decrease operations (Drummond 1980, p. 38).

But high fees and cheating by doctors are only a partial explanation for the rising cost of medical care. More important is the fact that medical care has become a very profitable big business.

> Medical care has uniquely attractive features which it shares with only certain sectors of the economy.
>   These features have attracted the presence of large-scale financial and industrial institutions in recent years.
>   Such institutions are subjecting medical care to the same "logic" (profitablility through perpetual expansion) that they have already imposed on other spheres of the economy (McKinlay 1978, p. 40).

Conglomerates such as Firestone and Atlantic-Richfield are entering the drug and medical technology field. There are huge profits to be made in drugs, health, insurance, and hospital equipment. Profits are high, since what costs a few pennies to make sells for dollars. The cost of making 100 five-milligram tablets of Valium was 24 cents (1975), but druggists were charged $6.95, a 2800 percent markup. Drug firms spend 25 percent of money taken in for advertising, much more than they spend on research. In short, as health care has become an industry, there has been a movement away from low-cost, outpatient, preventive medicine toward expensive machines for treating rare diseases, expensive drugs, and long hospital stays, where great profits are guaranteed (Klaw, pp. 27–30; Ehrenreich and Ehrenreich 1970, p. 97).

Hospital stays have become very expensive. In 1950, they cost $15 per day but in 1976 had increased to $150. While the cost of living went up 125 percent, hospital stays went up 1000% (Elrod 1978, p. 316). There are four reasons for the drastic increase in costs: The men and women who cook and clean in hospitals are unionizing and no longer make starvation wages (though this is not yet true in all hospitals). But workers' wages account for a small part of the increase. Much more important are excess beds, expensive medical technology, and doctors' salaries. Also, at a minimum, there are 100,000 surplus hospital beds, at a cost of $1 to $2.5 billion (Klaw, p. 13). Hospitals are engaged in empire-building. To finance larger bed capacity and prestigious but rarely used technology, hospitals need only to raise their rates—and they do. In 1950, national health expenditures were $12.66 billion, with $3.85 billion going for hospitals (30.4 percent of the total) and $2.75 billion for physicians' services. By 1978, of $192.4 billion, $76 billion (39.5 percent) went for hospitals and $35.3 billion (18.3 percent) went for physicians' fees. Hospital care takes by far the largest part of national health expenditures. Expensive medical technology also has contributed to the cost of hospital care as have laboratory, X-ray, and physicians' fees, many for unnecessary or never-performed services (*Statistical Abstract* 1977, p. 95; 1979, p. 101). Abuses of Medicare and Medicaid have also added to the burgeoning cost of medical care. The creation of Medicare in 1965 made it possible for profit-making nursing homes to appear. Many try to care for their patients in a humane way, but much evidence has shown that many other nursing homes neglect their patients to save costs and increase profits. A number of news accounts (Kotelchuck 1976, pp. 122-31) have revealed the incredible cheating of nursing homes. Many owners with political connections escape any inspection of their facilities and records. One owner charged to Medicare $40,000 luxuries like Persian rugs, liquor, and trips. Nursing home care accounted for 1.5 percent of national health expenditures in 1950, but for 8.2 percent of in 1978 ($15.8 billion) (*Statistical Abstract* 1979, p. 101).

Clinics profiting from Medicaid rise in many poor neighborhoods. Those running them charge for tests that are never performed, make patients come for endless visits, and make unnecessary referrals to specialists within the group. Profits are maximized and care minimized (see Caress, in Kotelchuck 1976, pp. 324 ff., for details).

## Human Relations in Medical Care

Such immense costs might be justified if health and medical care were improving. In fact, many studies show that the quality of care and the human relations between patients and those providing the care are worsening.

Ehrenreich and Ehrenreich outline the basic problems of dealing with the medical system: "finding a place where the appropriate care is offered at a reasonable price"; "finding one's way amidst the many available types of medical care"; "figuring out what they are doing to you"; "getting a hearing if things don't go right"; "overcoming the built-in racism and male chauvinism of doctors and hospitals." In short, we are treated cursorily; we are not told much of what is being done to us; and in the process we are being controlled and dehumanized (1970, pp. 3-10).

This impersonal treatment begins at birth in modern hospitals. Whereas it is true that medical advances have helped women with birth complications, for most women they have meant the transformation of a human experience into a medical problem controlled by doctors. Haire outlines "some of [the] common practices from early pregnancy to postpartum which have served to warp and distort the childbearing experience in the United States." These include: "Withholding information of the disadvantages of obstetrical medication.... Requiring all normal women to give birth in the hospital.... Separating the mother from familial support during labor and birth.... Confining normal laboring women to bed.... Shaving the birth area.... Professional dependence on technology and pharmacological methods of pain relief.... Routine electronic fetal monitoring.... Chemical stimulation of labor.... Requiring the mother to assume the lithotomy position (back flat, with knees drawn up and spread wide apart by 'stirrups') for birth.... The routine use of regional or general anesthesia for delivery." These and other practices serve only for the convenience of doctors and hospitals; they are not meant to serve the human and emotional needs of mother, child, and family. The lithotomy position, for example, makes the doctor's work easier, but it tends to "adversely affect the mother's blood pressure, cardiac return and pulmonary ventilation" and have other undesirable effects (1978, pp. 188 ff.; see also Shaw 1974).

The control of birth by doctors becomes even more clear when we look at the increase in Caesarian births in the 1970s. While women are struggling to liberate birth from medical control, doctors are finding new ways to retain and increase their dominance. In the years 1953–62, 3.7 percent of total United States births were by Caesarian; in 1965, 4.5; in 1970, 5.5; in 1975, 10.5; and in 1978, 13.9. This increase is due in part to the greater profitability of Caesarians (they cost three times what normal births cost), but it reflects other realities even more. It is another aspect of the medical tendency to dominate nature and people and not to observe and accommodate to natural processes. Doctors increasingly make the mother a passive observer, not a participant (Corea 1980; Drummond 1980).

After they are born, children in the United States still suffer from the quality and availability of medical care. The United States infant mortality rate was 17.5 (per 1,000 live births) in 1973, the worst of any industrial nation (Sweden has the best rate, 9.6), and 14.1 in 1977. Within the United States, mortality rate varies by class, race, and region. Many black ghettoes and rural areas have rates of 50 and higher. During the years 1968–1973, if the United States infant mortality rate had been as low as that of the Netherlands (11.6 in 1973), 120,000 babies would not have died. Klaw relates the story of a six-week-old baby who was not treated at the hospital where her mother took her, because the mother could not pay. The baby was sent home where she died from dehydration. Our pediatrician told me that in 1976, fully 80 percent of children in this country had not had all the vaccinations the health system could have made available (see below the contrast with socialist countries) (Kotelchuck 1976, p. 6; Klaw 1975, pp. 35–37).

One of the reasons for poor, hurried, or unavailable care is the concentration of doctors in certain states and in large cities. Counties with under 10,000 residents have 47.5 doctors per 100,000 people; counties with 5 million or over have 232.6 doctors per 100,000 people. Also, some areas of cities have few or no doctors and others have too many. Increasingly more doctors go into surgery and other specialties rather than general practice. As a result, the quality of care for routine illnesses has been decreasing.

Even for middle-class people, medical care has become a problem in availability and quality. Long waits for appointments and at the office, short visits with the doctor, and no house calls are common experiences for most people. There is little personal contact with doctors. Efficiency experts advise doctors in some cases to spend no more than nine minutes and fourteen seconds with each patient. Laboratories are doing most of the work. After the brief exam, people are given drugs, sent to specialists, and charged high prices. Preventive medicine is not practiced. Medical school education focuses on treating unusual illnesses and on research (the income is greater in those areas, too). There is no prestige in treating or preventing everyday ailments of people (Kotulak 1977; Klaw, pp. 82-83).

Students who question the direction of medical education face expulsion. Gilma Ramirez was threatened with expulsion from Tufts medical School

> ... because of what [was] described as "inappropriate behavior" and failure "to appreciate her limits as a student" during a nine-week surgery rotation ... at St. Elizabeth's Hospital in Brighton.... Ramirez and her supporters acknowledge that she is "outspoken" and "forceful" and that she asks questions, sometimes embarassing questions, of professors and supervising doctors. She also has been accused of identifying too closely with patients. "I'm concerned about patients, about their families, their jobs," Ramirez says. "I won't capitulate to the impersonal, mechanistic view of medicine" (McCain 1978b).

For a long time, of course, poor people have not been seeing doctors. They have had to go to hospital emergency rooms, where quality is poor and care impersonal and bureaucratic. But now even middle-class people resort to hospital emergency rooms at night because their doctors are not available at night. For a long time, medical care for most people has not resembled anything like the care shown on *Marcus Welby* and other TV shows.

Two doctors did a follow-up study of 141 people who went into the emergency room of Baltimore City Hospital (spring 1969). All had complained of stomach pains, were examined and X-rayed. The doctors concluded that "only 38 of the 141 had gotten effective care" (Klaw, pp. 41-42).

The fiscal crisis of many cities in the late 1970s began to diminish even the availability of medical care in hospitals. In New York, St. Louis, and elsewhere, municipal hospitals have been closing, leaving large sections of those cities, populated by poor and black people, with even more limited access to medical care (Lacefield 1979; Gentry 1980).

As doctors talk less with patients to see what is going on in their lives, they increasingly resort to drugs and technology. Antibiotics and vitamin $B_{12}$ injections are administered commonly, even when "there is little or no chance of their helping the patient." Evidence shows that up to 1.5 million people annually are hospitalized because of adverse reactions to drugs they should never have been given. Some of these prescriptions reflect incompetency, but more probably result from impersonal medical practices and blind faith in drugs and technology. So, dangerous drugs are prescribed for all sorts of conditions; often the side effects of the drugs are more dangerous than the illness they try to cure (Klaw, pp. 24-26, 116).

Enid Blaylock, who left nursing in 1968 and returned to it for a while in 1978, described how technology and control by doctors made it difficult for nurses to relate to people humanely:

> For instance, nursing tradition did not permit me to respond to patients' inquiries in an open, straightforward manner. Whenever a patient asked a pertinent question about the treatments that I was administering, my programmed response was, "You'll have to check with your doctor." I could not even tell the patient that his temperature was 100.2, or that his blood pressure was 180-90. Neither could I tell him that the medicine I was giving him is called Thorazine, and that it was prescribed to keep his blood pressure down. I did not like having to withhold information that patients needed, and to which they had every right.

Technology had made nursing even more impersonal in 1978:

> It seems that today nursing is one of the least humane of the helping professions. Patients die alone and uncomforted because nurses are too busy regulating the machines and gadgets that medical technology has spawned. Patients experiencing severe anxiety crises are put on hold because giving them the time they require would disrupt the medical assembly line.
>
> Today, nurses concentrate more on legal than on moral responsibilities. Too often, if a patient falls while trying to get to the bathroom because no one was around to assist him, the nurse's immediate concern is to protect the institution against possible lawsuits. Safety measures are based on legal need rather than on deep concern for patients' well-being (Blaylock 1978).

There is much evidence showing a decline in the quality of medical care. For example, in the 1950s, a study of eighty-eight general practitioners showed that more than half prescribed drugs to people with hypertension but never inquired about the causes for the condition.

A burgeoning of medical services and irrelevant or harmful practices prevent effective care. Procedures have been added beyond the simple necessities, and our encounter with the doctor has become impersonal and fleeting. It has become impossible for us as patients to distinguish the superfluous treatments from the necessary, and doctors are not about to enlighten us (McKinlay 1978, pp. 41-42).

Nor will they monitor each other for ineffective or dangerous care, or for cheating. Chapter 4 showed how doctors, like other professionals, protect incompetent colleagues and refuse to discipline them. The evidence is great (see Chapter 4). From 1968 to 1972, seven states having 23,000 doctors "reported no disciplinary actions of any kind, not even a reprimand." Grievance committees do exist, but many doctors do not know of them. Doctors known to be incompetent are safe if no patients bring complaints (Klaw, p. 97). In the early 1970s two New York obstetricians (twin brothers) had become drug addicts and were known to be in no condition to examine patients or enter the operating room. Yet, for at least three years, nothing was done to prevent them from practicing. We cannot know how long they would have been allowed to go on practicing, since they were found dead of overdoses.

Disciplining incompetent and dishonest doctors would begin to raise questions about all doctors' expertise and knowledge. Thus, doctors foster authoritarian relationships, wanting us to listen and obey their orders (supposedly) based on science and knowledge. In a sense, patients also want to believe in medical invincibility. Transference of the problem to the doctor relieves us of the burden of being responsible for ourselves. This is another consequence of living under capitalism, where, increasingly, responsibility and autonomy are taken away from us in all areas of life (see Chapter 4). The myth of medical expertise is used to increase the doctors' power, not to serve people (Ehrenreich 1978, pp. 59-60).

This poor medical care leads to increased costs. People have begun to sue doctors for obvious cases of malpractice (although most people, still under the cloud of medical invincibility, do not sue when they should). To protect themselves in case they are sued for malpractice, doctors order unnecessary X-rays and lab tests as a legal cover. So the cost of medical care increases further (Bodenheimer, in Kotelchuck 1976, p. 423).

Ehrenreich calls the above two kinds of critiques of the medical system *political economic* and *cultural* critiques. The political economic critique focuses on problems of cost, distribution, and availability of medical care. It assumes that medicine is beneficial in itself, but that problems arise when doctors abuse it and when it is not available to everyone. As Ehrenreich puts it: "The political economic critique challenges the poor distribution of an otherwise admirable service; the cultural critique disputes the value of the services themselves" (1978, p. 4). This section on the quality of medical care has been exploring issues raised by the cultural critique (see "Sources of Health and Illness," below). Although all socialists subscribe to the political economic critique, the cultural critique also is indispensable to a socialist perspective on health. The latter focuses on human meaning and consequences, on the social relations involved, when professional domination prevents the provision of health and curing of illness.

The cultural critique raises questions about the nature, functions, and consequences of the doctor-patient relationship—its frequently authoritarian nature and its mystique. That relationship often reinforces conditions in the larger society (domination, sexism, passivity). The medical model today avoids the large questions that deal with the quality of life and its effects on our health (Ehrenreich 1978, p. 15).

*Medicine as Social Control*

The cultural critique can be extended to a logical extreme and deny that any benefits derive from medical care (Illich, *Medical Nemesis,* 1975). I do not think we should deny the benefits of medicine; rather, we should focus on the ways it is used, for whose benefit and at what cost.

Doctors and the medical system as a whole do not hold absolute power, nor are they in the higher circles of the ruling class. Whereas it is true that we are witnessing "the medicalization of society" (Zola, quoted in Ehrenreich 1978, pp. 80-100), we must not confuse it with the power of the ruling class that shapes the course of society. Rather, the medicalization is a consequence of life under capitalism.

More human actions are falling within the province of medicine. Children's colds and marital problems were once handled in the community, with relatives and friends helping, but now medical specialists have expropriated this service. Two powerful books—Schrag and Divoky, *The Myth of the Hyperactive Child,* and Schrag, *Mind Control*—show how medicine is being extended to control ordinary human actions. In their book on hyperactivity, Schrag and Divoky document the use of drugs to control school children. A biological diagnosis ("learning disabilities;" "hyperkinesis"), limited to a few children, has been generalized to millions; medicine has provided the drugs to discipline these children. Social and human issues are masked under the guise of medical expertise.

> Traditional methods of management and control (threats, punishment, school suspensions) have been replaced by an accumulation of psychosocial and psychochemical techniques and by an ideology of "early intervention" which regards almost every form of undesirable behavior, however benign, as a medical ailment requiring treatment. Among the components are the prescription of psychoactive drugs to make children manageable in the classroom; the growing fashion for giving ordinary children ill-defined or meaningless pseudo-scientific labels like "learning disabled," "hyperkinetic," "behaviorally dysfunctional" or "predelinquent" and using them to justify segregation in special programs (Schrag and Divoky 1975, p. xi).

In his later book, Schrag explores the use of drugs, behavior modification, scientific-sounding labels, and other techniques used against people of all ages. Instead of open and admitted punishment for undesirable behavior, medicine has invented techniques that sound neutral, scientific, and beneficial, but which are really subtle, insidious methods of control. Revelations of CIA-sponsored research on mind control are but one chapter in the use of mind control (Shrag 1978).

In other ways, the very nature of the authoritarian doctor-patient relationship allows doctors to communicate many political and moral messages. For example, despite the lack of any evidence showing children in day care get more colds and illness, doctors make that claim, thus discouraging mothers from working (Ehrenreich and Ehrenreich, in Ehrenreich 1978, p. 64). Surely doctors have no special expertise in the making of moral and social choices. Which illnesses should or should not be treated, what patients should be told, and whether treatment should cease are not choices that can be backed by objective evidence. But the aura of expertise allows psychiatrists, for example, to commit people and prescribe behavior-modifying drugs, when, as anyone knows who has ever known a psychiatrist outside his or her office, they have no more (and often less) knowledge of human relations and emotions than any of us.

## The Growth of the Medical System

Today, the medical system is characterized by the increase in government payments, the rise of hospital empires that have replaced doctors as the center of power, group practice and specialization, and the growth of large corporations selling drugs and hospital equipment. The historical process that has led to this modern medical system is instructive.

For centuries, medicine and health care were the province of women and working people. Midwives and others took care of the needs of the vast majority of people. But in the nineteenth century, women were gradually being replaced by men and medicine became a profession.

Early in the twentieth century, medical education and practice were still unregulated. In the 1910s, a series of reforms of medical education led to the closing of many medical schools and a decrease in the number of doctors. The American Medical Association (AMA) was given the power to accredit schools and license doctors. One stated purpose was to raise the quality of training and care, but an equally important result was to create a shortage of doctors and a monopoly or sellers' market for those doctors still practicing.

Consider some data. In 1904, before the AMA took over control of medical education, there were 28,000 medical students. By 1927, after the reforms, the country increased by 34 million people, but the number of medical students decreased to 20,000. By 1949, there were fewer graduates than in 1930. In the late 1960s, as federal funding became available, more medical schools were started; and there were 9,500 first-year medical students in 1967 and 14,700 in 1974 (Klaw, p. 21).

An important development which began to change the whole medical system was the creation of Blue Cross in the 1930s. It began the shifting of medical care to hospital settings. Hospitals, wanting to insure payment of their bills, set up Blue Cross as a pre-payment plan. In a sense, people paid their bills before entering the hospital. Blue Cross is still dominated by hospitals, and it raises rates in mere anticipation of rising hospital costs.

Since the 1940s, three new forces have entered medicine: "academic medical empires (medical schools dominating large hospital complexes), health-care financiers (predominantly Blue Cross), and health-care profiteers (ranging from hospital supply and drug companies to nursing home entrepreneurs)" (Kotelchuck 1976, p. 2).

These groups and institutions began to grow when the federal government started funding medical care through Medicare and Medicaid (1966). As a result,

> Vast sums of money ostensibly for patient care poured virtually without government controls into hospitals and other health-care institutions, ranging from nursing homes and community mental health centers to drug and alcohol treatment centers.... Medical empires developed from academic medical centers, swallowing up public and smaller private hospitals through a variety of affiliation agreements. Hospitals grew by leaps and bounds, building new facilities, adding new beds, staff and equipment and expanding outpatient services into the surrounding communities. Health-care costs skyrocketed (Kotelchuck 1976, pp. xii–xiii).

One set of figures shows the trend to government funding. In 1950, public expenditures were 25 percent ($3 billion) of all national health expenditures. (This covers any spending related to health: research, Medicare, and so on.) In 1978, public expenditures were 40.5 percent ($78 billion) of national health spending. Medicare, which began in 1966, accounts for $26 billion of the 1978 public expenditures (*Statistical Abstract* 1979, p. 100).

Now, power in the medical system centers around large corporations and the "medical empires," large hospitals affiliated with major medical schools. These empires are replacing the AMA as the dominant group in medicine. The new centers of power have arisen despite AMA opposition to the funding sources—Blue Cross and government money—that now dominate health spending. Sole practitioners paid by their patients are rapidly disappearing, replaced by doctors paid by public and insurance payments, groups of doctors and nursing homes. And just as doctors once arranged it so that their profits and power were more important than good care, so are the new powers in medical centers and corporations arranging the system this way (Ehrenreich and Ehrenreich 1970, pp. 30–31; Millman 1977, p. 208).

Two features characterize the workforce within this new medical setting. Male doctors are at the top of the hierarchy, and specialization and professionalization are rampant. Doctors are mostly white men (over 90 percent); most registered nurses are white women; most licensed practical nurses, orderlies, and cleaning and cooking personnel are minority people. The class backgrounds typically are: upper and upper-middle class for doctors, lower-middle class for nurses, and the poor or working-class for other hospital staff (Krause 1971, p. 126).

Women not only occupy the lower-prestige occupations, they also make less when they have exactly the same jobs as men. Male X-ray technicians made $131 weekly (1969), female technicians made $116.50; male practical nurses $108.50, female $98.50 (Reverby, in Kotelchuck 1976, p. 173).

Finally, there is increasing specialization and the rise of new health professions (see the readings in Kotelchuck, pp. 206-248). At one time, there were four different groups in medicine: physicians, dentists, nurses, and pharmacists. Now there are at least twenty-two licensed occupations, each fighting to define clearly and defend its turf, by increasing credentials (see Chapter 4). Most of these credentials are only meant for public impressions and are not related to actual job requirements. For example, in the next few years all nurses will have to have a bachelor's degree, and those RNs now without it must go back to school to get it in order to advance. Surely nurses now get adequate training for their work; the addition of the bachelor's requirement will only make it more difficult for many women to enter nursing. Raising educational requirements only creates the impression of "professionalism" and is not related to the work (*Dollars and Sense*, November 1978, pp. 6-8).

Two new specialties illustrate some of the basic problems in medicine. Physician assistants (men) and nurse practitioners (women nurses) have appeared in the last few years. They are meant to practice medicine at some low level, but it is unclear what they are allowed to do, and doctors insist that both new specialties practice only under a doctor's supervision. In addition, sexism arises in that the physician assistants, who seem to carry more prestige than nurse practitioners, are mostly men, whereas it would seem that nurses would be the most logical group to elevate in medical skills. At the moment, doctors seem clearly in command of medical care, and they are resisting any laws to expand the role of nurses (hearings in Massachusetts in November 1978 brought out this resistance clearly).

## SOURCES OF HEALTH AND ILLNESS

The medical system is but one contributor to people's health. It is not the most important one. Medical care becomes necessary when the quality of life worsens and we need help. Health is not the absence of illness or something that doctors give us. Health is what we enjoy when we live in an environment that enhances well-being. Body and mind interact with the physical and social surroundings to produce a total effect of health or illness.

### Illness from the Physical Environment

Today, the food we eat often endangers our health. Processed food lacking in roughage causes digestive problems, even cancer of the colon. Pesticides and other chemicals used to grow much of our food may cause problems we do not even know about. As we consume large amounts of meat, and as the raising of animals becomes big business, we meet another source of danger to our health. The raising of cows has become big business, so they are kept and fed under crowded, assembly-line conditions, where cleanliness is difficult. Antibiotics are used to fight their inevitable diseases. But these huge quantities of antibiotics create bacteria that are resistant to antibiotics, and when we eat the meat with those bacteria, we are endangered. One study found salmonella contamination in 50 percent of chickens. It is estimated that seven of ten cases of after-dinner headaches and nausea may be due to salmonella poisoning. No one knows the cumulative effect of contaminated meat, full of hormones. Antibiotics and hormones are totally unnecessary when cattle are raised under clean conditions. But chemicals, hormones, and antibiotics have become a permanent fixture of corporate, profit-making farming (Zwerdling 1973).

There are still more connections between food and illness. Some doctors have found that symptoms of children diagnosed as "hyperactive" disappear permanently when these children eat food free of artificial colors and flavors and of sugar. Paralleling the rise of artificial additives in recent years is a rise in the number of children diagnosed as "hyperkinetic," according to one estimate (by California allergist Ben Feingold) an increase of from 2 to 25 percent of all children. Junk food and much other food abound with additives:

> The average child's breakfast, he says, will include a cereal "loaded" with nonessential flavors and colors, and perhaps frozen waffles or frozen French toast dyed with tartrazine. "At school, he says, "the same ritual is continued at lunch," where nitrate-laden hot dogs, luncheon meats, ice cream and other heavily preserved and otherwise chemicalized foods are served (Feltman 1974a, p. 111).

The environment also affects our health. The previous chapter discussed the effects of air pollution. Look specifically at cancer. It is the second leading killer of people between twenty-four and sixty-five (heart disease is first). Cancer strikes 25 percent of Americans and kills 400,000 people yearly. Scientists are coming to believe that 90 percent of cancers are caused by environmental pollution (although social conditions, described below, may also contribute to cancer deaths). According to writer Al Goodman, at this point the problem of cancer is "political and economic, not scientific." That is, we know much of what causes cancer; the issue is whether we will change the political conditions that lead to damage of the environment. For example, the American Cancer Society and most cancer research focus on curing cancer after it arises, not preventing it (Goodman 1978; Epstein 1978; Moss 1980).

Radiation is one cause of cancer. Radiation levels that had been assumed safe are now found to be too high. They are ten times higher than the really safe levels. People who have been exposed to "safe" levels have died from cancer and other illnesses. When scientists began exposing these effects, the government tried (with some success) to suppress their findings (Kohn 1978).

Recently we have learned of the unusually high rates of cancer and other illnesses found among people in Utah exposed to radiation from the Nevada testing grounds for nuclear weapons and among United States soldiers who went into Hiroshima and Nagasaki after the bomb explosions.

> Since the testing, residents of the area have died at alarming rates here. One recent study published in the *New England Journal of Medicine* examined the incidence of leukemia deaths in children 15 and under who were born in the southern half of Utah while the testing was going on. It concluded there were 2.4 times more leukemia-induced deaths among this sample than among children living in the same area who were born before and after the tests (Bradlee 1979a).

United States soldiers exposed to radiation in Japan have been in very poor health:

> There is indisputable evidence that U.S. Marines who participated in Nagasaki cleanup operations later fell victim to an extraordinary high incidence of bone marrow cancers and blood disorders. . . .
>
> [Seven men were located who spent time in Nagasaki.] Among the seven, some strikingly similar ailments have occurred. Hodge, Good, Quigley, Gender, and Crews suffered severe lung ailments, at times requiring surgery and in all cases causing chronic breathing problems beginning decades ago. Constant intestinal attacks, often within a few months after leaving Nagasaki, became long-term realities of life for Hodge, Zotter, Quigley, Gender, and Crews; each of those men also experienced persistent problems with their legs. And a pronounced pattern of unusual, chronic weeping skin sores or ulcerations has been suffered by Hodge, Zotter, Good, Quigley, and Gender (Solomon 1979, pp. 21, 24).

Nuclear power presents dangers at every stage: mining uranium, processing it, disposing of nuclear waste. Radiation from nuclear byproducts will last for about 500,000 years; since no safe storage method has yet been found, we will face an enormous health danger for a long time (Caldicott 1979).

The nuclear age is claiming more victims every day. Joe Harding worked for eighteen years in a uranium enrichment plant in Kentucky. The last few years of his life he suffered inoperable stomach cancer, massive blood clots in his legs, and other ailments. To the day he died, he worked for a government investigation of the dangers to which he and his co-workers had been exposed. His wife and friends are carrying on the fight (Moore 1980).

It is no wonder that the people of Three Mile Island are worried about the effects on their health of the radioactivity released there in March and April 1979. Many people are torn by fears, partly of what they are not being told (as the people in Utah were never told about the dangers to which nuclear explosions exposed them). "We feel . . . like characters in . . . a horror movie"; "many of us will never feel safe . . . again"; pregnant women are anxious about possible effects on their unborn children (Mills 1980).

They have reason to fear. A year after the accident at Three Mile Island, there was a sharp rise in the rate of hypothyroidism among newborn babies in adjacent areas (hypothyroidism is a condition that leads to physical and mental retardation) (Sternglass 1980).

People were not the only victims of this accident, however. Ever since the nuclear plant began operating at Three Mile Island in the mid-1970s, area farmers have noted strange happenings among their animals. In one farm 290 duck eggs were laid in 1978, but not one hatched. Horses, cows, sheep, cats, and other animals have been born deformed or sterile, or died without explanation (Wasserman 1980).

Other studies reveal that even low levels of lead ingested by children cause long-term damage. All children get some lead from the air (lead gets into the air from automobile gasolines); some children get more from lead paint. Up to now, the concern has been with those who get acute poisoning from lead paint. Evidence is now showing that many children with lead in their blood are affected in subtle ways ("hyperkinetic" behavior, for example). Elevated levels of lead, short of acute poisoning, have been found, nationally, in "6.5 percent of children tested in seventy-seven screening projects, . . . and the findings were confirmed by repeated testing." Cities with air pollution from automobile traffic show up to 20 percent of children with elevated levels (Huebner 1978, p. 22; Harris 1979).

A recent study in the *New England Journal of Medicine* (March 30, 1979) reported that children exposed to "safe" levels of lead who had had no obvious symptoms of lead poisoning showed "psychological effects." These included "increased distractability, increased daydreaming, lack of persistence, inability to follow directions, and lack of organization." (Teachers made the evaluations, but they "did not know which of their students had been recorded as having high or low lead exposure.") These effects must be studied more carefully, but the possible implications are frightening, given the amount of lead present in the air and everywhere else (Cooke 1979b).

Lately, we have come to know the dangers of exposure to materials containing asbestos. No level of exposure is safe. In the last thirty years, 4.5 million people have been exposed in shipyards alone. It can take up to thirty to forty years before the effects kill people. Even people who were exposed indirectly (women who may have shaken out their husbands' work clothes) have died from asbestos poisoning (Knox 1978; Caldwell 1979).

A man named Joe Ruggieri was dying of cancer in 1979. His case shows how asbestos exposure, leading to cancer years later, begins:

> Every day, for four months, a 19-year-old Navy seaman named Ruggieri helped overhaul the [tanker] Sabine, scraping, painting, cleaning. Above and around him, others tore covers from pipes and sandblasted the hull.

> Asbestos dust filled the ship. Day and night, Joe inhaled it. Millions of fibers pierced the soft, moist air sacs in his lungs, and over the decades, turned them to useless leather.... HEW estimates 67,000 Americans will die from asbestos disease every year for 30 years, the legacy of decades of negligence in the workplace (Patinkin 1979).

In the late 1970s former employees began to sue asbestos companies for hiding the dangers of asbestos from them. Documents that became available during those lawsuits show a continuing effort to keep scientific findings secret that proved the dangers of asbestos. For example, there were "documents and statements from former asbestos officials that the industry spent thousands of dollars setting up research projects at a Saranac Lake, N.Y., laboratory in the 1930's and 1940's and then prevented the researchers from publishing findings indicating possible asbestos danger to humans" (Richards 1978, p. 44).

Asbestos is only one of many deadly substances to which many of us are being exposed. Dioxin ("Agent Orange"), a chemical contained in defoliants, has been publicized since the late 1970s. American soldiers were exposed to it when they sprayed it in Vietnam, and many are now reporting debilitating diseases. Of course the Vietnamese were even more exposed, and the evidence is piling up in Vietnam: birth deformities, miscarriages, and sterility are occurring at much greater rates among Vietnamese exposed to Agent Orange than they are among those not exposed (Woollacott 1980).

But dioxin was not used only in Vietnam. People in rural Maine and Oregon were exposed to it through aerial spraying near their homes. Winds carried the spray onto farms and gardens. Soon after, vegetables had "grotesque growths"; people experienced unexplained breathing difficulties, bleeding gums, and numbness in fingertips. In Maine in 1978 the state birth defect rate was 1.8 percent, but it was 5.35 percent in the sprayed area (Blake 1980).

Similar dangers have been hidden from other Americans. Two years after a company in St. Louis, Michigan, knew of the potential dangers of PBB (polybrominated biphenyl), it had not told its workers. They were exposed to the dust and told it was safe enough to eat. One of those affected by PBB was Tom Ostrander: exposure left him weak and lethargic. He lost forty pounds. "He has not worked in 18 months, since he became too weak to do anything for more than two hours at a stretch except sleep." Even more tragically, PBB dust brought home in the workers' clothes seems to have affected some of their children (Clary and Thompson 1978).

PCBs (polychlorinated biphenyls), of which PBB is a close relative, have invaded the environment widely (see Chapter 10). PCBs have been incorporated into many products: soaps, food packaging, and paints. The PCB in these products affects the environment when they are dumped. The effects of PCB will be long-term because it does not become harmless with time. One oceanographer has concluded that PCBs are "present in varying concentrations in every species of wildlife on the earth." Indeed, the Environmental Protection Agency estimates that about half of us have accumulated "several parts per million" PCBs in our fatty tissues. The EPA has set a standard of fifty parts per million as cause for immediate action, but in North Carolina, some people near PCB spill sites were found to have 7,000 parts per million. These were fieldworkers in a tobacco farm, so even people in rural areas cannot avoid chemical poisoning (Jacobs 1980).

*Illness from the Social Environment*

Capitalism affects our health not only by changing the physical environment. Chapter 7 tried to show how capitalism decreases our sense of community: such isolation impoverishes our social and emotional lives but also damages our health.

In his book *The Broken Heart,* James Lynch has tried to document the relationship. He focuses on heart disease, the leading cause of death for people twenty-four to sixty-five. In a series of tables Lynch shows that people who are more socially isolated (single, divorced, widowed) suffer twice the death rate from heart disease as married people. For example, white divorced men as a group had 362 deaths per 100,000 per year (1959–1961); white married men had 176. Black married men had 142, black divorced men 298. The same rates, at lower numbers, hold true for women (1977, pp. 17, 41–51).

Lynch cites a remarkable study done in 1971, in which Dr. George Engel investigated carefully the sudden deaths of 170 people. In 101 of these cases, he found that some profound personal loss preceded the death:

1. After the collapse or death of a close person ... 36 people
2. During a period of acute grief (within 16 days) ... 35 people
3. Threat of the loss of a close person ... 16 people
4. After loss of status or self-esteem ... 9 people
5. During mourning or the anniversary of some event ... 5 people
(pp. 59–60).

It is not only being married or divorced or suddenly losing someone close that affect health. Community life that is stable and intimate also contributes to health; and the decrease in such community life leads to the deterioration of health. People in Roseto, Pennsylvania (see Chapter 7) in 1960 had diets of high cholesterol but a close community life: they had one-third as many heart attacks as nearby communities. But when they became more isolated and social mobility increased (by the early 1970s) Roseto's people were afflicted with the same rates of heart disease and other illness as their neighbors.

Framingham, Massachusetts, whose residents' health has been studied intensively since the 1940s, had one-third fewer people with heart problems than had been expected. According to Lynch, the lower heart disease rate came about because community life was closer in Framingham, which shows less of the deterioration of social relations than most cities (pp. 25–27).

Indeed, there is some evidence to show that the quality of existence under capitalism can shorten life. In a fifteen-year study done by the department of Health, Education, and Welfare, it was found that work satisfaction was the most important predictor of a long, healthy life. But as we have seen (Chapter 5), most people do not find satisfaction in their work; their health and life suffer (*Work in America* 1973; Navarro 1976, p. 39).

A *New England Journal of Medicine* study on death rates in different sections of the Greater Boston area shows how the social-class system pervades our existence, even to our death. The study showed that "economically deprived people die far more frequently from causes that are not likely to kill those better off in housing, nutrition, family stability, access to medical care, educational level and level of stress in their everyday lives." An area of Boston populated by poor people (mostly blacks) had a death rate in 1972 and 1973 30 percent higher than the statewide average and 50 percent higher than affluent suburbs a few miles away.

> The area had a mortality ratio two or more times the Commonwealth as a whole for respiratory diseases, infectious and parasitic diseases, cirrhosis of the liver, cancer of the esophagus, mental illness-related deaths, heart disease, diseases of the veins (mainly blood clots), pneumonia, digestive diseases, perinatal (fetal and newborn) deaths, fire-related deaths, homicides and other injuries (Knox 1977, pp. 1, 16).

Thus, social isolation, competition, economic insecurity and deprivation, and other social conditions combine with a polluted environment and unsafe food to make us ill, even kill us.

*Health*

Some conditions of our society, however, improve health. In contrast to the early stages of industrialism, life expectancy today is considerably longer. Conventional wisdom attributes the increase to progress in medicine and drugs. But most diseases began to decline before immunization shots and other medical treatments came about: a study by McKeown showed that tuberculosis, typhoid, and other diseases disappeared because of improvements in living (housing and nutrition), better sanitation, and "personal medical care" (quoted in Ehrenreich 1978, p. 12). (The poor are less poor.) Starr argues that better medical services have had a "positive effect on health" but concludes that "environment and behavior are the principal determinants of health and life expectancy; medical care plays a relatively small part" (1976, p. 54; see also Renaud 1975, pp. 103–104: Ehrenreich 1978, pp. 1–35; Drummond 1980; Chapin and Wasserstrom 1980).

Whereas our health or illness derive from the interaction of body, mind, and the social and physical environments, medicine today ignores the living conditions caused by industrialism: stress, social isolation, pollution, and so on. Rather, medicine focuses on individual pathology. This focus is based on the belief that each disease has its own specific cause and the view of the human body as a machine independent of the mind. In short, medicine under capitalism focuses on treating illness, not the social conditions that cause illness (Renaud, pp. 106–109; Ehrenreich, p. 12).

## CAN MEDICINE HEAL ITSELF?

The flaws of the medical system are obvious, even to liberal critics of the system who do not hold a socialist perspective. What solutions do liberals propose?

Since they see the trouble as a chaotic nonsystem, liberals propose the careful, systematic organization of medical institutions. Group practices (especially health maintenance organizations—HMOs) and some form of national health insurance (NHI) are their basic proposals.

### Health Maintenance Organizations

People who join HMOs pay to have all their health needs covered (drugs, eyeglasses, and a few other items usually are excluded). Our family belongs to the Harvard Community Health Plan (HCHP), for which we paid over $1,200 a year in 1979 (some of this was covered by my employer). Membership includes hospital insurance and visits to doctors (there is a fee of $1 for each visit). Belonging to Blue Cross–Blue Shield would cost about $150 more per year.

HMOs claim to operate on the principle of dealing early with illness and preventing major hospital costs. Data do show that HMOs cut costs by sending fewer people to hospitals than the rate for the population in general; HMOs also perform fewer surgeries. In both cases, at least some of the reduction is due to the elimination of unnecessary hospitalization and surgeries rather than preventive medicine. In 1973, in a study conducted in Southern California, an average-size family paid $447 for all their medical needs if they belonged to Blue Cross–Blue Shield; $364 if they had commercial insurance; and $323 if they belonged to a group-practice, HMO organization (Klaw 1975, pp. 166–68).

Klaw mentions that long waits for appointments and for service are common to HMOs. But, disagreeing with socialist critics, he does not believe HMOs cut back on services. If they did, he argues, people would not remain in them (pp. 171–72).

Other studies show that HMOs have neither reduced costs nor improved the quality of medical care. After initial cost savings, HMOs increase in cost as fast as other forms of insurance (in our family's case, premiums went up $10 a month in the second year). Also, the cost savings of HMOs are underestimated because they do not enroll old, poor, or chronically ill people. More important, the quality of care has not improved. Kaiser, one of the better known HMOs, has lower ratios of doctors per 100,000 people than the state average: in Northern California, Kaiser has a ratio of 102 versus the 161 state ratio. Thus, fewer personnel, fewer and shorter visits, and long waits for appointments are common. Studies show that 50 percent of HMO members are unhappy with service; people come to clinics rather than personal doctors; doctors themselves feel rushed. Service, in short, is neither personal nor careful. For those who are not persistent and insistent, HMOs provide little medical care (Kotelchuck 1976, pp. 345–86).

Our family's experience with HCHP generally supports these criticisms. During a bad case of flu for our older daughter, we spoke to four doctors, three nurses, and three receptionists. Each time we had to restate the symptoms and what we had done. We live about ten miles from the HCHP center, and the travel distance and impersonal contacts over the phone left us very unhappy. HMOs are not like good neighborhood health clinics providing personal care (see next section).

## National Health Insurance

Another major proposal to reduce health care costs is some form of national health insurance. Many bills have been proposed, providing various degrees of coverage. Although NHI is a controversial political issue, it seems inevitable that it will become a reality, in some form, over the next few years.

Of all the proposed bills, the Kennedy-Griffiths Health Security Act is the most liberal. It covers virtually all medical costs. It would be financed 50 percent from special taxes and 50 percent from general revenue funds. A national board would be set up to oversee operations, and there would be ten regional boards. Cost limits are included: the system could not spend more than the funds raised by taxes. In addition, there would be provisions (such as financial incentives) to encourage the creation of more HMOs and other changes in the delivery of care (Lander 1978, pp. 300–313).

But nothing in this bill, or any other proposal for NHI, guarantees better care. Doctors, hospitals, and HMOs could adjust to the limits on money for medical care by cutting back on services (as HMOs are doing now). Giving money to private groups committed to profit would only repeat the experience of Medicare and Medicaid—huge profits for doctors, hospitals, and corporations, but no better care. In 1968, the elderly paid the first $40 of their bills under Medicare; in 1978, they paid the first $144. Thus, "despite Medicare, elderly people pay more out of their own pockets for medical care today than they did before the program existed." All this has been going on while the share paid by the government has skyrocketed (Kotelchuck 1976, p. 289).

NHI is an insurance program and does not even attempt to deal with the important issue of quality of care. Even if government regulations aimed at "eliminating fraud, duplication, and waste meet with the wildest success," they cannot begin to improve health if they leave untouched the model of medical care based on high technology, specialization, and in-hospital care. The public now equates good medical care with this model (Kotelchuck, p. 207).

*Beyond Liberal Reform*

This section will look briefly at two proposals that do aim to change the quality and delivery of care.

Marilyn Elrod, a congressional legislative assistant, proposes a "comprehensive health service." Whereas NHI would finance the cost of services provided by doctors, hospitals, and others who remain private businesspeople, Elrod proposes socialized medicine in a capitalist society. All health personnel would work for regional government health centers for a salary. These centers would be run by elected representatives of local communities and would be financed through progressive taxes. There would be savings, obviously, with elimination of the profit motive. What about quality?

> Comprehensive, high-quality health care would become the right of everyone with no restrictions on eligibility or benefits. All services would be provided on a no-fee-for-service basis by salaried health workers, stressing the maintenance of good health and the prevention of illness (Elrod 1978, p. 317).

Even if passed (very unlikely while the United States remains capitalist), such a plan would have only limited success. While the rest of the society operates on the motives of profits and competition, how could medical personnel be motivated by service to their fellow citizens? Socialism cannot be partial, in one institution. Moreover, how would this plan deal with the social, political, and environmental causes of illness?

Finally, Ivan Illich, among others, proposes "self-care and lifestyle changes" as the only solutions. (In 1978, many people have been wearing T-shirts with "Health Thyself" written on them.) However, such proposals present no threat to corporate control; they imply clearly that individuals are the cause of the problem, and not the conditions of poor nutrition, alienating work, and lack of preventive care. For example, as individuals we can do little about poor nutrition. Conglomerates produce the super-processed, chemicalized food that is the cause of much poor nutrition. Collective political action is necessary to take the profit out of food production and remove control from the conglomerates (Illich 1975; Navarro 1976, pp. 43–45).

## SOCIALIST MEDICINE

The changes instituted in socialist societies, described briefly in previous chapters, have begun to improve health and medical care. In fact, some of the most dramatic changes under socialism have been in medicine. These changes are even more notable in light of the often widespread poverty, illness, and lack of any medical care before the coming of socialism.

### Some Principles

Socialized medicine, as in Great Britain and some other capitalist societies, and even to a degree in socialist societies, is not *socialist* medicine. Socialist medicine seeks to transform the social relations involved in health and treatment of illness (Ehrenreich 1978, p. 12).

It involves a focus on the causes and prevention of illness. Once people see that certain social and environmental conditions lead to illness, they can seek to eliminate them.

When illness arises its treatment can differ under a socialist medical system. The mystique of doctors' professionalism must be struggled against. Skills can become widespread, the limits of doctors' knowledge acknowledged, and all people involve themselves in being healthy and in curing themselves when they become ill. As individuals and in groups of all sizes, people must be participants in their own health. A democratic socialist society is the only guarantee of a truly healthy people.

### The Soviet Union and China

The Soviet medical system, according to Krause, is far superior to that of the United States. Soviet delivery of health services, he writes, cannot be equalled in any western country. Others, however, have found that the Soviet and East European health systems suffer from excessive bureaucracy. "The dehumanizing and alienating manifestations of bureaucracy have made themselves felt in many socialist countries which have tried to establish effective health care systems.... As a result, patients often must face cumbersome procedures which inhibit their ability to obtain the health care they seek" (Krause 1971, p. 139; Waitzkin and Waterman 1974, pp. 109–110).

To avoid bureaucratic control and professional domination by doctors, in 1965 the Chinese began to make significant changes in their system, a system that already had eliminated epidemic diseases and other ills. (The following description applies from 1965 to the early 1970s. Medical care, like other institutions, may be changing with the dismantling of the cultural revolution after 1976.)

Before 1949, China "was plagued with almost every known form of nutritional and infectious disease." Cholera, leprosy, tuberculosis, plague, syphilis, and other diseases were widespread. From 1950 to 1965, the Chinese people managed to abolish all these plagues and diseases.

> Cholera, plague, smallpox, and most nutritional illnesses quickly disappeared; opium addiction was eliminated, largely through community-based efforts; venereal disease took somewhat longer, but by a combination of social and medical techniques was reportedly almost completely wiped out in most of China by the early 1960's. Through the Great Patriotic Health Movements, the people were mobilized against "four pests" (at first, flies, mosquitos, rats, and sparrows, with the sparrows later being replaced in the list of public enemies by bedbugs) (Sidel and Sidel 1973, p. 23).

In fighting against syphilis, the social causes of prostitution were eliminated: prostitutes were trained to work, and, as with other diseases, a national campaign was launched to screen for syphilis, educate people, and treat it (Burchett and Alley 1976, p. 235).

But China still did not have a developed socialist medical system. In 1965, there were serious continuing defects. Medical care was still concentrated in the cities. In a statement on June 26, 1965, Mao urged that medical education become shorter, that research focus on common not exotic illnesses, and that the health needs of rural people (80 percent of the population) be met. Since then, according to Sidel and Sidel, the Chinese have worked to develop a socialist medical system that provides basic care for all. Local self-reliance is emphasized; however, there are still "referral pathways and specific lines of authority and responsibility"; traditional medicine (acupuncture is most famous in the West) is being integrated with western medicine; prevention is stressed; many types of medical personnel are being trained; "emphasis is placed on skills rather than on credentials"; continuing education is provided; and there is a stress on service to people rather than personal reward. For example, the pay differentials of health care workers have been reduced (Sidel and Sidel, pp. 28–29, 192–97).

This is the ideal of socialist medicine, and like all other socialist institutions, it is not completely embodied in reality. It appears, however, that much has been achieved. Resistance (see Chapter 4) has come from those at the top of the hierarchy, and a shift to professional and political domination may be undoing socialist principles and practice in medical care.

The health care institutions created parallel the social organization of Chinese society. In the country, communes (about 50,000 people in each) are divided into brigades and brigades into teams (about 1,500 people). Each team has a public health worker (known as a "barefoot doctor" because he or she works in the fields with other workers), who provides basic health care on a part-time basis. Each brigade has a health station, and each commune has a clinic. More complicated care is provided in the higher levels of the networks. There are over one million barefoot doctors in China (Chu Li and Tien Chieh-yun 1974, p. 196).

In cities, each workplace has one or more "worker doctors," the equivalent of barefoot doctors. For those who do not work and for children, there are "red medical workers" (usually women) in the residents' committees (about 2,000 people). Neighborhoods (about 50,000) and districts (about 500,000) provide services in clinics and hospitals.

The barefoot doctors, worker doctors, and the red medical workers provide basic health care. Their training is short (six months to a year), but they receive continuous training and education. The following is an account of the training of a thirty-eight-year-old housewife (barefoot doctors and worker doctors undergo similar training):

> During the training period she and her fellow housewives learned history-taking and simple physical examination techniques, such as blood-pressure determination. They were taught the uses of a number of Western and herb medicines and techniques of acupuncture and of intramuscular and subcutaneous injection. Preventive measures, such as sanitation, immunization, and birth-control techniques, were an important part of the curriculum. But the most important part, according to Comrade Yang, was that she and her colleagues were taught that there are no barriers between them and the acquisition of medical knowledge other than in their own fears. Once these are overcome, in part by sessions in which the "bitter past" and the feelings of students are shared and discussed, the housewives feel it is indeed possible to become medical personnel. Comrade Yang continues to learn from a doctor from the neighborhood hospital who visits residents' committee health station three times a week, from her own periodic visits to the hospital about a patient or for instruction, and from the bi-weekly or monthly meetings of all the Red Medical Workers of the neighborhood (Sidel 1974, p. 86).

In the Fengsheng neighborhood of Peking three women staffed the health station in 1972. Open from 8–11 a.m. and 3–5:30 p.m., the health workers focused on "preventive work, the treatment of minor illness, health education, and sanitation work." They made sure children received all immunizations. They provided birth control information. In addition, they follow up on patients released from the hospital. In factories, worker-doctors gave careful annual physical examinations to all workers (Sidel, p. 85; Sidel and Sidel, pp. 50, 73).

But most people live in communes. There, people benefit from the care provided by the barefoot doctors. In addition, since 1967, most new doctors have gone to work in clinics and hospitals serving the communes. Barefoot doctors are in close contact with other doctors, they get refresher courses a few times a year, they receive special training if an illness becomes widespread in their district, and they are taught new cures (Burchett and Alley 1976, p. 233). Two Chinese writers describe the work of the barefoot doctors of one commune:

> Whether in the popularization of family planning, or the prevention and cure of disease, the "barefoot doctors" are indispensable. In fact, they are the mainstay of rural medical and health work. Most of them are young people of

poor and lower-middle peasant background, with a fairly high degree of socialist consciousness and at least a junior middle-school education. They are accepted for training on the basis of nomination by the masses and confirmation by the Party branch.

"Barefoot doctors" participate in farm work in the busy seasons. ... Locally born and bred, they know best who is ill and what diseases to watch out for at various seasons. ... One of them, Liang Tseng-hsueh of the Lungchuan brigade, became quite skilled in acupuncture after years of diligent study. He used it successfully on many cases of facial paralysis, newly contracted hemiplegia and infantile bronchitis. Commune members with stubborn ailments come scores of kilometers to seek treatment from him. Liang has also carried out more than fifty painless tooth extractions using acupuncture anesthesia.

When Li Liang-tung, a "barefoot doctor" of the Liuchuang brigade, treats patients who were poor and lower-middle peasants in old society, he acquaints himself not only with their case histories, but also with the past bitterness of their life. This helps him see that many chronic diseases are the result of toil as human beasts of burden in the old society. An old woman who used to eke out a livelihood by fluffing cotton has suffered from bronchitis ever since (Chu Li and Tien Chieh-yun 1974, pp. 201-207).

This extensive medical care is free to workers, free to some commune members (depending on the commune), and others pay minimal fees. Sidel and Sidel claim these fees are very low and provide no hardship to anyone (pp. 74-75).

Sidel concludes that medical care exemplifies best the socialist principles of Chinese society:

> ... a strong belief in mass involvement; recruitment of health workers from among those who live in the community to be served; short periods of training to minimize alienation from the community; a minimum of social distance between the helper and the helped; attempts to demystify as much of medicine as possible; decentralization; and motivating people through altruism rather than through prestige or material incentives (otherwise known as "fame and gain") (p. 96).

*Cuba*

A brief reading on the Cuban medical system shows a system similar to the Chinese (Wald 1978, ch. 4). Before the Cuban revolution, disease was widespread. Poverty and starvation led to illness and prevented its treatment. Most people simply never received any medical care. Most doctors, 65 percent, worked in Havana. Most were specialists who stayed away from daily care: treating colds, delivering babies, and giving shots. In contrast, each doctor now learns how to provide all basic services, and doctors no longer congregate in Havana, and those who do work there also spend some time working in the country (pp. 78-82).

The emphasis is on education, prevention, proper nutrition, hygiene, and local community care. A "polyclinic" delivers health care to the approximately 30,000 people in its area. Nurses, general practitioners, and most specialists staff each polyclinic; about 80 percent of treatments take place here. More complicated problems are referred to hospitals.

Polyclinics send nurses to newborns and their mothers (not to "parents," revealing the great changes in sex roles still needed). In addition, a local commission made up of representatives from many organizations works with the polyclinic. They explain to the staff what people want and explain to people how they may use the clinic; the clinic uses the commission in conducting mass health campaigns (e.g., immunizations). Generally, Cuba has fewer technical resources than the United States and other industrial societies (it is still a poor country in some ways), but the distribution of health care throughout the society and educational and preventive efforts are far superior to those in the United States (Wald ch. 4).

Professionalism is struggled against. One doctor told Wald:

> "The main orientation we give [doctors] is in respect to treating the patients humanely. In the past we had seen how, even when patients received all the medication they needed, their families would still feel the treatment was unsatisfactory, because the doctor was rude to them or some such thing. It came from an attitude that the doctor is always right. We tell the students that when mothers have questions about their children's care, they are generally right. Even if at first one thinks that she is making too much of it, it usually turns out that the mother was right.
>
> "One of our first tasks at the beginning of the Revolution was to get rid of the old sense of 'professionalism,' and the class distinction that used to exist between doctors and nurses, and between them and orderlies and attendants. We try not to make any distinctions or give any privileges. Today's medical students not only work in hospitals as observers and assistants—they also spend time cleaning the floors, changing sheets and bedpans" (Wald, pp. 99–100).

People are encouraged to care for themselves, to live and eat well so they will stay healthy. Also, "diabetic children learn to inject themselves, asthmatics how to use a respiratory apparatus." Mentally retarded people are taught to feed and dress themselves. This may seem a small achievement until we read of conditions in United States institutions, where people are force-fed in three minutes, and many die from pneumonia because food gets into their lungs (Wald, pp. 93, 108).

I do not mean to imply that medical and health care is perfect in socialist societies. But two conclusions are obvious: in light of where they began, China and Cuba (others too) have made enormous progress, especially in providing basic, preventive care to all people. Whereas we cannot copy their system, we can learn much from what they have done and begin to apply it to our own situation.

# CONCLUSIONS

It is difficult to be objective in an evaluation of medical care. There are many destructive effects and also many benefits in modern medicine.

Medicine today can reduce daily discomfort (although we all must learn to live with some discomfort occasionally). It reduces fear and anxiety, for example, in childbirth; in 1940 when 50 percent of births took place in hospitals, 5,000 women died during childbirth, but in 1973, with 99 percent of babies born in hospitals, 500 women died (again, not all women need go to hospitals, and childbirth can become much more humane than it is now). Also, specific diseases have declined (such as tuberculosis and the flu) (Starr 1976, pp. 51–52).

However, it is not the knowledge and techniques of modern medicine that are the problem, but their delivery. Demystified medical practice, available to all, controlled by the community instead of for the benefit of doctors and corporations, along with education and prevention, are the desirable ways to use medicine.

Cuba and China are not denying modern medicine, they are organizing to use it for the health of all people.

We tend to forget the importance of the mind, social relations, and the environment for the health of our body. Tribal societies were acutely aware of the important role the mind plays. We dismiss tribal healers as witch doctors and shamans, but they understood much. Consider a contemporary example (late 1960s). Louis Whiton, an anthropologist, had suffered for two years "from lameness and severe pain in [his] right leg and hip, originally caused by acute trochanteric bursitis." Western medical specialists were unable to help him. A so-called witch doctor in Surinam, South America offered to cure him. Not convinced, Whiton gave him a try. After a very colorful, intense ceremony (described in detail by Whiton), the pain and lameness went away and had not returned in two years. Doctors hypothesized that the conviction of Raineh (the witch doctor) and the power of the ceremony broke the pattern of pain which had been sending messages through Whiton's spinal cord to his brain. This episode shows that we must pay attention to the health of the whole person:

> Science and the medical profession have attempted to explain the success of treatments such as Raineh's. But some doctors I have talked to about this subject have expressed regret that the great advances in surgical practices and the use of drugs during the last thirty years have obscured the importance of the mind in curing bodily ills. A professor at one medical school told me that much more attention is now being given to psychosomatic factors in treating physical symptoms. There is obviously much to learn about such phenomena (Whiton 1971, p. 16).

Any health system, if it is to be effective, must focus on (1) prevention; (2) education for people to lead healthy lives and cure their own illness as much as possible; (3) providing basic care to all people; (4) removing the mystique of medicine and doctors; and (5) the other changes discussed in this chapter.

Many critics of medicine seem to think that doctors and the medical system have great independent power and are the source of many of our troubles. The medical system reflects capitalist values, but it is not the source of oppression. Doctors, after all, only imitate the orientation of a capitalist economy, where profits are always more important than people's real needs. We cannot ask doctors to be benevolent and caring when the economy operates for profit and when success means material possessions. Problems of professional domination are inherent under capitalism and continue in socialist societies.

We must first change the economics of medicine; thus we must organize to change political conditions. But as the Chinese experience shows, the workers who provide basic medical care must be freed from professional dominance and gain the self-confidence they must have. Changes in "how people perceive themselves, their bodies, their relationships to others" require the "unleashing" of their imaginations, which can only begin to happen "under conditions of massive involvement in a social movement" (Ehrenreich 1978, p. 25).

---

**STRUGGLES: The Women's Health Movement**

*More than any other group, the women's movement has challenged capitalist health care. Self-help centers, created by and for women, have changed the traditional doctor-patient relationship. The following reading shows how such centers teach people to assume control of their bodies and themselves.*

Since the establishment of the first Feminist Women's Health Center in Los Angeles by Carol Downer and Lorraine Rothman in 1971, at least 50 women-run clinics have been founded in the United States. They offer a range of services including basic gynecological care, and in some cases abortions, prenatal care, and counseling. Most employ physicians on a part-time basis, but the doctors are usually confined to very narrow responsibilities (performing abortions, prescribing medications) and are restricted to a minimum of patient communication. The bulk of a patient's encounter, from the initial intake to the final counseling, is with women like herself—lay women who have learned their skills in self-help courses. That in itself had a consciousness-raising effect, since female patients are used to entering a medical system in which women are at the bottom of the hierarchy, occupying roles which offer very little opportunity for meaningful communication with patients.

But the point is not merely to replace the doctor with more socially compatible, sympathetic providers. Within feminist health clinics, an attempt is being made to completely redefine the patient and provider roles. The patient is taught how to examine her own cervix and breasts and, in some cases, how to interpret her own lab tests. For example, in the 14 Feminist Women's Health Centers throughout the United States, women assist in their pregnancy tests

*Source:* Excerpted from Helen I. Marieskind and Barbara Ehrenreich, "Toward Socialist Medicine: The Women's Health Movement," *Social Policy* 6:2 (September–October 1975), pp. 34–40. Copyright 1975 by Social Policy Corporation, New York, New York 10036.

*(continued)*

**The Women's Health and Movement** *(continued)*
and interpret the result based on the instructions contained within each pregnancy detection kit. In this process as in others, the woman is not the object of care but an active participant; not the recipient of a commodity but a coproducer of health care. As Gartner and Riessman have argued, involving patients in the service process not only changes the traditional roles of provider and receiver but also increases the productivity of the service delivery system.

The Feminist Women's Health Centers in Los Angeles and Oakland have taken an even further step away from traditional roles in their new "participatory clinics." In a participatory clinic a group of six to eight women experience care collectively: they discuss their histories (called "herstories") as a group, learn to examine each other, share their contraceptive or pregnancy experiences, take test smears from each other, etc. In this case the role of the provider becomes that of a mere facilitator; the significant healing relationships are formed between the patients. Instead of being a totally private and individual matter, health maintenance becomes a collective endeavor.

A change in the social relationships involved in health-care production necessarily implies a change in the relationship of people to technology. In conventional medical practice, medical technology and expertise are the property of the physician, and in a lesser degree, of his ancillary technicians. The physician essentially owns the means of production—the technology as well as the less tangible healing aspects of care; patients are only the material to which the technology is applied. Their relationship to the technology therefore is alienated. No matter whether the technology is accepted trustingly or reluctantly because of fear, it is frequently experienced as an invasion or imposition. When, as in the self-help clinics, patients are encouraged to master elements of the technology—when care is in fact defined as a sharing of knowledge and skills—the alienation is replaced by self-confidence and pride.

But once the technology has been wrested from the exclusive control of those who use it to oppress, the next step is to then take a critical look at the technology itself. This has been a major focus of the women's health movement. In the last six years a series of feminist exposes have provoked wide-scale skepticism about the safety and efficacy of the technology applied to women's care: Barbara Seaman on the hazards of the birth control pill; Ellen Frankfort on unnecessary, and unnecessarily radical, breast surgery; Kay Weiss on the dangers of DES (diethylstilbesterol), used in the "morning-after pill"; Doris Haire on the irrationalities of medically managed childbirth. The effect of these and other exposes was to confirm the idea within the women's health movement that there was nothing in medical science which could not or should not be questioned.

# 12

# Crime: Danger at Work and in the Streets

## WHAT IS CRIME?

In 1978, about 20,000 people died from homicides. In the same year, over 115,000 people (estimated) died from accidents at work (about 15,000) and diseases contracted at work (about 100,000). Millions more suffer from accidents and diseases that cripple, maim, and limit their lives (*Statistical Abstract* 1979, p. 177).

Why is one condition seen as a social problem but not the other? Why is homicide considered murder, but not death at work? Today we are learning that many corporations have known for years of the dangers to which they exposed their workers but allowed them to continue working under such conditions; such a policy is actually murder for the sake of profit.

But violence and murder are not limited to work. The operations of the corporate economy and the government (dominated by the ruling class) harm people daily (see Liazos, "The Poverty of the Sociology of Deviance: Nuts, Sluts, and Preverts," 1972). Numerous examples show that our lives and health are threatened much more by the corporations and the government than they are by street criminals (see Chapter 7, the destruction of Buffalo Creek; Ermann and Lundman, *Corporate and Governmental Deviance*, 1978; Swanson, *Focus: Unexplored Deviance*, 1978).

There are more examples. During the "oil crisis" of 1973-74 there were many stories of old people whose electricity was turned off because they could not pay the bills. Some people were found frozen to death in their unheated homes. Although such stories were much in the news, no one was prosecuted for these deaths; in this society, profit considerations are legal, even if not moral or humane. But such conditions are daily occurrences in many areas—people who do not eat enough or do not receive medical care, children exposed to lead-painted apartments, the victims of urban renewal —the list is endless. In each case, health and lives are endangered because of the operations of a capitalist society. The suffering and death are needless because there are enough resources to meet everyone's needs, but under capitalism, profits come before people. Consider the consequences of urban renewal. When people's homes are destroyed for hospitals, highways, and luxury apartments, the people are forced to move to crowded slums, where crime is greater and health endangered. Many displaced old people die when they are forced to leave homes and apartments in which they have lived for years. Those pushing for urban renewal are committing crimes—not by current legal definitions, of course, but surely crimes by any moral standard (Worthy 1976, pp. 51-52).

## Kinds of Crimes

Most of us think that crime comes in the standard forms discussed by the mass media and social scientists. Homicide, rape, robbery, assault, larceny, burglary, and auto theft are the acts counted by the FBI; they are known by the collective label of street crime.

But it is mostly the actions of poor, working-class, and minority people that are defined as crimes and for which people are stigmatized and punished. The much more serious harmful acts of corporations and the government are mostly ignored. Also, the street crime that does exist (and it is a serious problem) arises out of the conditions in which people live under capitalism. Poverty, insecurity, and alienation all affect people, who then strike out (mostly against other poor, working-class, or minority people).

There is also white-collar crime. First developed by Edwin Sutherland in the 1940s, the concept of white-collar crime seems to refer to illegal acts committed by corporations. Lately, it seems to have been expanded to include illegal acts by the government (made well known during and since Watergate, but prevalent for decades). For example, corporations fix prices or produce defective goods; the government violates civil rights and imprisons people illegally. Police corruption could also be included in an expanded definition of white-collar crime. All of these acts and more are violations of some law, and thus are crimes under a legal definition. But the perpetrators of these acts, and their superiors in corporations and governments, rarely are caught; if caught and prosecuted, their penalties are usually limited to fines and, very rarely, short prison sentences. Even those few who are imprisoned are not stigmatized as criminals. When they leave prison, they return to lucrative corporate careers or, as with Watergate, write books and go on lecture tours. They are not perceived as real criminals.

Here are some examples of the lenient treatment of such criminals. A drug manufacturer who "diluted an antidote for poisoned children with a worthless, look-alike substance" got a year's probation (no prison sentence) and a $10,000 fine. The president of a group of nursing homes cheated stockholders out of $200 million and got a year in prison. And a Texas state senator, who for twenty-one years embezzled state funds, got ten years' probation. Watergate criminals received similarly light or no prison sentences. All these people cause much more damage to our society than do street criminals (Reiman 1979, pp. 121–25).

I argue here that a third type of acts, beyond street crime and white-collar crime, are also crimes. Indeed, they are the most dangerous: the acts of ruling-class control that threaten us daily. Such acts are not prohibited legally; the ruling class that dominates our society also determines what the law defines as criminal. An alienated youth who robs an old person is called a dangerous criminal; an electric company that shuts off electricity for old people who then suffer or die, is considered to be only looking out for investments; after all, profit is the essence of its existence. For these reasons, I argue that the greatest source of crime in our society is capitalism itself. Such acts will be referred to here as crimes of capitalism.

Examples are cited throughout the book. A recent and dramatic case involved the executives of the Ford Motor Company. In the early 1970s they designed the Pinto as an inexpensive competitor to imported cars. Just before they began to produce it, internal Ford memos argued that the Pinto's gas tank design was more likely to result in fire and explosion in low-speed crashes than other available designs. Ford's own estimates concluded that about 180 people would die from such explosions if the design was not changed. But Ford did not make the change. They wanted to save the extra cost ($11 per car) and the approximate year's delay in producing the car necessary to correct the faulty design (Strobel 1979; Hoch 1980; Dowie 1977).

Art Buchwald's column, reprinted here, shows how much more destructive corporate actions are than the actions of street criminals. It also shows a failure to understand this danger and punish capitalist criminals.

You may argue that corporate leaders do not knowingly kill people. Why, then, do they allow conditions such as those that led to the Buffalo Creek disaster (see Chapter 7)? There are three possible explanations. The directors and managers of corporations do not care about people; they are

**Drawing the Line in the World of Crime—By Art Buchwald**

Washington—"Sergeant Riley, Fifth Precinct, Homicide Division, speaking."

"Sergeant, I would like to report a crime. Someone tried to poison my entire family."

"Are you sure?"

"I'm certain. I had my water and food analyzed by a laboratory and they were full of pesticides. Someone dumped the poison in our wells and rivers and not only my loved ones but all our neighbors may be croaking at this very moment."

"This is serious. Anybody have any grudges against you?"

"No one that I know of. Certainly we don't have enemies who would want to poison us."

"Maybe it's a crazy person who has some beef against the community. We better put out a dragnet."

"It's possible, but the person would have to have access to a lot of poison. Our pigs and cows are all sick and our horses are dying too."

"Let me get this straight. You think there is a mass murderer in your neighborhood?"

"Sergeant, I think there is a mass murderer in the county."

"You're not a kook, are you?"

"No sir. If you check my record I am a very respectable person and have never been in trouble with the law."

"Okay, do you have suspects?"

"Well, the Frankenstein Chemical Co. is about two miles from my house and they've been dumping all sorts of sludge in the river.

"Sometimes it's green, sometimes a dark red and other times it's a deep brown. They do it mostly at night so no one will see them."

"Wait a minute, the Frankenstein Chemical Co. is a multimillion dollar corporation with plants all over the United States. I know the men running the one in this county. They're lodge brothers of mine. Are you accusing them of poisoning people?"

"I know it sounds hard to believe, Sergeant, but I have this niece who works in the company's office and she has memos signed by two of the officers instructing the Frankenstein employees to dump all the waste in the river at night. The memos say that if anyone questions them about it to deny they did it, because if they get caught Frankenstein will have to close down the plant and they'll all be out of jobs."

"So what's the crime?"

"They're knowingly poisoning all of us. Isn't that a felony?"

"No, that's an environmental problem."

"Let me ask you something, Sergeant. If someone came into your house and started sprinkling arsenic on your food and fed your dog DDT and poured cyanide into your children's milk, would you arrest him?"

"Damn right I would, and I'd see he got sent up for life."

"What's the difference between that and a company doing the same thing to an entire community?"

"The police only deal with individual crime. We have no authority to arrest company officials just because they have no way of getting rid of their pesticides."

"Then you mean the average citizen has no recourse when a large corporation knowingly tries to kill him?"

"If the government thinks they're doing anything wrong they have ways of punishing people who dump their waste in the wrong place."

"What's the punishment?"

"I think it's a $5000 fine. It could be less. But you better be careful before you make wild charges such as you have."

"Why?"

"I can arrest you for harassing a respectable business establishment."

*Source:* Reprinted from *Boston Globe,* August 26, 1979, p. A5.

ignorant of the consequences of their actions (a difficult argument to make); the pressure for profits pushes corporate leaders to save money, and thus they cannot spend money to repair dangerous working conditions. In light of how the capitalist system operates, this last explanation seems the most plausible. In addition, the lack of personal contact with the people they kill and injure makes it easier to act as they do. They do not personally do the actual killing or injure people at work, so they (and we) do not see what they do as a crime.

Understood in this broader context, crime touches the lives of most of us. We may be victims of street crime, or we may fear it; most of us are hurt by white-collar and capitalist crime, since they are so pervasive.

## EXTENT AND EFFECTS OF CRIME

Of the three forms of crime—street, white-collar, and capitalist crimes—statistics are kept only on the first. I know of no official counts of white-collar crimes. The American Bar Association has estimated that white-collar crime amounts to about $40 billion annually (Connolly 1977). Of course, we cannot even begin to conceive how we could count crimes of capitalism.

*Street Crimes*

Official statistics on this phenomenon are collected by the FBI yearly, through reports by police departments of "offenses known to the police." In 1978, there were 11.14 million such offenses (1,062,000 defined as "violent," 10,080,000 as "property crime"). This is a 90 percent increase from the 5.9 million for 1967 (*Statistical Abstract* 1979, p. 177).

But much crime is not reported to the police. To overcome this deficiency, social scientists have tried other means of measuring street crimes. One method simply asks people, in anonymous questionnaires, to list the illegal acts they have committed. Virtually all such studies have been done with juveniles. They show that most juveniles break some law, with about 25 percent committing serious crimes.

More recently, large samples of people have been asked to check off the crimes committed against them. These victimization reports, of which the most important have been financed by the Law Enforcement Assistance Administration (LEAA), part of the Department of Justice, have given the most complete picture of street crime and its victims. Although no method can give a truly precise count, victimization reports are more accurate than official counts or self-reports.

In the years 1973-76, the sample of people interviewed for victimization reports showed that there were about 160 million "completed and attempted victimizations." Table 12.1 gives a percentage breakdown of the kinds of offenses: 14.5 percent involve some violence, and 85.5 percent are property crimes (*Myths and Realities about Crime* 1978, pp. 4-5; henceforth, *Myths*).

Completed and attempted victimizations do not cover all of this level of crime. Shoplifting, vandalism, and child abuse seem not to be included. It

**TABLE 12.1** Percent of Victimizations, by Type, 1973–76

| Type | Percent |
| --- | --- |
| Personal larceny | 39.9 |
| Assault | 10.5 |
| Rape | .4 |
| Personal robbery | 2.9 |
| Commercial robbery | .7 |
| Commercial burglary | 3.8 |
| Household burglary | 16.6 |
| Motor vehicle theft | 3.4 |
| Household larceny | 21.9 |
|  | 100 |

Source: *Myths and Realities about Crime* 1970, p. 5.

is estimated that only 3 percent of shoplifters are caught and that losses from shoplifting reach $8 billion a year (McCaghy 1980, p. 166; Barlow 1981, p. 187). Vandalism against schools alone cost $500 million in 1975; destruction in parks and other public places increase the cost. Child abuse, reflecting the pressures, insecurities, and isolation of family life, has become a great concern in the late 1970s.

Of all these victimizations, 48 percent were reported to the police. Of personal offenses, fewer than a third were reported, and only 38 percent of "household incidents" were reported (*Myths*, pp. 10–11).

Weapons were used in far fewer than half (39 percent) of the personal crimes of rape, robbery, and assault. As Table 12.2 shows, only in commercial robbery was a weapon commonly used.

The LEAA publication *Myths and Realities about Crime* concludes that crime did not increase during the years 1973–76. The data presented (summarized in Table 12.3) bear out that conclusion, although the numbers also show that much street crime does exist.

Most crimes reported to the police are not solved (or "cleared," in the LEAA term). Of serious crimes, 52.9 percent of violent offenses were cleared (1979), and only 19.3 percent of property offenses (which are most of the serious offenses) were cleared (*Statistical Abstract* 1979, p. 184). (Such low clearance rates may explain why most victimizations are not reported to the police.)

Self-reports of juveniles show that the offense rate is the same for people of all classes (Williams and Gold 1972; Reiman 1979, ch. 3). Arrest rates, however, are much higher for poor and minority people. In 1978, for example, black people accounted for about 11 percent of the population but for about 26.4 percent of persons arrested and 42 percent of those in jails (in 1972). Generally, studies have shown that the police, courts, and prisons discriminate against poor, working-class, and minority people. For example, black and poor juveniles get more severe sentences, for equally serious

**TABLE 12.2** Percent of Incidents in Which the Offenders Used Weapons, 1973–76

| Type | Percent |
| --- | --- |
| Rape | 26 |
| Assault | 35 |
| Personal robbery | 48 |
| Commercial robbery | 71 |

Source: Myths and Realities about Crime, pp. 24–25.

**TABLE 12.3** Victimization Rates

| Type of crime[a] | 1973 | 1976 | 1978 |
| --- | --- | --- | --- |
| Crimes of violence[b] | 32.6 | 32.6 | 33.7 |
| Crimes of theft[b] | 91.1 | 96.1 | 96.8 |
| Household burglary[c] | 91.7 | 88.9 | 86.0 |
| Household larceny[c] | 107.0 | 124.1 | 119.9 |
| Motor vehicle theft[c] | 19.1 | 16.5 | 17.5 |
| Commercial burglary[d] | 203.7 | 217.3 | — |
| Commercial robbery[d] | 38.8 | 38.5 | — |

[a] Includes completed and attempted victimizations. In most large categories, over 75 percent are completed.
[b] Per 1,000 people over twelve.
[c] Per 1,000 households.
[d] Per 1,000 businesses.
Source: Myths and Realities about Crime, p. 3; U.S. Department of Justice 1979.

offenses, than do whites and middle-class juveniles. Other studies have shown that police are more likely to harass and arrest poor and black juveniles (Chambliss 1973; *Statistical Abstract* 1977, pp. 177, 190; Galliher and McCartney 1977, chs. 4 and 5).

Although most offenses are not solved and even fewer offenders are sent to prison, keep in mind that a poor and minority person who commits serious and frequent offenses (usually property offenses) has a good chance of ending up in prison. George Jackson wrote (1970) that young black men grow up with the expectation of spending some time incarcerated. At the end of 1977, there were 278,141 people in federal and state prisons, an increase from 196,000 in 1972. Adding the number in jails (141,600 in 1972), means there are about 400,000 people in prison at any given time. However, different people are incarcerated at different times, and since it is mostly the lower classes who are so punished, a poor or minority person has a good chance of spending some time in prison over a lifetime (*Statistical Abstract* 1979, p. 195).

Indeed, statistics of inmates show this fact clearly. In mid-1972, 23 percent of those in jails had eight or fewer years of schooling; 43 percent more had nine to eleven years. Before their arrest, 44 percent had an annual income of less than $2,000, 11 percent had $2,000-$2,999, and 31 percent were in the $3,000-$7,499 range. Moreover, a recent investigation showed that in Massachusetts blacks convicted of the same crimes as whites "receive longer sentences and serve more time in prison than whites" (*Survey of Inmates of Local Jails,* pp. 16-17; Spotlight 1979).

## The Concern with Crime

It is very difficult to determine how much of a problem crime is. Politicians and the media can manipulate public opinion, and polls of attitudes do not always reflect what really concerns people. In the late 1960s and early 1970s public-opinion polls listed crime as the most commonly named concern, and today it remains among the top two or three issues named.

Look at the results of victimization surveys. When asked "Is there anything you don't like about this neighborhood?" 38 percent said "yes." Of those, 26 percent (10.5 percent of people asked) said street crime, and 26 percent named environmental deterioration (surveys done in the middle 1970s). When asked how safe they felt when they were out alone in the daytime, 11 percent of people of twenty-six central cities said (1974-75) very or somewhat unsafe. But for night time, 45 percent said they felt very or somewhat unsafe. As to any changes in activities because of the fear of crime, 46 percent said they had done so themselves, and 63 percent said they thought people in the neighborhood had changed activities (*Myths,* pp. 14-19).

The media and politicians express even more concern and fear about crime. We can trace public alarm about delinquency to at least the 1820s. Recent headlines of newspaper and magazine articles give an indication of the current perception of the problem of delinquency: "The Youth Crime Plague"; "The Rising Tide of School Crime"; "Gangs on the Corners, Strife in the Streets." A 1978 series in the *Boston Globe* opened with alarming words: ". . . a generation of street-corner teenagers . . . have seized control of the sidewalks and parks after dark, converting them to their own use. It has become a nuisance of startling proportions. Boston police call it their number one problem. Suburban officials spend inordinate time searching for solutions." In 1975, Boston police received 68,000 complaints about such groups of teenagers. The series reported that they terrorized citizens, especially old people in some Boston neighborhoods (Liazos 1974; *Time* 1977; Katz 1976; Kenney and Taylor 1976; Larkin and Taylor 1978).

But vandalism, theft, and terror are not limited to the cities. Vandalism in suburban schools constitutes a large part of the over $500 million annual cost. Larkin and Taylor write of teenagers shooting out $3,000 worth of windows in Belmont, a Boston suburb. There is general property destruction: cars, playgrounds, mailboxes, and the like.

No doubt there is much overreaction and sensationalism. But we must not dismiss a very serious problem. The concern with crime and the numbers of street crimes, as reported in the victimization reports, are real and serious. The forty million street crimes a year (murder, rape, assault, armed robbery, theft, auto theft, and burglary) lead to the deterioration of community and people's trust in one another. It is true that white-collar crimes and crimes of capitalism are even more destructive, but that reality does not diminish the threat of street crimes (Platt 1978).

Victimization surveys are limited, however. They report only street crime and do not touch white-collar and capitalist crimes, which endanger lives and diminish the quality of life. The effect of these crimes is seen indirectly in surveys that ask about people's trust in government, business, and other institutions (Institute for Social Research 1979). These surveys reveal a steady decrease in people's faith in corporations, the media, labor unions, and government. So why are the harmful acts of these institutions not perceived as crimes? Or perhaps they are seen as crimes in some unconscious way, but social scientists and the media refuse to explore this perception and the wider existence of crime arising from the nature of life under capitalism.

## WHY IS THERE CRIME?

In 1978, I attended a conference on delinquency. Sociologists, psychologists, law professors, and people working to reform juvenile justice were present. There were long, detailed, and fascinating discussions on new laws to deal with delinquency and on present and proposed reforms of the juvenile justice system. But there was an almost complete absence of any discussion on the causes of delinquency. The social, political, and economic conditions that lead young people, of all classes, to commit street crimes were not explored. It was a discussion in a vacuum, concerned largely with legal and technical issues.

*An Outline of Perspectives*

Traditional explanations of crime and delinquency vary widely. Basically, they fall in three categories. (1) Many people have seen street criminals as possessing biological or psychological differences. They have argued that they are born different, inheriting genetic or personality qualities that dispose them to crimes. A variation of the conservative view is the argument that the culture of some groups leads people to crime. For example, poor self-control and an orientation to the immediate present are said to lead to crime (a variation of the theory of the culture of poverty). (2) More liberal views on crime have focused on social conditions of all types (poverty; unemployment; unequal education). (3) Socialists too discuss these conditions, but in two different respects: unlike liberals, socialists see these conditions not as unfortunate but changeable conditions, but as inherent in the nature of capitalism. The socialist position also sees crimes other than street crimes as more dangerous.

The following discussion focuses on the causes of delinquency, since most street crimes are committed by people under thirty. In 1976, of people arrested, 60 percent were twenty-four or under, and 82 percent were thirty-four or under (*Statistical Abstract* 1977, p. 177).

Although this section focuses on street crime, the rest of this text, in a sense, explains the reasons for white-collar and capitalist crimes—the necessary result of a society dominated by competition, profit, and the lack of community.

*Capitalism, Alienation, and Crime*

Socialism focuses on material conditions, the political economy and its changes. Socialists do not see crime as merely a mechanical response to economic conditions: the political economy of capitalism creates material inequalities and physical suffering; it also destroys communities and human relations. People do not relate to each other as people but as competitors and strangers. Where there is no sense of community, people can justify stealing from each other, since they feel alienated and thus do not help each other. Pervasive alienation, powerlessness, and distrust can only diminish the quality of life and drive people to crimes. Thus we can understand the crimes people commit against their own group, the extensive vandalism by juveniles of all classes, and the terrorizing of old people. These are not the acts by people who live in real communities. They arise from lack of community and destroy further any remnants of it (Quinney 1977).

As many writers have noted, about 90 percent of reported street crimes involve theft or destruction of property. The other 10 percent, involving personal violence, are important because they destroy human relations. Crimes against property also destroy trust and community, and thus they contribute to the deterioration of the quality of life, to fear and distrust (Platt 1978).

David Gordon has written that crime, organized crime, and white-collar crime are a rational response to life under capitalism. Since 90 percent of crimes are property-related, we see that people resort to crimes to optimize their economic conditions. Gordon argues that poor people steal, pimp, and so on because they can make more money this way than by most legitimate jobs available (or not available) to them; organized crime markets various goods and services to earn high profits; and businesspeople resort to white-collar theft and price-fixing in order to maximize profits (maximization of profits is the first priority of a capitalist economy) (Gordon 1973).

These are true statements, but limited. As I have said, crime is not a mechanical response to economic conditions. Amounts stolen are usually small, under $100, and vandalism and similar acts result in no economic gain. Crime is a response to the bad social conditions created by capitalism (Platt 1978).

One of those conditions is alienating and demeaning work. Many books have shown the social, personal, and emotional destructiveness of work, foremost among them Harry Braverman's *Labor and Monopoly Capital* (1974), and Barbara Garson's *All the Livelong Day* (1975) (also see Chapter 5).

Many poor and working-class youths openly reject the limited lives they face:

> Reform schools often try to rehabilitate by training kids for socially accepted and useful jobs. But these kids already view the jobs in question—and we would agree—as dead-end occupations. For the most part these are working-class kids who are being trained to stay in working-class jobs. Their parents, neighbors, and schools are working-class, and these kids have found the life surrounding them oppressive and intolerable. They want out, and society tells them there is no way out (Blum and Smith 1972, p. 98).

For many teenagers (especially black ones) there are no jobs at all, and, as discussed in Chapter 9, widespread unemployment among young people was one of the causes of the uprising in the black areas of Miami in 1980. Official unemployment among black teenagers is 40–50 percent, but in fact in many areas it reaches 90 percent as in Charlotte, North Carolina. The result is predictable:

> As an example of the city's unemployed and underemployed black teenagers, Cleo is far from unique. That becomes clear after three weeks of hanging out with other Cleos on street corners, in chilly, dark housing-project parking lots, and on rocky, red clay clearings that pass for basketball courts and baseball diamonds. There the acrid, depressing stench of cheap marijuana blends with the gloom of corroding lives.
>    Black teenagers in housing projects like Dalton Village, Earle Village and Boulevard Homes, sitting in groups on cars or concrete apartment steps, are mistrustful of strangers, fearful of police harassment, angry, idle, frustrated, not really sure if they are criminals, as adults say they are, or the victims (Rich 1976, p. 594).

It is for alienating work that schools prepare youth. The vandalism and other crimes that worry school authorities result from youth's reaction to this socialization for demeaning and exploitative work. Such schools, work, and general quality of life conspire to produce juvenile delinquency (Liazos 1978).

Boredom and aimlessness are predictable. An eighteen-year-old woman said that she and her friends hang around in street corners because they have nothing to do. "If there was something else to do, we wouldn't be here." They think little of the future, "just looking for something to do," and "they complain of being excruciatingly bored" (Larkin and Taylor 1978).

In a recent study of increasing violence in San Francisco's Chinatown, Takagi and Platt provide another exploration of the political economy of juvenile delinquency. They show that the increased violence is not caused by gangs in Chinatown or by conflicts between Chinese and American culture:

> Delinquency is on the increase in Chinatown, and peer group formations among Chinese youth are quite common. But there is no evidence to support the argument that *the violence* is related to youth gangs. Organized violence appears to be related to the business of protection rackets and political intimidation of progressive organizations rather than to an "irrational" youth "subculture" (italics in original) (1978, p. 22).

Chinese youth resort to crime in reaction against the exploitation of their community and the degrading conditions in which they live.

> Chinatown was created and is sustained by capital to accumulate profit. Its cheap labor force creates superprofits for the garment industry and contributes to San Francisco's reputation as a profitable convention center.... With the exception of a very small bourgeoisie and petty bourgeoisie, Chinatown is a community of superexploited labor: women in the sweatshops, men in the restaurants and able-bodied youths out of work and on the streets. With long hours of work for little pay, both parents working to make ends meet, crowded and inadequate housing, few recreational facilities and regular police sweeps to keep the streets clear for tourists, it is not surprising that there is an increase in family fights and tensions, and in petty theft and vandalism among adolescents. Under these conditions, individualism replaces reciprocity as the basis of social relations (1978, pp. 22–23).

The crimes committed by the youth of Chinatown, like crimes by people anywhere else and of any age, are rarely political. They are individual responses, not conscious political statements. But they do reflect political conditions. It is thus that we must understand street crime. We must neither romanticize it as political rebellion nor dismiss it as meaningless and politically irrelevant (Platt 1978).

This explanation would seem to cover crimes committed by poor, minority, and working-class youths. What explains the equally pervasive crime in suburbs among middle-class youths? The answer has three parts: youth of all classes are powerless (Gross and Gross 1977); the deterioration in the quality of life and the loss of community are not limited to the poor in cities but are found everywhere (the special isolation of suburban life creates alienation and delinquency—in fact, there is less of a community in most suburbs than in many ethnic and working-class neighborhoods (Wynne 1977); above all, the distinctions we make between the "middle-class" on the one hand and the poor, minorities, and working-class on the other are, I believe, false. First of all, most jobs, not only typical working-class ones, are alienating. To be sure, factory work may be more destructive to mind and body than the work of a doctor or lawyer, but most people are not doctors or lawyers, or top managers. As Terkel shows, the typical "white-collar" job is very alienating. All young people see the pressures under which their parents work, and these pressures affect family and community life.

Secondly, most famiies do not earn enough to live the life-style defined as "comfortable" by the U.S. Bureau of Labor Statistics. In 1978, about 80 percent of families made under $27,420, which is where the supposed comforts of middle-class life begin (see Chapter 2).

In short, all youth are exposed to life under capitalism. Very poor youths are affected by sheer poverty and the exploitation of their community; suburban youths experience meaninglessness, alienation, competition, and insecurity; all youths suffer diminished status, and, like adults, live without community.

## CONTROLLING CRIME

Efforts to control crime have been limited to street types of crime, and have not been directed to eliminating causes. Since most street crimes are committed by working-class people against other working-class people who do not present a direct threat to the ruling class, they are an indirect indictment of life under capitalism. They expose the deterioration of human relations caused by capitalism. In this respect, the ruling class must deal with street crime in order to maintain legitimacy and authority.

This section will take a brief look at the history of crime control and then examine some recent efforts at crime prevention. A socialist critique of the latest reforms will follow.

You may find it helpful to keep in mind these three different approaches to controlling crime:

1. Solutions may focus on the *causes* of crime. If, for example, we think that class inequalities, alienating work, and the profit motive drive people to crime, then we should work to eliminate these conditions.

2. Many solutions focus on *reforming criminals*. Reform solutions deal with crime after it has been committed.

3. A third approach seeks to prevent crime through *deterrence*, not by eliminating the causes. This approach makes it difficult for people to commit crimes, through more police, neighborhood patrols, locked doors and windows, and longer sentences for prisoners.

Whereas any society must use all three approaches, I think that in the long run the only way to deal with crime is to understand and eliminate its causes. Lately, it seems that in the United States we have focused on the second and third approaches, with the emphasis moving to the third.

## Criminal Justice and Law as Social Control

Justice in any society reflects material conditions. It is "an integral part of the social, economic, and political structure of a society" (Quinney 1977, p. 1). In a capitalist society torn by profound conflicts, justice becomes another weapon in the class struggle. The justice system becomes capitalism's final line of defense after other institutions—family, school, church, communications media—have failed. But the ideology of equal justice and due process hides the actual repressive operations of the criminal justice system (for material that shows the real workings of capitalist justice, see Lefcourt 1971; all issues of the journal *Crime and Social Justice;* Wolfe 1978).

Laws are written, changed, and enforced to serve the interests of capitalists, protect private property, and regulate lives and labor according to capitalist demands. For example, the vagrancy laws, from the fourteenth century on, helped meet the labor needs of rising commercial capitalists. First the laws forced people to work; later they were modified in order to control the victims of rising capitalism who threatened it through crime and robberies. Studies of specific laws and of the capitalist legal system show how they were used to control people in order to enhance capitalist needs (Chambliss 1964; Hall 1952; Tigar and Levy 1977).

The system also works to regulate the destructive effects of capitalism and to legitimate capitalist society. The poor, an inevitable byproduct of capitalism, threaten it because they often resort to violence and crime, both against each other and the working class. Thus the system seeks to legitimate itself through the apparent protection of the working class from the poor, by minimizing and controlling the dangers of street crime. Street crime, although by no means the most serious threat to life, is a real danger for the poor and the working class. All the major reforms of the criminal justice system undertaken by the federal government since the 1960s, especially those initiated by the President's Commission on Law and the Administration of Justice and carried out by the Law Enforcement Assistance Administration, are a response to the perceived threat to capitalist legitimacy. Those setting policy and creating the reforms are clearly people from the ruling class, or agents of the state who are controlled by the ruling class. But since crime and delinquency reflect material conditions, which reforms of the criminal justice system leave untouched, crime cannot be controlled through any of these reforms (see Liazos 1974, 1978; Quinney 1974).

The argument can be made that the criminal justice system, controlled by ruling class institutions, focuses on street crime and its punishment as a means of diverting attention away from white-collar and capitalist crimes. The mass media tend to show only street criminals committing dangerous acts. When someone dies in a street crime, media accounts call the event a murder. When a mine company does not fix unsafe working conditions and twenty-six miners die, their death is called an accident. Thus we are trained to fear street crimes but not corporate crimes (Reiman 1979 develops this argument at length; see p. 45).

Finally, the use of justice as a weapon in the class struggle is also evident in the rise and function of the police. From the beginning, the police have been used as a buffer or mediator in the conflict between capitalists and workers. For example, the Buffalo police were used to prevent and control labor unrest in the late nineteenth century. In later times, public and private police have been used to control labor unrest and the protests of oppressed people. The police in the South of the United States are still used to fight worker unionization by protecting strikebreakers and by other means.

The call for police reform, for professionalization and more training, reflects an admission that the police have not done well in the task of controlling the oppressed. With the changing structure of capitalism and the higher cost of public policing, we now see much greater use of cheaper private police for the protection of private property (Center for Research on Criminal Justice 1975; Harring and McMullin 1975; Spitzer and Scull 1977).

*Reforms in Juvenile Justice*

The criminal justice system is vast, including lawmakers, police, courts, prisons, social workers and psychiatrists, and many prevention programs. Although people in the system have good intentions to help people, the institutions, created by the ruling class, function to define street crimes as the only dangerous crimes and thus help to maintain capitalism. A brief examination of juvenile justice may illustrate how the criminal justice system works (Liazos 1974; Quinney 1974).

From the very first institutions for delinquents in the United States in the 1820s (called "houses of refuge"), juvenile justice has taken the children of the lower classes and trained them to accept limited lives. Programs of all sorts, public or private, in or out of institutions (reformatories; training schools), have aimed to teach work habits ("industriousness") in various forms. Most of these programs have focused on work skills and attitudes as central to the reformation of delinquents. An 1847 report on reform schools in Massachusetts argued that they should make their inmates "industrious, useful, and virtuous citizens." The language has varied but the intent has not. The specific work given by institutions to young people and the jobs for which they have been trained show how youths have been socialized to be happy with dead-end jobs. Many have been trained for factory work, which requires only minimal skills and is deemed "realistic" in relation to the supposed limited abilities of the children. Other graduates of reform schools have become maids, gas station attendants, and farm workers (see Liazos 1974, for a detailed description of reforms since the 1820s).

You may think such programs represent a bygone era, that we have progressed since then. In fact, the search for effective programs in juvenile justice continues because old reforms did not reduce street crime.

## The Characteristics of Reforms

The terms "diversion" and "community alternatives" seem to characterize all reform programs. They keep juveniles away from courts and penal institutions and work to rehabilitate them in the community. The programs provide counseling, education, work training, and other services. Frequently, juveniles are assigned people who work with them, known as "volunteer probation officers" or by other names. In many cases, especially in the last three to four years, rehabilitation consists of some form of restitution or community service, such as the cleaning of a pond by a group of sentenced delinquents (Beha, Carlson, and Rosenblum 1977; Longcope 1977; Calhoun 1978; Kenney 1978).

Most of these programs deal with adolescents after they have committed offenses, usually serious offenses. Little is still done about prevention. Also, most programs are small, dealing with under a hundred people. Finally, LEAA funding (partial or total) is very common.

Work is central to most of these programs—actual paid work, work training, or the development of proper attitudes about work. However, the primary concern of many work programs is the prevention of trouble by idle teenagers. The headlines of three *Boston Globe* stories are revealing: "Job Plan Urged to Curb Violence"; "Jobs for Youth Needed to Avert Violence" (in summer); and "Summer in the City: Few Jobs for Young, Time for Trouble" (Cohen 1976; Jordan 1977; Barnicle 1978).

## The Massachusetts Department of Youth Services

One of the better-known reforms has been taking place in Massachusetts. It involves the closing down of institutions and the use of many other approaches to delinquency control.

The history of the Massachusetts experiment has been written in many places, and the controversy still rages. Many people are still angry at Youth Services Commissioner Jerome Miller for closing down the "training institutes" (reform schools) in 1972. Massachusetts is the only state to have done so, and the state still has places for about a hundred youths deemed dangerous and in need of imprisonment. This is called by other names—"secure detention," etc.—and many want to expand the program (Calhoun 1978, p. 16).

After he was hired in 1969, Miller decided soon that reform of the old reform schools was hopeless. So, even though alternative programs and places were not yet available for many youths, he closed down the reform schools, obviously on the theory that anything, even the absence of programs, would be better.

In 1978 in Massachusetts, the 2,000 youths committed to the Department of Youth Services were in the following programs: Six hundred were "at home receiving case work services"; five hundred and fifty were receiving "nonresidential services," such as "on-the-job training programs and alternative schools"; another five hundred and fifty were in "residential care," meaning foster homes, group homes, and halfway houses; sixty-nine were in locked settings ("secure care," meaning imprisoned); thirty-five were in a forestry camp; and the rest were in foster care or shelter care (e.g., YMCAs) (Calhoun 1978, pp. 13-14).

The Massachusetts experiment has received close attention. LEAA awarded $500,000 to Lloyd Ohlin and Harvard Law School to study the effects of the closing down of institutions and the change to community treatment. A preliminary report, comparing 1968 and 1974 recidivism rates, concluded that there had been neither a "substantial increase" nor a "substantial decrease." The authors noted that some regions of the state did show a substantial decrease (and others an increase), and that "youth from secure care recidivate at a faster rate than youth in less secure programs." In short, as the *Boston Globe* said in an editorial, the recidivism rate did not increase after the closing down of the reform schools (Ohlin, Miller, and Coates 1977).

*Exemplary Projects and Others*

Project New Pride and the Adolescent Diversion Project were two special projects distributed by LEAA; both claimed success.

New Pride provided four types of services to improve "the youth's typically very low esteem for themselves and others." The four services were education, which includes an "alternative school" providing personal, supportive teaching and a "learning disabilities center"; counseling, involving counselors who work closely with youth and their family; employment, which includes the teaching of skills, attitudes, and "realistic appraisals of career ambitions and requisite skills"; and cultural education, which includes sports events, restaurant dinners, and "many other educational and recreational events" (Blew, McGillis, and Bryant 1977, pp. 2-6).

The project served 200 youths from 1973 to 1976. The recidivism rate was 27 percent, and a control group had a rate of 32 percent (pp. 8, 51-63).

The Adolescent Diversion Project was run by the University of Illinois. It was conceived and administered by faculty and graduate students, but the work was carried out by undergraduates. Forty-nine juveniles were each assigned an undergraduate (adolescents were referred to the program by the police, instead of being turned over to the courts).

The youngster and assigned volunteer typically spent several weeks getting to know each other. Once the two had established a relationship, the volunteer assessed the needs and problems of the client and, with the help of peers and supervisor, developed a program using one or a combination of techniques known as *behavioral contracting and child advocacy.* Volunteers using behavioral contracting would monitor and mediate written contractual agreements between the youth and the parents concerning real-life issues such as privileges to be available to the child in return for complying with curfews; house chores; and personal appearance. Contracts with teachers were also frequently drawn up. The principle of a behavioral contract is that clearly detailed responsibilities must be fulfilled by the youngster as well as by the other participants in the contract. The volunteers using child advocacy would personally act to secure the rights of their clients when the clients faced crises, such as suspension from school. Moreover, the advocate would introduce the child to available educational, welfare, health, mental health, and vocational resources that could be used on the child's behalf. In each of the intervention strategies, the students attempted to ensure that their clients could serve as their own monitors and advocates after the students' involvement in the project had ended (Ku and Blew 1977, pp. 3-4).

One- and two-year followups showed much lower recidivism for this group than for a control group. For example, a year later youths in the 1973-1974 group had an 0.76 average number of police contacts per child versus 1.75 contacts for the twelve youths in the control group (p. 7).

It must be stressed that the samples were small and the time lapsed (two years) too short and that the authors do not know the reasons for the positive effects. They were unsure whether the effects came from a particular counseling technique or from "just having a sympathetic and helping figure" (p. 72).

Many other programs could be cited: youths tried by their peers; forestry camps which end in a three-day experience surviving on one's own (these show substantial reductions in recidivism). But all these programs show the poverty of capitalist solutions. Walter Miller "quietly harbors an . . . innovative approach, one he calls his 'pie in the sky' idea. 'It's a recreational program that would involve risk for kids. Maybe a demolition derby out in an isolated place where it wouldn't bother anyone. We could wean them away from the corners with it' " (Larkin and Taylor 1978, part 4).

Most of the same principles of reform apply to programs for adult street criminals. Since most are men under thirty, diversion, community alternatives, and work training are deemed essential so the men will not continue committing crimes. Even though the prison population is increasing, various programs similar to the two so-called exemplary projects described above have mushroomed (LEAA has funded many of them). At the same time, for those unwilling or unable to participate in such reform programs, new and old techniques of control await. Behavior modification, drugs, even brain surgery ("psychosurgery") to eliminate supposed inherent violence, are among the tools of oppression (Speiglman 1977, Schrag 1978).

Such programs are meant for people already in criminal careers of various degrees. Reform programs focusing on work are meant for those considered still changeable. Still other programs are aimed at the general community. They aim to prevent crime by improving detection and policing and to deal with minor disputes at the local level.

*Community Crime Prevention*

Burglary and other property crimes account for the vast majority of criminal acts. Many programs (inspired or sponsored by LEAA) aim to reduce the opportunities to commit such thefts, especially in high-crime areas. They focus on three goals: to help residents make their homes safer by inspecting doors, windows, and other parts of the house, thus making their homes more difficult to enter; to identify (mark) personal property so that thieves cannot sell it, or so that, if sold, it can be recovered; and, most important (according to those running prevention programs), to set up "block watches":

> To augment the "range of vision" of traditional police preventive patrol, CCPP [Community Crime Prevention Program] organizes neighborhood burglary prevention groups, familiarly known as *Block Watches.* A Block Watch typically consists of 10 to 15 families on a block who are willing to exchange information about their schedules and habits, watch each others' homes, and report suspicious activities to each other and to the police. CCPP considers the Block Watch the citizen's most important weapon against burglary (Cirel et al. 1977, pp. 5-6).

Block watches are considered the only effective protection, since there are not enough police to patrol every house and neighborhood.

How effective are these community crime prevention programs? Results have been mixed, but one (Seattle, Washington) claims clear success:

> - CCPP is successful in reducing the burglary victimization of the program participants. The victimization surveys reveal a 48 to 61 percent reduction in burglaries of households which have used CCPP services, or approximately four fewer burglaries per 100 households per year.
> - The two surveys found no evidence of displacement. The decrease in burglaries of households receiving CCPP services apparently did not produce an increase in burglaries of their non-participating neighbors or in adjacent census tracts not serviced by CCPP. . . . *A survey conducted by program staff in late 1975 indicates that an impressive percentage of households acted upon the recommendations of home service technicians.* Of residents responding, 39 percent said they had actually made one or more of the suggested improvements to their home security and another 11 percent said they intended to make improvements (Cirel et al. 1977, pp. 7-8; italics in original).

## Citizen Dispute Settlement (CDS)

In order to reduce court loads, cut costs, and avoid criminal records, programs have been created in many cities to settle disputes outside courts. Again, many are funded by LEAA.

The following is a summary of CDS aims and procedures from one city, Minneapolis:

> An alcoholic husband assaults his wife. A daughter on drugs becomes violent toward her parents. One neighbor threatens another because of his barking dog.... [to deal with such problems, a CDS program was set up]. Its main objectives are to (1) resolve disputes as quickly as possible; (2) provide support services for victims; (3) reduce violence in domestic relations; and (4) ease the burden of the court system.... If both parties (in the dispute) are agreeable to program participation, each is counseled individually about the problem. A mediation session is then scheduled and held within a week of the initial counseling. Based on the theory that there usually is a degree of fault on both sides, parties are told to think about what they want from the other party and what they in return are willing to give.
>
> At the mediation session both parties air their grievances and ultimately reach a mutually agreed upon solution which is then written in the form of a contract. Both parties must follow the set of conditions called for in the contract. These conditions may involve joining a community alcoholic treatment project or personal counseling program (TARGET 1977, pp. 5–6).

*Citizen Dispute Settlement*, a manual published by LEAA, lists the following as benefits of CDS: it enables people to meet each other and settle their own disputes; it reduces the court load and the cost per case; it provides a link with other community services; and it removes the stigma of a criminal record (p. 2). CDS goes on to claim that in Columbus, Ohio, all but 3.6 percent of the people who discussed their cases in mediation court did not file criminal complaints in regular court, and the cost per case was $20 vs. $100 in regular court (p. 7).

## Doing Good, Not Time

Another recent practice has been to "punish" criminals either by requiring them to repay the victim in some way, or to perform some community service (work in mental hospitals, clean up parks, and so on). The claim for one community service program involving delinquents is that it "helped youths develop a sense of community responsibility, ... involved the community in the problem of juvenile crime, [and] involved the victim in the case ... (TARGET 1975, 1977; Galaway 1977; Wood 1977, p. 22; McCain 1978a).

In Massachusetts, many judges have been sentencing young street criminals to repay victims for property that was stolen or destroyed. Sometimes the young offender must find a job and save enough so that he or she can repay. But in some communities courts have set up programs to find jobs for young offenders and provide counseling to them. "Earn-It" (in Quincy, Lowell, and elsewhere) has achieved some fame.

There were eleven restitution programs in 1978 in Massachusetts, with more planned. In 1977, "670 adults and 323 juveniles repaid a total of $81,713 to the victims of crimes they had committed. This year, the repayment will be more than $100,000." Restitution is meant to "humanize" the crime, to make people understand the consequences of their acts and meet the people they harm. It is considered most effective with young first offenders. In a survey of employers providing jobs to youths in restitution programs, thirty-five of fifty employers rated the program favorably and said they wanted to "help the kids." Some critics have noted, however, that most jobs in restitution programs are menial and transient (McCain 1978).

*A Socialist Critique*

Careful readers of this chapter, and of the book as a whole, can anticipate the socialist perspective on these reform programs. Even though many people who create and run them mean well and genuinely care for victims and victimizers, they cannot hope to make a substantial reduction in crime, or to "reform" street criminals. The history of reforms shows clearly none has ever worked, not on any large scale. They have failed because the causes of street crime have not been touched. Alienated people have been asked to adjust to an unjust society.

In essence, the continual search for new programs is an admission of failure of old ones. No prevention or control program has proved successful. Most "successes" turn out to be exaggerations or badly done studies (Krisberg and Takagi, in Krisberg and Austin 1978, p. 460), or are limited in scope and of short duration.

Dixon examined reports of nine types of programs: volunteers, counseling, street workers, and the like. Programs examined had to have included some way to evaluate their effectiveness. He concluded that all of these programs had little or no effect in reducing delinquency among those they worked with (Dixon 1975).

Another survey of delinquency programs came to the same conclusion. Most programs did not even study their own effectiveness, and those which did did not seem to have reformed delinquents at any greater rate than was true for delinquents who were in no programs at all. The authors concluded that delinquency reform programs should assume failure (they did not, however, ask why all reforms are doomed to fail) (Lundman and Scarpitti 1978).

Indeed, Joan McCord, who followed the boys of a famous Cambridge-Somerville project thirty years after counseling ended, argues there may have been a negative effect on those in the experimental group. Those who "received the most intensive treatment were 'slightly more' likely than those in the untreated control group to have committed at least one serious crime, were more likely to show signs of mental illness...." Even though some may dispute these findings, no one can claim that the Cambridge-Somerville study prevented delinquency and crime (Bruzelius 1978; McCord 1978).

Conservatives too have noted that the liberal reforms instituted since the late 1960s have not reduced crime much. Their recommendation has been to become stricter with street criminals. They have urged that the few "incorrigible" criminals who supposedly account for most crime get longer sentences. Under that approach, criminals will not be reformed, nor will the causes of crime be confronted (conservatives argue that "causes" are difficult to find), although criminals cannot steal if they are not out in the streets. But conservatives seem to ignore that the prison population is growing, and that the United States has the longest prison sentences of any western country, with no visible effect on the street crime rate.

Why have all efforts at prevention and reform failed? Simply stated, they have not confronted the causes of crime outlined above. The juvenile justice system is part of a larger system of control, aiming to perpetuate a capitalist society and its inequalities. Welfare, prisons, courts, schools, and mental health programs all work to oppress, not liberate (Liazos 1974).

Also, the skills and attitudes taught to youths in the juvenile justice system are preparation for low-prestige, low-paying jobs and limited lives. Wellman shows in detail how one antipoverty program functioned as "cooling-off" socialization for low-paying jobs or unemployment. And Project New Pride, with its claim of success, was no exception. "Most positions [of New Pride graduates] are janitorial or in the service industries" (service industry jobs are the lowest-paying of all jobs) (Wellman 1968; Blew et al., 1977, p. 46).

No type of work is, in itself, demeaning. But under capitalism the jobs for which delinquents are trained have low prestige and are low paying. Occupational prestige studies, in which people rate the prestige of each of a hundred jobs, show clearly that the jobs for which youth in the juvenile justice system have been, and are, prepared are low in prestige and pay, and thus alienating and demeaning (Terkel 1974; Braverman 1974; Garson 1975; Landis 1977, p. 145).

Moreover, there is no real commitment to change. In fact, most people in the criminal justice system are still processed in the usual punitive bureaucratic ways. Despite their publicity, reform programs affect few people—victims or offenders. And the programs meant to involve citizens in crime prevention are in fact limited, since ultimate authority rests with the police and the courts. At most, community prevention and citizen dispute resolution are meant to do no more than reduce the case load of police and the courts (and enable them to improve in their control and repression).

None of these reforms confront white-collar and capitalist crime. These crimes are inherent in the capitalist system, and no reform is impossible.

Another fundamental critique of reform programs goes beyond disputing their effectiveness. Not only do they fail on a large scale, but even for those who are "reformed," the real issue is the quality of lives they lead. What happens to reformed offenders, to those who engage in transitory delinquent behavior but do not become official delinquents, and to those who never commit any offenses? Schools and the juvenile justice system consider them successful people. But our vision is limited and distorted if all we expect of people is law-abiding behavior. Our essential concern should be the quality of the life most people lead. Terkel's book *Working* is populated by men and women who, at least outwardly, have accepted their fates and have settled down to the jobs our economy provides. But what kinds of lives do they lead; what does their work do to them? When Terkel listened to people talk about their buried feelings and aspirations, the wounds and hurts and discontent poured out. Those who "succeeded" by accepting degrading work as necessary are as oppressed as those who "fail." The discontent, safely buried most of the time, does arise on some occasions. One man asked Terkel to replay their taped talk. In amazement he said, "I never realized I felt that way."

Everyone is happy that most working-class youths eventually get a job and settle down and would like all youths to do the same. But what do these jobs do to young workers?

## CRIME AND SOCIALISM

When you enter China, you feel the almost physical dropping off of weights that you hadn't even realized you were carrying around, you had become so used to being laden down by them. In a matter of hours (literally) you've stopped checking your purse to make sure your wallet hadn't somehow disappeared. You've become accustomed to having no key for your door; it doesn't occur to you that one might be necessary. . . .

If there is such a thing as culture shock, it comes when you cross the border *leaving* China. Yes, it's a shock when those weights suddenly impose themselves again. They were so easy to forget. But in an instant you are their slave again. Is my wallet still there? How many bags was I carrying? One, two, three, four, yes, they're all here. Why must that poor ragged old woman in the train station carry that healthy young man's parcels on the carrying pole suspend on her bent shoulder, the baskets sagging low and hardly swaying from the heaviness? Why is that child crying, and why is that hysterical-looking woman screaming at him? Why must those painted, mini-skirted women hang around waiting for customers? Why is that man muttering to himself? One, two, three, four, they're still all here (Gamberg 1976, pp. 289-90).

## The Reduction of Crime

Gamberg's experience parallels the experiences of many other residents and visitors to China and Cuba who have concluded that these countries have very little crime. For example, Cuba claims there were only 100,000 crimes in 1968, compared to 200,000 in 1958 (the year before socialism came to Cuba). Murders were reduced from 2,650 to 475. Although crime has been reduced significantly in socialist countries, some does exist. Murders, rapes, and thefts do occur. Indeed, as long as classes and alienation still exist under socialism, we can expect some serious and some less serious crimes to exist (Chen 1975; Burchett and Alley 1976; Wald 1978; Kapp 1978).

To be sure, much crime has been eliminated, even in the less democratic socialist societies like the Soviet Union. Abject poverty has been eliminated, work is guaranteed to everyone, and, at least in some socialist societies, there is a continuing struggle to give dignity and prestige to all work and eliminate classes (see Chapters 2 and 4). Prostitution and drug addiction, so pervasive before 1949, are virtually nonexistent in China (on the Soviet Union, see Connor 1972).

Not only is street crime reduced significantly, white-collar and capitalist crimes also are reduced, even disappear. When the quest for profit no longer rules, people do not starve, or die at work, or are denied the essentials of life. All three types of crime have been reduced, a notable achievement.

Why does some crime persist, however? If, as socialist societies claim, they have eliminated the causes of crime, why would anyone steal? Briefly, although abject poverty and exploitation have disappeared, classes, inequalities, professional domination, alienation (especially at work) and other problems persist. When these are struggled against, crime can be reduced still more.

For now, alienation and other problems persist. There is alienation at work, where workers still toil under the same hierarchical conditions as before. To be sure, the product of their labor is not used for the benefit of a capitalist ruling class, but a form of ruling class does exist (Chapter 3). Moreover, workers still only execute the demands of managers, they have no control over the conception of their work. At least some of the alcoholism, crime, and delinquency in the Soviet Union may be attributed to the alienation of work. The following quote from Connor reads as if it could apply to the United States. Many youths in the bottom social classes, facing boring, limited jobs, are driven to delinquency. The absence of starvation, the guarantee of some type of job, the free medical care, are not enough for them.

> The adolescent from a working-class family will frequently find that, for a variety of reasons, he may not do so well in school as his peers from more culturally advantaged backgrounds. Dropping out after six or seven years of school with an indifferent or poor record, he finds only menial jobs available with little perceived opportunities for advancement; and even these jobs are

scarce. Entering a trade school, he may find the instructors unqualified, uninterested, and incapable of dealing with a population of students similar in many ways to himself. Neither he nor his peers will find museums, theaters, or hobby circles—approved forms of leisure—very attractive. He has little to offer by way of marketable knowledge or skills to Soviet society, and it offers him correspondingly little. Is it going too far to speculate that his frustrations and boredom may find some outlet in delinquent behavior, whether aimed at the acquisition of goods he does not possess or violent, aggressive behavior with no particular aim in view? This, at least, must be a partial explanation (Connor 1972, p. 112).

In 1979 the Soviet press was running stories about serious crimes committed by street gangs. There is much official concern about the extent and seriousness of the crimes, according to these news stories (Finke 1979). There are additional explanations for continuing crime. At times, some material deprivations reappear, and the measures created to deal with them (like the rationing in Cuba) lead to new forms of crime (cheating on rations). As important as any of these reasons is the perpetuation of old habits, customs, institutions, and morality. Liberal critics of socialism seem to ridicule this explanation of capitalist remnants as a cause of crime, but let them think about the difficulties of changing basic values and institutions in any society. Socialist societies must not only combat capitalist remnants within their own societies, but also existing examples in other societies. At any rate, it is obvious that the old order does not die easily, and the new order adds its own problems (Hinton 1972; Bettelheim 1978).

*Criminal Justice under Socialism*

To combat the continuing crime (old forms of crime and new crimes against the socialist order), new institutions must be created. The old criminal justice institutions served the capitalist ruling class; to serve the new ruling class, the workers, there is a need for new institutions.

What I describe below is an ideal. It has existed in part at times, and parts persist (in China and Cuba). It is not a blueprint for actual practice, for practice creates its own principles and theory. The fundamental guiding principles involve *community* and *control by the people*. (For the case of China in the late 1960s and early 1970s, see Brady 1977.)

As before, some basic principles are listed with little elaboration. Those interested should see some of the longer studies (Berman 1969; Brady 1977; Salas 1978, 1979).

Most crimes in socialist society are not handled in formal legal institutions. Neighborhood groups and committees, whose functions include more than dealing with crime, detect cases of minor crime or people who are heading for crime and try to reeducate them, without coercion. The same nonpunitive justice operates in workplaces and schools. The prevention and control of crime are the concern of all citizens, not of experts (Li 1973).

## Controlling Crime under Socialism

The aim of a socialist system of justice is to resolve most crimes, disputes, and conflicts at the local level. Social conflict is to be mediated, discussed, and resolved by working people (not by professionals) where people live or work. That is the ideal. My knowledge of criminal justice in socialist countries is limited, but what I have studied indicates that this ideal has been approached somewhat in China, to a lesser degree in Cuba, and hardly at all in the Soviet Union (I have not read about other socialist societies). Unless indicated otherwise, the following discussion is based on China.

Crime and criminals, as many United States police officials have noted, can never be detected and apprehended adequately by police. But if crimes are committed in real neighborhoods and communities, neighbors respond and capture the criminals. (You cannot steal your neighbor's bicycle when everyone knows it is his or her bicycle. You cannot go to another neighborhood and steal easily, since you would be recognized as an outsider.) In stable communities, crimes and criminals are detected fairly easily (Burchett and Alley 1976, p. 34).

Once crimes are committed, or disputes and conflicts arise between any two parties, they are handled locally. The committees so prevalent at the local level and at workplaces in China resolve most coflicts. It is only in rare cases when a dispute or crime cannot be resolved locally that formal agents of the courts and police are called upon; even then, the trial is held at the location of the group or committee involved (Pepinsky 1978, p. 20; Johnson 1978; Bell 1978).

A young man in a commune rode his bicycle carelessly and hit an old man, breaking his leg. It was an accident, but it resulted from carelessness and someone had suffered. The police were never called in.

> While the old man's leg was being set at the commune hospital the public-security committee deliberated and came up with the sentence which the young chap cheerfully accepted: "the old man lives on his own, so you had better move in and look after him until he gets well. You can cycle to work from here." So the lad moved in with the old man, and bought and cooked his food for him. Apart from the fact that the old man liked meat while the young chap was vegetarian, they got on famously together. When the leg was mended they parted but have remained fast friends ever since. Throughout the communes one finds such examples of common law in action—people settling their own affairs without interference by the 'law' as it is understood in most societies (Burchett and Alley 1976, p. 36).

Cases of child abuse, marital disputes, and petty theft are resoved in similar fashion.

Cases of more serious conflict or crime, whether resolved at the local level or whether sent to formal court trial, are investigated carefully.

Friends, neighbors, and coworkers all get a chance to express their opinions. Anyone can give evidence.

When a crime occurs or a dispute arises, a conciliation committee of neighbors and fellow workers conducts an investigation. It is an open search for facts, free of legal technicalities. The defendant is given a chance to present his or her side. The final trial takes place in a neighborhood spot convenient to people, and it is attended by neighbors. If the accused confesses to the crime, the local mediation group discuss his or her sentence. Such sentences aim at rehabilitation, not punishment. If the accused claims innocence, he or she can appeal to the People's Court, which is more formal but still allows for neighbors, friends, co-workers, and others to participate (Crockett 1976; Lowe 1978; these are accounts by United States judges and lawyers who made three-week visits to China in 1976 and 1977).

At the trial discussed by Lowe, the presiding magistrate was a judge by training, but the other two people were lay judges. In the Popular Tribunals of Cuba, all the judges (as of the late 1960s) were local workers who had received very minimal legal training. These are examples of the socialist principle to demystify and deprofessionalize the process of justice, to make it understandable by all. In the long run, the legal profession would be abolished. For some years during the cultural revolution, legal training (and lawyers) did not exist (former lawyers were not killed; they simply did not function in that capacity). With the beginning return of professionalism (see Chapter 4) and with the lessening of the struggle to eliminate social classes, lawyers are reappearing. In Cuba, lawyers were required to do one month a year of manual labor, and their training aimed to avoid elitism (Pepinsky 1978; Berman 1969).

The resolution of conflict, at all levels, aims to educate and rehabilitate, not punish people. With rare exceptions, rehabilitation is done by neighbors and co-workers, not in prisons and other punitive institutions. (Pepinsky thinks the Chinese may have the lowest incarceration rate in the world.) A young man stole a car (a rare and serious crime in China) and rode it for a few hundred yards, knocking down a bicyclist in the process. He was apprehended by passersby and, after a trial, he was given a two-year suspended sentence. The judge said to him:

> The court holds that this defendant deliberately stole the car and violated the law. The defendant confessed and showed willingness to repent. According to our policy of leniency to those who confess and harsh treatment to those who resist, you are sentenced to two years of imprisonment and suspension of sentence while you are transformed through labor and study of the works of Chairman Mao. You are under the supervision and direction of the Revolutionary Committee of this factory.
>
> If you are not satisfied with this judgment, you may appeal within ten days after your receive a written copy of the judgment by filing two copies of your appeal with the People's Higher Court of Peking. Take the defendant away (Lowe 1978, p. 16).

Trials, investigations, mediations, and discussions aim to find out what happened and why; to show the accused or parties in dispute why they are not acting in the proper cooperative manner; to educate not only the parties involved but all those in the audience. For example, the Cuban Popular Tribunals heard many cases of cheating in the rationing system. It was important to show the seriousness of such cheating and the necessity for it in a society struggling for equality. All had to learn from the incident, not only the direct participants.

Thus, the mediation and resolution of crime and conflict become another instance of local community action which aims to create a just society.

Most crimes are handled locally, but serious crimes (such as murder) and political crimes are handled at more formal, higher levels. Political crimes (sabotage; plotting to overthrow socialism) are punished severely, with fairly long prison sentences. Even in these cases, the Chinese claim that people are helped to change and rehabilitate themselves.

As we might expect from the lessening of the struggle against elites, domination, and classes in China (see Chapter 4) law and justice are changing. It is evident in the changes since 1976 that formal legal procedures are gaining at the expense of lay participation and neighborhood dispute resolution. Edwards cites current policy statements in which "courts are ... urged to assume jurisdiction over contradictions among the people (civil disputes) which have generally been handled outside court since the mid-1960s." A *Beijing Review* article on the present Chinese legal system and on planned changes never mentions mediation and local dispute resolution. The focus is on developing laws, formal procedures, and control by legal experts. With the explanation that there is need to curb abuses committed during the cultural revolution, the present Chinese leaders are moving the legal system away from any commitment to class struggle and popular control. Once more, law and criminal justice are shaped by and reflect class domination and class conflict (Edwards 1978, p. 96; *Beijing Review* January 12, 1979, pp. 25-32; see other issues of *Beijing Review* throughout 1979).

The revised legal system in China (which took effect on January 1, 1980) seems to have created a system very similar to the American one. There are three bodies: the police, who investigate and arrest accused criminals; the People's Procuratorate (district attorney's office), who investigate further and prosecute the cases; and the courts, which conduct trials and sentence people. The accused are guaranteed lawyers and provided with other legal safeguards. Like the United States system, in theory it protects people from injustice. But we have seen that the United States criminal justice system discriminates against the poor and the working class, it does not prosecute serious capitalist crimes, and is, in fact, a system of injustice.

It should be clear that a legal system cannot insure justice merely by the formal procedures it creates. It is the implementation that shows how

> *The criminal justice system in the United States is subtle and sophisticated in its persecution and imprisonment of political prisoners. Martin Sostre, a man who he and his supporters argue was falsely imprisoned for political activities, not for any crime he committed, points to the oppressive system of justice in the United States:*
>
> *"The difference between America and other countries is money," Sostre said. "In this country, they can spend $100,000 or more on court expenses just to imprison one political dissident. If you were in Argentina, you would just disappear. You'd be walking down the street and a carload of goons would grab you, put a blanket on your head, take you to a basement, and someone would get your nuts or your hand or your toes in a vise and keep it up until you signed a confession saying what they want you to say.*
>
> *"But here they can afford to make everything legal, keep up a semblance of law and justice. They can pick juries, pay off witnesses, tie up the courts for years. They have the money to play around with so they can say they don't have any political prisoners. They can frame you up on ciminal charges so that way you won't be able to prove that you're a political prisoner."*
>
> *Source:* Dobrin 1980, p. 35.

just a legal system is—whether it protects people from serious dangers. A society divided by classes and inequalities cannot provide justice, no matter what the legal formalities. If China continues to move to greater inequalities (see Chapters 2, 3, 4, and 5), no formal legal system can provide justice for people. In any society, the legal system—the ways of handling crimes and disputes—reflects the equalities and inequalities (Pincus 1979).

The issue of political prisoners disturbs many people in the West. Note, however, that we have had political prisoners in the United States—the criminal justice system is obviously oppressive against working people, since it tends to prosecute and punish only street criminals. In socialist societies, there are some people who plot and attempt to overthrow socialism (such as those who invaded Cuba in 1961). No socialist government can close its eyes to such threats.

But what about socialist citizens who only criticize the state? They are of two types: those who oppose socialism, and those who support it but criticize the current leaders and their programs. Clearly, both must be given freedom to speak. And in fact all socialist governments do formally provide for such freedom of speech. But there have been violations in practice. It is a disturbing issue to people who support socialism. Mao Ze-dong often said that there is no clear line between the critical supporters (who may be mistaken) and the enemies of socialism who want to sabotage the creation of a just society. In the midst of struggle and turmoil, injustices do occur. So long as they are recognized and rectified, there is hope. It is when repression of critics becomes systematic, and when it is practiced by a bureaucratic elite and a new ruling class, that there are fundamental violations of socialist principles.

## Comparisons with the United States

Careful readers will have noticed formal similarities between the Cuban, Chinese, and United States legal systems. However, the contexts within which these systems operate make a significant difference.

Work and work training is essential to the rehabilitation of delinquents in Cuba. It is also a goal in the rehabilitation of delinquents in the United States. What then is the difference? For one thing, jobs are available to all Cuban youth; they are not available to many United States youth, delinquents or nondelinquents. Also, American delinquents are socialized for low-prestige and low-paying jobs. Cuban youth live in a society where all jobs pay enough to cover the necessities of life and where there is a real struggle to give dignity and prestige to all work. Generally, American delinquents live in a society with much inequality, alienation, and oppression, all of which are struggled against in Cuba (Liazos 1974, 1978; Wald 1978).

There are other apparent similarities. Restitution is a new movement in United States justice. Does not the case of the young man in China who cared for the old man whose leg he broke with his bicycle deal with the same principle of restitution? Restitution is still only an experiment (as are all United States reforms discussed above), not an established practice. Restitution cannot become a workable practice where people are alienated and exploited; it is only possible, morally and practically, when there is a serious struggle for equality and democracy. The impressive achievements of the Chinese people have made it possible to make the moral argument to people that they should not steal. In the United States, where exploitation and theft abound at the highest levels of the government and the economy, how can we make a moral argument against theft, and for restitution to young people?

In a very powerful book (*On the Take: From Petty Crooks to Presidents* 1978), Chambliss documents the pervasive corruption in American politics and business. Politicians at all levels, businesspeople, police, and organized criminals cooperate to profit from gambling, prostitution, drugs, and other illegal activities. On a regular basis, most politicians receive "contributions" from businesses and organized crime. Corruption is everywhere.

Similarly with mediation and citizen dispute resolution. They are possible, and on a significant scale, only when community exists. Mediation in the United States legal system is conducted by professionals who live outside people's communities, not by neighbors and co-workers. Can any of us conceive of a divorce trial in most American communities where neighbors and co-workers speak about and to the divorcing couple? When there is no responsibility for one another, artificial institutions cannot be set up which play at such caring about our fellow citizens. Bell describes a Chinese divorce trial, which aims not to find guilt or innocence, but to reconcile. Here, neighbors and coworkers can speak and recommend because there is true communal responsbility. Such an event is inconceivable in our context (Bell 1978).

## Socialist Struggles in the United States

Each chapter in this book has argued that equality and justice are impossible under capitalism and difficult under socialism. But struggles for equality and justice do make some improvements in our lives, and they may be steps to the eventual creation of a new society committed to community and equality.

It is no different in the area of criminal justice. Some struges for justice are discussed below. Some of the participants acted out of a socialist perspective, some not; all were searching for ways to change the present unjust system.

There have been three types of movements to achieve equal justice. In the past and present, many minority communities have organized for self-defense against racist institutions and groups (police; the KKK). The Black Panthers began as such a group. Another group, the "Defenders," organized a group of blacks in a Southern town to defend themselves from KKK intimidation and violence. Women's antirape groups are another example; and groups of prisoners who became politicized and turned to political action (such individuals as Malcolm X and George Jackson, and former delinquent gangs like the Young Lords and the Black Crusaders) are the third type (Brady 1977; Nelson 1967; Browning 1970; Helmreich 1973).

Consider the problem of delinquency more specifically. Struggles for community control of delinquency prevention, of the political transformation of young people (especially delinquents), and for a change in the status of youth constitute some general principles of a socialist strategy to delinquency prevention. But they must take place within a general movement to a socialist society to improve the quality of life for everyone.

According to Krisberg and Austin, there have been only three efforts at community control of delinquency prevention. Two were attacked as "communist-inspired" and in time destroyed (the authors do not mention the fate or effectiveness of the third). All three sought to improve the quality of life for the people in the area.

> The community-controlled approach to delinquency emphasized placing power and resources at the disposal of those people closest to the needs and problems of youth. Community programs generally seek to assist children in their growing-up process through support and encouragement. Since such programs recognize the contributions of poverty, racism, and sex discrimination to delinquency, they challenge the existing structure of privilege on behalf of youth. Misbehavior by children is treated firmly, but with the compassion nurtured by a communality of persons who view the child as an individual (Krisberg and Austin 1978, p. 573).

It does not seem that any of these programs were based on a socialist ideology or strategy. Thus, their inevitable failure must have been very frustrating, for the people involved did not realize that no solutions are possible under capitalism, only steps to eventual solutions.

**STRUGGLES: The Political Transformation of Street Gangs**

*There have been many efforts at delinquency prevention and reform. The following account describes a rather unusual reform of delinquents: the transformation of a street gang from a fighter of other gangs into a group working to improve conditions for themselves and their community. The Young Lords in this story were prominent in 1969–70; they have not been much in the news since 1971. I do not know whether or when the organization has disbanded.*

The Lords, until 1967 just another gang, have become the most potent revolutionary organization of Puerto Rican youth in the United States. The Lords are not prodigal sons, returned from suburbia to organize the ghetto. Less romantically, they started out operating in fundamentally the same style as in *West Side Story*. That history sets them apart from the vast majority of radical organizations around the country. They have negotiated peace pacts among nearly all of Chicago's white and Latin gangs, convincing them to fight, not against each other, but against the system which oppresses them. Influenced by the Lords, the 3000-member Latin Kings, the city's largest Puerto Rican gang, have begun to organize themselves politically and have started their own breakfast-for-children program. At the same time, the Lords have battered constantly at West Lincoln Park's established institutions to make them serve poor people.

In the fall of 1968 they took over the Armitage Street Methodist Church—now the People's Church—to found their headquarters and begin a day-care program.

In the spring of 1969 they led hundreds of their Puerto Rican brothers down the street to an empty lot which was to be made into $1000-membership private tennis courts, and transformed it into a children's park.

By summer they had built a coalition with several other community organizations to fight an Urban Renewal plan that envisioned West Lincoln Park as an "inner-city suburb" for middle-income whites. That battle still wears on as the Lords and their allies have joined with architects and lawyers to present their own plans for poor people's housing.

Last winter they opened a free health clinic in the basement of the People's Church, initiating the first attack on the health problems of the entire Puerto Rican community.

The Chicago YLO has inspired the formation of similar groups in Puerto Rican communities in other cities. By far the most significant of these is the New York City Young Lords. A political split between the two organizations which occurred in June has so far been free of the usual acrimony. The two groups, as is clearly revealed in their parallel development, are in any case bound together by common roots—a bond which they now express with the phrase "revolutionary compañeros."

Once their political conversion began, it took no more than six months to establish YLO's revolutionary outlook. Dennis Cunningham, one of several Movement lawyers in Chicago who have handled cases for the Lords and the Latin Kings for several years, points to the Lords' early and continuing affiliation with the Black Panthers as fundamental to their political development. . . .

Up to about six months ago the YLO was completely dependent upon Jose (Cha Cha) Jimenez, chairman and head of the gang since long before its politicization. . . . Cha Cha went on trial again early in August on a mob action charge stemming from demonstrations against the city's Urban Renewal plans. When that trial is over he faces seven more charges.

While serving time earlier, Cha Cha discovered how full the jails were of Puerto Ricans—not just gang members, but old and middle-aged people, workers and welfare mothers. It became clear to him that the real enemy was not the Latin Kings or the Paragons or the Black Eagles; the real enemy was Daley's Chicago Urban Renewal, local Alderman George McCutcheon, and the U.S. government, whose imperial colonization policy has so mangled

*Source:* Reprinted from Frank Browning, "From Rumble to Revolution: The Young Lords," *Ramparts* (October 1970), pp 19, 20, 22. Copyright 1970 by Ramparts Magazine, Inc. Reprinted by permission.

*(continued)*

> **The Political Transformation of Street Gangs** *(continued)*
>
> Puerto Rico that he and his family had been forced to leave just to survive. . . .
>
> Alberto, a third-year medical student at Northwestern University, runs the health clinic, a program of free medical service to the community staffed by doctors, medical and nursing students and professional health workers. The clinic, which opened in February with a handful of patients, now receives nearly 50 people each Saturday afternoon, with services from prenatal care to eye examinations.
>
> At first many women were afraid to go to the clinic. They were wary of the old gang image and frightened by what they had read in the city's newspapers. Then health workers started canvassing door-to-door, asking people if anyone needed medical care and making arrangements for them to come to the clinic. If they failed to appear, they were sent a personal letter inviting them to come in the next week. Sometimes members of the Health Ministry and doctors go to the homes of people who can't come to the clinic.

Political transformation of individuals and gangs has led to the abandonment of crime and delinquency. George Jackson and Malcolm X are primary examples. Groups like the Black Panthers, the Young Lords, and the Black Crusaders have been very effective in reducing delinquency, at least of their members. Involved in a struggle to improve their condition and that of others, their lives gained meaning, and they saw the futility and destructiveness of crime. Efforts to feed hungry children, rid the community of drugs, and provide protection from crime became the best solutions to delinquency. In time, of course, all such groups have failed (in part through sabotage and infiltration), as they could be expected to fail under capitalism. They did teach, however, the way to delinquency prevention: young and old, delinquents and others, must all unite to fight for a better life. Delinquency may not have ended, nor justice have been achieved. But if the struggle is, and is seen as, part of a total socialist strategy, progress will have been made.

## SUMMARY

The main points of a socialist perspective on crime can be stated briefly:

1. *Street crime* is the focus of most discussions on crime, and more harmful crimes are ignored (both acts defined as crimes but enforced rarely (white-collar crimes) and acts not even defined as crimes (capitalist crimes at workplaces, in the environment, and so on).
2. Street crimes cannot be explained without understanding the situation under capitalism. Poverty, exploitation, alienation, insecurity, competition, and the destruction of community all contribute to cause theft, vandalism, and violence. People who lead fulfilling lives, have the necessities of life, and care for each other

are not likely to steal or to attack others. To the degree that inequalities and alienation persist under socialism, there will be some crime and conflict. (Whether any society can ever be totally free of crime and conflict is a theoretical question that cannot be explored here. It is clear that violent, destructive crime has been reduced under socialism; even if no more is achieved, that is something worth striving for.)

3. Solutions to crime are impossible under capitalism. The struggle for equality and community eliminates much crime. What crime does persist must be resolved within a local, community context (as is the case for solving all problems in a socialist society).

# 13

# *Education: Fitting People in an Unfit Society*

THE CHANGING SCENE

Many times in the United States history, the poor, minorities, and the working class have seen education as the vehicle for social mobility. What Greer calls *The Great School Legend* held that with study and perseverance, people could—and did—improve their social and economic positions.

The 1960s represent the latest example of these hopes. This time, it was thought that education would end the poverty of poor blacks and other minorities. The Headstart program, federal money for urban schools, other new programs, tutoring and remedial education—these are but a few examples of programs that were intended to provide poor people the opportunity to shed their poverty (see Carnoy 1978, pp. 250-51 for a list of these programs).

That time, so vivid to many of us who went to college and began working in the 1960s, now seems long ago, a period of hope and innocence. The 1970s have been a period of disillusionment and entrenchment. Not only has there been an end to most programs for poor people, but most of the liberal reforms of middle-class, suburban schools are being undone. The talk now is of moving "back to basics." Open classrooms, open high school campuses, less stress on grades, and other innovations are being eliminated for a stricter, traditional education.

Indeed, in many suburban communities voters have been greatly reducing education budgets and in many cases closing schools for weeks and months. Taxes have been going up as a percent of people's income, and since property taxes, which pay for education, are the only taxes over which people have some control, more revolt against education costs seems inevitable (Ciancanelli 1978, pp. 200–201).

What accounts for the almost total failure of the hopes of the 1960s? White ethnic groups have used education to advance themselves, so why are blacks and minorities now unable to get ahead through education? The answer that radical social scientists have been developing since the late 1960s is that schools did not really provide an avenue to success for any group. They did not because they were never meant to provide such a means to social mobility. In fact, they have always been structured so as to keep most people in their place, but, by giving them failing grades in school, to convince them that their low social and economic position is their fault, because of their supposed limited abilities and motivation.

The following pages explore three related, but somewhat different, critiques of the functions of education in the United States. First, many books in the late 1960s exposed the discrimination and brutality visited upon black and other minority students by urban schools. Kozol's *Death at an Early Age,* Kohl's *36 Children,* and Herndon's *the Way It Spozed to Be* showed the racism, lack of teaching materials, and total unconcern with teaching that pervaded urban schools. Other critiques showed that even the "good" schools of middle-class suburbia oppressed their students. Holt's *How Children Fail,* Friedenberg's *Coming of Age in America,* and other books argued that schools fostered competition, conformity, and obedience, and repressed exploration and real learning. Some critics argued that blacks and others were never taught any skills and could not make it in the United States economy; others questioned the price people paid for acquiring such skills and success. The developing radical Marxist critique (to be discussed here) holds that schools have in fact succeeded in their real function: to support the existing division of classes, provide workers for capitalism, and keep people in their place.

There are three related concerns in the libertarian, socialist critique of education: schools teach blind obedience to the national government (which is dominated by the ruling class); they train people to "accept work which is monotonous, boring, and without personal satisfaction"; and they create the myth that education provides opportunities for social mobility (Spring 1975, pp. 13–14).

This critique of education parallels somewhat the political economic and cultural critiques of health care. Not only does it concern the poor education of and discrimination against the lower classes, but it also questions the process and content of education. Specifically, capitalist education enhances negative human relations; it values authoritarianism, obedience, elitism, and control, instead of learning, exploration, and growth. Even those who supposedly benefit by education (white children of the upper classes) in fact are taught conformity, routine, and obedience.

These are the main issues in education. They are explored below in some detail, along with educational alternatives in the United States and educational policy in some socialist societies. The problems of education, like those of work, health and illness, the environment, and professional domination are not limited to a few people. They touch the lives of most of us, since we all must go to school, where class discrimination, boredom, and control by others will be our experience. Schooling is also related to work alienation, since it is meant to prepare us for work (see Chapters 4 and 5).

## THE RISE AND FUNCTIONS OF PUBLIC EDUCATION

Public schools were established to preserve social order and benefit the ruling class. Reforms in public education are meant to enhance that purpose, not to change it. As capitalist industrialism grew, it needed trained workers. "Workers needed to be punctual, obedient, passive and willing to accept their work and position" (Spring, pp. 22–23). Decorum and obedience, in addition to minimal reading skills, are desirable traits in workers.

### *Training for Obedience*

Much historical research has shown that those who set up public education were clear in their motives. The work of Samuel Bowles and others has shown that public education emerged in the United States to meet the needs of business and corporations, not to educate and enlighten people, and certainly not to provide opportunities for personal and social improvement. As industrialism expanded in the early 1800s, old ideologies and socializing processes making for allegiance to the established order began to crumble. A new tool was needed. The solution in most capitalist societies was the creation of free public education, which soon became compulsory (Bowles 1971a; Bowles and Gintis 1976).

Certainly, much teaching in the schools has focused on content and skills, but the larger concern has been with traits considered desirable by employers. Among these traits have been punctuality, unquestioning acceptance of rules, willingness to do boring and repetitive tasks, and allegiance to work itself (work which alienates people by requiring the use of only their bodies, not their minds). In their essential features, schools have copied the environment and organization of factories (*Work in America* 1973). Even today, when a high school diploma is irrelevant to the ability to perform many jobs, it is still required. "In the employer's mind, a high school graduate (as opposed to a dropout) will be more likely to show up daily, submit to orders, and not to cause trouble" (Carnoy 1972, p. 5). (For details on the changing labor force, see Chapter 5.)

Many of those in the past who worked to implement mass public education were very revealing in their comments on what they expected from the schools. For example, a manufacturer wrote in 1841:

> I have never considered mere knowledge as the only advantage derived from a good Common School education. . . . [Workers with more education possess] a higher and better state of morals, are more orderly and respectful in their deportment, and are more ready to comply with the wholesome and necessary regulations of an establishment. . . . In times of agitation, on account of some changes in regulations or wages, I have always looked to the most intelligent, best educated and the most moral for support (in Katz 1968, p. 88).

On the other hand, in 1880 Charles Francis Adams, Jr. characterized the schools as factories and prisons:

> Most of you, indeed, cannot but have been part and parcel of one of those huge, mechanical educational machines, or mills, as they might more properly be called. They are, I believe, peculiar to our own time and country, and are so organized to combine as nearly as possible the principal characteristics of the cotton-mill and the railroad with those of the model state's prison (in Katz, p. 162).

The same interests that motivated persons such as the manufacturer quoted above, although more obviously, motivated Southern industrialists who urged education for blacks. In the late nineteenth century, an Alabama iron manufacturer said of such education, "If the labor was better educated I am satisfied our labor here would be much more reliable." William H. Baldwin said at an educational conference in 1899 that education was a means to get black people to "willingly fill the more menial positions and do the heavy work, at less wages" than the white workers (Anderson 1975, pp. 24, 33).

Those sentiments were shared by some leading businessmen and educators of the past and are retained by many in the present. But how do we know that schools do, in fact, teach these values? The writings of Jules Henry and Edgar Friedenberg, among others, have shown some of the ways in which obedience is taught. A more recent and more focused study by Kathleen Wilcox and Pia Moriarty shows in detail how schools socialize young people (Henry 1963; Friedenberg 1965; Wilcox and Moriarty 1976).

A distinction must be made. All people, including most people in higher management, must learn to do the work that is alienating to their spirits and destructive of human relationships. But management people

> . . . probably are socialized so as to internalize authority and act without direct and continuous supervision to implement goals and objectives relatively alienated from their own personal needs (Bowles and Gintis 1976, p. 145).

In their work, they have much autonomy within the context of the internalized authority values. Workers, on the other hand, must be taught to follow the external directions of others: they must become "reliable" and obedient employees.

In their study of two elementary schools, one containing upper-middle-class students and the other filled with lower-middle-class youngsters, Wilcox and Moriarty showed how people are trained to fit into the different jobs awaiting them. In the upper-middle-class school, students were taught to become autonomous in the context of internalizing certain values.

> In an internal interaction, the teacher throws the responsibility back to the child to think and shape activity in a manner that promotes or relies upon internalized values, self-images, standards or goals.

Here are two examples of teacher comments: "Tommy, talk to yourself quietly and tell yourself where you are and what's expected of you." "You really goofed off. Why do you do this to yourself?" (p. 210).

At the lower-middle-class school, teachers used commands and orders. The teacher

> ... treats the child as a person who is expected to follow certain standard rules, procedures or directions laid down by herself and made solvent by her authority and direct power.

The following teacher comments show clearly the direction of the socialization process: "You have a responsibility to get that paper done and I want it done now." "You have an assignment. Sit down and get busy" (pp. 209–10). Both groups of students are being socialized to do what is expected of them—those headed for managerial positions will do it at their own direction; those destined for manual labor and clerical jobs will perform their work at the direction of others.

Thus, from the very beginning, schools have consistently worked to prepare students for deadening jobs that provide no possibility of financial or social improvement. It has also been imperative that this process of preparing a few for high positions and limiting the lives of most people be seen as the objective result of the differing personal qualities and individual abilities of the students.

## *The Myth of Social Mobility*

In my ten years of teaching I have often heard the following comment. "We (Italians, Irish, Polish, or other people) came to the United States, we went to school and worked hard, and we made it. Why can't they (blacks and other minorities) do the same? Why do they do so poorly in school? Either they can't do any better or they don't care. Why are they coddled with special education programs other groups never had?"

In such comments, people express their version of the legend of education for social mobility, a legend held by most social scientists, as Greer shows (1972, chs. 1–3). Most everyone writing on the topic has said or implied that the high failure and dropout rates of black students were not typical of public education. But Greer, simply by examining the performance record of urban schools (which ethnic groups and minorities have attended) shows that in fact from the very beginning urban public schools have failed to teach large numbers (often majorities) of their students: Irish, Italian, Polish, blacks, and Puerto Ricans. Instead of helping them to get better jobs and improve socially, schools have consistently failed most poor and minority children, and sent them out to the labor market of unskilled and semiskilled workers.

It is not that success in school leads to economic improvement; rather, when a group "succeeds" economically (moves out of poverty), this group puts pressure on the schools to educate their children. Thus, those immigrant poor who improved themselves did so despite, not because of, compulsory education. Most failed and were made to feel it was their fault for failing. What schools do to black people today is what schools have always done to ethnic and poor groups, and to most working-class people (Gans, in Greer 1972, pp. xii–xiii).

The facts gathered by Greer are instructive. From 1890 on, a large percentage of students have done poorly and dropped out. At most, only 60 percent of students have tested at their grade level (p. 108). Urban schools were crowded, run down, and not conducive to learning. In New York City,

> At the turn of the century 1,100 willing children were refused admission to any school for lack of space. Pupils in part-time classes had increased from almost 10,000 to 45,000 since 1898, and in 1902 they numbered 70,000; by 1906, over 14 percent of the elementary school registers were on such sessions with the heaviest strain on first-grade classes (p. 118).

Conditions and results did not improve with time. "One investigation committee in 1914 concluded that the public school system in New York City had 'abandoned . . . 80 percent of 14–16 year olds.'" Despite laws to keep children in school, many were given work permits and allowed to leave before reaching the minimal legal age. But as unskilled jobs became more scarce, schools responded by giving fewer work permits. In 1919, Chicago gave 10,000 permits, but only 987 in 1930. Thus, schools added to their function by acting as babysitting institutions, hiding both their failure to teach and the lack of jobs (Greer pp. 122, 109).

By the 1920s, all American cities had the same "serious deficiencies in academic performance, the same overcrowding, unsanitary conditions, and serious financial problems. . . ." A 1910s study of New York City high schools found that of those entering high school, the following percent graduated: less than 0 percent Italian; 0.1 percent of Irish; 10 percent native whites; 10.8 percent of British children; 15 percent of those from Germany; and 16 percent of Russian (mostly Jewish) children.

Things have not changed totally in New York, for in 1970, more than one-third of elementary school graduates did not complete their first year of high school (Greer, pp. 112–14). Also in that year, between the middle of their junior year and high school graduation, 30 percent of white students, 50 percent of black students, and 60 percent of Puerto Rican students dropped out of New York City high schools. And in 1979, at least 45 percent of students who began the ninth grade three years earlier in New York City had dropped out before graduation (Trimberger 1973, p. 33; Higgins 1980). The problem has not been only those who drop out. Those in school have been taught poorly. In New York in 1943, one study found that of 6,909 students entering high school, "almost 90 percent scored below the norm, despite the fact that each had been awarded an elementary school diploma." Thus, we can understand why half of the the high school freshmen did not graduate during the 1940s. In Detroit during the 1950s 50 percent of students dropped out before they completed the twelfth grade. But even those who stay on and get a high school diploma are not certified to have reading and other skills. Many read at seventh- or eighth-grade level. Such poor education is found not only in urban schools, but many rural areas, such as Appalachia (Greer, p. 127; Sexton 1961, p. 153; Caudill 1963).

Given these statistics on dropouts and poor education, we can see that education has not been the great elevator to success. In 1950, 80 percent of New York and New Jersey residents of Irish, Italian, and Slavic descent worked in unskilled or semiskilled jobs. In 1970, nationwide statistics revealed similar findings. Data from the 1920-1969 Census reports show that most sons of fathers without college do not attend college (Greer, p. 86).

Not only has education not been the road to success for blacks, it has not been for most white ethnics, to this day.

*Poverty, Education, and Jobs*

More education has not eliminated poverty. In 1960, about one-quarter of the population was in school: 29 million 6-13 year olds and 86 percent of the 11.2 million 14-17 year olds; 3 million were in college. Despite those numbers, poverty persisted. In 1979, even more people were in college (about 10 million), and schooling had increased to a median of 12.4 school years completed in 1978 (0-4 years—3.6 percent; 5-7—8-9—6.7 percent; 9 percent; 1-3 years high school—14.8 percent; high school—36.1 percent; 1-3 years college—14.1 percent; and 4 or more years college—15.7 percent). Most of us have experienced economic difficulties in the 1970s despite increased schooling (in years at least, if not in greater knowledge gained) (Carnoy 1978, pp. 249-50; *Statistical Abstract* 1979, p. 145).

The myth that more schooling leads to success was tested severely during the 1960s. By all accounts, the educational reforms and programs of the 1960s failed. They neither led to more learning nor to economic improvement. In the 1970s, educational conditions are worse. Schools are even more disorderly and less able to teach the basics; in many places, schools have closed (temporarily) because of tax revolts; urban schools have become the dumping grounds for the poor (Ciancanelli 1978, p. 196).

The economic crisis that began in 1973 has increased the loss in faith that schools lead to social mobility. The ruling class has responded in two ways: it has interpreted the failure of the schools as the students' failure (they supposedly are inferior and can't learn); and the movement to cut educational expenditures has been made to appear as the wish of the people (which it is, but only in the sense explained above). In constant dollars, of course, educational expenditures have not increased dramatically, $51 billion in 1967-68 to $63 billion in 1976-77 (this with an 8 percent increase in student enrollment). But cutting back on education, as on all social services, is a necessity so capitalism can deal with the worldwide crisis of capitalist countries in the 1970s (Union of Radical Political Economists 1978; Ciancanelli 1978).

Today, Greer argues, schools still "succeed" in their real function, which is to fail many students and send them "back into the cheap labor market. But today these jobs just aren't there" (p. 116). Many others have made the same argument, that today there is less demand for unskilled labor than, say, thirty to forty years ago. But actually, most jobs today demand little skill. Rather, there are fewer jobs than people who need them, and most employers have raised the educational qualifications required to hold the same old unskilled jobs. Indeed, to the extent that schools are giving more degrees and diplomas, they are creating a severe problem of educational inflation and unmet expectations, since three-quarters of the jobs available are essentially unskilled (working-class jobs at low pay) (Braverman 1974, pp. 438 ff.).

The connection between education and social mobility is deceptive (see statistics in next section on income and years of schooling). More education cannot improve our economic condition. There is in fact a shortage of jobs; women and blacks make less money than white men at all educational levels; and many jobs require no education, thus, more education would not change the situation. So, whereas it is true that some people may get better jobs by more education, they are likely to do so by displacing others (Carnoy 1978, pp. 252-53).

## CLASS AND EDUCATION

This section will examine in more detail how education has worked to train people for work and life under capitalism. Generally, there has been a class bias in education. It is seen in tracking, expenditures, teacher biases, and other ways.

### The Control of Educational Policy

As we saw above, the people who were active in setting up public education said specifically that they wanted schools to train people for work under industrial capitalism. They were leading capitalists who valued workers who were obedient and punctual and also possessed minimal skills.

Members of the upper classes (some from the ruling class, others from professional groups) have dominated school boards and other bodies that control education. In elementary and secondary education, studies throughout this century have shown that "elected school boards were controlled by a business and professional elite." Most school board members (60 percent and over) have been businessmen and professionals; only 10 percent have been workers (Spring 1975, p. 21; Useem and Useem 1974, p. 5).

It has not been different with college and university boards of trustees. Before the rise of industrial capitalism, in the early nineteenth century, colleges were religious institutions and the boards were populated by clergymen. But as the century progressed, businessmen replaced them on the boards of trustees, mirroring business's takeover of the society and economy. Examine the board of trustees of your college and you will see its professional and business domination. One study of 4,000 board members showed that 50 percent were lawyers or corporate officials, with only 100 (2-5 percent) being labor leaders (no workers here, only labor leaders) (Useem and Useem 1974, p. 9).

The ruling class and professionals dominate education in other ways. For example, today they distribute free materials (booklets, films, kits) to many schools. The contents subtly (or not so subtly) propagate corporate ideology, such as the claim that nuclear power is safe and good (*Dollars and Sense*, November 1978, pp. 12-13). Corporations also fund commissions and foundations that study the problems of education and recommend changes and new programs. The Carnegie Commission on Higher Education has been influential. One of its major recommendations has been its endorsement of community colleges and technical training (Darknell 1975; Wolfe 1974).

*School Expenditures*

Wealthy members of the ruling class send their children to private schools. But even in public education, financed by tax money, since communities differ in wealth and since property taxes pay most school costs, richer communities spend more money per student than do poorer communities. Even within the same city, "better" neighborhoods have more money to spend on their children.

In the 1950s in Detroit, schools attended by the lower-class students had older buildings and fewer and inadequate materials. Schools in the poorest areas averaged forty-five years in age, whereas schools in the most affluent areas averaged ten years (Sexton 1961, p. 215).

In 1970, Detroit, by then largely black, discriminated against black students. K-6 schools which were 10 percent or less black spent $495 per pupil. Those schools 90 percent and over black spent $430 per student (Michelson, in Carnoy 1972, p. 171).

Within states, expenditures vary widely. In 1974, in Massachusetts there was a range from $454 per student in some communities to $2,243 in others. In New York the range was $936 to $4,215. The same condition holds when we compare states. Generally, the higher the per capita personal income in the state, the higher the per capita school expenditures. In 1977, Mississippi, with per capita income of $5,736 spent $1,220 per student (data for elementary and secondary public schools); New York, on the other hand, with per capita income of $8,267, spent $2,527 per student (Ciancanelli 1978, p. 201; *Statistical Abstract* 1979, p. 157).

*Different Training for Different Classes*

Schools not only spend less money on the lower classes, but, more importantly, according to some people, they educate differenly, tracking students into different careers and teaching them different values and attitudes, corresponding to the jobs they are expected to hold. Bowles argues that the families of the children of different classes also value different attitudes, those of the working class valuing obedience, and those of the middle-class valuing initiative. Thus, school, family, the community, and the economy cooperate to teach children of different classes the values they will need to survive in the work they will do: managers will give orders and workers will follow them (Bowles 1971a).

But this "correspondence" analysis is too mechanical. It makes the ruling class all-powerful, as if they could manipulate education completely to produce the kinds of workers they want. They try to, of course, but changing conditions and people's resistance do not allow for total control. The constant changes in educational policy show the limits of control by the ruling class. School violence and other problems show how students reject the socialization of the schools (see Chapter 12).

The limits of control work this way: when capitalists push for more education, costs go up, so later the capitalists work to cut costs and thus starve education. At times they have pushed for vocational training, but the workers trained may have obsolete skills by the time they have entered the labor market. Capitalist needs often create problems and contradictions (Gorelick 1977; *Work in America* 1973).

In addition, Gorelick argues that working-class parents do not *value* strict education and authoritarianism. They may simply see that reforms such as open classrooms may become euphemisms for educational neglect of their children. They have neither the money, nor the education themselves, to compensate for the learning their children may not get in open classrooms (open classrooms are ideal—but only for people who see a reason to learn and are given a real chance to learn; like many reforms, they can assume different realities when they are applied to working-class and poor people).

Finally, a look at the schools for the ruling class shows them to be very authoritarian (racist and sexist, too). The correspondence of working-class education with authoritarianism and middle- and upper-class education with initiative and freedom, is less than complete. In fact, under capitalism the essence of most education is control, conformity, and obedience (Gorelick, p. 26).

*Tracking*

Under the guise of providing different educational programs for each student's ability, schools have assigned them to programs ("tracks") which keep them from going to college (poorer students are now often guided to community colleges—see below).

Since the 1920s, under the claimed policy of preparing students for later life and providing for differing student needs, tracking has become widespread.

> In the 19th century, public schools were established to train immigrants to work in the factories of New England. In the 1920's when there was a need for a more differentiated labor force, public education responded by developing a tracking system based on a student's "ability level." Students who were defined as "bright," most of whom also happened to be white and upper-middle class, were in the upper tracks and went on to college. The "slow" students, most of whom were also immigrants and working class, had to be satisfied with vocational programs leading to semi-skilled work. The large group of "average" students, most of whom were working and lower middle class, would be able to enter skilled blue collar and lower level white collar jobs (Pincus 1974, p. 29).

Defenders of tracking argue that it insures that workers will be available (and trained) to do all the jobs that need to be done. But in distributing students to different tracks, and therefore to different jobs and lives, tracking parallels the class system: students from the lower classes are assigned disproportionately to the lower tracks (Duberman 1976, p. 212). Hollingshead's *Elmtown's Youth* was one of several studies to show that in the 1940s, the children of the upper classes were mostly in the college track and those of the lower classes in the vocational track (Spring 1975, p. 28).

In the late 1950s, Sexton found that Detroit students were highly tracked by family income. As Table 13.1 shows, the higher the income, the more likely that a student would be in the college track (Sexton 1961).

A track leading to college education has insured a better job and higher income. Duberman asks, of course, "is a college degree necessary for *doing* a job or merely for *getting* a job?" (1976, p. 204). The answer is that it is only necessary to get the job, for the abilities of college students are not necessarily higher. But the entrance requirement of a college degree for many jobs has insured these jobs for the children of the upper classes.

Table 13.2 shows clearly the relation of education and income. College graduates, over their lifetime, make twice as much as high school dropouts—because for professional and managerial jobs the college diploma is

TABLE 13.1  Curriculum Enrollment in Detroit Schools (Late 1950s), by Family Income

| Income | College preparatory | Business and vocational | General |
|---|---|---|---|
| $5,000 | 19 | 33 | 48 |
| $6,000 | 25 | 46 | 29 |
| $7,000 | 40 | 31 | 29 |
| $8,000 | 57 | 21 | 23 |
| $9,000 | 79 | 11 | 10 |

Source: Sexton, *Education and Income*, 1961, p. 177.

TABLE 13.2  Lifetime Income for Men, by Years of School Completed, from Eighteen to Death (1972)

| Years of school | Lifetime income |
|---|---|
| fewer than 8 | $280,000 |
| 8 | $344,000 |
| 9–11 | $389,000 |
| 12 | $479,000 |
| 13–15 | $543,000 |
| 16+ | $758,000 |

Source: *Statistical Abstract of the United States* 1979, p. 144.

an entrance requirement. Of people with a high school deploma only 7 percent were in professional and managerial jobs; people with one to two semesters of college, 13 percent; three to four semesters, 28 percent; five to seven semesters, 32 percent; but of those with a college degree and higher education, fully 82 percent were in professional and managerial jobs. A 1976 study of high school graduates from 1972 also showed the relationship of education to income. In the three income groups of these graduates, as defined by the study, the following percentages had received a bachelor's degree four years later: low income—3.5; middle income—13; and high income—38 (*Dollars and Sense*, February 1980, p. 14). School tracking clearly influences the jobs we get and incomes we make (Karabel 1972, p. 119).

The system becomes perpetuated because when people make less income than others, their children have a lower chance of going to college. A study from the 1950s showed that if your father was a blue-collar worker, you had an 8 percent chance of graduating from college; if he was a salesman or clerk, your chances were 15 percent; if a businessman, 19 percent; and if a professional, 43 percent. William Sewell and his associates compared students of the *same academic abilities* but from different classes. Among other things they found that "an upper-class student's chances for education or training beyond high school are 2½ times greater than those of a lower-class student; chances for college are 4 to 1; for graduation, 6 to 1; and 9 to 1 for a postgraduate degree" (Duberman 1976, pp. 207, 210).

Sewell's data refer to 1957 graduates in Wisconsin. College attendance is also clearly related to income. In 1967, for example, only 19.8 percent of high school graduates from families with incomes under $3,000 attended college, whereas 86.7 percent of those from families with incomes over $15,000 attended (Bowles 1971a, p. 48).

Conditions had not changed in the late 1970s. In 1977, 22.6 percent of eighteen to twenty-four-year-olds from families making under $9,000 were in college; but of those from families making over $27,000, 59.8 percent were enrolled *(Statistical Abstract* 1979, p. 163).

The data presented so far may seem dated. After all, with the vast expansion of public higher education since the 1960s and the increasing percentage of high school graduates going to college (around 50 percent since the early 1970s), it may seem that class may no longer be related to college attendance. Tracking and lower education for working people still exist, but at a new level. Not only do more students from the lower classes still drop out of high school, or end their education with a high school diploma, but of those who go to college, fewer go to the better schools, and fewer finish.

The rise of the community college represents the latest form of tracking. It is a solution to educational inflation. When working people got high school diplomas, a college degree became a requirement for most good jobs. When working people realized this and demanded college education, the ruling class, which dominates educational policy, responded with the community college (Karabel 1972, p. 121).

Community colleges were created to offer the illusion of college but the reality of vocational training. Business people and the Carnegie Foundation supported community colleges as a means of training workers at public expense. The colleges have two types of programs: transfer programs, where students take liberal arts courses, receive an associate degree (A.A.), and transfer to four-year colleges; and terminal programs, where students get vocational training in many fields (X-ray technicians, secretaries, dental hygiene assistants, and the like). The plan was for most students to enroll in terminal programs, but students, knowing the occupational realities, flocked to the transfer programs (two-thirds, around 1970). Studies showed that most students wanted to transfer and get a B.A. In doing so, they would sabotage the purpose of community colleges, so the colleges created mechanisms to "cool out" these students and direct them to vocational programs. For example, counselors would keep reminding students of their low grades and of other realities. Generally, the administrations of community colleges and the foundations supporting community-college education have been concerned about too many students in transfer programs (data given below show a projected increase of college students in community colleges) (Karabel 1972, p. 129–130; Pincus 1974, p. 27; Clark 1960).

The objection many people raise is not to any inherent difference between an X-ray technician and a doctor. Both may be necessary and both deserve prestige and reward. Rather, the issue is that in *this society* doctors have much more prestige and make much higher income.

Generally, the children of the higher classes attend universities (those from the ruling class mostly attend elite private universities); children from the middle classes generally attend state colleges; and from the lower classes, community colleges. Table 13.3 and 13.4 provide some data. These tables refer to students entering and attending college; the figures become more unfavorable to the lower classes when we consider graduation from college, and graduation from what type of college.

Thus, students from working-class and poor families attend community colleges disproportionately. For example, "while blacks are 13% of the students in two-year colleges, they are only 5.9 percent of four-year students" *(Dollars and Sense,* February 1980, p. 14). Once in these colleges, there is further tracking by class. The lower the family income, and the more that the father's occupation is unskilled or semiskilled, the more likely a student will be in the technical or vocational programs (rather than in transfer programs) (Karabel 1972, p. 127.)

**TABLE 13.3** Median Income of Families of College Freshmen, 1972

| In Public Higher Education | |
|---|---|
| Community college | $11,000 |
| Four-year college | $12,800 |
| University | $14,450 |

| In Private Higher Education | |
|---|---|
| Four-year college | $15,500 |
| Universities | $17,850 |

*Source:* Pincus 1974, p. 25.

**TABLE 13.4** Family Income by Type of College Entered (Percentages)

| | Family income | | | | |
|---|---|---|---|---|---|
| Type of College | Under $8,000 | $8,000–12,499 | $12,500–20,000 | Over $20,000 | Total |
| Public two-year | 27.2 | 34.8 | 26.4 | 11.5 | 100 |
| Public four-year | 25.4 | 31.7 | 28.3 | 14.7 | 100 |
| Public university | 15.1 | 29.7 | 32.8 | 22.3 | 100 |
| Private university | 10.6 | 20.4 | 27.3 | 41.8 | 100 |

*Source:* table in Karabel 1972, p. 123.

Community colleges are safety valves, directing students away from more selective institutions while providing the illusion of equal opportunity for college education. The data above show clearly that higher education favors the children of the higher classes. Studies show that when we compare students of the same social class and academic abilities, those who entered community colleges "were *less* likely to receive the B.A. degree than those entering four-year schools." Also those states in the United States with the most developed community-college system had the lowest percentage of students completing four or more years of college. Thus community colleges act as a deterrent to college education for the children of the lower classes (Pincus 1974, p. 28; Karabel 1972).

The 1970s open-admissions policy in New York City became a path to lower-prestige colleges and high dropout rates. There was little motive to stay and finish when students saw how few good jobs awaited those who did finish (Trimberger 1973, pp. 35–39).

The trend in higher education is clearly toward the community colleges. The enrollment figures for 1975, and the projections for 1980 and 1985, show this trend (see Table 13.5). In 1975, in terms of full-time-equivalent enrollment, about 26 percent of students were in community colleges; the projection is for 31 percent to be in community colleges by 1985.

This trend reflects the goals of policy makers. They want to direct students from different classes to different educations and careers. And they spend less money for the students in community colleges. Around 1970, California public schools spent $1,000 to educate a student in a community college, $3,000 in a four-year college, and $5,000 in a university (Duberman 1976, p. 213). These figures are similar to those across the nation.

**TABLE 13.5a** Full-Time Equivalent Enrollment in Degree-Credit Institutions (in Millions)

| Year | Total | 4-year | 2-year |
|---|---|---|---|
| 1975 | 9.73 | 7.22 | 2.5 |
| 1980[a] | 11.14 | 7.9 | 3.25 |
| 1985[a] | 11.00 | 7.53 | 3.47 |

**TABLE 13.5b** Two-Year College Enrollment (Public Community College and Private Junior College) (in Millions)

| Year | Total | Part-time | Full-time | Public |
|---|---|---|---|---|
| 1975 | 3.87 | 2.16 | 1.7 | 3.74 |
| 1980[a] | 5.22 | 3.08 | 2.15 | 5.07 |
| 1985[a] | 5.74 | 3.5 | 2.25 | 5.58 |

[a] Projected estimates.
Source: *Yearbook of Higher Education* 1977–78, pp. 585, 586.

Thus, public tax money is spent disproportionately on the children of different classes. The states spend more money on the children of the higher classes to assure them of "better" education and jobs, thus higher incomes.

## I.Q. and Academic Ability

Many people have argued that the differences in educational attainment represent differences in abilities among students, not class discrimination. This issue will now be explored in more detail, expecially the uses (and abuses) of I.Q. scores.

The history of I.Q. testing shows that from the very beginning the scores were meant to discriminate against the lower classes and immigrants. In the 1910s, I.Q. tests were administered to immigrant groups, and they showed, according to those who administered them, that in each group 80 percent or more of the people were "feeble-minded." Such dubious findings were used to argue for the "inferiority" of immigrants and to end immigration. The makers and users of I.Q. tests were motivated politically, as Kamin has shown in detail (1974).

I.Q. scores in the 1910s showed 50 percent of soldiers scoring at the thirteen- to fifteen-year-old level, which would have meant they were retarded. That was obviously impossible and no one paid attention to these findings. But attention was paid to the findings that Irish and Jews had much lower I.Q. scores than did Protestants (now, all these groups have the same range of scores). Today, people seem to find it significant that blacks have I.Q. scores on the average fifteen points lower than whites, ignoring the earlier "findings" showing feeble-mindedness in Italians, Jews, Polish, Chinese, and others. Most people think I.Q. scores refer to inherent mental ability. In fact, I.Q. scores only tell what information people have been exposed to, not what they are capable of knowing (Gartner, Greer, and Riessman 1974, pp. 105-116).

A series of fascinating experiments by Haggard also indicate that our ability to recall what we know is highly influenced by the setting in which we are given the I.Q. tests. Poor and black students simply feel uncomfortable in the presence of white psychologists. Before administering the tests, Haggard socialized with the children; he talked with them and made them feel at ease. Only then did he give them the tests. He found that the scores of lower-class and black children went up fifteen to twenty points, and those of middle-class children increased less (Gartner, Greer, and Riessman, pp. 2, 206-212).

Many people have argued, in addition, that I.Q. scores penalize those who are curious and exploring, stressing instead the principle that there is only one right answer. (The test's emphasis is on correct answers, not on the method used to get the answer.) Haggard, in one of his studies, found that not one of thirty-five children who chose a correct analogy chose it for the reasons assumed by the test makers (Riessman, in Gartner et al. 1974, pp. 214, 218).

The vast majority of people, in any class or situation, are creative enough to live under the conditions imposed on them. Riessman reports studies showing that workers always beat incentive systems unfavorable to them, even "foolproof" ones. As another example of creativity, he cites the boys in a poor neighborhood who took a fruit basket, removed its bottom, and tied it to a fire escape so they could play basketball (p. 220).

For those who are not biased, it is almost too obvious to point out that children and adults learn to adapt and survive in their cultures or environment. Few people are retarded when judged by the criteria and conditions of *their* world:

> The Guatemalan child . . . knows less than the American child about planes, computers, and fractions. However, he knows much more about how to make rope and tortillas, how to tell the weather from cloud formations, and how to burn an old milpa for the June planting. The American middle-class child knows how to play chess and Scrabble, while the poor ghetto child knows how to play the "dozens" and dupe teachers and police. Each knows what is necessary for his life space. There are only a few dumb children in the world if you classify them from the perspective of the community of adaptation, but millions of dumb children if you classify them from the perspective of another society (Kagan 1974, p. 130).

The educational system discriminates against the lower classes and minorities in other ways. Sexton cites statistics from Detroit showing that 50 percent of the top 10 percent (in grades) of high school graduates did not go on to college. Most came from the lower classes (1961, p. xvii). Sewell's study of high school graduates in 1957 who had graduated from college by 1964-65 showed that, comparing only students from the top intelligence levels who came from different classes, the following percentages had graduated: lower class—20.1 percent; lower-middle—34.4 percent; upper-middle—46.7 percent; high—64 percent. Even if we accept the validity of I.Q. scores and grades we still find that the educational system discriminates against those from the lower classes (Duberman 1976, p. 208).

Using statistics I cannot reproduce here, Bowles and Gintis show that what determines "success" in life (income and occupation) is neither I.Q. score nor education. Rather, it is class background. That is, comparing people with the same I.Q. scores, but from different classes, those from the higher classes have a much greater chance of success in life (in Gartner et al. 1974, pp. 29-30).

But there are tables that correlate I.Q. scores with job success. That is, people in some occupations (factory workers, for example) do have lower I.Q. scores than people in other occupations (doctors and lawyers). But "correlation does not equal causation" (McClelland, in Gartner et al. 1974, p. 169). If I.Q. scores correlate with job success, it is probable that both I.Q. and job success are determined by the class to which we belong.

One very important cause of lower I.Q.s, lesser academic achievement, and low self-esteem is teacher expectations. Teachers, like most of us, are influenced by the society in which they live, which denigrates the abilities and motivations of poor and black people. Holding such low expectations of their students, teachers do seem to treat them as inferior and expect less of them. And these expectations are fulfilled.

Many studies have documented this self-fulfilling prophecy. The most famous of these studies was done by Rosenthal and Jacobson (1968). They told elementary school teachers that special tests given to some of their students had shown they were bright and likely to bloom academically. In fact, the tested students were chosen at random from the class lists. But in the following year these "bright" students did in fact improve dramatically, both in I.Q. scores and grades. Similar results were found in other studies. Significantly, in Rosenthal and Jacobson's study the effect was most dramatic in grades 1 and 2; in grades 5 and 6 "bright" students did not improve much. It would seem that by that time, both the perceptions of teachers and the self-concepts of students had already been established and were not likely to be changed by knowledge of a supposed hidden talent likely to bloom soon (Ryan 1976, p. 308).

Class affects the education of everyone in many ways. Schools are among the institutions in the United States that function to keep people in their class. This is the opposite of the legend, that schools provide an opportunity for social mobility.

## THE CULTURE OF EDUCATION

The criticism of schools as keepers of the class system is only one part of the socialist critique of education. For schools also oppress (though in different ways) those students they seem to favor. Education as constituted under capitalism stifles creativity, exploration, and real learning in children of all classes. The argument developed by Holt in *How Children Fail* (about one of the "best schools") and by many others accuses schools of creating a fear of failure, of perpetuating authoritarian and elitist human relations, and focusing on *control* of students rather than allowing real learning to go on.

### *Fear and Control*

Children do learn, teachers do teach. Schools cannot destroy the innate love and need of learning and growing. Most children manage to survive the anxiety and fear that schools and teachers create in them. Many do not, however.

In my classes, we often have a free-floating discussion of our school memories. People mention their teachers' punishments and habits, and their feelings about them. This discussion is always very animated; there is no lack of material to discuss. For we all experienced what Holt called "fear and failure." One day he asked his class, "what do you think, what goes through your mind, when the teacher asks you a question and you don't know the answer?" After a long silence, Ben said in a loud voice, "Gulp!"

> He spoke for everyone. They all began to clamor, and all said the same thing, that when the teacher asked them a question and they didn't know the answer they were scared half to death. I was flabbergasted—to find this in a school which people think of as progressive; which does its best not to put pressure on little children; which does not give marks in the lower grades; which tries to keep children from feeling that they're in some kind of race.
> 
> I asked them why they felt gulpish. They said they were afraid of failing, afraid of being kept back, afraid of being called stupid, afraid of feeling themselves stupid. Stupid. Why is it such a deadly insult to these children, almost the worst thing they can think of to call each other? Where do they learn this?
> 
> Even in the kindest and gentlest of schools children are afraid, many of them a great deal of the time, some of them almost all the time (Holt 1964, pp. 38–39).

Dennison, after describing some public-school students whose interest in learning had been destroyed by the fear, shame, anxiety, and self-contempt they had felt in their former schools, concluded that "the school child's chief expense of energy is self-defense against the environment" (1969, p. 85).

What Holt, Dennison, and many others have shown is that our conception of ourselves, as stupid or bright, is shaped by our school experiences; "education teaches individuals about their own personal ability and character traits. People learn to think of themselves as stupid or bright, as being worthy or as being failures" (Spring 1975, p. 29; paraphrasing Illich). For example, as Emma Goldman argued, the history we study in school focuses on rulers and governments, not on the lives of people like ourselves. The implied lesson is that presidents, kings, big businessmen, and others are important people who matter; we are mere pawns. In fact, the lives, struggles, and actions of working people are important and should not be ignored. They are ignored now, and the effect is to denigrate the worth of working people (Spring 1975, p. 46).

The daily experience of a student is of being controlled. Despite supposed changes in the late 1960s to early 1970s (see next section), most students in most schools did, and still do, attend schools where they are controlled by teachers and rules. Friendenberg detailed some of the controls: the need for permission to go to the bathroom, off-limits places, lack of privacy. Perhaps most of us do not consciously see schools as restrictive and oppressive because, from the day we were born, they were just there, part of our environment as air and earth are parts of our environment, not to be questioned. In interviews, students told Friedenberg that their high school was essentially benign and necessary (1965, pp. 28–34, 82).

Students had been socialized to express the proper sentiments to adults (and Friedenberg was an adult to them), but their daily experiences in school revolved around obedience and control. The very existence of laws compelling young people to go to schools that raise fears and anxieties in them is the first evidence that students are under control.

> What high school personnel become specialists in, ultimately, is the control of large groups of students even at catastrophic expense to their opportunity to learn. These controls are not exercised primarily to facilitate instruction, and, particularly, they are in no way limited to matters bearing on instruction. At several schools in our sample boys had, for example, been ordered by the assistant principal—sometimes on the complaint of teachers—to shave off beards. One of these boys, who had played football for the school all season, was told that, while the school had no legal authority to require this, he would be barred from the banquet honoring the team unless he complied. Dress regulations are another case in point (Friedenberg 1965, p. 46).

In addition, challenge of authority, questioning of dogma and teachers, and truly open debates are scarce in schools. After ten years of college teaching I have come to see that real debates are difficult, even in college, when one person (teacher) holds the power of grading. Far too often, either students will say nothing about an issue, or they will tell you what they think you want for an answer (and far too often, we teachers do have an answer in mind that we want).

Questions are allowed only within certain limits. For example, in my high school, a student once said in an English class that perhaps God only existed because we need to believe in God. He was told never to say anything like that again. Most students never are reprimanded that way because they learn to avoid topics that schools, teachers, and the powerful institutions make taboo. Socialism and the real history of class oppression are such taboo topics. We are shaped both by what we are taught and by what we are not taught.

## The Mirage of Change

Friedenberg's and my own school experiences are now twenty years old, during the years around 1960. Since then, we have gone through two changes of school environments. First came the supposed liberalizing of rules, regulations, and controls (late 1960s–early 1970s), followed by the undoing of some of the changes: dress codes, closed campuses, and general restrictiveness around the schools.

It is difficult to know how much change from the conditions of 1960 did take place, and how extensive any changes were. The great confrontations of the late 1960s over length of hair (in boys), dress codes, uncensored school newspapers, and so on indicate the social unrest of the times, with the Vietnam war affecting all sections of the society. So a liberalizing effect no doubt took place. But it is important to note that the essential structure of schools has remained unchanged: children have to attend school, by law; most of the time they learn what teachers and administrators decide they need to learn; most still sit in rows of desks and chairs; most are tested and required to memorize; most never learn their real history. And even the limited reforms are gradually being undone. For schools have continued to perform the real functions described in the previous three sections: to control and channel people, keep everyone in their social class, and control rather than liberate. (The alarm over declining reading scores for the last fifteen to twenty years may indicate that students are rejecting the socialization imposed on them; or, it may indicate that schools are losing their ability to teach even minimal skills in the face of their oppressive and controlling functions.)

*People Do Learn*

Many of the critics of the 1960s do not seem to have realized that schools were never meant to educate. Failing to see the class control of schools, these critics first exposed the destructiveness of school (see Holt 1964; Kozol 1967). Many went on to run schools or conduct classes that showed clearly that all people can learn when they are not controlled and oppressed. Below I will describe some of these learning situations. It is important to realize first, however, as Kohl was forced to admit, that real learning can only be of short duration in an oppressive class society. That is, it is possible to run a liberating and open school, where students can learn and grow free of fear and self-contempt, but if students must still live in a society with unemployment, alienating jobs, and social-class inequities, the effects of liberating education will be limited (which is not to say entirely worthless). In addition, such liberating education must be limited to few students in a few experiments. The education system as a whole cannot become liberating under capitalism.

There have been many reports of liberating situations in schools. Two of the most inspiring have been Kohl's *36 Children* (1967) and Dennison's *The Lives of Children* (1969). They are ample evidence that children want to and can learn. (I read these books in 1970. Later, when our own children were born, I began to see that curiosity, interest in the world, and love of learning are inherent in people. The most difficult learning task we ever have is learning to speak. Yet we all accomplish it with a minimum of teaching. By age two and one-half both our children had learned to form the past tense by adding -ed to the present tense; no one ever taught them this rule.)

Kohl ran a sixth-grade class in Harlem, with thirty-six black children who had already been declared failures. Dennison was active in running an alternative school with twenty-three students, of various ages, whom the public school system had also declared failures (one-third black, one-third Puerto Rican, one-third white).

Kohl's students came alive when they began to talk of important things: their lives, poverty, and their feelings. The short essays describing their lives were vivid and moving. Kohl, by not carping on grammar and not requiring the students to show him what they wrote, created an environment where the children began to write, think, debate, question. When he asked them to write about the block they lived on, they wrote with anger and passion. Here is one essay:

> I live on 117 street, between Madison and 5th avenue. All the bums live around here. But the truth is they don't live here they just hang around the street. All the kids call it "Junky's Paradise." Because there is no cops to stop them. I wish that the cops would come around and put all the bums out of the block and put them in jail all their life. I would really like it very much if they would improve my neighborhood. I don't even go outside to play because of them. I just play at the center of someplace else (pp. 46-49).

One boy of eleven, a supposedly slow learner, wrote a short novel that showed imagination and talent (Kohl, pp. 77-100). Generally, by the end of the year the children had grown immensely, writing many essays, exploring the origins and history of words, visiting places around New York. There was an excitement to their learning, since they were exploring their real world and expressing their thoughts and feelings.

Dennison's book too, shows children who came alive once they were freed from public schools. (Their school, with three teachers and twenty-three students, but no administration, cost no more than public schools did.) All the children had failed. Their parents were not really interested in an experimental school, but they were willing to try it since public schools had failed their children. In time, the parents became believers when they saw their children learning.

What Holt, Dennison, Freire (1970) and many others have shown is that real learning takes place when people are trying to understand what really matters to them, when they get validation for the way they live, when they get skills and knowledge that can expand their world. Such learning is exciting and liberating. When my daughter of eighteen months first understood that we attach symbols (words) to objects, she would point to objects (my nose, I remember vividly) and call them by name. She would sit there and repeat "nose," fifteen to twenty times. There was wonder, thrill, and excitement in her eyes.

Students learn best to read and write when the words chosen are meaningful in their lives. Freire even teaches illiterate peasants in South America by beginning with emotional words, writing them and examining them. Understanding these words became part of social and political liberation for the group, for they could begin to use their new skill to understand their poverty and oppression.

> For instance, one might teach reading in a middle-class suburb by beginning with some thematic representation of a community problem—pollution, perhaps, or, on a more unsophisticated level for small children, one might take up

such everyday themes as play, fights, or family problems. The leader and the children engage in a dialogue about the nature of the problem. From this initial dialogue words are taken that begin to form the basic text for reading. The children then work to solve the problem, reflect on their attempted solutions, add new words and stories to their readers and attempt to develop theories about the situation. In a poor urban area themes dealing with crime, poverty, family problems, and pollution could be used. In both examples the actual themes would not be chosen until after careful investigation. In this manner action, learning and consciousness would develop together (Spring 1975, p. 78).

We learn what we want to learn, what really matters to us. In a sense, even teaching techniques may not matter much. If a group of people are intensely interested in learning about slavery, for example, even the standard technique of lecturing may do well for them. An open classroom, as desirable as it may be, can teach little to people who see no reason to learn, whereas someone who wants to learn music (or a language, or any skill) can do so by "imitation and drill" (Feinberg and Rosemont 1975, p. 65). The motivation for learning may be more important than specific educational techniques.

## EDUCATION IN SOCIALIST COUNTRIES

The socialist critique of education contains many parts. Under capitalism, the lower classes get less and inferior education; the schools function to perpetuate the class system; and education is oppressive to all students, discouraging real learning and exploration.

Socialist countries seem to have solved some of these problems, but not all. Access to, and equality of, education exist. Once largely illiterate societies have abolished illiteracy (except for about 2–5 percent, mostly old people who grew up in pre-revolutionary days). The children of workers now can and do get good education for good jobs. By any standard, the accomplishments are noteworthy. But serious problems remain. In all socialist countries, especially in East Europe and the USSR, the children of professionals, party leaders, and other privileged people have a clear advantage in getting more education (university education especially). Some people are aware of this violation of socialist principles, but do not know what can be done (Dobson 1977). Even when education is equally open to everyone, socialist countries often have special schools for very gifted students (especially in the sciences), and there is the clear danger that people graduating from these schools will become a new elite.

In addition, teaching methods and student-teacher relations continue the authoritarian, competitive manner found under capitalism. Certainly, true liberation must come in education before democratic socialism can prevail. There has been some challenge to authoritarian education, limited mostly to China (during the years of the cultural revolution) and less so to

Cuba, and its extent and effectiveness seem limited. The problems of persisting class inequalities, elite domination, and limited democracy are reflected in education.

## General Conditions

Marquit provides a very positive account of education in socialist countries. All education is free. Grants are available to those who need them while they are in school. After the universal elementary education, there are two types of high schools: a general one (leading to university studies) and a technical-vocational one. Marquit claims that even those in vocational schools can go to college if they do well in their studies (1978, pp. 128–32).

Higher education is available to the children of all classes. In 1973, in the German Democratic Republic 40 percent of college and university students were the children of production workers; 7 percent of cooperative farmers; and 24 percent of office workers. But Marquit does not give the percentages of these groups in the population so we cannot judge the meaning of such data. What if production workers are 60 percent of the population (p. 130)?

Evening, correspondence, and part-time courses are also extensive. In Cuba, for example, where students are student-workers, workers are worker-students, since they are encouraged to study after work.

Marquit's account generally presents the educational accomplishments of socialist countries but none of the serious persisting problems. Below, China and Cuba are examined in some detail.

## China

In 1949, China had a literacy rate of 15 percent. It was estimated that 80–90 percent of its people were literate in 1975. Of elementary-school-age children, 90 percent were in school; of children of middle-school-age (roughly comparable to high school), 80–90 percent in cities and 60–75 percent in rural areas were in school. Thus, the change is enormous, but obviously many children are not in school (Gamberg 1977, p. 41). Neither Gamberg nor any other writer says what children out of school are doing.

Serious problems persisted during the early 1960s. During the cultural revolution, there were three basic criticisms of education: it discriminated against workers and peasants (especially peasants); the methods of education were authoritarian and nonsocialist; and the content and purpose of education furthered inequalities and elitism. For example, there were still monetary charges in school, and even though they were small, the cost was too much for many peasants. Education at higher levels was still the province of the children of professionals and bureaucrats (Bastid 1970, pp. 590–91).

The methods of education were also criticized in the 1960s. School took too many years, with a very heavy course load and an emphasis on memorization. Students listened passively to lectures and rarely questioned or debated. Most of the teachers had come from bourgeois backgrounds and perpetuated old ideologies.

In order to enter a university, students were required to pass very difficult exams. This system favored the children of the elite. Once admitted, many workers and peasants were flunked out. Difficult exams were given in order to fail and expel students who had difficulty; there was no effort to help them improve so they could continue. The teaching atmosphere at the university level, too, was strict, competitive, with an accent on memorization. In a society composed largely of workers and peasants, in many universities only 40 percent of the students came from such families (Gamberg 1977, pp. 147–48, 57).

Given these realities, the criticism of educational methods and schools during the cultural revolution often was severe. Many changes followed. (Again, since Mao's death in 1976, as in many areas, in education too many changes are being undone. For example, strict exams are returning [*Beijing Review* January 7, 1980, pp. 17–27]).

There was a conflict in the ranks of critics. Some wanted to abolish schools entirely, and others wanted to reform them and turn control over to workers and peasants. In time, the reformists won the day. But they made large demands on education. They called upon it to abolish all differences between city and country, worker and peasant, and mental and manual labor (Hinton, in Gamberg, p. xii).

Educational opportunities now are available to peasants and workers alike. (The present tense here is used for convenience, reflecting Gamberg's and Bastid's accounts.) In rural China, brigades direct their own schools to meet their own educational needs. In cities, workers also run the schools (the details are complicated; see Bastid, p. 598).

Before the cultural revolution, there were too many courses offered, requiring too much studying and memorization. Courses have been reduced, with time left to discuss and question, and also to have fun. Physical and mental development are both stressed. Education is becoming more rooted in reality. When some students were reading a Mao poem on snail fever, they went to the countryside and talked with the peasants (many of whom had been afflicted with snail fever), learning about their lives. Students were then able to discuss the poem much more vividly. Children are taught to share and cooperate (through song and practice in school), and this value is reinforced by what they see in their communities (Gamberg, pp. 134–42).

Since the cultural revolution, there are new policies on university study. Students have to work for two years after finishing high school. Then they can apply for admission to a university. They get in not by taking competitive examinations, rather by the recommendation of their co-workers. Academic achievement is only one criterion for admission. Candidates are interviewed, and their social, political, and cultural outlook are discussed along with their academic file (Gamberg, pp. 63-64).

Once in a university, students are encouraged to cooperate with each other. Exams are given not to fail people, rather, to find out their weaknesses and help them. Students can and do cooperate in writing exams. In some places, students choose the topics they will write on, or they write a summary of what they have learned. Listening to lectures passively is discouraged. Mao especially urged youth to criticize boring lectures, to ask questions, to rebel. Teachers are urged to learn from their students, to listen to criticisms (Gamberg,. pp. 147-55).

Work is part of all education. Children do not play at work. They produce food or make items people eat and use. There is a heavy stress on the unity of theory and practice. Theory (a program only of study) without contact with the outside world is limiting; practice is insufficient if not explained by theory. Practice, however, is more basic. Also, work and practical activities help to avoid the creation of an elite who despise work. A Chinese report said:

> "China is a state where the working people are the masters, it is inconceivable that the working class should run colleges to turn out people who look down upon physical labour and the labouring people. Of course the working class requires its own intellectuals who master science, technology and other knowledge, but in the first place, schools and colleges should turn out true revolutionaries who are faithful to the cause of the working class and who always remain one with the working people" (quoted in Bastid, p. 592).

Creativity is seen as practiced by all people, not merely artists. Workers who improve or invent machinery and peasants who increase yields are, and are seen as, creative artists (Gamberg, p. 129).

Education is becoming widespread. It goes on everywhere. Neighborhoods and factories set up their own courses and schools for people of all ages. People study politics (Marx, Lenin, and Mao in the original) and learn technical skills. University faculty go out to factories and neighborhoods to teach workers courses on all subjects: weather and politics, for example. Peking University offers such courses for 30,000 people (Gamberg, pp. 67, 271).

This is a somewhat idealized account of Chinese education. Except for continuing material shortages (a lack of teachers, leading to large classes, is one example), Gamberg points to no other problems. The main danger that I can see is the failure to provide for, and encourage, dissent, debate, and questioning. It is true, as Gamberg argues, that all of us are molded by our surroundings. The Chinese, she says, choose to make this process clear and direct, teaching openly their values of sharing and cooperation. These are admirable values, and the essence of socialism. But how can the society ensure that students be able to criticize those who violate these and other socialist principles? There is no "student power" in China, says Bastid. Students are consulted, but the schools are run by the community to give education deemed essential to the community. The Chinese did not want to replace the older elite with a student elite free of community control. Again, an admirable goal. But what is done to prevent the setting-in of conformity? If parents, teachers, cadres, and students cooperate in running the schools, in reality this could mean great pressure against those who may criticize the acts of leaders and others for not being socialist. Despite all my urging of students in my classes to dissent and debate, few do, from both lack of interest and the power inequalities of the situation. Gamberg's description of education in China does not show any awareness of the danger of such conformity, and of course no discussion of ways to avoid it. Too much control seems to remain.

And even such incomplete educational changes are now in danger of being eliminated. Many professors told Gamberg they welcomed the new educational policies, but many must have opposed them (even if they did not speak out), for now entrance examinations for university admission are returning.

Recent reports leave no doubt that there is an intensive campaign to select a few bright students and provide them with an elite education. Moreover, student work requirements are being relaxed. Hinton, however, does not think China will go back to the old teaching methods; he believes the Chinese are trying to improve the quality of education to provide the skilled and trained personnel needed by an industrializing society. In education as in other institutions, it seems that the struggle for democracy and equality is losing to the new priority for rapid "modernization" (Hinton 1979; Beecher 1979; *Monthly Review* May 1979).

A *Beijing Review* article contains some data on Chinese education and includes the Chinese leaders' perspective on education for the 1980s. Some changes instituted during the cultural revolution persist. Students help each other, and they are required to do some physical labor. But other changes are being undone. For example, competitive examinations have returned. There also seems to be an emphasis on student discipline rather than on questioning and challenging teachers. Generally, the mood is one of disciplined hard work (some of which is necessary, no doubt, if people are to acquire the necessary skills), not one of exploration, challenge, and creativity. There may be an inherent tension between discipline and challenge, and we cannot tell now whether the Chinese (or any society) will be able to work out the proper balance between the two. (See *Beijing Review* January 7, 1980, pp. 17–27, for details on education in China.)

*Cuba*

In Cuba, too, there have been impressive accomplishments, but also the possibility of creating an educational elite and the problem of persisting authoritarian methods.

Before 1959, about 25 percent of the people in Cuba were illiterate. In 1953, only 56 percent of six- to fourteen-year-olds were in school. Between age thirteen and eighteen, only 10 percent were. This compares to 1977 figures of 98.3 percent for six- to twelve-year-olds, and 82 percent of thirteen- to sixteen-year-olds. Education, especially the lower levels, was expanded tremendously. In 1968-69, 20 percent of productive capacity was devoted to formal schooling (Bowles 1971b, pp. 284-86; Ward 1978, p. 110).

Children immediately benefited from the expansion of education. But there were still many illiterate adults. The revolution could not afford to train more teachers for them (many teachers had left for the United States). To meet this need, someone had a stroke of genius: about 100,000 children (mostly ages twelve to fourteen) were sent to the countryside in 1961 to teach reading and writing to illiterate peasants. In about six months illiteracy was virtually eliminated. But the benefit was not to the peasants alone. The children who taught them also learned. They saw first-hand the life of the peasants, their hardships and the need for improvement. The experience was a profound one for most of the children (Wald 1978, pp. 156-57; Bowles 1971b, p. 289; Kozol 1978b).

Since its early days, the government has continually changed the educational system to meet the needs of the economy. There was a serious need for improvement of material conditions, and education was changed according to the changing economic situation. When labor shortages developed in the late 1960s, students were moved to the countryside (for forty-five days). In time, as education costs increased, schools were moved to the countryside, where the program for students combines work and study all year, not just work for forty-five days. These schools are largely self-sufficient. (This movement has involved students of junior-high-school age. By 1972 only 11 percent of them were in such schools, but the figure had increased by 1977, with just about all students attending them by 1980) (Carnoy and Werthein 1977, pp. 577-79).

As of 1973 (and still mostly true, with more schools moving to the countryside), Wald gives this account of the educational system:

> The structure of the educational system remains fairly simple. Children may attend childcare centers from [age] forty-five days to four years of age. From four to six is pre-school, which may be conducted in the circulo or in the primary school. From first to sixth grade children attend primary school. This may be a normal, or National, school, which children attend from seven a.m. to five p.m., returning home for lunch. It may be a semi-internado, or semi-boarding school, in which the children receive lunch and sometimes other meals. Or it may be an internado or boarding school in which the children live all week, returning home to their families on weekends. The internados are considered scholarship schools, or becas, and the students are often referred to as becados.
>
> After completing sixth grade, students go on to secondary school (Escuela Secondaria Basica) which may be normal, semi-boarding, or the new School in the Countryside. Since this period (from seventh to tenth grade) is consid-

ered very formative, the emphasis is on building more and more secondary schools in the countryside or near other work-sites where students can combine work with studies.

The equivalent of our high school is the pre-university, from eleventh to thirteenth grades, and then students may attend four- or five-year university programs. At the high school level (and sometimes earlier) students may elect to go to special technological, pedagogical, or vocational schools, or may be chosen for the Camilo Cienfuegos Military School or the Lenin (advanced science) Vocational School. There are also school shops for thirteen- to sixteen-year-olds who drop out of school and wish to learn a trade.

At every level there are also specialized schools for sports, the arts, and language, as well as schools for mentally or physically disabled children (p. 159).

Work has become a daily part of the program of all Cuban schools. All junior high schools combine three hours of work with five hours of study. Students work in the fields, in nearby factories, or produce goods on school grounds. Some fourth graders begin to do two daily hours of farm work, and soon kindergarten, and first, second, and third graders said they too wanted to work. They now work two to six hours a week. In addition, the students do all the cleaning in secondary schools; there are no janitors (Wald 1978, pp. 346–64; Ward 1978, p. 101). Students study together and help each other. But despite this collective study, individual exams and grades exist. Moreover, partly because of teacher shortages, older students often teach the younger ones. This is serious work which helps both groups of students. "Interest circles" are encouraged and spreading: students with the same interest (electronics, for example) get together for cooperative study and exchange of information (Wald, pp. 169–72).

But problems persist, most of them discussed openly by the Cubans themselves. Teachers work hard, they are dedicated revolutionaries, and they are held in high respect. They work too hard, in fact. The job is too demanding, especially for the many younger teachers (late teens) pressed into service to meet the teacher shortages (Wald, pp. 235–38).

Until 1973, there were serious physical problems: old, crowded buildings, scarcity of teaching materials, and so on. Such shortages began to ease after 1973 (Wald, p. 182).

In the late 1960s to early 1970s, there was a problem of dropouts. Of 59,000 students in the seventh grade in 1966–67, only 29 percent were in the tenth grade three years later, and only half of them passed that grade. Fidel Castro often spoke of this problem in the early 1970s. (I do not know whether it persists.) He attributed it to the shortages described above, the lack of awareness of the importance of education, and the enormous historical legacy of ignorance (Carnoy and Werthein 1977, p. 582).

But the dangers of creating a new elite are far more serious. In order to improve the economy and the standard of living, gifted students are sent to special schools. But despite the fact that these students share in doing manual labor, they are clearly special and may pose a problem (as such people do in all capitalist societies, where they are seen, and see themselves, as better than most workers). Immediate economic needs must be balanced against the long-term interests in a classless society and a liberating education.

Finally, educational methods in Cuba still seem unchanged. All accounts reveal traditional teaching methods: grades, discipline, teachers standing in front of the room. Wald does report an experiment begun in 1975, where teachers in grades 1–4 would give no traditional grades. And the Lenin School for science students is doing away with formal classes and grades, creating situations for individual students to direct their own studies, working with teachers and workers in their fields. But most students, in the mid-1970s, were in classrooms that would be familiar to most readers of this book (Wald 1978, pp. 165, 363; Bowles 1971b; Carnoy and Werthein 1977).

But Wald insists that there are important differences from United States educational methods: "despite the discipline and order, I didn't find these children repressed in any sense." The children respect and like their teachers, who are very dedicated and hard-working and who obviously care for the children. What seems like an ordinary classroom situation in fact has important differences. Teachers and students are friendly and work for the same goal; teachers work with students in the fields; janitors and cooks participate in school meetings: and school days begin with the reading of national and international news (pp. 172, 232, 241–42).

The differences cannot be denied. The children feel they are participants in a great revolution, and it is probably true that they are greatly motivated. In this context, educational methods may not matter much when students and teachers share the same goals. For example, a sixteen-year-old, who may not be a very trained teacher, may infuse younger students with the enthusiasm that leads to the internal discipline for learning. But in time, some of the adventure of starting a new society will fade, and institutions must be created that guarantee freedom, exploration, and learning outside the classroom. If new, liberating methods are not created, the present ones may become institutionalized and make learning more difficult. If truly democratic relations are to develop, schools are a good place to begin teaching them. Students, teachers, and everyone must participate in the development and growth of education. For now, it appears that there has been some popular discussion in Cuba of the changes in education, but the ultimate power and decisions rest in the hands of the government and the Cuban Communist party. Unless true power to control daily events does lie in the hands of the people (students, teachers, community), in education, work, government, and all areas, the rise of elites and bureaucrats can undo much of the progress toward a classless society. The system of education is crucial in the process toward democracy, for there people acquire habits of thought, of social relations, and of solving problems that set the stage for participation in society. It is not enough to teach skills; democratic human relations also must prevail.

# CHANGES IN THE UNITED STATES

Each chapter in this book has outlined some proposed ways to change the problem discussed. The suggested changes are from a socialist perspective applied to a society still under capitalism. They are not the whole solution socialists seek, but they would make for some improvement in people's lives and may enhance the movement to a socialist society. The danger, of course, is that some of these changes will become mere reforms and help to solidify capitalism. Despite the danger, however, we must struggle for changes, for without such a struggle capitalism is certain to continue.

Education too presents the same promises and dilemmas. Below, I outline some actual efforts and some proposals for changing the educational system. I do not consider them the best or the only proposals, but examples of what is being done and considered. I encourage you to think of more, and also to try some changes.

Dollar and Parker reported on "Project Enterprise" in Marshfield, Massachusetts:

> Project Enterprise's action focus is the restoration and recreation of historic buildings in the Marshfield community. The program got its start when a member of the local community arts society informally asked the school superintendent if it would be possible to involve high school students in an effort to rescue a 150-year-old church that was badly in need of repairs.... The project was designed as a full-time, self-contained, interdisciplinary program. Enterprise students (who now number about 60) take all their classes—Math, History or Government, English, and Problems in Construction—from Enterprise teachers on Mondays, Tuesdays, and Wednesdays. Thursdays and Fridays are then spent at work sites in the community, with teachers and students taking part side by side. This arrangement enables classroom subjects to relate directly to the work experience, both informing it and being informed by it. A central precept of the program, in fact, is that certain separations to which we have become accustomed—school life from community life, academic study from practical experience, student learning needs from community service and development needs—need to be bridged.

The program was funded with federal funds and began with thirty-five students and four teachers. It has been very successful in restoring old buildings, students and teachers are committed to the program and its philosophy, and the program may soon become self-sustaining. It is certainly an example for those who wish to combine work and study and to bring education back to the community (1977, p. 70).

Many people have proposed "community control" of the schools. If schools are to serve the interests and needs of black people (or any poor, minority, and working-class people), the community should control the schools and determine what and how subjects are taught. Some efforts at community control have been opposed by teachers' unions and other groups (as in the famous teachers' strike (Ocean Hill-Brownsville) in New York in 1968). Generally, there seems to have been no case of real community control; local people have often been consulted, but ultimate control stays in the hands of various government bodies (Levin 1971).

Carnoy and Levin argue that the best strategy for change is for teachers and students to take control away from the school administration. Once they control education they could change what is taught and how it is taught. It is imperative that teachers and students cooperate, rather than teachers alone having total control. Carnoy and Levin describe how teachers' unions may proceed to demand control of education (1977).

Spring outlines a series of related changes. Compulsory education should be abolished; the economic dependence of youth should end; the power of the educational bureaucracy should end, and it should not be allowed to control education. Ending compulsory education would certainly not hurt people, given the record of schools in educating them. But it would not help, either, if there were no accompanying political and economic changes. The major difficulty with Spring's proposal (made by many other critics of education) is the lack of strategies to implement them. How possible is it to end compulsory education? What would more unemployed youth do in an economy that already does not have enough jobs for those out of school? At present, although schools must function as baby-sitting institutions, there would be strong opposition to ending compulsory education (Spring 1975, pp. 136–140).

Some critics have despaired of any significant changes in public education and have set up "free schools." Some of them were set up in poor communities, raised money in any way they could, and were indeed free to poor people. Others were primarily for the children of professionals and provided a libertarian, open-classroom education. Some had a mixed student body (see Dennison 1969 and Kozol 1972). All observers of free schools report profound changes in the lives and learning of the students. But free schools are no long-term solution for the vast majority of students. Although many have arisen, each one has demanded great energy to set up and fund, and there simply is not enough money or energy (under capitalism) to create enough such schools for all children (see Stretch 1972 for a brief discussion of free schools and their problems). In the 1970s, "alternative" schools became more common than "free" schools.

## THE INTEGRATION OF LEARNING AND LIFE

This chapter has focused on education in the United States, its functions and possibilities. In conclusion, a long-term perspective on socialist, liberating education will suggest what can be achieved.

1. Formal schooling is relatively new in human history. But the ability to learn is not only innate in human beings, it is probably essential to the survival of any species. It has been said that schools arose in order to enable people to learn the great amount of knowledge needed to survive in modern

## STRUGGLES: Free Schools and Alternative Schools

Many people saw "free schools" as the great educational promise of the late 1960s and early 1970s (the term refers to small private schools opposed to traditional teaching methods). In fact, some people were predicting an explosion of free schools. But for various reasons, such as the enormous financial and other burdens necessary to start free schools, the number soon began to decline.

But the desire for a liberating education did not die. Parents sought to institute the principles of free schools within the regular school system. "Alternative schools" arose. These are schools in a public school system (sometimes separate schools, sometimes part of a traditional school) run on free-school principles. " 'Free school' meant a school that encouraged student participation in governance, parent and community involvement, work in the outside world, student choice in curriculum, more social and personal 'relevance' in subjects and projects, and opposition to conventional attitudes about authority and discipline in schools." Alternative schools are run on similar principles: "maximum freedom, participatory decision-making, self-motivation, concern with the emotional and personal, and so on" (Graubard 1979, pp. 49, 54).

(Even most regular schools no longer reflect traditional strict discipline and sole concern with teaching the three Rs. Whereas most older parents support discipline and a "return to basics," most younger parents [thirty and under] do not.)

Alternative schools enroll a very small minority of students. A survey in 1974 found about 600 alternative schools in public-school systems, with, at most, about 100,000 students. Others make higher estimates. Even these estimates, however, include no more than about 2 percent of all students in public schools. If that estimate changed in the late 1970s, it only decreased.

Why has the growth of alternative schools slowed? There seem to be two reasons. Real change is very difficult. After the initial hopes and some success, the realization comes that educational problems are "rooted in a society's culture and politics." Schools cannot change society. At best, schools can change with society. Secondly, the recession of the middle 1970s, unemployment, and competition for jobs forced both students and parents to be more concerned with basic skills than with liberating education.

Below is a brief account of how one alternative school (in Cambridge, Massachusetts) was begun. This account, and the preceding discussion, are based on Allen Graubard, "From Free Schools to 'Educational Alternatives,' " in John Case and Rosemary Taylor, eds., Coops, Communes, and Collectives (New York: Pantheon, 1979), excerpts from pp. 51–53).

In Cambridge, Massachusetts, . . . a group of parents of small children gathered together in the fall of 1971. Like many other such groups meeting in many living rooms throughout the country, they were committed to the spirit of educational reform articulated in the writings of people like Paul Goodman, John Holt, and George Dennison. They were graduate students, junior faculty, single mothers; most had participated in the antiwar movement. The organizers of the group had been part of two parent-controlled, integrated preschools, both infused with a spirit of informal, nonauthoritarian pedagogy and parent participation in all aspects of school life. Now that their children were reaching school age, they faced the prospect of sending them to traditional public schools. . . .

The group considered starting an independent free school for their children. But . . . the difficulties of founding and nurturing a new free school were becoming all too apparent. Tuition would have to be charged. Teacher salaries were bound to be low, and job security for teachers would be virtually nonexistent. Buildings that met city codes for schools were hard to find and hard to maintain. Public funding would have another benefit too. Without it, a school would have a hard time appealing to poor and minority-group parents. With it, the integration that these reform-minded middle-class people believed in might become a reality.

So the Cambridge parents launched a campaign for an alternative public school, calling for open education, effective parent control, and serious attention to issues like racism and sexism. Calling

*(continued)*

**Free Schools and Alternative Schools** *(continued)*
themselves the Committee for an Alternative Public School (CAPS), they recruited more parents, printed brochures, organized petition campaigns, lobbied school-committee candidates, gave talks and slide shows, and entered into frustrating negotiations with a generally unsympathetic school bureaucracy. After two years, however, their work paid off. The school committee voted 5 to 2 in favor, and an alternative public school—kindergarten through second grade, scheduled to grow a grade a year—came into being.

The first years were difficult, as was often the case in such experiments. Participants felt dissatisfied, confused, argumentative; there were serious staff and director problems. Unsympathetic school-department administrators, including the superintendent who had vehemently opposed the idea of this parent-controlled alternative school, made survival even more problematic. But the school survived, grew, stabilized, and found a new building. . . .

By 1975 the school had become a complete elementary school, through the eighth grade, with a racially and economically mixed student body of over two hundred. The school has special bilingual and vocational programs, and its racial mix makes it eligible for various sorts of federal and state "magnet school" grants, including state aid in the construction of its own building. . . . The policy of parent participation and power has been maintained, and there are more applicants than the school can accept. . . .

Although the first of the alternative high schools in Cambridge had to withstand intense pressure from conservative school-board members who wanted to close it down after its first year, by now the idea is generally accepted.

---

society. The history of education does not support that argument, for schools arose to socialize (and control) workers, not necessarily to teach them. People in tribal societies had to learn much more in order to survive than most of us probably do. They needed to know about hundreds of plants and animals; or they had to learn about the land, the weather, and domestic animals, if they were agriculturalists. People learned all these things, and much more, in the context of everyday life. Learning was integrated into all of life's activities, not segregated in special places. Today we still learn much outside the classroom, without grades and controls. We learn language in everyday interaction with family and others.

2. We need to reunite learning with daily life, to take it out of the classroom. We can, of course, meet in formal situations (for lectures and discussions) when these are voluntary and free of control. But we can also learn primarily from the people who practice what we want to know (apprenticeship). When we are ready to learn a new skill, we can find practitioners of that skill (we can also learn more by reading, courses, and so on). Also, when we want to explore philosophy, politics, human relations, we can get together with others to discuss these topics.

Throughout the world, people are learning outside the classroom. There are the worker-students in China, Cuba, and elsewhere. In the United States, most continuing education has been operated with formal schools and grades, but some people organize courses and groups without controls and grades. In Boston, you can learn how to build and play musical instruments, study the history of working people, or repair your car. Some learn through courses offered by schools, others just get together. This movement has a history. Workers in the United States, from about 1900 on, set up their own classes and groups to study political economy, to understand how their society really works. Some groups still continue. No grades, degrees, or recognitions are necessary, people get satisfaction and joy and growth from the learning itself (Katz and Bender 1976, pp. 21-22).

3. We have instituted all sorts of irrelevant tests and degree requirements before people can practice most occupations. If we want to know how well a person can do something (drive a car, cook, be a firefighter, be a nurse), we should test the person's ability to do that task and not require people to pass tests with verbal analogies, since few occupations require word analogies. We should not require nurses to get B.A.s and take sociology, philosophy, or English because we think nurses need them, and because educational requirements function today to raise the prestige of occupations and to keep people out. In fact, requiring sociology is the best way to make someone *not* learn it. It is when people want to and genuinely need to study something that they can study (without grades or requirements) and really benefit (McClelland, in Gartner et al., 1974, p. 179).

4. Education and learning can be liberating tools. They enable us to understand and survive in our world, to control our lives.

5. There is the danger of transforming radical educational methods into controlling mechanisms. Without a clear goal of a liberated, egalitarian, socialist society, "radical" methods can be used for oppression.

> Radical experiments in education tend to be trivialized as they are developed. Paulo Freire's techniques are adopted by the Peace Corps and the free school methods of Summerhill are introduced into the classrooms of the public school without any relationship to their underlying radical ideology. What begins as a radical movement is quickly absorbed by the existing system; new techniques are used, but only to accomplish the old objectives of control and discipline. The Summerhillian approach, trivialized within the public school classroom, becomes a warm, loving, and free method of teaching the same subject matter and producing the same character structure (Spring, p. 133).

6. Education is not neutral. Either it socializes people to fit into capitalist society, or it liberates them. Even arithmetic, supposedly neutral and objective, can be used for either oppression or liberation:

> Francisco Ferrer argued in the late nineteenth century that a knowledge of arithmetic could either become a tool for individual use or a tool of enslavement to the industrial system. If arithmetic were taught in terms of the ideology of capitalism—dealing with such things as problems of interest rates, business computations, and other techniques for functioning within the capitalist system—knowledge became a tool for enslavement. On the other hand, if arithmetic problems involving the development of new economic systems were presented, it became a tool of freedom and action (Spring, p. 34).

7. The autonomy we derive from liberating education cannot mean rampant individualism, "doing your own thing." Martell criticizes Friedenberg for focusing entirely on autonomy and individualism and neglecting a

sense of community, justice, and equality. Education cannot be a process of learning to survive in isolation; it is necessary that we learn how to be autonomous in cooperation with others, committed to justice and equality (Martell 1970).

8. Finally, I want to stress that liberal critics of education focus on the wrong causes. They blame teachers and administrators for racist, boring, and destructive education, as if all we need to do is retrain teachers. But schooling arose to socialize people for alienating work under capitalism; the cause is political and economic, not individual. So, in restructuring education, we must work against a system that requires oppressive schools.

# 14

# *Equality, Community, Ecology: Toward a Humane Society*

In this closing chapter, I try to provide a summary of the socialist perspective; a conclusion uniting the different topics I have covered in some detail; and a brief discussion of what has been and is being done to pave the way for a just and humane society.

## SOCIAL PROBLEMS ARE RELATED

The socialist perspective maintains that the existence of classes, inequalities, and the profit motive (three different aspects of the same reality) are what cause social problems. Sometimes the cause is direct, sometimes indirect.

Therefore, although we can only discuss one problem at a time, we must remember that we are not studying separate problems; rather, we are confronting the central reality of social classes and inequalities under capitalism. Different parts of the text have shown how problems are related to each other and to the ultimate cause, capitalism.

For example, people suffer from asbestosis and other diseases caused by exposure to dangerous substances. But this situation arises because of capitalism's needs for greater profits (see discussions on work, the environment, and health, Chapters 5, 10, and 11). The problem also relates to the effect of class on our daily lives (Chapter 2).

The problem of alienation (not discussed as a separate chapter) appears in many chapters. It is central to work. It is also related to crime, for alienation leads to anger and feelings of worthlessness, therefore to destructive actions. In education, too, we find alienation, as schools prepare youth for work that does not meet either personal or economic needs.

The problem of professional domination and elites also pervades all areas: the domination of children and women; the division of managers and workers; the elitism and "expertise" of doctors and teachers; and the control of law by legal experts.

Thus, the study of separate problems is a convention for convenient discussion; in reality, we are exploring different aspects of the same problems of classes, inequalities, and the profit motive. I am sure many more connections than I have mentioned have occurred to you as you have been reading this book.

## DRUGS, PROSTITUTION, ALCOHOLISM, AND OTHER FORMS OF DEVIANCE

Some of you may have noticed that this book does not discuss some conditions many people perceive as problems. Drugs, alcoholism, and mental illness are three problems included in most social-problems texts. (Older texts included prostitution, but I have not seen it in any recent text. Prostitution has not disappeared, but current problems texts do not mention it.)

A brief look at topics covered by social-problems texts shows both change and continuity. In the 1920s and 1930s, texts were overtly moralistic and directed at individual pathologies, not at social and political conditions. Prostitution, family problems, alcoholism, divorce, and suicide were the staple of those texts. One text (published in 1939) included a whole section on "the control and care of the defective classes." There were chapters on "feeble-minded and epileptics, insane, blind, deaf-mute, cripples, and eugenic and hereditary defectives." Another text (also in 1939) contained a section on the "pathology of domestic relationships," with chapters on "unmarried, widowhood, divorce and desertion, dependent and neglected childhood, unmarried parenthood, immorality and vice." (See Mills 1943 for a critique of those older texts.)

Those older topics, and even prostitution and suicide, no longer populate social problems texts. Some of the topics appear under new names (mental illness and mental disorder have replaced talk of the insane and the epileptic), others are new issues. Today, most social-problems texts include chapters on racism, sexism, work, ecology, medicine, crime and some aspect of classes and poverty. (These topics are covered here.) Drugs, alcoholism, mental illness, and aging are found in many texts. Some texts cover one or more of the following: war, urban problems, sexual behavior (or sexual deviance, or problems in human sexuality), family disorganization, overpopulation, and violence.

Drugs, alcoholism, mental illness, aging, and most of the other topics are valid concerns. They affect many people and cause profound suffering and pain. Why do I not include them here?

Perhaps the most honest response is to point out no one can cover all, or even most, topics one considers important. I have taught a course on mental illness (which both my students and I found very stimulating and challenging). But it is simply not possible to cover all problems.

Nevertheless, when a choice is made and some topics are included and others excluded, some criteria are used in making the choice. I believe that the topics I have included are the primary problems in a capitalist society. For example, it is the problems of work, inequality, economic insecurity, social isolation, and racism, in combinations or alone, that lead many people to drink in excess and become alcoholic. (Most of the problems not discussed here also derive, in my opinion, from the inequities of capitalism.)

Most people are not drug addicts or alcoholics (although many people drink), and most people manage to cope somehow without spending time in a mental hospital. But the stresses and anxieties we all suffer from life under capitalism will not improve much while we all must live under capitalism. All of us are shaped by the conditions of living in a capitalist society—by sexism; by ecological destruction; by relations of domination; and by the alienation of work. Therefore, I have explored those issues. Alcoholism and drug addiction are not discussed here because, important as they are, they really result from more fundamental conditions: the consequences of a society ruled by classes, inequalities, and the profit motive.

## PRINCIPLES FOR SOCIALIST STRUGGLE

This book has tried to explore and analyze the interrelated causes of social problems from a socialist perspective. Some principles that must guide our efforts to create a socialist and just society will be summarized here. If we stray from them, not only will we lessen the struggle to eliminate social classes and exploitation, we may even endanger the long-term survival of human beings (perhaps even of most life on earth).

## Community

It is quite probable that no just, classless society is possible unless we can re-create true communities. Cooperation, equality, and the solution of many problems (crime, mental illness, insecurity, work alienation,) cannot come about permanently if people live in large, anonymous groups. Groups must simply become smaller, on a human scale.

Bodley points out that small size is inherent to the existence and functioning of communities:

> It has been suggested that a truly egalitarian society can only be maintained within a continuously interacting, face-to-face population of no more than approximately 250-500 persons which has common goals to pull it together. As population densities increase, not only do people have a more difficult time keeping track of their relationships simply because there are now too many to sort out, but the probability of conflict over everyday irritations becomes much more likely. Invariably, population densities greater than 500 in a single social unit either break up into antagonistic factions, and/or they become hierarchically ordered (1976, p. 13).

Given the nature of urban industrial societies, and the domination of the car in the United States and elsewhere, we are talking about a fundamental transformation of human groups and relations. Even to begin the process will require a great struggle and much creativity and imagination. But unless we can create groups and situations where we relate to others personally, where we can have some control, no democratic and just society is possible. As the large extended family was the center of life in tribal societies, for us neighborhoods and small workplaces can re-create the same type of human relations in a world necessarily larger.

## Continuous Struggle

The road to socialism has never been easy. The establishment of a socialist state marks only the beginning of the long and continuous struggle to create a socialist society. Even if socialism ends the worst forms of exploitation, it will still have to fight against social classes. Also, work that is satisfying and not alienating; justice carried out by people, not experts; the end of sexism, and the creation of communities are not guaranteed by a socialist state. Socialism only gives us a greater chance to achieve these goals. As we have seen (Chapter 4, the discussion on China after Mao), classes and domination reappear, both in old and new forms, even under socialism. Therefore, we must be aware that the fight to eliminate classes will be long and uneven. I do not know that we can ever predict the total elimination of classes, but even a substantial lessening of class differences is a worthy goal.

## The Quality of Life

Socialism's goal is not affluence. It is to provide all people with the essentials of life, to end exploitation, and to create a society where cooperation, community, sharing, and improved human relations prevail. Socialism must also be guided by the ecological wisdom we need to survive (see Chapter 10).

In this sense, socialism is not a materialistic philosophy, nor does it posit economic determinism. Rather, it seeks to free us from a system where material rewards and competition are the central values. It seeks to find human meaning in our relations with each other. Consumption and monetary success will not be goals to emulate. Satisfying, creative work; relations of equality; small, democratic, personal groups—these are the goals we seek. Rather than two cars for everyone (an impossible goal, at any rate, leading to pollution, exhaustion of resources, and social isolation), we can search for ways to bring work, home, and play closer to each other—and thus bring people closer to each other. Burchett and Alley's book on *China: The Quality of Life* puts the proper stress on the quality of human relations under socialism.

## Freedom and Democracy

Marquit discusses the different meanings people have given to the words *freedom* and *democracy:*

> Let us consider the expression free world as encountered in our daily press. Certainly there is no way of considering South Africa with its white-racist regime as a free country, but it is embraced by the term free world. The same can be said of Chile under the junta headed by General Pinochet, or South Korea under General Park. It should be clear that in this sense, the word free in free world has a class character, namely, free to engage in capitalist investment, or more generally, free to engage in the exploitation of labor in one form or another. . . . Thus the meaning of the terms democracy and freedom cannot be examined independently of the social context in which they are used, and their meanings depend on the social or class position of the person or groups of persons using them. . . . Freedom as a social concept cannot properly be viewed as simply freedom from any kind of constraint (e.g., freedom to harm another person) or freedom for random behavior (e.g., freedom to make faces at one's self in a mirror). The concept of freedom as the ability to acquire knowledge of one's needs and the ability to act to satisfy these needs on the basis of such knowledge constitutes this thread of meaning of freedom common to the various social conditions to which it is applied. Insofar as the needs are restricted to an individual and must be acted upon individually, the freedom in question is individual freedom. Insofar as the needs are common to a large part of society and must be acted upon together by members of society in cooperation with one another, then the freedom is social freedom or the free-

dom of society. Democracy, then, refers to the form of social organization which provides access to knowledge of social needs (e.g., the right to education, freedom of the press and discussion) and provides the organizational and technological means of acting to satisfy these needs. Thus, limiting the concept of political democracy to the right of the people to elect a president who says he will keep us out of a war without the people having the power to stop him from involving the country in that war surely leaves something lacking. In the same sense, a society in which one has to work as a condition for the maintenance of life cannot be considered a democratic society if one simply has the right to look for work (recognition of needs), but not the right to find work (that is, to act to satisfy those needs). The right to hire labor power and then appropriate whatever is produced by it is indeed a vital freedom for capitalists as a class, for without it they cannot exist, but the right to retain the products of one's labor is a vital freedom for the workers as a class, a freedom which comes into direct conflict with the capitalist or bourgeois concept of freedom (1978, pp. 54-56).

This argument is a valid one. Freedom means both being free from constraints and controls, and also being able to work, study, grow, and have the essentials of life. Certainly, the legal freedom possessed by millions in America (often violated even in its own limited context) means little when they cannot get jobs.

But Marquit, I think, overlooks a serious problem. It seems that in socialist countries the Communist party, with a membership of only about 10 percent of the population (and often really ruled by a small minority of top leaders), works in the name and interests of the working class, but the working class as a whole does not rule yet; the people do not run the institutions in which they live and work; they do not make the ultimate political decisions. There are historical reasons for the "dictatorship of the proletariat," but it and the state should eventually disappear. Although popular control has expanded in many institutions, it is clear that ultimate power remains in the hands of the leadership of the Communist parties. In some cases (as in the USSR), popular control is minimal and new classes and rulers are arising.

In making this observation I do not mean to imply that real freedom exists under capitalism; freedom is mostly available to capitalists to exploit and rule (see Chapter 3).

But so far socialism has yet to develop processes and institutions that will lead to true and total control by all people. Serious, unresolved issues remain. One is the matter of size, how democracy can be made possible in large-scale societies (it is for this reason, among many, that the creation of small groups and communities is essential). Another problem involves freedom of the press. How is it possible when there is no private means of printing and distributing? The wall posters of China, begun during the cultural revolution (banned in 1979), are one means of guaranteeing free expression, but they are not enough. So long as some people run the press (even in the name of "the people"), they can and do censor ideas. There are few answers. Formal constitutional guarantees of free expression (as in the Soviet constitution) mean little when the actual opportunity is absent, or when people are punished for using it.

McMahon, for example, argues that one of the reasons nuclear power is relatively safer in the United States than in the USSR is the stifling of dissent in the Soviet Union. Opponents of nuclear power there have no access to technical information or government policy, and they cannot organize openly against government policy. United States opponents of nuclear power have also been persecuted by the government and the nuclear industry, however, as Solomon shows in some detail. Some organizers against nuclear power have even been shot at, and a few killed (McMahon 1979; Solomon 1980).

Lens, while pointing to the profound difficulties socialist revolutions have encountered when they took power, also points to the repression and many problems in socialist societies. But he thinks we should first see these revolutions in their historical contexts. We need not repeat the mistakes or apologize for them. Commoner's perspective seems a fair summary of the issue of freedom and democracy. While socialism has meant some denial of political democracy, we should remember that capitalist societies also have great limits in democracy. The governments of many of the poorer nations in the imperialist system, such as Chile, Brazil, and Indonesia are openly and totally repressive. In the United States (see Chapter 3), control is less openly repressive and there are possibilities for dissent, but the ruling class clearly holds most power. Also, in relation to the political conditions before socialism, socialist societies are an improvement in political freedom. We need not be limited by the experience of other societies (Lens 1979; Commoner 1976).

*Against Domination by the Elite*

Whether in work, education, or health, domination by elites and experts prevails under capitalism, and its ending must be a constant goal in a socialist society. We are talking about transforming human relations, so that all people have dignity and the chance to grow and create. Even the economic goal of providing life's essentials to all becomes endangered when an elite dominate and become a new ruling class. (In January 1979, with classes and elitism emerging again in China, there were media reports of peasants and workers protesting for more food and other essentials. When elites pay $1,600 for color TVs—see Chapter 4—working people must do without essentials.)

*New Values*

It is perhaps incorrect to label cooperation, responsibility for each other, ecological living, and the other socialist values "new." For they prevailed in many tribal societies (Radin 1953; Lee 1959; Bodley 1975, 1976; many anthropologists would not agree with these, and other, authors who portray tribal societies as essentially communistic and egalitarian). For us today, however, these values would be new. Their implementation in the context of large industrial societies would be a new stage in human history. In fact, their implementation is essential to human survival, and since societies do often shape themselves to enhance human survival, cooperation and ecological living in a new context are not impossible.

*Time* magazine, reflecting the cynicism of American capitalism, doubts that people can be cooperative.

> The socialist vision, which in its Marxist version is cloaked as a "scientific" law of history, suggests that under a right and just system all men can become the secular equivalent of saints, choosing to work in harmony for a common goal. The quintessential capitalist, whether or not he is religious, rejects the idea of man's perfectibility on earth and asks the socialist this question: If and when men become saints, socialism might indeed be able to fulfill its promise; but if sanctity were universal, would there be any need for socialism? (*Time* March 13, 1978, p. 36).

Socialists never claimed that people are saints or perfect. That is an invention of the defenders of capitalism. In fact, it is not saintliness that would dictate ecological living and cooperation; rather, it is survival—our own and that of our children. It is the recognition that our own happiness and survival are impossible without cooperation that should make us adopt new values and struggle for socialism, not any concern with saintliness. We shall all survive together, or we will perish together.

## THE PROSPECTS FOR SOCIALISM IN THE UNITED STATES

Socialist revolutions in various stages are found throughout the world. That is a fact we cannot ignore. Their development affects us directly. But we must also ask, what are the possibilities for socialism in the United States? Some of you may look forward to a socialist movement here; others may be unsure; still others no doubt dread it. However you feel, you may want to know about the future of our society and whether socialism is possible.

### *The Conditions for Revolution*

Historians and others have studied revolutions (socialist and otherwise) to find out what conditions lead to revolution. Today, socialist revolutions predominate, so we study their causes (see Szymanski 1978, ch. 13 for a good summary of issues and the literature on revolutions).

According to Szymanski, suffering in itself does not lead to revolution. People may suffer because their natural environment is poor. Or, even in an exploitative society, if people see their exploitation as "natural" and destined, they will not rise to change conditions. It is only when people suffer and are exploited under conditions of plenty (or the possibility of plenty) for all, and when they become conscious of their exploitation as unnecessary and avoidable, that one necessary condition for revolution arises. People must see that they need not suffer before they can begin to struggle to end their suffering. This struggle must be collective, planned, and long-term, or it cannot succeed.

But an equally important precondition for revolution, according to Szymanski, is a political, social, and economic crisis that calls into question the ability of the ruling class to rule. Under such conditions, if the ruling class becomes split, and if it begins to lose its ability and will to rule, the society will have the second precondition for revolution.

It is important to understand that both preconditions must exist. Capitalism will not fade away by itself because of its internal contradictions if a revolutionary party does not exist to lead a struggle against the ruling class.

Inequality and exploitation have existed in the United States for decades. Crises have also existed; the Depression of the 1930s was the most recent one, and we are living through another crisis now. At various times, socialist parties have begun to grow and make their presence known. They have never come close to taking power away from the ruling class, however. It may be that previous crises were not fundamental, or that the socialist parties were not strong, committed, or resourceful enough; or that the ruling class was able and determined to outlast the crisis. At any rate, history clearly shows that when socialist parties became strong, they were severely repressed and destroyed by the ruling class. In the 1920s and 1950s, there was an extensive and severe repression of socialist parties; this repression was a large part of the failure of socialism (URPE collective 1978, p. 334).

### The Crisis of the 1970s

We are now living through another crisis which may provide opportunity for revolutionary change. This crisis is severe and international. It is most obvious in declining living standards, the deterioration of social relations, and people's increasing loss of confidence in the ruling institutions.

Let us look at some of the evidence indicating the depths of the crisis. As corporations compete with each other (nationally and internationally), as profits decline because of this competition, and as other capitalist contradictions catch up with them, corporations have been shifting the burden of taxation onto working people. In 1954, corporate taxes were 30.4 percent of federal revenues, but only 13.8 percent in 1976. Looking at taxes from another perspective, we find that working people paid 9.2 percent of their income in federal taxes in 1954, and 16 percent in 1974. Corporations, on the other hand, have reduced the taxes they paid on profits, from 43.3 percent in 1954 to 31.8 percent in 1974 (Ciancanelli 1978, p. 201). At the same time, state and local property taxes have also increased, but real income has not. In 1967 dollars, the median net weekly income was $90 in 1967, and $84.60 in February 1980. So, people are caught in a serious financial problem. (See the Union for Radical Political Economics reader, *U.S. Capitalism in Crisis*, for a detailed account of the economic crisis.)

But the crisis is not only economic. Over the last twenty years, national opinion polls have shown a steady decrease in faith in government, business, the media, and other institutions. For example, in a 1966 poll 55 percent of those questioned expressed confidence in people who run major corporations; only 16 percent did so by 1976, however. Similarly, in the same ten-year span confidence in the military decreased from 62 to 29 percent; in the Congress, from 42 to 13 percent. Similar decreases in confidence have taken place for other institutions (Parenti 1979; Zinn 1980).

The low number of those voting (barely over 50 percent of those eligible to vote in national elections, as low as 25 percent in local elections) is another sign of the crisis, as are the problems described throughout the book.

Moreover, as people try to cope with their problems, as they make demands that the government cannot meet and that business opposes, the more will people realize the extent of the crisis. More loss in faith will follow.

The crisis is not the result of any lack of needs to be met or insufficient production. While millions are unemployed, and factories and other resources are used only partially, serious needs exist: housing and mass transit, for example. The crisis, rather, results from inadequate profits. Capitalism does not produce housing because it wants more profits than housing provides. In their search for higher profits corporations move overseas to cheap labor, leading to unemployment and lower wages in the United States. But American workers now have less money to buy the goods corporations make. Thus, the contradiction: corporations must grow, and to grow they need more profits, which can only come from exploiting the labor of workers, who do not have the money to buy (or, who borrow to buy, thus creating the present dangerous situation of increasing consumer debt). Corporate profits also are endangered by competition from other corporations (national and international), thus creating more pressure to find higher profits by exploiting workers (e.g., by using cheap labor in poor countries).

Another difficulty leading to the crisis is the spread of socialism. As more countries become socialist, capitalism has fewer places, people, and resources to exploit. The competition between capitalist countries for the diminishing resources and cheap labor leads to problems.

## What Can We Do?

What are people doing, and what can people do, to increase the chances for a socialist society?

Here is an answer given by the editors of *Monthly Review* (a socialist journal) to a thirteen-year-old.

> Recently we received the following letter: "I am writing to you in the hope that you can answer a question which has been put to me on several occasions but to which I can never give or find a good answer. I am 13 years old and despite my age am now a convinced Marxist. I am a subscriber to MR and buy MR books regularly. My question is, 'How do I earn money and not become compromised in a society I abhor?' This question has been thrown at me by several people who doubt my revolutionary sincerity. They say, 'When you get older and have to work to live, then what?' You were the only ones I could think of to turn to for an answer. Please answer this very important question as soon as possible. Thank you." Here is what we answered: "Perhaps the best way we can answer your question, which we agree is a very important one, is to tell you the story of a meeting one of us had with a group of economists in Paris a few years ago. When asked what they were doing, one of them replied: 'During the day we work for the government, and at night we work against the government.' And that's the way it has to be for most of those whose objective in life is to see capitalism over-thrown and replaced by socialism. They work for a living like everyone else, and then on their own time they work for the movement. Naturally there is more to it than that. They try to train themselves to get jobs which will give some satisfaction and enable them to work with and for people (teaching, public health, etc.), and they use any available opportunities to educate fellow workers and those they deal with. But as a rule such work on the job has to be quiet and discreet—which does not mean that it cannot be effective. Finally, there are some who manage to combine earning a living with work for the cause, e.g., through writing, publishing books, etc. In some countries where there is a strong working-class movement, there are jobs in the party or the unions which allow such a combination of earning a living and working for the cause. But there is also the danger that those holding such jobs will acquire an interest in preserving the existing system rather than overthrowing it. This is in fact one of the historical roots of reformism and revisionism (*Monthly Review*, March 1977, Notes from the Editors).

Many people are working to make changes. The media are deceiving us, in a way. Now that the confrontations and demonstrations of the 1960s are gone, the media do not have dramatic events to cover. But work toward change is going on, even if not covered by television and newspapers. The activity of the 1970s (and probably also in the 1980s) is of a different sort. Some with a socialist perspective, others just unhappy with social conditions and their suffering and insecurity, people are organizing on various fronts: tenants' organizations are trying to control increasing rents and improve housing conditions; self-help groups abound, giving strength and a new life to their participants (see Katz and Bender, *The Strength in Us*); ex-mental patients are using their own strength to do away with professionalism; food coops are becoming established and widespread; women are denying the mystique of medicine and educating themselves about their own bodies (Katz and Bender 1976; Dellinger 1978; Zwerdling 1980, p. 27).

Political activity was prevalent in the 1970s and continues into the 1980s. There are more organizations now working at all levels for change than there were in the 1960s. Many are not socialist, of course, but all seek to change the present system toward greater equality and justice. These are "grassroots" organizations, in which working people are trying to stop profiteering by the oil and electric companies, to create a more just tax system, to insure the basic necessities for everyone, and so on. In short, unlike the 1960s groups that focused on one or two issues (war, welfare, etc.), today's groups focus on many broad issues that affect most people's lives. More and more, they focus on capitalism as a whole system (DeLeeuw, Ansara, and Rathke 1979).

Most of the organizations working for social change are based in local communities and are run on an open and democratic basis. People from all walks of life belong to them. Some are only neighborhood groups, others include whole cities, a few are state organizations, and at least one is national; The Association of Community Organizations for Reform Now (ACORN). It has 26,000 members in nineteen states, and in 1979 it had a national convention in which it stated its principles and goals. ACORN and other organizations have been able to mobilize many people and they have achieved some significant goals (Adamson 1980).

There are some groups still organized around one issue. Tenant organizations are one type. They continue to grow as people find they cannot afford to buy houses, and as rents are increasing. The demands of tenant organizations are extensive, and the struggles to achieve them are radicalizing people.

> Within their buildings, neighborhoods, cities, and states, tenants are engaging in rent strikes, court suits, lobbying, mass rallies, picketing, and sit-ins to force landlords, banks, and the government to act on grievances. The issues involved include: rent increases, inadequate building, maintenance and security, one-sided leases that favor landlords, displacement, the lack of tenant voice in management policies, and racial and financing discrimination (Atlas and Dreier 1980, p. 16).

But the change in political consciousness involves more than the people who belong in organizations. During the 1970s, polls showed that 80 percent of those questioned thought the tax system favors the rich and that two-thirds favored government action to curb water and air pollution. In another area, both labor union strikes and political demonstrations continued through the 1970s and now continue into the 1980s. The fact that the media pay less attention to such activities than they did in the 1960s does not diminish their significance. The 1970s was not the silent decade; indeed, it was a "radical decade" (Parenti 1979).

Moreover, individuals and groups are more open in their study of socialism and Marxism. The *Time* story on socialism, inaccurate and belittling as it may be, is also an indirect admission that socialism is establishing itself as a viable alternative (*Time*, March 13, 1978; Parenti 1979).

Many people, in groups of various sizes, are spreading the socialist perspective. For example, some work actively in the labor unions of their workplaces and struggle both to make concrete improvements there and also to share with co-workers their socialist perspective on the current crisis. In this way, people hope to make unions effective tools in defending workers from paying the price for the crisis caused by capitalism. For example, unions can fight against speeding up production, unsafe working conditions, and other means employers use to increase profits at the expense of workers.

I have described some of the groups and what they are doing to improve conditions. Some groups work from a socialist perspective; many do not. All, however, are clearly dissatisfied with present conditions. In the long run, if the work of individuals and groups in the current crisis is to lead to socialism, a political instrument is needed, a socialist party. All socialists accept this need and many groups are working to realize it. But at this moment, there is no agreement on the nature of the party that is needed. There are many parties, often in strong disagreement with each other, trying to become the party that will organize working people into a socialist opposition (see URPE Collective 1978, p. 339; O'Brien 1977–78; Ackerman 1978).

There seem to be three approaches to the nature of the party socialists should form. Some people argue that socialists should try to take over the Democratic party and run candidates in Democratic primaries, from a populist-socialist perspective. Domhoff made this proposal, and occasionally some people do attempt it. Tom Hayden ran in the California senate primary in 1976; he lost, but he received a large vote (Domhoff 1974a).

Generally, most socialists do not find that approach promising. A large, open socialist party has been a second alternative. One such party is the New American Movement (NAM), which is gathering many political activists of the 1960s. It has not become a large party, but people in it are searching for ways to expand, organize, and attract people to a socialist movement.

"Leninist" parties are a third alternative. "The central core of Leninism is the disciplined political party, in which internal debate may be allowed but whose members unite in carrying out the party's agreed-upon program." Leninist parties aim to serve as the leadership of the working class in the creation of a socialist society. In this way, they may be smaller and more disciplined and organized than a mass party aims to be. (People in

Leninist parties argue that a small, tightly organized party is the only effective way to overthrow capitalism when the capitalist crisis grows and intensifies.) O'Brien lists the parties, their history, and their current status (1977-78).

McAfee, in describing the work of City Life, a socialist organization, argues that the means used in struggling for socialism are as important as the ends; indeed, many of these means are in fact the goals of democracy and control of our lives by all of us.

> Another essential ingredient for socialism that can only be developed through mass struggles is working class leadership and the confidence among working people that we can take over and run things better. To us in City Life, socialism means that the working class is in power at all levels of society. But the power to govern is not something we can just "take"; it has to be created through struggle, mass participation and over a long period of time. This is why we say the means of struggle are as important as the ends. In any particular battle, the extent to which people are mobilized, take collective risks, break through old patterns of individualism, sexism, and racism, gain a sense of their potential power, and strengthen the skills and accountability of leadership is as important as whether the particular demand is won or lost.
>
> This is a point on which we disagree with both the populists and with the traditionalist "ML" [Marxist-Leninist] groups, and where we think the two approaches have a lot in common. Both the populist and the current party-building groups, from what we have seen, tend to rely on hierarchical forms of organization and on methods of struggle which do little to increase the confidence, decision-making ability, and leadership potential of rank and file members (McAfee 1979, pp. 51-52; See also Rowbotham 1979, Hunter and Gordon 1979).

What we may need, above all, is an openness and willingness to adapt as conditions change. The history of all revolutions seems to show that the strategies, parties, and means used to overthrow capitalism have always been changed to meet present needs and conditions. Flexibility and close study of changing conditions seem essential. One approach works at some times, but not at others.

At present, in part because of the difficulties and frustrations in organizing a socialist movement, different groups and parties often take their frustrations out on each other instead of the common enemy, capitalism. It is imperative that we cooperate to realize our common goal.

As of now, much is happening. The crisis is intensifying. Groups everywhere are searching for alternatives. Changes are occurring. The crisis is world-wide; all capitalist countries experience it. But in the United States, unlike most other countries, there is no strong socialist party leading the struggle to overthrow capitalism. We can and must learn from socialist revolutions everywhere, but we cannot merely copy them. It seems that each revolutionary party had to develop its own strategies in response to its own conditions. In this country, while always aware of the international character both of the crisis and of socialist struggles, we need to fashion our

## STRUGGLES: A Socialist Organization

*Socialist individuals and groups use many approaches to work for the creation of a socialist society. McAfee below describes the work of one such socialist group, City Life. The first three paragraphs summarize the work of the group in 1973-76. The people in City Life reorganized in the following year, and the rest of this reading describes the three committees that were the focus of City Life activity in 1978-79.*

Since the Vietnam war was at its height, our first project was the production of an anti-war newsletter, the J.P. *Weekly War Bulletin,* which we handed out every Saturday at supermarkets and laundromats. The response was generally sympathetic, and as we met more local people through the *Bulletin,* we looked for ways to organize more directly around the material conditions of people's lives.

Housing seemed the obvious answer. Even a glance at the situation—acute shortage of apartments, worsening conditions, higher rents, replacement of homeowners by speculators, urban renewal and "gentrification" at the expense of working class residents—made it clear that the system of housing for profit was a disaster for all but the profiteers. We were also influenced by the half dozen or so tenants organizations in the Boston area, some founded by ex-student leftists, which were mobilizing to defend rent control legislation, block evictions, and promote rent strikes. . . .

Between 1973 and 1976 our efforts yielded some respectable results: several tenant unions formed, many rent increases defeated, repairs won, and evictions stopped. There were three cases in which our group, along with other local activists, helped to organize human blockades to prevent the eviction of an old woman, the demolition of a house, and the violent harassment of several Puerto Rican families by white neighbors. Less dramatic but just as important was the increased awareness in the community of tenants' rights, and of the anti-working class policies of the city and federal government and the local banks. . . .

*Tenants Committee:* Although we sometimes go door-knocking in buildings owned by targetted slumlords, most of the tenants we work with are people who get in touch with us for help. We get as many as 100 calls a month from people who hear about us from friends, the *CommUnity News,* or radio ads. We give advice to everyone, but we put the most energy into helping people who are working class and who are willing to work collectively with neighbors. As we work with people, we try to persuade them that each major rent increase, eviction, or demolition of a sound house is a blow to the whole working class community, and that homeowners as well as tenants have an interest in defending working-class housing. We try to get white people to recognize the effects of racist housing policies and to understand their own interests, as working class people, in supporting black and Latin struggles.

When we give aid to a tenant, we usually ask the person to reciprocate by doing something for the group (like answer phones) or for another tenant (like help someone contact a housing inspector). This helps to counteract the idea that we are some kind of social service agency. If the new person shows some initiative and interest in the group we encourage her to come to a tenants committee meeting. The next step would be to talk to the person about City Life and invite them to actually join the committee.

We haven't given up on tenant unions; in fact, a few of the groups we helped organize still exist. But we found that functioning tenant unions are hard to sustain, especially when there is a high turnover of residents in the building or development. We have also found that often the hardest thing to ask a new person to do as a first step is to organize her own neighbors. But by joining the committee, new people can get support in their own situations, experience in working collectively, exposure to socialism and the idea of building a working class movement, and the skills and confidence they need to go back and organize in their own buildings or neighborhoods.

*Source:* Excerpted pp. 40, 41, 48, 49, 50 in from Kathy McAfee, "City Life: Lessons of the First Five Years," in *Radical America* Vol. 13 #1, Jan.-Feb. 1979. 38 Union Sq., Somerville, MA 02143.

*(continued)*

**A Socialist Organization** *(continued)*

Most of the other Boston area tenants groups from the early 70s have fallen apart (as TAG probably would have had we remained a single-issue organization), and thus the tenants movement has ceased to exist. But we think there is the potential to rebuild city-wide resistance on a *class* basis to gentrification and neighborhood deterioration, and so we are trying to strengthen our ties with working class people and groups in other parts of the city. We also spend some time discussing ruling class plans for housing and the city and trying to formulate a socialist alternative.

*Education Committee:* This committee is made up of parents of kids in Boston public schools. The impulse for starting it arose from the need to deal with our children's problems at school as well as from a desire to organize other parents. So far the committee's work has centered around the Racial-Ethnic Parents Councils, parents advisory groups set up in each school as part of the desegregation plan. By giving parents a foot in school doors, the REPCs have aided the growth of a city-wide parents movement, responding to worsening conditions and struggling over a variety of issues ranging from transportation and classroom size to racist administrators. Often immediate problems, such as the lack of basic supplies, are so pressing that it is hard to get to the more fundamental issues.

The City Life Education Committee members play an active role in these immediate struggles and in doing so, try to relate them to the broader issues of race and class. They also try to increase the participation, class consciousness and power of working class parents within the movement, such as by forming support groups of working class parent activists, and by challenging the notion that the education "experts" know what is best for our kids. Another way the committee tries to reach new parents and get its view across is by writing a regular column in the *CommUnity News.* We use the column to expose the racist, sexist, and anti-working class bias in school structures and curricula, and to give a sense of what education *could* be like if working class people were in control of it.

*The Workplace Committee:* The membership of this committee reflects the economic base of Boston. Some members work in manufacturing, transportation, or printing, but as many have clerical or service jobs in industries such as health and education. This is City Life's newest committee, and we are still too small to concentrate people in any one industry or to carry out a city-wide strategy. Most of the committee members, however, are rooted in organizing at their own workplaces, and the committee functions as a support group for them. The committee has also mobilized support for a variety of local workers' struggles, and is beginning to set up events and study groups to which members can invite the people they get to know at work.

But primarily, at this stage, the job of this committee is to formulate a City Life strategy for our workplace organizing in Boston. Among the questions the committee has been discussing are: What is the role of socialists in union organizing drives and union shops? What are the peculiarities of organizing in service industries? What are the boundaries of, and divisions within the U.S. and the local working class? How can we promote struggles that build the *positive* side of class consciousness, i.e., workers' desires to take pride in and have control over our own work?

own party and strategy, for our conditions are different. It may be, as some people have argued, that the United States will be the last capitalist country. Whatever may happen, in the next few years we will experience profound crises and dislocations, and we can stop them only if we unite and fight for our common good. (See the essay by the URPE Collective, 1978, for an excellent discussion of the crisis and of strategies.)

# THE LONG STRUGGLE

As I near the end of this book, I see many changes even in the time it has taken me to write it (from the summer of 1977 to January 1979).

In the United States, the crisis is becoming more permanent and pervasive. Both inflation and unemployment continue high. President Reagan proposed a budget that will hurt middle-class, poor, and working people. Attempts at tax reform make our take-home pay no larger. Politicians, sensing the obvious rebellion against the burden of taxes, propose to stop it with promises of tax cuts but make no attack on the inequities of the tax system. The tax cuts will eliminate needed services, not the wastes of military spending or the business waste of money from government contracts.

Internationally, events are equally revolutionary (and puzzling). The United States government had to abandon another of its imperialist allies when the Shah of Iran retired on the millions he had stolen from the Iranian people. The United States interests tried in vain to find some solution to protect imperialist interests in Iran. The outcome will affect millions of people.

We in the United States do not know the background to the overthrow of the Shah. He represented the interests of the Iranian ruling class and imperialist nations. The wealth from the oil fields benefited primarily those interests, not the vast majority of Iranian people. A long struggle and protest, uniting conflicting religious, nationalist, social, and political groups led to the overthrow of the Shah. This defeat of imperialism was somewhat unusual because it was accomplished without a long armed struggle. Demonstrations and protests simply made it impossible for the Shah to rule. But as Sweezy and Magdoff, and Abrahamian show, the future of Iran is very uncertain. Many differing groups are vying for control of the society. The overthrow of the Shah shows that the power of imperialism is limited. Widespread, organized opposition can overthrow imperialism. But it is obvious, also, that the defeat of an imperialist-supported ruling class does not lead automatically to socialism (Abrahamian 1979; Sweezy and Magdoff 1979a).

In China, the undoing of the cultural revolution seems full-scale. Coca-Cola, industrial machinery, and other symbols of capitalist "progress" are heading for China. It is clear that American corporations look on the Chinese millions as a great market and a solution to their problems. It is less clear what the Chinese think will benefit them from trade with the United States. The machinery that the new leaders in China want to import so they can industrialize and modernize rapidly will be bought at a high price. Not only will United States corporations sell at high prices (to increase profits) but China may become trapped in the capitalist net of debt and interest payments. The new elite and ruling class will also come to want more of the consumerism and materialism of the West, thus taking away the resources for essential goods needed by the masses.

The invasion of Cambodia by Vietnam (1980) is another new reality, and one difficult to assess. Whatever else it means, it is clear that it shows much conflict and turmoil within the socialist world.

In other areas, the Soviet Union is engaged in actions with a mixed potential. On the one hand, with the cooperation of Cuba, it aided the Angola liberation forces and liberation movements elsewhere. But it is clear that their motives were mixed and that they are engaged in a new form of imperialism. The actions of the Chinese leaders are no less abhorrent at times. On the principle of opposing whatever the Soviet Union does, China sided with repressive regimes in Chile, Zaire, and other places.

The revolutionary potential and actions of people throughout the world are spreading. People are rebelling against the continued, and increasing, suffering imposed on them by imperialism and their own ruling classes. The events of the last few years in China, Cambodia, and Africa; the conflicts between socialist countries; the changing relationships between socialist and capitalist countries—all these complicate immensely our ability to understand what is happening. At times, we may even throw up our hands in hopelessness. But we should be clear that both here and abroad the world is changing. It is not moving in straight or uncomplicated paths, so we must struggle to understand and change it. Events anywhere in the world affect us.

Most people in the United States are not starving. Many are, however. Millions face physical suffering. But most of us suffer in other ways, from insecurity, domination, and exploitation. And things are worsening.

I have written this book in order to help myself and you understand the crisis we are undergoing. If I have only helped you begin to think critically, if I have given you a glimpse of a different world, I will have accomplished my goal. If I have seemed to offer easy solutions and simple explanations, I apologize. Reality, I have come to understand, allows no easy solutions. That does not mean, however, that we must resign ourselves to capitalist conditions. The absence of perfection and easy solutions only means we must always strive for improvements, even if serious problems will always remain. As Frederick Douglass wrote over a hundred years ago, we cannot expect change without turmoil and struggle and the end is uncertain, but continuing insecurity, exploitation, and destructive human relations *are* certain if there is no struggle.

> If there is no struggle, there is no progress. Those who profess to favor freedom, and yet deprecate agitation, are [people] who want crops without plowing up the ground. They want rain without thunder and lightning. They want the ocean without the awful roar of its many waters. This struggle may be a moral one; or it may be a physical one; or it may be both moral and physical; but it must be a struggle. Power concedes nothing without a demand. It never did and never will. . . . [People] may not get all they pay for in this world; but they must certainly pay for all they get (In Bennet 1966, p. 274).

# References

Abrahamian, Edward (1979). "Political forces in the Iranian revolution." *Radical America*, 13:3, May-June, pp. 45-55.

Ackerman, Frank (1978). "Dare to struggle, dare to influence people." *Radical America*, 12:3, March-April, pp. 56-51.

Ackerman, Jerry (1980). "Dumping nuclear waste—the sea is no solution." *Boston Globe*, May 4, pp. 1, 24.

Adamson, Madeleine (1980). "Born-again democracy." *Progressive*, May, pp. 40-41.

Agee, James, and Walker Evans (1941). *Let Us Now Praise Famous Men*. Boston: Houghton Mifflin.

Agee, Philip, and Louis Wolf (1978). *Dirty Work: The CIA in Western Europe*. New York: Lyle Stuart.

—— (1980). *Dirty Work II: The CIA in Africa*. New York: Lyle Stuart.

Allen, Ernest (1977). "Detroit: I do mind dying: A review." *Radical America*, 11:1, January-February, pp. 69-73.

Alperovitz, Gar, and Jeff Faux (1977). "Energy, capital, and socialism." *Social Policy*, 7:4, January-February, pp. 58-61.

Anderson, Charles (1974). *Toward a New Sociology* (2nd ed). Homewood, IL: Dorsey.

—— (1976). *The Sociology of Survival*. Homewood, IL: Dorsey.

——, and Jeffry Gibson (1978). *Toward a New Sociology* (3rd ed). Homewood, IL: Dorsey.

Anderson, James D. (1975). "Education as a vehicle for the manipulation of black workers." In W. Feinberg and H. Rosemont (eds.) 1975, *Work, Technology, and Education*. Urbana, IL: University of Illinois Press.

Anderson, Peter (1979). "A stab at self-sufficiency." *Boston Globe*, December 25, pp. 29, 35.

Andors, Stephen (1977). *Work in Revolutionary China*. White Plains, NY: M. E. Sharpe.

Appleseed, Jack (1976). "On the work ethic." *Monthly Review*, 28:5, October, pp. 61-62.

Arnesen, Eric (1979). "Hazardous wastes bubble up in Bay State." *Citizen Advocate* (Boston), November, p. 5.

Arnold, Alison (1978). "Those old school ties remain strong despite changing society." *Boston Sunday Globe,* February 19, p. B3.

Aronowitz, Stanley (1974). *Food, Shelter, and the American Dream.* New York: Seabury.

Ashford, Nicholas (1976). *Crisis in the Workplace.* Cambridge, MA: MIT Press.

Associated Press (1978). "Affirmative action called failure." *Boston Globe,* March 6, p. 10.

Atlas, John, and Peter Dreier (1980). "The housing crisis and the tenants' revolt." *Social Policy,* January-February, pp. 13-24.

Babson, Steve, and Nancy Brigham (1975). *Why Do We Spend So Much Money?* (2nd ed.) Somerville, MA: Popular Economics Press.

———— (1978). *What's Happening to Our Jobs?* (2nd ed.) Somerville, MA: Popular Economics Press.

Bachrach, Peter, and Morton Baratz (1970). *Power and Poverty.* New York: Oxford.

Bader, Michael (1979). "Hustling drugs to the third world." *Progressive,* December, pp. 42-46.

Baker, George (1973). "Multinational farmers: Good climate for agribusiness." *Nation,* November 5, pp. 456-62.

————, and R. Taylor (1972). "The conglomerate green giant." *Nation,* March 13, pp. 332-35.

Baldridge, J. Victor (1975). *Sociology.* New York: Wiley.

Baldwin, Deborah (1979). "Off the track." *Progressive,* July, pp. 12-17.

Balzer, Richard (1976). *Clockwork.* Garden City, NY: Doubleday.

Ban, John, and L. Ciminillo (1977). *Violence and Vandalism in Public Education.* Danville, IL: Interstate Printers and Publishers.

Barkan, Joanne (1979). "Worker turmoil in Italy." *Progressive,* June, pp. 46-49.

Barlow, Hugh D. (1981). *Introduction to Criminology* (2nd ed). Boston: Little, Brown.

Barnes, Peter (ed.) (1975). *The People's Land.* Emmaus, PA: Rodale Press.

Barnet, Richard J., and R. Müller (1974). *Global Reach: The Power of the Multinational Corporations.* New York: Simon and Schuster.

Barnicle, Mike (1978). "Summer in the city: Few jobs for young; time for trouble." *Boston Globe,* July 13, p. 17.

Baron, Harold (1971). "The demand for black labor." *Radical America,* 5:2, March-April, pp. 1-46.

Bass, Liz (1979). "Runaway plants leave workers out in the cold." *Citizen Advocate* (Boston), March, pp. 1, 12.

Bastid, Marianne (1970). "Economic necessity and political ideals in educational reform during the cultural revolution." In Karabel and Halsey 1977, pp. 589-607.

Baxandall, Rosalyn, Elizabeth Ewen, and Linda Gordon (1976). "The working class has two sexes." *Monthly Review,* 28:3, July-August, pp. 1-9.

————, Linda Gordon, and Susan Reverby (1976). *America's Working Women.* New York: Random House.

Bayles, Fred (1979). "How employees saved Clinton firm." *Boston Globe,* May 6, p. 43.

Bedell, Ben (1979). "Sexual harassment, a federal case." *Guardian*, December 12, p. 2.
Beecher, William (1979). "China today." *Boston Globe*, May 8, pp. 1, 8, 9.
Beha, James, Kenneth Carlson, and Robert Rosenblum (1977). *Sentencing to Community Service*. Washington, DC: U.S. Dept. of Justice, LEAA. U.S. Government Printing Office.
*Beijing Review* (1979). "China's socialist legal system." January 12, pp. 25-35.
Bell, Derrick (1978). "Inside China: conformity and social reform." *Juris Doctor*, 8:4, April, pp. 23-31.
Bennett, Leamon J. (1979). "When employees run the company." *Harvard Business Review*, January-February, pp. 75-90.
Bennett, Lerone (1966). *Before the Mayflower: A History of the Negro in America, 1619-1964*. Baltimore: Penguin.
Benson, Susan Porter (1978). "The clerking sisterhood." *Radical America*, 12:2, March-April, pp. 41-55.
Berman, Daniel (1978). *Death on the Job*. New York: Monthly Review Press.
Berman, Jesse (1969). "The Cuban popular tribunals." *Columbia Law Review*, 69, pp. 1317-1354.
Bernstein, Paul (1974). "Run your own business: Worker-owned plywood firms." *Working Papers*, 2:2, Summer, pp. 24-34.
Bernstein, Peter J. (1977). "Detroit's chemical warfare." *Nation*, April 9, pp. 422-25.
Bettelheim, Charles (1974). *Cultural Revolution and Industrial Organization in China*. New York: Monthly Review Press.
———— (1978). "The great leap backward." *Monthly Review*, 30:3, July-August, pp. 37-130.
Biffle, Christopher (1975). "A ton of onions keeps you even." *Nation*, September 25, pp. 269-71.
Bini, Obi (1979). "Brazil: Economic miracle?" *Guardian*, June 20, p. 12.
Blake, Andrew (1980). "Frightened—and ill." *Boston Globe*, January 23, p. 2.
Blau, Francine D. (1975). "Women in the labor force: An overview." In Jo Freeman, 1975. (Reprinted in Skolnick and Currie 1976.)
Blaylock, Enid (1978). "Technology has dehumanized nursing." *Boston Globe*, September 11, p. 16.
Blew, Carol Holliday, D. McGillis, and G. Bryant (1977). *Project New Pride*. Washington, DC: U.S. Government Printing Office (sponsored by LEAA).
Blum, Jeffrey D. and Judith Smith (1972). *Nothing Left to Lose*. Boston: Beacon.
Bodley, John (1975). *Victims of Progress*. Reading, MA: Cummings.
———— (1976). *Anthropology and Contemporary Human Problems*. Reading, MA: Cummings.
Bonavich, Edna (1976). "Advanced capitalism and black-white relations in the United States." *American Sociological Review*, 41:1, February, pp. 34-51.
Boughey, Howard (1978). *The Insights of Sociology*. Boston: Allyn and Bacon.
Bowles, Samuel (1971a). "Unequal education and the reproduction of the social division of labor." *Review of Radical Political Economics*, 3, Fall. (Reprinted in Carnoy 1972, pp. 36-64.)
———— (1971b). "Cuban Education and the revolutionary ideology." *Harvard Educational Review*, 41:4, Fall. (Reprinted in Carnoy 1972, pp. 272-303.)

_____ (1977). "Have capitalism and democracy come to a parting of the ways?" *Progressive,* June, pp. 20-23.
_____, and Herbert Gintis (1976). *Schooling in Capitalist America.* New York: Basic Books.
Bradlee, Ben (1979a). "The plight of 'Fallout City.'" *Boston Globe,* June 14, p. 2.
_____ (1979b). "800,000 in Salt Lake City live in 'microwave oven.'" *Boston Globe,* June 21, p. 3.
_____ (1980). "A warning from Miami." *Boston Globe,* May 25, p. 11.
Brady, James (1977). "Political contradictions and justice policy in People's China." *Contemporary Crises;* 1, pp. 127-62.
Brandon, William (1974). *The Last Americans.* New York: McGraw-Hill.
Braverman, Harry (1974). *Labor and Monopoly Capitalism: The Degradation of Work in the Twentieth Century.* New York: Monthly Review Press.
Brecher, Jeremy (1972). *Strike.* San Francisco: Straight Arrow Books.
Brown, E. Richard (1977). "Public health and imperialism." *Monthly Review,* 29:4, September, pp. 21-34.
Brown, Michael (1980). "Is Love Canal just the start?" *Boston Globe,* June 22, pp. A1-A2. (Excerpts from *Laying Waste,* New York: Pantheon, 1980.)
Browning, Frank (1970). "From rumble to revolution: The Young Lords." *Ramparts,* October, pp. 19-25.
_____ (1975). *The Vanishing Land.* New York: Harper and Row.
Bruzelius, Nils J. (1978). "Did counseling 40 years ago harm boys?" *Boston Globe,* January 10, pp. 1, 7.
Bularzik, Mary (1978). "Sexual harassment at the workplace: historical notes." *Radical America,* 12:4, July-August, pp. 25-43.
Burchett, Wilfred, and Reui Alley (1976). *China: The Quality of Life.* Baltimore: Penguin.
Burma, John, and Joseph Leon (1978). "The Mexican Americans." In Joseph Collier (ed.), *American Ethnics and Minorities.* Los Alamitos, CA: Hwong, pp. 97-132.
Burnett, Richard (1979). "Illegal aliens come cheap." *Progressive,* October, pp. 44-46.
Burnette, Robert, and John Koster (1974). *The Road to Wounded Knee.* New York: Bantam.
Burnham, Sophy (1978). "Why the rich don't care." *The Washington Monthly,* April, pp. 11-19.

Caldicott, Helen (1979). "Health hazards of nuke power." *Guardian,* May 3, p. 9.
Caldwell, Carol (1977). "You haven't come a long way, baby." *New Times,* June 10.
Caldwell, Jean (1979). "Asbestos: the public health issue of the '80's?" *Boston Globe,* October 25, pp. A1-A2.
Calhoun, John C. (1978). *Department of Youth Services Annual Report, 1977.* Commonwealth of Massachusetts.
Carnoy, Martin D. (ed.) (1972). *Schooling in a Corporate Society.* New York: McKay.
_____ (1978). "The role of the federal budget for education in alleviating poverty." In Raskin 1978, pp. 249-56.
_____, and Henry M. Levin (1977). "A strategy for education." In Raskin 1978, pp. 257-63.

———, and Jorgen Werthein (1977). "Socialist ideology and the transformation of Cuban education." In Karabel and Halsey 1977, pp. 573-89.

Caudill, Harry M. (1963). *Night Comes to the Cumberlands.* Boston: Atlantic–Little, Brown.

Center for Research on Criminal Justice (1975). *The Iron Fist and the Velvet Glove.* Berkeley, CA.

Cereseto, Shirley (1977). "On the causes and solution to the problem of world hunger and starvation: Evidence from China, India, and other places." *The Insurgent Sociologist,* 7:3, Summer, pp. 33-52.

Chambliss, William J. (1964). "A sociological analysis of the law of vagrancy." *Social Problems,* 12:1, Summer, pp. 67-77.

——— (1973). "The saints and the roughnecks." *Society,* 11:1, November-December, pp. 24-31.

——— (1978). *On the Take: From Petty Crooks to Presidents.* Bloomington, IN: Indiana University Press.

———, and Thomas Ryther (1975). *Sociology: The Discipline and Its Direction.* New York: McGraw-Hill.

Chapin, Georgeanne, and Robert Wasserstrom (1980). "A bitter harvest." *Progressive,* March, pp. 31-34.

Chen, Jack (1975). *Inside the Cultural Revolution.* New York: Macmillan.

Chen Muhua (1979). "Controlling population growth in a new way." *Beijing Review,* November 16, pp. 17-20.

Ch'en, Jerome (1979). "On China since Mao," *Monthly Review,* 31:1, May, pp. 21-34.

Chesler, Phyllis (1972). *Women and Madness.* Garden City, NY: Doubleday.

Chiñas, Beverly (1973). *The Isthmus Zapotecs: Women's Roles in Cultural Context.* New York: Holt, Rinehart, and Winston.

Chu Li and Tien Chieh-yun (1974). *Inside a People's Commune.* Peking, China: Foreign Languages Press.

Ciancanelli, Penelope (1978). "Politics and public school reform." In URPE 1978, pp. 194-204.

Cirel, Paul, P. Evans, D. McGillis, and D. Whitcomb (1977). *Community Crime Prevention.* Washington, DC: U.S. Government Printing Office (for LEAA).

Clairborne, Robert (1971). "Future Schlock." *Nation,* January 25, pp. 117-120.

Clark, Burton (1960). "The 'cooling-out' function of higher education." *American Journal of Sociology,* 65:6, May, pp. 569-76.

Clary, Mike and Jon Thompson (1978). "Your money and your life." *Seven Days,* December 18, pp. 21-24.

Cleaver, Eldridge (1968). *Soul on Ice.* New York: McGraw-Hill.

Cleverdon, Stephanie (1975). "On the brink: Three attempts to liberate women." *Working Papers,* 3:1, Spring, pp. 28-36.

Cluster, Dick (1978). "Clash in worker-owned asbestos mine." *Seven Days,* August, p. 26.

Cohen, Muriel (1976). "Job plan urged to curb violence." *Boston Globe,* October 17, p. 1.

Coles, Robert (1970). *Uprooted Children.* New York: Harper and Row, 1971.

——— (1977). "The children of affluence." *Atlantic Monthly,* September, pp. 52-66.

Collins, Sheila (1978). "Class, family, forgiveness." *Christianity and Crisis,* 38:5, April 17, pp. 82-88.

Committee on the Judiciary (1972). *Hearings Before the Committee, U.S. Senate, Ninety-Second Congress, Second Session—on Nomination of Richard G. Kleindienst, of Arizona, to be Attorney General* (Parts 1, 2, and 3). Washington, DC: U.S. Government Printing Office.

Committee on Labor and Public Welfare, U.S. Senate (1972). *Worker Alienation, 1972.* Washington, DC: U.S. Government Printing Office.

Commoner, Barry (1971). *The Closing Circle.* New York: Knopf.

———— (1976). *The Poverty of Power.* New York: Knopf.

Connolly, Richard J. (1977). "White-collar crime: A strain that costs us $40 billion." *Boston Globe,* May 1, p. 20.

Connor, Walter, D. (1972). *Deviance in Socialist Society.* New York: Columbia University Press.

Conrad, Thomas (1979). "East Germany in ferment." *Progressive,* June, pp. 50-52.

*Consumer Reports* (1979). "Proposition 13: who really won?" September, pp. 546-48.

Cook, Fred J. (1979). "How big oil turned off the gas." *Nation,* July 28-August 4, pp. 54ff.

Cook, Robert (1968). "The police." *The Bulletin of the American Independent Movement* (New Haven, CT), 3:6, pp. 1-6.

Cooke, Robert (1979a). "Ancient bones show lead danger greater now." *Boston Globe,* April 26, p. 68.

———— (1979b). "Lead poisoning warning issued." *Boston Globe,* March 30, p. 25.

Corea, Gena (1980). "The Caesarian epidemic." *Mother Jones,* July, pp. 28-35.

Corwin, Miles (1979). "Ancient Greece used solar energy." *Boston Globe,* May 23, p. 2.

Cox, Oliver C. (1976). *Race Relations.* Detroit: Wayne State University Press.

Crockett, George W., Jr. (1976). "Judge Walter Crockett, Jr., looks at China's legal system." *New China,* June 28, pp. 27-29.

Croll, Elizabeth J. (1976). "Social production and female status: women in China." *Race and Class,* 18:1, pp. 40-51.

Curtin, Sharon (1972). *Nobody Ever Died of Old Age.* Boston: Little, Brown.

Dahl, Robert (1961). *Who Governs?* New Haven, CT: Yale University Press.

Darknell, Frank (1975). "The Carnegie Council for Policy Studies in Higher Education: A new policy group for the ruling class." *Insurgent Sociologist,* 5:3, Spring, pp. 106-114.

Davin, Delia (1976). *Women-Work: Women and the Party in Revolutionary China.* NY: Oxford.

Dean, William, and Simon Breines (1975). "Footpower in the cities." *Nation,* September 27, pp. 271-74.

DeCormis, Anna (1979a). "Oil firms dominate nuke industry." *Guardian,* May 9, p. 6.

———— (1979b). "Economic parity eludes third world." *Guardian,* May 16, p. 24.

———— (1979c). "Sweatshops: A thriving business." *Guardian,* October 31, p. 2.

———— (1980). "Third world debt deepens further." *Guardian,* June 4, p. 15.

de Jesus, Carolina Maria (1962). *Child of the Dark.* New York: Signet, 1963.

DeLeeuw, Berk, Michael Ansara, and Wade Rathke (1979). "Perspectives on grassroots organizing." Presentations and discussion at the Society for the Study of Social Problems convention, August 27, Boston.

Dellinger, Dave (1978). "The seed beneath the snow." *Seven Days,* December 8, pp. 11–12.
Denby, Charles (1978). *Indignant Heart.* Boston: South End Press.
Denman, Scott, and Ken Bossong (1979). "Power politics: Big business." *Seven Days,* June 29, pp. 6–7.
Dennison, George (1969). *The Lives of Children.* New York: Random House.
Diamond, Norma (1975). "Collectivization, kinship, and the status of women in rural China." In Reiter 1975, pp. 372–395.
Dixon, Michael (1975). *Juvenile Delinquency Prevention Programs.* Nashville, TN: Peabody College for Teachers.
Dobrin, Arthur (1980). "An American prisoner of conscience." *Progressive,* May, pp. 35–39.
Dobson, Richard (1977). "Social status and inequality of access to higher education in the U.S.S.R." In Karabel and Halsey 1977, pp. 254–275.
Dolbeare, Kenneth, and Patricia Dolbeare (1976). *American Ideologies* (3rd ed.). Chicago: Markham.
Dollar, Bruce, and Thomas Parker (1977). "Students as producers of their own learning." *Social Policy,* 8:3, November-December, pp. 69–72.
Domhoff, G. William (1967). *Who Rules America?* Englewood Cliffs, NJ: Prentice-Hall.
―――― (1970). *The Higher Circles.* New York: Vintage.
―――― (1974a). "Blueprints for a new society." Ramparts, February, pp. 13–16.
―――― (1974b). *The Bohemian Grove and Other Retreats.* New York: Harper and Row.
―――― (1978a). *Who Really Rules?* New Brunswick, NJ: Transaction.
―――― (1978b). *The Powers That Be.* New York: Random House.
Douglass, Frederick (1855). *My Bondage and My Freedom.* New York: Dover, 1969.
Dowie, Mark (1977). "Pinto madness." *Mother Jones,* September–October.
―――― (1979). "The corporate crime of the century." *Mother Jones,* November.
Draper, Patricia (1975). "!Kung women: Contrasts in sexual egalitarianism in foraging and sedentary contexts." In Reiter 1975, pp. 77–109.
Dreier, Peter (1975). "Power structures and power struggles." *Insurgent Sociologist,* 5:3, Spring, pp. 233–44.
Dreyfuss, Joel (1978). "The new racism." *Black Enterprise,* January.
Drummond, Hugh (1980). "Playing doctor." *Mother Jones,* July, pp. 36–41.
Duberman, Lucille (1976). *Social Inequality.* Philadelphia: Lippincott.
Dumanoski, Dianne (1979). "The insidious killer called 'acid rain.'" *Boston Globe,* November 18, pp. A1–A2.
DuRand, Cliff (1979). "China: Workers' self-management." And "China battles unemployment." *Guardian,* December 12, p. 17; December 26, p. 16.
Dwyer, Timothy (1979). "Conversion: The despair of the elderly." *Boston Globe,* December 3, pp. 17, 19.

Edwards, Richard C., Michael Reich, and Thomas E. Weisskopf (eds.) (1978). *The Capitalist System* (2nd ed.). Englewood Cliffs, NJ: Prentice-Hall.
Edwards, R. Randle (1978). "Formal law begins a comeback in post-Mao China." *Contemporary China,* 2:2, Summer, pp. 92–102.
Ehrenreich, Barbara (1974). "Democracy in China." *Monthly Review,* 26:4, September, pp. 17–32.

_____, and John Ehrenreich (1970). *The American Health Empire.* New York: Vintage, 1971.
_____ (1977). "The professional-managerial class." *Radical America,* 11:2, March–April, pp. 7–32.
_____, and Deirdre English (1973). *Disorders and Complaints: The Sexual Politics of Sickness.* Old Westbury, NY: Feminist Press.
_____ (1978). *For Her Own Good.* Garden City, NY: Doubleday.
Ehrenreich, John (ed.) (1978). *The Cultural Crisis of Modern Medicine.* New York: Monthly Review Press.
Eitzen, D. Stanley (1980). *Social Problems.* Boston: Allyn and Bacon.
Elam, Frank (1979). "Chemical dumps: Legacy of greed." *Guardian,* May 2, p. 4.
_____ (1980). "Black youth unemployment—open secret." *Guardian,* March 12, p. 5.
Elrod, Marilyn (1978). "Comprehensive health service: An alternative answer to the health care crisis in the United States." In Raskin 1978, pp. 315–18.
England, Richard (1978). "Environmental gains going up in smoke." In URPE 1978, pp. 152–55.
Epstein, Samuel S. (1978). *The Politics of Cancer.* San Francisco: Sierra Club Books.
Erikson, Kai T. (1976). *Everything in Its Path.* New York: Simon and Schuster.
Ermann, M. David, and Richard Lundman (eds.) (1978). *Corporate and Governmental Deviance.* New York: Oxford.
Etra, Donald, and David Leinsdorf (1974). *Citibank.* New York: Grossman.
Ewen, Stuart (1976). *Captains of Consciousness.* New York: McGraw Hill.

Fallows, James (1975). "What did you do in the class war, daddy?" *Washington Monthly,* October, pp. 5–19.
Fan, K. H., and K. T. Fan (eds.) (1975). *From the Other Side of the River.* Garden City, NY: Doubleday-Anchor.
Feinberg, Walter, and Henry Rosemont, eds. (1975). *Work, Technology, and Education.* Urbana, Ill.: University of Illinois Press.
Feltman, John (1974a). "Food additives make problem children." *Organic Gardening and Farming,* 21:1, January, p. 111.
_____ (1974b). "Safe food—at a glance." *Organic Gardening and Farming,* 21:9, September, pp. 97–98.
Finke, Nikki (1979). "Street gangs growing problem for Soviets." *Boston Globe,* May 24, p. 2.
Firth, Raymond (1936). *We, The Tikopia.* Boston: Beacon Press, 1963.
Floss, Joe (1979). "N-plants: Stockpiles of disaster." *Guardian,* December 5, p. 7.
Frappier, Jon (1977). "Chase goes to Harlem." *Monthly Review,* 28:11, April, pp. 20–33.
Freeman, Jo (1970). "The building of the gilded cage." *Second Wave: A Magazine of the New Feminism,* 1:1, Spring. (Reprinted in Skolnick and Currie 1976.)
_____ (ed.) (1975). *Women: A Feminist Perspective.* Palo Alto, CA: Mayfield.
Freire, Paulo (1970). *Pedagogy of the Oppressed.* New York: Herder and Herder.
Freitag, Peter J. (1975). "The cabinet and big business." *Social Problems,* 23:2, December, pp. 137–52.
Freund, Ron (1979). "The politics of hunger." *Progressive,* December, pp. 38–39.
Frieden, Jeff (1977). "The trilateral commission: Economics and politics in the 1970's." *Monthly Review,* 29:7, December, pp. 1–17.

Friedenberg, Edgar Z. (1965). *Coming of Age in America.* New York: Vintage, 1967.
Friedman, Milton (1978). *The Economics of Freedom.* Pamphlet published by Standard Oil of Ohio.
Fromm, Erich (1955). *The Sane Society.* New York: Holt, Rinehart, and Winston. (Portion reprinted in Josephson 1962, pp. 56–73.)


Galaway, Burt (1977). "The use of restitution." *Crime and Delinquency,* 23:1, January, pp. 57–67.
Galbraith, John K. (1958). *The Affluent Society.* Boston: Houghton Mifflin.
Galdston, Ken (1978). "Poison in the Love Canal." *Progressive,* November, p. 43.
Galeano, Eduardo (1978). "Open veins of Latin America." *Monthly Review,* 30:7, December, pp. 12–35.
Gallaher, Art Jr. (1961). "Urbanizing influences on Plainville." In Olson 1963, pp. 187–204.
Galliher, John, and James McCartney (1977). *Criminology: Power, Crime, and Criminal Law.* Homewood, IL: Dorsey.
Galper, Miriam, and Carolyn Kot Washburne (1976). "A woman's self-help program in action." *Social Policy,* 6:5, March–April, pp. 46–52.
Gamberg, Ruth (1977). *Red and Expert.* New York: Schocken.
Gandy, Ross (1976). "More on the nature of Soviet society." *Monthly Review,* 27:10, March, pp. 11–14.
Gannon, James (1979). "The Pad V conspiracy." *Nation,* August 11–18, pp. 97, 113–116.
Gans, Herbert (1962). *The Urban Villagers.* New York: Free Press.
Garson, Barbara (1975). *All the Livelong Day: The Meaning and Demeaning of Routine Work.* New York: Penguin, 1977.
Garson, G. David (1975). "Worker participation in Europe in the 1970's." Unpublished paper.
Gartner, Alan, Colin Greer, and Frank Riessman (eds.) (1974). *The New Assault on Equality.* New York: Harper and Row (Perennial Library).
Gatto, Patricia (1979). "Town finding water contaminated." *Boston Globe,* June 3, pp. 25, 38.
Gedicks, Al (1977). "Raw materials: The Achilles heel of American imperialism." *Insurgent Sociologist,* 7:4, Fall, pp. 3–13.
Gentry, Margaret (1980). "The inner-city hospital battle." *Nation,* March 15, pp. 301–303.
Geschwender, James (1977). *Class, Race, and Worker Insurgency: The League of Revolutionary Black Workers.* New York: Cambridge.
Gitlin, Todd, and Nancy Hollander (1970). *Uptown: Poor Whites in Chicago.* New York: Harper and Row.
Goff, Kristin (1978). "More women in U.S. labor force." *Boston Globe,* June 5, p. 12.
Goffman, Erving (1959). *The Presentation of Self in Everyday Life.* Garden City, NY: Doubleday-Anchor.
Gold, Martin (1978). "Scholastic experience, self-esteem, and delinquent behavior: A theory for alternative schools." *Crime and Delinquency,* 24:3, pp. 290–308.
Gold, Michael (1930). *Jews Without Money.* New York: Avon, 1965.
Goodman, Al (1978). "Coming: Politics of cancer." *Boston Globe,* June 4, p. A2.
_____ (1979). "Farewell to the skilled worker." *Progressive,* January, pp. 36–37.

Good Tracks, Jimm G. (1973). "Native American non-interference." *Social Work,* 18:6, November, pp. 30–35.

Gordon, David (1973). "Capitalism, class, and crime in America." *Crime and Delinquency,* 19:1, April, pp. 163–186.

_____ (1975). "Recession is capitalism as usual." *New York Times Magazine,* April 27.

Gordon, Linda (1973). "The fourth mountain: Women in China." *Working Papers,* 1:3, Fall, pp. 27–39.

Gorelick, Sherry (1977). "Undermining hierarchy: Problems of schooling in capitalist America." *Monthly Review,* 29:5, October, pp. 20–36.

Green, Jim (1978). "Holding the line: Miners' militancy and the strike of 1978." *Radical America,* 12:3, May–June, pp. 3–27.

Greenbaum, Joan (1976). "Division of labor in the computer field." *Monthly Review,* 28:3, July–August, pp. 40–55.

Greene, Patricia (1979). "Visions of economic democracy." *New Roots,* 6, May–June, pp. 22–29.

_____, and Barbara Putnam (1980). "Heating your home with the sun." *New Roots,* 11, May–June, pp. 34–40.

Greenwood, Ray (1980). "Black rebellion engulfs Miami." *Guardian,* May 28, pp. 1, 6.

Greer, Colin (1972). *The Great School Legend: A Revisionist Interpretation of American Public Education.* New York: Penguin, 1976.

Greer, Edward (1976). "Racism and U.S. Steel, 1906–1974." *Radical America,* 10:5, September–October, pp. 45–64.

Greer, Scott (1958). "Individual participation in the mass society." In Olson 1963, pp. 327–336.

Greider, William (1978). "World energy 'crisis' disputed by some." *Boston Globe,* July 30, pp. 49–50.

Griffin, John Howard (1961). *Black Like Me.* New York: Signet, 1962.

Griffin, John P. (1978). "The job outlook in brief." *Occupational Handbook,* Spring, pp. 1–36.

Gross, Beatrice and Ronald Gross (eds.) (1977). *The Children's Rights Movement.* Garden City, NY: Doubleday.

Gross, Ronald and Paul Osterman (eds.) (1972). *The New Professionals.* New York: Simon and Schuster.

Grossman, Rachael (1980). "Women's place in the integrated circuit." *Radical America,* 14:1, January–February, pp. 29–50.

Guillette, Richard (1978). "A broken finger, four visits." *Boston Globe,* November 14, p. 18 (letter to the editor).

Gyllenhammer, Pehr (1977). "How Volvo adapts work to people." *Harvard Business Review,* July–August, pp. 102–113.

Haire, Doris (1978). "The cultural warping of childbirth." In John Ehrenreich 1978, pp. 182–200.

Hall, Jerome (1952). *Theft, Law and Society* (2nd ed.). Indianapolis: Bobbs-Merrill.

Hall, Richard H. (1975). *Occupations and the Social Structure* (2nd ed.). Englewood Cliffs, NJ: Prentice-Hall.

Hammond, Dorothy, and Alta Jablow (1976). *Women in Cultures of the World.* Reading, MA: Cummings.

*Handbook of Labor Statistics* (1977). U.S. Department of Labor, Bulletin 1966. Washington, D.C.: U.S. Government Printing Office.

Harring, Sidney (1976). "The development of the police institution." *Crime and Social Justice*, 5, Spring-Summer, pp. 54-59.

―――, and Lorraine McMullin (1975). "The Buffalo police 1872-1900: Labor unrest, political power, and the creation of the police institution." *Crime and Social Justice*, 4, Fall-Winter, pp. 5-14.

Harris, Michael (1979). "Getting the lead out." *Progressive*, October, p. 27.

Harrison, Barbara (1973). " 'Bestial until victory'—winning hearts and minds." *Nation*, January 22, pp. 117-19.

―――  (1974). *Unlearning the Lie: Sexism in School.* New York: Morrow.

Hartman, Chester (1978). "San Francisco's International Hotel: Case study of a turf struggle." *Radical America*, 12:3, May-June, pp. 47-58.

Helmreich, William B. (1973). "Black Crusaders: The rise and fall of political gangs." *Society*, 11:1, November-December, pp. 44-50.

Henry, Alan P. (1978). "Inner city rebuilding: The wealthy move in, the poor get pushed out." *Boston Globe*, August 21, pp. 1, 9.

Henry, Jules (1963). *Culture Against Man.* New York: Random House.

Herman, Peter (1974). "Workers, watches, and self-management." *Working Papers*, 1:4, Summer, pp. 18-25.

Herndon, James (1968). *The Way It Spozed to Be.* New York: Simon and Schuster.

Hicks, Nancy (1977). "Life after 65." *Black Enterprise*, May. (Reprinted in *Readings in Social Problems, 1978-79*. Guilford, CT: Dushkin, 1978, pp. 141-143.)

Higgins, Richard (1980). "New York's 45% school dropout rate called 'devastating.' " *Boston Globe*, January 10, p. 3.

Hill, Judah (1975). *Class Analysis.* San Francisco: Synthesis Publications.

Hinton, William (1972). *Turning Point in China: An Essay on the Cultural Revolution.* New York: Monthly Review Press.

Hoch, Nancy (1980). "Ford Motor Co. goes on trial for murder." *Guardian*, January 16, p. 6.

Hochschild, Arlie (1975). "Inside the clockwork of male careers." In Skolnick and Currie 1976, pp. 251-66.

Hoffman, Charles (1975). "Worker participation in Chinese factories." Second international conference on self-management, Cornell University, June 6-8.

Hoffman, William (1971). *David: Report on a Rockefeller.* New York: Dell, 1972.

Hollingshead, A. B. (1949). *Elmtown's Youth.* New York: Wiley.

Holstein, William J. (1978). "U.S. stake in Africa: Raw materials are key." *Boston Globe*, June 4, pp. 47, 50.

Holt, John (1964). *How Children Fail.* New York: Dell.

Hoos, Ida R. (1961). *Automation in the Office.* Washington, DC: Public Affairs Press.

Horowitz, David and David Kolodney (1969). "Charity begins at home." *Ramparts*, April, pp. 33-48.

Hoxha, Enver (1979). *Imperialism and the Revolution.* Tirana, Albania: "8 Nentori" Publishing House.

Huberman, Leo, and Paul Sweezy (1968). *Introduction to Socialism.* New York: Monthly Review Press.

Huebner, Albert (1977). "The environmental menace." *Nation*, September 10, pp. 218-20.

\_\_\_\_\_ (1978). "Childhood's hidden epidemic." *Nation,* March 4, pp. 242–44.
Hunnius, Gerry, G. David Garson, and John Case (eds.) (1973). *Workers' Control.* New York: Vintage.
Hunter, Allen, and Linda Gordon (1979). "Feminism, Leninism, and the U.S.: A comment." *Radical America,* 13:5, September–October, pp. 29–36.

Illich, Ivan (1975). *Medical Nemesis.* New York: Pantheon.
Institute for Social Research (1978). "Earnings advantage enjoyed by white males not explained by differences in qualifications." *Institute for Social Research* newsletter, Spring, p. 7.
\_\_\_\_\_ (1979). "Deepening distrust of political leaders is jarring public's faith in institutions." *Institute for Social Research* newsletter, Autumn, pp. 4–5.
Intelligence Report (1978). "Carter and his Harvardians." *Parade* (*Boston Sunday Globe*), May 14, p. 18.
Iwańska, Alicia (1962). "Without love for the land." In Olson 1963, pp. 205–19.

Jackson, George (1970). *Soledad Brother.* New York: Bantam.
Jacobs, Berry (1980). "The poisoned land." *Progressive,* July, pp. 43–47.
Jacobs, Paul, and Saul Landau (1971). *To Serve the Devil* (2 vols.) New York: Vintage.
Jacoby, Neil H. (1971). "What's a social problem?" *Center Magazine,* July–August, pp. 35–40.
Jalée, Pierre (1968). *The Pillage of the Third World.* New York: Monthly Review Press.
Jenkins, David (1973). *Job Power.* Baltimore: Penguin, 1974.
Jin Zhou (1979). "Housing China's 900 million people." *Beijing Review,* November 30, pp. 17–27.
Johnson, Beverly, and Howard Hayghe (1977). "Labor force participation of married women, March 1976." *Monthly Labor Review,* June, pp. 32–36.
Johnson, Elmer H. (1973). *Social Problems of Urban Man.* Homewood, Ill.: Dorsey.
Jordan, Robert A. (1977). "Jobs for youth needed to avert violence." *Boston Globe,* April 27, p. 19.
Josephson, Eric, and Mary Josephson (eds.) (1962). *Man Alone: Alienation in Modern Society.* New York: Dell.
Julian, Joseph (1977). *Social Problems* (2nd ed.). Englewood Cliffs, NJ: Prentice-Hall.

Kagan, Jerome (1974). "What is intelligence?" In Gartner *et al.,* 1974, pp. 114–130.
Kamin, Leon (1974). "The science and politics of I.Q." *Social Research,* Autumn, pp. 387–425.
Kapp, Robert (translator) (1978). "Documentation, chronology, and bibliography" [of crimes and punishment in China]. *Contemporary China,* 2:2, Summer, pp. 103–118.
Karabel, Jerome (1972). "Community colleges and social stratification." *Harvard Educational Review,* 42, November, pp. 521–62 (Reprinted in Useem and Useem 1974, pp. 117–45.)
\_\_\_\_\_, and A. H. Halsey (eds.) (1977). *Power and Ideology in Education.* New York: Oxford.
Katz, Alfred, and Eugene Bender (eds.) (1976). *The Strength in U.S.: Self Help in the Modern World.* New York: New Viewpoints.

Katz, Michael (1968). *The Irony of Early School Reform.* Cambridge, MA: Harvard University Press.
Katz, Tonnie (1976). "The rising tide of school crime." *Boston Globe,* May 23, p. 3.
Kelley, Kevin (1979). "U.S. prepares 'quick-strike force.' " *Guardian,* December 19, pp. 1, 3.
_____ (1980). "The U.S. blockade and Cuba's emigres." *Guardian,* June 11, p. 17.
Kellogg, Mary (1974). "Hawaii without the pineapple." *Nation,* March 16, pp. 338–340.
Kenney, Michael (1978). "Youths earn money to pay back victims." *Boston Globe,* May 7, p. 3.
_____ and Jerry Taylor (1976). "Gangs on the corners, strife in the streets." *Boston Globe,* September 5, p. 11.
Killian, Michael (1979). "The paraphernalia of the rich." *Boston Globe,* October 8, p. 68.
Kimble, Joseph (1970). "Night thoughts of a police chief." *Nation,* April 27, pp. 490–492.
Kinloch, Graham (1979). *The Sociology of Minority Group Relations.* Englewood Cliffs, NJ: Prentice-Hall.
Kinzer, Stephen (1980). "Cuba: All talk is of exodus." *Boston Globe,* May 25, p. 6.
Kirchheimer, Anne (1978). "Working women and sexual harassment." *Boston Globe,* December 7, p. 33.
Klare, Michael (1975). "Rent-a-cop: The boom in private police." *Nation,* November 15, pp. 486–91.
_____ (1980). "Is Exxon worth dying for?" *Progressive,* July, pp. 21–26.
Klaw, Spencer (1975). *The Great American Medicine Show.* New York: Penguin.
Knight, Michael (1980). "Pollution is an old neighbor in Massachusetts town." *New York Times,* May 16, p. A16.
Knox, Richard (1977). "Medical study finds an 'excessive death zone' covering central Boston, other sections of the city." *Boston Globe,* June 9, pp. 1, 16.
_____ (1978). "The killer that came home with the paycheck." *Boston Globe,* July 14, p. 3.
Kohl, Herbert (1967). *36 Children.* New York: Signet, 1968.
Kohn, Howard (1978). "The government's quiet war on scientists who know too much." *Rolling Stone,* March 23, pp. 42–44.
Kolko, Gabriel (1963). *The Triumph of Conservatism.* Chicago: Quandrangle, 1967.
Kolko, Joyce (1974). *America and the Crisis of World Capitalism.* Boston: Beacon.
Kotelchuck, David (ed.) (1976). *Prognosis Negative: Crisis in the Health Care System.* New York: Vintage.
Kotelchuck, Ronda (1978). "Health cost control strategies: futile monitors." In URPE 1978, pp. 205–209.
Kotulak, Ronald (1977). "Are doctors ripping us off?" *Boston Globe,* February 13, p. A3.
Kozol, Jonathan (1967). *Death at an Early Age.* Boston: Houghton Mifflin.
_____ (1972). *Free Schools.* Boston: Houghton Mifflin.
_____ (1978a). "Revolution still alive for children of Cuba." *Boston Globe,* August 6, pp. A1, A4.
_____ (1978b). *Children of the Revolution.* New York: Delacorte.
Krause, Elliott (1971). *The Sociology of Occupations.* Boston: Little, Brown.
Krisberg, Barry, and James Austin (eds.) (1978). *The Children of Ishmael: Critical Perspectives on Juvenile Justice.* Palo Alto, CA: Mayfield.

———, and Paul Takagi (1978). "Ethical issues in evaluating criminal justice demonstration projects." In Krisberg and Austin 1978, pp. 454-63.
Ku, Richard and Carol Blew (1977). *The Adolescent Diversion Project.* Washington, DC: Government Printing Office (for LEAA).

Lacefield, Patrick (1979). "Cut hospitals on critical list." *Seven Days,* August 14, pp. 9, 10, 34.
Lall, Sanjaya (1977). "Medicines and multinationals." *Monthly Review,* 28:10, March, pp. 19-30.
Lamb, Robert (1980). " 'We'll sell where we can.' " *Boston Globe,* March 30, p. A3.
Lander, Louise (1978). "National Health Insurance." In Raskin 1978, pp. 287-313
Landis, Judson R. (1977). *Sociology* (3rd ed.). Belmont, CA: Wadsworth.
Lane, David (1971). *The End of Inequality?* Baltimore: Penguin.
Langer, Elinor (1970). "The women of the Telephone Company." *New York Review of Books,* March 12, pp. 16, 18, 20-24; March 26, pp. 14, 15-21.
Langner, Paul (1979). "1200 protest chemical dump in East Taunton." *Boston Globe,* June 3, pp. 25, 37.
Lansford, Henry (1979). "Acid from the sky." *Mosaic,* July-August.
Lappé, Frances Moore, and Joseph Collins (1977). *Food First: Beyond the Myth of Scarcity.* Boston: Houghton Mifflin.
Larkin, Al, and Jerry Taylor (1978). "The street corner generation." *Boston Globe,* July 9-12 (Parts 1-4).
Lasch, Christopher (1977). "The siege of the family." *New York Review of Books,* November 24 (Reprinted in *Sociology 79/80.* Guilford, CT: Dushkin, 1979, pp. 154-57.)
Lasch, Robert (1980). "War fever." *Progressive,* July, pp. 14-18.
Lasson, Kenneth (1971). *The Workers.* New York: Bantam.
Law Enforcement Assistance Administration (1974). *Citizen Dispute Settlement.* Washington, DC: U.S. Government Printing Office.
Lawler, Edward (1977). "Workers can get their own wages—responsibly." *Psychology Today,* February, pp. 109-111.
Lederer, Edith (1978). "In China, a new luxury." *Boston Globe,* August 18, pp. 1, 10.
Lee, Dorothy (1959). *Freedom and Culture.* Englewood Cliffs, NJ: Prentice-Hall.
Lee, Richard B. (1969). "Eating Christmas in the Kalahari." *Natural History Magazine,* December, pp. 14ff.
Lefcourt, Robert (ed.) (1971). *Law Against the People.* New York: Vintage.
Leiken, Robert (1979). "On China since Mao." *Monthly Review,* 31:1, May, pp. 34-44.
Lens, Sidney (1979). "On the contradictions of socialism." *Progressive,* March, pp. 24-26.
——— (1980). "Hot cargo: The growing menace of nuclear transportation." *Progressive,* June, pp. 29-31.
Lenski, Gerhard (1966). *Power and Privilege.* New York: McGraw-Hill.
Leon, Carol, and Robert Bednarzik (1978). "Profile of women on part-time schedules." *Monthly Labor Review,* October, pp. 3-12.
Lessinger, Hanna (1979). "Doctors: Treatment sexist." *Guardian,* June 13, p. 10.
Levey, Robert (1976). "The 13 steps of metro Hub's social ladder." *Boston Globe,* February 22, p. B2.
——— (1978a). "Why a Northern Cheyenne tribe said no to a coal mining plan on its reservation." *Boston Globe,* September 3, p. 21.

_____ (1978b). "I want my kids out of here." *Boston Globe,* December 10, pp. 1, 9; December 11, p. 2.

Levin, Henry (1971). "The case for community control of the schools." In Carnoy 1972, pp. 193–210.

Levin, Myron (1977). "Steering OSHA back on course." *Boston Globe,* June 25, p. 15.

Levison, Andrew (1974). *The Working-Class Majority.* Baltimore: Penguin, 1975.

Lewin, Leonard (1978). "Publishing goes multinational." *Nation,* May 13, pp. 567–70.

Ley, Camara (1954). *The Dark Child.* New York: Farrar, Straus, and Giroux.

Li, Victor (1973). "Law and penology: Systems of reform and corrections." *Proceedings of the Academy of Political Science,* 31:1, March, pp. 144–56.

Liazos, Alexander (1972). "The poverty of the sociology of deviance: Nuts, sluts, and preverts." *Social Problems,* 20:1, Summer, pp. 103–120.

_____ (1974). "Class oppression: The functions of juvenile justice." *Insurgent Sociologist,* 5:1, Fall, pp. 2–23.

_____ (1978). "School, alienation, and delinquency." *Crime and Delinquency,* 24:3, July, pp. 355–70.

Liebow, Elliot (1967). *Tally's Corner.* Boston: Little, Brown.

Lipinski, Ann Marie (1979). "Working women... the struggle goes on." *Boston Globe,* May 29, p. 29.

Litwak, Eugene, and Ivan Szelenyi (1969). "Primary group structures and their functions: Kin, neighbors, and friends." *American Sociological Review,* 34:4, August, pp. 465–81.

Longcope, Kay (1977). "Young offenders working things out." *Boston Globe,* November 12, p. 3.

Longo, Tony (with John C. Raines) (1978). "The view from below." *Christianity and Crisis,* April 17, pp. 88–92.

López y Rivas, Gilberto (1973). *The Chicanos.* New York: Monthly Review Press.

Lotta, Raymond (ed.) (1978). *And Mao Makes 5.* Chicago: Banner Press.

Lowe, Mary Johnson (1978). "The trial of Ran Kao-chien." *Juris Doctor, 8:4, April,* pp. 12–16.

*Lundman, Richard J., and Frank R. Scarpitti (1978).* "Delinquency prevention: Recommendations for future projects." *Crime and Delinquency,* 24:2, April, pp. 207–220.

Lydon, Christopher (1977). "Jimmy Carter revealed: He's a Rockefeller Republication." *Atlantic Monthly,* July, pp. 50–57.

Lynch, James (1977). *The Broken Heart: The Medical Consequences of Loneliness.* New York: Basic Books.

Lynd, Robert, and Helen Lynd (1929). *Middletown.* New York: Harcourt, Brace.

_____ (1937). *Middletown in Transition.* New York: Harcourt, Brace.

Lynd, Staughton (1973). "Blue-collar organizing." *Working Papers,* 1:1, Spring, pp. 28–32.


McAfee, Kathy (1979). "City life: Lessons of the first five years." *Radical America,* 13:1, January–February, pp. 39–59.

McCaghy, Charles (1980). *Crime in American Society.* New York: Macmillan.

McCain, Nina (1978a). "Criminals: Doing good instead of time." *Boston Globe,* October 22, pp. A1, A4.

_____ (1978b). "Medical school and student in confrontation." *Boston Globe*, October 29, p. 33.

McCarthy, Terence (1974). "An age of scarcity: Oil is only the beginning." *Ramparts*, May, pp. 28–32, 53–54.

_____ (1975). "Capitalism in one country?" *Ramparts*, May–June, pp. 32–36.

Maccoby, Michael (1975). "Changing work: The Bolivar project." *Working Papers*, 3:2, Summer, pp. 48–55.

McCord, Joan (1978). "A thirty-year follow-up of treatment effects." *American Psychologist*, 33:5, March, pp. 284–89.

MacEwan, Arthur (1976). "Capitalist expansion and the sources of imperialism." In Edwards et al., 1978, pp. 481–92.

_____ (1979). "On China since Mao." *Monthly Review*, 31:1, May, pp. 44–48.

McKinlay, John (1978). "On the medical-industrial complex." *Monthly Review*, 30:5, October, pp. 38–42.

McLean, Deckle (1975). "Volvo brings 'team' idea to the land of assembly line." *Boston Globe*, June 30, p. 28.

McLuhan, T. C. (1971). *Touch the Earth: A Self-Portrait of Indian Existence*. New York: Pocket Books, 1972.

McMahon, Bob (1979). "U.S. nukes safer than Soviet plants." *Guardian*, June 20, p. 20.

McManus, John F. (1977). "Does U.S. really have an energy shortage?" *Boston Globe*, May 5, p. 19.

McMillan, Gary (1980). "To be old, cold, hungry." *Boston Globe*, May 22, pp. 1, 28.

McNall, Scott G. (1975). *Social Problems Today*. Boston: Little, Brown.

McNamara, Robert S. (1977). "A world crisis that won't go away." *Boston Globe*, January, 9, pp. A1, A3.

Magdoff, Harry (1969). *The Age of Imperialism*. New York: Monthly Review Press.

_____ (1977). "How to make a molehill out of a mountain." *Insurgent Sociologist*, 7:2, Spring, pp. 106–112.

_____ (1979). 'The U.S. dollar, petro-dollars, and U.S. imperialism." *Monthly Review*, 30:8, January, pp. 1–13.

Malcolm X (1965). *The Autobiography of Malcolm X*. New York: Grove Press, 1966.

Mann, Fred (1978). "Solar energy is a reality in California homes, commerce." *Boston Globe*, November 12, pp. 65, 70.

Marable, Manning (1978). "Thoughts on the political economy of the new South since the civil rights movement." *Radical America*, 12:5, September–October, pp. 9–21.

Marden, Charles, and Gladys Meyer (1978). *Minorities in American Society* (5th ed.). New York: D. Van Nostrand.

Marine, Gene (1973). "Scoreboard on the environment." *Ramparts*, December, pp. 18–20.

Marquit, Erwin (1978). *The Socialist Countries*. Minneapolis: Marxist Educational Press.

Martell, George (1970). "High school: No place to find who you are." In Satu Repo (ed.), *This Book Is About Schools*. New York: Vintage, 1970, pp. 94–114.

Massey, Thomas (1978). "China and India and me." *Washington Monthly*, March, pp. 45–50.

Mathews, Jay (1979a). "Hunan assails Deng for straying too far." *Boston Globe*, May 29, p. 8.

_____ (1979b). "Economic discontent gnaws at China's worker." *Boston Globe*, July 16, p. 8.
_____ (1979c). "Privilege in China—a new scandal." *Boston Globe*, August 30, p. 3.
Mattera, Philip (1979). "Hot child in the city." *Radical America*, September-October, pp. 49-60.
Mead, Margaret (1935). *Sex and Temperament in Three Primitive Societies.* New York: Morrow.
Meier, August, and Elliott Rudwick (1970). *From Plantation to Ghetto.* New York: Hill and Wang.
Miller, Wayne (ed.) (1972). *A Gathering of Ghetto Writers.* New York: New York University Press.
Millman, Marcia (1977). *The Unkindest Cut.* New York: Morrow.
Mills, C. Wright (1956). *The Power Elite.* New York: Oxford.
Mills, Susan (1980). "Voices from Three Mile Island." *Progressive,* June, pp. 16-24.
Mintz, Beth (1975). "The president's cabinet 1897-1972: A contribution to the power structure debate." *Insurgent Sociologist,* 5:3, Spring, pp. 131-48.
Mitchell, John (1980). "The Bedford syndrome." *Massachusetts Audubon,* 19:4, January, pp. 3-6.
Mitchell, Juliet (1971). *Women's Estate.* New York: Pantheon. (Parts reprinted in Skolnick and Currie 1976, pp. 198-215.)
Molotsky, Irvin (1980). "Damage to chromosomes found in Love Canal tests." *New York Times,* May 17, pp. 1, 28.
*Monthly Review* Editors (1977). "Notes from the editors." *Monthly Review,* 28:10, March.
Moore, Taylor G. (1980). "Nuclear casualty." *The Progressive,* May, pp. 32-33.
Morris, David (1978). "Energy, democracy, and the Carter energy plan." In Raskin 1978, pp. 265-86.
Morris, Robert (1977). "Jimmy Carter's ruling class." *Harper's,* October, pp. 37-45.
Moss, Ralph W. (1980). "The cancer establishment." *Progressive,* February, pp. 14-18.
Mostert, Noel (1974). *Supership.* New York: Knopf.
Munson, Richard (1979). "Ripping off the sun: Big business moves in on solar power." *Progressive,* September, pp. 12-15.
*Myths and Realities About Crime* (1978). U.S. Department of Justice, LEAA.

Nader, Ralph, and Ronald Brownstein (1980). "Beyond the Love Canal." *Progressive,* March, pp. 28-31.
Nadler, Eric (1980a). "Chemical garbage strewn across U.S." *Guardian,* June 11, p. 5.
_____ (1980b). "Burger giants give help a raw deal." *Guardian,* June 11, p. 8.
Navarro, Vincente (1976). "The fetishism of industrialization: A critique of Ivan Illich." *Monthly Review,* 28:5, October, pp. 36-46.
Nelson, Harold (1967). "The defenders: A case study of an informal police organization." *Social Problems,* 14:2, Fall, pp. 124-47.
Nettler, Gwynn (1976). *Social Concerns.* New York: McGraw-Hill.
*New Albania* (1979). "Facts and figures about Albania." (Published in Tirana, Albania.) No. 2, p. 17.
Newfield, Jack (1973). "Lindsay and the developers: Rape of the cityscape." *Village Voice,* January 19, p. 1.

———, and Paul DuBrul (1977). *The Abuse of Power: The Permanent Government and the Fall of New York.* New York: Viking.
Nichols, David (1974). *Financing Elections: The Politics of an American Ruling Class.* New York: New Viewpoints.
Noble, David (1979). "The chemistry of risk." *Seven Days,* June 5, pp. 23–26, 34.
Norbeck, Edward (1971). "Men at Play." *Natural History Magazine,* December, pp. 48–53.
Novak, Jeremiah (1977). "The trilateral connection." *Atlantic Monthly,* July, pp. 57–59.

O'Brien, Jim (1977–78). "American Leninism in the 1970's." *Radical America,* 11:6 and 12:1, November–February, pp. 27–62.
Ohlin, Lloyd E., Alden D. Miller, and Robert B. Coates (no date, probably 1977). *Juvenile Correctional Reform in Massachusetts.* Washington, DC: U.S. Government Printing Office (for LEAA).
Olson, Philip (ed.) (1963). *America as a Mass Society.* New York: Free Press.
O'Reilly, Jane (1980). "In Manhattan: Mink is no four-letter word." *Time,* February 18, p. 6.
Orleans, Leo, and Richard Suttmeier (1970). "The Mao ethic and environmental quality." *Science,* 170, December 11, pp. 1173–76.
Ouyang, Hyiyun (1979). "Marked results in China's most populous province." *Beijing Review,* November 16, pp. 22–24.

Packard, Vance (1972). *A Nation of Strangers.* New York: McKay.
Parenti, Michael (1979). "Radical decade." *Nation,* December 8, pp. 580–81.
Patinkin, Mark (1979). "The fight of his life." *Boston Globe,* April 8, pp. 25, 38.
Patry, Bill (1978). "Taylorism comes to the social services." *Monthly Review,* 30:5, October, pp. 30–37.
Payer, Cheryl (1976). "Third world debt problems." *Monthly Review,* 28:4, September, pp. 1–19.
Pelletier, Wilfred (1970). "Childhood in an Indian village." In Satu Repo (ed.), *This Book Is About Schools.* New York: Vintage, 1970, pp. 18–31.
Pepinsky, Harold (1978). "On the correct handling of contradictions." *Juris Doctor,* 8:4, April, pp. 16–22.
Perelman, Michael, and Hugh Gardner (1975). "Hidden dimensions of the energy crisis." In Barnes 1975, pp. 122–24.
Petras, James F. (1977). "Chile and Latin America." *Monthly Review,* 28:9, February, pp. 13–24.
——— (1979a). "Political change, class conflict, and the decline of Latin American fascism." *Monthly Review,* 31:2, June, pp. 26–37.
——— (1979b). "Whither the Nicaraguan revolution?" *Monthly Review,* 31:5, October, pp. 1–22.
———, and James Morley (1975). *The United States and Chile: Imperialism and the Overthrow of the Allende Government.* New York: Monthly Review Press.
Pfeffer, Richard M. (1973). "Leaders and masses." *Proceedings of the Academy of Political Science,* 31:1, March, pp. 157–74.
——— (1979). *Working for Capitalism.* New York: Columbia University Press.
Phelps, Robert (1978). "One man updates his Shanghai notebook." *Boston Globe,* January 11, pp. 1–2.

Pincus, Fred (1974). "Tracking in community colleges." *Insurgent Sociologist,* 4:3, Spring, pp. 22-35.
Pine, Art (1980). "U.S. unemployment rate soars." *Boston Globe,* June 7, pp. 1, 9.
Pinkney, Alphonso (1975). *Black Americans* (2nd ed.). Englewood Cliffs, NJ: Prentice-Hall.
Piven, Frances Pox, and Richard Cloward (1971). *Regulating the Poor: The Functions of Public Welfare.* New York: Vintage.
Plaste, Richard, Georgie Dullea, and Angela Taylor (1974). "Low income: Getting by becomes still more difficult; Middle income: the fun is gone; High income: Time to take note of the grocery bill." *New York Times,* February 14.
Platt, Anthony (1978). "Street crime—a view from the left." *Crime and Social Justice,* 9, Spring-Summer, pp. 26-34.
Pollard, Gayle (1979). "Life with toxic wastes." *Boston Globe,* May 13, pp. 68, 73.
Pollin, Robert (1980). "The multinational mineral industry in crisis." *Monthly Review,* 31:11, April, pp. 25-38.
Popenoe, David (1974, 1977). *Sociology* (2nd and 3rd eds.). Englewood Cliffs, NJ: Prentice-Hall.
Primack, Phil (1977). "The great strip mine flood." *Nation,* June 4, pp. 691-92.

Quinney, Richard (1974). *Critique of Legal Order.* Boston: Little, Brown.
_____ (1977). *Class, State, and Crime.* New York: McKay.

Radin, Paul (1953). *The World of Primitive Man.* New York: Grove Press, 1960.
*Ramparts* editors (1970). *Eco-Catastrophe.* New York: Harper and Row.
Raskin, A. H. (1977). "The heresy of worker participation." *Psychology Today,* February, p. 111.
Raskin, Marcus (ed.) (1978). *The Federal Budget and Social Reconstruction.* New Brunswick, NJ: Transaction.
Reddick, L. D. (1976). "Black history as a corporate colony." *Social Policy,* 7:1, May-June, pp. 36-40.
Regal, Kim C. (1976). "Bad days on the reservation." *Nation,* November 20, pp. 525-30.
Reich, Michael (1972). "Economic theories of Racism." In Carnoy 1972, pp. 67-69.
Reiman, Jeffrey (1979). *The Rich Get Richer and the Poor Get Prison.* New York: Wiley.
Reiter, Rayna (ed.) (1975). *Toward an Anthropology of Women.* New York: Monthly Review Press.
Renaud, Marc (1975). "On the structural constraints to state intervention in health." In Ehrenreich 1978, pp. 101-120.
Reuter (1978). "Some Chinese excused from labor." *Boston Globe,* November 11, p. 41.
Rich, Cynthia Jo (1976). "Young, black, and no place to go." *Nation,* May 15, pp. 592-95.
Rich, Spencer (1980). "Financial power in the U.S. interlocked, study says." *Boston Globe,* May 3, p. 45.
Richards, Bill (1978). "Company files tell of asbestos danger coverup." *Boston Globe,* November 13, p. 44.
Richards, Carol, and Jonathan Rowe (1977). "Restoring the city: Who pays the price?" *Working Papers,* 4:4, Winter, pp. 54-61.

Ridgeway, Jim (1979). "The local approach to energy options." *Boston Globe*, August 19, pp. A1, A2.

Robinson, Joan (1979). "On China since Mao." *Monthly Review*, 31:1, May, pp. 48–56.

Rodriguez, Richard (1975). "On becoming a Chicano." *Saturday Review*, February 8, pp. 46–48.

Roose, Diana (1975). "Top dogs and top brass: An inside look at a government advisory committee." *Insurgent Sociologist*, 5:3, Spring, pp. 53–63.

Rose, Arnold (1967). *The Power Structure.* New York: Oxford.

Rose, Thomas (ed.) (1969). *Violence in America.* New York: Vintage.

Rosenbaum, Walter (1977). *The Politics of Environmental Concern* (2nd ed.) New York: Praeger.

Rosenthal, Robert, and Lenore Jacobson (1968). *Pygmalion in the Classroom.* New York: Holt, Rinehart, and Winston.

Rosenthal, Robert J. (1979). "Water: An endangered species." *Boston Globe*, September 9, 10, and 11.

Roth, Julius (1965). "Hired hand research." *American Sociologist*, 1:1, November, pp. 190–96.

Rowbotham, Sheila (1979). "The women's movement and organizing for socialism." *Radical America*, 13:5, September–October, pp. 9–28.

Rowen, James (1972). "Conglomerate beef: Greyhound steak, sauce oppenheimer." *Nation*, June 5, pp. 714–19.

Ruben, Albert (1976). "The anachronism of the work ethic." *Monthly Review*, 27:8, January, pp. 61–64.

Rubin, Lillian Breslow (1976). *Worlds of Pain: Life in the Working-Class Family.* New York: Basic Books.

Ryan, William (1971, 1976). *Blaming the Victim.* New York: Vintage.


Sacks, Karen (1976). "Class roots of feminism." *Monthly Review*, 27:9, February, pp. 28–48.

Salas, Luis (1978). "Popular courts in Cuba." Unpublished paper.

―――― (1979). "Juvenile delinquency in postrevolutionary Cuba." *Cuban Studies*, 9:1, January, pp. 43–56.

Satchell, Michael (1979). "Superbugs: A new biblical plague." *Parade (Boston Sunday Globe)*, September 30, pp. 8–9.

Sattel, Jack (1978). "Harry Braverman's sociology of work." *Insurgent Sociologist*, 8:1, Winter, pp. 35–40.

Sawyers, Larry (1977). "Urban planning in the USSR and China." *Monthly Review*, 28:10, March, pp. 34–48.

Scheier, Ronni (1980). "Arson epidemic spreads like wildfire." *Guardian*, April 2, p. 6.

Schrag, Peter (1978). *Mind Control.* New York: Pantheon.

―――― , and Diane Divoky (1975). *The Myth of the Hyperactive Child.* New York: Pantheon.

Schumacher, E. F. (1973). *Small Is Beautiful.* New York: Harper and Row.

Schurman, Frantz, and Sandy Close (1979). "The emergence of Global City, U.S.A." *Progressive*, January, pp. 27–29.

Schwartz, Janet S. (1979). "Women under socialism: Role definitions of Soviet women." *Social Forces*, 58:1, September, pp. 67–88.

Schwerin, Jules (1979). "Piled high and deep." *Seven Days,* October 26, pp. 22-24.
Scobel, Donald N. (1975). "Doing away with the factory blues." *Harvard Business Review,* November-December, pp. 132-42.
Scull, Andrew (1977). *Decarceration.* Englewood Cliffs, NJ: Prentice-Hall.
Seifer, Nancy (1976). *Nobody Speaks for Me: Self-Portraits of American Working-Class Women.* New York: Simon and Schuster.
Selden, Mark (1979). "China's uninterrupted revolution." *Monthly Review,* 31:5, October, pp. 34-36.
Sexton, Patricia Cayo (1961). *Education and Income.* New York: Viking.
Shabecoff, Philip (1979). "U.S. urged to lead drive to control fluorocarbons." *New York Times,* December 22, p. 44.
Shaiken, Harley (1979). "Numerical control of work: Workers and automation in the computer age." *Radical America,* 13:6, November-December, pp. 25-39.
Shaw, Nancy (1974). *Forced Labor.* New York: Pergamon.
Sherrill, Robert (1973). "Invisible empires: The multinationals deploy to rule." *Nation,* April 16, pp. 488-95.
Sidel, Ruth (1974). *Families of Fengsheng: Urban Life in China.* Baltimore: Penguin.
────── (1976). "Self-help and mutual aid in the People's Republic of China." In Katz and Bender 1976, pp. 216-28.
Sidel, Victor, and Ruth Sidel (1974). *Serve the People.* Boston: Beacon.
Singer, Max, and Paul Bracken (1976). "Should rich nations take the blame for poverty in others?" *Boston Herald American,* November 17, pp. A1, A5.
Skolnick, Richard, and Elliott Currie (eds.) (1976). *Crisis in American Institutions* (3rd ed.). Boston: Little, Brown.
Smith, Ruth Bayard (1979). "No money for oil, but N.H. family can't get fuel aid." *Boston Globe,* December 9, pp. 1, 29.
Smoot, Bill (1977). "Life on the job." *Nation,* July 23, pp. 81-84.
Snell, Bradford (1973). "American ground transport." In Skolnick and Currie 1976, pp. 304-26.
Solomon, Norman (1979). "Nagasaki's other victims." *Progressive,* July, pp. 21-27.
────── (1980). "Nuclear big brother." *Progressive,* January, pp. 14-21.
Sonquist, John, and Thomas Koenig (1975). "Interlocking directorates in the top U.S. corporations." *Insurgent Sociologist,* 5:3, Spring, pp. 196-230.
Spector, Malcolm, and John I. Kitsuse (1977). *Constructing Social Problems.* Reading, MA: Cummings.
Speiglman, Richard (1977). "Prison psychiatrists and drugs: A case study." *Crime and Social Justice,* 7, Spring-Summer, pp. 23-39.
Spitzer, Stephen, and Andrew Scull (1977). "Privatization and capitalist development: The case of the private police." *Social Problems,* 25:1, October, pp. 18-29.
Spotlight (1979). "Blacks receive stiffer sentences." *Boston Globe,* April 4, pp. 1, 50, 51.
Spradley, James, and Brenda Mann (1975). *The Cocktail Waitress.* New York: Wiley.
Spring, Joel (1975). *A Primer of Libertarian Education.* New York: Free Life Editions.
Starr, Paul (1976). "The politics of therapeutic nihilism." *Working Papers* 4:2, Summer, pp. 48-55.
────── (1977). "A coming doctor surplus?" *Working Papers,* 4:4, Winter, pp. 18-19, 100-102.

States News Service (1980). "Study shows jobs scarce for youths." *Boston Globe,* March 1, p. 3.
*Statistical Abstract of the United States (1977, 1979).* U.S. Department of Commerce, Bureau of the Census. Washington, DC: U.S. Government Printing Office.
Stein, Maurice (1960). *The Eclipse of Community.* Princeton, NJ: Princeton University Press.
Steinberg, Jon (1978). "China's cultural counterrevolution." *Seven Days,* September 29, pp. 30–32.
Steiner, Stan (1976). *The Vanishing White Man.* New York: Harper and Row.
Stern, Gerald M. (1976). *The Buffalo Creek Disaster: The Story of the Survivors' Unprecedented Lawsuit.* New York: Random House.
Stern, Philip (1972). *The Rape of the Taxpayer.* New York: Random House.
Sternglass, Ernest (1980). "Three-Mile Island fallout." *Boston Globe,* March 23, p. A3.
Stevenson, Paul (1974). "Monopoly capital and inequalities in Sweden." *Insurgent Sociologist,* 5:1, Fall, pp. 41–58.
Stranahan, Eileen (1976). "Why 115,000 workers will die this year." *Boston Globe,* March 21, pp. A1, A4.
Stretch, Bonnie Barrett (1972). "The rise of the 'free school.'" In Carnoy 1972, pp. 211–223.
Strobel, Lee (1979). "Ford study: Price tag on human lives." *Boston Globe,* October 14, pp. 65, 70.
Subcommittee on Oversight and Investigations (of the U.S. House Committee on Interstate and Foreign Commerce) (1976). *Cost and Quality of Health Care: Unnecessary Surgery.* Washington, DC: U.S. Government Printing Office.
Suhor, Mary Lou (1980). "Cuba pays its 'debt to humanity.'" *Progressive,* July, pp. 38–42.
Sun Chief (Leo Simmons [ed.]) (1942). *Sun Chief: The Autobiography of a Hopi Indian.* (Parts reprinted in James Spradley and George McDonough [eds.], *Anthropology Through Literature.* Boston: Little, Brown, 1973.)
Sung Ching-Ling (1975). "Women's liberation in China." In Fan and Fan 1975, pp. 32–36.
Supek, Rudi (1975). "Problems and experiences of Yugoslav workers' self-management." Second International Conference on Self-Management, Cornell University, June 6–8.
*Survey of Inmates of Local Jails* (no date). Washington, DC: U.S. Department of Justice. LEAA.
Swados, Harvey (1957). "The myth of the happy worker." In Josephson 1962, pp. 105–114.
———— (1959). "The miners: Men without work." In Olson 1963, pp. 232–243.
Swanson, Charles (ed.) (1978). *Focus: Unexplored Deviance.* Guilford, CT: Dushkin.
Sweezy, Paul (1951). "The American ruling class." *Monthly Review,* May–June. (Reprinted in Maurice Zeitlin [ed.], *American Society, Inc.* Chicago: Markham, 1970, pp. 356–71.
———— (1969). "Thoughts on the American system." *Monthly Review,* February.
———— (1977). "Theory and practice in the Mao period." *Monthly Review,* 28:9, February, pp. 1–12.
———— (1978). "Is there a ruling class in the USSR?" *Monthly Review,* 30:5, October, pp. 1–17.

_____ (1979). "On the new global disorder." *Monthly Review*, 30:11, April, pp. 1-9.

_____, and Harry Magdoff (1977). "Comment by the editors." *Monthly Review*, 29:7, December, pp. 19-22.

_____ (1979a). "Iran: The new crisis of American hegemony." *Monthly Review*, 30:9, February, pp. 1-24.

_____ (1979b). "China: New theories for old." *Monthly Review*, 31:1, May, pp. 1-19.

_____ (1980). "U.S. foreign policy in the 1980's." *Monthly Review*, 31:11, April, pp. 1-12.

Szasz, Thomas S. (1961). *The Myth of Mental Illness*. New York: Harper and Row.

Szymanski, Albert (1974). "Race, class, and the working class," *Social Problems*, 21:5, June, pp. 706-25.

_____ (1976). "The socialization of women's oppression." *Insurgent Sociologist*, 6:2, Winter, pp. 31-58.

_____ (1977). "Capital accumulation on a world scale and the necessity of imperialism." *Insurgent Sociologist*, 7:2, Spring, pp. 35-53.

_____ (1978). *The Capitalist State and the Politics of Class*. Cambridge, MA: Winthrop.


Takagi, Paul, and Tony Platt (1978). "Behind the gilded ghetto: An analysis of race, class, and crime in Chinatown." *Crime and Social Justice*, 9, Spring-Summer, pp. 2-24.

Tanzer, Michael (1978). "The state and the oil industry in today's world." *Monthly Review*, 29:10, March, pp. 1-14.

*TARGET* (1975). "Maryland juveniles perform community service work." 4:12, December.

_____ (1976). "Misdemeanants perform community service." 5:5, July.

_____ (1977). "Minneapolis settling disputes out of court." 6:1, January.

Taylor, Ronald B. (1973). *Sweatshops in the Sun: Child Labor on the Farm*. Boston: Beacon.

Terkel, Studs (1970). *Hard Times*. New York: Avon, 1971.

_____ (1974). *Working: People Talk About What They Do All Day and How They Feel About What They Do*. New York: Avon, 1975.

Thomas, Gail, and Will B. Scott (1979). "Black youth and the labor market: The unemployment dilemma." *Youth and Society*, 2:2, December, pp. 163-189.

Thomas, Jack, (1978). "Life forms may vanish, report says." *Boston Globe*, July 23, p. 10.

_____ (1979). "A West Coast tug-of-war." *Boston Globe*, November 21, p. 2.

_____ (1980). "For Maine widow, a daily nightmare." *Boston Globe*, March 16, pp. 1, 28.

Thompson, E. P. (1964). *The Making of the English Working Class*. New York: Pantheon.

Thornberry, Terrence (1973). "Race, socio-economic status, and sentencing in the juvenile justice system." *Journal of Criminal Law and Criminology*, 64, pp. 90-98.

Thurow, Lester (1976). "Not making it in America: The economic progress of minority groups." *Social Policy*, 6:5, March-April, pp. 5-11.

Tigar, Michael (with Madeleine Levy) (1977). *Law and the Rise of Capitalism*. New York: Monthly Review Press.

*Time* (1977). "The youth crime plague." July 11, pp. 18-28.

_____ (1978). "Socialism: Trials and errors." March 13, pp. 24-36.
Titmus, Richard M. (1971). *The Gift Relationship.* New York: Pantheon.
Toedtman, Jim (1979). "Disposing a national hazardous problem." *Boston Globe,* May 13, p. 73.
Toffler, Alvin (1970). *Future Shock.* New York: Random House.
Torrey, William (1978). "Doctors and ethics: Patience runs out." *Boston Globe,* July 30, pp. A1, A4.
Trausch, Susan (1979). "Inflation and the working poor." *Boston Globe,* July 29, pp. 61-62.
Trimberger, Ellen Kay (1973). "Open missions: A new form of tracking." *Insurgent Sociologist,* 4:1, Fall, pp. 29-43.
Turkel, Gerald (n.d.). Personal communication.
Turnbull, Colin (1961). *The Forest People.* New York: Simon and Schuster.
Turner, Steve (1976). "Work can be dangerous to your health." *Boston Globe Magazine,* May 2.
Tyler, Patrick, and Jonathan Neumann (1979). "Imports up during the oil crisis." *Boston Globe,* August 30, pp. 1, 8.

*Union for Radical Political Economics* (URPE) (eds.) (1978). *U.S. Capitalism in Crisis.* New York: URPE.
United Nations (1978). *Statistical Yearbook.* New York: United Nations.
United Press International (1977). "Poor better food shopper than middle class, U.S. official says." *Boston Globe,* September 25, p. 20.
URPE Editorial Collective (1978). "Toward a people's movement in the United States." In URPE 1978, pp. 331-42.
U.S. Bureau of the Census (1978). *Consumer Income—Money Income in 1977 of Families and Persons in the U.S.* Washington, DC: U.S. Government Printing Office.
U.S. Department of Justice (1979). *Criminal Victimization in the United States: Summary Findings of Crime and of Trends Since 1973.* Washington, DC: LEAA.
U.S. Department of Labor (1976). *The Earnings Gap Between Women and Men.* Washington, DC: U.S. Department of Labor, Women's Bureau.
_____ (1978a). Bureau of Labor Statistics, news release of July 24 (USDL 78-638).
_____ (1978b). *Employment in Perspective: Working Women.* Bureau of Labor Statistics, no. 3, third quarter 1978, September.
_____ (1978c). Bureau of Labor Statistics, news release of October 12 (USDL 78-842).
_____ (1978d). Bureau of Labor Statistics, news release of July 3 (USDL 78-581).
_____ (1979a). Bureau of Labor Statistics, news release of April 29 ("Autumn 1978 Urban Family Budgets").
_____ (1979b). *Occupational Injuries and Illnesses in 1977: Summary.* Washington, DC: Bureau of Labor Statistics, Report 561.
_____ (1980). *Employment in Perspective: Working Women—1979 Summary.* Washington, DC: Bureau of Labor Statistics, Report 587.
*U.S. News and World Report* (1976). "New, second thoughts about the environment." January 19, pp. 52-53.
Upton, Letitia, and Nancy Lyons (1972). *Basic Facts: Distribution of Personal Income and Wealth in the U.S.* Cambridge, MA: Cambridge Institute.

Useem, Elizabeth, and Michael Useem (eds.) (1974). *The Education Establishment.* Englewood Cliffs, NJ: Prentice-Hall.
Useem, Michael (1978). "The inner group of the American capitalist class." *Social Problems,* 25:3, February, pp. 225–240.

Vanek, Jaroslav (1975). *Self-Management: Economic Liberation of Man.* New York: Penguin.
Vidich, Arthur, and Joseph Bensman (1958). *Small Town in Mass Society.* Princeton, NJ: Princeton University Press.
Vocations for Social Change (1976). *No Bosses Here: A Manual on Working Collectively.* Boston: Vocations for Social Change.
von Ranson, Jonathan (1980). "Water Politics." *New Roots,* 11, May–June, pp. 28–32.

Waitzkin, Howard, and Barbara Waterman (1974). *The Exploitation of Illness in Capitalist Society.* Indianapolis: Bobbs-Merrill.
Wald, Karen (1978). *Children of Ché: Childcare and Education in Cuba.* Palo Alto, CA: Ramparts Press.
Ward, Fred (1978). *Inside Cuba Today.* New York: Crown.
Warner, W. Lloyd (1963). *Yankee City.* New Haven, CT: Yale University Press.
\_\_\_\_\_, Marchia Meecker, and Kenneth Eells (1960). *Social Class in America.* New York: Harper and Row.
Warren, Ellen (1980). "She badgers the biggies." *Boston Globe,* June 18, p. 2.
Washington Post (1978). "Experts debate effects of ozone reduction." *Boston Globe,* November 23, p. 60.
Wasserman, Harvey (1980). "What is happening to the animals?" *Progressive,* June, pp. 25–28.
Weir, David (1979). "The boomerang crime." *Mother Jones,* November.
Weisberg, Barry (1971). *Beyond Repair: The Ecology of Capitalism.* Boston: Beacon.
Weisel, Jonas (1978). "Boston's backyard press." *New England* (magazine of *Boston Globe*), August 20, pp. 10ff.
Weissman, Steve (1973). "The multinationals assemble: A new ruling class for the world." *Nation,* October 15, pp. 358–60.
Wellman, David (1968). "The wrong way to find jobs for Negroes." *Transaction,* April, pp. 9–18.
Whiton, Louis C. (1971). "Under the power of the Gran Gadu." *Natural History Magazine,* August–September, pp. 14–16ff.
Wilcox, Kathleen, and Pia Moriarty (1976). "Schooling and work: Social constraints on equal educational opportunity." *Social Problems,* 24:2, December, pp. 204–213.
Williams, Eric (1944). *Capitalism and Slavery.* New York: Capricorn Books, 1976.
Williams, Jay R., and Martin Gold (1972). "From delinquent behavior to juvenile delinquency." *Social Problems,* 20:2, Fall, pp. 209–29.
Williams, Lynora (1980a). "Gentrification stampede is on." *Guardian,* April 2, p. 7.
\_\_\_\_\_ (1980b). "Miami reflects national frustration." *Guardian,* May 28, p. 7.
Wilson, James Q. (1975). *Thinking About Crime.* New York: Basic Books.
Winn, Peter (1980). "Is the Cuban revolution in trouble?" *Nation,* June 7, pp. 682–85.

Winship, Thomas (1975). "China's corporate man: He's one of the workers." *Boston Globe,* July 9.
Withorn, Ann (1980). "Helping ourselves: The limits and potential of self-help." *Radical America,* 14:3, May-June, pp. 25-40.
Wolfe, Alan (1974). "Carnegie again." *Social Policy,* 5:4, November-December, pp. 60-62.
_____ (1978). *The Seamy Side of Democracy.* New York: Longman.
Wood, John B. (1977). "Community Justice." *New England* (magazine of *Boston Globe*), March 20, pp. 18-26.
Wooden, Kenneth (1976). *Weeping in the Playtime of Others.* New York: McGraw-Hill.
Woodward, C. Vann (1957). *The Strange Career of Jim Crow.* New York: Oxford.
Woollacott, Martin (1980). "Poisonous legacy in Vietnam." *Boston Globe,* June 4, p. 3.
*Work in America* (1973). Report of a special task force to the Secretary of Health, Education, and Welfare. Cambridge, MA: MIT Press.
Worthy, William (1976). *The Rape of Our Neighborhoods.* New York: Morrow.
Wright, Richard (1945). *Black Boy.* New York: Harper and Row, 1966.
Wynne, Edward (1977). *Growing Up Suburban.* Austin, TX: University of Texas Press.

Yanowitch, Murray (1977). *Social and Economic Inequality in the Soviet Union.* White Plains, NY: M. E. Sharpe.
Yates, Michael (1979). "On China since Mao." *Monthly Review,* 31:1, May, pp. 56-60.
*Yearbook of Higher Education* (1977-78). Chicago: Marquis Academic Media.
Young, John, and Jan Newton (1980). *Capitalism and Human Obsolescence: Corporate Control Versus Individual Survival in Rural America.* Montclair, NJ: Allenheld, Osmun.
Young, L.C. (1974). "Mass sociology: The Chinese style." *American Sociologist,* 9:3, August, pp. 117-25.
Young, Michael, and Peter Willmott (1957). *Family and Kinship in East London.* Baltimore: Penguin, 1962.

Zaretsky, Eli (1978). "The effects of the economic crisis on the family." In URPE 1978, pp. 209-218.
Zeitlin, Maurice (1970). "Inside Cuba: Workers and revolution." *Ramparts,* March, pp. 10-11ff.
_____ (1974). "Corporate ownership and control: The large corporation and the capitalist class." *American Journal of Sociology,* 79:5, March, pp. 1073-1119.
_____ (1978). "Who owns America?" *The Progressive,* June, pp. 14-21.
Zhou Jinghua (1979). "Interview with a specialist on population." *Beijing Review,* November 16, pp. 20-22.
Zimbalist, Andrew (1975). "Worker participation in Cuba." *Challenge,* November-December, pp. 45-54.
Zimmerman, Mitch (1973). *International Run-Away Shop* (2nd ed.). San Francisco: United Front Press.
Zinn, Howard (1980). "A showcase of repression." *Progressive,* June, pp. 35-39.

Zweigenhaft, Richard (1975). "Who represents America?" *Insurgent Sociologist,* 5:3, Spring, pp. 119-30.
Zwerdling, Daniel (1973). "Drugs in the meat industry." *Ramparts,* June, pp. 37-41.
_____ (1974). "Managing workers." *Working Papers,* 2:3, Fall, pp. 9-18.
_____ (1975). "The food monopolies." *Progressive,* January, pp. 13-17.
_____ (1978). "Curbing the chemical fix: Organic farming—the secret is it works." *Progressive,* December, pp. 16-25.
_____ (1980). "The food monsters." *Progressive,* March, pp. 16-27.

# Glossary

**Alienation.** In its general meaning, it refers to feeling estranged from others and from one's own emotions and feelings. It is also the belief that we have no control over our lives. In relation to work, alienation refers to the lack of control over what we do and how we do it, to the separation of conception from execution. According to Marx and others, alienation is inherent in capitalism.

**Class.** In Marxist tradition, class is defined by people's relation to the means of production—whether they own and control the major means of producing goods and services in their society, or whether they work for those who own the means of production. Socially, class is defined by the people one associates with, primarily whom he or she marries. According to Sweezy, a social class is made up of "freely intermarrying families."

There are five classes in American society. (a) Ruling class—under capitalism, it is the class that dominates and controls the major means of production (corporations, banks, factories, and so on) and the political institutions. Also, directly or indirectly it influences most other institutions. People in this class derive most of their income from property they inherit (stocks, bonds, real estate), not from their jobs. (b) Professional-managerial class—doctors, managers, engineers, psychologists, and other professionals and business management people belong to this class. They do not own the major means of production; rather, they work for and manage the business of the ruling class. This class also serves to lessen and compensate for some of the suffering people inevitably suffer under capitalism. (c) Small business owners—owners of businesses of various types and sizes (restaurants, hardware stores, pharmacies, and so on) that are not the major means of production. Individuals within this class vary widely in income, beliefs, and life-styles. A very few eventually make it into the ruling class, most do not, and many eventually lose their businesses. This class has been declining steadily in the twentieth century. (d) The poor—unemployed people, those on welfare, and those who work at or close to the minimum wage. They are usually unskilled. Their income is too low for even the necessities of life in the United States. (e) Working class—those people who do not fit into the other four classes, meaning most people in the United

427

States. Workers in factories, restaurants, hotels, offices, and stores fall in this class. They vary in income, life-style, and expectations, but none lives in affluence; indeed, many barely manage and are not far from poverty.

**Collective.** A workplace owned and run equally by all the workers. There are no bosses or managers. Usually, all jobs are rotated on a regular basis and decisions are made by consensus—discussion continues until everyone feels comfortable with that decision.

**Colonialism.** The direct political and economic control of one nation by another. During the colonial era (now almost completely gone) the United States and some European nations exploited the resources and labor of nations in Africa, Asia, and Latin America. (England also colonized Ireland.)

**Community.** Usually a small group of people who share common values, interests, and activities, show concern and responsibility for each other, and live in the same area. As capitalist values and institutions (profit motive, individualism, and competition) have come to dominate, they have been weakening the sense of community and often destroying communities.

**Conglomerate.** A corporation that makes two or more different products. As it does so, it expands its power and wealth. Conglomerates are coming to dominate the United States economy. For example, CBS owns a radio and a television network, radio and television stations, a publishing company, and a record company. Most large United States corporations are conglomerates.

**Conservatism.** A social and political philosophy that holds that, if people were left alone to pursue their own personal interests, their needs and the needs of the whole society would be met in the most efficient manner. Government should perform very limited functions (such as enforcing laws). Conservatives vary in their belief in government noninterference.

**Contradiction.** This arises in a society when the achievement of some goals automatically means other goals cannot be met. In capitalist society the central contradiction is between the ruling class, who want to retain and increase their wealth and power, and the workers who struggle to meet their own physical, social, and psychological needs. The high profits of the ruling class are gained at the expense of workers.

**Crimes of capitalism.** Acts that are not necessarily illegal, but which cause much more harm than does street crime. For example, unsafe working conditions that *could be eliminated* kill and injure many more people than does street crime.

**Cultural revolution.** The ten-year period of China (1966–1976) during which some groups struggled to diminish the power of experts, professionals, and elites, and sought to establish popular control over all institutions. There has been a long debate and disagreement about the nature and goals of the cultural revolution.

**Domination.** In modern society, experts and professionals (doctors, teachers, managers, psychologists, and others) tend to use their positions to exercise power and control over their clients. Domination has increased with the spread of professionalism.

**Ecology.** Nature places limits on us, and we need to live within those limits. Industrial capitalism, in its search for greater profits and a consumer society, has been destroying the environment by going beyond those limits. We suffer as the environment is being polluted and destroyed.

**Imperialism.** The capitalist nations of the world are integrated in one economic system. The ruling classes of the dominant capitalist nations, often with the cooperation of the ruling classes of the poorer nations, control this economic system. The rest of the people, especially in the poorer nations, suffer under this system.

**Interlocking directorate.** More and more, directors serve on the boards of two or more corporations at the same time. Therefore, it comes about that a few people control the major corporations, and these major corporations are able to coordinate their activities for the benefit of each other.

**Liberalism.** The social and political philosophy that accepts the basic premises of conservatism, but sees the need for some government actions to provide services for individuals and communities. Without such government actions, some people would suffer and some needs would not be met. Liberals vary widely in the degree of government action they espouse.

**Means of production.** The land, raw materials, factories, machinery, and other resources used by the people in a society to produce the goods and services they need to survive. In capitalist society, the ruling class controls the major means of production and uses them primarily for its own benefit, rather than for meeting social needs.

**Monopoly.** One company controls the entire market for a product or a service. In most places, the telephone, electric, and gas companies are monopolies.

**Multinational.** A corporation with plants or branches in two or more countries. Most major United States corporations are multinationals with major investments overseas (see **imperialism**). Multinationals are becoming powerful world institutions.

**National planning.** In a socialist society the use and distribution of its resources (land, labor, materials, and money) is planned on a regional and national scale. The goal is to insure the most rational and beneficial use of a country's limited resources. Theoretically, all people should participate in forming such plans.

**Neocolonialism** (see **colonialism**). Direct political and economic control and exploitation of poor natives by richer ones no longer exists, but exploitation continues in other ways. For example, richer capitalist societies buy raw materials cheaply from the poorer ones, and they sell to them expensive manufactured products. In addition, poorer nations are in heavy debt to richer ones.

**Oligopoly.** A few corporations that control the market for a product or service. In many instances, four or fewer corporations control almost the entire market; for example, in steel, autos, and breakfast cereals.

**Professionalism.** As professionals define themselves, they are people who, after long training and education in a field, acquire special knowledge, theory, and techniques. In compensation for their long training and service to clients, professionals receive high prestige and rewards. Professionals also set their own standards for entering the field. The socialist critique of professionalism disputes many of these claims. It argues that the required degree of special knowledge and training is exaggerated, and that professionals create a mystique of special knowledge in order to control the public and to profit themselves.

**Racism.** A belief that people of one race or group are inherently inferior to other races or groups. In relation to black people, racism arose as an ideology to rationalize the economic exploitation of slaves (and later also of free blacks).

**Ruling class.** The social class, at most one percent of the population, that owns and controls the major means of production. In addition, in various degrees it controls and shapes the political and educational systems, the mass media, and other institutions.

**Self-help.** The movement to reassert control over our lives. Experts, professionals, and managers have come to dominate many areas of life, a situation self-help seeks to change. The term means that we provide for and help each other to meet our needs and solve our problems. For example, ex-mental patients form their own groups to help each other cope. Self-help may be seen as a movement of people to do for themselves many things that they did in the past.

**Socialism.** The social and political philosophy that sees an inevitable conflict between the power of the ruling class and the needs of the rest of the people. It argues that people's needs can be met only through cooperation, sharing, concern for the common good, the control of the means of production by communities, the workers, and the government, and a long struggle against the domination of social classes.

**Socialist medicine.** It seeks to provide the available medical services equally to everyone, but also to transform the nature and quality of those services. It focuses on preventive medicine, on improving the quality of people's lives, and on overcoming the mystique and control of doctors and other medical personnel.

**Social problem.** There are two definitions. (a) A social problem arises when society, a large group, or a powerful minority defines a social condition as a problem that must be changed. (b) A social condition is a problem when it causes physical, psychic, or social injury to people, even if they have not yet perceived or defined it as a problem.

**Street crime.** Theft, murder, assault, and vandalism are the acts we have been socialized to fear as dangerous crimes. In the socialist view, however, although street crimes are seen as dangerous, white-collar crimes and crimes of capitalism (see definitions) are more dangerous to our individual and collective well-being.

**Surplus value.** The difference between the value of the goods or services workers produce, and what they get paid. This is the "profit" of the capitalist owners. Workers struggle to decrease the size of the surplus value, and owners to increase it.

**White-collar crime.** Illegal acts committed by managers and other people in high positions in businesses and organizations. A classic example happened in 1961, when officials from General Electric, Westinghouse, and other corporations were convicted of getting together and fixing the prices of some products at high levels, thus increasing their profits.

**Workers' control.** The workers should conceive, plan, and execute the decisions about work in a workplace. There are different versions of workers' control, in capitalist and socialist settings; but in all of them the ultimate goal is for all workers to participate equally in both the conception and execution of the work.

# Index

Accidents, job-related, 102
Accumulation of capital, 9
Acid rain, 250
Advertising, 63–64
Advisory commissions, 67–69
Affluence, 3, 24
Afghanistan, Soviet invasion of, 159
Africa (*see also* South Africa)
  land use in, 150
  rebellion against imperialism in, 398
  Socialist revolution in, 161
  as source of slaves, 217
  U.S. involvement in, 141
"Agent orange" (Dioxin) poisoning, 296
Agribusiness, 160
Air pollution (*see* Pollution)
Albania, 42, 43, 49, 216
Algeria, 150
Alienation of workforce (*see* Workers, alienation of)
Alternative schools, 377–378
American Bar Association, 315
American Cancer Society, 293
American Indians (*see* Native Americans)
American Medical Association (AMA), 290
American Telephone and Telegraph Co. (AT&T), 59
Anderson, Charles, 56, 265, 271

Angola, Socialist revolution in, 161, 162, 163
Antinuclear protest movement, 246
Antitrust laws, 7
Antiwar demonstrations, 22 (*see also* Vietnam War)
Appalachia
  background of, 174
  community in, 174–179
  education in, 350
  oppression in, 216
  poverty in, 38
  strip mining of, 61, 175
  unemployment in, 100
Argentina, 147, 155
Armed forces, U.S., 24, 34, (*see also* Vietnam War)
Arson for profit, 2
Assembly line work, 107, 113
Association of Community Organizations for Reform Now (ACORN), 392
Atlantic-Richfield Corporation, 62, 283
Atomic Energy Commission, Los Alamos Scientific Laboratories, 248
*Automation in the Office*, Ida R. Hoos, 112
Automobile industry, 144
  corporate executives, 59

  economic domination of, 254–256
  manufacturers in, 253–254

Babson, Steve, 58, 59, 61, 72
Baltimore City Hospital, 286
Ba Mbuti (tribe), 191
Bangladesh, 148
Bank-America Corporation, 59
Banks, U.S., 157, 160
"Barefoot doctors" (China), 303–304
*Beijing Review*, 151–152, 338, 370–371
Belgian Congo, 138
Bernstein, Paul, 126, 132
Bethlehem Steel Company, 116
Bettelheim, Charles, 43, 74, 92, 130
Black Americans (*see also* Minorities)
  education of, 220
  in the labor force, 223–225
  racism against, 216, 221
  unemployment rates of, 100, 231
"Black capitalism" in Nixon administration, 241
Black Crusaders (gang), 341, 343
Black lung disease, 73
Black Muslims, 240 (*see also* Malcolm X)
Black Panthers, 243

*431*

432    INDEX

Blue Cross–Blue Shield, 290, 291, 299
Bodley, John, 42, 138, 139, 245, 248, 258
Bohemian Grove, 55
Boston, Massachusetts, 81, 181, 182, 186, 318
Boston Edison Company, 59
*Boston Globe*, 318, 326
Bourgeoisie (*see* Ruling class)
Bowles, Samuel, 347, 361
Braverman, Henry, 111, 113, 116, 118, 119, 120, 170, 321
Brazil, 144, 153, 155, 156, 234, 387
Brigham, Nancy, 58, 59, 61, 72
Brooks, Congressman Preston, 3
Browning, Frank, 61, 264
Brzezinski, Zbigniew, 65
Buchwald, Art, 313–314
Buffalo Creek, West Virginia, 4, 81, 176, 178, 180, 187, 313, 325
Bureaucratization of society, 79
Bureau of Indian Affairs, 242
Burnham, Sophy, 54, 56
*Business Week*, 60

California
  corporation-owned land in, 61
  Proposition 13, 56
Cambodia, 398
Cambridge, Massachusetts, 182, 332, 377–378
Canada, 142, 144, 145
Cancer, from the environment, 293
Capitalism, 68, 71, 103, 298
  exploitationist policies of, 390
  future collapse of, 165
  racism under, 231–233
  socialist analysis of, 8
  socialist critique of, 7
  technology in, 264
  unemployment in, 100
  victims of, 27
  work principles, 121
Carnegie Commission on Higher Education, 353
Carnegie Foundation, 357
Cars (*see* Automobile industry)
Carter, President Jimmy, 47, 65, 66, 159, 260
Castro, Fidel, 373
Center for Democratic Information, 159
Center-periphery metaphor, 135–136
Central America, 155
Central Intelligence Agency (CIA), U.S., 17, 92, 155, 159, 164, 265, 289
Cereseto, Shirley, 148, 151
Chase Manhattan Bank, 242
Chase Manhattan Corporation, 57, 59, 69
Chavez, Cesar, 242
Chicago, Illinois, 102, 168, 175–176, 350–351
Chicanos (*see* Mexican-Americans)
Child-rearing, professionalization of, 83
Chile, 17, 71, 147, 148, 154, 398
  CIA in, 159
  overthrow of socialist government in, 153
  political persecution in, 155, 156
  repressive societies in, 387
  U.S. arms shipment to, 160
  U.S. bank loans to, 160
  U.S. capital investments in, 143
China, 44, 74, 75, 92, 103, 207–208
  communes in, 151
  community in, 173, 184
  crime control in, 322, 336
  crime rates in, 337
  cultural revolution in, 43, 74, 75, 84–88, 118, 131, 369–370, 397
  economic problems, 44
  education in, 7
  environmental concern of, 265
  feeding of people in, 151, 164
  labor force in, 104, 126, 127, 130, 132
  legal system of, 338, 340
  population control in, 151–152
  reforestation in, 150
  socialist society in, 42, 43, 265–266
  socialized medicine in, 302, 303–304, 306–308
  U.S. racism against, 216
  women in, 205–206
Chiñas, Beverly, 191, 193
Christianity, 263
Christian Science Church, Boston, 182
Chrysler Corporation, 61, 62
Church, Senator Frank, 159
Cincinnati, Ohio, 168
Citicorp, 57, 59, 145
"City Life" (organization), 394–396
Civil War, U.S., 220
Clamshell Alliance of New England, 277
Class structure, 7, 8, 354, 355
Coca-Cola Company, 160, 397
Colby, William F., 159
Coles, Robert, 39, 40
Collectives, 16
Collins, Joseph, 138, 148, 151, 270
Colonialism, 136, 137, 139–140, 141, 142
Columbia Broadcasting System (CBS), 62
Commercialism, effect on community, 171
Commoner, Barry, 247, 263, 264, 271, 387
"Common Ground" (restaurant), Vermont, 124–126
Communications Workers (union), 47
Communist parties, 208
Community, 167–187, 384
Community colleges, 359
Community Crime Prevention Plan (CCPP), 329–330
Competition, human values affected by, 10, 11
Compromise of 1877 (Civil War), 220
Condominium conversion, 2
Conglomerates, 62
Congress of Industrial Organizations (CIO), 240
Connally, John, 68
Connecticut River, pollution of, 275
Conservative politics, 17–19
Consumer credit, 100
Consumerism, 63, 261–262
Co-op City, New York, 92
Corporate Data Exchange, 57
Corporations, 3, 57–60, 101
Council of Environmental Quality, 262
Council on Foreign Relations (CFR), 68
Crime
  Citizen Dispute Settlement, LEAA manual, 330
  community prevention of, 329–330
  conservative viewpoint of, 19
  effect on society of, 315
  legal system for, 4, 324
  ruling-class, 313–314
  socialist critique about, 331–333
  white-collar, 312–313
Crime and delinquency, 319–323
Crisis of the 1970s, 389, 390
Cuba, 4, 75, 76, 89, 156, 243, 398
  Communist party in, 374
  crime in, 334
  education in, 368, 371
  history of, 372

legal system in, 340
living conditions in, 45
popular tribunals in, 337, 338
U.S. expansion into, 229
women in labor force in, 7, 206
workers liberation in, 129

Dashee, Alvin, 248, 249
Davis, California, energy
　consumption in, 275
Day care, 208, 209, 210
DDT pollution, 249–250
Delinquency (see also Crime and
　delinquency)
　causes, 319–323
　controls of, 323–324
　juvenile justice reforms for, 325
　prevention of, 341
　recidivism of, 327
Del Monte Foods, 63, 149
Democracy, 17, 51, 74, 76,
　385–386
Democratic Party, 64, 74, 242,
　393
Dennison, George, 363, 365, 366
Depression of the 1930s, 25, 26,
　72, 120, 171, 175, 228
Detergents, as pollutants, 251
Detroit, Michigan, 168, 226
Diet, affected by environment,
　258
Doctors (see Medical profession)
Domhoff, G. William, 53, 55, 58,
　64, 66, 68, 70, 71, 72, 74, 393
Domination of the ruling class,
　77–93 (see also Ruling class)
Douglass, Frederick, 219–220,
　234, 236, 238, 398
Dreier, Peter, 52, 73, 74
Drugs, sold by U.S., 155
Duberman, Lucille, 40, 41, 48,
　355
DuBois, W.E.B., 243
DuPont Corporation, 52, 62
DuRand, Cliff, 44, 131

Eastern European Socialist
　societies, 129
East Germany (see German
　Democratic Republic)
Eastman Kodak, 65
Eaton Corporation, 122, 123, 124
Economic institutions,
　domination of, 7
Ecosystem, 247–248
Education, 70, 345–380
　alternative schools for, 377–378
　changes in, 364–365
　community control of, 375

culture of, 362–367
discrimination in, 346, 353
effect of capitalism on, 362
I.Q. testing in, 360–362
long-term strategies for, 376
Marxist critique of, 346
minorities in, 350
oppression of capitalism in, 362
poverty in, 351
public, 347
rise of, 347
social class effects on, 352
Egypt, 103
Ehrenreich, Barbara, 34, 35, 198,
　284, 308–309
Ehrenreich, John E., 34, 35, 190,
　284, 288, 308
Electricity, costs of, 71
Elitism, 77–93
Employment, 4, 21, 173 (see also
　Labor Force; Unemployment;
　Workers)
Energy
　consumption of, 253, 273
　corporations, 245, 255, 271
　shortages of, 245, 271
　sources of, 252
　waste of, 253, 254
England, 140, 141
Environment, 245–278
　cancer from, 293
　crisis of, 248
　laws for protection of, 266, 272
　liberal reforms for, 271, 272, 273
　pollution of, 3, 249–253
Environmental Protection
　Agency (EPA), 259, 260, 272,
　297
Erikson, Kai T., 176, 177, 178
Ethics, professional, 80
Europe, U.S. investments in, 144
European Common Market, 140
Exxon Corporation, 59, 63, 160

Family, social class of, 33
Federal Bureau of Investigation
　(FBI), 243, 315
Federal Housing Act, 73
Firestone Tire Company, 255,
　283
First National City Bank, 59, 69,
　160
Food additives, 248
Food and Drug Administration,
　66
Food First (see Collins; Lappé)
Ford, Henry, 103
Ford Motor Company, 59, 62,
　145

Foreman, Carol, 35
"Four Corners," air pollution of,
　250
Framingham, Massachusetts,
　health studies, 297
France, 140, 182, 207
Fraser, Douglas, 47
Free schools (see Alternative
　schools)
Frei, Eduardo, 159
Friedenberg, Edgar, 346, 348,
　363, 364
Friedman, Milton, 228, 262
Fuel crisis, 3
Functionalist theory of
　inequality, 41

Galbraith, John Kenneth, 96
Galeano, Eduardo, 154, 155
Gamberg, Ruth, 333–334, 368,
　370–371
General Electric, 101, 145
General Knitwear Factory,
　Peking, 130
General Motors Corporation, 59,
　141, 145, 255
German Democratic Republic, 43,
　74, 207–208, 368
Ghana, 145
Ghettoes (urban), 234–235
Gordon, David, 205, 207, 320
Great Depression (1930s), 25, 26,
　72, 120, 171, 175, 228
Greece, 103, 141, 157, 177, 190,
　263
Greer, Colin, 345, 350, 352
Greyhound Corporation, 62
Griffin, John Howard, 236
Gross National Product (GNP),
　249, 280
Guatemala, 149
Guinea Bissau, Socialist
　revolution in, 161
Gulf and Western Oil
　Corporation, 62, 161

Haiti, 45
Harlan County, Kentucky, 47
Harrison, Barbara, 197, 210, 212
Harvard University, 24, 36, 54,
　182, 299
Havana, Cuba, 305
Headstart Program, 345
Health
　definition of, 292
　improvement of, 294
Health care, 301, 308–309
Health hazards, 259, 294–296

Health Maintenance Organizations (HMOs), 299-300
Heart disease, 297-298
Hill, Judah, 34, 53, 60
Hiroshima, 294
Hispanics, in the labor force, 223
Holt, John, 346, 362-363, 366
Honduras, 164
Hong Kong, 101, 144
Hooker Chemical Company, 259-261
Hopi, 249 (see also Native Americans)
Hospital care, cost of, 283-284
Housing, shortage of, 2
Human relations, 10, 11
Hungary, 43
Hunger, 147, 148, 164

Illinois, University of, 327
Illegal aliens, 228
Illness, 293, 294-298
Imperialism
  definition of, 135
  effects of, 153-160
  present forms, 137
  Socialist revolution defeat of, 161
Imprisonment, alternatives to, 330-331
Income, 55
Income taxes, 71
India
  hunger in, 151
  labor in, 103
  overpopulation in, 151
  petroleum resources of, 164
Indians, U.S. (see Native Americans)
Individualism, conservative ideology of, 18
Indonesia, 158
Industrialization, 173
Industrial Revolution, 96, 115
Infant formulas, 150-151, 157
Inflation, 25
Institute for Social Research, 319
Intelligence Quotient (IQ) testing, 360-362
International Business Machines (IBM), 160
International Telephone and Telegraph (ITT), 62
Interstate Commerce Commission (ICC), 66
Iran, 158-159, 397
Ireland, 219

Irish immigrants, U.S., 222, 231, 234-237
Israel, 132, 210
Italian immigrants, 222, 230
Italy, 48

Jackson, George, 234, 235, 317, 341, 343
Jacksonian era, 88
Japan, 140, 141, 263
Jenkins, David, 120, 129
Jim Crow laws, 220
Journal of the American Medical Association, 198

Kaiser Aluminum, 145
Kaiser HMO, 300
Kennedy, Edward, 54, 66, 97
Kennedy, Joseph, 72
Kennedy, Robert, 242
Kennedy-Griffiths Health Security Act, 300
Kissinger, Henry, 68, 159
Klaw, Spencer, 285, 299
Kleindienst, Richard, 68
Kohl, Herbert, 346, 365
Kolko, Joyce, 66, 165
Korea, 101, 158
Ku Klux Klan (KKK), 244, 341
!Kung (tribe), 88-89, 105, 191, 192, 193, 209, 210

Labor force, 47, 116, 223 (see also Employment; Unemployment; Women; Workers)
Labor unions, 62, 163 (see also Trade unions)
Lake Baikal (USSR), 265
Land, abuse of, 149, 257, 258
Lappé, Frances Moore, 92, 138, 148, 149, 151, 164, 270, 274
Lasson, Kenneth, 51, 104
Latin America, 145, 147, 148, 154
Law Enforcement Assistance Association (LEAA) 315, 324, 325, 327, 328, 329, 330
Lead poisoning, 295
League of Revolutionary Black Workers (LRBW), Detroit, 243
Lee, Dorothy, 92, 169
Lee, Richard, 88, 104
Lenin, V.I., 370
Leninist parties, 393
Lenin School, Cuba, 374

Levison, Andrew, 32, 108, 236
Liberal politics, 17, 19-20
Lindsay, John, 69
Logan Airport, East Boston, 277
London, 168, 172
Los Angeles, 255-256
"Love Canal" chemical dump site, 259-260
Lowell, Massachusetts, 100
Lumpen-proletariat, defined by Marx, 32
Lynd, Helen and Robert, 33, 170, 171

McAfee, Kathy, 394-399
McCord, Joan, 331, 332
McDonald's Corporation
McNamara, Robert, 152, 165-166
Magdoff, Harry, 143, 144, 397
Malcolm X, 234, 235, 240, 241, 343 (see also Black Muslims)
Malnutrition, 150
Manual labor, 103-104, 132 (see also Work)
Manufacturers-Hanover Trust Corporation, 59, 160
Mao Zedong, 74, 75, 86, 89, 265, 303, 339, 369-370
Marcos, Ferdinand, Philippine president, 155
Marcus Garvey movement, 240
Marieskind, Helen I., 308-309
Marquit, Erwin, 43, 205, 206, 207, 208, 368, 385
Marx, Karl, 32, 73, 105, 370
Marxism, 32, 74, 393
Massachusetts, Department of Youth Services, 182, 326, 327
Massachusetts Fair Share, 243
Mead, Margaret, 190
Media, used in capitalism, 392
Medicaid, 25, 284, 291, 300
Medical care, China, 86 (see also China)
Medical care, U.S., 299-306
  birth practices of, 285
  cost of, 280
  decline in quality of, 286-288
  dehumanization of, 284, 285
  history of system of, 290
  "medical empires" in, 291
  social control of, 289-290
  socialist perspective on, 288-289
  socialized, 301, 302, 305-308, 309
  specialization in, 283, 291
  women in, 292, 308-309
*Medical Economics*, 282

Medical profession, 81-82, 280-281, 288, 290
Medicare, 284, 291, 300
Mental Patients Association, Canada, 90
Mexican-Americans, 216, 221, 223, 227-228
Mexico, 101, 144, 149, 153, 156, 158, 164
Miami, Florida, riots in, 226
Middletown (Muncie, Indiana), 33, 114
Migrant workers, 38 (see also Workers)
Militarism, 143, 158
Miners for Democracy, 47
Mineworkers, working conditions of, 73
Minorities, 4, 22, 71, 101, 222-223, 241, 317
Mobil Oil Corporation, 59, 61, 145, 160
Model Cities Program, 241
Mondale, Walter, 66
Monopolies, 60
*Monthly Review,* 391
Morgan, J. P., 57, 59
Moriarty, Pia, 348, 349
Mozambique, 161
Multinational corporations (MNCs)
  definition of, 62-63
  domination of economies by, 154-156
  imperialism of, 140, 141
  manufacturing overseas by, 144
  perpetuation of wars by, 160
  protection by U.S. of, 158

NAACP, 240
Nader, Ralph, 66
Nagasaki, 294
National Health Insurance, 300-301
National Highway Trust Fund, 256
Native Americans, 61, 62, 89, 138, 139, 163, 164, 217, 268 (see also Minorities)
  ecology concerns of, 248
  exploitation of, 223, 227
  land taken from, 227
  racism against, 216, 233
  reforms to aid, 242
  woman in tribes of, 191
Neocolonialism, 100, 156-157
Nevada, nuclear testing ground in, 294
New American Movement, 393

New England, 100, 250
*New England Journal of Medicine,* 295, 298
New Hampshire, 259, 271
New Jersey, 61, 230
New York, New York, 4, 9, 69, 157, 160, 229, 234, 272, 274, 350-351
New York Stock Exchange, 56, 65
Nicaragua, 4, 161
Niger, 150
"9 to 5" (group), 213
Nixon, Richard, 11, 68, 159, 241
Noise pollution, 248, 277
Non-Marxists, 32
Nuclear energy, 62, 246, 265, 271, 353, 387
  accidents with, 252-253
  protests against, 276-277
  testing of, 294
  wastes from, 251

Occupational Safety and Health Act, 73, 102
Oil corporations, 18, 62, 72, 256
Oil exploration, 164
OPEC (Oil Producing and Exporting Countries), 140, 165
"Operation Bootstrap" (Puerto Rico), 229
Overpopulation, 151-152

Payer, Cheryl, 159-160, 164
Pelletier, Wilfred, 89, 92
"People's Park" (Berkeley, California), 275
People's Republic of China (see China)
Petit bourgeoisie, definition of, 32
Petroleum resources, 72, 141, 164
Philippines, 63, 155, 229
Poland, 208
Polaroid Corporation, 123
Pollution, 249-252, 260 (see also Energy; Environment)
Portugal, 140, 161, 162, 163, 164
Poverty, 26, 35, 152
Power elite, domination by, 387
Prescription drugs, 283, 289
Presidency, U.S., 64, 67 (see also Carter; Nixon; Reagan)
President's Commission on Law and the Administration of Justice, 324
Professionalization of labor force, 79, 80, 292
Professional-Managerial Class (PMC), 34

"Project Enterprise," 375
Proletariat, 32, 34, 69 (see also Workers)
Proposition 13, 56
Psychiatry, 290
Publishing industry, conglomerate control of, 62
Puerto Rican immigrants, U.S.
  emigration sites, 230
  exploitation of, 229-230
  in labor force, 223
  racism against, 216
  resources of, 163, 164

Racism, 20, 136, 215-244 (see also Black Americans; Minorities; Native Americans; Puerto Rican immigrants)
Railroads, 61, 256-257
Reagan, Ronald, 65, 397
Recession, 1970s, 25, 26
Republican Party, 64, 68
Revolution, 74 (see also China, cultural revolution in)
Rhodesia, 138 (see also Zimbabwe)
Robeson, Paul, 243
Rockefeller, David, 23, 65, 241
Rockefeller family, 23, 52, 59, 69, 139, 140, 220, 272
Roosevelt family, 54
Rubin, Lillian Breslow, 25
Ruling class
  case history of, 67
  definition of, 32, 34, 52, 53
  economic control of, 55, 70
  Marxist definition of, 32
  open door policy within, 67-69
Rumania, 43
Ryan, William, 242-243

Seabrook, New Hampshire, 277 (see also Nuclear energy)
Seattle, Washington, 275
Seifer, Nancy, 197, 211
Self-employment, 35, 114
Self-help, 89-92
Senegal, 150
Sexton, Patricia Cayo, 355, 361
Shah of Iran, 397
Slavery, history of, 2, 13, 217-222
Social class, 7, 23-49, 352
  divisions of, 30-38
  effects on education of, 352
  Marxist theory of, 33
Socialism, 76, 83, 151, 159, 230, 231, 390
  alternatives offered by, 13

Socialism (*continued*)
  control of, 336–337
  crime under, 333–344
  definition of, 128
  labels against, 7
  U.S. prospects for, 387, 388–396
  women in, 190, 206–208
  work principles of, 121, 128
Socialist analysis of capitalism, 7–10
Socialist revolutions, 161, 205, 388–389
Socialist societies, 263–264, 367, 368, 381, 383–388 (*see also* China; USSR)
Socialized medicine (*see* Medical care, socialized)
Social justice, 341
*Social Registers*, 53
Social Security, 228
Solar energy, 273–274
South Africa, 138, 145, 155, 228
South Korea, 144
Spain, 140, 229
Standard Oil of California, 255
Strip mining, 252, 257–258, 265
Swados, Harvey, 92, 175
Sweezy, Paul, 33, 36, 43, 48, 52, 397
Szymanski, Albert, 143, 209, 389

Taiwan, 146, 158
Tanzania, 164
Taylor, Frederick, 116
Taylor's Principles, 118, 120
Technology, 119, 261, 264
Tenant organizations, 392
Tenneco, 62
Terkel, Studs, 45, 51, 59, 98, 106, 108, 109, 269, 323
Thailand, 63
Third parties, 74
Three Mile Island, 252–253, 277, 294–295
Tikopia, 99, 133
*Time* (magazine), 62, 388, 393
Trade unions, 221 (*see also* Labor unions)
Transportation, 173, 253–257
Tribal societies, 42, 267–268, 307
Trilateral Commission, 65–66, 72
Tufts Medical School, 286
Turkey, 141

Unemployment, 99–101, 153
Union for Radical Political Economics, 390
Urban renewal, 180
USSR (Union of Soviet Socialist Republics)
  assistance to Cuba, 156
  environmental concerns of, 264–265
  imperialist actions of, 398
  invasion of Afghanistan by, 159
  nuclear power in, 265, 387
  socialist society of, 42, 43
  women in labor force of, 206–208
  working conditions in, 129, 265
United Auto Workers, 45, 47, 123, 243
United Farmworkers Union, 242
United Mineworkers Union (UMWA), 46, 47
United Nations, 153
United States Bureau of Labor Statistics, 323
United States Central Intelligence Agency (CIA) (*see* Central Intelligence Agency)
United States Department of Agiculture, 35
United States Department of Defense, Industry Advisory Council, 68, 71
United States Department of Health, Education and Welfare, 97, 120, 121, 298, 347, 354
United States Department of Housing and Urban Development, 81
United States Department of the Interior, 141
United States Department of Labor, 27, 36
United States House of Representatives, Subcommittee on Oversight, 282
United States of America (*see also* Capitalism; Democracy; Imperialism)
  banking in, 144
  coal reserves of, 252
  colonialist power of, 140
  foreign relations of, 68
  imperialism in, 157
  imports of, 141, 142
  independence of, 17
  multinational corporations of, 145, 155
  overseas investments of, 144–147
  surplus foods of, 149
  taxes in, 56, 66, 256
  trade relations of, 143, 144
  women in, 207 (*see also* Women)
*U.S. News and World Report*, 246
U.S. Steel, 59, 222, 240
Utah, nuclear fallout in, 294–295
Utopian ideals, 13, 76
Uzbek region (USSR), 205

Valium, 283
Vandalism, 4 (*see also* Crime and Delinquency; Delinquency)
Vega factory strike, 97
Vietnam War, 22, 24, 158, 161, 164, 187, 227 398
Volvo experiment, 123, 261

Wages, 100, 101, 153
Wald, Karen, 207, 306, 374
Warner, W. Lloyd, 30, 31, 119
Waste pollution (*see* Pollution)
Watergate scandal, 11, 70, 312, 313
Watts riots, 226
Wealth, 55, 56
Welfare system, U.S., 100, 231
West Virginia, 61, 250
White-collar labor, 28, 96, 110–113
Women, 4, 22, 191, 193–196
  liberation of, 205, 207
  oppression by psychiatry of, 198
  oppression of, 189–214
  sex roles determined, 192, 196
  socialist revolution and, 205
  strengths of, 193
Women in the labor force, 195, 196, 292
  changes in, 211
  corporate oppression of, 203
  lower salaries of, 201–202
  pressure on, 203
  sexual harassment of, 204
Women's Health Movement, 308–309
Work, 95–133
  hazardous conditions in, 102
  liberal reforms of, 120
  schedules of, 122
  socialist system of, 128
Workers
  alienation of, 4, 21, 97, 105, 114–120
  collectives of, 127
  control of conditions by, 120, 128, 129
  effect of imperialism on, 160

exploitation of, 79
management teams of, 130
ownership by, 124
specialization of, 132
strikes by, 97
Working class, 34, 69
World Bank, 156
World Trade Center, 69
World War II, 195, 231

Worthy, William, 81, 92, 181, 185
Wright, Richard, 231, 234

Yankee City (Newburyport, Massachusetts), 30, 31, 69, 114, 119
Young Lords (gang), 341, 343
Yugoslavia, 43, 123, 129, 132

Zaire, 398
Zapotec (tribe), 193
Zeitlin, Maurice, 51, 60
Zimbabwe, 4, 17
Zimbalist, Andrew, 43, 44, 75
Zimmerman, 101, 157
Zwerdling, Daniel, 61, 274, 275

**Acknowledgments** *(continued from p. ii):*

*Pages 138, 149, and 171:* Frances Moore Lappé and Joseph Collins, *Food First.* Copyright 1977 by Ballantine Books, a Division of Random House, Inc.

*Page 157:* Copyright © 1974 by Richard L. Barnet and Ronald E. Müller. Reprinted by permission of SIMON & SCHUSTER, a Division of Gulf & Western Corporation.

*Pages 177, 177-178, and 179:* Copyright © 1976 by Kai T. Erikson. Reprinted by permission of SIMON & SCHUSTER, A Division of Gulf & Western Corporation.

*Pages 196-197, 212, and 214:* Reprinted from *Unlearning the Lie, Sexism in School,* by Barbara Grizzuti Harrison, with permission of Liveright Publishing Corporation. Copyright © 1973 by Barbara Grizzuti Harrison.

*Pages 304 and 305:* Ruth Sidel, *Families of Fengsheng: Urban Life in China* (New York: Penguin Books, 1974). Copyright © Ruth Sidel, 1974. Reprinted by permission of Penguin Books.

*Pages 306 and 372-373:* Reprinted with permission from *Children of Che* by Karen Wald. © 1978 by Ramparts Press, Palo Alto, CA.

*Page 391:* Copyright © 1977 by Monthly Review, Inc. Reprinted by permission of Monthly Review Press.

*Pages 395-396:* Excerpted from "City Life: Lessons of the First Five Years," in *Radical America,* Vol. 13, #1, Jan.-Feb. 1979. 38 Union Sq., Somerville, MA 02143.

*Page 12:* From *The Lives of Children,* by George Dennison. Copyright © 1969 by George Dennison. Reprinted by permission of Random House, Inc.

*Page 67:* From *The Powers That Be,* by G. William Domhoff. Copyright © 1978 by G. William Domhoff. Reprinted by permission of Random House, Inc.

*Pages 75, 161, and 203:* Reprinted by permission of *Dollars and Sense,* Somerville, MA.

*Pages 85-86 and 336:* Reprinted from Wilfred Burchett with Rewi Alley. *China: The Quality of Life* (Pelican Books, 1976), pp. 36, 191-192. Copyright © Wilfred Burchett, 1976. By permission of Penguin Books Ltd.

*Pages 106, 106-107, 108, 109, 112, and 123:* From *Working: People Talk about What They Do All Day and How They Feel about What They Do,* by Studs Terkel. Copyright © 1972, 1974 by Studs Terkel. Reprinted by permission of Pantheon Books, a division of Random House, Inc.

*Pages 248, 248-249, and 268:* Reprinted by permission of Curtis Brown, Ltd. Copyright © 1976 by Stan Steiner.

*Pages 257-258, 261-262, and 384:* Reprinted by permission of Benjamin/Cummings Publishing Company.

*Page 297:* Reprinted by permission of Enid Blaylock.

*Pages 377-378:* From "Free Schools to Educational Alternatives," by Allen Graubard. From *Co-ops, Communes, and Collectives,* edited by John Case and Rosemary C. R. Taylor. Copyright © 1979 by John Case and Rosemary C. R. Taylor. Reprinted by permission of Pantheon Books, a division of Random House, Inc.